The Lessons of the
Temporal Cycle and the Principal Feasts
of the Sanctoral Cycle
According to the Monastic Breviary

Compiled and adapted for the
Office of the Brothers of
St. Meinrad's Abbey

ST. MEINRAD'S ABBEY
ST. MEINRAD
INDIANA
1940

IMPRIMI POTEST

☩ IGNATIUS ESSER, O.S.B.
Abbot of St. Meinrad

IMPRIMATUR

☩ JOSEPH E. RITTER, D.D.
Bishop of Indianapolis

May 12, 1940

This present translation is lovingly dedicated to those devout souls who are desirous of reading and meditating upon the words of the Fathers of the Church, but have been hindered from so doing by an insufficient knowledge of Latin.

Feast of Our Lady's Nativity
September 8, 1940

Ut In Omnibus Glorificetur Deus

THE TEMPORAL CYCLE

I SUNDAY IN ADVENT

I Nocturn

Beginning of the Prophecy of Isaias, c. 1, 1 - 11

II Nocturn

Sermon of St. Leo, Pope

When the Savior would instruct His disciples concerning the coming of the kingdom of God and of the end of the world and of time, and teach the whole Church in the person of the Apostles, He said: Take heed lest your hearts be weighed down by surfeiting and drunkenness and the cares of this life. Dearly beloved, we know indeed that this warning applies more especially to us, for though that day which our Lord foretold is at present hidden from us, yet we doubt not that it is near.

Let every man then make himself ready for the coming of the Lord, lest it find him a slave to gluttony, or entangled in worldly cares. For we see by daily experience, dearly beloved, that fulness of drink blunts the keenness of the mind, and excess of food weakens the will. Moreover, to eat as much as one desires is contrary to the health of the body, unless temperance withstands desire, and the momentary pleasure of indulgence is checked by the thought of future discomfort.

Although the body has no desires apart from the soul, and its feelings come from the same source as its movement: yet it is the function of the same soul to deny things to the body which is subject to it, and, acting on its interior conviction, to keep the outer man from things unseemly. Then will the soul, more often free from bodily lusts, sit at leisure in the inner court of the mind, meditating on divine wisdom. There, where the turmoil of earthly cares is stilled, will it feed on holy thoughts and find joys in pleasures that will never end.

Even in this life, if something is difficult to carry out, it can be done more easily if done frequently; so we ought to be occupied for longer times and oftener with the spiritual things than with the temporal. And as with more exalted cares our morals are the better, so our temporal actions also turn into incorruptible riches.

R.† I look from afar, and, behold I see the power of God coming, and a cloud covering all the earth. * Go ye out to meet Him, and say: Tell us if Thou art He, who shall rule over the people of Israel. Both the earth-born and the sons of men, rich and poor together. Go ye out to meet Him and say. Give ear, O Thou who rulest Israel, Thou that leadeth Joseph like a sheep. Tell us if Thou art He. V. Lift up your gates, O ye princes, and be ye lifted up, O eternal gates, and the King of Glory

†These responses are not taken in order but are chosen arbitrarily.

shall enter in. R. Who shall rule over the people of Israel. Glory be to the Father, and to the Son, and to the Holy Ghost. *Then is repeated.* R. I look from afar, and behold I see the power of God coming, and a cloud covering all the earth. Go ye out to meet Him, and say: Tell us if Thou art He who shall rule over the people of Israel.

III Nocturn

The reading of the holy Gospel according to St. Luke

At that time: Jesus said to His disciples: There shall be signs in the sun, and in the moon, and in the stars: and upon the earth distress of nations. And so forth.

Homily of St. Gregory, Pope

Our Lord and Redeemer, wishing to find us ready, foretells the evils about to come on the world as it grows old, that He may wean our hearts from earthly affections. He makes known to us the great convulsions which will come before the end, that if we will not fear God when we are at peace, at least we may be so impressed by these terrible happenings as to dread His judgment when it is at hand.

A little before the passage which has just been read to you from the Gospel are found these words of our Lord: Nation shall rise against nation, and kingdom against kingdom: and there shall be great earthquakes in divers places, and pestilences and famine. After a few more verses come the words you have just heard: There shall be signs in the sun and in the moon and in the stars, and upon the earth distress of nations, by reason of the confusion of the roaring of the sea and of the waves. Some of these things indeed, have come to pass: others, we fear, are not far off.

In these our days we see nation rise against nation, and their distress over all the earth, more than we ever read of in books. You know also how often we have heard of earthquakes overwhelming countless cities in other parts of the world. We ourselves suffer pestilences without end. As yet we do not actually see signs in the sun, moon and stars, but the very change of the atmosphere warns us that we may look for them before long.

Finally, there has not yet arisen any new confusion of the sea and of the waves. But since many prophecies have already been fulfilled, there is no doubt but that the few which remain shall also follow; for our certitude of that which is to follow is the accomplishment of that which went before. For this cause do we speak these things, most dear brethren, so that your minds might give heed to the study of diligence, lest feeling secure they remain inactive, and being ignorant they become weak; but in all things let on the one hand fear rouse them up, and on the other, solicitude for doing good strengthen them.

R. I beseech thee, O Lord, send whom Thou wilt send: behold the affliction of Thy people: * As Thou hast spoken, come, and deliver us. V. Give ear, O Thou that rulest Israel, Thou that leadest Joseph like a sheep, Thou that sittest upon the Cherubim. As. Glory. As.

Here is said the Hymn Te Deum

✠ Continuation of the holy Gospel according to St. Luke.—At that time: Jesus said to His disciples: There shall be signs in the sun, and in the moon, and in the stars; and upon the earth distress of nations, by reason of the confusion of the roaring of the sea and of the waves: men withering away for fear and expectation of what shall come upon the whole world. For the powers of heaven shall be moved. And they shall see the Son of Man coming in a cloud with great power and majesty. But when these things begin to come to pass, look up and lift up your heads, because your redemption is at hand. And He spoke to them a similitude: See the fig tree and all the trees: when they now shoot forth their fruit, you know that summer is nigh. So you also, when you shall see these things come to pass, know that the kingdom of God is at hand. Amen, I say to you, this generation shall not pass away till all things be fulfilled. Heaven and earth shall pass away: but My words shall not pass away. R. Amen.

LET US PRAY

Arouse Thy power and come, we beseech Thee, O Lord, that Thou mayest protect and save us from the threatening dangers of our sins: Who livest and reignest with God the Father, in the unity of the Holy Ghost, one God, world without end. R. Amen.

II SUNDAY IN ADVENT
I Nocturn
From Isaias the Prophet, c. 11, 1 - 13
II Nocturn
From the Exposition of St. Jerome, Priest, on Isaias the Prophet.

And there shall come forth a rod out of the root of Jesse. Up to the beginning of the vision, or burden of Babylon, which Isaias the son of Amos saw, all this is a prophecy concerning Christ: we will explain it part by part lest the memory of the reader should be confused if we commented on the whole at once. The Jews interpret rod and flower of the root of Jesse as the Lord Himself: because forsooth the power of a ruler is indicated by the rod, by the flower, his beauty.

But let us understand the rod from the root of Jesse to signify the holy Virgin Mary, who had no shoot belonging to her; of whom we read above:

Behold a virgin shall conceive and bear a Son. And for the flower, let us take it to mean the Lord and Savior, who says in the Canticle of Canticles: I am the flower of the field, and the lily of the valley.

Therefore upon this flower, which shall suddenly come forth from the stock and root of Jesse through the Virgin Mary, the Spirit of the Lord shall rest: for truly in Him all the fulness of the Godhead was pleased to dwell corporeally: the Spirit was not poured out upon Him by measure, as it was upon the other Saints: but, as we read in the Hebrew Gospel used by the Nazarenes: The whole fountain of the Holy Ghost shall be poured forth upon Him. For the Lord is a Spirit; and where the Spirit of the Lord is, there is liberty.

In the same part of St. Matthew's Gospel we read: Behold My Son whom I have chosen; My elect, in whom My soul is well pleased; I shall place My Spirit over Him and He will meet out judgment to the gentiles; (the phrase) in Him rests the Spirit of the Lord, in that He remained in the eternal abode (of the Trinity), is to be understood of the Savior.

R. Behold there cometh the Lord, our defender, the Holy One of Israel, * Wearing the royal crown upon His head. V. And His power shall be from sea to sea, and from the rivers even to the ends of the earth. Wearing. Glory. Wearing.

III Nocturn

The reading of the holy Gospel
according to St. Matthew

At that time: When John had heard in prison the works of Christ, sending two of his disciples, he said to Him: Art Thou He that art to come, or look we for another? And so forth.

Homily of St. Gregory, Pope

They who had seen so many signs and mighty works should not have been scandalized, but awestruck. And yet these very works were a stumbling block to the unfaithful when they saw dying Him who had wrought so many miracles. Hence Paul says: But we preach Christ crucified, unto the Jews indeed a stumbling block, and unto the Gentiles foolishness.

Foolish indeed did it seem to men that the Author of life should die for men: and thus they took scandal against Him for having done that very thing by which He laid them under the greater debt. For the greater the humiliation God has undergone for the sake of men, the more worthy is He of being glorified by men.

What, therefore, means the saying: Blessed is he who shall not be scandalized in Me; unless it clearly points to the abjection and shame of His death? As if He should openly say: I do indeed work wonders, but I do not refuse to endure shame. When then I come to die like other men, let those who now worship Me because of the miracles I work, take heed lest they despise Me because of My death.

The disciples of John having gone their way, let us hear what Jesus said to the multitude concerning this same John: What went you out into the desert to see? A reed shaken by the wind? Clearly He did not infer that this was so, but rather the contrary. For, let but a breath of air blow upon a reed and it bends over to the other side. What then does a reed signify but a carnal mind, which sways in one direction or the other as it meets with praise or blame?

R. Jerusalem, thou shalt plant a vineyard in thy mountains: Thou shalt rejoice, for the day of the Lord will come: arise, O Sion, and turn unto the Lord thy God: rejoice and be glad, O Jacob: * For thy Savior cometh from the midst of the nations. V. Rejoice greatly, O daughter of Sion: shout with gladness, O daughter of Jerusalem. For. Glory. For.

✠ Continuation of the holy Gospel according to St. Matthew.—At that time, when John had heard in prison the works of Christ, sending two of his disciples, he said to Him: Art thou He that art to come, or look we for another? And Jesus making answer, said to them: Go and relate to John what you have heard and seen. The blind see, the lame walk, the lepers are cleansed, the deaf hear, the dead rise again, the poor have the gospel preached to them: and blessed is he that shall not be scandalized in Me. And when they went their way, Jesus began to say to the multitudes concerning John: What went you out into the desert to see? A reed shaken with the wind? But what went you out to see? A man clothed in soft garments? Behold they that are clothed in soft garments are in the houses of kings. But what went you out to see? A prophet? Yea, I tell you, and more than a a prophet. For this is he of whom it is written: Behold I send My Angel before Thy face, who shall prepare Thy way before Thee.

LET US PRAY

Arouse our hearts, O Lord, to prepare the way for Thy only begotten Son, that by His coming we may be worthy to serve Thee with minds that have been purified; Who liveth and reigneth with Thee in the unity of the Holy Ghost, one God, world without end. R. Amen.

Watch ye therefore, because
you know not the day nor
the hour.

Matthew 25, 13.

III SUNDAY IN ADVENT

I Nocturn

From Isaias the Prophet, c. 26, 1 - 14

II Nocturn

Sermon of St. Leo, Pope

The season of the year with its customary devotions reminds us, dearly beloved, that it is our duty as shepherd of your souls to exhort you to the observance of the December fast. Now that all the fruits of the earth have been gathered in, it is most fitting that this sacrifice of abstinence should be offered to God who has so bountifully bestowed them upon us.

And what can be more useful to this end than fasting? For by its observance we draw near to God, we resist the devil, and overcome the allurements of vice. Fasting has ever been the support of virtue. From abstinence spring chaste thoughts, reasonable desires, and salutary counsels. By voluntary mortifications the lusts of the flesh are extinguished, and the soul receives new strength.

But since fasting alone will not obtain health for our souls, let us add to our fasting works of mercy to the poor. Let us spend in good works what we deny to indulgence. Let the abstinence of him who fasts become the support of the poor. Let us be zealous in the protection of widows, in the support of orphans; let us strive to comfort the afflicted, to reconcile those who are at variance. Let us receive the stranger, and succor the oppressed; let us clothe the naked, and care for the sick. And then may every one of us who shall have spent himself in offering this sacrifice of piety to God, the author of all good, merit to receive from Him the reward of the heavenly kingdom.

Therefore, let us fast on Wednesday and Friday; and on Saturday let us keep vigil at the church of blessed Peter the Apostle: that through his merits we may obtain what we ask, through our Lord Jesus Christ, who with the Father and the Holy Ghost liveth and reigneth forever and ever. Amen.

R. Behold the Lord shall appear upon a white cloud, * And thousands of His Saints with Him: and He shall have on His vesture, and on His thigh written: King of kings, and Lord of lords. V. He shal appear at the end, and shall not lie; though He tarry, wait for Him, because He will surely come. And thousands. Glory. And thousands.

III Nocturn

The reading of the holy Gospel
according to St. John

At that time: The Jews sent from Jerusalem priests and levites to John, to ask him: Who art thou? And so forth.

Homily of St. Gregory, Pope

In the words we have just heard, dearly beloved brethren, the humility of John is to be commended. He was of such courage that he might have been held to be Christ Himself, but he preferred to be taken for what he really was than to let others vainly esteem him. For he confessed and did not deny: and he confessed: That I am not the Christ. But when he said: I am not; he did indeed openly declare what he was not, but he did not deny what he was; so that, speaking the truth, he might become a member of Him whose name he would not falsely assume.

By refusing to take to himself the title of Christ, he became a member of Christ. Because he humbly strove to confess his own littleness, he truly merited to share in the greatness of Christ. But when we call to mind what our Redeemer declared in another place, a very knotty question arises from the words of this lesson. When our Lord was asked by His disciples about the coming of Elias, He replied: Elias is come already, and they knew him not, but have done unto him whatsoever they had a mind. And: If you will receive it, John is Elias.

But when John was asked, he answered: I am not Elias. What does this mean, dearly beloved, for the Truth affirms what the prophet of truth denies? Between: He is, and: I am not, there is a very great difference. How is John the prophet of truth if He contradicts Him who is Truth Itself? Let us inquire more minutely into the meaning of these words, and we shall find that they are not really contradictory.

The Angel said to Zachary concerning John: He shall go before Him in the spirit and power of Elias. John is said to be coming in the spirit and power of Elias, because he comes before the first advent of the Lord as Elias will come before His second advent. As Elias will be the forerunner of the Judge, so John is the forerunner of the Redeemer. John, therefore, was Elias in spirit but not in person. And thus our Lord asserts of the spirit what John denies of the person.

R. Bethlehem, city of the most high God, out of thee shall come forth the Ruler of Israel, whose going forth is from the beginning of the days of eternity, and He shall be magnified in the midst of the whole earth: * And there shall be peace in our land when He cometh. V. He shall speak peace unto the Gentiles, and shall have dominion from sea to sea. And there shall be peace. Glory. And there shall be peace.

✠ Continuation of the holy Gospel according to St. John.—At that time: the Jews sent from Jerusalem priests and levites to John, to ask him: Who art thou? And he confessed, and did not deny; and he confessed: I am not the Christ. And they asked him: What then? Art thou Elias? And he said: I am not. Art thou the Prophet? And he answered: No. They said therefore unto him: Who art thou, that we may give an answer to them that sent us? What sayest thou of thyself? He said: I am the voice of one crying in the wilderness, Make straight the way of the Lord, as said the Prophet Isaias. And they that were sent were of the Pharisees. And they asked him, and said to him: Why then dost thou baptize, if thou be not the Christ, nor Elias, nor the Prophet? John answered them, saying: I baptize with water: but there hath stood one in the midst of you, whom you know not. The same is He that shall come after me, who is preferred before me: the latchet of whose shoe I am not worthy to loose. These things were done in Bethania, beyond the Jordan, where John was baptizing.

LET US PRAY

We beseech Thee, O Lord, listen to our prayers, and by the grace of Thy visit to us enlighten the darkness of our minds; Who livest and reignest with God the Father, in the unity of the Holy Ghost, one God, world without end. R. Amen.

WEDNESDAY IN EMBER WEEK

The reading of the holy Gospel
according to St. Luke

At that time: The Angel Gabriel was sent from God into a city of Galilee, called Nazareth, to a virgin espoused to a man whose name was Joseph, of the house of David: and the virgin's name was Mary. And so forth.

Homily of St. Ambrose, Bishop

The divine mysteries are indeed hidden from us, nor, as the prophet says, can anyone easily come to the knowledge of God's designs. Yet from what we do know of the words and works of our Lord and Savior, we may gather that for some weighty reason she who was especially chosen to bring forth the Lord, was espoused to a man. Why did she not become pregnant before she was espoused? Perhaps lest it should be said that she had conceived in adultery.

And the Angel came in unto her. That she was a virgin we may learn from her behavior, from her modesty, from her speech, from the mystery. It is the part of a maiden to be timid, to shrink from the society of all men, to avoid their addresses. Let women learn to imitate this example of modesty. She whom no man might look upon was alone in her chamber, and the Angel alone found her. She is saluted by the Angel when alone, without a companion, without a witness, lest she should suffer harm from profane conversation.

A message so great and full of mystery must needs be uttered not by the mouth of man, but by an Angel. This day for the first time are heard the words: The Holy Ghost shall come upon thee. They are heard and believed. Then she says: Behold the handmaid of the Lord: be it done unto me according to thy word. Consider her humility and her devotion. She whom the Lord has chosen for His mother calls herself His handmaid; she is not forthwith lifted up on account of the promise made to her.

FRIDAY IN EMBER WEEK

The reading of the holy Gospel
according to St. Luke

At that time: Mary rising up, went into the hill country with haste into a city of Juda. And so forth.

Homily of St. Ambrose, Bishop

All who ask to be believed are expected to give reasons why they should be believed. Therefore, when the Angel had announced what should come to pass, he made known to the Virgin Mary, as a reason for believing in him, that an old and barren woman had conceived. This he did to assure her that whatever was pleasing to God was also possible. When Mary heard this, she set out for the hill country, not because she did not believe the an-

nouncement or was incredulous of the messenger,
or doubted the example of Elizabeth, but cheerfully,
as if to fulfil a vow; with devotion, as to a religious
duty, in haste for very joy. Whither, indeed, if
not to greater heights, should she who was now full
of God make her way with haste? The grace of
the Holy Ghost knows no languid efforts.

Do you also, O holy women, learn what attention
you ought to bestow on your kinsfolk when they
are with child. The virgin modesty of Mary did
not hold her back from mixing with the crowd,
though till then she had lived alone in the strictest
privacy; nor did the roughness of the mountain
ways abate her zeal, nor the length of the journey
keep her back from doing a kindness. The virgin
set out in haste into the hill country, a virgin
mindful of her duty, unmindful of mishaps, urged
on by affection, heedless of the delicacy of her sex,
leaving her home behind her. Learn, O virgins,
not to run about to the houses of strangers, not to
loiter in the streets, not to spend time talking with
others in public. Mary who moved quietly about
her own home, in haste only on the public roads,
abode three months with her kinswoman.

You have learned, O virgins, the modesty of
Mary: learn also her humility. She went as a relative to her relative, the younger to the elder: and
not only did she come, but she first saluted Elizabeth. For the more chaste a virgin is, the more

humble should she be. She will know how to submit to her elders. She who professes chastity should be mistress of humility. For humility is the root of piety, and the very rule of its teaching. It is to be noted, that the superior comes to the inferior that the inferior may be assisted, Mary comes to Elizabeth, Christ to John.

SATURDAY IN EMBER WEEK

The reading of the holy Gospel

according to St. Luke

In the fifteenth year of the reign of Tiberius Caesar, Pontius Pilate being governor of Judea. And so forth.

Homily of St. Gregory, Pope

The date at which the Forerunner of our Redeemer entered on his task of preaching is indicated by the name of the ruler of the Roman State and by those of the kings of Judea. The time of his preaching is indicated by these names because he had come to preach Him who was to be the Redeemer of some Jews and many Gentiles. The manner in which these earthly rulers are named clearly shows that the Gentiles were to be gathered together and the Jews to be scattered for their perfidy; for we find that one ruler is ascribed to the Roman State, whilst the kingdom of Judea is divided among four princes.

These are the words of our Redeemer: Every kingdom divided against itself shall be brought to desolation. Evidently the kingdom of Judea was about to come to an end, since its territory was divided among so many kings. It is fitting also that mention should be made not only of the kings under whom John the Baptist began to preach, but also of the priests, since He whom he announced was to be both King and Priest. Therefore did Luke the Evangelist indicate the date of his preaching by the names of kings and priests.

And he came into all the country about the Jordan, preaching the baptism of penance for the remission of sins. It is evident from these words that John not only preached, but also administered the baptism of penance: yet he could not give baptism unto remission of sins. For remission of sins is granted to us through the baptism of Christ alone. Let us observe, therefore, what is said: Preaching the baptism of penance for the remission of sins; that is to say, he preached the baptism which was to loose sins, though he himself could not give it. Even as he went before the incarnate Word of the Father with the word of preaching, so with his baptism, which could not remit sin, he was to foreshadow that baptism of penance which was able to remit sin.

IV SUNDAY IN ADVENT

I Nocturn

From Isaias the Prophet, c. 35, 1 - 10

II Nocturn

Sermon of St. Leo, Pope

If, dearly beloved, we rightly and wisely understand the beginning of our creation, we shall find that man was made in the image of God, to the end that he might imitate his Creator; and the natural dignity of our race consists in this, that the goodness of the divine nature should be reflected in us as in a mirror. Daily the grace of our Savior helps us to regain this dignity, for that which fell in the first Adam, in the second Adam is raised up.

It is nothing but the mercy of God that is the cause of our restoration, for we could not love Him unless He had first loved us and scattered the darkness of our ignorance by the light of His truth. Thus the Lord declared by the holy Isaias, saying: I will lead the blind into the way that they knew not, and I will make them tread the paths that they have not known. I will make darkness light for them and crooked things straight. These things will I do to them, and will not forsake them. And again: I was found by them that sought Me not; I was made manifest unto them that asked Me not.

We learn from the Apostle John how this was fulfilled where he says: We know that the Son of

God is come, and He hath given us understanding that we may know the true God and may be in His true Son. And again: Let us therefore love God, because He first loved us.

By loving us, therefore, God restores us to His image: and that He may find in us goodness after the pattern of His own, He enables us to do what He does, kindling, as it were, the lamps of our souls, and inflaming us with the fire of His charity, that we may love not Him only, but also whatever He loves.

R. Blow ye the trumpet in Sion, call together the nations, tell it among the people and say: * Behold God our Savior cometh. V. Tell it, and make it to be heard; speak aloud, and cry. Behold. Glory. Behold.

III Nocturn

The reading of the holy Gospel according to St. Luke

In the fifteenth year of the reign of Tiberius Caesar, Pontius Pilate being governor of Judea. And so forth.

From a Homily of St. Gregory, Pope

John said to the multitudes that went forth to be baptized by him: Ye offspring of vipers, who hath showed you to flee from the wrath to come? Now this wrath to come is the chastisement of the last day of vengeance, from which the sinner will not be able to escape unless he has recourse now to the mourning of penance. Observe that wicked children who follow their parents in doing evil are called the offspring of vipers: for they envy the righteous and persecute them; they return evil for good; they seek how they may injure their neighbors; and since in all these ways they imitate their carnal parents, they are, as it were, the envenomed offspring of envenomed parents.

But seeing that we too have sinned, that we are entangled in evil habits, let him tell us what we are to do if we would flee from the wrath to come. He continues: Bring forth fruits worthy of penance. Here we must take note that the friend of the bridegroom exhorts us to bring forth not only fruits of penance, but fruits worthy of penance. For it is one thing to bring forth fruits of penance, and another, to bring forth fruits worthy of penance.

To speak first of fruits worthy of penance, we must know that whoever has refrained from what is forbidden is rightly allowed to make use of what is permited; and such a one may devote himself to works of piety without being obliged to give up the things of the world. But if any one has fallen into the sin of fornication or, perhaps, into the more serious sin of adultery, he ought to refrain in some degree from things lawful to make up for his indulgence in things unlawful.

For he who has sinned less is not bound to bring forth the fruit of good works to the same degree as he who has sinned more; nor is he who has not fallen at all bound to do as much as he who has fallen, be his sins few or many. Let every one to whom there may be applied these words: Bring forth fruits worthy of penance, act according to his conscience, so that he who has incurred greater losses by his sins may by penance acquire greater riches of good works.

R. I must decrease, but He must increase: He it is who coming after me is preferred before me: * The latchet of whose shoe I am not worthy to loose. V. I have baptized you in water: He shall baptize you in the Holy Ghost. The latchet. Glory. The latchet.

✠ Continuation of the holy Gospel according to St. Luke.—Now in the fifteenth year of the reign of Tiberius Caesar, Pontius Pilate being governor of Judea, and Herod being tetrarch of Galilee, and Philip his brother tetrarch of Iturea and the country of Trachonitis, and Lysanias tetrarch of Abilina, under the high priests Annas and Caiphas: the word of the Lord was made unto John, the son of Zachary, in the desert. And he came into all the country about the Jordan, preaching the baptism of penance for the remission of sins, as it was written in the book of the sayings of Isaias the prophet: A voice of one crying in the wilderness: Prepare

In the

brightness

of the

saints,

from

the womb

before the

day star I begot Thee.   (Psalm 109, 3)

ye the way of the Lord: make straight His paths: every valley shall be filled: and every mountain and hill shall be brought low, and the crooked shall be made straight, and the rough ways plain: and all flesh shall see the salvation of God.

LET US PRAY

Arouse, we beseech Thee, O Lord, Thy power and come; assist us by Thy great strength that through the help of Thy grace what our sins keep back from us may be quickly granted by Thy goodness and mercy; Who livest and reignest with God the Father, in the unity of the Holy Ghost, one God, world without end. R. Amen.

VIGIL OF THE NATIVITY

The reading of the holy Gospel
according to St. Matthew

When Mary, the mother of Jesus, was espoused to Joseph, before they came together, she was found with Child, of the Holy Ghost. And so forth.

Homily of St. Jerome, Priest

Why was He conceived of a virgin that was betrothed, rather than of one that was free? Firstly, that by the genealogy of Joseph, the lineage of Mary might be shown. Secondly, lest she should be stoned by the Jews as an adulteress. Thirdly, that she might have a guardian when she had to flee into Egypt. To these the martyr Ignatius has added a fourth reason why the Lord should be conceived by one betrothed: namely, that the birth should be concealed from the devil, since he would suppose that our Lord would be born, not of a virgin, but of a married woman.

Before they came together, she was found with child of the Holy Ghost. She was found by Joseph, but by no one else. He had a future husband's right to know all that concerned her. But the words: Before they came together; do not imply that afterwards they did so. The scripture merely indicates that up to that time they had not done so.

Whereupon Joseph her husband, being a just man and not willing publicly to expose her, was minded to put her away privately. If anyone is joined to an adulteress, he becomes one body with her, and according to the Law, not only those who commit a sin, but also those who have knowledge of it are held guilty. How, then, could Joseph be described as just if he had concealed the sin of his wife? But this is rather a testimony to Mary's purity, for Joseph, knowing her chastity yet wondering what had happened, kept silence about the mystery he did not understand.

NATIVITY OF OUR LORD

I Nocturn

*The four following Lessons from Isaias
are read without a title.*

Chapter 9, 1 - 6

At the first time the land of Zabulon, and the
land of Nephtali was lightly touched: and at the
last the way of the sea beyond the Jordan of the
Galilee of the Gentiles was heavily loaded. The
people that walked in darkness have seen a great
light: to them that dwelt in the region of the
shadow of death, light is risen. Thou hast multiplied the nation, and hast not increased the joy.
They shall rejoice before Thee as they that rejoice
in the harvest, as conquerors rejoice after taking a
prey, when they divide the spoils. For the yoke of
their burden, and the rod of their shoulder, and the
scepter of their oppressor thou hast overcome, as
in the day of Madian. For every violent taking of
spoils, with tumult, and garment mingled with
blood, shall be burnt, and be fuel for the fire. For
a Child is born to us, and a Son is given to us, and
the government is upon His shoulder: and His name
shall be called Wonderful, Counsellor, God the
Mighty, the Father of the world to come, the
Prince of Peace.

R. This day the King of heaven was pleased to be born to us of a virgin, that He might bring back to heaven man who was lost: * There is a joy among the hosts of Angels: because eternal salvation hath appeared unto men. V. Glory to God in the highest, and on earth peace to men of good will. R. There is joy among the hosts of Angels: because eternal salvation hath appeared unto men. V. Glory be to the Father and to the Son and to the Holy Ghost. R. This day the King of heaven was pleased to be born to us of a virgin that He might bring back to heaven man who was lost: There is joy among the hosts of Angels: because eternal salvation hath appeared unto men.

Chapter 40, 1 - 8

Be comforted, be comforted, My people, saith your God. Speak ye to the heart of Jerusalem, and call her: for her evil is come to an end, her iniquity is forgiven: she hath received of the hand of the Lord double for all her sins. The voice of one crying in the desert: Prepare ye the way of the Lord, make straight in the wilderness the paths of our God.

R. This day is the true peace come down to us from heaven: * This day throughout the whole world the skies drop down honey. V. This day is the daybreak of our new redemption, of the restoring of the old, of everlasting joy. * This day throughout the whole world the skies drop down honey.

Every valley shall be exalted, and every mountain and hill shall be made low, and the crooked shall become straight, and the rough ways plain. And the glory of the Lord shall be revealed and all flesh together shall see that the mouth of the Lord hath spoken. The voice of one, saying: Cry. And I said: What shall I cry? All flesh is grass, and all the glory thereof as the flower of the field. The grass is withered, and the flower is fallen, because the spirit of the Lord hath blown upon it. Indeed the people is grass: The grass is withered, and the flower is fallen: but the Word of our Lord endureth for ever.

R. Whom have you seen, O shepherds? speak, and tell us, who has appeared on earth? * We saw the new born Child, and the choirs of Angels loudly praising the Lord. V. Speak, what have ye seen? And tell us of the birth of Christ. * We saw.

Chapter 52, 1 - 6

Arise, arise, put on thy strength, O Sion, put on the garments of thy glory, O Jerusalem, the city of the Holy One: for henceforth the uncircumcised and unclean shall no more pass through thee. Shake thyself from the dust, arise, sit up, O Jerusalem: loose the bonds from off thy neck, O captive daughter of Sion. For thus saith the Lord God: My people went down into Egypt at the beginning to sojourn there: and the Assyrian hath oppressed them without any cause at all. And now what have I here, saith the Lord: for my people is taken away gratis? They that rule over them treat them unjustly, saith the Lord, and my name is continually blasphemed all the day long. Therefore my people shall know my name in that day: for I myself that spoke, behold I am here.

R. The true God, begotten of the Father, descended from heaven and entered into the womb of a Virgin, so that He might appear visibly to us, clothed with human flesh as were the first parents: * And He, being God-man, the Light, Life and Maker of the world, came forth from a closed door. V. As a bridegroom coming forth from the bride chamber. And He. Glory. And He.

II NOCTURN

Sermon of St. Leo, Pope

Today, dearly beloved brethren, was our Savior born: let us rejoice. For it is not right that sadness should find a place among those who are keeping the birthday of Life, which swallows up the fear of mortality, and brings us gladness on account of the promise of eternity. No one is shut out from sharing in this gladness: all have one common cause of joy. For as our Lord, the destroyer of sin and death, finds no one free from guilt, so is He come to set all free.

R. O great mystery and wonderful sacrament, that animals should see the new-born Lord lying in a manger: * Blessed is that Virgin, whose womb deserved to bear Christ our Lord. V. Hail, Mary, full of grace: the Lord is with thee. * Blessed.

Let the saint exult, for he draws nigh to the palm; let the sinner rejoice, for he is invited to forgiveness; let the Gentile take heart, for he is called unto life. For according to that fullness of time which the unsearchable depth of the divine counsel ordained, the Son of God took on Him the nature of mankind in order to reconcile it to its Maker, that the devil, the inventor of death, might be conquered through that very nature which had been conquered by him.

R. Blessed is Mary, the Mother of God, who remained a Virgin undefiled: * This day she hath brought forth the Savior of the ages. V. Blessed is she that hath believed: because all those things are accomplished which were told her from the Lord. * This day.

And this conflict, which He entered upon for our sakes, He waged upon a principle of great and wondrous equity; for the almighty Lord does battle with that most cruel enemy, not in His own majesty, but in our lowliness; opposing him with the very same form, and the very same nature, which shared indeed our mortality but was free from all sin. For this nativity has no concern with what we read of all others: no one is clean from defilement, not even an infant, whose life on earth is but one day old. Nothing, therefore, of the lust of the flesh has passed into this peerless nativity, nothing of the law of sin has entered it. A virgin of the royal race of David is chosen to be pregnant with the sacred embryo, and to conceive the divine and human offspring, first in mind, and then in the body. And, lest in ignorance of the heavenly counsel, she should tremble at this unwonted manner of speech, she learns by conversing with an Angel what is to be wrought in her by the Holy Spirit. Nor does she believe it to be any loss of modesty that she is soon to be the Mother of God.

R. O holy and spotless virginity, how to proclaim thy praises, I know not: * For thou hast borne in thy bosom Him whom the heavens cannot contain. V. Blessed art thou amongst women, and blessed is the fruit of thy womb. * For.

Let us then, dearly beloved, give thanks to God the Father, through His Son, in the Holy Spirit; who for His great love, wherewith He loved us, has had pity upon us; and when we were dead in sins, has quickened us in Christ, that in Him we might be a new creature and a new work of His hands. Let us therefore put off the old man with his deeds, and having obtained a share in Christ's birth, let us renounce the works of the flesh. Acknowledge, O Christian, thine own dignity; and having been made partaker of the divine nature, do not by degenerate conduct return to thine old baseness. Bethink thee of what a head and of what a body thou art a member. Remember that thou hast been snatched from the power of darkness, and translated into the light and kingdom of God.

R. The angel said to the shepherds: I announce to you a great joy which is for all people; because today is born for us the Savior, * Who is Christ, in the city of David. V. You shall find the Infant wrapped in swaddling clothes, and laid in a manger. Who is. Glory. Who is.

III NOCTURN

The reading of the holy Gospel

according to St. Matthew

"The book of the generation of Jesus Christ, the Son of David, the Son of Abraham. Abraham begot Isaac. And Isaac begot Jacob. And so forth.

Homily of St. Jerome, Priest

In Isaias we read: "His generation who shall declare?" Let us not think that the Evangelist contradicts the Prophet when He begins to narrate what the Prophet had declared impossible to say: for the Prophet spoke of the generation of His Divine Nature while St. Matthew spoke of His Incarnation. He begins therefore, with that which is carnal so that through man we may begin to know God. "The Son of David, the son of Abraham." An inverted (impossible) order, but necessarily so changed. For if Abraham had been placed first, and then David, it would have been necessary to again repeat Abraham in order to form the exact geneological order.

R. Behold the Lamb of God, behold Him Who taketh away the sins of the world, behold Him of whom I spoke to you: He Who cometh after me was made before me: * The latchet of whose shoe I am not worthy to loose. V. He who is of the earth speaks of the earth: He Who cometh from heaven, is above all. * The latchet.

The reading of the holy Gospel according to St. Luke

At that time: There went out a decree from Caesar Augustus, that the whole world should be enrolled. And so forth.

Homily of St. Gregory, Pope

Since by the favor of the Lord we are about to celebrate the solemn office of the Mass three times

today, we cannot speak at length on this passage
of the Gospel; and yet this very Birthday of our
Redeemer compels us to say something, however
brief. Why then is it that, when the Lord was to
be born, the whole world was enrolled? Was it not
to show clearly that He, who now appeared in the
flesh, would one day enroll His elect in life eternal?
But to the reprobate the prophet says: Let them
be blotted out of the book of the living, and with
the just let them not be written. It was fitting
that the Lord should be born in Bethlehem; for
Bethlehem signifies a house of bread, and the Lord
Himself said: I am the living bread which came
down from heaven. The place, then, where our
Lord was born, was already called the house of
bread, because there He was to appear who would
refresh the souls of the elect with a spiritual banquet. Not in the house of His parents was He born,
but away from home, in order to show that by the
human nature which He had taken He was born, as
it were, in a foreign country.

R. Blessed is the womb of the Virgin Mary,
which gave suck to Christ the Lord: * Who this
day hath been pleased to be born of a Virgin for
the salvation of the world. V. This day which is
dawning for us is holy: O come ye Gentiles and
adore the Lord. * Who this day.

The reading of the holy Gospel
according to St. Luke

At that time: The shepherds said to one another.
Let us go over to Bethlehem, and see this word
that is come to pass, which the Lord hath showed
to us. And so forth.

Homily of St. Ambrose, Bishop.

Behold the beginning of the rise of the Church.
Christ is born, and shepherds begin to watch, so
as to herd into the Lord's fold that Gentile flock,
which had hitherto lived like brute animals, lest it
should suffer from the inroads of spiritual beasts
of prey in the thick darkness of the night. And
well do those shepherds watch whom the Good
Shepherd instructs. The flock, then, is the people;
the night is the world; the shepherds are the
priests. Or perhaps he too is a shepherd to whom
it is said: Be watchful and strengthen. For God
has ordained to watch over His flock, not only
bishops, but also the Angels.

R. In the beginning was the Word and the Word
was with God and the Word was God: * This was
in the beginning with God. V. All things were
made by Him and without Him was made nothing.
* This was.

The reading of the holy Gospel
according to St. John

In the beginning was the Word, and the Word was with God, and the Word was God. And so forth.

Homily of St. Augustine, Bishop

Lest you should think of something worthless, such as is wont to come into your mind when you hear human words, hearken to what you should ponder on: The Word was God. Now perhaps some Arian unbeliever will come forward and say that the Word of God was made. How can it be that the Word of God was made when God made all things by the Word? If the very Word of God was also made, by what other word was It made? But if you say that there is a word of the Word, I say that That by which it was made is Itself the only Son of God. But if you do not say there is a word of the Word, then admit that That was not made by which all things were made. For that by which all things were made could not be made by Itself. Therefore believe the Evangelist.

R. The Word was made flesh and dwelt with us: * And we saw His glory, the glory as of the Only Begotten of the Father, full of grace and truth. V. In the beginning was the Word and the Word was with God and the Word was God. And we saw. Glory. And we saw.

(Then is said the Hymn) Te Deum.

✠ The beginning of the holy Gospel according to St. Matthew.—The book of the generation of Jesus Christ, the Son of David, the Son of Abraham. Abraham begot Isaac; and Isaac begot Jacob; and Jacob begot Judas, and his brethren; and Judas begot Phares and Zara of Thamar; and Phares begot Esron; and Esron begot Aram; and Aram begot Aminidab; and Aminidab begot Naason; and Naason begot Salmon; and Salmon begot Booz of Rahab; and Booz begot Obed of Ruth; and Obed begot Jesse; and Jesse begot David the King. And David the king begot Solomon, of her who had been the wife of Urias; and Solomon begot Roboam; and Roboam begot Abia; and Abia begot Asa; and Asa begot Josaphat; and Josaphat begot Joram; and Joram begot Ozias; and Ozias begot Joatham; and Joatham begot Achaz; and Achaz begot Ezechias; and Ezechias begot Manasses; and Manasses begot Amon; and Amon begot Josias; and Josias begot Jechonias and his brethren in the transmigration of Babylon. And after the transmigration of Babylon, Jechonias begot Salathiel; Salathiel begot Zorobabel; and Zorobabel begot Abiud; and Abiud begot Eliacim; and Eliacim begot Azor; and Azor begot Sadoc; and Sadoc begot Eliud; and Eliud begot Eleazar; and Eleazar begot Mathan; and Mathan begot Jacob; and Jacob begot Joseph, the husband of Mary, of whom was born Jesus, who is called Christ. R. Amen.

LET US PRAY

Grant, we beseech Thee, O almighty God, that the new birth of Thy Son as Man may deliver those whom the old servitude held under the yoke of sin. Through the same Jesus Christ, Thy Son, our Lord Who liveth and reigneth with Thee in the unity of the Holy Ghost, one God, world without end. R. Amen.

December 26
ST. STEPHEN, THE FIRST MARTYR

I Nocturn
From the Acts of the Apostles, c. 6, 1 - 10 and 7, 54 - 60

II Nocturn
Sermon of St. Fulgentius, Bishop

Yesterday we celebrated the birth in time of our eternal King; today we celebrate the victory, through suffering, of His soldier. Yesterday our King, clothed in a robe of flesh, coming forth from the Virgin's womb as from a palace, was pleased to visit the world; today His soldier, going forth from the tabernacle of the body, enters heaven in triumph. The one, without losing the majesty of the everlasting Godhead, girded Himself with flesh as a servant and entered into the battlefield of this world; the other, laying aside the corruptible covering of the body, ascends to the heavenly mansion to reign there forever. The one comes down and is veiled by His birth; the other goes up and is glorified by his death.

As the one comes down amid the jubilation of Angels, so the other goes up amid the stoning of the Jews. Yesterday the holy Angels rejoiced and sang: Glory to God in the highest; today they joyfully received Stephen into their company. Yesterday the Lord came forth from the Virgin's womb; today His soldier leaves the prison of the body.

Yesterday Christ for our sakes was wrapped in swaddling bands; today He clothes Stephen in a robe of immortality. Yesterday a narrow manger held the new-born Christ; today the boundless heavens receive the victorious Stephen. The Lord came down alone that He might raise up many; our King humbled Himself that He might exalt His soldier. Yet we should consider, brethren, with what arms Stephen was able to overcome the cruelty of the Jews so as to merit a blessed triumph.

Now Stephen had no other arms than charity, and this it was that enabled him to conquer on all sides so as to deserve the crown which his name signified. The love of God strengthened him against the cruelty of the Jews; the love of his neighbor led him to pray even for them that stoned him. Through love he rebuked the wandering that they might amend their ways; through love he prayed for them that stoned him that they might not suffer punishment. By the might of his charity he overcame Saul, his cruel persecutor, and won for a comrade in heaven the very man who had been his enemy on earth.

III Nocturn

The reading of the holy Gospel according to St. Matthew

At that time: Jesus said to the scribes and Pharisees: Behold I send to you prophets and wise men and scribes: and some of them you will put to death and crucify. And so forth.

Homily of St. Jerome, Priest

We have already said that the words: Fill ye up the measure of your fathers, may refer to the person of the Lord whom the Jews afterwards put to death. They may also be applied to His disciples of whom He goes on to say: Behold I send to you prophets and wise men and scribes. Here observe that, as the Apostle writes to the Corinthians, there are diversities of gifts among the disciples of Christ. Some are prophets, foretelling things to come; some are wise men, who know when they ought to speak; others are scribes, most learned in the law. And from among these Stephen was stoned, Paul was put to death, Peter was crucified, and the disciples, of whom mention is made in the Acts of the Apostles, were scourged.

We ask, who is this Zacharias, son of Barachias; for we read of many persons of this name. But here is added, in order to prevent any mistake: Whom you killed between the temple and the altar. I have read different opinions upon this question in various authors; and I set them down here. Some say that Zacharias, the son of Barachias, was the eleventh of the twelve prophets, and this opinion is supported by the name of his father. But the Scriptures nowhere tell us that this prophet was slain between the temple and the altar; especially as there were scarcely even ruins of the temple in his day.

Some maintain that this Zacharias was the father of John, relying on certain dreams of apocryphal writers, who declared that he was slain for having preached the coming of the Savior. Others again will have it that this was the Zacharias who was slain by Joas, king of Juda, between the temple and the altar, of whom we read in the history of the Kings. But it is to be noticed that Zacharias is there said to be not the son of Barachias but of Joiada the priest; whence it is said in the Scriptures: Joas remembered not the kindness which Joiada his father had done to him.

Since, then, we hold that the Zacharias spoken of in the Gospel was the son of Joiada and the place of his death confirms our opinion, the question arises, why is he called the son of Barachias and

not of Joiada? In our tongue Barachias signifies
Blessed of the Lord, and the righteousness of the
priest Joiada is implied by this Hebrew name. In
the Gospel used by the Nazarenes we find that son
of Joiada is written instead of son of Barachias.

December 27
ST. JOHN, APOSTLE AND EVANGELIST

I Nocturn
From the first Epistle of St. John, the Apostle,
c. 1, 1 - 10

II Nocturn

From the book of St. Jerome, Priest, on
Ecclesiastical Writers

The Apostle John, whom Jesus loved exceedingly,
was the son of Zebedee, and the brother of the
Apostle James, whom Herod beheaded after the
Lord's Passion. He wrote his Gospel the last of all,
at the request of the bishops of Asia, against Ce-
rinthus and other heretics. Especially was he compelled to declare the divine birth of Christ, since
the Ebionites had begun to teach that Christ did
not exist before Mary.

In the fourteenth year of Domitian, who stirred
up the second persecution after that of Nero, John
was banished to the island of Patmos. There he
wrote the Apocalypse, which has been explained by
Justin, the Martyr, and Irenæus.

But when Domitian was murdered, the senate annulled all his acts on account of their excessive cruelty and John returned to Ephesus during the reign of Nerva. Remaining there until the reign of Trajan, he founded and governed all the churches of Asia. Worn out with old age, he died sixty-eight years after the Lord's Passion and was buried near the same city of Ephesus.

From the Commentaries of the same on the Epistle to the Galatians

The blessed John the Evangelist lived at Ephesus even to extreme old age, until he could scarcely be carried to church by his disciples. Not being able to make a long discourse, he used simply to say at each meeting: Little children, love one another. At last his disciples and the brethren who were present grew weary of always hearing the same words and said: Master, why do you always say the same thing? The answer John gave was worthy of him: Because it is the commandment of the Lord; do this alone, and it is enough.

R. Most worthy of honor is blessed John who leaned upon the Lord's breast at the supper: * To whom Christ on the cross committed His Mother, a virgin to a virgin. V. A virgin is chosen by the Lord and beloved above all the rest. To whom. Glory. To whom.

III Nocturn

The reading of the holy Gospel
according to St. John

At that time: Jesus said to Peter: Follow Me. Peter turning about, saw that disciple whom Jesus loved following. And so forth.

Homily of St. Augustine, Bishop

The Church knows of two kinds of life divinely set before her and commended to her. In the one we walk by faith, in the other by sight; the one is the pilgrimage of time, the other the abode of eternity; the one is a life of labor, the other of repose; in the one we are on the road, in the other, in our own country; the one is spent in the toil of action, the other in the recompense of contemplation.

The one turns away from evil and does good; the other has no evil from which to turn away but rather has a great good to enjoy. The one fights with an enemy, the other reigns and has no enemy. The one succors the needy, the other dwells where none are needy. The one forgives the sins of others that its own may be forgiven; the other neither has anything to forgive nor does anything which calls for forgiveness.

The one is chastened by evils lest it be uplifted in good things; the other is so filled with grace as to be free from all evil that so it may cling to the highest good without temptation to pride. Wherefore the one is good but still wretched; the other is better and blessed. The Apostle Peter is a type of the former kind of life, the Apostle John of the latter.

All that belongs to the one continues here as long as this world lasts and only then comes to an end; the other waits for its completion in the hereafter and continues forever in the world to come. Therefore is it said unto the one: Follow Me. But of the other: If I will that he tarry till I come, what is that to thee? Follow thou Me. What do these words mean? As far as I can understand, what do they mean but this? Follow thou Me by imitating Me in bearing earthly sorrow; let him tarry until I come to render everlasting rewards.

R. He that shall overcome I will make him a pillar in my temple, saith the Lord: * And I will write upon him My name and the name of the city, the New Jerusalem. V. To him that overcometh I will give to eat of the tree of life, which is in the paradise of my God. And. Glory. And.

✠ Continuation of the holy Gospel according to St. John.—At that time: Jesus said to Peter: Follow Me. Peter turning about saw that disciple whom Jesus loved following, who also leaned on His breast at supper and said: Lord, who is he that shall betray Thee? Him therefore when Peter had seen, he saith to Jesus: Lord, and what shall this man do? Jesus saith to him: So I will have him to remain till I come, what is it to thee? Follow thou Me. This saying therefore went abroad among the brethren, that that disciple should not die. And Jesus did not say to him: He should not die; but: So I will have him to remain till I come: what is it to thee? This is that disciple who giveth testimony of these things, and hath written these things: and we know that his testimony is true. R. Amen.

LET US PRAY

O Lord, mercifully enlighten Thy Church; that illumined by the teachings of blessed John, Thy Apostle and Evangelist, It may attain the eternal rewards. Through our Lord.

December 28

THE HOLY INNOCENTS, MARTYRS

I Nocturn

From Jeremias the Prophet, c. 31, 15 - 23

II Nocturn

Sermon of St. Augustine, Bishop

Today, dearly beloved brethren, we keep the birthday of those children who, as the Gospel tells us, were put to death by the cruel king Herod. Therefore let the earth rejoice with exceeding joy, for she is the fruitful mother of the great host of heavenly soldiers. The favor of the wicked enemy could never have done such service to these blessed little ones as did his hatred. For the holy feast we are keeping today clearly shows that as iniquity abounded against these little ones, so much the more were heavenly blessings poured out upon them. Blessed art thou, O Bethlehem in the land of Juda, who didst suffer the cruelty of king Herod in the slaughter of thy children, but at the same time who was found worthy to offer to God an innocent troop of helpless children.

Yet we may well keep the birthday of those who were more blessed in leaving earth for heaven than in being born from their mother's womb. For scarcely had they entered on this present life when they obtained the dignity of life unending.

We esteem as precious the death of those Martyrs who have deserved praise for their confession, but these delight us by their death alone. Scarcely had life dawned upon them when the very destruction which brought it to a close became for them the beginning of glory. They whom the wickedness of Herod tore from their mother's breasts are rightly called the flowers of the Martyrs. Hardly had these early buds of the Church pushed above the ground in the winter of unbelief than the frost of persecution destroyed them.

III Nocturn

The reading of the holy Gospel
according to St. Matthew

At that time: An Angel of the Lord appeared in sleep to Joseph, saying: Arise and take the Child and His mother and fly into Egypt: and be there until I shall tell thee. And so forth.

Homily of St. Jerome, Priest

When he took the Child and His Mother and fled into Egypt, he took them by night and in darkness. And that darkness signified the night of ignorance in which He left the unbelievers from whom He fled. But when He returned into Judea, the Gospel makes no mention of night or darkness; for at the end of the world the Jews shall be enlightened and shall receive the faith again as once they received Christ returning from Egypt.

That it might be fulfilled which the Lord spoke by the prophet, saying: Out of Egypt have I called my Son. Let those who deny the truth of the Hebrew scriptures tell us where this is to be found in the Septuagint. And as they will not find it there, we tell them it is written in the prophet Osee as can be proved from the texts we have recently published.

Then was fulfilled that which was spoken by Jeremias the prophet, saying: A voice in Rama was heard, lamentation and great mourning, Rachel bewailing her children. Rachel was the mother of Benjamin and Bethlehem does not belong to his tribe. Why then, you ask, does Rachel weep, as for her own, for the children of Bethlehem who are of the tribe of Juda?

We will answer briefly, that she was buried near Bethlehem in Ephrata; and because a resting-place was found there for the body of this mother, the place became known by her name. Or it may be that the two tribes of Juda and Benjamin were joined together and Herod had ordered that the children were to be slain not only in Bethlehem but in all its borders.

SUNDAY WITHIN THE OCTAVE OF CHRISTMAS

I Nocturn
From the Epistle of St. Paul, the Apostle, to the Romans, c. 1, 1 - 19

II Nocturn
Sermon of St. Leo, Pope

Dearly beloved brethren, the greatness of God's work far exceeds the capacity of human utterance and therefore it is most difficult to speak, although there is reason for not being silent. The words of the prophet: Who shall declare His generation?

point not only to the divine essence in Christ Jesus
the Son of God, but also to His human nature.

Unless faith believes, words cannot explain how
both substances are united in one Person. And so
the matter of praise ever outruns the powers of expression of him who praises. Therefore let us rejoice that this mystery of mercy is greater than we
can utter; and let us be convinced that it is good
for us to fail when discourse falls short of the sublimity of our salvation.

No one comes nearer to the knowledge of the
truth than he who sees clearly that, however far
he penetrates into the things of God, he will never
wholly grasp them. For he who imagines that he
has attained to that which he seeks after has not
indeed found it but has rather failed in his search.
But lest we should be troubled at these hindrances
arising from our infirmity, we have the words of
the Gospels and the prophets to help us. And these
are able so to enkindle and instruct us that we seem
to look upon the birth of our Lord, wherein the
Word was made flesh, not as a thing past but as
present before our eyes.

The message of the Angel to the shepherds as
they watched their flocks rings in our ears also. To
this end we are set over the Lord's flock that we
may keep in our heart the word revealed from heav-
en and say to you as it will be said today: I bring

you tidings of great joy that shall be to all the
the people, for this day is born to you a Savior who
is Christ the Lord in the city of David.

R. Whom have you seen, O shepherds? speak
and tell us who has appeared on earth? * We saw
the new-born Child and choirs of Angels loudly
praising the Lord. V. Speak, what have you seen?
And tell us of the birth of Christ. We saw. Glory.
We saw.

III Nocturn

The reading of the holy Gospel
according to St. Luke

At that time: Joseph and Mary the mother of
Jesus were wondering at those things which were
spoken concerning Him. And so forth.

Homily of St. Ambrose, Bishop

You see that grace is abundantly poured forth
on all by the birth of the Lord and that the gift
of prophecy, if denied to the unbelieving, is not
withheld from the righteous. Behold, Simeon
prophecies that the Lord Jesus Christ has come for
the fall and the resurrection of many; that is to
say, He will consider the merits of the good and of
the wicked; and as a true and just judge He will
decree punishment or reward, according as our
deeds shall have deserved.

And thy own soul a sword shall pierce. There is no record or tradition that Mary passed out of this life by a violent death. A material sword can pierce the body only, not the soul. By these words therefore, he shows that Mary was not ignorant of the heavenly mystery.

For the Word of God is living and powerful and sharper than the sharpest sword, penetrating even to the dividing of the soul and spirit, of the joints too, and marrow; it searches the thoughts of the heart and the secrets of the soul, for all things are naked and open to the Son of God from whom the secrets of our conscience are not hidden.

Before Simeon prophesied, a virgin and also one who was married had prophesied. Now a widow was to prophesy so that every state and each sex might bear witness. Anna is brought forward as giving such an example of a good life and well-spent widowhood that we may believe her to have been entirely worthy to announce the coming of the Redeemer of all. As we have spoken elsewhere of her merits when addressing widows, we will not repeat here what we have already said because we wish to hasten to another subject.

R. O King of heaven who is served by such fitting homage: He who holds the world in His hand is laid in a stable: * He lieth in a manger and reigneth in heaven. V. Unto us is born this day a Savior in the city of David who is Christ the Lord. He lieth. Glory. He lieth.

✠ Continuation of the holy Gospel according to St. Luke.—At that time: Joseph and Mary the mother of Jesus were wondering at those things which were spoken concerning Him. And Simeon blessed them and said to Mary His mother: Behold, this Child is set for the fall and the resurrection of many in Israel: and for a sign which shall be contradicted: and thy own soul a sword shall pierce, that out of many hearts thoughts may be revealed. And there was one Anna a prophetess, the daughter of Phanuel, of the tribe of Aser: she was far advanced in years and had lived with her husband seven years from her virginity. And she was a widow until fourscore and four years: who departed not from the temple, by fastings and prayers serving night and day. Now she, at the same hour, coming in, confessed to the Lord: and spoke of Him to all that looked for the redemption of Israel. And after they had performed all things according to the law of the Lord, they returned into Galilee to their city of Nazareth. And the Child grew and waxed strong, full of wisdom: and the grace of God was in Him.

LET US PRAY

Almighty and eternal God, guide our actions according to Thy own good pleasure; that we may merit to abound in good works in the name of Thy dearly beloved Son; Who liveth and reigneth with Thee in the unity of the Holy Ghost, one God, world without end. R. Amen.

December 29

FIFTH DAY WITHIN THE OCTAVE OF THE NATIVITY

I Nocturn

The reading of the holy Gospel according to St. Luke

At that time: The shepherds said one to another: Let us go over to Bethlehem and let us see this word that is come to pass which the Lord hath showed to us. And they came with haste. And so forth.

Homily of the Venerable Bede, Priest

The shepherds indeed hurried with a blessed joy to see what they had heard about; and they merited to find their Savior because they sought Him with such ardent love. And the shepherds of an intelligent flock have shown equally by their actions and words with what intentness all the faithful must seek Christ. Let us go over to Bethlehem, they said, and let us see this word that is come to pass. Dearest brethren, let us, too, go over even to Bethlehem, the city of David by thinking and lov-

ingly studying what in that Word was made flesh;
and how we may celebrate His Incarnation with
becoming honors. With all fleshly concupiscence
cast aside, and with minds aflame with desire, let
us pass over to that heavenly Bethlehem, which is
the house of the living Bread, not made by the
hands of man but which is eternal in heaven, and
there recall with love that the Word was made
Flesh. Thither did He ascend in the flesh; there
He is sitting on the right hand of the Father. By
the steady practice of virtue and with earnest
chastisement of the heart and body, let us follow
Him thither so that we may deserve to see reigning from the throne of the Father Him whom we
now see in that crib so distant from His throne.

And coming with haste they saw Mary and
Joseph and the Infant lying in a manger. The
shepherds came hastening and found the God-man
born, together with those who ministered to that
birth. My brethren, let us, too, hasten, not indeed
with the steps of the feet but with the performance of good works to see that same glorified humanity together with the ministers of His service,
repaid with a becoming reward. Let us hasten to
see Him all resplendent with His Father's and His
own majesty. Let us hasten, I say, because there
is no happiness in a languid and half-hearted seeking; Christ's footsteps must, on the contrary, be
followed with great alacrity. Having placed His

hand in ours He himself wishes to quicken our
steps and to hear from us these words: Draw us
after Thee and we shall run in the odor of Thy
ointment. Let us increase our pace towards virtue
all the more, that we may be fit to go with Him.
Let no one be converted to the Lord tardily, let no
one put off from day to day to pray before all and
through all that He direct our step according to
His word and that all injustice be taken from us.

Seeing, they understood the word that was
spoken to them about this Child. So also, dearest
brethren, let us hasten to receive with devout faith
and filled with love, embrace that Word spoken to
us about our Savior, true God and man; so that we
may merit to understand it with perfect comprehension in the future. This is the true and only
life for both angels and men,—to look for all eternity into the face of their Creator, that face which
the psalmist so ardently desired when he said: My
soul hath thirsted for the living God, when shall
I come and appear before the Face of God? He
meant that by the vision of that Face alone, and not
by any earthly advantage could his desire be satiated; he said again: I shall be satiated when Thy
glory shall be manifested. And truly he assures
that not those who are lazy or half-hearted, but
those who laboriously take hold on works of virtue
will be worthy of the divine contemplation: But
with justice shall I appear in Thy sight.

December 30

SIXTH DAY WITHIN THE OCTAVE
OF THE NATIVITY

I Nocturn

The reading of the holy Gospel
according to St. Luke

At that time: The shepherds said one to another:
Let us go over to Bethlehem and let us see this
word that is come to pass which the Lord hath
showed to us. And they came with haste. And so
forth.

Homily of St. Ambrose, Bishop

See how the shepherds come with haste. So must
every one put away sloth who would seek Christ.
Mark how the shepherds believed the Angel; and
wilt not thou believe Father, Son, and Holy Ghost,
Angels, Prophets and Apostles? Take note how
carefully the Scripture weighs the exact force of
each word. They came with haste, it says, to see
the Word. For to see the flesh of the Lord is to
see the Word, which is the Son.

Because the shepherds were of humble origin let
not this example of their faith seem to thee a
trifling thing. Truly, though poor in learning, they
were very rich in faith. The Lord sought not for
schools crowded with wise men but for a people

of a simple mind, incapable of enlarging upon or embellishing what they hear. He seeks such as are simple; He cares not for ambition.

Think not meanly then of the shepherds' words. For by the shepherds even the faith of Mary is strengthened and by the shepherds the people are gathered together to the worship of God. All that heard wondered at those things that were told them by the shepherds. But Mary kept all these words, pondering them in her heart. Let us learn modesty of the holy virgin, who, chaste in speech as in body, pondered in her heart the evidences of her faith.

January 1

CIRCUMCISION OF OUR LORD

AND OCTAVE OF THE NATIVITY

I Nocturn

From the Epistle to the Romans, c. 4, 1 - 17

II Nocturn

Sermon of St. Leo, Pope

Dearly beloved brethren, he who would keep this day's festival with true reverence and pious observance must neither think falsely of the Lord's incarnation nor unworthily of His Godhead. For it is as dangerous an evil to deny that Christ has really taken upon Himself our nature as to refuse to believe that He is equal to the Father in glory.

When, therefore, we attempt to probe the mystery of Christ's birth, wherein He was born of a virgin Mother, let us rise above the clouds of human reason and let the mists of worldly wisdom be dispelled from the enlightened eye of faith.

Divine is the authority on which we believe; divine is the teaching which we follow. For whether we lend an ear to the witness of the law or to the sayings of the prophets or to the trumpet of the Gospel, that is true which John proclaimed when filled with the Holy Ghost: In the beginning was the Word, and the Word was with God, and the Word was God. All things were made by Him and without Him was not anything made.

That also is true which the same preacher added: The Word was made flesh and dwelt among us, and we saw His glory, the glory as it were of the only-begotten of the Father. Therefore in both natures it is the same Son of God, taking what is ours and not losing what is His own. He appears as man to restore men but abides unchangeable in Himself.

For the Godhead, which is His in common with the Father, suffered no loss of omnipotence, nor did the form of a servant dishonor the form of God. The most high and everlasting Being, bending down to save the human race, did indeed lift us up into His own glory, yet ceased not to be what He was. When then the only-begotten Son of God

confesses Himself less than the Father and yet
calls Himself equal, He shows the truth of either
nature in Himself; for, that He is less than God
proves His manhood; and that He is equal to God
proves His Godhead.

R.   Behold the Lamb of God, behold Him who
taketh away the sins of the world: behold Him of
whom I said to you: He that cometh after me is
preferred before me: * The latchet of whose shoe
I am not worthy to loose.   V.   He that is of the
earth speaketh of the earth: He that cometh from
heaven is above all. The latchet. Glory. The latchet.

III Nocturn

The reading if the holy Gospel
according to St. Luke

At that time: After eight days were accomplished, that the Child should be circumcised; His name
was called Jesus.   And so forth.

Homily of St. Ambrose, Bishop

So the Child is circumcised.   Who is this Child
unless it is He of whom it is said: A Child is born
to us, a Son is given to us; and: For He was made
under the law that He might redeem them who
were under the law; and: That they might present
Him to the Lord?   Here I might explain what it
means to be presented to the Lord in Jerusalem
if I had not already done so in my commentary on

Isaias. He that is circumcised from vice is held worthy of the Lord's favor; for: The eyes of the Lord are upon the just.

You will notice that all through the old law are found types to be fulfilled in the new; and so circumcision signifies the cleansing of the soul from sin. But since the body and mind are frail and so addicted to their inclination to sin as to become entangled in vice, the eighth day, which was that of the circumcision, typifies the complete cleansing from sin which will be ours at the resurrection. This is the meaning of the words: Every male opening the womb shall be called holy to the Lord. These words of the law contain the promise that a Virgin should bring forth. Truly He that opened her womb was holy, since He was altogether spotless.

And lastly, the Angel showed who was signified by the law when he repeated almost the same words, saying: The Holy one which shall be born of thee shall be called the Son of God. Among all that are born of woman the Lord Jesus alone is holy. He alone, through His immaculate birth, felt no touch of human corruption and it came not near Him because of His heavenly majesty.

For how can we take the words of the law literally and say that every male is holy, when we know that many have been very wicked? Was Achab holy? Were the false prophets holy who were consumed by the avenging fire from heaven at the prayer of Elias? But He is indeed holy who was signified by these pious ceremonies of the divine law, themselves a figure of future mysteries. And He alone might open the secret womb of spotless fecundity that holy Church, as a chaste virgin, might bring forth the people of God.

R. A holy day dawns upon us: come, ye Gentiles, and adore the Lord: * Because today a great light has come down upon the earth. V. This is the day which the Lord hath made; let us rejoice and be glad therein. Because. Glory. Because.

✠ Continuation of the holy Gospel according to St. Luke.—At that time: After eight days were accomplished, that the Child should be circumcised: His Name was called Jesus, which was called by the Angel before He was conceived in the womb.

LET US PRAY

O God, Who hast given the reward of eternal salvation to the human race by the fruitful virginity of the Blessed Mary; grant, we beseech Thee, that we may be assisted by her intercession through whom we have received the Author of life, Jesus Christ, Thy Son our Lord, who liveth and reigneth with Thee in the unity of the Holy Ghost world without end. R. Amen.

THE MOST HOLY NAME OF JESUS

I Nocturn

From the Acts of the Apostles, c. 3, 1 - 16

II Nocturn

Sermon of St. Bernard, Abbot

Not without reason does the Holy Ghost compare the name of the bridegroom to oil when He teaches the bride to say to the Bridegroom: Thy name is as oil poured out. For oil provides light, nourishment, and anointing. It feeds fire, it nourishes the body, it soothes pain; it is a light, a food, and a medicine. Consider now that all this is true of the Bridegroom's name. To speak of it gives light, to think of it is the food of the soul, to call upon it calms and soothes the heart. Let us take each point separately. What, think you, has made the light of faith to shine so brightly and so suddenly in the whole world but the preaching of the Name of Jesus? Is it not in the light of this Name that God has called us into His marvellous light? To us, being thus enlightened, and in that light, does Paul truly say: You were heretofore darkness, but now light in the Lord.

This is the Name which the same Apostle was biden to carry before kings and Gentiles and the children of Israel. And he carried that Name as a light and enlightened his country and everywhere he cried: The night is passed and day is at hand.

Let us therefore cast off the works of darkness and put on the armor of light; let us walk honestly as in the day. To all he pointed out that candle set upon a candlestick, preaching in every place Jesus, and Him crucified.

How did that light shine forth, blinding every eye that beheld it, when it came like lightning from the mouth of Peter and gave strength to the soles and feet of the lame man and enlightened many who were spiritually blind? Did he not cast fire when he said: In the Name of Jesus of Nazareth, arise and walk?

Not only is the Name of Jesus light; it is also food. Are you not strengthened as often as you call it to mind? What else so fattens the soul of him who ponders over it? What is there with such power to refresh the wearied senses, to strengthen courage, to help men to lead good and holy lives, to cherish chaste affection? The soul finds every food dry that is not moistened with this oil; everything tasteless, if not seasoned with this salt. Nothing you write has any interest for me unless I hear the Name of Jesus. That Name is like honey in the mouth, like music in the ear, like gladness in the heart. It is a healing balm also. Is any sad among us? Let the thought of Jesus come into his heart and thence leap to his mouth. When the light of that Name begins to dawn, it scatters every cloud and brings back calm. Does any one fall into sin and through despair come nigh to the brink of death? If he but call on that life-giving Name, he shall quickly come back to life.

R. Behold thou shalt conceive and bring forth a Son and thou shalt call His Name Jesus: * For He shall save His people from their sins. V. His Name was called Jesus, which was so named by the Angel before He was conceived in the womb. For. Glory. For.

III Nocturn

The reading of the holy Gospel
according to St. Luke

At that time: After eight days were accomplished that the Child should be circumcised, His Name was called Jesus. And so forth.

Homily of St. Bernard, Abbot

Behold, a great and wonderful mystery! The Child is circumcised and is called Jesus. What is the connection between these two things? It would seem that circumcision should rather be for the saved than for the Savior and that it would be more fitting for the Savior to circumcise than to be circumcised. But behold the mediator between God and men, how even from His very birth He joins the things of God to the things of men, the highest to the lowest. He is born of a woman but the womb that bore Him loses not the flower of virginity. He is wrapped in swaddling clothes but even these are made honorable by angelic praises. He is hidden in a manger but is made known by a star shining in the heavens. So also His circumcision proved the reality of the manhood He had taken; and the Name, which is above every name, proclaims the glory of His majesty. He is circumcised like a true son of Abraham; He is called Jesus as the true Son of God.

My Jesus bears not this Name as an empty and meaningless title as did others before Him. In Him it is not the shadow of a great name but the reality itself. That His Name was revealed from heaven is attested by the Evangelist, for he says that He was called by the Angel before He was conceived in the womb. Observe the deep meaning of these words: after Jesus was born, men called Him Jesus but He was called Jesus by the Angel before He was conceived in the womb. He is Savior both of angels and men; but of men since the Incarnation, of angels since they were created.

His name was called Jesus, says the Gospel, which was called by the Angel. Therefore by the mouths of two or three witnesses, every word is corroborated; and that word which the Prophet speaks of as being cut short is made manifest in the Gospel as the Word made flesh.

Justly indeed is the Child Who is born for us called Savior when He is circumcised; because from

that moment He began to work for our salvation
by shedding for us that most pure blood. Nor
should Christians need to ask why the Lord Christ
willed to be circumcised. He was circumcised for
the same reason for which He was born and for
which He suffered. He desired none of these things
for Himself but all for the elect. He was neither
born in sin nor circumcised from sin nor did He
die for His own sin; but rather, He did all because
of our sins. Which was called, says the Gospel, by
the Angel before He was conceived in the womb.
This Name was not merely attributed to Him; He
was truly what He was called, for it was His from
the very beginning. He was Savior by His very
nature; and this Name was natural to Him, not
given to Him by any creature, man or angel.

R. Blessed is Thy Name, O God of our fathers,
for in Thy wrath thou wilt remember mercy, * And
in the time of tribulation Thou dost forgive sins.
V. And blessed be the name of Thy majesty forever, Thou who alone dost wonderful things. And
in. Glory. And in.

✠ Continuation of the holy Gospel according to
St. Luke.—At that time: After eight days were
accomplished that the Child should be circumcised,
His Name was called Jesus, which was called by
the Angel before He was conceived in the womb.

LET US PRAY

O God, Who didst appoint Thy only begotten Son as Savior of the human race and didst command His Name to be called Jesus: mercifully grant that we, who honor His holy Name on earth, may enjoy the vision of Him in heaven. Through the same Lord.

January 5

VIGIL OF THE EPIPHANY
I Nocturn

The reading of the holy Gospel according to St. Matthew

At that time: When Herod was dead, behold an Angel of the Lord appeared in sleep to Joseph in Egypt saying: Arise and take the Child and His mother and go into the land of Israel. And so forth.

Homily of St. Jerome, Priest

From this passage we may understand that Herod was not alone in seeking the death of the Lord but the priests and scribes had sought it at the same time. And Joseph arose and took the Child and His mother. It is not written: He took his son and his wife; but the Child and His Mother. He is spoken of as guardian, not as husband.

But hearing that Archelaus reigned in Judea in the place of Herod his father, he was afraid to go thither. Because of their ignorance of history, many fall into the error of thinking this Herod, who is here said to be dead, to be the same as he who mocked the Lord in His Passion. But the Herod who afterwards made friends with Pilate was the Son of this Herod and the brother of Archelaus.

He shall be called a Nazarene. If he were quoting a definite passage of Scripture, he never would have said: Which was said by the prophets; but simply: Which was said by the prophet. But as he speaks of prophets in the plural, it is clear that he has taken the sense of the Scriptures, not any particular passage. Nazarene signifies holy; and the whole of Scripture declares that the Lord was to be holy. We can likewise say that it is written in Isaias, in the Hebrew version even in the same words, that: There shall come forth a rod out of the root of Jesse and a Nazarene shall rise up out of his root.

January 6

THE EPIPHANY OF THE LORD

I Nocturn

From Isaias the Prophet, c. 55, 1 - 4, c. 60, 1 - 6, c. 61, 10 - 11, c. 62, 1

II Nocturn

Sermon of St. Leo, Pope

Rejoice in the Lord, dearly beloved, again I say, rejoice; for but a short time has passed since the

solemnity of Christ's birth and now the feast of
His manifestation has dawned upon us. On that
day the Virgin brought Him forth; on this, the
world knew Him. Jesus, the Word made flesh, so
ordered the beginnings of His life in our flesh that
when He was born, He was manifested to those who
believed in Him but hidden from His enemies.

Already the heavens declared the glory of God
and the sound of truth went forth into all lands
when the angelic host appeared to the shepherds
and announced the birth of the Savior and the
guiding star led the Magi to adore Him, that from
the rising of the sun to the going down thereof the
birth of the true King might shine forth, the kingdoms of the East might learn the truth of what had
taken place from the wise men, and His birth might
not be concealed from the Roman rulers.

The very cruelty of Herod, in striving to put an
end to the newly-born King whom he feared, un-
wittingly served this dispensation. Intent on this
atrocious crime, he sought to destroy a child he
did not know in an indiscriminate slaughter of in-
fants, while the marvellous story was everywhere
repeated about the ruler whose birth had been announced from heaven. The novelty of this heavenly
sign together with the wickedness of the cruel persecutor caused the story to spread more quickly
and more widely. Then too was the Savior carried

into Egypt that this people, still given up to their ancient errors, might be prepared by a hidden grace for the salvation so near at hand; and though as yet they had not freed themselves from superstition, already they were to receive the Truth as a guest among them.

Therefore, dearly beloved brethren, let us recognize in the Magi who adored Christ the first-fruits of our own vocation and faith, and let us celebrate with joy of heart the dawn of a blessed hope. For henceforth we begin to enter into our eternal heritage; henceforth the hidden sayings of Scripture reveal Christ to us and the truth, which the Jews in their blindness did not receive, has sent forth its light upon all nations. Let us then honor this sacred day on which the Author of our salvation was made manifest and let us adore Him whom the Magi worshipped as a Child in the manger and who now reigns almighty in heaven. As they opened their treasures and offered mystic gifts to the Lord, so let us look into our hearts and bring forth gifts worthy of God.

R. This day when the Lord was baptised in the Jordan, the heavens were opened and the Spirit in the form of a dove rested upon Him and the voice of the Father was heard saying: * This is My beloved Son in whom I am well pleased. V. The Holy Ghost descended in bodily shape as a dove upon Him and a voice came from heaven. This is. Glory. This is.

III Nocturn

The reading of the holy Gospel according to St. Matthew

When Jesus was born in Bethlehem of Juda in the days of King Herod, behold, there came wise men from the East to Jerusalem saying: Where is He that is born King of the Jews? And so forth.

Homily of St. Gregory, Pope

Dearly beloved brethren, as you have heard in the lesson from the Gospel, when the King of heaven was born, an earthly king was troubled. For earthly greatness is brought to confusion when the might of heaven appears. But let us ask why it was that an Angel appeared to the shepherds in Judea when Christ was born; yet not an Angel but a star led the Magi from the East to adore Him.

Truly to the Jews, as rational beings, a rational creature, that is, an Angel, had to proclaim the good news; but the Gentiles, who knew not how to reason, were led to know the Lord not by a voice but by signs. Hence St. Paul ssys: Prophecies are given to believers, not to unbelievers; but signs are given to unbelievers, not to believers. And so here we read that prophecies were given to believers and not to unbelievers, and that signs were given not to those who believed but to those who believed not.

We must also take note that to these same Gentiles the Apostles preach our Redeemer when He had reached the perfect age; but when He was yet a babe and unable to speak, He is announced to the nations by a star. For right reason demands that when He had Himself begun to speak, He, Whom dumb elements proclaimed when as yet speechless, should be made known to us by speech. In all the signs that accompanied the Lord's birth or death let us consider how exceedingly hard of heart were those Jews, since neither prophecies nor miracles led them to recognize Him.

All the elements indeed bore witness to the coming of their Creator. Let me speak of them after the manner of men: The heavens knew that He was God for they sent a star forthwith. The sea knew Him and became solid under His feet. The earth knew Him for it trembled when He died. The sun knew Him and hid the rays of its light. The rocks and walls knew Him for they were rent at the time of His death. Hell knew Him and gave up the dead that were in it. And yet even now the hearts of the unbelieving Jews refuse to recognize Him as God whom all the senseless elements felt to be their Lord. But the Jews are harder than stones and will not be rent by repentance.

R. The kings of Tharsis and the islands shall offer presents: * The kings of the Arabians and of Saba shall bring gifts to the Lord God. V. All they from Saba shall come, bringing gold and frankincense. The kings of the Arabians. Glory. The kings of the Arabians.

✠ Continuation of the holy Gospel according to St. Matthew.—When Jesus was born in Bethlehem of Juda in the days of King Herod, behold there came wise men from the East to Jerusalem saying: Where is He that is born King of the Jews? For we have seen His star in the East and are come to adore Him. And King Herod hearing this was troubled and all Jerusalem with him. And assembling together all the chief priests and the scribes of the people, he inquired of them where Christ should be born. But they said to him: In Bethlehem of Juda. For so it is written by the Prophet: And thou Bethlehem, the land of Juda, art not the least among the princes of Juda: for out of thee shall come forth the Captain that shall rule My people Israel. Then Herod, privately calling the wise men, learned diligently of them the time of the star which had appeared to them and sending them into Bethlehem, said: Go and diligently inquire after the Child, and when you have found Him, bring me word again that I also may come and adore Him. Who having heard the king went their way. And behold the star, which they had seen in the East, went before them until it came and stood over where the Child was. And seeing the star, they rejoiced with exceeding great joy. And entering into the house, they found the Child with Mary His mother, *(here genuflect)* and falling down they adored Him. And having received an answer in sleep that they should not return to Herod, they went back another way into their own country.

LET US PRAY

O God, Who on this day by the guidance of a star didst reveal Thy only begotten Son to the Gentiles; mercifully grant that we, who already know Thee by faith, may be led to behold the beauty of Thy Majesty. Through the same Lord.

SECOND DAY WITHIN THE OCTAVE OF THE EPIPHANY

The reading of the holy Gospel according to St. Matthew

When Jesus was born in Bethlehem of Juda in the days of King Herod, behold, there came wise men from the East to Jerusalem, saying: Where is He that is born King of the Jews? And so forth.

Homily of St. Gregory, Pope

When Herod heard of the birth of our King, he had recourse to cunning and, lest he should be deprived of his earthly kingdom, he asks to be told where the Child may be found and pretends that he himself would like to come and worship Him. This he did so that if he could find Him he might put Him to death. But of what avail is the malice of man against the counsel of God? For it is written: There is no wisdom nor understanding nor counsel against the Lord. So the star that appeared to the Magi led them on; they found the newborn King and offered their gifts; then they were warned in a dream that they should not return to Herod. And thus it came about that Herod could not find Jesus when he sought Him. Is he not a type of all hypocrites who never deserve to find the Lord since they only pretend to seek Him?

Here we may remark that the Priscillianist heretics hold that every man is born under the influence of the stars and in confirmation of their error they bring forward this instance of a new star appearing when the Lord was born in the flesh; and this star, because it was then first seen, they look upon as influencing His destiny. But let us consider the words of the Gospel concerning this star: Until it came and stood over where the Child was; that is, the Child did not come to the star but the star came to the Child; and so we may say that the star was not the destiny of the Child but the Child was the destiny of the star.

But let not the faithful ever think or say that any such thing rules their destiny. For the life of man on this earth is subject to that Founder alone who created it. Neither was man made for the stars but the stars for man; and if we say that a star rules the destiny of man, we thereby declare that man is dependent on their ministry. Certainly when Jacob, coming out of the womb, took hold of his elder brother's heel with his hand, the elder could by no means have entirely come forth unless the younger had begun to come forth; and yet their lot in after-life was far from being the same though the mother brought them forth both at the same time and at the same moment.

THIRD DAY WITHIN THE OCTAVE
OF THE EPIPHANY

The reading of the holy Gospel
according to St. Matthew

When Jesus was born in Bethlehem of Juda in the days of King Herod, behold, there came wise men from the East to Jerusalem, saying: Where is He that is born King of the Jews? And so forth.

Homily of St. Gregory, Pope

The wise men brought gold, frankincense, and myrrh. Gold is a fitting gift for a king, incense is offered in sacrifice to God; with myrrh are embalmed the bodies of the dead. The Magi therefore, by their mystic gifts, proclaim Him whom they adore; they offer gold as to a king, incense as to God, and myrrh as to a mortal man. There are certain heretics who believe Him to be God but refuse to believe that He reigns over all. These indeed offer incense to Him but withhold the gold. Again there are others who look upon Him as King but not as God. These offer Him gold but keep back their incense.

And some there are who confess Him to be both God and King but deny that He took upon Himself our mortal flesh. These offer to Him both gold and incense but will not offer the myrrh of the mortal nature which He took upon Himself. But let us offer gold to our new-born Lord as confessing that He reigns over all; incense, as believing that He who appeared in time was God before all time; myrrh, as believing that He who cannot suffer in His Godhead was yet mortal in our flesh.

Gold, frankincense, and myrrh may also bear another meaning. For gold signifies wisdom as Solomon says: In the mouth of the wise abideth a treasure to be desired. But incense, which is burnt in God's honor, signifies the virtue of prayer as the Psalmist says: Let my prayer be directed as incense in Thy sight. Myrrh is indeed a figure of our bodily death; therefore holy Church says

of her laborers who strive for God even unto death:
My hands have dropped myrrh.

FOURTH DAY WITHIN THE OCTAVE
OF THE EPIPHANY

The reading of the holy Gospel
according to St. Matthew

When Jesus was born in Bethlehem of Juda in
the days of King Herod, behold, there came wise
men from the East to Jerusalem, saying: Where
is He that is born King of the Jews? And so forth.

Homily of St. Gregory, Pope

The wise men teach us a great lesson in that they
returned into their own country by another way.
By thus doing as they had been warned, they make
known to us what we too should do. Our country
is paradise and we are forbidden to return thither
along the same way by which we left it since we
now know Jesus. For we departed from our own
country by the way of pride, of disobedience, of
love of things which are seen, of tasting the forbidden food, but we must return thither by the way
of tears, of obedience, of despising things which
are seen, and of curbing the desires of the flesh.

Let us then return to our own country by another
way; and since we left the joys of paradise for the
sake of pleasure, we are bidden to regain them by
pain. And therefore, dearly beloved, we must ever

be fearful, ever on the watch, as we set before the eyes of our heart on the one side, our guilty deeds, on the other, the severity of the last judgment. Let us consider how severe a Judge is coming who even now threatens us unseen; who strikes terror into sinners and nevertheless still bears with them and delays to come quickly for this reason that when He does come, He may find less to condemn.

Let us expiate our sins with tears and, in the words of the Psalmist, let us come before His presence with thanksgiving. Let no appearance of pleasure deceive us; let no vain joy seduce us. For the Judge is at hand who said: Woe to you that now laugh; for you shall mourn and weep. Hence did Solomon say: Laughter shall be mingled with sorrow; and: mourning taketh hold of the end of joy. And again: Laughter I counted error and to mirth I said: Why art thou vainly deceived? And yet again: The heart of the wise is where there is mourning and the heart of fools where there is mirth.

FIFTH DAY WITHIN THE OCTAVE OF THE EPIPHANY

The reading of the holy Gospel
according to St. Matthew

When Jesus was born in Bethlehem of Juda in the days of King Herod, behold, there came wise men from the East to Jerusalem, saying: Where is He that is born King of the Jews? And so forth.

Homily of St. Jerome, Priest

We have seen His star in the East. The star rose in the East that the Jews might be put to shame when they heard of the birth of Christ from the Gentiles. That this star was to appear they knew from the prophecy of Balaam, whose successors they were. Read the book of Numbers. Guided by the star, the Magi are brought into Judea that the priests, having been asked by them where Christ was to be born, might not be able to plead ignorance of His coming.

But they said to him: In Bethlehem of Judea. This is a mistake of copyists. For I am of the opinion that what the Evangelist wrote in the original must have been: of Juda, as we read in the Hebrew text, and not of Judea. For what other Bethlehem is there in any other nation that this one should be described as of Judea for the sake of distinction? But he did well to write Bethlehem of Juda since there is another Bethlehem in Galilee. Read the book of Josue the son of Nun. Finally, the passage quoted from the prophecy of Micheas runs thus: And thou Bethlehem, the land of Juda.

And opening their treasures, they offered Him gifts: gold, frankincense and myrrh. Juvencus the Priest has excellently expressed the mysteries hidden under these gifts in one couplet: Frankincense, myrrh and gold they bring, as gifts to God made man, their king. And having received an answer in sleep that they should not return to Herod, they went back another way into their own country. They had offered gifts to the Lord and therefore they had received an answer, not from an angel but from the Lord Himself, by a privilege no less great than that of Joseph. And they went back another way: that they might not come into contact with the infidelity of the Jews.

SIXTH DAY WITHIN THE OCTAVE
OF THE EPIPHANY

The reading of the holy Gospel
according to St. Matthew

When Jesus was born in Bethlehem of Juda in the days of King Herod, behold, there came wise

men from the East to Jerusalem, saying: Where is
He that is born King of the Jews? And so forth.

Homily of St. Ambrose, Bishop

What are these gifts of true faith? Gold, as to
a king; incense, as to God; myrrh, as to a dead
man. For the first is a mark of royal dignity, the
second is a symbol of divine power, and the third
is a decent observance used in burial which does
not corrupt the body of the deceased but preserves
it. Let us who hear and read these things, my
brethren, also make similar gifts out of our treasures. For we have treasures, although in earthen
vessels. If therefore thou oughtest to admit that
this treasure is not from thyself but from Christ,
how much more art thou bound to confess that
what thou hast in Christ is not thine own, but His.

So the wise men offered gifts from their treasures. Would you know how well they were reward-
ed? They see the star: it disappears where Herod
is and is seen again where Christ is and shows the
way to Him. This star then is the way and the
way is Christ; because, according to the mystery of
the Incarnation, Christ is called a star: For a
star shall rise out of Jacob and a man shall spring
up from Israel. Indeed, where Christ is there is
the star also. He is Himself the bright and morning star. By His own light then He declares Himself.

Receive another proof. The Magi came by one way and returned by another. They had seen and had known Him; therefore they went back better off than they came. Now there are two ways: one which leads to destruction, another which leads to the kingdom. The way of sin leads to Herod; the other way is Christ and by this Way we return to our fatherland. For this life is an exile as it is written: My soul hath been long a sojourner.

SUNDAY WITHIN THE OCTAVE OF THE EPIPHANY

I Nocturn

From the First Epistle of blessed Paul the Apostle to the Corinthians, c. 1, 1 - 13

II Nocturn

Sermon of St. Leo, Pope

It is the right and reasonable duty of true piety, dearly beloved, on the days which bear witness to the works of divine mercy, to rejoice with the whole heart and to celebrate with all honor the things which have been wrought for our salvation: for the very law of recurring seasons calls us to such devout observance and has now brought before us this feast of the Epiphany, consecrated by the Lord's appearance soon after the day on which the Son of God, coeternal with the Father, was born of a Virgin.

Herein the providence of God has established a great safeguard to our faith so that, while the worship of the Savior's earliest infancy is repeated year by year, the origin of the true man's nature in Him might be attested by the original proofs themselves.

For this it is that makes the ungodly just; this it is that makes sinners into saints; to wit, the belief in the true Godhead, whereby being before all ages in the form of God He is equal to the Father: the Manhood, whereby in later days He is united to man in the form of a servant.

For the confirmation therefore of this faith, which was to be forearmed against all errors, it was a wondrous loving provision of the divine plan that a nation which dwelt in the far-off country of the East and was cunning in the art of reading the stars should receive the sign of that Infant's birth who was to reign over all Israel. For the unusual splendor of a bright new star appeared to the wise men and filled their minds with such wonder as they gazed upon its splendor that they did not think that they ought to neglect what was announced to them with such distinctness.

R. Be enlightened, be enlightened, O Jerusalem, for thy light is come: * And the glory of the Lord is risen upon thee. V. And the nations shall walk in thy light and kings in the brightness of thy rising. And the glory. Glory. And the glory.

III Nocturn

The reading of the holy Gospel
according to St. Luke

When Jesus was twelve years old, they going up to Jerusalem according to the custom of the feast and having fulfilled the days, when they returned, the Child Jesus remained in Jerusalem. And so forth.

Homily of St. Ambrose, Bishop

We read that when He was twelve years old the Lord began to dispute. The number of His years was the same as the number of the Apostles whom He afterwards sent forth to preach the Faith. He Who, as touching His Manhood, was filled with wisdom and grace from God, was not unmindful of the parents of the same Manhood, and after three days was pleased to be found in the Temple: thereby foreshadowing that after the three days of His victorious Passion, He Who had been reckoned with the dead would present Himself, living, to our faith in His heavenly Kingship and Divine Majesty.

How is it that you sought Me? Christ has two Generations: one from His Father, another from His Mother. That from His Father is His Eternal Generation as God the Son; that from His Mother is that whereby He came to work for us and minister to us. Therefore, those acts of His which are above nature, beyond His age, and different to His custom, proceeded not from the strength of His Manhood but from the power of His Godhead.

On another ocasion His Mother moves Him to work a miracle; here He answers her because she treats that which was of the Godhead as though it were of the Manhood. On this ocasion it is said that He was twelve years old but on the other He already had disciples. His mother had seen His wonders on the earlier occasion and had learnt from her Son to call on the mightier nature for a work of power.

And He came to Nazareth and was subject to them. For what is a teacher of virtue unless he fulfill the duty of affection? And do we marvel how He Who was subject to His Mother was about His Father's business? His subjection to His Mother proceeded not from weakness but from dutiful affection. Nevertheless, the false serpent lifts its head from its cruel lair and spits poison from its venomous breast. The heretic says that as the Son was sent by the Father, therefore the Father is greater than the Son and if the Father be greater than the Son, then the Son is less; yea, that He Who is sent hath of necessity need of some strengthening from outside Himself. He was subject to His Mother. Was He less than she? God forbid!

R.   The Holy Ghost appeared in the form of a
dove and the voice of the Father was heard: * This
is my beloved Son in Whom I am well pleased.
V.   The heavens were opened above Him and the
voice of the Father was heard.   This is.   Glory.
This is.

✠ Continuation of the holy Gospel according to
St. Luke.—When Jesus was twelve years old, they
were going up into Jerusalem according to the custom of the feast, and having fulfilled the days,
when they returned, the Child Jesus remained in
Jerusalem and His parents knew it not. And thinking that He was in the company, they came a day's
journey and sought Him among His kinsfolks and
acquaintance.   And not finding Him, they returned
into Jerusalem seeking Him.   And it came to pass
that after three days they found Him in the Temple,
sitting in the midst of the doctors, hearing them
and asking them questions.   And all that heard
Him were astonished at His wisdom and His answers.   And seeing Him they wondered.   And His
mother said to Him: Son, why hast Thou done so
to us?   Behold Thy father and I have sought Thee
sorrowing.   And He said to them: How is it that
you sought Me?   Did you not know that I must be
about My Father's business?   And they understood
not the word that He spoke unto them.   And He
went down with them and came to Nazareth and
was subject to them.   And His mother kept all

these words in her heart. And Jesus advanced in
wisdom and age and grace with God and men.

LET US PRAY

Receive, we beseech Thee, O Lord, by Thy heavenly goodness, the prayers of Thy people who pray
to Thee; that they may both see what must be done
and have the strength to perform the same.
Through our Lord.

OCTAVE DAY OF THE EPIPHANY

I Nocturn

*From the First Epistle of blessed Paul the Apostle
to the Corinthians, c. 1, 1 - 13*

Sermon of St. Gregory Nazianzen

I cannot restrain the transports of joy but I am
mentally elevated and deeply moved and forgetful
of my own meanness; I long and strive to follow
the great John in his office, or rather, service.
Though not like him a forerunner, yet I come from
the desert. Christ is enlightened, or rather He enlightens us with His own splendor; Christ is baptised; let us also go down with Him that with Him
we may likewise ascend.

John is baptising and Jesus draws nigh: perhaps
indeed that He may sanctify him by whom He was
baptised, but without doubt that He may bury the
old Adam in the waters. Above all, He comes to

sanctify the waters of the Jordan that as He was
spirit and flesh, so also the effect of that sanctification might be imparted to them who should be
baptised in the spirit and in the water. The Baptist suffers Him not; Jesus contends with him. I,
he says, have need to be baptised by Thee, says the
Lamp to the Sun, says the Voice to the Word.

Jesus comes up out of the water leading forth
and upraising the world which in a sense had been
submerged: and He beholds the heavens which
Adam had closed to himself and to us his posterity,
not merely cleft but opened, just as Paradise had
been closed with a fiery sword.

The Holy Ghost bears witness to Him Who is
like unto Himself. Testimony cometh down from
heaven for from thence was He to whom testimony
was given.

R. All they from Saba shall come bringing gold
and frankincense and showing forth praise to the
Lord, * Alleluia, alleluia, alleluia. V. The kings
of Tharsis and the islands shall offer presents, the
kings of the Arabians and of Saba shall bring gifts.
Alleluia. Glory. Alleluia.

III Nocturn

The reading of the holy Gospel
according to St. John

At that time: John saw Jesus coming to him
and he saith: Behold the Lamb of God, behold
Him who taketh away the sins of the world. And
so forth.

Homily of St. Augustine, Bishop

Before the Lord came to be baptised by John in
the Jordan, John already knew Him as we perceive
by his words: Comest Thou to me to be baptised?
Rather ought I to be baptised by Thee. But behold, he knew the Lord, he knew the Son of God.
How do we prove that he already knew that it was
He who should baptise with the Holy Ghost? Before the Lord came to the river when many hastened to John to be baptised, he said to them: I indeed baptise you with water; but He that cometh
after me is greater than I, the latchet of whose
shoe I am not worthy to loose; He shall baptise you
with the Holy Ghost and with fire. This, then, he
already knew.

What, therefore, did John learn from the appearing of the dove, lest he should seem afterwards to
have been a liar (which God forbid that we should
think), unless this, that there was a certain peculiar attribute in Christ reaching into the future,

so that although many ministers were to baptise, some of them just, some unjust, yet the holiness of baptism was to be attributed to Him only upon whom the dove descended, of whom it is said: It is He who baptises in the Holy Ghost. Whether Peter baptises, or Paul, or Judas, it is Christ who baptises.

For if the holiness of baptism depended on the degree of merit in him who baptised, then baptism would not have the same merit in all cases and anyone might think that he had received something better if he had received it from a better minister. Now the saints themselves (by whom are meant, brethren, the good men who belong to the dove, who have part and lot in the city of Jerusalem, the good themselves in the Church, of whom the Apostle says: The Lord knoweth who are His) have not the same graces, they are not all equal in merit.

Some are holier than others, some better than others. If then, for example, one person is baptised by a just and holy man and another by a man of less merit before God, of a lower rank, of less strict continence, of a less holy life, and yet both receive the same thing, how can this be, unless it is Christ who baptises?

R. The star which the Magi had seen in the East went before them until they came to the place where the Child was: * And when they saw it, they rejoiced with great joy. V. And entering into the house, they found the Child with Mary His mother, and falling down they adored Him. And. Glory. And.

✠ Continuation of the holy Gospel according to St. John.—At that time: John saw Jesus coming to him and he saith: Behold the Lamb of God, behold Him who taketh away the sin of the world. This is He of whom I said: After me there cometh a man who is preferred before me because He was before me. And I knew Him not, but that He may be made manifest in Israel, therefore am I come baptising with water. And John gave testimony saying: I saw the Spirit coming down as a dove from heaven and He remained upon Him. And I knew Him not: but He who sent me to baptise with water said to me: He upon whom thou shalt see the Spirit descending and remaining upon Him, He it is that baptiseth with the Holy Ghost. And I saw and I gave testimony that this is the Son of God.

LET US PRAY

O God, whose only begotten Son appeared in the substance of our flesh, grant, we beseech Thee, that we may be inwardly reformed by Him whom we recognize to have been outwardly like unto ourselves: Who liveth and reigneth with Thee.

II SUNDAY AFTER THE EPIPHANY

I Nocturn

*From the second Epistle of blessed Paul the Apostle
to the Corinthians, c. 1, 1 - 14*

II Nocturn
Sermon of St. John Chrysostom

As I listen intently to the reading of St. Paul's Epistles, often two or three or four times a week, whenever we commemorate the holy martyrs, I am filled with joy, delighting in the sound of that spiritual trumpet. And as I recognize the voice of a friend, I am roused and enkindled with love so that I almost seem to see him present and to hear him speaking. But nevertheless I grieve and am troubled that all do not know this great man as he deserves to be known. Indeed, many are so ignorant as not even to know how many Epistles he wrote. But this ignorance is not due to a want of intelligence on their part but because they will not carefully study the writings of this blessed man.

For what we know, if we know anything, we do not know it owing to any superlative talent or penetration but, being strongly drawn towards this great man, we never cease from reading his works. For it is so that those who love anyone usually know better than others what he whom they love has done because they take the trouble to learn all about him. The blessed Paul himself shows that this is so when he says to the Philippians: As it is meet for me to think this for you all: for that I have you in my heart and in my bands and in the defence and confirmation of the Gospel.

And so if you also will diligently attend to the reading, you will have no need of other instruction. Most true are those words of Christ: Seek and you shall find; knock and it shall be opened unto you.

For the rest, since many of those who are assembled here are charged with the care of a wife and providing for a family and the bringing up of children and therefore cannot devote themselves wholly to this study, yet let them at least bestir themselves to receive what others have gathered, showing as much eagerness in listening to what is said about him as in acquiring wealth. For though it is unseemly to demand from you no more than this, yet it is to be wished that you do this at least.

R. Thou hast made known to me, O Lord, the ways of life: * Thou shalt fill me with joy with Thy countenance: at Thy right hand are delights forevermore. V. Thou art He that will restore my inheritance unto me. Thou shalt fill. Glory. Thou shalt fill.

III Nocturn

The reading of the holy Gospel
according to St. John

At that time: There was a marriage in Cana of Galilee: and the mother of Jesus was there. And Jesus also was invited, and His disciples, to the marriage. And so forth.

Homily of St. Augustine, Bishop

Apart from any mystical meaning, the Lord, by the very fact of His being invited and going to the marriage, willed to show clearly that He was the author of marriage. For those of whom the Apostle spoke who forbade to marry and declared that marriage was a wicked thing and that the devil was the author of it were yet to come. And yet we read in the Gospel that the same Lord, being asked whether it was lawful for a man to put away his wife for any cause, answered that it was not lawful except for the cause of fornication. And in His reply, if you remember, He says: What God hath joined together, let not man put asunder.

They who are well instructed in the Catholic faith know that God is the author of marriage; and as the marriage-bond is from God, so divorce is from the devil. But it is lawful to put away a wife on account of adultery because she who has been unfaithful to her husband has herself first refused to be a wife.

Those women who have vowed their virginity to God and thus are in a higher degree of honor and sanctity in the Church are not deprived of marriage, for they have part in the marriage of the whole Church in which Christ Himself is the Bridegroom.

Thus our Lord, being invited, came to the marriage that conjugal chastity might be strengthened and the sacrament of matrimony clearly displayed; for the bridegroom in that marriage, to whom it was said: Thou hast kept the good wine until now, represented the person of the Lord. For Christ has kept the good wine, that is, the Gospel, until these latter days.

R. The earth is the Lord's and the fulness thereof: * The world and all they that dwell therein. V. He hath founded it upon the sea and hath prepared it upon the rivers. The world. Glory. The world.

✠ Continuation of the holy Gospel according to St. John.—At that time: there was a marriage in Cana of Galilee: and the mother of Jesus was there. And Jesus also was invited, and His disciples, to the marriage. And the wine failing, the mother of Jesus saith to Him: They have no wine. And Jesus saith to her: Woman, what is that to Me and to thee? My hour is not yet come. His mother saith to the waiters: Whatsoever He shall say to

you, do ye. Now there were set there six water-
pots of stone, according to the manner of the purifying of the Jews, containing two or three measures
apiece. Jesus saith to them: Fill the water-pots
with water. And they filled them up to the brim.
And Jesus saith to them: Draw out now and carry
to the chief steward of the feast. And they carried
it. And when the chief steward had tasted the
water made wine, and knew not whence it was, but
the waiters knew who had drawn the water: the
chief steward calleth the bridegroom and saith to
him: Every man at first setteth forth good wine:
and when men have well drunk, then that which is
worse: but thou hast kept the good wine until now.
This beginning of miracles did Jesus in Cana of
Galilee and manifested His glory; and His disciples believed in Him.

LET US PRAY

O almighty and eternal God, Who dost govern
all things both in heaven and upon the earth; mercifully hear the prayers of Thy people and grant
the gift of Thy peace in our times. Through our
Lord.

III SUNDAY AFTER THE EPIPHANY

I Nocturn

*From the Epistle of blessed Paul the Apostle to the
Galatians, c. 1, 1 - 14*

II Nocturn

From the Commentary on the Epistle to the
Galatians of St. Augustine, Bishop

The reason why the Apostle wrote to the Galatians was this: to explain how the grace of God
had so worked in them that they were no longer
under the law. For when the grace of the Gospel
had been preached to them, there were not wanting
some of the circumcision who, although Christians
in name, did not yet appreciate that great benefit
of grace. These still desired to bear the burdens
of the law which the Lord God had laid not upon
such as follow after righteousness but upon such
as serve sin. The law itself was righteous but was
given to the unrighteous to make manifest their
sins, not to take them away. For sin is taken
away by the grace of faith alone which works by
love.

Those of the circumcision wished that the Galatians, who had received this grace, should submit
to the yoke of the law and they declared that the
Gospel would profit them nothing unless they were

circumcised and kept the other carnal observances of the Jewish rite.

The Galatians therefore began to suspect the Apostle Paul, who had preached the Gospel to them, of not holding to the teaching of the other Apostles, who compelled the Gentiles to observe the Jewish law.

This very question is discussed in the Epistle to the Romans also, but with this difference, that there the Apostle put an end to the contention and settled the dispute which had arisen between the Jewish and Gentile converts. The Jews thought that the Gospel had been given to them in reward for their observance of the law and they were unwilling that it should be given to the uncircumcised who, so they thought, had done nothing to deserve it; whereas the latter loudly declared that they were superior to the Jews, who had put to death the Lord. But in this Epistle St. Paul writes to those who were already excited by the authority of those Jews who were circumcised and who wished to compel the observance of the law.

R. O Lord, rebuke me not in Thine anger nor chastise me in Thy wrath: * Have mercy upon me, O Lord, for I am weak. V. Fear and trembling are come upon me and darkness hath covered me. Have mercy. Glory. Have mercy.

III Nocturn

The reading of the holy Gospel
according to St. Matthew

At that time: When Jesus was come down from
the mountain, great multitudes followed Him: and
behold a leper came and adored Him. And so forth.

Homily of St. Jerome, Priest

When the Lord came down from the mountain,
He was met by crowds of people who had not been
able to follow Him to the heights. First there
came a leper; on account of his disease he had not
been near enough to hear the long sermon of the
Savior on the mount. Take notice that he is the
first whose cure is specially mentioned; the second
is the centurion's servant; the third is Peter's
wife's mother who was sick of a fever at Capharnaum; in the fourth place are those who were brought
to Him possessed with devils from whom He cast
out the spirits by His word, and at the same time
He healed all that were sick.

And behold a leper came and adored Him saying (It is right that, after the preaching and teaching of our Lord, an occasion should present itself
for a sign that the power of a miracle might confirm the truth of what He had just said): Lord,
if Thou wilt, Thou canst make me clean. He prays
the Lord to be willing; therefore he doubts not
His power.

And Jesus stretching forth His hand, touched him saying: I will: Be thou made clean. As soon as the Lord put forth His hand, the leprosy departed. Observe how humble and free from boasting is the Lord's answer. The leper said: If Thou wilt; the Lord replied: I will. To the leper's assertion: Thou canst make me clean, the Lord answers and says: Be thou made clean. These words are not therefore to be joined together and read thus: I will to cleanse, as many Latins think; but they are to be read separately; first the Lord says: I will; then He commands: Be thou made clean.

And Jesus said to him: See thou tell no man. Truly, what need was there to publish abroad what his body showed to all? But go, show thyself to the priest. For several reasons He sent him to the priest; firstly, because of His humility that He might show reverence for the priests. For the law commanded that such as were cleansed from leprosy should offer gifts to the priests. Secondly, that when the priests saw the leper cleansed, they might either believe in the Savior or refuse to believe. If they believed, they would be saved; if they believed not, they would have no excuse. And lastly, He did this lest He might seem to break the law, an accusation so often brought against Him.

R. Two Seraphim cried one to another: * Holy holy, holy is the Lord God of hosts: All the earth

is full of His glory.   V.   There are three who give
testimony in heaven: the Father, the Word, and
the Holy Ghost: and these three are one.   Holy.
Glory.   Holy.

✠ Continuation of the holy Gospel according to
St. Matthew.—At that time: When Jesus was come
down from the mountain, great multitudes followed Him: and behold a leper came and adored Him
saying: Lord, if Thou wilt, Thou canst make me
clean.   And Jesus stretching forth His hand, touched him saying: I will.   Be thou made clean.   And
forthwith his leprosy was cleansed.   And Jesus
saith to him: See, thou tell no man: but go, show
thyself to the priest and offer the gift which Moses
commanded for a testimony unto them.   And when
He had entered into Capharnaum, there came to
Him a certain centurion beseeching Him and saying: Lord, my servant lieth at home sick of the
palsy and is grievously tormented.   And Jesus saith
to him: I will come and heal him.   And the centurion making answer said: Lord, I am not worthy
that Thou shouldst enter under my roof: but only
say the word and my servant shall be healed.   For
I also am a man subject to authority, having under
me soldiers; and I say to this: Go, and he goeth;
and to another: Come, and he cometh; and to my
servant: Do this, and he doeth it.   And Jesus hearing this marvelled and said to them that followed
Him: Amen I say to you, I have not found so great

faith in Israel. And I say to you that many shall
come from the east and the west and shall sit down
with Abraham and Isaac and Jacob in the kingdom
of heaven: but the children of the kingdom shall be
cast out into the exterior darkness: there shall be
weeping and gnashing of teeth. And Jesus said
to the centurion: Go, and as thou hast believed, so
be it done to thee. And the servant was healed at
the same hour.

LET US PRAY

O almighty and eternal God, mercifully behold
our weakness and extend the right hand of Thy
Majesty to protect us. Through our Lord.

IV SUNDAY AFTER THE EPIPHANY

I Nocturn

From the Epistle of blessed Paul the Apostle to the
Philippians, c. 1, 1 - 18

II Nocturn

From the Book of Morals of St. Gregory, Pope

We satisfy the body with food lest it should become weak and fail; we weaken it with abstinence
lest, being overnourished, it should importune us;
we arouse it by movement lest it should be destroyed by the rust of laziness; but very soon we stand
still again lest in its very activity it should faint.

We cover it with garments lest the cold should harm it; and we cast off these garments lest the heat should consume it.

Among all these contraries, expending so much care in humoring the body so as to help it to bear up against the pressing weight of weakness and decay, what do we do but pander to all that which must perish? Well, therefore, does Paul say: For the creature was made subject to vanity, not willingly, but by reason of him that made it subject, in hope. Because the creature also itself shall be delivered from the servitude of corruption into the liberty of the glory of the children of God.

The creature was not made subject to vanity willingly: for when man, of his own will, abandoned the state of unchangeableness in which he was born, the just sentence of death weighed heavily upon him, and against his will he became subject to the corruption of change. But the creature itself shall be delivered from the servitude of corruption when it shall rise again incorruptible and be taken up into the glory of the children of God.

Here, then, the elect are encompassed with miseries, being still subject to the penalty of corruption; but when we shall have put off this corruptible flesh, we shall be loosed from these bonds in which we are at present held fast. For though we long to appear before God, we are still entangled, as it were, in the net of this mortal body. Rightly, therefore, are we called prisoners, since we are not yet free to go to God as we desire; and well might Paul cry out, yearning as he did after things eternal while still bearing the burden of his corruptible body: I desire to be dissolved and to be with Christ. For he would not have sought to be loosed unless he had felt himself undoubtedly a captive.

R. O God, who sittest upon the throne and judgest justice, be Thou the refuge of the poor in tribulation: * For Thou alone considerest labor and sorrow. V. To Thee is the poor man left, Thou wilt be a helper to the orphan. For Thou. Glory. For Thou.

III Nocturn

The reading of the holy Gospel according to St. Matthew

At that time: When Jesus entered into the boat, His disciples followed Him: and behold a great tempest arose in the sea, so that the boat was covered with waves, but He was asleep. And so forth.

Homily of St. Jerome, Priest

The Lord did the fifth sign when, departing from Capharnaum, He commanded the winds and the sea. The sixth was when, in the country of the Gerasenes, He gave the devils power over the swine. The seventh, when, coming into His own city, He cured the man sick of the palsy, lying on a bed. The first paralytic whom He cured was the centurion's servant.

But He was asleep: and they came to Him and awakened Him saying: Lord, save us. We find a type of this sign in the book of Jonas, for when the others were in danger, he was safe, and he fell asleep and was awakened. Then ordering those who had awakened him to throw him into the sea, he delivered them by the mystery of his own suffering.

Then rising up, the Lord commanded the winds and the sea. From these words we understand that all things created recognize their Creator; for these things felt the power of Him who rebuked and commanded them. Now these things, which pay no heed to us, obeyed Him not because they were endowed with life, as the heretics wrongly imagine, but as discerning the majesty of their Maker.

But the men wondered, saying: What manner of man is this, for the winds and the sea obey Him? It was not His disciples who wondered, but the sailors and others that were in the ship. If anyone wishes to dispute this point and to maintain that only the disciples wondered, we shall answer that those who did not yet know the power of the Savior were rightly called merely men.

R. I will love Thee, O Lord, my strength: * The Lord is my support and my refuge. V. My deliverer, my God, my helper. The Lord. Glory. The Lord.

✠ Continuation of the holy Gospel according to St. Matthew.—At that time: When Jesus entered into the boat, His disciples followed Him: and behold a great tempest arose in the sea, so that the boat was covered with the waves, but He was asleep. And His disciples came to Him and awakened Him saying: Lord, save us, we perish. And Jesus saith to them: Why are you fearful, O ye of little faith? Then rising up, He commanded the winds and the sea, and there came a great calm. But the men wondered, saying: What manner of man is this, for the winds and the sea obey Him?

LET US PRAY

O God, Who dost know that we who live amid such great dangers are unable to stand firm because of our human frailty, grant us health of soul and body that aided by Thy grace, we may overcome the things we suffer for our sins. Through our Lord.

V SUNDAY AFTER THE EPIPHANY

I Nocturn

*From the Epistle of blessed Paul the Apostle to
Timothy, c. 1, 1 - 16*

II Nocturn

Sermon of St. Augustine, Bishop

This is a saying made for man and worthy of all
acceptation that Christ Jesus came into the world
to save sinners. Listen to the Gospel: The Son of
man is come to seek and to save that which is lost.
If man had not been lost, the Son of man would
not have come. Man then was lost; God came, being made man, and man was found. Man had perished by his own free-will; the God-man came by
the grace which was to set man free.

Do you ask how free-will can do evil? Call to
mind a sinner. Do you ask what God made man
can do to help him? Consider that in Him is the
grace that sets man free. What the will of man
can do, when, ruled by pride it tries to avoid evil
without the help of God, could never be better or
more clearly shown than in the first man.

Behold, the first man perished, and where would
he have been if the second man had not come? Because he who was lost was a man, therefore He who
came to save him was made man; that was why we

said it was a saying made for man. And neither
does the sweetness of grace and the generosity of
God's almightiness anywhere appear so clearly as
in the man Christ Jesus, mediator between God and
man.

For what do we say, my brethren? I speak to
those brought up in the Catholic faith as well as
to those who have been won to Catholic peace. We
know and we hold that the mediator between God
and men, the man Christ Jesus, inasmuch as He
was man, was of the same nature as we are. For
our flesh is not of another nature than His flesh;
nor is our soul of another nature than His soul. He
took upon Himself this nature which He had determined to save.

R. The Lord is at my right hand that I be not
moved: * Therefore my heart hath been glad and
my tongue hath rejoiced. V. The Lord is the portion of my inheritance and of my cup. Therefore.
Glory. Therefore.

III Nocturn

The reading of the holy Gospel
according to St. Matthew

At that time: Jesus spoke this parable to the
multitudes: The kingdom of heaven is likened to
a man that sowed good seed in his field. And so
forth.

Homily of St. Augustine, Bishop

When they who were set over the Church grew careless, or when the Apostles slept the sleep of death, the devil came and oversowed those whom the Lord designates as wicked children. But, you ask, are these heretics, or Catholics living bad lives? For even heretics might be called the children of the wicked one, who, although they have sprung up from the seed of the Gospel and have been begotten in the name of Christ, have turned aside to false doctrines through listening to erroneous opinions.

When it is said that they were sown among the wheat, it would seem that only those are meant who are of the same communion with us. Yet since the Lord interpreted this field as signifying, not the Church, but the world, the cockle may well be understood to mean heretics because in this world they are mingled with the good, not in the fellowship of the one true Church or of the one faith, but only as sharing the name of Christian.

But the wicked who are of the same faith are to be considered as straw rather than cockle; for the straw grows up together with the wheat and has one common root. By the net in which were gathered together both good and bad fish, bad Catholics may reasonably be understood.

For, on the one hand, the sea is a more fitting symbol of the world; and, on the other hand, the net seems to point to the communion of one faith or of one Church. The difference between heretics and bad Catholics is that the former believe false doctrine, while the latter, though believing aright, do not live according to their faith.

R. To Thee, O Lord, have I lifted up my soul: * In Thee, O my God, I put my trust, let me not be ashamed. V. Keep Thou my soul and deliver me. In Thee. Glory. In Thee.

✠ Continuation of the holy Gospel according to St. Matthew.—At that time: Jesus spoke this parable to the multitudes: The kingdom of heaven is likened to a man that sowed good seed in his field. But while the men were asleep, his enemy came and oversowed cockle among the wheat and went his way. And when the blade was sprung up and had brought forth fruit, then appeared also the cockle. And the servants of the goodman of the house coming, said to him: Sir, didst thou not sow good seed in thy field? Whence then hath it cockle? And he said to them: An enemy hath done this. And the servants said to him: Wilt thou that we go and gather it up? and he said: No, lest perhaps, gathering up the cockle, you root up the wheat also together with it. Suffer both to grow until the harvest, and in the time of harvest I will say to the reapers: Gather up first the cockle and bind it into bundles to burn, but the wheat gather ye into my barn.

LET US PRAY

Protect Thy family, we beseech Thee, O Lord, by Thy constant goodness and care, that as it confides entirely in the hope of Thy heavenly grace, it may always be strengthened by Thy protection. Through our Lord.

VI SUNDAY AFTER THE EPIPHANY

I Nocturn

From the Epistle of blessed Paul the Apostle to the Hebrews, c. 1, 1 - 14

II Nocturn

Sermon of St. Athanasius, Bishop

If the heretics had but known the person, the matter, and the time of which the Apostle spoke, they would never have behaved so wickedly and foolishly towards Christ as to attribute human qualities to the Godhead. This will easily be seen if thou takest the beginning of the Lesson and go through it carefully a second time. The Apostle says: God, who at sundry times and in divers manners, spoke in times past to the fathers by the prophets, last of all, in these days hath spoken to us by His Son.

And a little further on: making purgation of sins, He sitteth on the right hand of the majesty on high: being made so much better than the angels as He hath inherited a more excellent name than they. The Apostle here makes mention especially of the time wherein God has spoken to us by His Son, when He made purgation of sins. But when did He speak to us by His Son, or when was purgation of sins made, or when was He born as man, if not after the Prophets, and in these last days?

The Apostle, when about to speak of the human dispensation of the Word and of these last days, naturally mentions that God had not been silent in times past but had spoken by the Prophets; and after the Prophets had fulfilled their office and the law had been given by the ministry of Angels, the Son also came down to us and entered on His ministry. Then at last the Apostle finds himself obliged to add: Being made so much better than the angels: wishing to show that as the Son was greater than a servant, so the ministry of the Son must have been better than the ministry and office of servants.

The Apostle, therefore, wishing to make a distinction between the ministry of the old law and that of the new law, uses great liberty in writing and speaking to the Jews. For this reason he was not speaking generally nor making use of a comparison, properly so called, when he said that He was greater and more worthy of honor; lest any should understand these words as meaning that

they and He were of the same nature and possessed
of similar qualities; but to this end he said that
He was better, in order to point out the difference
between the nature of the Son and that of all created things.

R. Mercy and judgment I will sing unto Thee,
O Lord: * I will sing and I will understand in the
unspotted way when Thou shalt come unto me. V.
I have walked in the innocence of my heart, in the
midst of my house. I will sing. Glory. I will sing.

III Nocturn

The reading of the holy Gospel
according to St. Matthew

At that time: Jesus spoke this parable to the
multitudes: The kingdom of heaven is like to a
grain of mustard-seed, which a man took and sowed
in his field. And so forth.

Homily of St. Jerome, Priest

The kingdom of heaven is the preaching of the
Gospel and the knowledge of the Scriptures which
leads to life; that kingdom concerning which it was
said to the Jews: The kingdom of God shall be
taken from you and shall be given to a nation yielding the fruits thereof. Therefore is this kingdom
like to a grain of mustard-seed which a man took
and sowed in his field.

By the man that sowed it in his field, many understand the Savior because He sows seed in the souls of them that believe.   Others understand it as of a man sowing in his own field, that is, in himself and in his own heart.   Who is this sower but our own mind and soul which, receiving the grain of preaching, nourishes that seed and, in the moisture of faith, makes it germinate in the soil of our breast?

The preaching of the Gospel is the simplest of all forms of teaching.   When a man preaches that God became man, that Christ died, and the shame of the cross, he is scarcely believed.   Compare this teaching with the doctrines of the philosophers, with their books, with the splendor of their eloquence and the style of their phrases, and you will see that the seed of the Gospel is the least of all seeds.

But when those other seeds grow up, there is nothing biting, nothing lively, nothing vigorous about them, but they spring up all drooping, fading and tender, into herbs and grass which quickly dry up and wither.   But this preaching, which seemed so insignificant in the beginning, when it shall have been sown in the soul of the believer or in the whole world, does not grow up into a herb but becomes a tree; so that the birds of heaven (by which we must understand the souls of the faithful, or the heavenly powers devoted to the service of God) come and lodge in its branches. I think that the branches of the Gospel-tree which have sprung from the grain of mustard are the various truths of religion which afford rest to these birds of which we have been speaking.

R. The Lord hath set my feet upon a rock and God hath directed my steps: * And He hath put a new song into my mouth. V. He hath heard my prayers: and hath brought me out of the pit of misery. And He hath. Glory. And He hath.

✠ Continuation of the holy Gospel according to St. Matthew.—At that time: Jesus spoke to the multitudes this parable: The kingdom of heaven is like to a grain of mustard seed, which a man took and sowed in his field: which is the least indeed of all seeds: but when it is grown up, it is greater than all herbs and becometh a tree, so that the birds of the air come and dwell in the branches thereof. Another parable He spoke to them: The kingdom of heaven is like to leaven, which a woman took and hid in three measures of meal, until the whole was leavened. All these things Jesus spoke in parables to the multitudes: and without parables He did not speak to them: that it might be fulfilled which was spoken by the Prophet, saying: I will open my mouth in parables, I will utter things hidden from the foundation of the world.

LET US PRAY

Grant, we beseech Thee, O almighty God, that always considering what is right, we may always please Thee by our words and actions. Through our Lord

SEPTUAGESIMA SUNDAY

I Nocturn

From the Book of Genesis, c. 1, 1 - 26

II Nocturn

From the Enchiridion of St. Augustine, Bishop

The Lord threatened man with the punishment of death if he should sin. Thus, while endowing him with free-will, He kept control over him by the fear of destruction. And so He placed him in the paradise of happiness, as it were, in a sheltered nook of life, whence he might have attained to a better life if he had remained righteous.

But man sinned and was driven out of paradise; and moreover he entailed upon his offspring the penalty of death and damnation, for, by his own sin, he had tainted it also at its very root. His wife too who had caused him to sin shared his sentence; so that all who were descended from them through fleshly desire, in which the penalty of disobedience is likewise paid, inherited original sin whereby they are drawn on through divers errors and sorrows to that last unending torment which they share with the fallen angels, their corrupters, masters, and partakers of their doom.

Thus by one man sin entered into the world, and by sin death; and so death passed upon all men, in whom all have sinned. By the world, the Apostle of course means in this place the whole human race. Thus, then, did matters stand. The whole mass of mankind was doomed; it lay in misery, or rather, wallowed in it and quickly fell from bad to worse and, together with that part of the angels who had sinned, it suffered the punishment it had merited by its impious apostacy.

For whatever the wicked willingly do through blind and unbridled lust, as well as the manifest or secret punishments which they suffer unwillingly, must evidently concern the just anger of God. The Creator in His goodness does not cease to minister even to the wicked angels life and vital power (which if He withdrew they would perish). As for men, although they are descended from a corrupt and doomed stock, He ceases not to give form and life to their seed, to fashion their members throughout the various periods of life and in various parts of the earth, to quicken their senses and to provide them with sustenance. For He preferred to draw good out of evil rather than not to permit evil.

R. In the beginning God created heaven and earth, and the Spirit of God moved over the waters:

* And God saw all things that He had made, and they were very good. V. So the heavens and the earth were finished and all the furniture of them. And God. Glory. And God.

III Nocturn

The reading of the holy Gospel according to St. Matthew

At that time: Jesus spoke to His disciples this parable: The kingdom of heaven is like to a householder who went out early in the morning to hire laborers into his vineyard. And so forth.

Homily of St. Gregory, Pope

The kingdom of heaven is compared to a householder who hired laborers to work in his vineyard. Who indeed is more justly likened to a householder than our Maker? He rules over those He has made and, as a lord is master of the servants in his own house, so He is master of His chosen ones in this world. His vine is evidently the universal Church which has sent forth as many branches, so to speak, as it has produced Saints, from the just Abel even to the last of the elect that shall be born unto the end of the world.

This householder, therefore, hired laborers to work in his vineyard early in the morning and again during the day at the third, sixth, ninth and eleventh hours; for from the beginning to the end of the world He does not cease to gather together preachers for the instruction of the faithful. The morning of the world was from Adam to Noe; the third hour, from Noe to Abraham; the sixth hour, from Abraham to Moses; the ninth hour, from Moses to the coming of the Lord; the eleventh, from the Lord's coming to the end of the world. At the eleventh hour the holy Apostles were sent to preach and, though coming late, they received full wages.

Therefore, for the instruction of His people, that is, for the cultivation of His vineyard, the Lord never at any time ceased to send laborers. First by the Fathers, then by the Doctors of the law and the Prophets, and last of all by the Apostles, He has striven to ennoble the conduct of His people, as if laboring at the cultivation of a vineyard by means of workmen; although anyone who joined right faith to the preaching of good deeds was in some degree and measure a laborer in His vineyard.

The workmen of the early morning and of the third, sixth, and ninth hours signify the ancient Hebrew people, that chosen race which from the very beginning of the world strove to worship God with true faith and thus did not fail to work in His vineyard. But at the eleventh hour the Gentiles are called and to them it is said: Why stand you here all the day idle?

R. Where is thy brother Abel? said the Lord to Cain. I know not, Lord, am I my brother's keeper? And He said to him: What hast thou done? * Behold the voice of thy brother Abel's blood crieth to Me from the earth. V. Cursed shalt thou be upon the earth which hath opened her mouth and received the blood of thy brother at thy hand. Behold. Glory. Behold.

✠ Continuation of the holy Gospel according to St. Matthew.—At that time: Jesus spoke to His disciples this parable: The kingdom of heaven is like to a householder who went out early in the morning to hire laborers into his vineyard. And having agreed with the laborers for a penny a day, he sent them into his vineyard. And going out about the third hour, he saw others standing in the market place idle and he said to them: Go you also into my vineyard, and I will give you what shall be just. And they went their way. And again he went out about the sixth and ninth hour and did in like manner. But about the eleventh hour he went out and found others standing, and he saith to them: Why stand you here all the day idle? They say to him: Because no man hath hired us. He saith to them: Go you also into my vineyard. And when evening was come, the lord of the vineyard saith to his steward: Call the laborers and pay them their hire, beginning from the last even to the first. When therefore they were come that

came about the eleventh hour, they received every
man a penny. But when the first also came, they
thought that they should receive more: and they
also received every man a penny. And receiving
it they murmured against the master of the house,
saying: These last have worked but one hour, and
thou hast made them equal to us that have borne
the burden of the day and the heats. But he answering said to one of them: Friend, I do thee no
wrong: didst thou not agree with me for a penny?
Take what is thine and go thy way: I will also
give to this last even as to thee. Or, is it not lawful for me to do what I will? Is thy eye evil because I am good? So shall the last be first, and
the first, last. For many are called, but few are
chosen.

LET US PRAY

Graciously hear, we beseech Thee, O Lord, the
prayers of Thy people, that we who justly suffer
for our sins, may be delivered for the glory of Thy
Name. Through our Lord.

SEXAGESIMA SUNDAY

I Nocturn

From the Book of Genesis, c. 5, 31; 6, 1 - 15

II Nocturn

From the book on Noe and the Ark
by St. Ambrose, Bishop

Thou readest that the Lord was angry. He did indeed know that man could not be without sin, placed as he was on earth and having a body (for the earth is a place of temptation, and the flesh is a bait for corruption). Yet man had a mind capable of reason and a soul with power to control the body and yet, without any reflection, he hastened to his fall from which he was unwilling to rise.

The thoughts of God are not as those of man; He does not follow after any new modes of thought nor does He grow angry like an unstable man. Therefore these things are to be read in order to express the grievousness of our sins whereby we have merited the divine wrath. When even God, who by His nature cannot be moved to anger, appears to be provoked to wrath, then we perceive to what an extent wickedness has increased.

Moreover, God threatened that He would destroy man. I will destroy, He said, everything, from man even to beasts, from creeping things even to the fowls of the air. What harm had the irrational creatures done? They had been made for man and, when man was destroyed, it followed that they too must share the same fate because they were no longer of any use. But there is a deeper meaning in this. Man is a mind capable of reason, for man is defined as a rational animal, living, yet subject to death. When, therefore, the highest power of man is gone, his every sense goes with it because there is nothing left to be saved when that power which is the basis of salvation is lost.

But in condemnation of the rest of men and to manifest the divine mercy, Noe is said to have found grace before God. We learn also that the sin of others does not cast its shadow on the just man when Noe himself is preserved to be the ancestor of the whole human race. He is praised, not for the nobility of his birth, but for his just and holy life. The descendants of a man of proved virtue inherit his virtue for, as men beget men, so souls beget virtues. A family is illustrious for the glory of its race but the comeliness of a soul is the luster of its virtue.

R. I will set my bow in the clouds, said the Lord to Noe: * And I will remember My covenant which I made with you. V. And when I shall cover the sky with clouds, my bow shall appear in the clouds. And I will. Glory. And I will.

III Nocturn

The reading of the holy Gospel
according to St. Luke

At that time: When a very great multitude was gathered together and hastened out of the cities unto Jesus, He spoke by a similitude: The sower went out to sow his seed. And so forth.

Homily of St. Gregory, Pope

Dearly beloved brethren, the reading from the holy Gospel which you have just heard needs not explanation, but exhortation to follow it. For what Truth Itself has explained, human weakness may not presume to comment upon. But there is something in this explanation given by the Lord which we ought carefully to consider. If we said to you that by the seed is signified the word, by the field the world, by the birds the devils, by the thorns riches, you might perhaps hesitate to believe us.

Therefore the Lord Himself has deigned to explain what He said that you may know how to interpret other parables of which He has not given the meaning. By the very fact of explaining what He said, the Lord shows that He spoke figuratively; as though He would give us confidence when, in spite of our incapacity, we lay open to you the hidden meaning of His words.

Who would ever believe me if I said that thorns signified riches? Especially as thorns are prickly and riches give pleasure. And yet riches are indeed thorns, for they tear the mind by the pricks of care. And when they draw us even into sin, they, as it were, make us bleed with the wounds they inflict. Clearly the Lord is speaking here not of riches in themselves, but of the vanity of riches, as we learn from another Evangelist.

Riches are vain since we cannot keep them with us for long; they are vain since they do not relieve the needs of our soul. Only those are true riches which make us rich in virtue. If then, dearly beloved brethren, you would be rich, desire the true riches. If you would rise to the height of true honor, strive after the kingdom of heaven. If you love the glory that belongs to dignities, make haste to be received into the heavenly court of the Angels. Let the words of the Lord, which you perceive by the ear, sink into your soul. For the word of God is the food of the soul, and as a sickly stomach cannot retain the food it receives, so it is with you when you do not retain in the bowels of your memory the words you have heard. But if a man cannot retain his food, his life is despaired of.

R. When a very great multitude was gathered together to Jesus and had hastened out of the cities unto Him, He spoke by a similitude: * The sower went out to sow his seed. V. And as he sowed,

some fell upon good ground and, being sprung up,
yielded fruit a hundredfold. The sower. Glory.
The sower.

✠ Continuation of the holy Gospel according to
St. Luke.—At that time: When a very great multitude was gathered together and hastened out of
the cities unto Jesus, He spoke by a similitude: The
sower went out to sow his seed: and as he sowed,
some fell by the wayside and it was trodden down,
and the fowls of the air devoured it. And other
some fell upon a rock: and as soon as it was sprung
up, it withered away because it had no moisture.
And other some fell among thorns and the thorns
growing up with it choked it. And other some fell
upon good ground: and being sprung up yielded
fruit a hundredfold. Saying these things, He cried
out: He that hath ears to hear, let him hear. And
His disciples asked Him what this parable might
be. To whom He said: To you it is given to know
the mystery of the kingdom of God, but to the rest
in parables: that seeing they may not see, and
hearing they may not understand. Now the parable is this. The seed is the word of God. And
they by the wayside are they that hear: then the
devil cometh and taketh the word out of their heart
lest believing they should be saved. Now they upon
the rock are they who, when they hear, receive the
word with joy; and these have no roots: for they
believe for awhile and in time of temptation they

fall away. And that which fell among thorns are they who have heard and, going their way, are choked with the cares and riches and pleasures of this life and yield no fruit. But that on the good ground are they who in a good and perfect heart, hearing the word, keep it and bring forth fruit in patience.

LET US PRAY

O God, Thou Who dost see that we do not trust in the merit of our own actions, mercifully grant that we may be preserved from all adversities by the protection of the Teacher of the Gentiles. Through our Lord.

QUINQUAGESIMA SUNDAY

I Nocturn
From the Book of Genesis, c. 12, 1 - 19

II Nocturn

From the Book of St. Ambrose, Bishop, on the Patriarch Abraham

Abraham was a truly great man and renowned for many virtues whom philosophy could not equal among its votaries. What philosophy has imagined falls short of what he did; and the simple faith of truth surpasses the ambitious lying of eloquence. Let us therefore consider of what kind was this man's piety.

For this virtue holds the first place as being the foundation of all others; and thus it was the first which God asked of him when He said: Go out from thy country and from thy kindred and from thy father's house. Would it not have been enough to have said: from thy country? For that would have been to leave his kindred and his father's house. But God made mention of each in particular that He might prove the love of Abraham; and also that he might not seem to undertake this journey rashly nor make any mistake as to the commandment he received from heaven.

So all the precepts were set down together that nothing might be concealed; and lest perchance he should despair, the rewards too were stated. He was tried as one that is strong; he was urged on as one that is faithful; he was called forth as being just; and he set forth as the Lord had commanded him. And Lot went forth with him. Thus did Abraham put in practice that celebrated saying of the Seven Wise Men: Follow God. He did this before their maxims were heard of; he followed God and went forth from his own country.

But since he had previously been of another country, that is, the land of the Chaldees from whence Thare, the father of Abraham, had gone forth and had migrated to Haran: and again, he to whom it had been said: Go forth from thy kindred, took with him also his nephew: let us consider whether to go forth from one's country may not perhaps be to go forth from a certain abiding in this land, that is, in our body, from which Paul went forth when he said: Our conversation is in heaven.

R. The Angel of the Lord called unto Abraham saying: * Lay not thy hand upon the boy for thou fearest God. V. When he stretched forth his hand to slay his son, behold the Angel of the Lord called unto him from heaven and said. Lay not. Glory. Lay not.

III Nocturn

The reading of the holy Gospel
according to St. Luke

At that time: Jesus took unto Him the twelve and said to them: Behold we go up to Jerusalem, and all things shall be accomplished which were written by the prophets concerning the Son of man. And so forth.

Homily of St. Gregory, Pope

Our Redeemer, foreseeing that His disciples would be troubled in their minds at His Passion, announced to them long before both the sufferings of His Passion and the glory of His Resurrection; so that when they should see Him dying, as He foretold, they might not doubt that He would rise again. But the disciples were still earthly-minded and by no means able to understand this mystery, so He worked a miracle. Before their eyes a blind man received his sight that they who could not understand His words concerning the heavenly mysteries might be strengthened in their faith by such deeds of heavenly power.

But the miracles of our Lord and Savior must be accepted in this manner, dearly beloved brethren, that we must believe that they actually took place and at the same time were intended to signify something to us. Indeed, the works of God not only manifest His power, but also speak to us of some mystery. For behold, who this blind man was of whom the story is told, we know not, but we do know what is signified by this miracle.

This blind man is indeed a figure of mankind, driven out from the joys of Paradise in the person of its first parent, knowing not the glory of the heavenly light and suffering the darkness of its condemnation. But nevertheless, he is enlightened in the presence of his Redeemer; so that now he possesses in desire the joys of inward light and by good works begins to walk in the way of life. We must take note that the blind man received his sight as Jesus drew near to Jericho. Jericho indeed signifies Moon and in holy Scripture the moon denotes the failing of bodily strength because, in waning every month, it signifies the decay of our mortal nature.

When therefore our Creator drew near to Jericho, the blind man returned to the light; for when the Godhead took upon Itself the weakness of our human nature, mankind again received the light it had lost. For God, through His suffering as man, raised up man to things divine. The blind man is rightly described as sitting by the wayside begging. For the Truth Itself says: I am the Way.

R. A blind man sat by the wayside as the Lord passed by and cried out to Him: and the Lord said to him: * What wilt thou that I do for thee? Lord, that I may receive my sight. V. And Jesus standing, commanded him to be brought unto Him: and when he was come near, He asked him saying. What. Glory. What.

✠ Continuation of the holy Gospel according to St. Luke.—At that time: Jesus took unto Him the twelve and said to them: Behold, we go up to Jerusalem and all things shall be accomplished which were written by the Prophets concerning the Son of Man. For He shall be delivered to the Gentiles, and shall be mocked and scourged and spit upon: and after they have scourged Him, they will put Him to death, and the third day He shall rise again. And they understood none of these things, and this word was hid from them, and they under-

stood not the things that were said. Now it came
to pass, when He drew nigh to Jericho, that a certain blind man sat by the wayside, begging. And
when he heard the multitude passing by, he asked
what this meant. And they told him that Jesus of
Nazareth was passing by. And he cried out saying: Jesus, Son of David, have mercy on me. And
they that went before rebuked him, that he should
hold his peace. But he cried out much more: Son
of David, have mercy on me. And Jesus standing,
commanded him to be brought unto Him. And
when he was come near, He asked him saying:
What wilt thou that I do to thee? But he said:
Lord, that I may see. And Jesus said to him: Receive thy sight, thy faith hath made thee whole.
And immediately he saw and followed Him, glorify-
ing God. And all the people, when they saw it, gave
praise to God.

LET US PRAY

Graciously hear our prayers, we beseech Thee,
O Lord, and having freed us from the bonds of our
sins, protect us from all adversity. Through our
Lord.

ASH WEDNESDAY

The reading of the holy Gospel
according to St. Matthew

At that time: Jesus said to His disciples: When you fast, be not as the hypocrites, sad. And so forth.

Homily of St. Augustine, Bishop

According to these precepts, it is clear that our every action should be aimed at acquiring joy within the soul; lest, in seeking external rewards, we be conformed to this world and lose that promise of blessedness, which is the more solid and stable as it is interior, by which God has chosen us to be made like to the image of His Son. What we must especially notice in this chapter is that pride is to be found, not only amid material pomp and splendor, but even in sadness and squalor; and it is then even more dangerous because it leads to error under the pretence of humble service of God.

Whoever, therefore, exhibits excessive refinement and apparel of the body, or splendor of any kind, is easily convicted by these very things of being a follower of the world and its pomps and he deceives nobody by this cunning pretence of sanctity. But when one, who makes profession of Christianity, attracts notice by an unusual squalor and filth, and when he does this of his own will and not of necessity, we can guess from his other actions whether he behaves thus out of scorn of needless refinement or from a certain ambition. For the Lord warned us to beware of wolves in sheep's clothing when He said: But by their fruits you shall know them.

If it happens that some trial falls upon them and these things, which under the pretence of sanctity they have obtained or wish to obtain, are taken away from them or denied them, then it will clearly appear whether they are wolves in sheep's clothing or sheep in their own. Nevertheless, Christians ought not to try to please the eyes of men by superfluous adornment merely because hypocrites, in order to deceive the unwary, often wear poor clothing and only what is absolutely necessary. For the sheep need not lay aside their skins, even if sometimes wolves may put them on.

THURSDAY

The reading of the holy Gospel
according to St. Matthew

At that time: When Jesus entered into Capharnaum, there came to Him a centurion, beseeching Him and saying: Lord, my servant lieth at home sick of the palsy and is grievously tormented. And so forth.

Homily of St. Augustine, Bishop

Let us see whether Matthew and Luke agree
about this servant of the centurion. Matthew says:
There came to Him a centurion, beseeching Him
and saying: my servant lieth at home sick of the
palsy. This seems to contradict what Luke says:
And when he had heard of Jesus, he sent unto Him
the ancients of the Jews desiring Him to come and
heal his servant. And when they came to Jesus,
they besought Him earnestly, saying to Him: He
is worthy that Thou shouldst do this for him, for
he loveth our nation and he hath built us a synagogue. And Jesus went with them, and when He
was now not far from the house, the centurion sent
his friends to Him saying: Lord, trouble not Thyself; for I am not worthy that Thou shouldst enter
under my roof.

For if it happened thus, how can what Matthew
says be true: There came to Him a certain centurion; since he did not come himself, but sent his
friends? But if we look closely, we shall see that
Matthew did not altogether depart from familiar
speech. For not only are we accustomed to say that
someone has approached even before he has reached
the place to which he is said to have approached:
whence we also speak of a person as making small
progress or great progress to that which he desires
to reach; but we also often speak of that contact,
which is made for the purpose of obtaining any-

thing, as actually made even if the person who approaches does not actually see him whom he is said to have approached, since he reaches him whose favor is necessary for him through the agency of a friend. This custom is so well-established that even in the vulgar parlance of our time, certain men are called "diplomats" who, in the practice of canvassing, reach the otherwise unapproachable minds of men of rank by the employment of suitable intermediaries.

Therefore it was not unreasonable for Matthew—a thing which even the vulgar can understand—in referring to the centurion's "approach" to the Lord (which was really effected by others), to have chosen to say concisely: There came to Him a centurion. Nevertheless, we must not fail to observe a certain mystical depth in the wording of the Evangelist in accordance with what is written in the Psalm: Come ye to Him and be enlightened. For in like manner, seeing that the Lord Himself commended the centurion's faith (by which faith he truly "approached" Jesus) when He declared: I have not found so great faith in Israel, the Evangelist wisely chose to speak as if the centurion himself had "approached" Christ, rather than to refer to those by whom he had sent the message.

FRIDAY

The reading of the holy Gospel
according to St. Matthew

At that time: Jesus said to His disciples: You have heard that it hath been said: Thou shalt love thy neighbor and hate thy enemy. And so forth.

Homily of St. Jerome, Priest

But I say to you: Love your enemies: do good to them that hate you. There are many who, measuring the precepts of God by their own weakness and not by the strength of the Saints, think it impossible to observe them and say that it is enough if the virtuous do not hate their enemies, but that to command that they should be loved is to ask what is beyond the strength of human nature. We must know, then, that Christ did not command us to do what is impossible, but to do what is perfect. David did so in regard to Saul and Absalom. Stephen, the Martyr, also prayed for his enemies who stoned him, and Paul desired to be anathema for his persecutors. Jesus not only taught this, but also practiced it when He said: Father, forgive them, for they know not what they do.

That you may be the children of your Father, who is in heaven. If, by keeping the commandments of God, one becomes a child of God, it is not, therefore, by nature that one is a child, but by one's own will. When, therefore, thou dost an alms-deed, sound not a trumpet before thee, as the hypocrites do in the synagogues and in the streets that they may be honored by men. He, then, is a hypocrite, who sounds a trumpet when he does an alms-deed. He too is a hypocrite who disfigures his face when he fasts that he may display the emptiness of his stomach in his countenance. He is a hypocrite also who prays in the synagogues and at the corners of the streets that he may be seen by men.

From all these examples it is to be concluded that they who do anything for the sake of being glorified by men are hypocrites. It seems to me that he was a hypocrite who said to his brother: Let me cast the mote out of thy eye; for it would appear that he did this out of self-esteem, wishing that he himself might be thought righteous. Therefore did the Lord say to him: Thou hypocrite, cast out first the beam out of thy own eye. It is not so much the act of virtue itself, as the motive of the act, that wins a reward before God. And if one turns aside ever so little from the straight way, it matters not whether one goes to the right or to the left.

SATURDAY

The reading of the holy Gospel according to St. Mark

At that time: When it was late, the ship was in the midst of the sea, and Jesus alone on the land. And so forth.

Homily of St. Bede the Venerable, Priest

Both the labor of the disciples in rowing and the contrary wind they encountered signify the many afflictions of holy Church who is striving, amidst the waves of a hostile world and the tempest of unclean spirits, to attain to the rest of the heavenly fatherland, as if making for a safe port. It is well said, that the ship was in the midst of the sea and Himself alone on the land; for the Church sometimes finds herself not only afflicted by the persecutions of the Gentiles, but even disfigured, so that it would seem, if that were possible, that her Redeemer had actually abandoned her for a time.

Whence there is that mournful voice (of the Psalmist), overtaken by the waves and tempests of overwhelming temptations and seeking the aid of divine protection: Why, O Lord, hast Thou retired afar off? Why dost Thou slight us in our wants, in the time of trouble? And further on in the Psalm he puts these words in the mouth of the

enemy: For he hath said in his heart: God hath
forgotten, He hath turned away His face not to see
to the end.

But God does not forget the prayer of the poor
nor turn away His face from them that hope in
Him. On the contrary, He helps them to conquer
in the combat with the enemy and He rewards their
victory with an eternal crown. That is why it is
expressly said in this place, that He saw them laboring in rowing. Indeed, the Lord saw them laboring in the sea, although He Himself was on
land; for even if He seems to delay for some time
before going to the help of those in trouble, He
does not fail to strengthen them with a merciful
look lest they should faint in their tribulations;
and sometimes He helps them visibly to overcome
their troubles, as He did when He walked on the
rolling waves and calmed them.

I SUNDAY IN LENT

I Nocturn

*From the second Epistle of blessed Paul the Apostle
to the Corinthians, c. 6, 1 - 16*

II Nocturn

Sermon of St. Leo, Pope

Dearly beloved, I am about to preach to you the
holiest and greatest of fasts, and what more suitable preface may I use than if I begin with the

words of the Apostle and tell you what has been read, wherein Christ said: Behold now is the acceptable time: behold now is the day of salvation? For although there is no season which is not full of divine gifts, or when access to the mercy of God is not granted to us by His grace, yet at this time the minds of all should be urged with greater earnestness towards spiritual progress and be animated with fuller confidence when the return of that day on which we were redeemed invites us to every work of piety: so that, cleansed in heart and body, we may celebrate that mystery which excels all others.

Such great mysteries should truly have given rise to an unending devotion and abiding reverence that we might ever remain in the sight of God as we ought to be found on the feast of the Pasch itself. But there are few who have the strength for this; and, because of the frailty of the flesh the more severe discipline is relaxed and moreover the attention is divided among the many actions of this life, even the hearts of religious men must of necessity become defiled by the dust of worldly things. Hence this most wholesome institution, divinely appointed, provides that in order to restore the purity of our minds, we should be corrected by the discipline of these forty days; and thus the faults of other times may be redeemed by the works of piety and be diminished by holy fastings.

And therefore, dearly beloved, as we are about to enter upon these mystic days, appointed in a most hallowed manner for the purification of both soul and body, let us take care to obey the apostolic commandments and cleanse ourselves from all defilement of flesh and spirit: that in the struggles which go on between our two natures, the soul, which under the guidance of God should govern the body, may uphold the dignity of its rule: so that, giving no offence to any man, we may not be exposed to the reproaches of those who revile us.

For we shall be justly blamed by unbelievers, whose wicked tongues will find in our misdeeds a weapon of attack against religion, if the conduct of those who keep the fast is not in accordance with the spirit of perfect continence. For our fasting does not consist merely in abstinence from food; it will not profit us to deprive the body of food if the mind be not recalled from wickedness.

R. The season of the fast opened to us the gates of heaven: let us enter therein with prayer and supplication: * That on the day of the resurrection we may rejoice with the Lord. V. In all things let us approve ourselves as the ministers of God in much patience. That. Glory. That.

The reading of the holy Gospel
according to St. Matthew

At that time: Jesus was led by the Spirit into
the desert to be tempted by the devil. And when
He had fasted forty days and forty nights, afterwards He was hungry. And so forth.

Homily of St. Gregory, Pope

Some are wont to consider it doubtful by what
spirit Jesus was led into the desert because of what
is said below: The devil took Him up into the
holy city; and again: He took Him up into a very
high mountain. But truly and beyond any question,
it may fitly be taken that we are to believe that He
was led into the desert by the Holy Spirit: for His
own Spirit led Him there where the devil should
find Him in order to tempt Him.

But behold, when it is said that the God-Man
was taken up either into a high mountain or into
the holy city by the devil, the mind refuses to believe it; men's ears dread to hear it. However, we
shall acknowledge that this is not incredible if we
think over what was done upon this and other occasions.

Truly, the devil is the head of all the wicked and
all the wicked are members belonging to this head.
Was not Pilate a member of the devil? Were not
the Jews who persecuted Christ and the soldiers
who crucified Him members of the devil? Why,

then, should we wonder that He allowed Himself to be taken up into a mountain by the devil, by whose members He even allowed Himself to be crucified? Therefore, it was not unfitting that our Redeemer, who came to be slain, should will to be tempted. It was indeed just that He, by His own temptations, should conquer our temptations even as by His own death He overcame our death.

But we ought to be aware that temptation passes through three stages: suggestion, delight in the temptation, and consent. And we men, when we are tempted, often fall into taking delight in the temptation or even into yielding our consent; for we, conceived of sinful flesh, even bear within us that whereby we suffer strife. But God, who took flesh in the womb of a Virgin and came into the world without sin, suffered no contradiction within Himself. He could, then, be tempted by suggestion but the delight in sin could never force a way into His mind. And therefore all those temptations of the devil were external to Him and were not from within.

R. God hath given His Angels charge over Thee to keep Thee in all Thy ways: * In their hands they will bear Thee up, lest Thou dash Thy foot against a stone. V. Thou shalt walk upon the asp and the basilisk and Thou shalt trample under foot the lion and the dragon. In their hands. Glory. In their hands.

✠ Continuation of the holy Gospel according to St. Matthew.—At that time: Jesus was led by the Spirit into the desert to be tempted by the devil. And when He had fasted forty days and forty nights, afterwards He was hungry. And the tempter coming said to Him: If Thou be the Son of God, command that these stones be made bread. Who answered and said: It is written: Not in bread alone doth man live, but in every word that proceedeth from the mouth of God. Then the devil took Him up into the holy city and set Him upon the pinnacle of the temple and said to Him: If Thou be the Son of God, cast Thyself down. For it is written: That He hath given His angels charge over Thee, and in their hands they shall bear Thee up, lest perhaps Thou dash Thy foot against a stone. Jesus said to him: It is written again: Thou shalt not tempt the Lord Thy God. Again the devil took Him up into a very high mountain and showed Him all the kingdoms of the world and the glory of them, and said to Him: All these will I give Thee if, falling dawn, Thou wilt adore me. Then Jesus saith to him: Begone, Satan! for it is written: The Lord thy God shalt thou adore, and Him only shalt thou serve. Then the devil left Him and behold, angels came and ministered to Him.

LET US PRAY

O God, who dost purify Thy Church by the annual observance of Lent, grant to Thy family that what it seeks to obtain from Thee by fasting, it may secure by good works. Through our Lord.

MONDAY

The reading of the holy Gospel according to St. Matthew

At that time: Jesus said to His disciples: When the Son of man shall come in His majesty and all the Angels with Him, then shall He sit on the seat of His majesty; and all nations shall be gathered together before Him. And so forth.

Homily of St. Augustine, Bishop

If the comandments have not been kept, is it possible to attain unto life by faith alone, which without works is dead? Then, how will that be reasonable which He will say unto those who are set on the left hand: Go ye into everlasting fire which was prepared for the devil and his angels? He does not rebuke them because they have not believed in Him, but because they have not done good works. For assuredly, lest anyone should promise himself eternal life by reason of his faith, which without works is dead, He went on to say that He would separate all nations which before had been mingled together and had used the same pastures, that it may be apparent that those who had believed in Him but had not taken pains to do good works will say to Him: Lord, when did we see Thee suffering such and such afflictions and did not minister to Thee? as though they could attain unto eternal life by means of that same dead faith.

Or can it be, perhaps, that they who have not done works of mercy will go into everlasting fire, while those shall not go who have stolen the goods of others or who have been unmerciful to themselves by defiling the temple of God within them? As though works of mercy could be of any profit without love, as the Apostle says: If I distribute all my goods to the poor and have not charity, it profiteth me nothing? Or how is it that anyone loves his neighbor as himself, if he does not love himself? For he that loveth iniquity hateth his own soul.

Neither can it be said concerning this, as many, deceiving themselves, say, that the fire indeed is everlasting but the burning itself is not everlasting. For they think that those souls, unto whom, on account of their dead faith, they promise that they "will be saved, yet so as by fire," will pass through the fire; so that the fire itself is everlasting but their own burning, that is, the action of the fire upon them, will not be everlasting; whereas the

Lord, foreseeing this also, ended His sentence thus, saying: Thus those shall go into everlasting burning, but the just into everlasting life. The burning, therefore, like the fire, will be everlasting; moreover, the Truth says that they, whom He charges with having failed not in faith, but in good works, shall go into it.

TUESDAY

The reading of the holy Gospel according to St. Matthew

At that time: When Jesus was come into Jerusalem, the whole city was moved, saying: Who is He? And so forth.

Homily of St. Bede the Venerable, Priest

That which He did in figure by cursing the barren fig-tree, the Lord soon afterwards showed more openly by casting the unrighteous out of the temple. For the tree had not sinned in that it had no fruit when the Lord was hungry, for the time for fruit was not yet come; but the priests who were carrying on worldly business in the house of the Lord had sinned and failed to bear that fruit of piety then due from them, for which the Lord was hungering. The Lord withered the tree with a curse that men, seeing this or hearing of it, might better understand how they are liable to be condemned by the divine judgment if, having borne no fruit of good works, they soothe themselves in the mere self-approval of their own religious discourses, as it were, with a rustling shelter of green leaves.

But because they had not understood, the Lord in vengeance necessarily meted out to them the punishment they had brought upon themselves; and what concerned trade in human affairs he cast out from that house in which, according to the commandment, only what was divine was to be done, that is, victims and prayers were to be offered to God, and the word of God was to be read, heard, and sung. And yet it is to be believed that only such things were found in the temple as were necessary to be bought or sold for the service of the temple itself, according to what we read as taking place on another occasion, when, entering into the same temple, He found there men buying and selling sheep, oxen, and doves. For we must certainly believe that those who came from a distance bought all these things from the inhabitants of the place only that they might offer them up in the house of the Lord.

If, therefore, the Lord would not have those things to be sold in the temple which were to be offered there according to His wish, and this no doubt because of the sin of avarice or fraud, which is a crime wont to be associated with trade, with how much greater severity, do you think, will He not punish those whom He may find spending their time in laughter or idle talk or giving themselves up to any other vice? For if the Lord will not suffer temporal business, which might be exercised freely elsewhere, to be carried on in His house, how much more shall those things that are not lawfully done in any place merit the wrath of heaven if they are done in temples consecrated to God? Truly, since the Holy Ghost appeared in the form of a dove upon the Lord, rightly by doves are signified the gifts of the Holy Ghost. And who are they who today sell doves in the temple of God, unless they be those who in the Church accept a price for the imposition of hands namely, by which the Holy Ghost is given from heaven.

EMBER WEDNESDAY

The reading of the holy Gospel according to St. Matthew

At that time: Some of the scribes and Pharisees answered Him saying: Master, we would see a sign from Thee. And so forth.

Homily of St. Ambrose, Bishop

After the people of the Jews were condemned, the mystery of the Church is plainly declared. For the penance of the Ninivites and the zeal of the Queen of the South for receiving knowledge signify that the Church is a body gathered together from all the ends of the earth to hear the words of the peaceful Solomon. For truly is the Church a queen whose kingdom is undivided, rising up out of divers and distant nations into one body.

Therefore, that is a great mystery concerning Christ and the Church, but nevertheless, this is a greater mystery: because before, the mystery was in figure, but now it is fully verified. For there, Solomon was the type; but here, we have Christ in His own Body. Accordingly, the Church is built up of two classes of people: those who know not sin and those who have ceased to sin. For penance wipes out sin and knowledge guards against it.

For the rest, the sign of Jonas is both a type of the Lord's Passion, and a proof of the great sins which the Jews committed. It is at once, we may observe, a declaration of the Lord's power and a token of His mercy. For by the example of the Ninivites both the punishment is foretold and a way of escape is pointed out. So that even the Jews need not despair of pardon if they are willing to do penance.

THURSDAY

The reading of the holy Gospel
according to St. Matthew

At that time: Jesus went forth and retired into the coasts of Tyre and Sidon. And so forth.

Homily of St. Jerome, Priest

Leaving behind Him His false accusers, the scribes and Pharisees, He passed over into the coasts of Tyre and Sidon that He might heal the Tyrians and Sidonians. And a woman of Canaan came out of those coasts, crying out that she might beseech Him to heal her daughter. Note that the daughter of the Canaanite was the fifteenth person to be healed. Have mercy upon me, O Lord, Thou Son of David. Hence she knew to call Him Son of David, for she had already come out of her country, and when she changed her home and her faith, she put away the errors of the Tyrians and Sidonians.

My daughter is grievously troubled by a devil. We may, I think, take this daughter of the woman of Canaan to be the souls of believers who, knowing not their God and adoring stones, were grievously troubled by the devil. Who answered her not a word: not out of pride, like that of the Pharisees, nor from disdain, as that of the scribes, but that He might not seem to contradict His own judgment wherein He had commanded: Go ye not into the way of the Gentiles, and into the city of the Samaritans, enter ye not. For He did not wish to give an occasion for His accusers, and also, He reserved the full salvation of the Gentiles to the time of His passion and resurrection.

And His disciples came and besought Him, saying: Send her away, for she crieth after us. The disciples, either because they were at that time ignorant of the Lord's secrets or because they were moved to pity or else wished to be freed from her importunity, for she was crying out repeatedly as though He were a harsh and not a merciful physician, pleaded for the woman of Canaan whom another Evangelist calls a Syro-Phenician. And He answering, says: I was not sent except to the sheep that are lost of the house of Israel. Not that He was not sent to the Gentiles, but that He was first sent to Israel: that, when they would not receive the Gospel, it might justly pass to the Gentiles.

EMBER FRIDAY

The reading of the holy Gospel
according to St. John

At that time: There was a festival day of the Jews and Jesus went up to Jerusalem. And so forth.

Homily of St. Augustine, Bishop

Let us see what He intended to signify in the case of that one whom He Himself, keeping the mystery of unity, deigned to heal out of so many sick folk. He found in the years of this man the number indicative, as it were, of debility: he had been eight and thirty years under his infirmity. How this number pertains rather to debility than to health must be somewhat more carefully expounded. I wish you to be attentive: the Lord will be at hand to help us that I may speak fitting words and that you may listen well. The number forty is commended to our notice as one consecrated by a kind of perfection: this, I suppose, is well known to you, beloved; the holy Scriptures do very often bear witness of it. You are well aware that fasting was consecrated by this number. For Moses fasted forty days and Elias the same; our Lord and Savior Jesus Christ Himself also fulfilled this number of fasting. By Moses is signified the Law, by Elias are signified the Prophets, by the Lord is signified the Gospel. And therefore all three appeared on that mountain where He showed Himself to His disciples in the brightness of His countenance and raiment; for He appeared in the midst, between Moses and Elias, even as the Gospel received testimony from the Law and the Prophets.

And therefore, whether it be in the Law or in the Prophets or in the Gospel, the number forty is brought to our notice in the matter of fasting. Now fasting, in its large and general import, is to abstain from sin and the unlawful pleasures of the world, and this is the perfect fast: That, denying ungodliness and worldly desires, we should live soberly and justly and godly in this world. What reward does the Apostle annex to this fast? He goes on to say: Looking for that blessed hope and manifestation of the glory of our blessed God and Savior, Jesus Christ. In this world, therefore, we celebrate, as it were, the forty days' abstinence when we live aright, that is, when we abstain from sin and unlawful pleasures; but since this abstinence will not be without reward, we look for that blessed hope and revelation of the glory of our great God and Savior, Jesus Christ. In that hope we are to receive our wages, a penny, when the reality of the hope shall have come to pass. For according to the Gospel this is the same wages paid to the laborers working in the vineyard, as I believe you remember, for everything need not be repeated, as if to persons ignorant and inexperienced. This penny, then, which takes its name from the number ten, is paid, and this conjoined with the forty makes up fifty; whence it is, that before Easter we keep the forty days of Lent with hardships, but the fifty days after Easter we keep with joy, as though having received our wages.

Remember what I propounded: the number thirty-eight of the years of this debilitated man. I wish to explain how this number of thirty-eight belongs rather to debility than to health. Therefore, as I was saying, charity fulfils the Law: in all works the number forty pertains to the completing of the Law. But in charity there are two commandments commended to us: Thou shalt love the Lord thy God with thy whole heart, and with thy whole soul, and with thy whole mind; and thou shalt love thy neighbor as thyself. On these two commandments dependeth the whole Law and the Prophets. With good reason did that widow place into the offerings of God two mites, all the living she had; with good reason did the innkeeper receive two pieces of money for the sick man, who had been wounded by robbers, that he might be restored to health; with good reason did Jesus spend two days among the Samaritans that He might confirm them in charity. For by this number of two, since it signifies something good, the twofold duty of charity is especially commended. If, then, in the number forty is contained the perfection of the Law, and the Law cannot be fulfilled but by the twofold precept of charity, why dost thou wonder that this man who was short of forty by two years, was debilitated?

EMBER SATURDAY

The reading of the holy Gospel according to St. Matthew

At that time: Jesus took Peter and James and John, his brother, and bringeth them up into a high mountain apart: and He was transfigured before them. And so forth.

Homily of St. Leo, Pope

The lesson from the Gospel, dearly beloved, which has reached the inner hearing of our minds through our bodily ears, calls us to the understanding of a great mystery, to which we shall more readily attain if, by the assistance of God's grace, we take into consideration the events that have been narrated a little above. For the Savior of mankind, Jesus Christ, in establishing that faith whereby the wicked are called back to justice and the dead to life, instructed His disciples, by the doctrines He taught them and by the miracles He wrought, to believe that the same Christ was the Only-begotten of God and likewise the Son of man. For one of these truths without the other would not have availed them unto salvation; it would have been equally as dangerous to believe that the Lord Jesus Christ was God alone and not man as that He was man alone and not God. Both truths, then, had to be confessed alike; for just as the true manhood was present in the Godhead, so was the true divinity present in the manhood.

In order, then, to confirm their knowledge of this faith so necessary to salvation, the Lord asked His disciples what, among the various opinions of other men, they themselves believed concerning Him, or what they thought upon the matter. Whereupon Peter, the Apostle, by the revelation of the Most High Father, rising above bodily things and passing beyond human things, saw with the eyes of his mind the Son of the living God and confessed the glory of the Godhead, for he looked beyond the substance of flesh and blood. And he became so pleasing by this sublime faith that he received the fulness of blessing and was endued with the holy firmness of an unbreakable rock: on which the Church should be built and prevail over the gates of hell and the laws of death. Moreover, in the case of binding and loosing of any person whatsoever, no sentence should be ratified in heaven other than that which was established by the judgment of Peter.

But, dearly beloved, the sublimity of Peter's recognition, which the Lord had praised, had to be founded upon the mystery of the lower nature: lest the faith of the Apostle, borne on high to confess the glory of the Godhead in Christ, should deem it unworthy and unfitting for the impassible God to assume our weakness, and thus should believe that the human nature in Christ was then so glorified that it could neither suffer pain nor be dissolved by death. And therefore, when the Lord said that He must go to Jerusalem and suffer many things from the ancients and scribes and the chief priests, and be put to death and rise again, blessed Peter, who, illumined by light from on high and burning in his ardent confession of the Son of God with, as he thought, a religious and generous hatred, had spurned the notion that the Lord should suffer the shame of such a mocking and the disgrace of so cruel a death, was corrected by Jesus with a kindly rebuke and was filled with the desire of sharing even His Passion.

II SUNDAY IN LENT

I Nocturn
From the book of Genesis, c. 27, 1 - 29

II Nocturn

From the book of St, Augustine, Bishop, against lying

What Jacob did at his mother's instigation, so as to seem to deceive his father, if it be considered diligently and faithfully, is not a lie, but a mystery. For if we are to call such things lies, all parables and figures signifying any things whatsoever that are not to be taken in their proper sense, but in which one thing is to be understood of another, must also be called lies; which is very far from being the case.

For he who thinks this can also, in regard to figurative expressions of which there are so many, impute this calumny to them; so that even that figure which we call a metaphor, that is, the irregular transferring of any word from its proper sense to another which it does not rightly possess, can also, by this reasoning, be called a lie. For it is the things that are signified that matter: that is what is really said; and they are accounted lies only because people do not understand that really the things that are signified are said, but believe that things which are false are uttered.

That this may be made clearer by an example, consider attentively that very thing Jacob did. Assuredly, he covered some part of his body with the skins of the kids. If we seek the immediate cause, we shall account him to have lied; for he did this that he might be taken for the man he was not. But if this deed be taken in reference to that for the signifying of which it was really done, then the skins of the kids stand for sins, and he who covered himself with them signified Him who bore, not His own, but the sins of others.

Therefore, the true signification cannot in any sense be rightly called a lie; as in deed, so also in word. For when his father said to him: Who art thou, my son? He answered: I am Esau, thy first-born. Now if this be taken in reference to those twin brethren, it will seem a lie; but, if in reference to that for the signifying of which those deeds and words were written: He (Christ) is here understood in His own body, which is His Church, who, speaking of this thing, saith: When you shall see Abraham and Isaac and Jacob and all the prophets in the kingdom of God, and you yourselves thrust out. And: They shall come from the east and the west and the north and the south, and shall sit down in the kingdom of God. And: Behold, they are last that were first, and they are first that were last. For so, in a manner of speaking, the younger brother did bear off the primacy of the elder brother and transferred it to himself.

R. The Lord shall be my God and this stone which I have set up for a title shall be called God's house: and of all that thou shalt give me, * I will offer tithes and peace-offerings to thee. V. If I shall return prosperously to my father's house. I will offer. Glory. I will offer.

III Nocturn

The reading of the holy Gospel according to St. Matthew

At that time: Jesus took unto Him Peter and James, and John his brother, and brought them up into a high mountain apart: and He was transfigured before them. And so forth.

From a Homily of St. Leo, Pope

Jesus took unto Him Peter and James, and John his brother, and going up with them apart into a very high mountain, He showed them the brightness of His glory. For although they understood concerning the majesty of God within Him, yet they knew not the power of the body in which the divinity was concealed. And it was for that reason that He had especially and distinctly promised that some of His disciples standing by should not taste death till they had seen the Son of man coming in His kingdom, that is, in the splendor of His royalty.

To these three men He willed to manifest this which pertained spiritually to the nature of man which He had assumed.

For they could by no means view and behold, while yet clothed in mortal flesh, that unspeakable and inaccessible vision of His Godhead which is reserved for the pure of heart in eternal life. When the Father said: This is My beloved Son in whom I am well pleased, hear ye Him, is it not plainly to be understood thus: This is My Son, who is of Me and with Me throughout all ages? For the begetter does not come before Him who is begotten, nor does He who is begotten, come after the begetter.

This is My Son, whom the Godhead doth not separate from Me, nor power divide, nor eternity set apart. This is My Son, not by adoption, but by nature; not created from another source, but begotten of Me; not made of another nature like to Me, but of My own being, born equal unto Me. This is My Son, by whom all things were made and without whom nothing was made: who does all things in like manner as I do them; and whatsoever I work, He worketh with Me, inseparably and without distinction.

This is My Son: the equality that He hath with Me, He seized not by robbery, nor did He unlawfully assume it; but, abiding in the form of My glory, He bowed down the unchangeable Godhead

even unto the form of a servant that our common
purpose, the restoration of mankind, might be fulfilled. Him, therefore, in whom I am well pleased
in all things and by whose preaching I am made
known to men, by whose humility I am glorified, the
same hear ye without delay: for He is the Truth
and the Way, He is My strength and My wisdom.

R. The Angel said to Jacob: * Let me go, for it
is break of day. And he said: I will not let thee
go except thou bless me. And he blessed him in the
same place. V. And when Jacob arose, behold a
man wrestled with him till morning, and when he
saw that he could not overcome him, he said to him.
Let me go. Glory. Let me go.

✠ Continuation of the holy Gospel according to
St. Matthew.—At that time: Jesus took Peter and
James, and John his brother, and brought them up
into a high mountain apart: and He was transfigured before them. And His face did shine as the
sun and His garments became white as snow. And
behold there appeared to them Moses and Elias
talking with Him. And Peter answering, said to
Jesus: Lord, it is good for us to be here: if Thou
wilt, let us make here three tabernacles, one for
Thee, and one for Moses, and one for Elias. And
as he was yet speaking, behold a bright cloud overshadowed them. And lo, a voice out of the cloud,
saying: This is My beloved Son, in whom I am
well pleased: hear ye Him. And the disciples hear-

ing, fell upon their face and were very much afraid.
And Jesus came and touched them and said to
them: Arise, and fear not. And they lifting up
their eyes saw no one, but only Jesus. And as they
came down from the mountain, Jesus charged them,
saying: Tell the vision to no man till the Son of
Man be risen from the dead.

LET US PRAY

O God, who seest that we are wholly without
strength; protect us in both body and soul that our
bodies may be defended from all dangers and our
minds cleansed from evil thoughts. Through our
Lord.

MONDAY

The reading of the holy Gospel
according to St. John

At that time: Jesus said to the multitudes of the
Jews: I go, and you shall seek Me: and you shall
die in your sin. And so forth.

Homily of St. Augustine, Bishop

The Lord spoke unto the Jews, saying: I go. For
to Christ the Lord, death was a going to that place
whence He had come, yet from whence He had
never departed. I go, He says, and you shall seek
Me, not for desire of Me, but for hatred. For after
He had passed away from the eyes of men, He was

sought both by them who hated Him and by them who loved Him: the former for the sake of persecuting Him, the latter for the desire of possessing Him. In the Psalms the Lord Himself says by the Prophet: Flight hath failed Me, and there in no one that hath regard to My soul. And again He says in another place in a Psalm: Let them be confounded and ashamed that seek after My soul.

He blamed those who sought Him not, He condemned those who did seek Him. For it is a good thing to seek after the soul of Christ, but only in the way that the disciples sought it; and it is also a bad thing to seek after the soul of Christ, that is, in the way that the Jews sought it; for the former sought to possess it, the latter to destroy it. Accordingly, because these men sought it thus in a wrong way, with a perverted heart, what next did He add? You shall seek Me; and lest you think you are seeking Me rightly, you shall die in your sin. This comes of seeking Christ in an evil way: to die in one's sin; this comes of hating Him, by whom alone you can be saved.

For while men whose hope is in God ought not to render evil, even for evil; yet these men rendered evil for good. Therefore, the Lord announced to them beforehand, and in His foreknowledge uttered the sentence, that they should die in their sin. And then He added: Whither I go, you cannot come.

He said this to His disciples also in another place;
yet to them He did not say: You shall die in your
sin. But what did He say? The same as what He
said to these men: Whither I go, you cannot come.
He did not deprive them of hope, but He foretold a
delay. For at the time when the Lord was speaking this to His disciples they were not able to come
whither He was going, but afterwards they were to
come; but these men, to whom in His foreknowledge He said: You shall die in your sin, were never
to come.

TUESDAY

The reading of the holy Gospel
according to St. Matthew

At that time: Jesus spoke to the multitudes and
to His disciples, saying: The scribes and Pharisees
have sat on the chair of Moses. All things therefore whatsoever they shall say to you, observe and
do, but according to their works do ye not. And so
forth.

Homily of St. Jerome, Priest.

Where shall we find one milder, one more gentle,
than the Lord? He was tempted by the Pharisees,
their snares were broken, and as the Psalmist says:
The arrows of children are become their wounds.
And nevertheless, because of the dignity of their
priesthood and title, He exhorts the people to be

subject to them, not having regard to their works, but to their teaching. For when He says: The scribes and the Pharisees have sat on the chair of Moses, by chair He gives them to understand the doctrine of the law. And therefore, as to what is said in the Psalm: Nor sat in the chair of pestilence; and again: He overthrew the chairs of them that sold doves, we must take it as signifying doctrine.

For they bind heavy and insupportable burdens and lay them on men's shoulders, but with a finger of their own they will not move them. This is spoken generally against all masters who order things to be done and will not themselves do the least of them. But it is to be noticed that shoulders, the finger, the burdens, and the bonds with which the burdens are tied are to be understood here in a spiritual sense. But all their works they do in order to be seen by men. Whosoever, therefore, does anything merely to be seen by men, he is a scribe and a Pharisee.

For they make their phylacteries broad and enlarge their fringes. They love also the first places at feasts and the first chairs in the synagogues, and salutations in the market-place, and to be called by men, Rabbi. Woe unto us miserable men, to whom the vices of the Pharisees have passed. When the Lord had given the commandments of the law by

Moses, He added at the end: Thou shalt bind them upon thy hand and they shall be fixed before thy eyes. And the meaning is this: Let My commandments be upon thy hand that they may be fulfilled in works; let them be before thy eyes that thou mayst meditate upon them day and night. The Pharisees, wrongly interpreting this passage, wrote out the decalogue of Moses, that is to say, the ten sentences of the law, upon skins and folding them, bound them upon their foreheads, making as it were a crown for the head; that thus the commandments might ever move to and fro before their eyes.

WEDNESDAY

The reading of the holy Gospel according to St. Matthew

At that time: Jesus, going up to Jerusalem, took the twelve disciples apart and said to them: Behold we go up to Jerusalem, and the Son of man shall be betrayed to the chief priests and the scribes, and they shall condemn Him to death. And so forth.

Homily of St. Ambrose, Bishop

Consider what it is that the mother of the sons of Zebedee is asking, together with and on behalf of her sons: she is verily a mother, the range of whose desires in her anxiety for the honor of her sons is indeed immoderate, but nevertheless pardonable. And especially as she, a mother advanced in years, deeply religious, deprived of consolation, who suffered her sons to be absent from her at the very time when she needed their efficient help and support, preferred her sons to receive the reward of those who followed Christ to considering her own comfort. For at the first call of the Lord (as we read) they left their nets and their father, and followed Him.

She, therefore, with all the tenderness of a mother's zeal, besought the Savior, saying: May these, my two sons, sit, the one on Thy right hand and the other on Thy left, in Thy kingdom. If this be a fault, then it is a fault of piety. For a mother's love knows no bounds: if she be covetous in her pleading, then such avarice may be forgiven her, for she is covetous not of money, but of grace. Nor is she overbold in her petition, for she is mindful not of herself, but of her children. Consider the mother, think well upon the mother.

Christ considered the love of the mother, whose consolation in her extreme old age was the thought of her sons' reward; and who, although spent with a mother's longing, endured the absence of these dear pledges of her love. Consider also that she was a woman, that is to say, one of the weaker sex which the Lord had not yet strengthened by His own Passion. Consider, I repeat, that she was an heiress of that Eve, the first woman, failing through the inheritance of immoderate desire transmitted to all; whom the Lord had not yet redeemed with His own Blood, from whose heart Christ had not yet washed away in the laver of His Blood the craving for undue dignity implanted in the hearts of all. Therefore, the woman was at fault, but it was an inherited weakness.

THURSDAY

The reading of the holy Gospel according to St. Luke

At that time: Jesus said to the Pharisees: There was a certain rich man who was clothed in purple and fine linen: and feasted sumptuously every day. And so forth.

Homily of St. Gregory, Pope

What, dearly beloved brethren, is to be understood by this rich man who was clothed in purple and fine linen and feasted sumptuously every day, if not the Jewish nation, who kept the observances of religion in their outward life, who used the refinements of the law they had received, for their own magnificence and not for their true advantage? What, again, is to be understood as expressed by Lazarus, the man full of sores, if not the Gentile people? For they, as soon as they were converted to God, were not ashamed to confess their sins, whence the sores in their skin. Indeed, it is through such wounds in the skin that poison is drawn out from the inward parts, and outwardly breaks forth.

What, then, is the confession of sins but the breaking-out, as it were, of sores? For in confession the poison of sin is laid wholesomely open, which before lurked balefully in the mind. Indeed, through wounds in the skin, the corrupt humor is drawn to the surface. And in the confession of sins, what else do we do but expose the evil that lay hidden within us? But Lazarus, full of sores, desired to be filled with the crumbs that fell from the rich man's table, and no one gave them to him: for this proud people did not deign to admit any of the Gentiles to the knowledge of the law.

As long as the teaching of the law inclined them not to love, but to pride, they swelled, as it were, with importance at the thought of the treasure they had received; and the words they let fall from their knowledge were like crumbs dropping from the table. But, on the other hand, the dogs licked the sores of the poor man as he lay there. Often, in holy Scripture, by dogs are to be understood preachers. Now dogs heal wounds by licking them with their tongues: even so, holy teachers, when they instruct us in the confessing of our sins, as it were, touch the wounds of our souls with their tongues.

FRIDAY

The reading of the holy Gospel
according to St. Matthew

At that time: Jesus spoke this parable to the
multitude of the Jews and the chief priests: There
was a man, a householder, who planted a vineyard
and made a hedge round about it. And so forth.

Homily of St. Ambrose, Bishop

Many and various are the interpretations given
of the term, vineyard: but Isaias said plainly that
the vineyard of the Lord of Sabaoth was the house
of Israel. Who else but God planted this vineyard?
It is He, then, that let it out to husbandmen and
went Himself into a strange country; not that the
Lord went from place to place, since He is present
everywhere, but that He is more especially present
with those who are diligent in His service and far
from those who are negligent. He was abroad for
a long time lest He should seem overhasty in what
He required. For where the more indulgent liberality has been shown, there obstinacy is the more
inexcusable.

Thus it is well said, according to Matthew, that
He made a hedge round about it, that is, He fenced
it in with the wall of divine protection, lest it
should too easily be open to the inroads of spiritual
wild beasts. And He dug in it a wine-press. How

shall we understand what is meant by this wine-press unless, perhaps, because certain Psalms are inscribed: For the presses; for in these Psalms the mysteries of the Lord's Passion seethe and brim over with the Holy Spirit like foaming new-made wine? Whence those men were thought to be drunk who were flooded with the Holy Spirit. And therefore, this man dug the wine-press into which the inward fruit of the reasonable grape should flow in a spiritual outpouring.

He built a tower, that is to say, He raised aloft the pinnacle of the law: and so He let out this vineyard, thus furnished, tended, and adorned, to the Jews. And, at the time of the fruits, He sent His young servants. It is well put: At the time of the fruits; not: At the vintage. For no fruit came forth from the Jews, no vintage from this vineyard, whereof the Lord says: I looked that it should bring forth grapes and it hath brought forth thorns. And therefore, these wine-presses did not run over with the wine of joy, the new-made wine of the spirit, but with the blood of the Prophets that were slain.

SATURDAY

The reading of the holy Gospel according to St. Luke

At that time: Jesus spoke to the Pharisees and scribes this parable: A certain man had two sons;

and the younger of them said to his father: Father, give me the portion of the substance that falleth to me. And so forth.

Homily of St. Ambrose, Bishop

Thou seest that the divine patrimony is given to those who ask for it. Do not attribute blame to the father because he gave to the younger son. In the kingdom of God, there is no period of feebleness; neither is faith weighed down by years. Certainly he judged himself fit to have it, since he asked for it. And indeed, if he had not left his father, he would not have found his age a hindrance. But, after he had left his father's house and gone abroad into a far country, he began to be in want. Truly, then, he has wasted his patrimony who has deserted the Church.

He went abroad into a far country. What farther can a man go than to depart from himself, to separate himself from the Saints, not by tracts of land, but by his own dispositions, to be separated, not by countries, but by his own ambitions; and thus to be cut off from them, as it were, by an intervening sea of worldly passion? For indeed, he who separates himself from Christ is an exile from his native land, he is a citizen of this world. But we are no more strangers and foreigners, but fellow-citizens with the Saints, and of the household of God. For we who were afar are brought nigh in the blood of

Christ. Let us not despise those returning from that far country; for we too once dwelt in a distant land, as Isaias teaches. For thou hast these words: Light is risen to them who sat in the region of the shadow of death. Therefore, this far-off region is the shadow of death.

But we, to whom Christ the Lord is as the breath of our nostrils, live in the shadow of Christ. And therefore the Church says: I desired Him and sat down under His shadow. This man, then, by living riotously, wasted all the beauty of his nature. And do thou who hast received the image of God, who bearest His likeness, waste it not by brutish foulness. Thou art the work of God; say not to a stock: Thou art my father; lest thou take upon thyself the likeness of a stock, for it is written: Let them that make them become like unto them.

III SUNDAY IN LENT

I Nocturn

From the Book of Genesis, c. 37, 2 - 28

II Nocturn

From the book of St. Ambrose, Bishop,
on holy Joseph

The lives of the Saints are a model for the lives of the rest of men. And therefore we have received a very well-arranged series of them in the Scriptures, that when in our reading we come to know Abraham, Isaac, Jacob, and other just men, by following in their footsteps we may tread, as it were, that path of innocence which is opened to us by their virtues. And now, since I have often treated of these matters, the story of holy Joseph is suggested to me today: in him, although there are virtues of very many kinds, yet that of chastity shines forth in a particular manner.

Therefore, when you discover in Abraham the tireless devotion of faith, in Isaac the purity of a sincere mind, and in Jacob singular patience of heart and endurance of labor, it is fitting that out of this common fund of virtues you should give your attention to the particular kinds of discipline you find practised there. Let us, then, set holy Joseph before us as a mirror of chastity. For modesty shines forth in his deeds and manner of life and, as though an attendant upon chastity, there shines the luster of his graceful bearing. And for this reason he was beloved by his parents above the rest of their sons.

But this gave rise to envy, which circumstance was not to be passed over in silence; for in this lies the whole argument of the story, by this we understand that the perfect man is neither moved by ill-will to avenge an injury, nor renders evil for evil. Whence also David says: If I have rendered evils to them that repaid me evils. How, then, should Joseph merit to be preferred above the rest of men if he had injured those who injured him and loved those who loved him? For most men do this. But it is a remarkable thing if thou lovest thine enemy, as the Savior teaches.

It is therefore truly marvellous that he acted thus before the coming of the Gospel, that he showed mercy to them who injured him; that he forgave them who attacked him; and when sold, he did not render evil to them, but paid back the insult with kindness. We who have received the Gospel have learnt all this, but cannot fulfil it. Let us learn, then, how the Saints have been hated that we may imitate their patience. And let us recognize that they were not by nature better than other men, but only more vigilant; that they were not free from faults, but amended them. And thus, if even Saints can be scorched by the fire of jealousy, how much greater care must sinners take lest they be burnt in the flame?

R. When Jacob saw Joseph's coat, he rent his garments and wept, and said: * An evil wild beast hath devoured my son Joseph. V. And his brethren took his coat and sent it to his father. And he knew it and said. An evil wild beast. Glory. An evil wild beast.

III Neturn

The reading of the holy Gospel according to St. Luke

At that time: Jesus was casting out a devil, and the same was dumb. And when He had cast out the devil, the dumb spoke, and the multitudes were in admiration at it. And so forth.

Homily of St. Bede the Venerable, Priest

This man possessed with a devil was, according to Matthew, not only dumb, but also blind; and he was cured by the Lord, we are told, so that he both spoke and saw. Three miracles, therefore, were wrought upon this one man at one and the same time: blind, he saw; dumb, he spoke; possessed, he was delivered from the devil. What was done then according to the flesh is accomplished daily in the conversion of believers: in the first place the devil is driven out and they behold the light of faith; then their mouths, that before were dumb, are set free to sing the praises of God.

But some of them said: He casteth out devils by Beelzebub, the prince of devils. This was not said by any among the multitude, but by the scribes and Pharisees who maligned Him, as the other Evangelists bear witness. For indeed this multitude, which would seem to be made up of those of little learning, ever marvelled at the Lord's doings. Those men, on the contrary, were laboring either to deny them or, if they could not deny them, to pervert them by putting an evil interpretation upon them, as though they were not wrought by the power of His divinity, but by an unclean spirit.

And others, tempting, asked of Him a sign from heaven. They desired that, as it had been with Elias, fire should come down from on high; or, as with Samuel, that in the summer time the thunder should peal, the lightning flash, the rain pour down: as though they could not have interpreted even that amiss and said that it had happened on account of various hidden disturbances in the sky. But thou who dost deny the truth which thou seest with thine eyes, holdest in thy hand and findest to be useful, what wilt thou do concerning those things which shall come from heaven? Assuredly thou wilt answer that the magicians in Egypt also wrought many signs from heaven. But He, seeing their thoughts, said to them: Every kingdom divided against itself shall be brought to desolation, and house upon house shall fall. He replies, not to their words, but to their thoughts; that thus they might be compelled to believe in His power since He could see what was hidden in the heart.

But if every kingdom divided against itself is brought to desolation, then the kingdom of the Father, the Son, and the Holy Ghost is not divided: for without any discord, without any possibility of being brought to desolation, it is to abide in everlasting steadfastness. But if Satan be divided against himself, how shall his kingdom stand; because you say that through Beelzebub I cast out devils? In saying this He wished it to be understood that, by their own confession, in not believing in Him they chose rather to be in the kingdom of the devil, which indeed could not stand since it was divided against itself.

R. We deserve to suffer these things because we have sinned against our brother: seeing the anguish of his soul when he besought us, and we would not hear him: * Therefore is this affliction come upon us. V. Ruben said to his brethren: Did I not say to you: Do not sin against the boy; and you would not hear me? Therefore. Glory. Therefore.

✠ Continuation of the holy Gospel according to St. Luke.—At that time: Jesus was casting out a devil, and the same was dumb. And when He had cast out the devil, the dumb spoke, and the multitudes were in admiration at it. But some of them said: He casteth out devils by Beelzebub, the prince of devils. And others, tempting, asked a sign from heaven. But He, seeing their thoughts, said to them: Every kingdom divided against itself shall be brought to desolation, and house upon house shall fall. And if Satan also be divided against himself, how shall his kingdom stand? because you say that through Beelzebub I cast out devils. Now if I cast

out devils by Beelzebub, by whom do your children
cast them out? Therefore, they shall be your judges.
But if I by the finger of God cast out devils, doubtless the kingdom of God is come upon you. When
a strong man armed keepeth his court, those things
are in peace which he possesseth. But if a stronger
than he come upon him and overcome him, he will
take away all his armor wherein he trusted, and
will distribute his spoils. He that is not with Me
is against Me: and he that gathereth not with Me
scattereth. When the unclean spirit is gone out of
a man, he walketh through places without water,
seeking rest: and not finding, he saith: I will return into my house whence I came out. And when
he is come, he findeth it swept and garnished. Then
he goeth and taketh with him seven other spirits
more wicked than himself, and entering in they
dwell there. And the last state of that man becomes worse than the first. And it came to pass,
as He spoke these things, a certain woman from the
crowd, lifting up her voice, said to Him: Blessed
is the womb that bore Thee, and the paps that gave
Thee suck. But He said: Yea rather, blessed are
they who hear the word of God, and keep it.

LET US PRAY

We beseech Thee, O almighty God, regard the desires of Thy humble servants and extend the right
hand of Thy Majesty to defend us. Through our
Lord.

MONDAY

The reading of the holy Gospel according to St. Luke

At that time: Jesus said to the Pharisees: Doubtless you will say to Me this similitude: Physician, heal Thyself: as great things as we have heard done in Capharnaum, do also here in our country. And so forth.

Homily of St. Ambrose, Bishop

No mean degree of envy was that which led these men to turn what should have been a reason for love into an occasion of bitter hatred, unmindful of the charity due to a fellow-citizen. In this passage it is shown both by example and by word that if thou enviest the fruits of virtue in other men, thou wilt look in vain for the assistance of heavenly mercy. For the Lord is a despiser of the envious: and from those who persecute other men for possessing divine benefits He turns away the wonders of His power. For the works of the Lord in His human nature are a manifestation of His divinity; and His invisible works are shown to us by means of those which are visible.

Not without reason, therefore, does the Savior excuse Himself because He worked no miracles of His power in His own country, lest perchance anyone should think that he owes little affection for his own country. Indeed, it was impossible for Him not to love His fellow-citizens, since He loved all men, but it was they themselves who, in giving way to envy, forfeited the love due to fellow-citizens. In truth I say unto you: there were many widows in the days of Elias. Not that the days belonged to Elias, but that they were the days in which Elias worked; or that Elias made day appear to them who saw in his works the light of spiritual grace and were converted to the Lord. And therefore heaven was opened to the beholders of the eternal and divine mysteries; it was shut, and there was a famine when there was no longer an abundance of the knowledge of God. But of this we spoke more fully when we wrote concerning widows.

And there were many lepers in Judea in the time of Eliseus the prophet: and none of them was cleansed but Naaman the Syrian. By these words the Lord and Savior clearly teaches and exhorts us to be zealous in our reverence for divine things: because no one is shown to be made whole and have his body free from the defilements of disease except he who seeks to be healed through the performance of religious duties. For God does not bestow His blessings on the slothful, but on those who observe His commandments. In another book we said concerning that widow to whom Elias was sent that she was set as a type that prefigured the Church. The people gathered together and formed the Church in order that other people might follow that which had been gathered together out of strange nations. The people that, before being baptized in the mystic waters, was previously leprous, was formerly defiled; that same people, after being washed from the stains of body and mind by the sacrament of baptism, was now no longer a leper, but a spotless virgin without wrinkle.

TUESDAY

The reading of the holy Gospel according to St. Matthew

At that time: Jesus said to His disciples: If thy brother shall offend against thee, go, and rebuke him between thee and him alone. And so forth.

Homily of St. Augustine, Bishop

Why dost thou rebuke him? Is it because thou art vexed that he has offended against thee? God forbid. If thou dost this for love of thyself, thou dost nothing; but if thou dost it for love of him, thou dost excellently. And thus, from these very words, mark well for whose love thou oughtest to do this, whether for love of thyself or of him. If he shall hear thee, He says, thou hast gained thy brother. Then do it for his sake, that thou mayst gain him. By so doing, thou gainest him; hadst thou not done it, he would have been lost. How is

it, then, that most men disregard these sins and
say: What great offence have I committed? I have
only sinned against man. Do not disregard these
sins, that thou hast sinned against man.

Wouldst thou know, that in sinning against man,
thou art lost? If he against whom thou hast sinned hath rebuked thee between thee and him alone
and thou shalt listen to him, he hath gained thee.
He hath gained thee: what does this mean, but that
thou hadst been lost, had he not gained thee? For
if thou wouldst not have been lost, how hath he
gained thee? Therefore, let no man disregard it,
when he sins against his brother. For the Apostle
says in a certain place: Now when you sin thus
against the brethren and wound their weak conscience, you sin against Christ; for this reason, because we have all been made members of Christ.
How dost thou, who sinnest against a member of
Christ, not sin against Christ?

Therefore, let no one say: I have not sinned a-
gainst God, but I have sinned against a brother; I
have sinned against a man, a light sin or no sin at
all. It may be, then, that thou sayest it is light because it is quickly remedied. Thou hast sinned a-
gainst a brother; make satisfaction and thou art
healed. Quickly thou didst this deadly thing; but
just as quickly hast thou found the remedy. Which
of us, my brethren, can hope for the kingdom of
heaven when the Gospel says: Whosoever shall say

to his brother, Thou fool, shall be in danger of hell
fire? This is terrible indeed, but behold in the same
place the remedy. If thou offer thy gift at the altar
and there thou remember that thy brother hath
anything against thee, leave there thy offering before the altar. God is not angered that thou de-
layest to offer thy gift; God seeks thee rather than
thy gift.

WEDNESDAY

The reading of the holy Gospel
according to St. Matthew

At that time: The scribes and Pharisees came
to Jesus from Jerusalem saying: Why do Thy disciples transgress the tradition of the ancients? And
so forth.

Homily of St. Jerome, Priest

The foolishness of the scribes and Pharisees is
amazing. They rebuke the Son of God because He
does not keep the precepts and traditions of men:
For Your disciples, they say, wash not their hands
when they eat bread. It is the hands, that is, the
works, not indeed of the body, but of the soul, that
are to be washed, that the word of God may be fulfilled in them. But He answering said to them:
Why do you also transgress the commandment of
God on account of your tradition? He refutes the
false charge by a true answer. While you neglect

the commandments of God, He says, on account of the tradition of men, why do you think My disciples are to be rebuked because they attach little weight to the ordinances of the ancients so as to fulfil the statutes of God?

For God said: Honor thy father and mother; and: He that shall curse father or mother, let him die the death. But you say: Whosoever shall say to father or mother: Whatever gift is from me shall profit thee; and he shall not honor his father or his mother. Honor in the Scriptures is not to be understood so much of greetings or of services rendered as of almsdeeds and the offering of gifts. Honor widows, says the Apostle, that are widows indeed. By honor here is to be understood a gift. And in another place: Priests are to be honored with a double honor, especially they who labor in the word and doctrine of God. And by this command we are ordered not to muzzle the ox that treadeth out the corn: and that the laborer is worthy of his hire.

The Lord had commanded that sons should honor their parents, even in supplying them with the necessities of life, out of consideration for their weakness, old age, or poverty. But the scribes and Pharisees, wishing to overrule this most prudent law of God and to encourage impiety under the name of piety, taught undutiful sons that if they would vow to God, who is indeed their Father, the things that they should rightly bestow on their parents, the oblation made to the Lord would be preferred above the gifts offered to parents. At any rate the parents themselves, by refusing the gifts which they perceive to have been dedicated to God lest they should incur the crime of sacrilege, are thus brought to suffer want. So it came about that the gifts offered by sons in honor of God and His temple went to the profit of the priests.

THURSDAY

The reading of the holy Gospel according to St. Luke

At that time: Jesus rising up out of the synagogue, went into Simon's house. And Simon's wife's mother was taken with a great fever. And so forth.

Homily of St. Ambrose, Bishop

Behold the mercy of the Lord and Savior: He is not moved to indignation nor is He vexed by evil doings, nor, outraged by insults, does He desert Judea: nay rather, unmindful of insult, but mindful of mercy, now by teaching, now by setting men free, now by works of healing, He softens the hearts of that faithless people. And well has St. Luke given the first place to the man delivered from the evil spirit and the second to the woman who was made whole. For the Lord came to heal both sexes: yet he ought first to be healed who was first created;

but she is not to be passed over who sinned rather from fickleness of mind than from actual malice.

That the Lord first began His works of healing upon the Sabbath day signifies that the new creature began where the old creature left off; and it shows further how the Son of God was not under the law, but above the law in the very beginning; and that the law was not destroyed, but fulfilled. For the world was not made by the law, but by the word, as we read: By the word of the Lord the heavens were established. Therefore the law was not destroyed, but fulfilled, that man, who had already fallen, might be restored. Whence also the Apostle says: Stripping off the old man from yourselves, put on the new man, who is created according to God.

Rightly, then, did He begin upon the Sabbath day that so He might show Himself as the Creator, carrying out His works in due order and succession, continuing what He had already begun: even as a builder, intending to restore a house, begins to remove the old masonry not from the foundations, but from the roof. And so He first sets His Hand to the place where He had left off: then He begins with the lesser things that He may come to those that are of more importance. For even men, by the word of God, can set others free from the devil; but to command the dead to rise again belongs to divine power alone. Perhaps again it may be that under the type of this woman, the mother-in-law of Simon and Andrew, is signified our flesh, sick with sundry fevers of sin and inflamed with the wanton promptings of all kinds of evil desires. And I would not say that the fever of love is less violent than the heat of a bodily fever. Therefore the one inflames the heart, the other, the body. For our fever is avarice; our fever is lust; our fever is luxury; our fever is ambition; our fever is anger.

FRIDAY

The reading of the holy Gospel according to St. John

At that time: Jesus came to a city of Samaria which is called Sichar, near the land which Jacob gave to his son, Joseph. And so forth.

Homily of St. Augustine, Bishop

Now the mysteries begin. For it is not in vain that Jesus is weary; not in vain is the power of God weary; for not without a purpose is He weary, by whom the weary are refreshed; not without reason is He weary, by whose absence we are wearied, by whose presence we are strengthened. Nevertheless, Jesus is weary, and weary from His journey; He sits down, and it is beside a well He sitteth; and it is at the sixth hour that He, being weary, sits down. All these things betoken something, are intended to intimate something; they make us eager, they exhort us to knock. May He Himself, then, open to us and to you, He who deigned thus to exhort us, saying: Knock, and it shall be opened unto you.

It was for thee that Jesus was wearied from His journey. We find Jesus, the mighty one; and we find Jesus, the weak one: both strong and weak. Strong, because: In the beginning was the Word, and the Word was with God, and the Word was God; the same was in the beginning with God. Wouldst thou see how strong is this Son of God? All things were made by Him and without Him nothing was made; and made, too, without labor. Then, what can be stronger than He, by whom all things were made without labor? Wouldst thou know Him weak? The Word was made flesh, and dwelt among us. The strength of Christ created thee, the weakness of Christ re-created thee. The strength of Christ created all things that what was not might exist: the weakness of Christ assumed our nature that what was already made should not perish. He created us by His strength, He sought us by His weakness.

He, therefore, becoming weak Himself, nourishes the weak as a hen her chickens, for He likened Himself to a hen. How often, He said to Jerusalem, would I have gathered thy children as the hen doth gather her chickens under her wings, and thou wouldst not? And you see, brethren, how the hen becomes weak with her chickens. For no other bird, when it is a mother, is recognized at once to be so. We see sparrows of all kinds building their nests before our eyes; daily we see swallows, storks, and doves making their nests; but, except when we see them on their nests, we do not at once recognize that they are parents. But the hen is so enfeebled over her brood that, even if the chickens are not following her, even if thou seest not her young ones, yet at once thou knowest her to be a mother.

SATURDAY

The reading of the holy Gospel according to St. John

At that time: Jesus went to Mount Olivet; and early in the morning He came again into the temple. And so forth.

Homily of St. Augustine, Bishop

Jesus went unto Mount Olivet, unto the fruitful mount, unto the mount of ointment, unto the mount of chrism. Where indeed could it be more fitting for Christ to teach than upon Mount Olivet? For the name of Christ is said to be from chrism; and *chrisma,* in Greek, is called in Latin *unctio,* anointing. And He has anointed us for this reason, because He has made us wrestlers against the devil. And early in the morning He came again into the temple, and all the people came to Him, and sitting

down, He taught them. And He was not laid hold
upon because He did not yet deign to suffer. And
now, mark how the Lord's meekness was tempted
by His enemies.

And the scribes and Pharisees bring unto Him a
woman taken in adultery, and they set her in the
midst and said to Him: Master, this woman was
even now taken in adultery. Now Moses in the law
commanded us to stone such a one. But what sayest Thou? And this they said tempting Him, that
they might accuse Him. Accuse Him of what? Had
they indeed caught Him in any crime? or was that
woman said to have been concerned with Him in
any way?

We understand, brethren, that there was a marvellous gentleness in the Lord. They perceived that
He was exceedingly meek, surpassingly gentle. Indeed, this had been long ago foretold of Him: Gird
Thy sword upon Thy thigh, O Thou most mighty.
With Thy comeliness and Thy beauty, set out, proceed prosperously, and reign: because of truth and
meekness and justice. And therefore, as a teacher,
He brought forth truth; as a deliverer, meekness;
as an advocate, justice. Because of these things,
the prophet, through the Holy Spirit, foretold that
He should reign. When He spoke, the truth was
acknowledged; when He was not strongly moved
against His enemies, His meekness was praised.
Whilst, therefore, in respect of these two things,

that is, His truth and His meekness, His enemies were tormented with envy and ill-will, they made a stumbling block of the third, that is, His justice.

IV SUNDAY IN LENT

I Nocturn

From the book of Exodus, c. 3, 1 - 15

II Nocturn

Sermon of St. Basil the Great

Moses, we know, went up fasting into the mountain: nor would he otherwise have dared to approach that smoking hill-top and to enter into its gloom unless he were protected by fasting. It was through fasting that he received the commandments written upon tables by the finger of God. Likewise on the heights of the mountain, fasting was the promoter of the spreading of the law. while in the depths below, gluttony drew the people on into idolatry and defiled them. The people, it says, sat down to eat and drink, and rose up to play. One drunken bout on the part of the people rendered fruitless and vain the labor and perseverance of forty days, in which the servant of God fasted and prayed without ceasing.

For drunkenness broke those tables, written by the finger of God, that had been granted to fasting; the most holy Prophet judged that this wine-soaked people were not fit to receive the law from God. In one moment of time, through gluttony, that people, who had been instructed in the worship of God by means of the greatest miracles, fell headlong into the most foul idolatry of Egypt. From this, if thou considerest both these facts together, it may be seen that fasting draws men to God while pleasures lead to the loss of salvation.

What was it that defiled Esau and made him the servant of his brother? Was it not a single portion of food, for which he sold his birthright? And Samuel, was he not granted to his mother's prayers through fasting? What was it that made the most mighty Samson invincible? Was it not fasting, through which he was conceived in his mother's womb? Fasting conceived him, fasting nurtured him, fasting made him the man he was. For thus indeed the angel commanded his mother, warning her, lest she touch anything whatsoever that came from the vine, nor drink wine, nor any strong drink. Fasting brought forth the prophets, it strengthens and confirms the mighty.

Fasting makes rulers wise; it is the sure guardian of the soul, a safe companion for the body, arms and defence to mighty men, training for athletes and wrestlers. Moreover, it is this that drives away temptations, that prepares us for loving service, that accompanies sobriety, and is the author of temperance. In war it brings courage, in peace it teaches gentleness. It sanctifies the Nazarene, it perfects the priest; for it is not fitting to approach the sacrifice without fasting, not only as regards the mystical and true adoration of God as we have it now, but also in respect of that adoration in which sacrifices were offered in figure according to the law. Fasting was the means of Elias beholding a great vision: for when he had cleansed his soul by fasting forty days, he merited to behold God, as far as this is right for man to do, from his cave. Moses, receiving the law for a second time, gave himself to fasting. The Ninivites, unless they and their beasts had fasted, would never have escaped the threatened calamity. And in the desert, who were they whose bodies were stricken? Were they not those who desired flesh-meat?

R. Let us sing to the Lord: for He is gloriously magnified: the horse and the rider He hath thrown into the sea: * The Lord is my strength and my praise, and He is become salvation to me. V. The Lord is as a man of war, Almighty is His name. The Lord is my strength. Glory. The Lord is my strength.

III Nocturn

The reading of the holy Gospel
according to St. John

At that time: Jesus went over the sea of Galilee, which is that of Tiberias, and a great multitude followed Him because they saw the miracles which He did on them that were diseased. And so forth.

Homily of St. Augustine, Bishop

The miracles that were wrought by our Lord Jesus Christ are indeed divine works and incite the mind of man to the understanding of God through visible things. But inasmuch as He is not such a substance as may be seen by the eyes, and His miracles, by which He rules the whole world and disposes every creature, are despised because they are always taking place, so that practically no man deigns to consider the astounding and marvellous works of God exhibited in a single grain of seed, He has, according to His great mercy, reserved to Himself certain works, beyond the usual course and order of nature, which He should perform on a fitting occasion that they, by whom His daily miracles are lightly esteemed, might be struck with astonishment at beholding miracles, not indeed greater, but more unusual.

Truly, it is a far greater miracle to govern the whole world than to satisfy five thousand men with five loaves. And yet at the one, no man wonders; at the other, men are in admiration, not because it is the greater miracle, but because it is a thing that seldom happens. For who is it that, even today, feeds the whole world, if not He who out of a few grains creates whole harvests?

Therefore, it was as God that He did this. For from the source whence He multiplies the harvest from a few grains, thence He multiplied the five loaves in His hands: for the power was in the hands of Christ. Moreover, these five loaves were as seeds, not indeed committed to the earth, but multiplied by Him who made the earth.

Here, then, was something brought before the senses that by it the mind should be roused to attention; there was something exhibited to the eyes that upon it the understanding should be exercised; so that we might be led to wonder at the invisible God by means of His visible works and, being lifted up to faith and cleansed by faith, we might desire to behold even that invisible Being Himself whom, though invisible, we came to know by the things that can be seen. But it is not enough to observe these points in the miracles of Christ. Let us ask those miracles what they have to tell us about Christ, for if we can only understand it, they have a language of their own. And since Christ Himself is the Word of God, even the deed of that Word must be a word to us.

R. Give ear, O My people, unto My law: * Incline your ear unto the words of My mouth. V. I will open My mouth in parables: I will utter sayings from the beginning of the world. Incline. Glory. Incline.

✠ Continuation of the holy Gospel according to St. John.—At that time: Jesus went over the sea of Galilee, which is that of Tiberias: and a great multitude followed Him, because they saw the miracles which He did on them that were diseased. Jesus, therefore, went up into a mountain and there He sat with His disciples. Now the pasch, the festival day of the Jews, was near at hand. When Jesus therefore had lifted up His eyes and seen that a very great multitude cometh to Him, He said to Philip: Whence shall we buy bread that these may eat? And this He said to try him, for He Himself knew what He would do. Philip answered Him: Two hundred pennyworth of bread is not sufficient for them, that every one may take a little. One of His disciples, Andrew, the brother of Simon Peter, saith to Him: There is a boy here that hath five barley loaves and two fishes, but what are these among so many? Then Jesus said: Make the men sit down. Now there was much grass in the place. The men, therefore, sat down, in number about five thousand. And Jesus took the loaves, and when He had given thanks, He distributed to them that were sat down: in like manner also of the fishes, as much as they would. And when they were filled, He said to His disciples: Gather up the fragments that remain, lest they be lost. They gathered up, therefore, and filled twelve baskets with the fragments of the five barley loaves which remained over and above to them that had eaten. Now those men, when they had seen what a miracle Jesus had done, said: This is of a truth the prophet that is to come into the world. Jesus therefore, when He knew that they would come to take Him by force and make Him king, fled again into the mountain, Himself alone.

Let Us Pray

Grant, we beseech Thee, O almighty God, that we who justly suffer for our sins may obtain relief by the consolation of Thy grace. Through our Lord.

MONDAY

The reading of the holy Gospel according to St. John

At that time: The Pasch of the Jews was at hand and Jesus went up to Jerusalem: and He found in the temple them that sold oxen and sheep and doves. And so forth.

Homily of St. Augustine, Bishop

What is this we have been hearing, brethren? Behold, that temple was still nothing more than a figure, and yet the Lord cast out from thence all that sought their own affairs, all who came there to trade. And what was it that they sold there? Things which men had need of for the sacrifices of that day. For you know, dearly beloved, that sacrifices were given to that people, because of the carnal temper and stony heart yet within them, to keep them from falling into idolatry: and so they offered there in sacrifice oxen, sheep, and doves. This you know, for you have read it.

It was, then, no great sin if they sold in the temple what was bought to be offered in the temple: and yet He cast them out from thence. But what would the Lord do if He found drunken men there? For He drove out those who were selling lawful goods and not doing anything contrary to justice (for what is honestly bought is not unlawfully sold), and He would not suffer the house of prayer to become a house of trade.

If the house of God ought not to become a house of trading, should it become a house of winebibbing? When we say this, they gnash their teeth against us; yet we are comforted by the Psalm which you have just heard: They gnashed upon me with their teeth. We know also that we hear therein how we may be healed; even when again and again the scourges fall upon Christ, whose own word is even now being scourged. Scourges were laid upon Me, says He, and they knew it not. He was scourged by the scourges of the Jews; He is scourged by the blasphemies of false Christians; they multiply scourges for the Lord their God, and they know it not. Let us, so far as He aids us, do as the Psalmist did: But as for me, when they were troublesome to me, I put on haircloth and I humbled my soul with fasting.

TUESDAY

The reading of the holy Gospel
according to St. John

At that time: About the middle of the feast Jesus went up into the temple and taught. And the Jews wondered. And so forth.

Homily of St. Augustine, Bishop

He who was in hiding now taught; He spoke openly and no man laid hands on Him. For that He hid Himself was for an example; that He manifested Himself was to show His power. But when He taught, the Jews marvelled. All of them, as I think, marvelled, yet all were not converted. And why did they marvel? Because many of them knew where He was born and how He had been brought up. They had never seen Him learning letters, but they heard Him disputing concerning the law, producing testimonies of the law, which no one could produce unless he had read, and no one could read unless he had learnt letters; and that was why they marvelled. But their marvelling was made an occasion to the Master of instilling the truth more deeply into their minds.

For verily, on account of their marvelling and their words, the Lord gave utterance to something of great depth and worthy of careful examination and discussion. What was it, then, that the Lord answered to them who were marvelling how He came to know letters, never having learnt? My doctrine, He says, is not Mine, but His that sent Me. Here is the first deep mystery, for it seems as if He had said contradictory things in these few words. For He does not say: This doctrine is not Mine; but: My doctrine is not Mine. If it be not Thine, how is it Thine? If it be Thine, how is it not Thine? For Thou sayest both: My doctrine, and not Mine.

But if we look carefully at what the same holy Evangelist says by way of introduction: In the beginning was the Word, and the Word was with God, and the Word was God, there lies the answer to this question. What is the doctrine of the Father if not the Word of the Father? Therefore, Christ Himself is the doctrine of the Father if He is the Word of the Father. But since the Word cannot be from no one, but must be of someone, He said both "His doctrine," namely, Himself, and also "not His own," because He is the Word of the Father. For what is so much "thine" as thyself? And what is so much "not thine" as thyself, if it be of someone else that thou art?

WEDNESDAY

The reading of the holy Gospel
according to St. John

At that time: Jesus, passing by, saw a man who was blind from his birth, and His disciples asked

Him: Rabbi, who hath sinned, this man or his parents, that he should be born blind? And so forth.

Homily of St. Augustine, Bishop

These acts of our Lord Jesus Christ, so astounding and wonderful, are both works and words: works, because they are deeds; words, because they are signs. Therefore, if we consider the meaning of this that was done, this blind man represents the human race. For this blindness fell upon the first man on account of sin and from him we all have derived the origin, not only of death, but of iniquity. If blindness, then, be unbelief, and enlightenment, faith, whom did Christ, at His coming, find a believer? Since indeed the Apostle, born as he was in the nation of the prophets, says: We also, in time past, were by nature children of wrath, even as the rest. If we were children of wrath, children of vengeance, children of punishment, children of hell, how is it said: By nature, if not that, by the sin of the first man, vice rooted itself in us as a nature? If evil has so taken root within us that it has become our nature, every man is born blind as regards his mind.

The Lord came: what did He do? He put forward a great mystery. He spat upon the ground, with the spittle He made clay, (for the Word was made flesh) and He anointed the blind man's eyes. He was anointed, but at first he saw not. He sent him to the pool which is called Siloe. But it was

for the Evangelist to call our attention to the name
of this pool, and he says: Which is interpreted,
Sent. Already you recognize who it is that was
sent, for unless he had been sent, none of us would
have been delivered from iniquity. So he washed
his eyes in that pool which is interpreted, Sent: he
was baptized in Christ. If therefore, when He, so
to speak, baptized the man in Himself, He thereupon enlightened him; when He anointed him, He
made him, so to say, a catechumen.

You have heard a great mystery. Ask a man:
Art thou a Christian? He will answer thee: I am
not. Art thou a pagan, then, or a Jew? And if he
shall answer: I am not, then thou wilt ask him further: Art thou a catechumen, or one of the faithful? If he shall answer thee: A catechumen, he
is anointed, not yet washed. But whence has he
been anointed? Ask, and he will reply. Ask him
who it is in whom he believes? By the very fact of
his being a catechumen, he answers: In Christ.
Mark that I speak, in a way, both to the faithful
and to the catechumens. What did I say in reference to the spittle and the clay? That the Word
was made flesh: the catechumens hear this, but
that to which they have been anointed is not all
they need: if they are seeking light, let them hasten to the font.

THURSDAY

The reading of the holy Gospel according to St. Luke

At that time: Jesus went into a city called Naim; and there went with Him His disciples and a great multitude. And so forth.

Homily of St. Ambrose, Bishop

This passage overflows with a double grace. In the first place, it gives us to understand how readily the divine mercy was moved by the lamentation of a widowed mother, especially of one who was distressed by the sufferings or death of an only son; nevertheless, it was the crowd of mourners that won for this widow that work of power. In the second place, we may well believe that this widow, surrounded by a crowd of people, stands for something more than a woman, whose tears earned for her the resurrection of this young man, her only son: for this reason, because holy Church recalls many young men to life, by the sight of her tears, from the funeral procession and the last rites of burial, she too is forbidden to weep for those who are to rise again.

The dead man was borne to the grave on a bier by the four elements of the material world; but he had hope of rising again because he was carried out upon wood. And though this had formerly been of no use to us, nevertheless, once Jesus had touched it, it began to avail us unto life: showing that salvation would be restored to the people by the gibbet of the cross. Therefore, when those grim bearers who were hastening the human body along in the deadly course of material nature heard the word of God, they stood still. Now what do we do but lie lifeless upon a certain bier, that is, something used for the last rites of the funeral, when either we are burned by the fire of inordinate desire, or bathed in a cold sweat, or when the vigor of our souls is deadened by the sloth of our earthly body, or when our mind is nourished by a spirit benumbed by sin and devoid of pure light? These are the bearers at our funeral.

But although the last rites accorded to the dead have banished all hope of life, and the lifeless bodies lie at the very threshold of the tomb; nevertheless, at the word of God, the dead corpses rise again, the voice returns, the son is restored to his mother, called back from the tomb, snatched from the grave. What is that tomb of thine but a wicked life? Thy tomb is faithlessness: thy sepulchre is thy throat. For: Their throat is an open sepulchre, whence deadly words come forth. Christ delivers thee from this sepulchre: thou shalt arise from this tomb if thou wilt listen to the word of God. And if thy sin be so grievous that thou canst not wash thyself with the tears of penitence, let thy mother the Church weep for thee, for she pleads for each one,

even as a widowed mother for her only son. She
grieves with a certain spiritual sorrow, keen as that
of nature, at the sight of her children borne on to
death by deadly sins.

FRIDAY

The reading of the holy Gospel
according to St. John

At that time: There was a certain man sick,
named Lazarus, of Bethania, of the town of Mary
and of Martha, her sister. And so forth.

Homily of St. Augustine, Bishop

In a former lesson, you remember, the Lord escaped out of the hands of them who would have
stoned Him and went away beyond the Jordan,
where John was baptizing. Then, while the Lord
was staying there, Lazarus fell sick in Bethania,
which was a town lying close to Jerusalem. And
Mary was she that anointed the Lord with ointment and wiped His feet with her hair, whose
brother Lazarus was sick. His sisters, therefore,
sent to Him. Now we understand whither it was
they sent, namely, where Jesus was, for He was
away, as you know, beyond the Jordan. They sent
messengers to the Lord, telling Him that their
brother was sick, in order that, if He deigned to do
so, He might come and deliver him from his sickness. The Lord delayed to heal that He might be
able to raise to life.

But what was the message sent by his sisters?
Lord, behold he whom Thou lovest is sick. They
did not say: Come; for to Him who loved him,
they had only to send the tidings. They did not
venture to say: Come and heal him; they did not
venture to say: Command there, and it shall be
done here. For why should not these women have
said this if the faith of that centurion is commended on this very account? For he said: I am not
worthy that Thou shouldst enter under my roof; but
only say the word and my servant shall be healed.
These women say none of these things, but only:
Lord, behold he whom Thou lovest is sick. It is
enough for Thee to know it; for Thou dost not love
and forsake.

Someone will say: How is it that by Lazarus is
signified a sinner, and yet he was so loved by the
Lord? Let such a one listen to Him when He says:
I came not to call the just, but sinners. For if God
loved not sinners, He would not have come down
from heaven to earth. And Jesus, hearing it, said
to them: This sickness is not unto death, but for
the glory of God, that the Son of God may be glorified. That He should be thus glorified was no gain
to Him, but only for our good. This, then, is what
He says: Is not unto death: because even that
death itself was not unto death, but rather unto the
working of a miracle whereby men might believe in
Christ and escape the true death. And mark how

the Lord, as it were, covertly, declares Himself to be God because of some who deny that the Son of God is God.

SATURDAY

The reading of the holy Gospel according to St. John

At that time: Jesus spoke to the multitude of the Jews, saying: I am the light of the world: he that followeth Me walketh not in darkness, but shall have the light of life. And so forth.

Homily of St. Augustine, Bishop

What the Lord saith: I am the light of the world, is clear, I think, to those who have eyes with which to share in this light; but they who have no eyes, save only those of the body, marvel at what is said by the Lord Jesus Christ: I am the light of the world. And perhaps there will not lack someone who will say within himself: May it not be that the Lord Jesus Christ is that sun which, in its rising and setting, causes the day? The Manicheans have thought Christ the Lord to be that sun visible to the eyes of the flesh, openly set forth to be seen, not only by men, but even by the beasts.

But the right faith of the Catholic Church disapproves of such an opinion and knows it to be the teaching of the devil; she not only by believing acknowledges it to be such, but also by reasoning proves it to whom she is able. Let us therefore reject this kind of error upon which Holy Church has set her anathema from the beginning. Let us not imagine the Lord Jesus Christ to be this sun which we see rising in the East and setting in the West; to whose course night succeeds, whose rays are obscured by a cloud; which goeth on its way by a fixed motion from place to place. This is not the Lord Christ. The Lord Christ is not the created sun, but He by whom the sun was created. For all things were made by Him and without Him nothing was made.

There is, then, a Light which made this visible light. Let us love this Light, let us earnestly desire to understand it, let us thirst for the same, that, by its own guidance, we may at length attain to it; let us so live in it that we may never die. For this is that light which of old went before the Israelites, of which the prophecy hath thus sung in the Psalm: For with Thee is the fountain of life, and in Thy light we shall see light. Mark ye what the ancient discourse of the holy men of God did promise concerning such a light. Men, saith it, and beasts Thou wilt preserve, O Lord: as Thou hast multiplied Thy mercy, O God.

PASSION SUNDAY

I Nocturn

From the book of Jeremias the Prophet, c. 1, 1 - 19

II Nocturn

Sermon of St. Leo, Pope

Among all the Christian festivals, dearly beloved, we are well aware that the Paschal mystery holds the first place: while the practices of all seasons prepare us for receiving it duly and worthily, these present days more especially solicit our devotion, seeing that they bring us so near to that sublime mystery of the divine mercy. Taught by the Holy Ghost, the holy Apostles ordained a strict fast to be kept upon these days; that, by sharing together in the cross of Christ, we too may take our part in some way in that which He did for us, as the Apostle says: If we suffer with Him, we shall also be glorified with Him. Sure and certain is the hope of promised bliss where there is a participation in the Passion of the Lord.

To no one is denied by circumstances, dearly beloved, a share in this glory, as if times of peace were devoid of occasions for the exercise of virtue. For the Apostle preaches, saying: All that will live godly in Christ shall suffer persecution; and therefore the trial of persecution shall never fail for those who never fail in works of godliness. For the Lord in His exhortations says: He that taketh not up his cross and followeth Me, is not worthy of Me.

And we ought not to doubt that this saying refers not only to the disciples of Christ, but to all the faithful and to the whole Church, who, in those who were then present, heard for all time the way to be saved. Therefore, just as it is required of the whole body to live piously, even so it is for the whole of time that the cross must be carried: each one is induced to bear this cross because it is accommodated to each one according to his own disposition and capacity. There is but one name for all forms of persecution, but the cause of the contest is not one and the same; and there is, moreover, far more danger to be feared from a foe who works in ambush than from an open enemy.

Blessed Job, well versed in alternate changes of good and evil in this world, said with truth and piety: Is not the life of man upon earth a temptation? For the faithful soul is not only assailed by corporal pains and sufferings, but also, when safe and sound as to his bodily members, he will be weighed down by grievous sickness if he be weakened by the delights of the flesh. But since the flesh lusteth against the spirit, and the spirit against the flesh, the rational mind is fortified by the defence of the cross of Christ, and does not con-

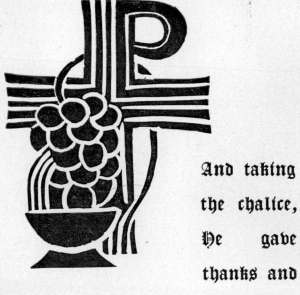

And taking the chalice, He gave thanks and gave to them, saying: Drink ye all of this. For this is My Blood of the new testament, which shall be shed for many unto remission of sins.

Matthew XXVI, 27, 28.

sent when enticed by evil desires, since it is pierced by the nail of continence and by the fear of God.

R. O Lord, my trouble is very near and there is none to help me; before they pierce my hands and my feet, deliver me from the mouth of the lion, * That I may declare Thy Name unto my brethren. V. O God, deliver my soul from the sword and my only one from the power of the dog. That I may.

III Nocturn

The reading of the holy Gospel according to St. John

At that time: Jesus said to the multitudes of the Jews: Which of you shall convince Me of sin? If I say the truth to you, why do you not believe Me? And so forth.

Homily of St. Gregory, Pope

Consider, dearly beloved brethren, the meekness of God. He had come to pardon sins, and He said: Which of you shall convince Me of sin? He does not disdain to prove by argument that He is not a sinner, He who in virtue of His Divinity was able to justify sinners. But what follows is indeed terrible: He that is of God heareth the words of God: therefore you hear them not because you are not of God. For if he who is of God hears the words of God, and anyone who is not of God cannot hear His words, let each one ask himself if he receiveth the words of God into the ears of his heart; and thus he will know whose he is.

The Truth commands us to long for the heavenly country, to bridle the desires of the flesh, to spurn the glory of the world, to refrain from coveting the goods of other men, and freely to give away our own. Let each one of you, therefore, ponder within himself whether this voice of God has made itself heard in the ear of his heart, for then he will learn whether he is of God. For there are some who disdain to receive the commandment of God even with their bodily ears. And there are others who indeed receive it with the ears of their body, but never fulfil it with the desire of their mind. And there are others who receive the words of God gladly and even shed tears of compunction, yet when the time of weeping is over, they turn again to iniquity.

Truly such as these hear not the words of God since they neglect to fulfil them in deeds. Set then, dearest brethren, your life before the eys of your mind, and earnestly considering yourselves, tremble at what has been pronounced by the lips of the Truth: Therefore you hear them not, because you are not of God. But what the Truth has to say concerning rejected sinners, they themselves make manifest by their evil deeds, for there follows: The Jews therefore answered, and said to Him: Do we not say well, that Thou art a Samaritan, and hast a devil?

But let us hear how the Lord replies on receiving such an insult: I have not a devil, but I honor My Father, and you have dishonored Me. Now Samaritan is interpreted: Watchman; and He is truly a watchman of whom the Psalmist says: Unless the Lord keep the city, they watch in vain that keep it. And to whom Isaias said: Watchman, what of the night? Watchman, what of the night? And so the Lord would not reply: I am not a Samaritan, but: I have not a devil. Truly, both these accusations were brought against Him; the one He denies, to the other, by His silence, He gives consent.

R. Who will give water to my head and a fountain of tears to my eyes, and I will weep day and night? for my nearest brother hath supplanted me, * And every friend hath dealt deceitfully against me. V. Let their way become dark and slippery: and let the Angel of the Lord pursue them. And.

✠ Continuation of the holy Gospel according to St. John.—At that time: Jesus said to the multitudes of the Jews: Which of you shall convince Me of sin? If I say the truth to you, why do you not believe Me? He that is of God heareth the words of God. Therefore you hear them not, because you are not of God. The Jews, therefore, answered and said to Him: Do not we say well, that Thou art a Samaritan, and hast a devil? Jesus answered: I have not a devil: but I honor My Father, and you have dishonored Me. But I seek not My own glory: there is One that seeketh and judgeth. Amen, amen, I say to you: If any man keep My word, he shall not see death forever. The Jews, therefore, said: Now we know that Thou hast a devil. Abraham is dead, and the prophets: and Thou sayest: If any man keep My word, he shall not taste death forever. Art Thou greater than our father Abraham, who is dead? and the prophets are dead. Whom dost Thou make Thyself? Jesus answered: If I glorify Myself, My glory is nothing; it is My Father that glorifieth Me, of whom you say that He is your God, and you have not known Him; but I know Him: And if I shall say that I know Him not, I shall be like to you, a liar. But I do know Him and do keep His word. Abraham your father rejoiced that he might see My day: he saw it and was glad. The Jews therefore said to Him: Thou art not yet fifty years old, and hast Thou seen Abraham? Jesus said to them: Amen, amen, I say to you, before Abraham was made, I am. They took up stones therefore to cast at Him: but Jesus hid Himself, and went out of the temple.

LET US PRAY

We beseech Thee, O almighty God, mercifully regard Thy family that our bodies may be ruled by Thy goodness and our souls protected by Thy care. Through our Lord.

MONDAY

The reading of the holy Gospel
according to St. John

At that time: The rulers and Pharisees sent ministers to apprehend Jesus. And so forth.

Homily of St. Augustine, Bishop

How could they apprehend Him if, as yet, He were unwilling? Since, then, they could not apprehend Him because He did not will it, they were sent that they might hear what He was teaching. And what was He teaching? Jesus, therefore, said to them: Yet a little while I am with you. What you wish to do now, you shall do hereafter; but not just now, for I do not will it now. Why am I now as yet unwilling? Because yet a little while I am with you and then I go to Him that sent Me. I must fulfil My charge, and thus come to My Passion.

You shall seek Me and shall not find Me; and where I am, thither you cannot come. Here He has already foretold His Resurrection: for they would not acknowledge Him when He was present with them, but afterwards they would seek Him, when they saw the multitude already believing in Him. For great signs were wrought, even when the Lord was risen again and ascended into heaven. For then mighty deeds were done by His disciples; but it was He, who also worked by Himself, that wrought these things through them; indeed, He Himself had

told them: Without Me you can do nothing. When
that lame man who sat at the gate rose up at the
voice of Peter and walked upon his own feet, so that
men marvelled, Peter thus addressed them, saying
that he had not done this by his own power, but by
the power of Him whom they themselves had slain.
Many, being stung with remorse, said: What shall
we do?

For they saw themselves bound by a monstrous
crime of impiety when they slew Him whom they
ought to have revered and adored; and this, they
thought, was beyond all pardon. It was indeed a
great crime, and to think upon it might bring them
to despair, yet they ought not to have despaired
since it was for them that the Lord was pleased to
pray while He hung upon the cross. For He had
said: Father, forgive them, for they know not
what they do. He saw among the many strangers
some who belonged to Him; He begged forgiveness
for these, from whom He was still receiving outrages. For He heeded not that He was dying at
their hands, but only that He was dying for them.

TUESDAY

The reading of the holy Gospel
according to St. John

At that time: Jesus walked in Galilee, for He
would not walk in Judea because the Jews sought
to kill Him. And so forth.

Homily of St. Augustine, Bishop

In this chapter of the Gospel, brethren, our Lord Jesus Christ more especially commends Himself, in regard to His humanity, to our faith. For indeed, He ever aimed at this in His deeds and words, that men might believe Him to be both God and man: God who made us, man who sought us: God with the Father always, man with us in time. For He could not have sought man whom He had made if He Himself had not become that which He had made. But remember this and never let it depart from your hearts: Christ was made man in such a way that He never ceased to be God. Still remaining God, He, who had made man, assumed man's nature.

Therefore, when as man He hid Himself, we must not think that He had lost His power, but only that He had given an example to the weak. For when He willed, He was apprehended; when He willed, He was slain. But because in time to come His members, that is, the faithful, would not have this power that He, our God, had, in that He kept Himself hid, in that He concealed Himself as if thereby to avoid being put to death, He indicated that His members were to do this in the future, those members of His in whom He truly lives.

For Christ is not merely in the head and not in the body: but the whole Christ is in the head and in the body. And therefore, He is what His members are; but His members are not necessarily what He is. Were His members not Himself, He would not have said to Saul: Why persecutest thou Me? For Saul was persecuting on the earth, not Him, but His members, that is, the faithful. And yet He did not choose to say, My saints, or My servants, or, more honorably still, My brethren, but: Me, that is, My members, of whom I am the head.

WEDNESDAY

The reading of the holy Gospel
according to St. John

At that time: It was the feast of the dedication at Jerusalem, and it was winter. And Jesus walked in the temple, in Solomon's porch. And so forth.

Homily of St. Augustine, Bishop

The Encenia was the feast of the dedication of the Temple. For in Greek, *kainon* signifies new. Whenever anything new was dedicated, it was called *encaenia*. And now this word has passed into common use. If a man puts on a new tunic, he is said to *encaeniare* (to renovate). This day, then, on which the temple was dedicated, was kept by the Jews as a solemn festival; they were keeping this same feast when the Lord spoke these words which we have just read.

It was winter, and Jesus walked in the temple, in Solomon's porch. The Jews, therefore, came round about Him and said to Him: How long dost thou hold our souls in suspense? If Thou be the Christ, tell us plainly. Not that they desired the truth, but they were planning a false accusation. It was winter, and they were cold: for they were loath to draw near to that divine fire. If to draw near is to believe, then he who believes draws near and he who denies, retires. The soul is not moved by the feet, but by the affections.

They had become icy cold in the charity that shows affection, and they burned with the desire to do an injury. They were far away, and yet were there: they did not draw near by believing in Him, yet they pressed close by persecuting Him. They sought to hear from the Lord: I am Christ; and perhaps they did understand something of Christ as regards His manhood. For the prophets had preached Christ; but the divinity of Christ, expressed both in the prophets and in the Gospel itself, is not grasped even by heretics: how much less, then, by the Jews, so long as the veil is upon their hearts.

THURSDAY

The reading of the holy Gospel
according to St. Luke

At that time: One of the Pharisees desired Jesus to eat with him; and He went into the house of the Pharisee, and sat down to meat. And so forth.

Homily of St. Gregory, Pope

Thinking upon the penitence of Mary Magdalen, I am more ready to weep than to say anything. For what heart of stone would not be softened to a like penitence by the tears of this sinner? She considered what she had done, and would not be moderate in what she was doing then. She broke in upon the guests, she came unasked, she brought her tears to the banquet. You may understand with what sorrow she burns, in that she is not ashamed to weep even at a feast.

But this woman, whom Luke calls a woman that was a sinner, is named by John, Mary; and we believe she was that Mary from whom, as Mark bears witness, seven devils were cast forth. And what is signified by seven devils, if not all the vices? For since all time is counted by periods of seven days, rightly by the number seven is signified completeness. Mary, then, had seven devils because she was full of all the vices.

But behold, when she saw the stains of her foulness, she ran to wash herself at the fountain of mercy, having no shame before the guests. Indeed, since she felt so much shame in herself, she counted it for nothing to be outwardly disgraced. Therefore, what shall we wonder at, brethren? That Mary came, or that the Lord received her? Received her, or shall I not rather say, drew her? But it were better to say: both drew her and received her: for in His mercy He drew her inwardly, and in His meekness He received her outwardly.

FRIDAY

The reading of the holy Gospel according to St. John

At that time: The chief priests and the Pharisees gathered a council against Jesus and said: What do we; for this man doth many miracles. And so forth.

Homily of St. Augustine, Bishop

The chief priests and the Pharisees took counsel together; and yet they did not say: Let us believe. For these abandoned men took more thought how to do harm in order to destroy Him than how to take counsel for themselves, that they might escape destruction; and yet they were afraid, and did in a manner take counsel together. For they said: What do we, for this man doth miracles? If we let Him alone so, all will believe in Him; and the Romans will come and take away our place and nation. They feared to lose temporal things and took no thought for eternal life, and thus they lost both together.

For after the Lord had suffered and had entered into glory, the Romans took away from them their place and nation by conquering them and carrying them away; which agrees with what was said elsewhere: But the children of the kingdom shall go into exterior darkness. But this was what they feared, that if all should believe in Christ, there would be none left to defend the city and temple of God against the Romans; for they imagined that the teaching of Christ was directed against that temple and against the laws of their fathers.

But one of them, named Caiphas, being the high priest that year, said to them: You know nothing; neither do you consider that it is expedient for you that one man should die for the people, and that the whole nation perish not. And this he spoke not of himself: but being the high priest of that year, he prophesied. From this we learn that even wicked men may foretell the future by the spirit of prophecy; this, however, the Evangelist ascribes to a divine sacrament, for this man was the pontiff, that is to say, the High Priest.

SATURDAY

The reading of the holy Gospel according to St. John

At that time: The chief priests thought to kill Lazarus also; because many of the Jews, by reason of him, went away and believed in Jesus. And so forth.

Homily of St. Augustine, Bishop

Having seen Lazarus as one raised from the dead (for the fame of so great a miracle wrought by the

Lord had been accompanied far and wide with so much evidence of its genuineness, as it had been so openly performed, that they could neither keep secret what had happened nor deny it), observe the plan which they devised. But the chief priests thought to kill Lazarus also. O foolish thought and blinded rage! Could not the Lord Christ, who could raise a dead man to life, raise one that was slain? When you inflict death upon Lazarus, will you, at the same time, rob the Lord of His power? And if it does seem to you that a dead man is one thing, a murdered man, another, behold, the Lord did both; He raised Lazarus who was dead, and He raised Himself who was put to death.

And on the next day a great multitude that had come to the festival day, when they heard that Jesus was coming to Jerusalem, took branches of palm trees and went forth to meet Him, crying: Hosanna, blessed is He that cometh in the Name of the Lord, the King of Israel. Palm branches are used as tokens of praise, to signify victory: for the Lord was about to overcome death by dying, and to triumph over the devil, the prince of death, by the trophy of the cross. And the exclamation used by the adulatory multitude is Hosanna, indicating, as some who understand the Hebrew tongue say, rather a state of mind than having any positive significance, just as in the Latin language there are words which are called interjections; as when we are sad we say, Alas! or when we are pleased we say, Aha!

The multitude was uttering these words of praise to Him: Hosanna, blessed is He that cometh in the name of the Lord, the King of Israel. What a cross of mental suffering for the envy of the Jewish rulers to endure when so great a multitude proclaimed Christ their King? But what was it to the Lord to be King of Israel? What great thing was it for the King of ages to become the King of men? For Christ was not King of Israel to exact tribute, or to arm a body of men with the sword, or to subdue visible forces; but King of Israel that He might rule souls and counsel them regarding eternity, that He might lead to the kingdom of heaven such as believe in Him, hope in Him, and love Him.

PALM SUNDAY

I Nocturn

From Jeremias the Prophet, c. 2, 12 - 22

II Nocturn

Sermon of St. Leo, Pope

What we have longed for, dearly beloved, and what the whole world desires, the festival of the Lord's Passion, has come, and will not suffer us to be silent amid the outbursts of our spiritual joy. And though it is difficult to discourse very often upon the same solemnity worthily and appropriately, yet in regard to so great a mystery of the divine mercy, the priest cannot leave unfulfilled the duty of preaching to the faithful people: since the subject itself, for the very reason that it is sublime, gives scope for speech: nor can there ever be a lack of something to say upon a matter concerning which enough can never be said.

Let our human weakness, then, sink under the glory of God and ever find itself unequal to the task of expounding the works of His mercy. Let us toil in thought, fail in insight, falter in utterance; it is good for us to feel how inadequate are our thoughts, even the thoughts which we rightly think concerning the majesty of the Lord. For since the prophet says: Seek ye the Lord and be strengthened, seek His Face evermore, no one should presume that he has found all he seeks lest, if he cease his endeavors, he fail to draw near.

And indeed, among all the works of God by which man's admiration is dazzled, what so delights and baffles our mind's gaze as the Passion of the Savior? In order to loose mankind from the bonds of the deadly transgression, He hid the might of His majesty from the fury of the devil, and opposed him with the weakness of our lowly nature. For if the proud and cruel enemy could have known the counsel of God's mercy, he would rather have striven to soften the hearts of the Jews into mildness than to fire them with unjust hatred, lest he should lose the thraldom of all his captives while attacking the liberty of one who owed him nothing.

Thus he was foiled by his own malice, for he brought upon the Son of God a punishment which turned to the healing of all the sons of men. He shed righteous blood, which became the ransom and the healing drink for the reconciliation of the world. The Lord took upon Himself what He had chosen according to the purpose of His own will. He submitted Himself to the impious hands of cruel men which, while busied with their own wickedness, were of service to the Redeemer. So great was the tender love He bore even towards His murderers that, praying to His Father from the cross, He asked not that He might be avenged, but that they might be forgiven.

R. O Lord, be not Thou far from me: spare me in the day of evil: let them be confounded that persecute me, * But let not me be confounded. V. Let all mine enemies that seek after my soul be confounded. But let.

III Nocturn

The reading of the holy Gospel
according to St. Matthew

At that time: When Jesus drew nigh to Jerusalem, and was come to Bethphage, unto Mount

Olivet: then He sent two disciples, saying to them. And so forth.

Homily of St. Ambrose, Bishop

It is beautifully shown that when the Lord had deserted the Jews that He might take up His abode in the hearts of the Gentiles, He went up into the temple. For this is the true temple wherein the Lord is adored, not according to the letter, but in spirit. This is the temple of God whereof He has laid the courses, not in stones built one upon another, but in faith. Thus they who hated Him are forsaken: they are chosen who will love Him. And so He comes to Mount Olivet, to plant upon the heights of virtue those slips of olive whose mother is that Jerusalem which is above.

In this mountain dwells the heavenly husbandman: and thus when all are planted in the house of God, each one of them can say: But I, as a fruitful olive-tree in the house of the Lord. And perhaps Christ Himself is this mountain. For who other than He could ever bear such a wealth of olive-trees, that is, not of trees weighed down with the abundance of their fruit, but of the Gentiles fruitful with the fulness of the spirit? He it is by whom we ascend, and He also to whom we ascend. He is the gate, He is the way, He it is that is opened and He also who opens: it is He that is knocked at by those who enter in, and He that is adored by those who have obtained their reward.

To return to the narrative: the colt was in the village, tied with the ass; he could not be loosed but by the Lord's command. It was an apostolic hand that set him free. Such is the work, such the life, such the grace. Be then thyself also such, that thou mayest loose them that are bound. Now let us consider who those were, who being detected in error and cast out of paradise, were consigned to the village. Thou seest also how those who have been driven out by death are called back again by life.

Therefore, according to Matthew, we read of an ass and a colt: this is because when man was banished, both sexes were represented; and now, as typified by these two animals, both sexes are recalled. There, then, in the mother-ass, is figured Eve as the mother of error : and here, too, in the colt is shown the multitude of the Gentile nations: hence He is seated upon the colt of an ass. And well is it said: On which no one hath sat: for, before Christ, no one called the people of the nations to the Church. Finally, according to Mark, thou findest these words: Upon which no man yet hath sat.

R. Liars have surrounded me: they have fallen upon me with scourges without cause: * But do Thou, O Lord, my defender, avenge me. V. For trouble is near and there is none to help. But do Thou.

✠ Continuation of the holy Gospel according to
St. Matthew.—At that time: When Jesus drew
nigh to Jerusalem, and was come to Bethphage, unto Mount Olivet, then He sent two disciples, saying
to them: Go ye into the village that is over against
you, and immediately you shall find an ass tied, and
a colt with her: loose them and bring them to Me:
and if any man shall say anything to you, say ye
that the Lord hath need of them: and forthwith he
will let them go. Now all this was done that it
might be fulfilled which was spoken by the Prophet,
saying: Tell ye the daughter of Sion: Behold thy
King cometh to thee meek, and sitting upon an ass,
and a colt the foal of her that is used to the yoke.
And the disciples going, did as Jesus commanded
them. And they brought the ass and the colt, and
laid their garments upon them and made Him sit
thereon. And a very great multitude spread their
garments in the way: and others cut boughs from
the trees and strewed them in the way; and the
multitudes that went before and that followed cried,
saying: Hosanna to the Son of David: Blessed is
He that cometh in the name of the Lord.

LET US PRAY

O almighty and eternal God, Who, to give the
human race an example of humility, didst decree
that our Savior shouldst assume our nature and endure the sufferings of the Cross; mercifully grant

that we may learn the lesson of His patience and share the blessings of His Resurrection. Through the same Lord.

MONDAY IN HOLY WEEK

The reading of the holy Gospel according to St. John

Six days before the Pasch Jesus came to Bethania, where Lazarus, whom Jesus raised to life, had been dead. And so forth.

Homily of St. Augustine, Bishop

Lest men should think that he had become a phantom because he had risen from the dead, Lazarus was one of them who reclined at table. He lived, he spoke, he feasted; the truth was made manifest and the disbelief of the Jews brought to confusion. Jesus, then, sat down to table with Lazarus and the rest; Martha, one of the sisters of Lazarus, served. But Mary, the other sister of Lazarus, took a pound of ointment of right spikenard, of great price, and anointed the feet of Jesus and wiped His feet with her hair; and the house was filled with the odor of the ointment. We have heard what was done: let us seek out the mystery.

Whosoever thou art, if thou wouldst be a faithful soul, anoint with Mary the feet of the Lord with precious ointment. That ointment signified justice, and therefore it was of the weight of a *libra* (pound; balance). It was, moreover, ointment of right spikenard, of great price. That it is called *pisticum*, we might understand as referring to some place from which this costly ointment came. But this does not exhaust its possible meanings, and it harmonizes well with a sacramental symbol. The Greek *pistis* is called in Latin *fides* (faith). You sought to work justice. The just man liveth by faith. Anoint the feet of Jesus; by a good life, follow the footsteps of the Lord. Wipe them with thy hair: what thou hast in superfluity, give to the poor, and thou hast wiped the feet of the Lord: for the hair of the body seems to be a superfluity. Here is something for thee to do with thy superfluous goods: they are superfluous to thee, but necessary to the feet of the Lord. It may be that the feet of the Lord upon earth suffer want.

For of whom, if not of His members, will it be said at the last: As long as you did it to one of these, My least brethren, you did it unto Me? You spent your superfluous riches: but you rendered a service to My feet. And the house was filled with the odor: the world was filled with the good fame; for, good odor signifies good fame. Those who live evil lives and are called Christians, do an injury to Christ: of such it is said that through them the Name of the Lord is blasphemed, through good men the Name of the Lord is praised. Listen to the Apostle: We are the good odor of Christ, he says, in every place.

TUESDAY IN HOLY WEEK

From Jeremias the Prophet, c. 11, 15 - 20,
c. 12, 1 - 4, and 7 - 11

WEDNESDAY IN HOLY WEEK

From Jeremias the Prophet, c. 17, 13 - 18,
c. 18, 13 - 23
For the remaining days of Holy Week, see special
Holy Week Manual

EASTER SUNDAY

I Nocturn

From the Epistle of blessed Paul the Apostle to the
Romans c. 6, 2 - 13

II Nocturn

Sermon of St. Gregory Nazianzen

I shall say the word Pasch and honor thereby the
Blessed Trinity. For the Pasch is for us the festivity of festivities, by far the most glorious celebration of all other celebrations, excelling not only
those of human and earthly origin, but also those
which are of Christ Himself and which are celebrated because of Him, as much as the sun out-
shines the stars. Yesterday the Lamb was sacrificed, the door-posts were anointed, and the first-

born of Egypt lived. As we too have been protected
by the Precious Blood (it being a warning sign to
terror and fear), the destroying angel passed us up
also.

Today we truly escape from Egypt and from
that pitiless master, Pharao (Satan), and from
those hard over-lords; we are freed from the clay
and from making bricks. (Note: The Israelites'
chief occupation in Egypt was handling the clay
and making bricks for Pharao.) There is no one
who can prohibit our celebrating the *exitus* (passage over) to our Lord God; and this celebrating
will not be in the old leaven of malice and iniquity,
but with the new bread of sincerity and truth, having in us none of the Egyptian and wicked leaven.
Yesterday I was hanging on the cross with Christ;
today I am glorified with Him. Yesterday I died;
today I live. Yesterday I was buried with Him; today I rise with Him.

Rightly let us offer gifts to Him who suffered
and rose for us. Perhaps you think of saying gold,
or silver, or fine cloth, or silk, or all manner of precious stones, or costly perfumes of the earth. These
remain things of earth, and the wicked, the servants of this world and the princes thereof, possess
the greater part of them. But let us offer ourselves,
that is, works most pleasing to God and such as are
most befitting. Let us render representative things
to the One represented. Let us recognize our dig-

nity. Let us gratify our exemplar with honor and understand the power of the mystery, and for what Christ died. Let us be as Christ is, for Christ is one of us. Let us become like gods because of Him, since He was made Man because of us.

He assumed what was inferior (human nature) so that He might give what was superior (Divinity). He became a beggar so that we might be benefited by His need. He took the form of a servant so that we might be brought to liberty. He was tempted so that we might overcome, became contemptible so that we might be glorious, died so that He might procure for us eternal life, ascended so that He might draw those who have fallen into sin to Himself. Whosoever gives all, gives it to Him who gave Himself as the price of Redemption for us and for the blotting out of our sins. No one, when he offers himself, can give as much to Him as he who rightly understands the reason of this mystery, and who, on account of it, knows that he should become all things to Him who became all things for us.

R. I am the true vine, and you the branches: * He that abideth in Me, and I in him, the same beareth much fruit, alleluia, alleluia. V. As the Father hath loved Me, I also loved you. He that. Glory. He that.

III Nocturn

The reading of the holy Gospel
according to St. Mark

At that time: Mary Magdalen and Mary, the mother of James, and Salome, brought sweet spices that coming, they might anoint Jesus. And so forth.

Homily of St. Gregory, Pope

You have heard, dearly beloved brethren, how the holy women who had followed the Lord came to the sepulchre, bringing sweet spices; Him whom they had loved in life, in death also they would serve with all care and tenderness. But all these things that were done signify something that in Holy Church we must do. And so it behooves us to hear what was done then, that we may consider what we have to do now by way of imitation. Now, therefore, if we, who believe in Him that was dead, come and seek the Lord, bearing with us the perfume of the virtues together with the repute of good works, we do indeed come to His sepulchre bringing sweet spices.

And those women, when they came with sweet spices, saw angels: for it is clear enough that the citizens of heaven may be readily beheld by such minds as, with the perfumes of the virtues, go forth to seek the Lord by holy desires. Moreover, we should do well to note why it was upon the right side that the Angel was seen sitting. What indeed is signified by the left, if not this present life? and what by the right hand, but the life eternal? Whence it is written in the Canticle of canticles: His left hand is under my head and His right hand shall embrace me.

Therefore, since our Redeemer had already passed beyond the corruption of this present life, rightly did the Angel who came to announce His eternal life sit upon the right side. He appeared clothed in a white robe: because he announced the joys of our feast. Truly, the whiteness of the raiment proclaims the splendor of our solemn festival. Ours, shall we say, or his? But, to speak more truly, we should say both his and ours. For certainly the Resurrection of our Redeemer was our feast, since it brought us back to immortal life; and it was the feast of the Angels because, when we were recalled to heaven, their number was filled up.

Therefore upon this, his feast and ours, the Angel appeared clad in white garments; because, when we are led back to our home above through the Lord's Resurrection, the losses in the heavenly country are made good. But let us hear why it was said to the women as they came near: Be not affrighted. It is as though he said openly: Let those fear who love not to see the citizens of heaven approaching; let them be exceedingly afraid who, weighed down by the desires of the flesh, despair of ever attaining to their fellowship. But as for you, why should you be afraid when you see your fellow citizens? Whence St. Matthew also, describing how the Angel appeared, says: His countenance was as lightning and his raiment as snow. Because lightning affrights and terrifies, but snow gives delight by its shining whiteness.

R. When the sabbath was passed, Mary Magdalen, and Mary, the mother of James, and Salome, brought sweet spices, * That coming, they might anoint Jesus, alleluia, alleluia. V. And very early in the morning, the first day of the week, they came to the sepulchre, the sun being now risen. That Glory. That.

✠ Continuation of the holy Gospel according to St. Mark.—At that time: Mary Magdalen, and Mary, the mother of James, and Salome bought sweet spices, that coming, they might anoint Jesus. And very early in the morning, the first day of the week, they came to the sepulchre, the sun being now risen. And they said one to another: Who shall roll us back the stone from the door of the sepulchre? And looking, they saw the stone rolled back. For it was very great. And entering into the sepulchre, they saw a young man sitting on the right side, clothed with a white robe, and they were astonished. Who saith to them: Be not affrighted; ye seek Jesus of Nazareth, who was crucified: He is risen, He is not here; behold the place where they laid Him. But go, tell His disciples, and Peter,

that He goeth before you into Galilee: there you
shall see Him, as He told you.

LET US PRAY

O God, who through Thine only begotten Son
hast on this day overcome death and opened to us
the gates of everlasting life; grant that our holy
desires, which already have been aroused within us
by Thy grace, may by Thy further aid be happily
fulfilled. Through the same Lord.

EASTER MONDAY

I Nocturn

*From the first Epistle of blessed Paul the Apostle
to the Corinthians, c. 15, 1 - 22*

II Nocturn

Sermon of St. Maximus, Bishop

Very appropriately, dearest brethren, is this
Psalm, in which the Prophet exults, commands, and
rejoices, read today. David invites all creatures to
the celebration of today's festivity. Today, through
the Resurrection of Christ, limbo is opened, through
the neophytes of the Church, the earth is renewed,
and through the Holy Spirit, heaven is reopened.

Limbo being opened gives up its dead, the earth
being renewed buds forth those who are arising,
the heavens being reopened receives those who are
ascending. The penitent thief ascends to heaven,

the bodies of the saints rise to the holy city. The dead are brought back to life and, by a certain dispensation in the Resurrection of Christ, they lift themselves to a higher element of life.

Limbo contains these, now it gives them up to the higher regions. The earth is their tomb, but now it gives them to heaven. Heaven receives them and gives them over to the Lord. By one and the same operation, the Passion and Death of the Savior elevates them from the deepest abyss, lifts them from the earth and places them into the Most High. The Resurrection of Christ is life to the dead, forgiveness for sinners, and glory to the Saints. Therefore, holy David invites all creatures to this feast. He says that there should be exulting and rejoicing on this day which the Lord has made.

Therefore we should exult on this holy day. Let no one withdraw himself from the social joy by a conscience laden with sin; let no one be held back from public worship by the votaries of crime. On this day the sinner need not despair of indulgence, for this particular prerogative is not the least of Easter's merits. For if the thief merited paradise, why should not the Christian receive pardon? And if the Master was merciful to the thief when He was crucified, how much more will He not be merciful to the Christian in His Resurrection? If the humility of the Passion meant so much to one who was penitent, how much more will the glory of the

Resurrection give to one who supplicates? As you yourselves know, the happy victory which ends captivity should stand out, then, with the greatest prominence.

R. With great power the Apostles gave * Testimony of the Resurrection of our Lord Jesus Christ, alleluia, alleluia. V. They were filled with the Holy Ghost, and they spoke the word of God with boldness. Testimony. Glory. Testimony.

III Nocturn

The reading of the holy Gospel according to St. Luke

At that time: Two of the disciples of Jesus went the same day to a town which was sixty furlongs from Jerusalem, named Emmaus. And so forth.

Homily of St. Gregory, Pope

You have heard, dearly beloved brethren, how the Lord appeared to two of the disciples as they were upon a journey, who did not as yet believe in Him, but at least they were talking of Him: but that He did not show Himself to them in His true likeness, for then they would have recognized Him. Therefore, what the Lord was working outwardly in respect of their bodily eyes, was precisely what was taking place inwardly in regard to the eyes of their heart. For inwardly they loved, and yet they doubted: outwardly the Lord was present with them, but did not show them who He was.

Thus, because they were speaking of Him, He manifested His presence to them: but because they doubted, He hid the countenance they would have recognized. Indeed, He took up what they were saying, He rebuked the dullness of their understanding, He laid open those mysterious passages of the sacred Scriptures that had been written concerning Him: and nevertheless, because He was not yet present in their hearts by faith, He feigned as though He would go further. For indeed, the Latin word *fingere* (to feign) has also the meaning of *componere* (to fashion): hence, those who fashion clay are called *figuli* (potters). Therefore, He who is Truth itself did nothing by duplicity: but He showed Himself to them in body, such as He appeared to them in mind.

But they were to be tried, to see whether, though they did not yet love Him as God, they would at least show a friendly feeling for Him as a stranger. But since these men with whom the Truth was walking could not be without charity, they invited Him to their lodging as though He were indeed a stranger. But why should we say: Invited: since it is there written: And they constrained Him? Without doubt we are to learn from this example, that strangers are not merely to be invited to share our hospitality, but even to be pressed to do so.

And so they set the table for Him and offered Him bread and meats: and then, in the breaking of bread, they recognized as God Him whom they knew not when He explained the sacred Scriptures. Therefore, in hearing the commandments of God, they were not enlightened, but in doing them they obtained light, for it is written: Not the hearers of the law are just before God, but the doers of the law shall be justified. Whoever, then, desires to understand the lessons he has heard, let him hasten to put into practice what he has already been able to hear. Behold, the Lord was not recognized while He was speaking, but deigned to be known when food was set before Him.

R. Mary Magdalen, and the other Mary went very early to the sepulchre. * Jesus whom you seek is not here, He is risen as He said, and goeth before you into Galilee: there you shall see Him, alleluia, alleluia. V. And very early in the morning, the first day of the week, they came to the sepulchre, the sun being now risen: and entering in, they saw a young man sitting on the right hand, who said to them. Jesus. Glory. Jesus.

✠ Continuation of the holy Gospel according to St. Luke.—At that time: Two of the disciples of Jesus went that same day to a town which was sixty furlongs from Jerusalem, named Emmaus. And they talked together of all these things which had happened. And it came to pass, that while they talked and reasoned with themselves, Jesus Himself also, drawing near, went with them. But their eyes were held that they should not know Him. And He said to them: What are these discourses that you hold one with another as you walk, and why are you sad? And the one of them whose name was Cleophas answering said to Him; Art Thou a stranger in Jerusalem, and hast not known the things that have been done there in these days? To whom He said: What things? And they said: concerning Jesus of Nazareth, Who was a prophet, mighty in work and word before God and all the people; and how our chief priests and princes delivered Him to be condemned to death, and crucified Him. But we hoped that it was He that should have redeemed Israel: and now, besides all this, today is the third day since these things were done. Yea, and certain women also of our company affrighted us who, before it was light, were at the sepulchre, and not finding His body, came, saying that they had also seen a vision of Angels, who say that He is alive. And some of our people went to the sepulchre, and found it so as the women had said, but Him they found not. Then He said to them: O foolish, and slow of heart to believe in all things which the Prophets have spoken! Ought not Christ to have suffered these things, and so to enter into His glory? And beginning at Moses and all the Prophets, He expounded to them in all the Scriptures the things that were concerning Him. And they drew nigh to the town whither they were going; and He made as though He would go farther. But they constrained Him, saying: Stay with us, because it is towards evening, and the day is now far spent. And He went in with them. And it came to pass, whilst He was at table with them, He took bread and blessed, and broke, and gave to them: and their eyes were opened, and they knew Him, and He vanished out of their sight. And they said one to the other: Was not our heart burning within us whilst He spoke in the way, and opened to us the Scriptures? And rising up the same hour, they went back to Jerusalem and they found the eleven gathered together, and those that were with them, saying: The Lord is risen indeed, and hath appeared to Simon. And they told what things were done in the way, and how they knew Him in the breaking of the bread.

LET US PRAY

O God, who through Thine only begotten Son hast on this day overcome death and opened to us the gates of everlasting Life; grant that our holy desires, which already have been aroused within us by Thy grace may by thy further aid be happily fulfilled. Through the same Lord.

EASTER TUESDAY

I Nocturn

Acts of the Apostles, c. 13, 25 - 37

II Nocturn

Sermon of St. John Chrysostom

All the solemnities, dearest brethren, which are celebrated to the honor of God are holy and venerable, but today, the Lord's Resurrection Day, has a festivity all its own. Because, whereas all other days have in them the joy of the living only, this day has in it the gladness of the dead.

This festivity is then common to the lowest and to the highest, because the Lord, rising from the dead, gave festivity to the place where He conquered death as well as to that place to which the Conqueror went from death. Well, therefore, does the Psalmist speak words which apply especially to this day: This is the day which the Lord hath made, let us exult and be glad therein.

For He says that the blessed day of exultation proclaims the Lord's Resurrection not only to the highest (the living), but also to the lowest (the dead.) By the Lord's descending into the confines of the darkness of hell (limbo), even that place, without any doubt, became a place of the greatest splendor wherever the Savior illumined it. The Evangelist beautifully says of this: The Light shined in the darkness and the darkness did not comprehend it. Because, although the Lord descended into the darkness, He did not experience the obscurity of the darkness.

He suspended the inviolable splendor of His Divine Nature, and thus the light was not overtaken by the night, but the night, by the light. Dearest brethren, let us therefore be glad and exult in the Lord because today there is given to us from the Lord the Light of salvation concerning which the same Psalmist says: The Lord God has enlightened us.

III Nocturn

The reading of the holy Gospel
according to St. Luke

At that time: Jesus stood in the midst of the disciples, and saith to them: Peace be to you: it is I, fear not. And so forth.

Homily of St. Ambrose, Bishop

It is wonderful how a corporeal nature could pass through an impenetrable body and be invisible in its entrance, yet visibly beheld; easily touched, but not easily defined. Hence the disciples were troubled, thinking that they saw a spirit. And therefore the Lord, in order to give us a tangible proof of His Resurrection, says: Handle, and see, for a spirit hath not flesh and bones, as you see me to have. It was not then with a spiritual nature, but with a glorious and risen body that He passed through what was solid and naturally impenetrable. For, what can be touched, must be a body: what can be handled, must be a body.

And we shall rise again in the body. For it is sown a natural body, it shall rise a spiritual body: but that body will be subtler, while this is denser, seeing that it still bears that density due to its earthly imperfection. For how should that which the Lord offered to be handled, in which still remained the marks of the wounds and the traces of the scars, be other than a body? In so doing, He not only strengthened our faith, but quickened our love, seeing that He would not part with the wounds which He had received for love of us, but willed to carry them into heaven that He might show to God the Father the price of our freedom. Such is He whom the Father hath set at His right hand, welcoming the trophy of our salvation; and such too, are those Martyrs yonder, whom He has shown us, bearing the crown of their scars.

And since our discourse has now reached this point, let us consider how it is that, according to John, the Apostles believed and were glad: according to Luke, they were, as it were, upbraided for their unbelief: according to John, they received the Holy Ghost; according to Luke, they were told to stay in the city, till they should be endued with power from on high.

It seems to me that the former (John), as an Apostle, touches upon great and deep matters, while the latter (Luke) gives the sequence of events of human circumstances: Luke writes with historical fulness, John abridges: for we cannot doubt him, who gives testimony of those things which he himself witnessed, and his testimony is true: on the other hand, we must certainly banish all suspicion of carelessness or untruthfulness in regard to one who was counted worthy to be an Evangelist. And therefore we hold both accounts to be true, and not to differ with regard to facts or persons. For even if Luke says at first that they did not believe, he shows later on that they did so: and if we consider what he says first, there is a contradiction; but if we examine what follows, we certainly find both accounts to be in agreement.

R. With great power the Apostles gave * Testimony of the Resurrection of our Lord Jesus Christ, alleluia, alleluia. V. They were filled with the Holy Ghost, and they spoke the word of God with boldness. Testimony. Glory. Testimony.

✠ Continuation of the holy Gospel according to St. Luke.—At that time: Jesus stood in the midst of His disciples, and saith to them: Peace be to you; it is I, fear not. But they, being troubled and frighted, supposed that they saw a spirit. And He said to them: Why are you troubled, and why do thoughts arise in your hearts? See My hands, and

My feet, that it is I Myself; handle Me, and see; for a spirit hath not flesh and bones, as you see Me to have. And when He had said this, He showed them His hands, and His feet. But while they yet believed not, and wondered for joy, He said: Have you here anything to eat? And they offered Him a piece of broiled fish, and a honey-comb. And when He had eaten before them, taking the remains, He gave to them. And He said to them: These are the words which I spoke to you while I was yet with you, that all things must needs be fulfilled that are written concerning Me. Then He opened their understanding, that they might understand the Scriptures. And He said to them: Thus it is written, and thus it behooved Christ to suffer, and to rise again from the dead the third day; and that penance and remission of sins should be preached in His name among all nations.

LET US PRAY

O God Who through Thine only begotten Son hast on this day overcome death and opened to us the gates of everlasting Life; grant that our holy desires, which already have been aroused within us by Thy grace may by Thy further aid be happily fulfilled. Through the same Lord.

WEDNESDAY IN EASTER WEEK

The reading of the holy Gospel
according to St. John

At that time: Jesus showed Himself again to
the disciples at the sea of Tiberias. And He showed Himself after this manner. There were together
Simon Peter, and Thomas who is called Didymus.
And so forth.

Homily of St. Gregory, Pope

The lesson from the holy Gospel that has just
been read aloud to you, my brethren, urges a question upon the mind, and yet, while urging it, indicates the value of discretion. For it may be asked
why Peter, who before his conversion was a fisherman, should, after his conversion, return again to
his fishing: and since the Truth says: No man putting his hand to the plough, and looking back, is fit
for the kingdom of God: why did he take up again
what he had once forsaken? But if we look into the
matter with discretion, the reason will soon appear:
for doubtless, since the business in which he was
engaged before his conversion was not a sinful one,
he could return to it again after his conversion
without committing any fault.

Now we know that Peter was a fisherman, and
Matthew a tax-gatherer: after his conversion,
Peter returned to his fishing, but Matthew sat no
more at the seat of the custom: for it is one thing

to seek a living by fishing, and quite another to amass wealth by profits gained in the gathering of taxes. There are indeed many trades that can hardly, or never, be practiced without sin. Of necessity, then, a man after his conversion may not apply himself again to such occupations as would involve him in sin.

Again it may be asked why, when the disciples were laboring on the sea, the Lord appeared after His Resurrection standing upon the shore, while before His Resurrection, He had walked upon the waves of the sea in the sight of His disciples. We shall soon see the reason of this if we consider the inner nature of the case. For what does the sea represent, if not this present world, surging with the tumult of its ever-shifting fortunes and with the billows of this corruptible life? What is signified by the solidity of the shore, if not the everlasting peace of eternity? Therefore, since the disciples were as yet surrounded by the billows of this mortal life, they were struggling on the sea: but since our Redeemer had already passed beyond the corruption of the flesh, after His Resurrection He was standing on the shore.

THURSDAY IN EASTER WEEK

The reading of the holy Gospel
according to St. John

At that time: Mary stood at the sepulchre without, weeping. Now as she was weeping, she stooped down and looked into the sepulchre; and she saw two angels in white, sitting. And so forth.

Homily of St. Gregory, Pope

Mary Magdalen, who had been a sinner in the city, washed away with her tears the stains of her misdeeds because she loved the truth: and the word of Truth was fulfilled which He spoke: Many sins are forgiven her, because she hath loved much. For she who first had remained cold through sin, afterwards burned with the violence of her love. For when she came to the sepulchre and found that the Lord's body was not there, she believed that it had been taken away, and also told the disciples: they coming, saw and believed it to be as the woman had said. And of them it goes on to say: The disciples, therefore, departed to their home; then is added: But Mary stood at the sepulchre without, weeping.

And here we should consider what a mighty force of love it was that kindled this woman's heart, so that even when the disciples had left the Lord's sepulchre, she did not leave it. She kept on seeking Him whom she had not found: seeking, she wept, and, consumed with the fire of her love, she burned with the desire of Him who, as she believed, had been taken away. And so it came to pass that she alone, then, who had remained to seek Him, saw Him: for indeed the virtue of a good work is perseverance; and the voice of Truth has said: But he that shall persevere unto the end, he shall be saved.

Mary, therefore, when she wept, stooped down and looked into the sepulchre. Surely she had already seen that the sepulchre was empty when she had announced that the Lord had already been taken away; why, then, does she again stoop down, and again desire to see? But for one who loves it is not enough to have looked once, because the strength of the love increases the will to seek. Therefore, she sought at first, and found not; she persevered in seeking, and at length succeeded in finding: and it happened that her baffled desires grew greater, and in growing, grasped what they had found.

FRIDAY IN EASTER WEEK

The reading of the holy Gospel
according to St. Matthew

At that time: The eleven disciples went into Galilee, unto the mountain where Jesus had appointed them. And so forth.

Homily of St. Jerome, Priest

After His Resurrection, Jesus was seen upon a mountain of Galilee, and there He was adored: and though some doubted, their doubts increase our faith. Then He showed Himself more openly to Thomas, pointing to His side, wounded with the spear, and the prints of the nails in His hands. Jesus, coming, spoke to them, saying: All power is given to Me in heaven and on earth. To Him is this power given, who, but a little while before, had been crucified, buried in the sepulchre, lain there dead, and afterwards had risen again. And power is given to Him in heaven and on earth; that He, who before had reigned in heaven, might now reign also on earth, through the faith of them that believe.

Going, therefore, teach ye all nations, baptizing them in the Name of the Father, and of the Son, and of the Holy Ghost. First they teach all nations, and then, having taught them, they baptize them with water. For the body cannot receive the sacrament of baptism, unless the soul has already received the truth of faith. They are baptized in the name of the Father, and of the Son, and of the Holy Ghost; that there may be oneness in the giving as there is oneness in the divinity: for the name of the Trinity is the name of the one only God.

Teaching them to observe all things whatsoever I have commanded you. This arrangement is important: He commanded the Apostles first to teach all nations, then to steep them in the sacrament of faith, and, after imparting faith and administering Baptism, to instruct them in the precepts they must observe. And lest we should think these precepts to be few in number and of small importance, He added: All things whatsoever I have commanded you; so that all those who had believed and been baptized in the Trinity, should do all those things that are commanded. And behold I am with you even to the consummation of the world. He, who promises to be with His disciples even to the consummation of the world, also shows them that they will live forever, and that He will never depart from those who believe in Him.

SATURDAY IN EASTER WEEK

The reading of the holy Gospel
according to St. John

At that time: On the first day of the week, Mary Magdalen cometh early, when it was yet dark, unto the sepulchre. And so forth.

Homily of St. Gregory, Pope

The lesson from the holy Gospel which you have just heard, brethren, is very plain as to its historical and superficial aspect: but it behooves us, however briefly, to seek its inner meaning. Mary Magdalen cometh, when it was yet dark, unto the sepulchre. According to the historical sense, the hour is noted: but according to the mystical meaning, it is to be understood of the mind of the seeker. For indeed, Mary was seeking in the sepulchre the Author of all things, whom she had seen dead in the flesh; and because she could not find Him there, she believed that He had been stolen away. Therefore, it was yet dark when she came unto the sepulchre. Running quickly, she told the disciples: but Peter and John, as they loved Him more than the others, so did they outrun the others.

And they both ran together: but John did outrun Peter. He came first to the sepulchre, yet did not dare to go in. Then cometh Peter following him, and went in. What, brethren, is signified by this running? Is it to be believed that so exact a description given by the Evangelist can be devoid of mystery? By no means. For John would not have said he was there first, and yet did not go in, if he had not believed there was a mystery in his own consternation. What, therefore, is signified by John, if not the synagogue: what by Peter, if not the Church?

Neither should it seem a strange thing that the synagogue is represented by the younger, and the Church by the elder man: although the synagogue was before the Church of the Gentiles as regards the worship of God, yet the multitude of the Gentiles preceded the synagogue in the order of nature, as Paul testifies, saying: Yet that was not first which is spiritual, but that which is natural. By Peter, then, the elder of the two, is signified the Church of the Gentiles: but by John, the younger, the synagogues of the Jews. They run both together: because from the sunrise to the sunset of their day, along a road common and equal to both, although not taken by both in a common and equal manner, Gentiledom ran together with the synagogue. The synagogue came first to the sepulchre, but by no means went in: because it had indeed received the commandments of the law and had heard the prophecies of the Passion of the Lord, yet, seeing Him dead, would not believe in Him.

LOW SUNDAY

I Nocturn

From the Epistle of blessed Paul the Apostle to the Colossians, c. 3, 1 - 17

II Nocturn

Sermon of St. Augustine, Bishop

The Paschal solemnity is concluded by the festival of today, and therefore today the Neophytes change their garments: in such manner, nevertheless, that the whiteness which is laid down with those garments is retained forever in their hearts. Now are the days of the Passover, that is, when pardon and remission have been granted, and therefore our duty is so to sanctify the recreation of these holy days that it may not tarnish the purity of our soul: yea, rather let us strive that our relaxation may be such that we hold ourselves aloof from all excess, drunkenness, and uncleanness: so that what we have not yet gained by bodily fasting, we may be able to seek after by purity of mind.

This discourse applies indeed to all who are under our care: but since today brings to an end the festival of these sacred mysteries, it is to you in particular that we address ourselves; you, the newly-grafted shoots of holiness, regenerated by water and the Holy Ghost, our tender buds, our new swarm, the flowers of our honor, the fruits of our labor, my joy and my crown, all you who stand fast in the Lord.

I address you in the words of the Apostle: Behold, the night is past and the day is at hand: cast off the works of darkness and put on the armor of light. Let us walk honestly as in the day: not in rioting and drunkenness, not in chambering and impurities, not in contention and envy: but put ye on the Lord Jesus Christ. We have, says he, the more sure prophetical word: whereunto you do well to attend, as to a light that shineth in a dark place, until the day dawn and the daystar arise in your hearts.

Let your loins, therefore, be girt and lamps burning in your hands: and you yourselves like to men who wait for the lord, when he shall return from the wedding. Behold, the days draw near of which the Lord says: A little while, says He, and you shall see Me. This is the hour of which He said: You shall be sorrowful, but the world shall rejoice; that is, in this life, filled as it is with temptations, while we are absent from Him. But I will see you again, He says, and your heart shall rejoice, and your joy no man shall take from you.

R. With great power the Apostles gave * Testimony of the Resurrection of our Lord Jesus Christ, alleluia, alleluia. V. They were filled with the Holy Ghost, and they spoke the word of God with boldness. Testimony. Glory. Testimony.

III Nocturn

The reading of the holy Gospel
according to St. John

At that time: When it was late that same day, the first of the week, and the doors were shut where the disciples were gathered together for fear of the Jews, Jesus came and stood in the midst and said to them, Peace be to you. And so forth.

Homily of St. Gregory, Pope

The first question that strikes the mind in this Gospel lesson is: how could the Lord's Body after the Resurrection be a true one if He could come in to His disciples when the doors were shut? But we must know that if the ways of God can be understood by our reason, they are no longer wonderful: and there is no merit in faith where a proof can be given by human reason. But those works of our Redeemer, which considered in themselves alone can never be understood, should be compared with other works of His, that wonderful things may be confirmed by the testimony of even greater wonders.

Thus the Lord's Body which came in to His disciples when the doors were shut was the same which, at His Birth, had come forth to the eyes of men through the closed portals of the Virgin's womb. What wonder, then, if He, who was now to live forever, should enter in through closed doors, who, when He came among us to die, came forth without opening the Virgin's womb. But because the faith of the onlookers was uncertain in regard to that body which they had been able to see, He quickly showed them His hands and His side; inviting them to handle that flesh which He had made to pass through closed doors.

In this He showed them two miracles which, according to human reason, seemed completely to contradict each other: for after His resurrection He proved that His body was incorruptible and yet, at the same time, capable of being handled. Now, of necessity, what can be handled, is liable also to corruption; and what cannot be corrupted, cannot be handled. But in a wonderful way, beyond our power of understanding, our Redeemer, after His resurrection, showed His body to be at once both incorruptible and capable of being handled: so that by showing it to be incorruptible He might invite men to share His reward; and by offering it to be handled, He might confirm their faith. Thus He showed Himself to be both incorruptible and capable of being handled; that He might make it clear that His body, after His resurrection, was unchanged in nature, though different in glory.

He said to them: Peace be to you. As the Father hath sent Me, I also send you; that is: As the Father, who is God, hath sent Me, who am God, I also, as a man, send you, who are men. The Father sent the Son, for He planned that the Son should become incarnate for the redemption of mankind. He willed indeed that the Son should enter the world to suffer: and yet He loved the Son, whom He sent to suffering. But the Lord sent forth His chosen Apostles, not to the joys of the world, but to suffer in the world, even as He Himself had been sent. Thus, as the Son is loved by the Father, and yet sent forth by Him to suffering, even so were the disciples loved by the Lord, who yet sent them out into the world to suffer. It is rightly said, therefore: As the Father hath sent Me, I also send you; that is to say: With the like charity do I love you, whom I send forth to be tempted by the persecutors, as that wherewith the Father loved Me, whom He sent forth to the endurance of suffering.

R. Purge out the old leaven that you may be a new paste: for Christ our Pasch is sacrificed * Therefore, let us feast in the Lord, alleluia. V. He died for our offences and rose again for our justification. Therefore. Glory. Therefore.

✠ Continuation of the holy Gospel according to St. John.—At that time: When it was late that same day, the first of the week, and the doors were shut where the disciples were gathered together for fear of the Jews, Jesus came, and stood in the midst and said to them: Peace be to you. And when He had said this, He showed them His hands and His side. The disciples, therefore, were glad when they saw the Lord. He said therefore to them again: Peace be to you. As the Father hath sent Me, I also send you. When He had said this, He breathed on them, and He said to them: Receive ye the Holy Ghost: whose sins you shall forgive, they are forgiven them; and whose sins you shall retain, they are retained. Now Thomas, one of the twelve, who is called Didymus, was not with them when Jesus came. The other disciples therefore said to him: We have seen the Lord. But he said to them: Except I shall see in His hands the print of the nails, and put my finger into the place of the nails, and put my hand into His side, I will not believe. And after eight days, again His disciples were within, and Thomas with them. Jesus cometh, the doors being shut, and stood in the midst and said: Peace be to you. Then He saith to Thomas: Put in thy finger hither, and see My hands, and bring hither thy hand and put it into My side; and be not faithless, but believing. Thomas answered and said to Him: My Lord and my God. Jesus saith to him: Because thou hast seen Me, Thomas, thou hast believed: Blessed are they that have not seen, and have believed. Many other signs also did Jesus in the sight of His disciples, which are not written in this book. But these are written, that you may believe that Jesus is the Christ, the Son of God; and that, believing, you may have life in His name.

LET US PRAY

Grant, we beseech Thee, O almighty God, that we who have celebrated the feasts of the Paschal solemnity, may retain their fruits in our life and actions. Through our Lord.

II SUNDAY AFTER EASTER

I Nocturn

From the Acts of the Apostles, c. 1, 1 - 26

II Nocturn

Sermon of St. Leo, Pope

Those days, dearly beloved, which elapsed between the Lord's Resurrection and Ascension, did not fruitlessly drift by, but in them great and sacred truths were confirmed, great mysteries were revealed. In those days the fear of awful death was taken away, and the immortality, not only of the soul, but also of the body, was made known. In those days, through the Lord's breathing upon them, the Holy Ghost was poured upon all the Apostles: and to the blessed Apostle Peter, above the rest, was entrusted, in addition to the keys of the kingdom, the care of the Lord's flock.

In those days, the Lord joined the two disciples as a third companion on the way and, in order to clear away all the darkness of our uncertainty, He rebuked the slowness of their cowardly and timorous hearts. The enlightened hearts catch the flame of faith, and, lukewarm as they have been, are made to burn while the Lord unfolds the Scriptures.

Moreover, in the breaking of bread, the eyes of them that sit at table with Him are opened; far more blessed is the opening of their eyes, to whom the glorification of their nature is revealed, than that of our first parents, on whom was heaped the confusion of their own transgression.

But among these and other wonders, when the disciples were harassed by anxious thoughts and the Lord appeared in the midst of them and said, Peace be to you, lest what was passing through their hearts might remain their fixed opinion (for they supposed they saw a spirit, and not flesh), He rebuked their thoughts which were at variance with

the truth; to the eyes of these doubters He presented the marks of the cross yet remaining in His
hands and feet and He invited them to handle Him
with attentive care. For the traces of the nails
and the spear were retained that the wounds of unbelieving hearts might be made whole; and thus
they might comprehend, not with a wavering faith,
but with a steadfast knowledge, that the nature
which had lain in the sepulchre was to sit on the
throne of God the Father.

R. After our Lord Jesus was risen, standing in
the midst of His disciples, He said: * Peace be to
you, alleluia: the disciples rejoiced at the sight of
the Lord, alleluia. V. On the first day of the week,
when the doors were shut where the disciples were
gathered together, Jesus came and stood in the
midst of them and said to them. Peace. Glory.
Peace.

III Nocturn

The reading of the holy Gospel
according to St. John

At that time: Jesus said to the Pharisees: I am
the good shepherd. The good shepherd giveth his
life for his sheep. And so forth.

Homily of St. Gregory, Pope

You have heard, dearly beloved brethren, in the
lesson from the Gospel, an instruction that concerns
yourselves, and you have heard of the dangers that

threaten us. For behold, He whose goodness comes not from any gift bestowed on Him, but who is Himself essentially good, says: I am the good shepherd. And He has added thereto a pattern of this goodness which we may imitate, for He goes on to say: The good shepherd layeth down his life for his sheep. He has done Himself what He foretold; He has accomplished what He commanded.

The good shepherd laid down His life for His sheep that in this, our sacrament, He might transform His Body and Blood, and satisfy, with the food of His own Flesh, the sheep that He has redeemed. We have been shown the way we should follow, that is, of despising death: the pattern has been set before us wherewith we should be stamped.

Our first duty is to spend our temporal goods in merciful care for His sheep; then afterwards, if need be, we should offer ourselves to die for those same sheep. Thus from the first and lesser gift we come to the greater. But since the spirit by which we live is beyond all comparison better than the earthly riches we outwardly possess, how shall a man lay down his life for the sheep if he will not give up his goods for them.

And there are some who, since they love their earthly riches more than the sheep forfeit the very name of shepherd: of such it is added forthwith: But the hireling, and he that is not the shepherd, whose own the sheep are not, seeth the wolf coming and leaveth the sheep and flieth. He who feeds the Lord's sheep, not from any inward love of them, but for temporal gain, is not called a shepherd, but a hireling. He is in truth a hireling who indeed holds the place of the shepherd, but seeks not the welfare of souls; he longs for earthly comforts, enjoys the honor of his position of authority, gratifies himself with temporal riches and rejoices in the reverence paid to him by other men.

R. The good shepherd who laid down His life for His sheep and deigned to die for His flock is risen again: * Alleluia, alleluia, alleluia. V. For Christ our Pasch is sacrificed. Alleluia. Glory. Alleluia.

✠ Continuation of the holy Gospel according to St. John.—At that time: Jesus said to the Pharisees: I am the good shepherd. The good shepherd giveth his life for his sheep. But the hireling, and he that is not the shepherd, whose own the sheep are not, seeth the wolf coming and leaveth the sheep and flieth: and the wolf catcheth and scattereth the sheep: and the hireling flieth, because he is a hireling and he hath no care for the sheep. I am the good shepherd: and I know Mine, and Mine know Me, as the Father knoweth Me and I know the Father: and I lay down My life for My sheep. And other sheep I have that are not of this fold: them also I must bring, and they shall hear My voice, and there shall be one fold and one shepherd.

Let Us Pray

O God, who hath raised up a fallen world in the humility of Thy Son, grant to Thy faithful servants eternal joy; that those whom Thou didst snatch from the dangers of eternal death may enjoy everlasting happiness. Through the same our Lord.

III SUNDAY AFTER EASTER

I Nocturn

From the Apocalypse of blessed John the Apostle, c. 1, 1 - 19

II Nocturn

Sermon of St. Augustine, Bishop

During these holy days dedicated to the Lord's Resurrection, we purpose to discourse, as far as we are able with His help, upon the resurrection of the flesh. For this is our belief: this gift bestowed upon the flesh of our Lord Jesus Christ has been promised to us and was shown beforehand in Him as an example of what we are to expect. For He wished not only to foretell, but even to demonstrate to us, what He had promised should come to us at the last. Those who were then present, when they saw Him and were frightened and supposed they saw a spirit, grasped the solid substance of His Body.

For He not only spoke to them in words they could take in with their ears, but also in a form their eyes could behold; and it was not enough for

Him to offer Himself to be gazed upon, but He must even yield Himself to be laid hold of and handled. For He says: Why are you troubled, and why do thoughts arise in your hearts? For they supposed they saw a spirit. Why are you troubled, He says, and why do thoughts arise in your hearts? See My hands and My feet: handle and see: for a spirit hath not flesh and bones, as you see Me to have.

But as men, they disputed this evidence. For what else would men do, who are sensible only of the things of men, but dispute thus about God, in spite of God? He is God, they are men. But God knoweth the thoughts of men, that they are vain. To a carnal man, the one rule that determines what he shall understand is daily experience. What they are accustomed to see, they believe; what they are unaccustomed to see, they do not believe. But God works miracles outside the ordinary course, because He is God.

It is indeed a far greater miracle that every day so many men should be born who did not exist, than that a few who did exist should have been raised from the dead; and yet these miracles are not recognized; on the contrary, they are disregarded because of their frequency. Christ rose again: that is a fact. He had a body, He took flesh; He hung upon the cross, He gave up the ghost, His flesh was laid in the sepulchre. He, who lived once more in the flesh, showed His living flesh. Why do we wonder? Why do we not believe? It is God who did this.

R. One of the seven Angels spoke with me saying: Come, and I will show thee the new bride, the spouse of the Lamb: * And I saw Jerusalem coming down from heaven, adorned with her jewels, alleluia, alleluia, alleluia. V. And he carried me away in spirit to a great and high mountain. And I saw. Glory. And I saw.

III Nocturn

The reading of the holy Gospel according to St. John

At that time: Jesus said to His disciples: A little while, and now you shall not see Me; and again a little while, and you shall see Me; because I go to the Father. And so forth.

Homily of St. Augustine, Bishop

It is but a little while, this whole space of time, in which the present dispensation of the world fleeteth by. And hence this same Evangelist says in his Epistle: It is the last hour. For in this sense also He added: Because I go to the Father: which is to be referred to the former sentence where He says: A little while, and now you shall not see Me; and not to that which comes after where He says: And again a little while, and you shall see Me. For, by His going to the Father, He was to bring it about that they should not see Him.

And on this account, therefore, His words did not mean that He was about to die, and that, until He should rise again, He would be withdrawn from their sight; but that He was about to go to the Father, which He did after He rose again and, after holding intercourse with them for forty days, ascended into heaven. It was, therefore, to those who saw Him then in the flesh that He said: A little while, and now you shall not see Me; because He was about to go to the Father; and henceforth they were not to see Him as a mortal man, such as they saw Him to be while He was speaking thus.

But what He added: And again a little while, and you shall see Me: He gave as a promise to the whole Church, just as to the whole Church He promised: Behold I am with you even to the consummation of the world. The Lord delayeth not His promise. A little while, and we shall see Him; where we shall no more have requests to make, because nothing shall remain for us to desire, nothing be hidden for us to seek out. This little while seems to us a long time because it is still going on; but when it shall be ended, then we shall realize what a little while it was.

Let not our joy, then, be like that of the world, whereof it is said: But the world shall rejoice. And yet let us not be sad and joyless in this travail of our desires, but, as the Apostle says: Rejoicing in hope: Patient in tribulation: for even the woman

in travail, to whom we are compared, has more joy
over the offspring so soon to be born, than sorrow
on account of her present pain. But let this be the
end of this discourse: for in what follows there is
a very difficult question which must not be com-
pressed into a short space, that, if the Lord wills,
it may be more befittingly explained.

R. Your sorrow, alleluia, * Shall be turned into
joy, alleluia, alleluia. V. And the world shall rejoice, yet you shall be made sorrowful, but your
sorrow. Shall be turned. Glory. Shall be turned.

✠ Continuation of the holy Gospel according to
St. John.—At that time: Jesus said to His disciples: A little while, and now you shall not see
Me: and again a little while and you shall see Me:
because I go to the Father. Then some of His disciples said one to another: What is this that He
saith to us: A little while, and you shall not see
Me; and again a little while, and you shall see Me,
and because I go to the Father? They said, therefore: What is this that He saith, A little while?
We know not what He speaketh. And Jesus knew
that they had a mind to ask Him. And He said to
them: Of this do you inquire among yourselves,
because I said: A little while, and you shall not
see Me; and again a little while, and you shall see
Me? Amen, amen, I say to you, that you shall lament and weep, but the world shall rejoice: and you
shall be made sorrowful, but your sorrow shall be

turned into joy. A woman, when she is in labor, hath sorrow because her hour is come; but when she hath brought forth the child, she remembereth no more the anguish, for joy that a man is born into the world. So also you now indeed have sorrow: but I will see you again and your heart shall rejoice: and your joy no man shall take from you.

LET US PRAY

O God, who dost show forth the light of Thy truth that the erring may return to the path of justice; grant that all who profess they are Christians, may reject whatever is opposed to that name and follow what is becoming to it. Through our Lord.

IV SUNDAY AFTER EASTER

I Nocturn

From the catholic Epistle of blessed James the Apostle, c. 1, 1 - 16

II Nocturn

From the Treatise of St. Cyprian, Bishop and Martyr, on the Boon of Patience

Since I am to speak to you, dearly beloved brethren, upon patience, and to set forth to you its merits and advantages, how could I better begin than by saying that I feel that your patience is necessary in listening to me at this moment; for this very thing, your hearing and learning, how can you do it without patience? For then only will this salutary discourse and doctrine be thoroughly mastered when what is said is listened to with patience. Nor do I find, dearly beloved brethren, among the many other ways of heavenly discipline along which, in order to obtain the divine reward of hope and faith, our footsteps are directed, one that could better aid us in the attainment either of life or of glory, than that we, who strive to keep the Lord's commandments in the obedience of fear and devotion, should maintain patience in everything that we do.

This doctrine philosophers also have professed to follow, but their patience is as false as their wisdom. For whence shall a man who knows nothing either of the wisdom or patience of God be either wise or patient? But we, dearly beloved brethren, who are philosophers, not in words, but in deeds, who show forth our wisdom, not in garb, but in truth; we who possess the inner consciousness of virtue rather than boast ourselves upon it; who speak not great things, but live rather as servants and worshippers of God: let us exhibit in our spiritual service that patience we have learned from our heavenly masters.

For this is a virtue we share in common with God Himself: thence does patience take its rise, thence is derived its glory and its dignity. Patience, in its origin and its greatness, proceeds from God as its author. That which is dear to God should indeed be loved by man. The good which He Himself loves,

the Divine Majesty commends to man. If God is
to us both Lord and Father, let us seek to imitate
His patience: for it behooves servants to be faithful in their service, and it is unbecoming for sons
to be unworthy of their parentage.

Patience it is that both commends and binds us
to God: this it is that restrains anger, that bridles
the tongue, governs the mind, maintains peace, reg-
ulates discipline, breaks the force of evil desires,
checks the violence of rising passions, quenches the
flame of hatred, controls the power of the rich, consoles the neediness of the poor, safeguards the
blessed integrity of virgins, the laborious chastity
of widows, the faithful love of relatives and married folk; this it is that makes men humble in prosperity, courageous in adversity, meek under insults
and injuries; it teaches us promptly to forgive of-
fenders, and, when we ourselves offend, to pray for
pardon long and earnestly; it overcomes temptations and crowns sufferings and martyrdoms with
success. This it is that mightily upholds the foundations of our faith.

R. With my whole heart, alleluia, have I sought
after Thee, alleluia: * Let me not stray from Thy
commandments, alleluia, alleluia. V. Blessed art
Thou, O Lord, teach me Thy justifications. Let me
not. Glory. Let me not.

III Nocturn

The reading of the holy Gospel
according to St. John

At that time: Jesus said to His disciples: I go
to Him that sent Me; and none of you asketh Me:
Whither goest Thou? And so forth.

Homily of St. Augustine, Bishop

When the Lord Jesus had foretold to His disciples the persecutions they would have to undergo
after His departure, He went on to say: But I
told you not these things from the beginning, because I was with you: and now I go to Him that
sent Me. The first thing to be noticed here is
whether He had not already predicted their future
sufferings. But the three other Evangelists make
it sufficiently clear that He had foretold these things
prior to the approach of the Supper; according to
John, it was when the supper was over that He
spoke thus, saying: But I told you not these things
from the beginning because I was with you.

Are we, then, to settle such a question in this
way, that they too relate that He was near His
Passion when He said these things? Then it was
not when He was with them at the beginning that
He so spoke, seeing that He was even now about to
depart, even now about to go His way to the Father.
And also, according to these other Evangelists, it
is true what is said here: But I told you not these
things from the beginning.

But what are we to make of the credibility of the Gospel according to Matthew, who relates that these things were made known to them by the Lord, not only when He was about to eat the Paschal supper with His disciples just before His Passion, but also at the beginning, when the twelve apostles were first mentioned by name and sent out upon their divine work?

What, therefore, can He mean by what He says here: But I told you not these things from the beginning, because I was with you: but that what He here says about the Holy Spirit, who was to come to them and to bear witness when they should have such ills to endure? this He said not unto them at the beginning, because He was with them. The Comforter, then, or Advocate, (for the Greek word Paraclete may be interpreted in both these senses), had become necessary after Christ's departure; and therefore He had not told them of the Holy Spirit at the beginning, while He Himself was with them, because they were consoled by His presence.

R. O God, to Thee I will sing a new canticle, alleluia: * On the psaltery of ten strings I will sing to Thee, alleluia, alleluia. V. Thou art my God, and I will praise Thee: Thou art my God, and I will exalt Thee. On the psaltery. Glory. On the psaltery.

✠ Continuation of the holy Gospel according to St. John.—At that time: Jesus said to His dis-

ciples: I go to Him that sent Me; and none of you
asketh Me: Whither goest Thou? But because I
have spoken these things to you, sorrow hath filled
your heart. But I tell you the truth: It is expedient to you that I go, for if I go not, the Paraclete will not come to you: but if I go, I will send
Him to you. And when He is come, He will convince the world of sin, and of justice and of judgment. Of sin, because they believed not in Me; and
of justice, because I go to the Father, and you shall
see Me no longer; and of judgment, because the
prince of this world is already judged. I have yet
many things to say to you: but you cannot bear
them now. But when He, the Spirit of truth, is
come, He will teach you all truth. For He shall not
speak of Himself: but what things soever He shall
hear He shall speak, and the things that are to
come He shall show you. He shall glorify Me: because He shall receive of Mine and shall show it to
you. R. Amen.

Let Us Pray

O God, who dost make the minds of the faithful
to be of one accord, grant that Thy people may love
what Thou dost command and desire what Thou
dost promise; that amidst the changes of this life
our hearts may ever remain fixed where the true
joys are to be found. Through our Lord.

V SUNDAY AFTER EASTER

I Nocturn

From the first Epistle of blessed Peter the Apostle,
c. 1, 1 - 12, and from his second Epistle, c. 1,   1 - 9

II Nocturn

From the Book of St. Ambrose, Bishop, on Faith in the Resurrection

Since it was impossible for the Wisdom of God to die and because what had never died could not rise again from the dead, the Lord took flesh, which was capable of death, so that when this died, as was natural to it, what had once been dead might rise again.   For there could not have been any resurrection, save by means of a man: for as by a man came death, so by a man came the resurrection of the dead.   Therefore, as man He rose again, because as man He died; it was a man who was raised from the dead, but He who raised Him was God. Then was He man according to the flesh; now, in every respect, God.   And now we no longer know Christ according to the flesh, but we hold the benefit of His flesh, in that we know Him to be the first-fruits of them that sleep, the first-born of the dead.

First-fruits are indeed of the same nature and kind as the rest of the crop; of these the earliest are offered as a gift to God, to win from Him a more abundant harvest; a sacred offering for all the rest, and, as it were, the homage of restored nature. Christ, therefore, is the first-fruits of them that sleep. Yet does this refer merely to His own followers who, as though having no share in death, are held, as it were, in a sweet sleep? or does it mean rather all the dead? But as in Adam all die, so also in Christ all shall be made alive.

As the first-fruits of death were in Adam, so also the first-fruits of the resurrection are in Christ; therefore, all shall rise again. But let no one despair, nor let the just grieve that all are to share alike in the resurrection, since they are looking for a special reward for their virtue. All indeed shall rise again, but, as the Apostle says, every one in his own order. The reward of the Divine Mercy is common to all, but different for every one is the order of his merits.

We observe how grave a profanity it is not to believe in the resurrection. For if we shall not rise again, then Christ died to no purpose, then Christ has not risen. For if it was not for us that He rose again, then indeed He has not risen, for He Himself had no reason to rise again. In Him the world rose again; in Him heaven rose again; in Him the earth rose again. For there shall be a new heaven and a new earth. But for Himself there was no need of a resurrection, for the bonds of death held Him not. For even though as man He died, He was yet free in hell. Dost thou wish to

know how He was free? I am become as a man
without help, free among the dead. And it is well
said, Free, of Him who could raise Himself up from
the dead, according as it is written: Destroy this
temple, and in three days I will raise it up. Well
again is it said, Free, of Him who descended there
that He might redeem others.

R. I will declare Thy name to my brethren, alleluia: * In the midst of the Church will I praise
Thee, alleluia, alleluia. V. I will give praise to
Thee, O Lord, among the people, and I will sing a
psalm to Thee among the nations. In. Glory. In.

III Nocturn

The reading of the holy Gospel
according to St. John

At that time: Jesus said to His disciples: Amen,
amen, I say to you: If you ask the Father anything in My name, He will give it you. And so
forth.

Homily of St. Augustine, Bishop

These words of the Lord have now to be discussed: Amen, amen, I say to you: If you ask the
Father anything in My name, He will give it you.
It has been said already, in the earlier portions of
this discourse of the Lord, concerning those who
ask anything of the Father in Christ's Name and
do not receive, that whatsoever is asked contrary
to the due order of salvation is not asked in the

Name of the Savior. For it is not the sound of the letters and syllables, but what the sound itself signifies and what by that sound is rightly and truly understood, that is to be taken as the Lord's meaning when He says: In My Name.

Hence, he who holds such opinions of Christ as ought not to be held concerning the only Son of God does not ask in His Name, even though he does not refrain from pronouncing the Name of Christ in so many letters and syllables: for he is asking in his name of whom he is thinking while he asks. But he who holds such opinions of Him as ought to be held, he does ask in His Name: and he receives what he asks, if he asks for nothing contrary to his own eternal salvation. He receives it, however, when it is right for him to receive it. For some things are not refused, but deferred, that they may be given at a suitable time.

Such is the true interpretation of what He says: He will give it you; so that thereby we may know that those benefits are signified which belong properly to those who ask for them. For indeed all the Saints are heard effectively in their own behalf, but are not so heard in behalf of all, whether friends or enemies, or any others, because it is not said in a general way: He will give it: but: He will give it you.

Hitherto, He says, you have not asked anything in My Name. Ask, and you shall receive, that your joy may be full. This full joy of which He speaks here is assuredly not carnal, but spiritual joy; and when it shall be so great that nothing more can be added to it, without doubt it will then be full. Therefore, if we understand the grace of God, if we truly desire that life of bliss, whatever is asked that has to do with the obtaining of this joy must be asked in Christ's Name. But if anything else is asked, nothing is asked: not that the thing itself is altogether nothing, but that in comparison with something so great as this, anything else that may be desired is nothing.

R. If I forget Thee, alleluia, let my right hand be forgotten: * Let my tongue cling to my jaws if I do not remember Thee, alleluia, alleluia. V. By the waters of Babylon there we sat and wept when we remembered Thee, O Sion. Let my tongue. Glory. Let my tongue.

✠ Continuation of the holy Gospel according to St. John.—At that time: Jesus saith to His disciples: Amen, amen, I say to you: If you ask the Father anything in My name, He will give it you. Hitherto you have not asked anything in My name: Ask, and you shall receive, that your joy may be full. These things I have spoken to you in proverbs. The hour cometh when I will no more speak to you in proverbs, but will show you plainly of the Father. In that day you shall ask in My name: and I say not to you that I will ask the Father for you: for the Father Himself loveth you, because you have loved Me and have believed that I came out from God. I came forth from the Father and am come into the world: again I leave the world and I go to the Father. His disciples say to Him: Behold, now Thou speakest plainly and speakest no proverb. Now we know that Thou knowest all things and Thou needest not that any man should ask Thee: by this we believe that Thou camest forth from God.

LET US PRAY

O God, from whom all good gifts come, grant to those who ask Thee that by Thy inspiration we may think what is right and by Thy guidance may also perform it. Through our Lord.

ROGATION MONDAY

The reading of the holy Gospel
according to St. Luke

At that time: Jesus said to His disciples: Which of you shall have a friend and shall go to him at midnight, and shall say to him: Friend, lend me three loaves. And so forth.

Homily of St. Ambrose, Bishop

This passage gives occasion for another teaching: that at every moment, not only by day, but by night as well, prayer should be offered up. For thou seest that this man who went at midnight to beg three loaves of his friend, and persisted in maintaining his petition, was not defrauded of what he asked. What are these three loaves but the food of heavenly mysteries? Which food, if thou lovest the Lord thy God, thou wilt merit to obtain, not only for thyself alone, but for others also. For who is more a friend to us than He who delivered up His Body for us?

From Him at midnight David begged bread, and received it. For he was asking this when he said: I rose at midnight to give praise to Thee. Thus he merited to receive those loaves which he has set before us to be eaten. He was asking this when he said: Every night I will wash my bed. For he did not fear lest he should rouse from sleep Him whom he knew to be ever wakeful. And therefore, bearing in mind what is written, persevering in prayer by day and by night, let us beg forgiveness for our sins.

For if so holy a man as David, who was occupied with the affairs of his kingdom, gave praise to the Lord seven times a day and never missed the morning and evening sacrifices, what ought we to do, who should beseech Him all the more earnestly since we transgress more often by reason of the weakness of our flesh and of our mind, that, when weary of our journey and tired out by the affairs of the world and the winding paths of this life, that bread of refreshment, which strengthens the heart of man, may not fail us? The Lord teaches us to be watchful, not only at midnight, but at almost every moment. For He comes at the evening hour, and in the second watch, and in the third: and He is wont to knock. Blessed, therefore, are those servants whom, when the Lord shall come, He shall find watching.

ROGATION WEDNESDAY

VIGIL OF THE ASCENSION

The reading of the holy Gospel
according to St. John

At that time: Jesus lifting up His eyes to heaven, said: Father, the hour is come; glorify Thy Son. And so forth.

Homily of St. Augustine, Bishop

Our Lord, the only begotten and coeternal with the Father, could, if need be, in the form of a servant and out of the form of a servant, pray in silence. But He willed to show Himself thus as praying to the Father that He might remember that He was our teacher. Accordingly, that prayer which He made for us, He also made known to us; seeing that it is not only the delivering of discourses to them by so great a master, but also His prayer for them to His Father, that is a means of edification for His disciples; and if for theirs who were present to hear His words, assuredly for ours also, who were to read those words when they had been written down.

And thus, what He says here: Father, the hour is come, glorify Thy Son: showed that all time, and every occasion, when He did anything or suffered anything to be done, was determined by Him who was Himself not subject to time: for all these things which were to take place at fixed future times have their efficient causes in the wisdom of God, with whom there are no distinctions of time. And so it must not be believed that this hour had come because urged on by fate, but rather, because ordained by God. Nor did any law of the heavenly bodies determine the Passion of Christ: far be it from us to imagine that the stars should compel the Maker of the stars to die.

By many it is understood that the Son was glorified by the Father in that He spared Him not, but delivered Him up for us all. But if He can be said to be glorified in His Passion, His humility rather than His glory is set forth, as the Apostle bears witness, saying: He humbled Himself, becoming obedient unto death, even to the death of the cross. And then he continues, and now speaks of His glorification: For which cause God also hath exalted Him, and hath given Him a Name which is above all names: that in the Name of Jesus every knee should bow, of those that are in heaven, on earth, and under the earth. And that every tongue should confess that the Lord Jesus Christ is in the glory of God the Father. This glorification of our Lord

Jesus Christ which took its beginning from His Resurrection.

THE ASCENSION OF THE LORD

I Nocturn

From the Acts of the Apostles, c. 1, 1 - 14

II Nocturn

Sermon of St. Leo, Pope

After the blessed and glorious Resurrection of our Lord Jesus Christ, wherein He raised up in three days that true temple of God which had been destroyed by the ungodly Jews, there is this day fulfilled, dearly beloved, that number of forty holy days which had been ordained by a most sacred dispensation and spent in giving us valuable instructions; so that, while the Lord permitted His bodily presence to tarry among us for this space of time, our faith in His Resurrection might be strengthened by needful proofs.

For the death of Christ had greatly disturbed the hearts of the disciples, and a certain lethargy of disbelief had crept over their grief-laden minds at His torture on the Cross, at His giving up the ghost, and at the burial of His lifeless body. Thus the most blessed Apostles and all the disciples, who had been full of fear at the final issue of the cross and uncertain in faith concerning the Resurrection, were so strengthened by the clear vision of the truth that, when the Lord was going up into the heights of heaven, they were not troubled by any sadness, but rather were filled with great joy.

And in truth it was a great and ineffable cause of rejoicing, when, in the sight of a holy multitude, human nature ascended above the dignity of all celestial creatures to pass above the ranks of the Angels, to be raised beyond the heights of the Archangels, and not to have any degree of loftiness set as a limit to its advancement short of the right hand of the eternal Father, where it should be associated to His royal glory to whose nature it was united in the Son.

Therefore, since Christ's Ascension is our own exaltation, and where the glory of the head has gone before, thither is the hope of the body summoned, let us, dearly beloved, exult with due rejoicing and be glad, devoutly giving thanks. For today, not only have we been confirmed in the possession of paradise, but in Christ we have penetrated even the heights of heaven; having gained, through the ineffable grace of Christ, far more than we lost through the malice of the devil. For those whom that virulent enemy cast down from the happiness of their first estate, these has the Son of God made to be one body with Himself, and placed them at the right hand of the Father; with whom He liveth and reigneth in the unity of the Holy Ghost,

God through all eternity. Amen.

R. Let not your heart be troubled: I go to the Father: and when I am taken from you, I will send you, alleluia, * The Spirit of truth, and your heart shall rejoice, alleluia. V. I will ask the Father, and He will give you another Paraclete. The Spirit. Glory. The Spirit.

III Nocturn

The reading of the holy Gospel according to St. Mark

At that time: Jesus appeared to the eleven disciples as they were at table: and He upbraided them with their incredulity and hardness of heart, because they did not believe them who had seen Him after He was risen again. And so forth.

Homily of St. Gregory, Pope

That the disciples were thus slow to believe in the Lord's Resurrection was not so much a matter of their weakness as, if I may say so, of our future stability. For the Resurrection itself was, on account of their doubt, demonstrated by many proofs, and when, as we read these proofs, we come to acknowledge the Resurrection, what else is it but that we are confirmed by their doubting? For Mary Magdalen, who soon believed, did less for me than Thomas, who long remained doubtful. For he, in his doubting, touched the scars of the wounds, and removed from our hearts the wounds of our doubts.

We should also observe what Luke, to allege the reality of the Lord's Resurrection, has recorded, saying: Eating together with them, He commanded them that they should not depart from Jerusalem. And a little further on: While they looked on, He was raised up, and a cloud received Him out of their sight. Note the words, mark the mystery. Eating together with them, He was raised up. He ate, and He ascended; clearly, in order that, by the fact of His eating, He might manifest the reality of His flesh.

But Mark mentions that, before the Lord ascended into heaven, He chided them for their unbelief and hardness of heart. In these things what have we to consider, but that the Lord chided His disciples, at the time when He was withdrawing His bodily presence from them, that the words which He spoke at parting might remain more deeply impressed in the hearts of the listeners.

He rebuked their hardness, then, and now let us hear what He says in admonishing them: Go ye into the whole world and preach the Gospel to every creature. Can it be, my brethren, that the holy Gospel is to be preached to senseless things and to brute beasts, that it should thus have been said to the disciples: Preach to every creature? But by the phrase, Every creature, is signified man. For man possesses something in common with every creature. Mere existence, he shares with stones;

life, with trees; feeling, with beasts; and understanding, with the Angels. If then man has something in common with every creature, man is in
some way, every creature. And therefore, the Gospel
is preached to every creature when it is preached to
man alone.

R. I will ask the Father, and He shall give you
another Paraclete, * That He, the Spirit of truth,
may abide with you forever, alleluia. V. For if I
go not, the Paraclete will not come to you: but if I
go, I will send Him to you. That He. Glory. That
He.

☩ Continuation of the holy Gospel according to
St. Mark.—At that time: Jesus appeared to the
eleven as they were at table: and He upbraided
them with their incredulity and hardness of heart,
because they did not believe them who had seen
Him after He was risen again. And He said to
them: Go ye into the whole world and preach the
Gospel to every creature. He that believeth and is
baptized shall be saved: but he that believeth not
shall be condemned. And these signs shall follow
them that believe: In My Name they shall cast out
devils; they shall speak with new tongues; they
shall take up serpents; and if they shall drink any
deadly thing, it shall not hurt them; they shall lay
their hands upon the sick, and they shall recover.
And the Lord Jesus, after He had spoken to them,
was taken up into heaven and sitteth on the right

hand of God. But they, going forth, preached everywhere, the Lord working withal, and confirming the
word with signs that followed.

Let Us Pray

Grant, we beseech Thee, almighty God, that as we
believe Thy only begotten Son, our Redeemer, hath
on this day ascended into heaven, we also in spirit
may abide in the heavenly places. Through the
same our Lord.

FRIDAY

The reading of the holy Gospel
according to St. Mark

At that time: Jesus appeared to the eleven as
they were at table: and He upbraided them with
their incredulity and hardness of heart, because
they did not believe them who had seen Him after
He was risen again. And so forth.

Homily of St. Gregory, Pope

He that believeth and is baptized, shall be saved:
but he that believeth not, shall be condemned. Someone, perhaps, will say to himself: I have already
believed, so I shall be saved. He says what is true,
if he maintains his faith by his works. For that
faith is true which does not belie in practice what
it professes in words. For hence it is that Paul
says concerning certain false brethren: They pro-

fess that they know God, but in their works they deny Him. Hence John says: He who saith that He knoweth God, and keepeth not His commandments, is a liar.

Since this is so, it behooves us to test the reality of our faith by a careful consideration of our lives. For then only are we truly faithful, when we fulfil in works what we promise in words. Assuredly, we promised on the day of our baptism to renounce all the works of our old enemy and all vain pomps. Therefore, let each one of you turn the eyes of his mind upon the consideration of himself; and if after baptism he still observes what he promised before baptism, let him rejoice, because he may know for certain that he is faithful.

But behold, if he has by no means kept what he has promised, if he has fallen back again into doing wicked deeds and desiring the vain pomps of the world, let us see if he knows how to bemoan his wrong-doing. For in the eyes of a merciful judge, that man is not held a liar who returns to the truth after his lying: for almighty God welcomes our repentance, and Himself, in His judgment, conceals our sin.

SATURDAY

The reading of the holy Gospel
according to St. Mark

At that time: Jesus appeared to the eleven as they were at table: and He upbraided them with their incredulity and hardness of heart, because they did not believe them who had seen Him after He was risen again. And so forth.

Homily of St. Gregory, Pope

And these signs shall follow them that believe: In My Name they shall cast out devils, they shall speak with new tongues, they shall take up serpents: and if they shall drink any deadly thing, it shall not hurt them; they shall lay their hands upon the sick, and they shall recover. Is this to say, my brethren, that since you do not work such signs as these, you do not believe? But these things were necessary when the Church first came into being. For in order that the multitude of believers might increase in the faith, it was nourished by miracles: even so, when we plant out young trees, we continue to water them until we see that they have taken root in the ground: and when once they are firmly rooted, the watering is given up. For hence it is that Paul says: Tongues are for a sign not to believers, but to unbelievers.

But there is in these signs and wonders something which we should do well to study more closely.

For of a truth, holy Church does every day in a spiritual sense what the Apostles did then in a bodily manner. For when her priests, in virtue of the power of exorcism, lay their hands upon believers and forbid evil spirits to dwell in their minds, what else do they but cast out devils? And the faithful likewise, when they forsake the worldly speech of their old life and give utterance to holy mysteries, setting forth, as far as they are able, the praise and power of their Creator, what else is this but speaking with new tongues? And when, by their own good admonitions, they draw out the evil from other men's minds, they are taking up serpents.

And when they hear mischievous suggestions, but yet are by no means to be enticed thereby into any evil action, it is verily a deadly draught that they drink; yet it will do them no harm. Whensoever they shall see their neighbors to be weak in welldoing, and shall help them with all their power, strengthening by the example of their own action the lives of those who are faltering in what they have to do, what else is this but laying hands upon the sick, that they may recover? Truly these are the greater miracles in that they are spiritual; they are so much greater inasmuch as by their means, not the body, but the spirit is restored.

SUNDAY WITHIN THE OCTAVE
OF THE ASCENSION

I Nocturn

From the first Epistle of blessed John the Apostle,
c. 1, 1 - 10; c. 2, 1 - 6

II Nocturn

Sermon of St. Augustine, Bishop

Our Savior, dearly beloved brethren, has ascended into heaven; then let us not be troubled here on earth. If our minds be there, we shall have peace here. Meanwhile, let our hearts ascend with Christ; when the day that He has promised shall come, our bodies too shall follow. But we must know, my brethren, that neither pride, nor avarice, nor luxury ascend with Christ; none of our vices ascend with our physician. And therefore, if we desire to follow our physician on high, we must lay aside our vices and sins.

For all such things hold us fast, as though with fetters, and strive to entangle us in a net of sins; and therefore, with God's help, according to what the Psalmist says: Let us break their bonds asunder: that we may confidently say to the Lord: Thou hast broken my bonds, I will sacrifice to Thee the sacrifice of praise. The Resurrection of the Lord is our hope, the Ascension of the Lord is our glorification.

Today we celebrate the feast of the Ascension. Therefore, if we are to celebrate the Ascension of the Lord fittingly, faithfully, devoutly, and in a holy and religious manner, let us ascend with Him and raise our hearts on high. But in ascending let us not be uplifted, presuming on our merits as though they were truly our own. For it is to the Lord that we must lift up our hearts. For a heart uplifted, but not to the Lord, is pride; but a heart uplifted to the Lord is a heart seeking safety. Behold, brethren, a wonderful miracle. The Lord is high: lift thyself up, and He will flee from thee; humble thyself, and He will descend to thee. Why is this? Because He is high and looketh on the low, and the high He knoweth afar off. They that are low He beholds from near at hand, that He may raise them up: they that are high, that is to say, the proud, He knoweth afar off, that He may thrust them down.

For Christ rose again to give us hope that man, who dies, rises again; He has given us confidence that in dying we may no more despair, nor suppose our life to end forever with our death. For we were anxious about the future of the soul itself: and He, by rising again, has reassured us as to the resurrection of the body. Believe, then, that thou mayest be made clean. First, it behooves thee to believe that afterwards, by faith, thou mayest deserve to see God. For dost thou wish to see God?

Hear what He says: Blessed are the clean of heart, for they shall see God. Think first, then, upon the cleansing of thy heart; remove thence whatsoever thou seest would offend God.

R. When Christ ascended on high, He led captivity captive, * He gave gifts to men, alleluia, alleluia, alleluia. V. God is ascended with jubilee, and the Lord with the sound of the trumpet. He gave. Glory. He gave.

III Nocturn

The reading of the holy Gospel
according to St. John

At that time: Jesus said to His disciples: When the Paraclete cometh, whom I will send you from the Father, the Spirit of Truth who proceedeth from the Father, He shall give testimony of Me. And so forth.

Homily of St. Augustine, Bishop

The Lord Jesus, in the discourse which He addressed to His disciples after the supper, now close upon His Passion, as it were, upon the eve of His departure from them and of depriving them of His bodily presence, while continuing His spiritual presence to all His disciples till the very end of the world, exhorted them to endure the persecutions of the wicked, whom He described by the name of the world. He also said, however, that it was out of the world that He had chosen the disciples themselves: that they might know that it was by the grace of God that they were what they were; and that it was by their own vices that they had been what they had been.

Then He clearly signified the Jews, as persecutors both of Himself and of His disciples that it might appear unmistakably that they also were to be included in the appellation of that damnable world that persecutes the saints. And after He had said of them that they knew not Him who had sent Him, and yet hated both the Son and the Father, that is, both Him who was sent and Him by whom He was sent, He came at length to say this: That the word may be fulfilled which is written in their law: They hated Me without cause.

And then He added, as though in consequence of what He had just said, the words we have now taken in hand to discuss: But when the Paraclete cometh, whom I will sent you from the Father, the Spirit of Truth who proceedeth from the Father, He shall give testimony of Me: and you shall give testimony, because you are with Me from the beginning.

What has this to do with what He had said: But now they have both seen and hated both Me and My Father; but that the word may be fulfilled which is written in their law: They hated Me without cause? Was it that the Paraclete, the Spirit of Truth, when He came, convinced by His clearer testimony these who had both seen and hated? Nay, rather, even some of those who had seen and till then had hated, He converted, by this manifestation of Himself, to that faith which works by love.

R. The Lord hath set all His beauty above the stars: * His loveliness is in the clouds of heaven and His Name endureth forever, alleluia. V. His going out is from the highest heaven, and His circuit even to the height thereof. His loveliness. Glory. His loveliness.

✠ Continuation of the holy Gospel according to St. John.—At that time: Jesus said to His disciples: When the Paraclete cometh, whom I will send you from the Father, the Spirit of truth, who proceedeth from the Father, He shall give testimony of Me: and you shall give testimony, because you are with Me from the beginning. These things have I spoken to you, that you may not be scandalized. They will put you out of the synagogues; yea, the hour cometh, that whosoever killeth you will think that he doth a service to God. And these things will they do to you, because they have not known the Father, nor Me. But these things I have told you, that, when the hour shall come, you may remember that I told you of them.

Let Us Pray

O almighty and eternal God, make us always to have a will that is devoted to Thee and to serve Thy Majesty with a sincere heart. Through our Lord.

MONDAY

The reading of the holy Gospel
according to St. Mark

At that time: Jesus appeared to the eleven as they were at table: and He upbraided them with their incredulity and hardness of heart, because they did not believe them who had seen Him after He was risen again. And so forth.

Homily of St. Gregory, Pope

And the Lord Jesus, after He had spoken to them, was taken up into heaven, and sitteth on the right hand of God. We have learned in the old Testament how Elias was caught up into heaven. But the aerial heaven of the terrestial atmosphere is one thing, and the ethereal heaven is another. For the aerial heaven is close to the earth: whence we speak of the birds of heaven, because we see them flying in the air. It was, then, into the aerial heaven that Elias was carried up, and he was suddenly borne away into some unknown region of the earth, where, in an unbroken calm of flesh and spirit, He might continue to live until he should return at the end of the world and pay the penalty of death. For he merely postponed his death, he has not escaped it; but our Redeemer, since He did not postpone it, overcame it, and, by rising again, utterly vanquished it, while by His Ascension He proclaimed the glory of His Resurrection.

It is further to be noticed that, as we read, Elias ascended in a chariot: and this, indeed, that it may be clearly shown that, as a mere man, he needed assistance from without. It was by the Angels that this help was given and these things were done: for, weighed down as he was by the infirmity of his own nature, he could not by his own power ascend even into the aerial heaven. But we do not read that our Redeemer was taken up in a chariot, or by the Angels: for He, who made all things, was certainly carried up above all things by His own power. For indeed, He was but returning where He had always been and He was going back to the place which He had never left; for when in His Manhood He ascended into heaven, in His Divinity He encompassed alike both earth and heaven.

And as Joseph, sold by his brethren, prefigured the betrayal and selling of our Redeemer: even so Enoch, who was carried away to another place, and Elias, who was taken up into the aerial heaven, foreshadowed the Lord's Ascension, one before the law was given, and the other under the law: until such time as He, who could truly ascend into heaven, should come. Hence also there is a difference in the manner in which each was lifted up. For it is recorded that Enoch was carried away to another place, whereas Elias was taken up into heaven: that later on He should come who should neither be carried away nor taken up, but should ascend by His Own power into the ethereal heaven.

TUESDAY

The reading of the holy Gospel according to St. Mark

At that time: Jesus appeared to the eleven as they were at table: and He upbraided them with their incredulity and hardness of heart, because they did not believe them who had seen Him after He was risen again. And so forth.

Homily of St. Gregory, Pope

We have to consider why it is that Mark says: He sitteth on the right hand of God; while Stephen says: I see the heavens opened and the Son of Man standing on the right hand of God. Why is it that Mark speaks of Him as sitting, whereas Stephen declares that he sees Him standing? Yet you are aware, brethren, that men sit when they give judgment, but stand when they fight or when they come to the assistance of others.

Therefore, because our Redeemer was taken up into heaven and is now judging all things, and at the last day will come as the Judge of all, Mark describes Him, after He was taken up, as sitting, for after the glory of His Ascension He shall be seen at the last as Judge. But Stephen, who was then in the stress of his own contest, saw Him standing, inasmuch as he knew Him for his helper: for in order that Stephen might overcome the treachery of his persecutors, Christ, by His grace, was fighting for him from heaven.

It goes on: but they going forth preached everywhere, the Lord working withal, and confirming the word with signs that followed. What have we to consider here, what have we to remember, but that obedience followed the command given, and signs followed the obedience rendered? But because, under the guidance of God, we are passing quickly through the lesson from the Gospel to explain it, it remains for us to say something further in consideration of so great a festival.

WEDNESDAY

The reading of the holy Gospel
according to St. Mark

At that time: Jesus appeared to the eleven as they were at table, and He upbraided them with their incredulity and hardness of heart, because they did not believe them who had seen Him after He was risen again. And so forth.

Homily of St. Gregory, Pope

But the first thing we have to consider is why, when the Lord was born, Angels appeared, and yet we do not read that they were seen in white garments; but when the Lord ascended into heaven, we read that Angels were sent down and appeared

robed in white. For so it is written: While they
looked on, He was raised up, and a cloud received
Him out of their sight. And while they were beholding Him going up to heaven, behold two men
stood beside them in white garments. Now white
garments betoken festivity and joy of mind. Why
else is it, then, that at the Lord's birth, they were
not in white garments, while at the Ascension of
the Lord, the Angels did appear in white garments:
was it not because it was for the Angels a day of
great festivity, when God, made man, entered heav-
en? For when the Lord was born, the divine nature seemed to be humiliated; but when the Lord
ascended, human nature was exalted. Now white
garments are better suited to exaltation than to
humiliation.

And thus, at His Ascension, the angels were duly
seen clad in white garments; because He, who at
His birth appeared as God, yet in lowliness, at His
Ascension was shown as man, but raised to loftiness. Yet, dearly beloved brethren, what we should
consider above all things in this solemnity is this:
that on this day the hand-writing of our condemnation was blotted out; the judgment by which we
were sentenced to corruption is reversed. For that
very nature to which it was said: Thou art earth,
and to the earth shalt thou return, has this day entered heaven. On account, then, of this exaltation
of our flesh, blessed Job, speaking figuratively,

called the Lord a bird. Because he saw that the Jews did not understand the mystery of the Ascension, He passed judgment on their infidelity in this figure, saying: he hath not known the path of the bird.

Now the Lord is rightly called a bird, for with His fleshly body He soared into the air. And whosoever does not believe in His Ascension, he has not known the path of this bird. Of this great feast it is said by the Psalmist: Thy magnificence is elevated above the heavens. And again he says: God is ascended with jubilee and the Lord with the sound of the trumpet. And once more he says: Ascending on high, He led captivity captive, He gave gifts to men. Verily, ascending on high, He led captivity captive; for He swallowed up our corruption. Of a truth He gave gifts to men, for having sent down the Spirit from on high, He gave to some the word of wisdom, to some the word of knowledge, to some the gift of power, to some the grace of healing, to some divers kinds of tongues, to some the interpretation of speeches.

OCTAVE DAY OF THE ASCENSION

I Nocturn

From the Epistle of blessed Paul the Apostle to
The Ephesians, c. 4, 1 - 21

II Nocturn

Sermon of St. Augustine, Bishop

Dearly beloved, all those wonders that our Lord Jesus Christ wrought in this world, having assumed our frail nature, are profitable to us. And when He carried up our humanity into the heights above, He showed to believers that heaven could be opened to them; and when He bore it aloft victorious over death into the heavenly places, He showed to such as should themselves win the victory whither to follow Him.

The Ascension of the Lord, then, was the confirmation of the Catholic Faith; for we may firmly believe that one day we too shall be given a share in this wondrous gift, the effect of which we have even now perceived. Thus, let every one that is faithful, having already received so much, learn to hope for what has been promised, on account of that which He knows to have already been given, and let him hold the goodness of God in the past and present as a pledge for what is yet to come.

That earthly body, then, is set on high above the heavens; those bones, lately shut up within the

narrow limits of the sepulchre, are borne aloft into
the assembly of the angels; mortal nature passes
over into the embrace of immortality. Thus the
sacred narrative of the lesson from the apostles
bears witness: And when He had said these things,
while they looked on, He was raised up. When thou
hearest that He was raised up, know that this service was rendered by the hosts of heaven; whence
today's festival has clearly shown us the mystery
of God and man. Under one and the same Person,
behold in Him who raises up, the power of the divinity; but in Him who is raised up, the substance
of humanity.

And so those baneful errors of the East which,
by an impious novelty, presume to assert that the
Son of God and the Son of man are of one nature,
are altogether to be detested. Whichever side they
take, either they say that He was merely man and
thus deny the glory of the Creator; or that He was
God alone and so deny the mercy of the Redeemer.
In this respect the Arian cannot well be possessed
of the Gospel truth, where we read of the Son of
God as now equal to, now less (than the Father).
The man who by a deadly error believes our Savior
to be of one nature alone, is forced to say either
that man only, or God only, was crucified. But it
is not so. God alone could not have suffered death,
and a mere man could not have overcome it.

R. Let not your heart be troubled: I go to the

Father; and when I am taken from you, I will send you, alleluia * The Spirit of truth, and your heart shall rejoice, alleluia. I will ask the Father, and He will give you another Paraclete. The Spirit. Glory. The Spirit.

III Nocturn

The reading of the holy Gospel according to St. Mark

At that time: Jesus appeared to the eleven as they were at table: and He upbraided them with their incredulity and hardness of heart, because they did not believe them who had seen Him after He was risen again. And so forth.

Homily of St. Gregory, Pope

Of the glory of the Lord's Ascension Habacuc too says: The sun was lifted up and the moon stood still in her course. Now what is signified by the name of the sun, but the Lord, and what by the name of the moon, if not the Church? For until the Lord ascended into heaven, His holy Church set at variance with the world, was full of fear; but after His Ascension she was strengthened, and openly preached what she inwardly believed. And thus the sun was lifted up and the moon stood still in her course; for when the Lord went to heaven, His holy Church came forth and preached with authority.

And hence, as though it were the Church herself

speaking, Solomon says: Behold He cometh leaping upon the mountains and skipping over the hills. For he had in mind the heights of His lofty achievements and says: Behold He cometh leaping upon the mountains. For indeed, in coming to redeem us, He did, so to say, make leaps. Will you know, beloved brethren, what were those leaps He made? From heaven He came to the womb, from the womb to the manger, from the manger to the cross, from the cross to the sepulchre, and from the sepulchre He went back to heaven.

Behold, that He might incite us to follow Him, the Truth, when manifested in the flesh, made certain leaps for our sake; for He hath rejoiced as a giant to run His way, that from our hearts we might say to Him: Draw us; we will run after Thee in the odor of Thy ointments. Wherefore, beloved brethren, it behoves us to follow Him thither in our hearts, where we believe Him to have ascended in the body.

Let us flee earthly desires; let nothing here below delight us longer since we have a Father in heaven. And we ought to consider this above all things: that He, who ascended in peace, will come again with terror; and whatsoever He taught us in gentleness, He will exact from us in severity. Let no one, then, make light of the time granted us for penance; let no one neglect the care of himself while he may yet exercise it; for then our Redeemer will judge us with all the more severity, since before the judgment He has treated us with so much patience.

R. When Christ ascended on high, He led captivity captive * He gave gifts to men, alleluia, alleluia. V. God is gone up in jubilation, and the Lord with the sound of the trumpet. He gave. Glory. He gave.

✠ Continuation of the holy Gospel according to St. Mark.—At that time: Jesus appeared to the eleven as they were at table: and He upbraided them with their incredulity and hardness of heart, because they did not believe them who had seen Him after He was arisen again. And He said to them: Go ye into the whole world and preach the gospel to every creature. He that believeth and is baptized shall be saved: but he that believeth not shall be condemned. And these signs shall follow them that believe: In My Name they shall cast out devils; they shall speak with new tongues; they shall take up serpents; and if they shall drink any deadly thing, it shall not hurt them; they shall lay their hands upon the sick, and they shall recover. And the Lord Jesus, after He had spoken to them, was taken up into heaven and sitteth on the right hand of God. But they going forth preached everywhere, the Lord working withal, and confirming the word with signs that followed.

LET US PRAY

Grant, we beseech Thee, O almighty God, that as we believe Thy only begotten Son, our Redeemer, hath on this day ascended into heaven, we also in spirit may abide in the heavenly places. Through the same our Lord.

VIGIL OF PENTECOST

The reading of the holy Gospel according to St. John

At that time: Jesus said to His disciples: If you love Me, keep My commandments. And I will ask the Father, and He will give you another Paraclete. And so forth.

Homily of St. Augustine, Bishop

When the Lord says: I will ask the Father, and He will give you another Paraclete, He shows that He is Himself a Paraclete. For in Latin, paraclete is called *advocatus* (advocate); and it is said of Christ: We have an advocate with the Father, Jesus Christ the just. And even as He said that the world cannot receive the Holy Ghost, so it is said also: The prudence of the flesh is an enemy to God; for it is not subject to the law of God, neither can it be; just as if we were to say: Injustice cannot be justice. For truly, in speaking here of the world, He signified the lovers of this world, which love is not of the Father. And therefore the love of this world which gives us enough to do to diminish and extinguish its power within us, is contrary to the love of God, which is poured forth in our hearts by the Holy Ghost, who is given to us.

The world, then, cannot receive Him, because it seeth Him not nor knoweth Him. For worldly love has not those invisible eyes with which the Holy Ghost may be seen, for He cannot be seen save in an invisible manner. But you, He says, shall know Him; because He shall abide with you, and shall be in you. He shall be in them, that He may abide; He shall not abide, that He may be in them; for, to abide in any place, it is necessary first to be there. Yet lest they should suppose that these words: Shall abide with you, were spoken in the same sense as that in which a guest usually abides with a man in a visible way, He explained what He said: He shall abide with you, by adding: And shall be in you.

Therefore He is seen in an invisible way. Nor can we have any knowledge of Him unless He be in us; for it is in a similar way that we come to see our conscience within us. For we see the face of another, but we cannot see our own; yet we do see our own conscience, but not that of another. Now our conscience is never anywhere save within ourselves; but the Holy Ghost can be also apart from us. In fact, He is given that He may also be

I will not

leave you

orphans;

I go,

and I come

again to you,

and your hearts shall rejoice.

John XIV, 18; XVI, 22.

in us; but He cannot be seen and known by us as
He ought to be seen and known, if He be not within
us. After making promise of the Holy Ghost, lest
any should think that the Lord was to give Him,
as it were, in place of Himself, in any such way as
that He Himself would not likewise be with them,
He added the words: I will not leave you orphans,
I will come to you. And therefore, although the
Son of God has made us to be the adopted sons of
His Father and willed that we should have by grace
the same Father as He has by nature, yet even He
Himself in some sort shows towards us a fatherly
affection when He says: I will not leave you orphans.

PENTECOST SUNDAY

I Nocturn

From the Acts of the Apostles, c. 2, 1 - 21

II Nocturn

Sermon of St. Leo, Pope

Dearest brethren, the hearts of all Catholics
know that today's Solemnity is to be placed among
the principal feasts. And no one can have any mis-
givings about our reverence for this day which the
Holy Spirit so admirably consecrated with the most
excellent of His gifts.

Indeed this is the tenth from that day in which
the Lord ascended above the heights of heaven

where He was to sit on the right hand of the Father, and the fiftieth day from the one on which He began for us, by His Resurrection, our salvation. This day recalls for us great mysteries of both old and new sacredness. By this it can be most safely declared that grace was prefigured by the law, and that the law was fulfilled through grace.

For just as the law was given to those Hebrews who had been delivered from the hands of the Egyptians on the fiftieth day after the immolation of the lamb, so also, after the Passion in which the true Lamb was slain, on the fiftieth day from His Resurrection, the Holy Spirit was sent upon the Apostles and believers, so that the loving Christian may more easily see that the beginnings of the Old Testament ministered to Evangelical beginnings, and that the second treaty, for which the first one was instituted, had been made.

On this day the trumpet of the preaching of the Gospel began to blow; from this day on the special gifts of the Holy Ghost (Charismata), the stream of blessings have watered the whole desert (this earth) and all that was parched, for the spirit of God moved over the waters for the purpose of renewing the face of the earth; and the flashes of new light shone brightly, with the splendor of parted tongues for the purpose of expelling the ancient darkness. For this reason the light-bearing and fire-laden Word of God would have appeal to the intellect, and consume sin as well as illuminate. It would also have the power of burning.

R. I do not now call you servants, but My friends; because you have known all that I have done among you, alleluia: * Receive ye the Holy Ghost, the Paraclete: He it is whom the Father has sent you, alleluia. V. You are My friends if you do the things I command you. Receive ye. Glory. Receive ye.

III Nocturn

The reading of the holy Gospel
according to St. John

At that time: Jesus said to His disciples: If any one love Me, He will keep My word, and My Father will love him, and We will come to him, and will make Our abode with him. And so forth.

Homily of St. Gregory, Pope

It would be well, beloved brethren, to run quickly through the words of the lesson from the Gospel, that afterwards we may have more time to spend in the consideration of this great festival. Today the Holy Spirit, with a sudden sound, came down upon the disciples and changed their carnal minds, filling them with love for Himself; and by the outward appearance of fiery tongues, inwardly their hearts were kindled into flame; for while they perceived God in that fiery vision, they sweetly glowed with love. The Holy Ghost Himself is love, whence

John also says: God is charity.

He then, that desires God with all his mind, in truth possesses Him already whom he loves. Neither can anyone love God if he does not possess Him whom he loves. But behold, if any one of you were asked whether he loved God, he would reply with confidence and conviction of mind: I do. But in the very beginning of this lesson you have heard what the Truth Himself says: If any one love Me, he will keep My word. The test of love, then, is its manifestation in practice. Hence, in his epistle St. John says again: He that saith, I love God, and keepeth not His commandments, is a liar.

For then do we truly love God and keep His commandments when we refrain ourselves from our own wanton pleasures. He who still abandons himself to unlawful desires certainly does not love God; since of his own will he opposes Him. And My Father will love him, and We will come to him and will make Our abode with him. Consider, beloved brethren, what a great honor it is to have God coming into our hearts as a guest.

Assuredly, if some rich or powerful friend were entering our dwelling, we should make all haste to have the house cleaned throughout, lest there should be anything to offend the eyes of our friend when He came in. Let him, then, who is preparing the house of his mind to receive God, cleanse away the grime of evil works. But mark what the Truth

Himself says: We will come and will make Our abode with him. For there are some whose hearts He enters, but does not abide there. This is because, although they have been brought to acknowledge God on account of something that has pricked them with remorse, yet in time of temptation they forget that very thing for which their conscience pricked them; and so they return to renew those offences as though they had never bewailed them.

R. When the days of Pentecost were accomplished, they were all together in one place, alleluia: and suddenly there came a sound from heaven, alleluia, * As of a mighty wind, and it filled the whole house, alleluia, alleluia. V. When therefore the disciples were gathered together for fear of the Jews, suddenly a sound from heaven came upon them. When therefore. Glory. When therefore.

✠ Continuation of the holy Gospel according to St. John.—At that time: Jesus said to His disciples: If any one love Me, he will keep My word, and My Father will love him, and We will come to him and will make our abode with him: he that loveth Me not keepeth not My words. And the word which you have heard is not Mine, but the Father's who sent Me. These things have I spoken to you, abiding with you. But the Paraclete, the Holy Ghost, whom the Father will send in My Name, He will teach you all things, and bring all things to your mind, whatsoever I shall have said to you. Peace

I leave with you, My peace I give unto you; not as the world giveth, do I give unto you. Let not your heart be troubled, nor let it be afraid. You have heard that I said to you: I go away, and I come unto you. If you loved Me, you would indeed be glad, because I go to the Father: for the Father is greater than I. And now I have told you before it shall come to pass: that when it shall come to pass, you may believe. I will not now speak many things with you. For the prince of this world cometh, and in Me he hath not any thing. But that the world may know that I love the Father, and as the Father hath given Me commandments, so do I.

LET US PRAY

O God, who on this day didst instruct the hearts of the faithful by the light of the Holy Spirit, grant that by the same Spirit we may always be truly wise and ever rejoice in His consolation. Through our Lord Jesus Christ Thy Son, who liveth and reigneth with Thee in the unity of the same Holy Spirit, one God world without end. Amen.

PENTECOST MONDAY

I Nocturn
From the Acts of the Apostles, c. 19, 1 - 12

II Nocturn

Sermon of St. Augustine, Bishop

Today's Solemnity makes remembrance of the Lord, the great God, and of the great grace which is poured over us. The solemn feast is kept to God lest the fact of what had taken place should be forgotten. The same is true of a solemnity as of other things which occur yearly: a river is called perennial because its bed is not dry during any part of the year. This is also true of a feast which is kept throughout the year.

Today we celebrate the coming of the Holy Spirit. The Lord sent the Spirit whom He promised down from heaven to the earth; and He sent Him because He promised Him. Christ said: He (the Spirit) cannot come unless I go, but if I go, I shall send Him to you. Christ suffered, died, rose and ascended, and saw to it that He fulfilled what He had promised.

His disciples and the Apostles, (their number having been completed) and one hundred and twenty others were waiting for the fulfilment. He chose the twelve, but into the hundred and twenty He sent His Spirit. They, therefore, waiting for the fulfilment, gathered in one house and prayed, because they desired with faith alone what could be accomplished only by prayer and spiritual desire. They were new bottles who awaited new wine from heaven; and it came. He (Christ) had been trodden upon (pressed out) and had become a great ferment, and He was glorified. We read in the Gospel: The Spirit had not as yet been given because He had not yet been glorified.

You have heard what great miracles took place. All who were there had learned but one tongue. The Holy Spirit came; they were filled and they began to speak with divers tongues of all nations which they neither knew nor learned: He entered; they were filled and He spoke. And then there was a great miracle: whosoever (not only the hundred and twenty) had received the Holy Spirit, was suddenly filled by the Spirit and spoke with the tongues of all.

R. Go ye into the whole world and preach the Gospel, alleluia: * Whosoever will believe and be baptized shall be saved, alleluia, alleluia, alleulia. V. They will cast out devils in My Name, they will speak with new tongues and walk upon serpents. Whosoever. Glory. Whosoever.

III Nocturn
The reading of the holy Gospel
according to St. John

At that time: Jesus said to Nicodemus: God so loved the world as to give His only-begotten Son;

that whosoever believeth in Him may not perish, but may have life everlasting. And so forth.

Homily of St. Augustine, Bishop

So far, then, as it lies in the physician, he is come to heal the sick. That man who will not obey the commands of his physician destroys himself. He is come, a Savior, into the world. Why is He called the Savior of the world, if not because He is come to save the world, and not to judge it? Thou art not willing to be saved by Him; thou shalt be judged by thine own act. And why do I say: Thou shalt be judged? Behold what He says: He that believeth in Him is not judged. But he that doth not believe; what dost thou expect shall be said to him, but: He is judged?

And He adds: Already, He says, he is judged; the judgment has not yet appeared; and the judgment has already taken place. For the Lord knoweth who are His; He knows them who are persevering towards a crown, and them who are persevering towards the flames. He knows the wheat on His threshing floor, and He knows the chaff; He knows the good grain, and He knows the cockle. He who does not believe is already judged. Why judged? Because he believeth not in the Name of the only-begotten Son of God.

And this is the judgment: because the light is come into the world, and men loved darkness rather than the light; for their works were evil. My brethren, whose works does the Lord find good? The works of none. He finds the works of all to be evil. How, then, did some of them do the truth, and come to the light? For this likewise follows: He that doth truth, cometh to the light.

But, He says, they loved darkness rather than the light. On that, He laid the emphasis. For many loved their sins; yet many confessed their sins; now he who confesses and rebukes his sins, thenceforth works with God. God rebukes thy sins; and if thou too rebuke thyself then art thou united with God. There are, as it were, two things: the man and the sinner. That thou art called man, was God's doing; that thou art called sinner, was man's own doing. Destroy what thou thyself hast made, that God may save what He has made. It behooves thee to hate thine own work in thyself, and to love God's work in thee. And when what thou hast done shall begin to displease thee, from that time is the beginning of thy good works, in that thou dost rebuke thy evil works. The beginning of good works, then, is the confession of evil works.

R. I will not now call you servants, but My friends; because you have known all things whatsoever I have done among you, alleluia: * Receive ye the Holy Ghost, who is your Comforter within you: the same is He whom the Father will send unto you, alleluia. V. You are My friends if you

do whatsoever I command you.   Receive.   Glory.
Receive.

✠ Continuation of the holy Gospel according to
St. John.—At that time: Jesus said to Nicodemus:
God so loved the world as to give His only-begotten
Son: that whosoever believeth in Him may not perish, but may have life everlasting.   For God sent
not His Son into the world to judge the world, but
that the world may be saved by Him.   He that believeth in Him is not judged; but he that doth not
believe is already judged: because he believeth not
in the Name of the only-begotten Son of God.   And
this is the judgment: Because the light is come
into the world, and men loved darkness rather than
the light: for their works were evil.   For every one
that doth evil hateth the light, and cometh not to
the light, that his works may not be reproved; but
he that doth truth cometh to the light, that his
works may be made manifest.

LET US PRAY

O God, who on this day didst instruct the hearts
of the faithful by the light of the Holy Spirit, grant
that by the same Spirit we may always be truly
wise and ever rejoice in His consolation.   Through
our Lord. . . . . in the unity of the same Holy Spirit.

PENTECOST TUESDAY

I Nocturn
From the Prophet Joel, c. 2, 23 - 32

II Nocturn

Sermon of St. John Chrysostom

Today the earth is made heaven for us not by the stars coming down to earth, but by the Apostles' ascending to heaven, because the abundant grace of the Holy Spirit was poured out, and the whole earth was made into a heaven, not by any change of nature, but by the amending of the will of man.

For the Holy Spirit found the publican and made of him an Evangelist; He found the persecutor and changed him into an Apostle; found a thief and led him into paradise; found a harlot and made her equal to virgins; found a magician and made him an Evangelist. He fled from malice and took to Himself benignity; exterminated servitude and brought in liberty; cancelled debts and brought the grace of God. He made earth a heaven. This do I say and will not cease to say.

And suddenly there came a sound as of a mighty wind coming, and it filled the whole house where they were sitting. And there appeared to them parted tongues, as of fire; not fire, but as of fire. If fire, how was it that they did not burn, the Jew asks? I also will ask the Jew: If the tongues were fire, how was it that they did not burn the brambles and the dry wood? What is more ravishing than fire? What more inflammable than brambles? And although the wood was not enkindled, the fire was not extinguished.

And how was it that the fire did not burn up the bodies of the three youths, but on the contrary, the blast furnace was changed into a refreshing dew and the coals became like roses? The conflict between the fire and the body was, nevertheless, won by the youths. It is fitting for me to interpret ancient things (although they are past), so that you may believe the truth. The Holy Spirit appeared under the form of fire in order to make an appeal to the quick grasping power of the mind. But not only on that account, but also to show that as quickly as fire consumes thorns, so also does the Holy Spirit expel sins. Daniel was sent into the den of the lions, and the Divine power repressed their ferocious hunger.

R. The Lord has taught them discipline and wisdom: He has confirmed the grace of His Spirit in them. * And He has filled their hearts with understanding, alleluia. V. Suddenly with a sound the Holy Spirit came over them. And He has filled. Glory. And He has filled.

III Nocturn

The reading of the holy Gospel
according to St. John
At that time: Jesus said to the Pharisees: Amen,

amen, I say to you; he that entereth not by the door
into the sheepfold, but climbeth up another way,
the same is a thief and a robber. But he that entereth in by the door is the shepherd of the flock.
And so forth.

Homily of St. Augustine, Bishop

The Lord has set forth in the lesson of today a
similitude of His own flock, and of the door by
which the sheepfold is to be entered. Let the pa-
gans therefore say: We lead good lives! If they
do not enter by the door, what does that profit them,
whereof they glory? For to this end ought good
living to benefit each individual, that it may be
granted him to live forever; for to whomsoever
eternal life is not given, of what use is it to live
well? Because they who either through blindness
are ignorant of the very end of all good living, or
through pride despise the same, cannot be said to
live well.

But no man has a true and certain hope of living
forever, unless he acknowledge the life which is
Christ, and enter by the door into the sheepfold.
Such men as these, therefore, for the most part
seek to persuade men to live well, and yet not to be
Christians. They wish to climb up another way, to
steal and to kill; not, like the good shepherd, to
keep and to save.

And so there have been certain philosophers, holding many subtle discussions upon the virtues and

vices; dividing, defining, reasoning out most acute conclusions, filling volumes, airing their own wisdom with loud mouth; who would dare to say to others: Follow us; keep our sect if you would live happily. But they did not enter by the door; they wished to destroy, to slay, to kill.

What shall I say of these men? Behold, the Pharisees themselves were wont to read, and, in that very reading, their voices re-echoed Christ; they hoped for His coming, and yet did not recognize Him while He was with them. They boasted that they themselves were among the Seers, that is, among the wise; but they denied Christ, and entered not in by the door. Therefore, such also, if they chanced to lead away others, would lead them away to slay and to kill them, not to deliver them. Let us leave these aside. Let us look to those who glory in the Name of Christ Himself, and see whether even they perchance are entering in by the door. For there are countless numbers who not only boast that they are Seers, but would have it appear that they are enlightened by Christ; yet they are heretics.

R. The Apostles spoke with divers tongues the wondrous works of God, * According as the Holy Ghost gave them to speak, alleluia. V. They were all filled with the Holy Ghost, and began to speak. According. Glory. According.

✠ Continuation of the holy Gospel according to St. John.—At that time: Jesus said to the Pharisees: Amen, amen, I say to you: he that entereth not by the door into the sheepfold, but climbeth up another way, the same is a thief and a robber. But he that entereth in by the door is the shepherd of the sheep. To him the porter openeth, and the sheep hear his voice, and he calleth his own sheep by name, and leadeth them out. And when he hath let out his own sheep, he goeth before them: and the sheep follow him, because they know his voice. But a stranger they follow not, but fly from him, because they know not the voice of strangers. This proverb Jesus spoke to them. But they understood not what He spoke to them. Jesus therefore said to them again: Amen, amen, I say to you, I am the door of the sheep. All others, as many as have come, are thieves and robbers; and the sheep heard them not. I am the door. By Me, if any man enter in, he shall be saved: and he shall go in and go out, and shall find pastures. The thief cometh not but for to steal, and to kill, and to destroy. I am come that they may have life, and may have it more abundantly.

LET US PRAY

O God, who on this day didst instruct the hearts of the faithful by the light of the Holy Spirit, grant that by the same Spirit we may always be truly wise and ever rejoice in His consolation. Through

our Lord Jesus Christ. . . .in the unity of the same
Holy Spirit.

EMBER WEDNESDAY

The reading of the holy Gospel
according to St. John

At that time: Jesus said to the Jews: No man
can come to Me except the Father, who hath sent
Me, draw him. And so forth.

Homily of St. Augustine, Priest

Do not think that thou art drawn against thy
will; the mind is drawn also by love. Neither
ought we to fear, lest perchance we be taken to
task, on account of this evangelic word of the holy
Scriptures, by men who study the words, but are
very far removed from the things to be understood,
most of all from divine things; and lest it be said
to us: If I be drawn, how can I believe of my own
free will? I say: It is little enough to be drawn
by the will; thou art drawn also by pleasure. What
is it, to be drawn by pleasure? Delight in the Lord,
and He will give thee the requests of thy heart.
There is a certain pleasure in the heart which
tastes the sweetness of that heavenly bread. Moreover, if it was right for the poet to say: Every one
is drawn by his own pleasure; not necessity, but
pleasure; not obligation, but delight; how much
more boldly ought we to say that a man is drawn
to Christ when he delights in the truth, delights

in blessedness, delights in righteousness, delights in life everlasting, all of which Christ is? Or is it the case that while the senses of the body have their pleasures, the mind is left without pleasures of its own? If the mind has no pleasures of its own, whence is it said: But the children of men shall put their trust under the covert of Thy wings; they shall be inebriated with the plenty of Thy house; and Thou shalt make them drink of the torrent of Thy pleasure. For with Thee is the fountain of life; and in Thy light we shall see light.

Give me one who loves, and he understands what I say; give me one who longs, give me one who hungers, give me one who is travelling in this wilderness, and thirsting and panting after the fountain of his eternal home; give me such a one, and he will know what I mean. But if I talk of this to a coldhearted man, he will not understand what I say. It was men of this sort who murmured among themselves. He whom the Father shall draw, He says, cometh unto Me. But what does this mean: Whom the Father shall draw, when Christ Himself draws? Why was He pleased to say: Whom the Father shall draw? If we are to be drawn, let us be drawn by Him, to whom it was said by one who loved Him: We will run after the odor of Thy ointments. But let us, brethren, give our attention to what He would have us understand, and let us

grasp it as far as we are able. The Father draws
to the Son such as believe in the Son, because they
consider that He has God for His Father. For God
the Father begot the Son equal to Himself; and he
who reflects, and, in virtue of his faith, perceives
and ponders in his mind that He in whom he believes is equal to the Father, him the Father draw-
eth to the Son.

Arius believed the Son to be a creature, he was
not drawn by the Father; for he that does not believe the Son to be equal with the Father is not
mindful of the Father. What sayest thou, O Arius?
What sayest thou, O thou heretic? What dost thou
tell us? What is Christ? Not true God, says he,
but one whom the true God has made. Thou art
not drawn by the Father; for thou hast not understood the Father, whose Son thou deniest. What
thou dost imagine is something else, it is not the
Son Himself; thou art neither drawn by the
Father, nor drawn to the Son. For the Son is one
matter, and what thou sayest is another. Photinus
says: Christ is only a man, He is not also God.
He who believes thus has not been drawn by the
Father. Whom has the Father drawn? Him who
said, Thou art Christ, the Son of the living God.
Hold out a green branch to a sheep, and thou draw-
est it. Nuts are shown to a boy, and he is enticed;
he is drawn by what he runs to, drawn without
hurt to the body, drawn by the bonds of the heart.

If, then, these things, which among earthly delights and pleasures are shown to those who love such things, have power to attract, since it is truly said: Every one is drawn by his own pleasure; does not Christ, as revealed by the Father, attract us? For what does the soul desire more earnestly than the Truth?

THURSDAY

The reading of the holy Gospel according to St. Luke

At that time: Jesus calling together the twelve apostles, gave them power and authority over all devils, to cure diseases. And so forth.

Homily of St. Ambrose, Bishop

What kind of man he who preaches the kingdom of God should be is clearly shown by the precepts given in the Gospel: He is to set forth without staff, without scrip, without shoes, without bread, without money; that is to say, not seeking the support of this world's goods, but strong in faith, he is to reckon that the less he seeks after such things, the more they will abound. Now we can, if we will, so interpret these things that this passage seems to bear a spiritual sense alone. For a man would seem to have stripped himself, as it were, of a bodily garment when he has not only rejected power and despised wealth, but has also renounced the allurements of his own flesh. To men such as these

is given in the first place a general commandment
of peace and stability, that they bring peace, that
they be steady in conduct, and observe the laws
laid down for guests. For it would ill befit a
preacher of the kingdom of heaven to be ever going from house to house in violation of the sacred
laws of hospitality.

But as the disciples are admonished to be grate-
ful for hospitality, so also are they bidden, when
they are not received, to shake off the dust of that
city and depart. We are taught, moreover, that
the reward of hospitality is no small good, since
not only do we bring peace to our hosts, but if they
are under the shadow of some faults of earthly
frailty, these are removed when they entertain
apostolic preachers. And it is not without reason
that, according to Matthew, the Apostles are told
to make a careful choice of the house they are to
enter, that there may be no reason to change their
host, and thus dissolve the bonds of hospitality. But
the same caution is not recommended to the host,
lest, in selecting his guest, his hospitality should be
lessened.

Yet as, in its literal sense, this passage instructs
us concerning the sacred rites of hospitality, so
also does it charm us with its inner meaning of
heavenly mystery. Now when the house is chosen,
a worthy host is sought for. Let us see whether
this does not signify that the Church and Christ

are to be preferred above all others. What house is more fit to receive the apostolic preacher than the Church? Or who is more worthy of our choice than Christ, who is wont to wash the feet of His guests, and does not allow those whom He has received into His house to remain there with unclean feet; but though their former life has been defiled, He deigns to cleanse them for the time to come? This is the one host from whom no man should depart nor seek a change of dwelling. And rightly is it said to Him: Lord, to whom shall we go? Thou hast the words of eternal life, and we believe.

EMBER FRIDAY

The reading of the holy Gospel according to St. Luke

At that time: It came to pass on a certain day that Jesus sat teaching; and there were Pharisees and doctors of the law sitting by, that were come out of every town of Galilee and Judea and Jerusalem, and the power of the Lord was to heal them. And so forth.

Homily of St. Ambrose, Bishop

The cure of this paralytic was not purposeless nor limited. It was for our sakes that the Lord prayed before healing him. Not indeed that He so prayed as pleading for his cure, but that He might give an example. He gave a pattern for others to imitate! He did not seek to make a display of His prayer. And when the doctors of the law had come together out of all Galilee and Judea and Jerusalem, among other cures of sick persons, the healing of this paralytic is described. Now, as we have said before, every sick man should in the first place, have those about him who will pray for his recovery; for thus our shattered lives and halting deeds may be restored by the medicine of heavenly doctrine.

Let the sick man, then, have some to counsel him, and to raise his mind to heavenly things, though he be languid because of the weakness of his body. By their aid he may readily be lifted up and set down before Jesus, worthy that the Lord should look at him. For the Lord does look upon humility; He regarded the humility of His handmaid. And when He saw their faith, He said: Man, thy sins are forgiven thee. Great is the Lord who forgives one on account of the merits of another, and in praising one, grants pardon to another. Why, O man, is your fellow-citizen worth nothing in your sight, while before God a slave has both the privilege of pleading and the right to obtain his request?

O thou that judgest, learn to forgive; thou that art sick, how to obtain thy cure. If thou are doubtful of pardon because thy sins are grave, call to thy aid such as will pray for thee; summon the Church whom, when the Lord seeth, He will grant that for-

giveness He might otherwise have denied thee. And
now, though we must not pass over the historical
truth that the body of this man, sick of the palsy,
was veritably healed, we must recognize, nevertheless, that the inner man also was made whole, when
his sins were forgiven him. And when the Jews
say that God alone can forgive sins, then, of a
truth, they confess Him to be God. They, who exalt
the work to deny the worker, reveal their perfidy
by this their own sentence.

EMBER SATURDAY

The reading of the holy Gospel
according to St. Luke

At that time: Jesus rising up out of the synagogue, went into Simon's house. And Simon's wife's
mother was taken with a great fever. And so forth.

Homily of St. Ambrose, Bishop

Behold the mercy of the Lord and Savior: He is
not moved to indignation nor is He vexed by evil
doings, nor, outraged by insults, does He desert
Judea: nay rather, unmindful of insult, but mindful of mercy, now by teaching, now by setting men
free, now by works of healing, He softens the
hearts of that faithless people. And well has St.
Luke given the first place to the man delivered from
the evil spirit and the second to the woman who was
made whole. For the Lord came to heal both sexes:

yet he ought first to be healed who was first created; but she is not to be passed over who sinned rather from fickleness of mind than from actual malice.

That the Lord first began His works of healing upon the Sabbath day signifies that the new creature began where the old creature left off; and it shows further how the Son of God was not under the law, but above the law in the very beginning; and that the law was not destroyed, but fulfilled. For the world was not made by the law, but by the word, as we read: By the word of the Lord the heavens were established. Therefore the law was not destroyed, but fulfilled, that man, who had already fallen, might be restored. Whence also the Apostle says: Stripping off the old man from yourselves, put on the new man, who is created according to God.

Rightly, then, did He begin upon the Sabbath day that so He might show Himself as the Creator, carrying out His works in due order and succession, continuing what He had already begun: even as a builder, intending to restore a house, begins to remove the old masonry not from the foundations, but from the roof. And so He first sets His Hand to the place where He had left off: then He begins with the lesser things that He may come to those that are of more importance. For even men, by the word of God, can set others free from the devil; but to command the dead to rise again belongs to divine power alone. Perhaps again it may be that under the type of this woman, the mother-in-law of Simon and Andrew, is signified our flesh, sick with sundry fevers of sin and inflamed with the wanton promptings of all kinds of evil desires. And I would not say that the fever of love is less violent than the heat of a bodily fever. Therefore the one inflames the heart, the other, the body. For our fever is avarice; our fever is lust; our fever is luxury; our fever is ambition; our fever is anger.

TRINITY SUNDAY

I Nocturn
From Isaias the Prophet, c. 6, 1 - 12

II Nocturn

From the book of St. Fulgentius, Bishop,
on Faith, addressed to Peter

The faith which the holy patriarchs and prophets received from God before the Incarnation of His Son, which the holy apostles heard from the Lord Himself when He became man, and, taught by the Holy Ghost, not only preached, but also set down in writing for the better instruction of those who should come after them, this same faith teaches us to worship God in three Persons, Father, Son, and Holy Ghost.

But if the Father, the Son, and the Holy Ghost were one and the same person, there would be no true Trinity. For if the Father, Son, and Holy Ghost were one person as they are one substance, there would be nothing which could be properly called a Trinity. Again, if the Father, Son, and Holy Ghost were of different nature as they are distinct Persons, there would indeed be a real Trinity, but that Trinity Itself would not be one God.

But because in this Trinity which is one God and the True God, it is essentially true, not only that there is one God, but also that there are three Persons; therefore, in this same true God there is Trinity of Persons and unity of nature. Through this unity of nature, the Father is wholly in the Son and the Holy Ghost, the Son is wholly in the Father and the Holy Ghost, and the Holy Ghost is wholly in the Father and the Son.

Of these three Persons none is in anything separate from the others; for none precedes the others in eternity, or excels them in greatness, or surpasses them in power. As to the unity of the divine nature, the Father is not older or greater than the Son or the Holy Ghost; nor is it possible that the Son should surpass the Holy Ghost in eternity or immensity.

R. Great is the Lord, and greatly to be praised; * And of His wisdom there is no end. V. The Lord is great, and great is His power: and there is no limit to His wisdom. And. Glory. And.

III Nocturn
The reading of the holy Gospel
according to St. Matthew

At that time: Jesus said to His disciples: All power is given to Me in heaven and on earth. Going, therefore, teach ye all nations, baptizing them in the name of the Father, and of the Son, and of the Holy Ghost. And so forth.

Homily of St. Gregory Nazianzen

Every Catholic knows that the Father is truly Father, the Son truly Son, the Holy Ghost truly Holy Ghost; as the Lord Himself says to the Apostles: Going, baptize all nations in the name of the Father, and of the Son, and of the Holy Ghost. This is the perfect Trinity in unity, which we profess to be of one substance.

For we cannot admit division in God as though He were a body; but according to the power of the divine nature, which is immaterial, we both believe there are truly distinct persons, and testify to the unity of the divinity. We do not say, as some have imagined, that the Son of God is the extension of some part of the divinity; nor do we hold that He is a word without reality, like the sound of a voice; but we believe the three names and three persons to be of one essence, majesty and power.

Therefore we confess one God: because the unity of majesty does not allow us to speak of several gods. Lastly, according to the Catholic faith we

speak of the Father and the Son; but we neither
can nor ought to say They are two Gods. Not indeed that the Son of God is not God, rather He is
true God of true God; but because we know that
the Son of God is from none other than the one
Father Himself, therefore we speak of one God.
This is the doctrine delivered to us by the prophets
and the apostles, and taught by the Lord Himself
when He says: I and the Father are one. When
He says: One, it refers to the unity of the divinity,
as I have already said: but the word: are, indicates
the persons.

The reading of the holy Gospel
according to St. Luke

At that time: Jesus said to His disciples: Be
ye merciful, as your Father also is merciful. And
so forth.

Homily of St. Augustine, Bishop

There are two works of mercy which set us free,
and these the Lord has briefly laid down in the
Gospel: Forgive, and it shall be forgiven you; this
refers to the pardoning of offences: Give, and it
shall be given to you; this refers to the giving of
alms. As to what He says of pardoning offences,
you desire to be forgiven for what you have done
wrong, and you have some one whom you on your
part can forgive. Again, as to what regards alms-
giving, a beggar asks something of you, and you
are a beggar of God. For when we pray, we are

all beggars of God; before the door of the great
Father of the family we stand. We even cast ourselves down and groan in prayer, wishing to receive something; and this something is God Himself. What does a beggar ask of you but bread?
And what do you ask of God except Christ, who
says: I am the bread of life which came down
from heaven? If you wish to be forgiven, do you
yourselves forgive others. Forgive, and it shall
be forgiven you. Do you wish to receive something?
Give, and it shall be given to you.

R. Let us bless the Father and the Son and the
Holy Ghost: * Let us praise and exalt Him above
all forever. V. Blessed art Thou, O Lord, in the
height of heaven: worthy of praise and glorious
forever. Let us. Glory. Let us.

℟ Continuation of the holy Gospel according to
St. Matthew.—At that time: Jesus said to His
disciples: All power is given to Me in heaven and
on earth. Going, therefore, teach ye all nations,
baptizing them in the name of the Father and of
the Son and of the Holy Ghost. Teaching them to
observe all things whatsoever I have commanded
you; and behold I am with you all days, even to the
consummation of the world.

LET US PRAY

O almighty and eternal God, who hath given Thy
servants to know the glory of the eternal Trinity
in the profession of the true faith, and to adore the

unity in the power of majesty, we beseech Thee, that by the firmness of the same faith, we may always be preserved from all adversity. Through our Lord.

THE FEAST OF CORPUS CHRISTI

I Nocturn

From the first Epistle of St. Paul to the Corinthians, c. 11, 20 - 32

II Nocturn

Sermon of St. Thomas Aquinas

The immense blessings bestowed by the divine mercy upon the Christian people confer upon it an inestimable dignity. There is not, nor ever was, a nation so great that has gods so nigh as our God is present to us. For the only-begotten Son of God, wishing to make us partakers of His divinity, took upon Himself our nature, that being made man, He might make men gods. And this Body that He took from us, He gave wholly for our salvation. For He offered His Own Body to God the Father upon the altar of the cross as a victim for our reconciliation, and He shed His Own Blood both to redeem and cleanse us, that we, being bought back from a wretched slavery, might be washed from all our sins. And then, that the memory of so great a benefit might abide in us, He left His Body to be our food and His Blood to be our drink, to be received by the faithful under the species of bread and wine.

O precious and wonderful banquet, healthgiving and full of all sweetness! What could be more precious than this banquet, in which no longer, as under the law, the flesh of calves and goats is eaten, but Christ the true God is set before us that we may receive Him? What could be more wonderful than this sacrament, in which bread and wine are substantially changed into the Body and Blood of Christ? And therefore Christ, perfect God and Man, is contained under the appearance of a little bread and wine.

He is eaten by the faithful, but not torn asunder; indeed, when the Sacrament is divided, He remains entire in each particle. The accidents subsist without a subject, that there may be room for faith when we receive visibly that which is invisible and hidden under an appearance not its own. Thus the senses are kept free from deception, for they judge of accidents known to them.

Of all the sacraments none is more healthgiving, for by it sins are washed away, virtues are increased, and the soul is fed with an abundance of all spiritual gifts. It is offered in the Church for the living and the dead, that all may profit by that which was instituted for the salvation of all. Lastly, no words suffice to describe the sweetness of this sacrament, in which spiritual delights are tasted

All we who partake
of one bread and
one chalice although
we are many, are
one bread and one
body.

at their very source, and the exceeding charity of Christ in His Passion is called to mind. It was in order to impress more deeply upon the minds of the faithful the boundless extent of His charity that, when He had kept the Pasch with His disciples and was about to depart out of this world unto His Father, Christ instituted this Sacrament as a perpetual memorial of His Passion, the fulfilment of the ancient figures, the greatest of all His miracles. To those who grieved at His absence, it was to be a special consolation.

R. I am the bread of life; your fathers did eat manna in the desert, and are dead: * This is the bread which cometh down from heaven, that if any man eat of it, he may not die. V. I am the living bread, which came down from heaven: If any man eat of this bread, he shall live forever. This. Glory. This.

III Nocturn

The reading of the holy Gospel
according to St. Mark

At that time: Jesus said to the multitudes of the Jews: My Flesh is meat indeed and My Blood is drink indeed. And so forth.

Homily of St. Augustine, Bishop

For whilst by food and drink men seek to attain to this end that they shall neither hunger nor thirst, there is nothing that truly affords this, except that food and drink which makes those who partake of it immortal and incorruptible, to wit, the very fellowship of the saints, where there will be peace and full and perfect unity. Therefore, indeed, it is even as men of God understood this before us, that our Lord Jesus Christ has commended unto us His Body and Blood in those things, which from being many are reduced to some one thing. For a unity (bread) is formed out of many grains; and another unity (wine) is made by the juice of many berries flowing together.

At length, He now explains how that, which He speaks of, comes to pass, and what it is to eat His Body and to drink His Blood. He that eateth My Flesh and drinketh My Blood, abideth in Me, and I in him. This it is, therefore, for a man to eat that food and to drink that drink, to abide in Christ and to have Him abiding in him.

Consequently, he who abides not in Christ, and in whom Christ abides not, without doubt does not spiritually eat His Flesh, nor drink His Blood, though he may, in the flesh and visibly, press with his teeth the sacrament of the Body and Blood of Christ; but rather does He eat and drink the sacrament of so great a thing to his own judgment, because he, being unclean, has presumed to draw near to Christ's sacraments, which no man taketh worthily, except that he be clean; of whom it is said: Blessed are the clean of heart, for they shall see God.

As, says He, the living Father hath sent Me, and
I live by the Father: so he that eateth Me, the
same also shall live by Me. As though He should
say: That I live by the Father, that is, that I ascribe My life to Him as to one greater than I, is
brought about by that emptying of Myself in which
He sent Me; but, that one lives by Me is effected
by that participation in which he eats Me. And
thus, I, being brought low, live by the Father;
while that man, being raised up, lives by Me. But
if it is said; I live by the Father; so as to mean
that He is of the Father; not the Father of Him,
it is said without disparagement to the equality between them. But on the other hand, by saying:
He that eateth Me the same also shall live by Me,
He did not signify equality between Him and ourselves, but He thereby showed the grace of the
mediator.

R. He that eateth My Flesh and drinketh My
Blood, * Abideth in Me, and I in him. V. There
is no other nation so great, that hath gods so nigh
to them, as our God is present to us. Abideth.
Glory. Abideth.

✠ Continuation of the holy Gospel according to
St. John.—At that time: Jesus said to the multitudes of the Jews: My Flesh is meat indeed, and
My Blood is drink indeed. He that eateth My Flesh,
and drinketh My Blood, abideth in Me, and I in
him. As the living Father hath sent Me, and I live

by the Father, so he that eateth Me, the same also shall live by Me. This is the bread that came down from Heaven. Not as your fathers did eat manna and are dead. He that eateth this Bread shall live forever.

LET US PRAY

O God, who hath left us a memorial of Thy Passion in this wonderful Sacrament, grant we beseech Thee, so to reverence the sacred mystery of Thy Body and Blood that we may always enjoy within our souls the fruit of Thy Passion. Who liveth and reigneth with God the Father.

FRIDAY

The reading of the holy Gospel according to St. John

At that time: Jesus said to the multitudes of the Jews: My Flesh is meat indeed and My Blood is drink indeed. And so forth.

Homily of St. Augustine, Bishop

We have heard in the Gospel the words of our Lord which follow the former discourse. From these, a sermon is due for your ears and understanding; and it is not unseasonable on this day, for it is concerning the Body of the Lord, which He said that He gave to be eaten for eternal life. And He explained the manner of this bestowal and gift of His, in what manner He would give them to eat His Flesh, when He said: He that eateth My

Flesh and drinketh My Blood abideth in Me, and I in him. The sign that a man hath eaten and drunk is this: that he abides, and is abided in; that he dwells and is dwelt in; that he adheres, so as not to be separated.

This, then, He has taught us, and admonished us in mystical words that we may be in His Body, in His members under Himself as head, eating His Flesh, not separating ourselves from union with Him. But many of those who were present were scandalized, by not understanding; for in hearing these things, they thought only of the flesh which they themselves were. For the Apostle says, and says truly: To understand according to the flesh is death. The Lord gives us His Flesh to eat; and to understand according to the flesh is death. Since He says of His Own Flesh that in it is eternal life, we must not think of this Flesh according to the flesh, as in these words that follow: Many, therefore (not His enemies, but His disciples), hearing it, said: This saying is hard, and who can hear it?

If His disciples found this saying hard, what must His enemies have thought? And yet it was meet that it should be so said, which should not be understood by all. A secret of God ought to make us attentive, not hostile; but these men quickly fell away when the Lord Jesus Christ spoke in this manner. They did not believe that He was speaking of something great, and that grace lay hidden

under these words; they understood only according
to their wishes, and after the manner of men, that
Jesus was able, or was determining this, to distribute that Flesh wherewith the Word was clothed,
piecemeal, as it were, to those who believed in Him.
This saying is hard, say they: who can hear it?

SATURDAY

The reading of the holy Gospel
according to St. John

At that time: Jesus said to the multitude of the
Jews: My Flesh is meat indeed, and My Blood is
drink indeed. And so forth.

From a Homily of St. Augustine, Bishop

We have said, brethren, that what the Lord has
commended to us in the eating of His Flesh and
the drinking of His Blood is that we should abide
in Him, and He in us. But we abide in Him when
we are His members; and He abides in us when we
are His temple. But, that we may be His members,
unity joins us together; and, that unity may join
us together, what can effect this, except charity?
And the charity of God, whence is it? Ask the
Apostle. The charity of God, he says, is poured
forth in our hearts by the Holy Ghost who is given
to us.

It is the spirit, therefore, which quickeneth; for
it is the spirit that makes the members to live; nor

does the spirit make any members to live unless they are united to the body, which the spirit itself also animates. For the spirit which is in thee, O man, by which it is evident that thou art a man, can it quicken a member which it finds cut off from the flesh? By thy spirit, I mean thy soul. Thy soul does not quicken thy members unless they are part of the flesh; if thou takest one away, it is no longer quickened by thy soul because it is not joined to the unity of thy body.

These things are said that we may love unity and dread division. For a Christian ought to fear nothing so much as to be cut off from the body of Christ. For if he is cut off from Christ's body, he is no longer a member of Christ; if he is not a member of Christ, he is not animated by His Spirit. For if any man saith the Apostle, have not the the Spirit of Christ, he is none of His. It is the spirit, therefore, which quickeneth, the flesh profiteth nothing. The words which I have spoken unto you, they are spirit and life. What does this mean: They are spirit and life? They are to be understood spiritually. Hast thou understood spiritually? They are spirit and life. Hast thou understood carnally? Even so, they are spirit and life, but are not so to thee.

SUNDAY WITHIN THE OCTAVE
OF CORPUS CHRISTI

I Nocturn

From the first Book of Kings, c. 1, 1 - 11

II Nocturn

Sermon of St. John Chrysostom

Since the Word says: This is My Body, let us be persuaded of the truth of these words; let us believe and look upon Him in this Sacrament with the eyes of our mind. For Christ hath not given to us sensible realities, but altogether intelligible ones, though under sensible things. It is the same in baptism; by means of a material element, namely, water, a gift is bestowed; but the intelligible reality performed is birth and renewal. If thou hadst no body, He would have given thee incorporeal gifts without any matter; but since thy soul is joined to a body, He bestows upon thee intelligible realities under sensible things. How many say: Would that I could see our Lord in His Body as He lived. His face, His garments, even His shoes! Behold, thou dost see Him, thou touchest and eatest Him. Thou indeed desireth to see His garments, but He grants thee not only to see, but to eat, to touch, and to receive Him within thyself.

Let no one, therefore, draw near with disgust or carelessly; let all come with eagerness, with fervor, and with love. The Jews ate the paschal lamb

in haste, standing, their feet shod, their staves in
their hands.   They indeed were to pass over into
Palestine, and therefore they did as travellers
would do; but thou must leave this earth for heaven.

This being so, thou must be ever on the watch,
for the punishment of them that receive unworthily
is no slight one.   Consider within thyself how thou
art filled with indignation against the betrayer of
the Lord and against those who crucified Him; and
then look to thyself lest thou also shouldst be guilty
of the Body and Blood of Christ.   They indeed put
to death that most sacred Body, but thou receivest
it with thy soul full of impurity, and that, too, after
the Lord has bestowed so many benefits upon thee.
For it was not enough for Him to became man, to
be buffeted, and to be crucified, but He must even
make Himself one with us; so that not by faith
only, but in very deed He makes us His Own Body.

Who should be more spotless than he who par-
takes of such a sacrifice?   Purer than a sunbeam
should be the hand which distributes that Flesh,
the mouth which is filled with that spiritual fire,
the tongue reddened by that Blood, awful beyond
compare.   Consider what an honor has been reserved for thee, at what a table thou art seated.
That whereon angels fear to look, nor dare to gaze
at steadfastly by reason of its dazzling splendor,
upon that we feed, to that we are joined, and are
made one body and one flesh with Christ.   Who

shall declare the powers of the Lord? Who shall
set forth all His praises? What shepherd feeds
his flock with his own blood? A shepherd, do I say?
Many mothers there are who after all the pains of
childbirth give their children to strangers to nurse.
But Christ could not endure that His children
should be fed by others. He nourishes us Himself
with His Own Blood, and in every way makes us
one with Himself.

R. Whilst they were at supper, Jesus took bread,
and blessed, and broke, and gave to His disciples,
and said: * Take ye and eat: this is My Body. V.
The men of my tabernacle said: Who will give us
of his flesh, that we may be filled. Take. Glory.
Take.

III Nocturn

The reading of the holy Gospel
according to St. Luke

At that time: Jesus spoke to the Pharisees this
parable: A certain man made a great supper and
invited many. And so forth.

Homily of St. Gregory, Pope

There is this difference, dearly beloved brethren,
between the pleasures of the body and the soul.
Bodily pleasures are greatly desired so long as we
do not yet enjoy them, but when they are partaken
of to the full, our liking for them soon turns to
disgust. Spiritual delights, on the contrary, are a

matter of indifference and scorn to us when we do not possess them, but when we begin to experience them, then we are filled with desire; and the more we partake of them, the more we desire them.

In the pleasures of the body desire is delightful, fruition, disappointing; in the pleasures of the soul desire is poor, fruition, very delightful. The former, when indulged in, soon bring disgust; but of the latter we can never have too much. When our souls are full of spiritual joy, we long for more; since by tasting it, we learn to desire it more eagerly. We cannot love what we do not possess because we have no experience of it. For who can love that of which he knows nothing?

Therefore the Psalmist admonishes us, saying: Taste and see that the Lord is sweet; as if to say plainly: You know not His sweetness if you have never tasted it; let the palate of your heart but taste the bread of life, that becoming acquainted with its sweetness, you may be able to love it. Now man lost these delights when he sinned in Paradise; he went out from thence when he no longer opened his mouth to taste the heavenly food which filled him with spiritual joy.

Thus it comes to pass that we too, born into the miseries of this exile, find ourselves here below filled with disgust for our true good, and not knowing what we ought to desire. Now this disgust is a malady which increases in us in proportion as the soul withdraws itself from partaking of that delicious food. For the longer the soul turns away from spiritual joys, the less it desires them. It pines away through disgust for this food, and is worn out because of its long fast; and, not wishing to taste of the spiritual sweetness which is offered to it, is so miserable as to love the hunger it endures.

R. A certain man made a great supper, and he sent his servants at the hour of supper to say to them that were invited that they should come, * Because all things were ready. V. Come, eat my bread, and drink the wine which I have mixed for you. Because. Glory. Because.

✠ Continuation of the holy Gospel according to St. Luke.—At that time: Jesus spoke to the Pharisees this parable: A certain man made a great supper, and invited many. And he sent his servant, at the hour of supper, to say to them that were invited, that they should come, for now all things were ready. And they began all at once to make excuse. The first said to him: I have bought a farm, and must needs go out and see it; I pray thee, hold me excused. And another said, I have bought five yoke of oxen, and I go to try them; I pray thee, hold me excused. And another said, I have married a wife, and therefore I cannot come. And the servant returning, told these things to his lord. Then the master of the house being angry, said to his servant: Go out quickly into the streets and lanes of the city, and bring in hither the poor, and the feeble, and the blind, and the lame. And the servant said: Lord, it is done as thou hast commanded, and yet there is room. And the lord said to the servant: Go out into the highways and hedges and compel them to come in, that my house may be filled. But I say unto you, that none of these men that were invited shall taste of my supper.

LET US PRAY

Grant us, O Lord, a constant love and reverence for Thy holy Name; for Thou dost never forsake in Thy care those whom Thou dost choose in Thy unchanging love. Through our Lord.

MONDAY

The reading of the holy Gospel
according to St. John

At that time: Jesus said to the multitude of the Jews: My Flesh is meat indeed and My Blood is drink indeed. And so forth.

From a Homily of St. Augustine, Bishop

This is the bread which cometh down from heaven. The manna was a sign of this bread; God's altar was a sign of this bread. Those things were sacraments; in the signs they are different; but in the thing which is signified they are alike. Hear the Apostle: For I would not, says he, have you ignorant, brethren, that our fathers were all under the cloud and all passed through the sea, and all in Moses were baptized in the cloud and in the sea, and all did eat the same spiritual food. Of course, the same spiritual food; for materially it was another; for since they ate manna, we, something other than that; but the spiritual food was the same as that which we eat; but it is: our fathers, not the fathers of those (Jews); those fathers to whom we are like, not those fathers to whom they were like. And he adds: And all drank the same spiritual drink. They drank one thing, we drink another, but in the visible form which, however, signified the same thing in its spiritual virtue. For how was it that they drank the same drink? They drank, says he, of the spiritual rock that followed them: and the rock was Christ. Thence the bread, thence the drink. The rock was Christ in figure, the true Christ is in the Word and in the Flesh. And how did they drink? The rock was struck twice with a rod; the double smiting signifies the two beams of the cross.

The faithful discern the Body of Christ if they do not neglect to be the body of Christ. Let them become the body of Christ if they desire to live by the Spirit of Christ. For the Spirit of Christ liveth not in any but the body of Christ. Understand, my brethren, what I would say. Thou art a man, and that is called the soul whereby it is evident that thou art a man; for man is made up of body and soul. For thou hast an invisible spirit and a visible body. Tell me, which gives life to the other? Does thy spirit live by thy body, or thy body live by thy spirit? Every man who is alive will answer; but he who cannot answer this question, I know not if he is alive. What will every man who is alive answer? Truly, it is my body that lives by my spirit. Wilt thou then also live by the Spirit of Christ? Then be thou in the body of Christ.

For, does my body live by thy spirit? My body lives by my spirit, and thine by thy spirit. The body of Christ cannot live except by the Spirit of Christ. Hence Paul the Apostle, explaining what this bread is, says: We, being many, are one bread, one body. O mystery of piety, O sign of unity, O bond of charity! He that would live, he hath wherein to live, he hath whereon to live. Let him draw nigh, let him believe, let him enter into that body, that he may be quickened. Let him not shrink from the society of its members; let him not be a decaying member, fit only to be cut off; let him not be a deformed member, whereof to be ashamed. Let him be a fair, useful, and healthy member; let him cleave to the body; let him live in God and by God. Let him labor now on earth that he may reign hereafter in heaven.

TUESDAY

The reading of the holy Gospel
according to St. John

At that time: Jesus said to the multitude of the Jews: My Flesh is meat indeed and My Blood is drink indeed. And so forth.

From a Homily of St. Augustine, Bishop

Not as your fathers did eat manna, and are dead. Why did they eat, and why did they die? Because they believed that which they saw; that which they saw not, they did not understand. Therefore were they your fathers, for you are like unto them. For so far, my brethren, as relates to this visible death of the body, do not we who eat of the bread coming down from heaven also die? They died just as we shall die, so far, as I said, as related to the visible and carnal death of this body.

But so far as relates to that death which the Lord threatens, that death which their fathers died: Moses ate the manna, and Aaron ate the manna, and Phineas ate the manna; many who were pleasing to the Lord ate of it and they did not die. Why? Because they understood spiritually the visible food; they hungered for it spiritually, they tasted it spiritually that they might be satisfied spiritually. For we likewise today receive a visible food; but the Sacrament is one thing, the power of the Sacrament another.

How many there are who receive of the altar, and die, even by the very receiving! Whence the Apostle says: He eateth and drinketh judgment to himself. Was the morsel given by the Lord poison to Judas? And yet he received it. And when he received it, the enemy entered into him; not because he received an evil thing, but because he, being evil, did in evil wise receive what was good. Look to it, then, brethren, eat ye spiritually the heavenly bread; bring innocence to the altar. Your sins, though they be daily, at least let them not be deadly. Before you draw near to the altar, mark well what you say: Forgive us our trespasses as we forgive them that trespass against us. If you forgive, then you shall be forgiven; approach without fear, it is bread, not poison.

WEDNESDAY

The reading of the holy Gospel according to St. John

At that time: Jesus said to the multitude of the Jews: My Flesh is meat indeed, and My Blood is drink indeed. And so forth.

Homily of St. Hilary, Bishop

When we speak of the things of God, it must not be according to the ideas and feelings of men or the world. Let us read what is written in the Scriptures, and let us understand what we have read;

and then, having a perfect faith, let us act accordingly. Unless we learn from Christ how to speak of the real truth of His abiding in us, we speak without judgment and without piety. For He Himself says: My Flesh is meat indeed, and My Blood is drink indeed. He that eateth My Flesh and drinketh My Blood abideth in Me, and I in him. He has left us no room to doubt of the truth of His Flesh and Blood.

For now we know by the declaration of the Lord and by our faith that this is truly His Flesh and Blood; and that, having eaten the one and drunk the other, we are in Christ and Christ is in us. Is not this true? He Himself is in us by His Flesh, and we are in Him, since our own nature is with Him in God. But that we are in Him through that Sacrament wherein His Flesh and Blood are communicated to us, He Himself testifies, saying: Yet a little while and the world seeth Me no more. But you shall see Me: because I live, and you shall live. For I am in My Father: and you in Me, and I in you.

That this union with us is real, Christ Himself has thus testified: He that eateth My Flesh and drinketh My Blood abideth in Me, and I in him. For no one abides in Him, in whom He does not abide; and only he who eats the Body of the Lord is made one body with Him. He had already taught that it was a Sacrament of perfect unity when He

said: As the living Father hath sent Me and I live
by the Father: so He that eateth My Flesh, the
same also shall live by Me.   He lives, then, by the
Father; and as He lives by the Father, so shall we
live by receiving His Body.

I Nocturn

*From the First Epistle of blessed Paul the Apostle
to the Corinthians, c. 11, 20 - 32*

II Nocturn

OCTAVE DAY OF CORPUS CHRISTI

Sermon of St. Cyril, Bishop of Jerusalem

The teaching of blessed Paul would seem to be
sufficient in itself to make your faith sure in the
divine mysteries; and, being prepared to receive
them worthily, you are made, so to speak, one body
and one blood with Christ.   You have just heard
the apostle declaring that our Lord Jesus Christ,
the same night in which He was betrayed, took
bread, and giving thanks, broke, and gave to His
disciples, saying: Take ye and eat: This is My
Body.   And taking the chalice and giving thanks,
He said: Take ye and drink: This is My Blood.
Since Christ Himself said, in speaking of this
bread: This is My Body, who could henceforth venture to doubt His words? And since He said so pos-
itively: This is My Blood, who could ever question

the truth of His words, and say it was not the Blood of Christ?

Once in Cana of Galilee Christ changed water into wine, a liquid which has some qualities in common with blood; and shall we esteem Him less worthy of belief when He changed wine into blood? He was invited to that marriage in which two persons were joined together, and He wrought this miracle to the amazement of all; and should not we be even more firmly convinced that He has given us His Body to eat and His Blood to drink, so that with absolute certainty we may receive them as His very Own Body and Blood?

For under the species of bread He gives us His Body, and under the species of wine He gives us His Blood; and so, when you receive, you eat of the Body and Blood of Christ, being made partaker of His Body and Blood. Thus are we made bearers of Christ, that is, we carry Christ in our bodies, when we receive His Body and Blood into our members. In this way we are made, as blessed Peter says, partakers of the divine nature.

On one occasion Christ said to the Jews: Except you eat My Flesh and drink My Blood, you shall not have life in you. But they did not take what He had said in a spiritual sense, and many went back; for they thought they were bidden to eat flesh. In the Old Testament there were loaves of proposition, but these have now come to an end, since they belonged to the Old Testament. The bread of the New Testament is heavenly, and the cup healthgiving, and by them both body and soul are sanctified. Therefore I would that you look upon this bread and wine not as mere common bread and mere common wine; for they are the Body and Blood of Christ. Even if your senses do not tell you that this is so, let your faith assure you of it. Judge not by the taste, but let faith make you believe without doubting that you are made worthy to become partakers of the Body and Blood of Christ.

R. You shall eat flesh, and you shall have your fill of bread: * This is the bread, which the Lord hath given you to eat. V. Moses gave you not bread from heaven, but My Father giveth you the true bread from heaven. This. Glory. This.

III Nocturn

The reading of the holy Gospel
according to St. John

At that time: Jesus said to the multitude of the Jews: My Flesh is meat indeed and My Blood is drink indeed. And so forth.

Homily of St. Cyril, Bishop of Alexandria

These are the words of Christ: He that eateth My Flesh and drinketh My Blood abideth in Me, and I in him. If into melted wax, other wax is thrown, the two are certain to get thoroughly mixed one with the other. In the same way, he who receives the Body and Blood of the Lord is so united with Him that he is to be found in Christ, and Christ in him.

You will find a somewhat similar comparison in Matthew. The kingdom of heaven, he says, is like to leaven, which a woman took and hid in three measures of meal. As Paul says: A little leaven corrupteth the whole lump; so also a little of this blessing draws the whole man into itself and fills him with its grace, and in this way Christ abides in us and we in Christ.

If, then, we wish to obtain eternal life, if we desire to have within us the giver of immortality, let us hasten gladly to receive this blessing. And let us beware, lest the devil lay a snare for us, suggesting that we should hold back through false reverence. What you tell me is quite true, he makes us say; nevertheless, we do not forget what is written, that he who eats of this bread and drinks of this chalice unworthily, eateth and drinketh judgment to himself. Therefore I prove myself and find myself unworthy. When wilt thou be worthy, whoever thou art, who speakest thus? When wilt thou offer thyself to Christ? For if thy sins render thee unworthy, and thou never ceasest to sin (for who can understand sins? says the Psalmist), thou wilt be deprived forever of this grace which gives life and sanctity.

I beseech you, therefore, cultivate holy thoughts;

be careful to live piously; and then partake of this blessing; for, believe me, it drives away not only death, but all diseases also. For when Christ abides in us, He calms the law of sin in our members which fights against the law of our souls; He strengthens piety, extinguishes the passions of the soul, cures our infirmities, heals our wounds; and like the good shepherd who lays down his life for the sheep, He raises us up after every fall.

R. As the living Father hath sent Me, and I live by the Father: * So also he who eateth Me shall live by Me. V. The Lord fed him with the bread of life and understanding. So also. Glory. So also.

FEAST OF THE MOST SACRED HEART OF JESUS

I Nocturn

*From Jeremias the Prophet, c. 24, 5 - 7; c. 30,
18 - 24; c. 31, 1 - 3 c. 31, 31 - 33*

II Nocturn

Among the wonderful developments of sacred teaching and piety, by which the plans of the Divine Wisdom are daily made clearer to the Church, hardly any is more manifest than the triumphant progress made by the devotion of the Most Sacred Heart of Jesus. Very often indeed, during the course of past ages, Fathers, Doctors, and Saints have celebrated our Redeemer's love: and they

have said that the wound opened in the side of
Christ was the hidden fountain of all graces. Moreover, from the Middle Ages onward, when the faithful began to show a certain more tender piety towards the Most Sacred Humanity of the Savior,
contemplative souls became accustomed to penetrate
through that wound almost to the very Heart Itself,
wounded for the love of men. And from that time,
this form of contemplation became so familiar to
all persons of saintly life that there was no country
or religious order in which, during this period, witnesses to it were not to be found. The monastic
order has at no time ceased to propagate this devotion. Of former times the virgins Elphian, Gertrude, and Mechtilde, from whose lives and actions
it is evident how great a devotion they practiced,
stand out most prominently. They sometimes glorify that Sacred Heart as being a treasury in which
all the riches of heaven are found; again, as a fount
from which flow a torrent of graces; then, as a
harp which when plucked by the Holy Spirit sounds
with a most ineffable melody; again, as a censer
giving forth a most sweet odor in the sight of God;
or as an altar on which the supreme High Priest,
Jesus Christ, immolates Himself. Finally, during
recent centuries, and most especially at that period
when heretics, in the name of a false piety, strove
to discourage Christians from receiving the Most
Holy Eucharist, the veneration of the Most Sacred

Heart began to be openly practiced, principally through the exertions of St. John Eudes, who is by no means unworthily called the founder of the liturgical worship of the Sacred Hearts of Jesus and Mary.

But in order to establish fully and entirely the worship of the Most Sacred Heart of Jesus and to spread the same throughout the whole world, God Himself chose as His instrument a most humble virgin from the order of the Visitation, St. Margaret Mary Alocoque, who even in her earliest years already had a burning love for the Sacrament of the Eucharist, and to whom Christ the Lord had very many times appeared and was pleased to make known the riches and the desires of the Divine Heart. The most famous of these appearances was that in which Jesus revealed Himself to her in prayer before the Blessed Sacrament, showed her His Most Sacred Heart, and, complaining that in return for His unbounded love, He met with nothing save outrages and ingratitude from mankind, He ordered her to have a care for the establishment of a new feast, on the Friday after the octave of Corpus Christi, on which His Heart should be venerated with due honor, and that the insults offered Him by sinners in the Sacrament of love should be expiated by worthy satisfaction. But there is no one who does not know how many and how great were the obstacles which the handmaid of God experienced in carrying out the commands of Christ: but, endowed with strength by the Lord Himself, and actively aided by her pious spiritual directors who exerted themselves with an almost unbelievable zeal, up to the time of her death she never ceased faithfully to carry out the duty entrusted to her by heaven.

At length, in the year 1765, the supreme Pontiff, Clement XIII, approved of the Mass and Office in honor of the Most Sacred Heart of Jesus; and Pius IX extended the feast to the universal Church. Thenceforward, the worship of the Most Sacred Heart, like an overflowing river, washing away all obstacles, has poured itself over the whole earth, and at the dawn of the new century Leo XIII, having proclaimed a jubilee, willed to dedicate the whole human race to the Most Sacred Heart. This consecration was actually carried out with solemn rites in all the churches of the Catholic world, and brought about a great increase of this devotion, leading to it not only nations, but even private families, who in countless numbers dedicated themselves to the Divine Heart, and submitted themselves to its royal sway. Lastly, the Sovereign Pontiff Pius XI, in order that by its solemnity the feast might answer more fully to the so greatly widespread devotion of the Christian people, raised the feast of the Most Sacred Heart of Jesus to the rite of a double of the first class with an octave;

and moreover, that the violated rights of Christ, the supreme King and the most loving Lord, might be repaired, and that the sins of the nations might be bewailed, he ordered that annually, on that same feast day, there should be recited an expiatory form of prayer in all churches of the Christian world.

R. All the nations whatsoever Thou hast made shall come * And shall adore before Thee, O Lord. V. And they shall glorify Thy name, for thou art great, and dost wonderful things. And shall. Glory. And shall.

III Nocturn

The reading of the holy Gospel
according to St. John

At that time: The Jews, because it was the parasceve, that the bodies might not remain upon the cross on the Sabbath day, for that was a great sabbath day, besought Pilate that their legs might be broken, and they might be taken away. And so forth.

Homily of St. Bonaventure, Bishop

That the Church might be formed from the side of Christ as He slept on the Cross, and the Scripture be fulfilled which says: They shall look on Him whom they pierced; it was permitted by divine ordinance that one of the soldiers should pierce that Sacred Side, opening it with a lance, in so far as, when the blood and water gushed forth, the price of

our salvation might be poured out, as if issuing
from the hidden fountain, as it were, of the Heart,
and might give power to the Sacraments of the
Church to bestow the life of grace; and, moreover,
might be as a saving drink of living waters, bub-
bling up to life eternal, to those who were already
living in Christ.   Arise, then, O soul, beloved of
Church to bestow the gift of grace; and, moreover,
drink the waters from the saving fountains.

For once we have found our way to that most
sweet Heart of the Lord Jesus, and it is good for us
to be here, let us not easily be torn away from It.
O how good and pleasant it is to dwell in this Heart.
Thy Heart, O most dear Jesus, is the good treasure,
the pearl of great price, which we find by digging
in the field of Thy Body.   Who would cast aside this
pearl?   Yea, rather I will give all my pearls, I will
exchange for it all my thoughts and affections and I
will purchase it for myself, turning all my thoughts
to the Heart of the good Jesus, and without fail It
will support me.

Therefore, O most sweet Jesus, finding this
Heart that is Thine and mine, I will pray to Thee,
my God: admit my prayers into the shrine of Thy
hearing: nay, draw me altogether into Thy Heart.
For to this end was Thy side pierced, that an entry
might be open to us.   To this end was Thy Heart
wounded, that in It we might be able to dwell secure from alarms from without.   And no less was

it wounded on this account that, through the visible wound, we might see the invisible wound of love. How could this ardor be better shown than by His allowing, not only His Body, but even His very Heart Itself, to be wounded by a lance? And so, the wound in His Flesh shows forth the wound in His Spirit.

Who does not love that Heart, so deeply wounded? Who would not return love for love to One so greatly loving? Who would not embrace One so pure? Let us, therefore, still abiding in the flesh, in so far as we are able, return love for love to that which loves us, embrace our wounded one whose hands and feet, side and Heart, have been pierced by wicked husbandmen; and let us pray that He may deign to bind our hearts, still hard and impenitent, with the chain of His love, and wound them with the dart thereof.

R. If I be lifted up from the earth, * I will draw all things to myself. V. Now this He said, signifying what death He should die. I will draw. Glory. I will draw.

✠ Continuation of the holy Gospel according to St. John.—At that time: The Jews, because it was the Parasceve, that the bodies might not remain upon the cross on the Sabbath day for that was a great Sabbath day, besought Pilate that their legs might be broken and that they might be taken away. The soldiers, therefore, came and broke the legs of the first, and of the other that was crucified with Him. But after they were come to Jesus, when they saw that He was already dead, they did not break His legs, but one of the soldiers with a spear opened His Side, and immediately there came out blood and water. And he that saw it hath given testimony and his testimony is true. And he knoweth that he saith true: that you also may believe. For these things were done that the Scripture might be fulfilled: You shall not break a bone of Him. And again another Scripture saith: They shall look on Him whom they pierced.

LET US PRAY

O God, who hath mercifully placed for us the infinite treasures of Thy love in the Heart of Thy Son, wounded by our sins; grant, we beseech Thee, that as we offer It the devoted reverence of our love, we may also fulfil the duty of a worthy atonement.

SATURDAY

The reading of the holy Gospel
according to St. John

At that time: The Jews, because it was the parasceve, that the bodies might not remain upon the cross on the sabbath day, for that was a great sabbath day, besought Pilate that their legs might be broken, and that they might be taken away. And so forth.

Homily of St. John Chrysostom

Seest thou how strong is truth? Through the zeal of the Jews the prophecy is fulfilled. Another prediction also receives fulfilment. For the soldiers, coming, broke the legs of the others, not so of Christ. But yet these men, to please the Jews, pierce His side with a lance, and treat the dead body with contumely. O wicked and accursed crime? But be not troubled or cast down, beloved. They, indeed, did it in ill-will, but they contended for the truth; for indeed the prophecy was: They shall look on Him whom they pierced. And not only this; but this crime served as a demonstration even for those faithless ones who were to come after, such as Thomas, and others like him. The ineffable mystery was consummated also to this end. For there came forth blood and water. Not without cause or by chance did these fountains flow, but because of the fact that the Church was founded from both of them.

This the initiated know, they who are regenerated by the water and nourished with the Flesh and the Blood. Thence do the Sacraments derive their origin, so that when thou dost approach to the awe-inspiring cup, thou shouldst come as if thou wert about to drink from this very side. And he that saw it, hath given testimony: and his testimony is true. That is to say: Not from others have I heard it, but I myself was present and saw it, and the testimony is true.

Deservedly indeed. He is speaking of an insult, not of something great and wonderful, else thou mightest doubt his testimony; but he, shutting the mouths of heretics and foretelling future mysteries, mindful of the treasure contained in them, also enumerates one by one the events that have taken place. And there was fulfilled that prophecy: They shall not break a bone of Him. For although this was said of the lamb of the Jews, nevertheless from the figure came forth the reality in which the prophecy was more completely fulfilled. That is why he brings the prophet to the fore.

Since the testimony he himself bears might not everywhere be held worthy of belief, he quotes Moses, to intimate that this thing was not done by chance, but had already long ago been foretold in writing. By Moses this was said: Not a bone of Him shall be broken. And again he rests his faith on the same Prophet. These things I have said, says he, that you may learn how great is the resemblance between the figure and the reality. Seest thou what great care he takes, that the body should be treated with contumely by the soldier was far worse than Its Crucifixion. But nevertheless, says he, I have both said these things and have said them most emphatically, that you may believe. Let no one, therefore, deny credence to these things, nor

for shame tamper with our beliefs. For those
things which seem to be the most dishonoring are
in fact our greatest pride.

SUNDAY WITHIN THE OCTAVE OF
THE FEAST OF THE SACRED HEART

The III Sunday after Pentecost

I Nocturn

From the first book of Kings, c. 9, 18 - 27; c. 10, 1

II Nocturn

From the Encyclical Letter of Pope Pius XI

Among all other proofs of the infinite kindness
of our Redeemer, this one is especially conspicuous,
that, as the love of the Christian believers grew
cold, He, Divine Love itself, was proposed to be
honored by a special devotion, and that the rich
treasures of His goodness were thrown wide open
by means of that form of worship with which we
honor the most Sacred Heart of Jesus, "in whom
are all the treasures of wisdom and knowledge."
For, as formerly God wished to give light to the
human race as they came out of Noe's ark by the
signal treaty of friendship, "a bow appearing in
the clouds," so in those most troublous times of a
more recent age, when that most subtle of all heresies, Jansenism, was everywhere creeping in, an
enemy of the love of God and of piety, preaching

that God was not so much to be loved as a father, as to be feared as an unrelenting judge, the most kind Jesus manifested unto the nations His Most Sacred Heart, borne on high like unto a banner of peace and love, an augury of certain victory in battle.

And it is indeed justly so; for in this most auspicious sign and in that which follows from it, is there not contained the highest model of piety of the whole of religion, and therefore the rule of the more perfect life, in as much as it leads our minds the more easily to a deeper knowledge of Christ the Lord and to a more vehement love of Him, and moves our souls more effectually to a more exact imitation of Him? Therefore, no one will be surprised that Our predecessors have continuously vindicated this most approved form of devotion from the accusations of cavillers, that they have extolled it with the highest praises, and have promoted it with the most ardent zeal, according as considerations of the period and of affairs in general have demanded. And it has come to pass, by the providence of God, that the devout affection of Christ's faithful people towards the Most Sacred Heart of Jesus obtains greater augmentations day by day.

But, indeed, among the different practices which directly accompany devotion to the most Sacred Heart, assuredly the foremost and most notable is the act of consecration by which we offer to the divine Heart of Jesus both ourselves and all that belongs to us recognizing that all we have comes to us from the infinite charity of the eternal Deity. Moreover, to all these expressions of veneration it is expedient that another be added; we refer to the act of expiation or atonement, as it is called, to be made to the most Sacred Heart of Jesus. For, if in the act of consecration the intention to repay, as it were, the love of the Creator with the love of the creatures stands out most prominently, there follows almost naturally from this another fact, namely, that if this same uncreated Love has either been passed over through forgetfulness or saddened by reason of our sins, then we should repair such outrages, no matter in what manner they have occurred: ordinarily, we call this duty atonement.

If we are urged to both these practices for the reason given, we are held to the duty of making reparation by the most powerful motives of justice and of love; of justice, in order to expiate the injury done to God by our sins, and to re-establish, by means of penance, the divine order which has been violated; and of love, in order to suffer together with Christ, patient and covered with opprobrium, so that we may bring to Him, in so far as our human weakness permits, some comfort in His sufferings. For it is our duty to honor God not only by the worship of adoration, whereby we adore His infinite Majesty, or by means of prayer, when we recognize His supreme dominion over us, or by acts of thanksgiving, when we praise His infinite generosity towards us; but it is necessary to do more than this. Since we are all sinners, burdened with many offences, we must also satisfy the just anger of God, "because of the numberless sins, offences and negligences" which have been committed. Therefore, we must add to the act of consecration, by virtue of which we offer ourselves to God and become thereby, as it were, sacred to God by reason of the holiness which naturally flows from an act of consecration, as the Angelic Doctor teaches, an act of expiation by means of which all our faults are blotted out, lest perchance the sanctity of infinite justice spurn our arrogant unworthiness, and look upon our gift as something rather to be rejected than to be accepted.

R. Let us therefore be followers of God, * And walk in love. V. As Christ also hath loved us and hath delivered Himself for us. And walk. Glory. And walk.

III Nocturn

The reading of the holy Gospel
according to St. Luke

At that time: The publicans and sinners drew near unto Jesus to hear Him. And so forth.

Homily of St. Gregory, Pope

You have heard, my brethren, in the reading from the Gospel how sinners and publicans approached our Redeemer; and how He received them, not only talking with them, but also eating with them. The Pharisees, seeing this, were scornful. From which occurrence you may gather that true justice hath compassion, but false justice hath scorn.

And, indeed, the just are rightly wont to be scornful of sinners: but that which is done in pride or haughtiness is one thing, and that which is done out of zeal for discipline is quite another thing. For truly they scorn, but are not scornful; they despair, but are not desperate; they initiate persecution, but they are affectionate: because although they multiply rebukes outwardly for the sake of discipline, nevertheless they maintain a pleasant disposition for the sake of charity.

In their own minds, they very often have a higher opinion of those they correct than they have of themselves, and they consider those whom they judge as better than themselves. It is clear that, acting thus, they guard those who are under them by discipline and themselves by humility. But on the other hand, those who, through false justice, are wont to be haughty, despise every one else, show no mercy to the weak, and, because they do not look upon themselves as sinners, for that reason become worse sinners.

Of which number assuredly the Pharisees were conspicuous, who found fault with the Lord because

He received sinners, and in the dryness of their own hearts rebuked the very fountain of mercy. But they were so sick that they failed to realize their sickness, and therefore, that they might become aware of what they really were, the heavenly physician healed them with an agreeable treatment, put before them a gracious example, and reduced the swelling of the wound in their heart.

R. The Lord is nigh to all that call upon Him, * to all that call upon Him in truth. V. The Lord is gracious and merciful, patient and plenteous in mercy. To all. Glory. To all.

✠ Continuation of the holy Gospel according to St. Luke.—At that time: The publicans and sinners drew near unto Jesus to hear Him: and the Pharisees and Scribes murmured, saying: This man receiveth sinners and eateth with them. And He spoke to them this parable, saying: What man is there of you that hath a hundred sheep, and if he shall lose one of them, doth he not leave the ninety-nine in the desert and go after that which was lost until he find it? And when he hath found it, lay it upon his shoulders rejoicing, and coming home, call together his friends and neighbors, saying to them: Rejoice with me, because I have found my sheep that was lost? I say to you, that even so there shall be joy in heaven upon one sinner that doth penance, more than upon ninety-nine just who need not penance. Or what woman having ten groats, if she lose one groat, doth not light a candle and sweep the house, and seek diligently until she find it? And when she hath found it, call together her friends and neighbors, saying: Rejoice with me, because I have found the groat which I had lost? So I say to you, there shall be joy before the angels of God upon one sinner doing penance.

LET US PRAY

O God, the protector of all who trust in Thee, without whom there is nothing good or holy, increase Thy mercy towards us; that by Thy guidance and assistance we may so use the temporal goods of this world that we lose not the eternal. Through our Lord.

MONDAY

The reading of the holy Gospel
according to St. John

At that time: The Jews, because it was the parasceve, that the bodies might not remain upon the cross on the sabbath day, for that was a great sabbath day, besought Pilate that their legs might be broken, and that they might be taken away. And so forth.

Homily of St. Laurence Justinian, Bishop

Therefore, after they were come to Jesus and saw that He was already dead, by no means did they break His legs, but one of those who stood by, hurling a spear, opened His side, and immediately there came out blood and water. Truly a great and unheard-of wonder, that from a lifeless body should come forth blood and water. But nevertheless, in what happened, the wisdom of God willed to put before us a very great mystery, namely, the oneness of His Church with Himself. For a figure of this spiritual union had gone before, when it is related that from the side of Adam, as he slept, one of his ribs was taken, and from it there was formed Eve, the mother of all, who was a type of the Church. The Holy Ghost then signified that there was to be a true and spiritual Adam, fashioned by the power of the Paraclete, from whose side, while He slept on the Cross, as the water and blood flowed forth, the Church would be formed, a comely spouse without spot or wrinkle.

For truly these are the Sacraments of the Church by which the whole body of the Church is washed and sanctified. Assuredly, in the laver of regenerating water, consecrated by the death of Christ, she is cleansed from original sin. And not only is she purified from every stain in the Blood of the Redeemer, but also the entrance to the heavenly kingdom is opened to her. Both these things are done at one and the same time, nor does one avail for salvation without the other; for no one is able to receive the inheritance of future bliss without the sacrament of baptism and the remission of sins.

This, all the world over, holy mother Church confesses, and it is confirmed by manifold testimonies of divine Scripture. Moreover, he too, who saw the water and blood flow forth from the side of Christ, bore witness, and his testimony is true. Now this is John the Apostle and Evangelist who was loved with an exceeding love by the Lord.

Actually, these things were done that the Scripture might be fulfilled which says: Thou shalt not break a bone of Him. For truly it had been commanded to Moses by the Lord, that in the sacrifice of the passover, in the celebration of the sacrificing of the lamb, no bone should be broken. But in that most innocent Lamb, the Lord Jesus, the truth of this figure was fulfilled. For in no wise were His legs broken, after the manner of what was done to the two rogues hanging with Him; but His side alone was opened, so that another Scripture might be fulfilled which says: They shall look on Him whom they pierced. Moreover, the Lord willed to retain the marks of the wounds in His Body, that it might incite the elect to devotion, and also be an unanswerable testimony of damnation to the reprobate. Thus all things were consummated in Christ, which had been long before declared by the oracles of the Prophets, that the Catholic Faith might be strengthened both in itself and against the errors of heretics.

TUESDAY

The reading of the holy Gospel
according to St. John

At that time: The Jews, because it was the parasceve, that the bodies might not remain upon the cross on the sabbath day, for that was a great sabbath day, besought Pilate that their legs might be broken, and that they might be taken away. And so forth.

Homily of St. Bernardine of Sienna

John continues: One of the soldiers with a spear opened His side, and immediately there came out blood and water. O love, Thou who meltest all things! How didst Thou leave our beloved for the sake of our redemption? For that this flood of love might spread everywhere, the great firmaments were rent above us, forsooth, the depths of the Heart of Jesus, which the cruel spear did not fail to pierce to its innermost recesses. There came out blood and water. Blood for redemption, but water also for cleansing flowed out; whence the Church was formed from the side of Christ that she might know herself to be ever the only beloved of Christ, and that she might realize how greatly sin displeased Him, seeing His Divine Blood thus flow forth from the God-man, both in life and in death. For if the divine Blood is shed for us, then we cost not a little.

The water did not flow forth literally mingled with the Blood. For if it had flowed forth actually mixed with the Blood, it could not have been perceived by simple folk. And, perchance, all the Blood flowed forth from that divine Body as a sign that all His love was poured out, after which a watery humor came forth. This indeed was done in token of a deep mystery, that first from that same Body might come forth the price of redemption, and then the water by which the redeemed multitude of the nations is signified. For many waters signify many people; yet all who belong to the Christian faith are one people in the faith, so that they are not waters, but the water which flowed from the side of Christ, as the Apostle says in the tenth chapter of the first epistle to the Corinthians: All we, being many, are one bread and one body, who partake of one bread and one cup. And again, in the fourth chapter of his letter to the Ephesians, he says: One God, one faith, one baptism.

Nevertheless, it is markedly deserving of attention that the side of Christ is said to be opened, not wounded; since a wound cannot properly be inflicted except upon a living body. For John the Evangelist says: One of the soldiers with a spear opened His side; that, through that open side, we might become aware of the love of His Heart even unto death, and that we might enter into that unutterable love of His through the same channel by which

it had come to us. Let us draw near, then, to His
Heart, a deep Heart, a hidden Heart, a Heart thinking of all, a Heart knowing all, a Heart loving all,
yea, even on fire with love; and let us recognize at
least in the vehemence of His love that the gate is
open; with our hearts made like unto His, let us
enter into that secret place hidden from all eternity,
but now in death revealed, as it were, through the
open side; for the opening of His side is a figure of
the opening of the eternal temple, where is consummated the everlasting happiness of every creature.

WEDNESDAY

The reading of the holy Gospel
according to St. John

At that time: The Jews, because it was the parasceve, that the bodies might not remain upon the
cross on the sabbath day, for that was a great sabbath day, besought Pilate that their legs might be
broken, and that they might be taken away. And
so forth.

Homily of St. Peter Canisius, Priest

Do thou with all diligence turn over in thy mind
how with unutterable charity He, who is God over
all, endured a most bitter death on the Cross in exceeding anguish of Heart, whilst the whole world
mocked Him, and all this for thee, a most paltry
little worm. Meditate on the immense generosity
which the Preserver displayed to all of His own

people. For at one time, standing in the midst of the people, He cried out thus: If any one thirst, let him come to Me and drink; showing that He was ready to come to the help of everyone in their every need. Consider how freely He gave thee to drink of His Heart's precious Blood, when His sacred side was opened, and He poured forth whatever Blood was left in His Body.

Wherefore, lest I should be utterly ungrateful, often I call up before my eyes those perennial fountains of gifts and of all good things, since from them that most sweet promise stands out: You shall draw waters with joy out of the Savior's fountains and you shall say in that: Praise ye the Lord. Thither will I flee, to those thrice-blest holes in the rock which can never be demolished; there will I build me a most durable nest, holding nothing better in all sorrows and perils that befall me than to think on the wounds of the Lord.

And in every trial do thou promptly flee to the lovable Heart of Christ, and call to mind His goodness and charity, setting them against thine own vileness, malice, unfaithfulness, and pride. For how great was the charity of Christ in calling all to Himself: Come to Me all you that labor and are burdened, and I will refresh you; with this intent He offers Himself to us, ready and desirous out of love for us to sustain the burdens of each and all! Do thou then cast thy sins with great confidence into the abyss of His charity, and straightway thou shalt find thyself lightened of thy load.

THURSDAY

The reading of the holy Gospel
according to St. John

At that time: The Jews, because it was the parasceve, that the bodies might not remain upon the cross on the sabbath day, for that was a great sabbath day, besought Pilate that their legs might be broken, and that they might be taken away. And so forth.

Homily of St. Cyril, Bishop of Alexandria

The blessed Evangelist does not say these things as though admitting any godliness in the savage and cruel Jews, but rather that he may show how foolishly and ignorantly they strained out a gnat and swallowed a camel, as Christ Himself had said. For they are found to make light of most grievous and awful crimes while they observe very carefully and anxiously the least trivialities, in both ways displaying their ignorance. This can readily be shown. For behold, having put Christ to death, they give honor to the great sabbath; and, with incredible insolence, they make a show of reverence for that law, whose author they have dishonored.

And they who have put to death the Lord of that great day pretend to show a special reverence for that great sabbath day; and they earnestly solicit a favor worthy of them alone, namely, that the legs of the crucified ones may be broken, inflicting an intolerable pain, a more bitter misfortune than death itself, on those already almost dead. The soldiers therefore came, and they broke the legs of the first, and of the other that was crucified with Him. The soldiers, sent at the request of the Jews, were laboring under a like cruel frenzy, so they break the legs of the two thieves, who were indeed found to be still alive. But when they found that Jesus had bowed His Head and concluded that He had already expired, they think it useless to break His legs, but still, not quite certain that He is yet dead, they pierce His side with a spear, whence blood mixed with water flowed out, a figure and also the first-fruits of the mystical banquet and of holy baptism.

And from these things which came to pass, the most wise Evangelist proves to his hearers that this is the Christ who was long ago foretold by holy Scripture; for all that happened agrees with what was divinely prophesied concerning Him. Thus, according to the Scriptures, not a bone of Him was broken, and He was pierced with the soldier's spear. The Evangelist does certainly say that the one who saw this thing was the same disciple who gave testimony concerning these things, and that he knew that his testimony was true: by this expression meaning not another, but himself.

OCTAVE DAY OF THE FEAST OF THE MOST SACRED HEART

I Nocturn

From Jeremias the Prophet, c. 27, 5 - 7; c. 30, 18 - 27; c. 31, 1 - 3 c. 31, 31 - 33

II Nocturn

From the Encyclical Letter of Pope Pius XI

Therefore, as the act of consecration proclaims and confirms our union with Christ, so the act of expiation, by purifying us from sins, is the beginning of such union; our participation in the sufferings of Christ perfects it, the offering we make to Him of our sacrifices for the welfare of our brethren brings such union to its final consummation. And this was precisely the design of the mercy of Jesus when He unveiled to our gaze His Heart, surrounded by the emblems of His Passion and aflame with the fire of love, that we, on the one hand, perceiving the infinite malice of sin, and on the other, filled with a knowledge of the infinite love of the Restorer, might detest sin more cordially and substitute for it an ardent love of Him. Inasmuch as when Christ revealed Himself to the sight of Margaret Mary, though He then insisted on the immensity of His love, at the same time, with sorrowful mien, He grieved over the great number of horrible outrages heaped upon Him by the ingratitude of mankind, He used then these words, words which should be graven on the hearts of all pious souls so as never to be forgotten by them: "Behold That Heart", says He, "which has so loved men, which has heaped upon them so many benefits; in return for which infinite love It finds no gratitude; instead, It meets with forgetfulness, indifference, outrages, and all this at times even from souls bound closely to it in the bounds of a very special love."

Now, anyone who uses his eyes and mind, if he but think of this world seated in wickedness, can see, as we stated above, how urgent especially in our own times is the need of expiation or atonement. For there come to Our ears from every side the cries of nations whose rulers or governments have actually risen up and have conspired together against the Lord and against His Church. Nor is that other spectacle less sad that, even among the faithful, washed as they have been by baptism in the Blood of the Lamb without spot and enriched by His grace, we encounter so many of every station in life who, ignorant of things divine, are poisoned by false doctrine and live a sinful life far from their Father's house, without the light of the true faith, without the joy of hope in a future life, deprived of the strength and comfort which come with the spirit of love, that one may say quite truthfully that they sit in darkness and in the shadow of death.

But there must be added to this accumulation of

evils the sloth and laziness of those who, like the
disciples asleep or fleeing, since they are not firmly
rooted in the faith, have shamefully abandoned
Christ, burdened with sorrows and attacked by the
satellites of Satan, as well as the perfidy of those
others who, following in the footsteps of Judas the
traitor, either with sacrilegious temerity approach
the sacrament of the altar, or go over to the camp
of the enemy. And there thus comes to mind, almost involuntarily, the thought that we have arrived at the hour prophesied by our Lord when He
said: And because iniquity hath abounded, the
charity of many shall grow cold. If the faithful,
burning with love for the sufferings of Christ,
should meditate on all these considerations, it would
be unthinkable that they should not expiate with
their greater zeal both their own faults and the
faults of others, and that they should not repair the
honor of Christ and be filled with zeal for the eternal salvation of souls.

Assuredly, we may adapt to our own age what
the Apostle wrote: Where sin abounded, grace did
more abound; for even though the sinfulness of
men has greatly increased, by the grace of the Holy
Ghost there has also increased the number of the
faithful of both sexes who most gladly try to make
satisfaction to the divine Heart for the numerous
injuries heaped on it; nay, they even joyfully offer
themselves to Christ as victims for sin. For truly,

anyone who has been considering in a spirit of love
all that has been revealed to his mind thus far, if
he has impressed these thoughts, as it were, on the
fleshly tablets of his heart, such a one assuredly
cannot but abhor and flee all sin as the greatest of
evils.   He will also offer himself wholly and entirely to the will of God, and will strive to repair the
injured divine Majesty by constant prayer, by voluntary penances, by patient suffering of all those
ills which shall befall him; in a word, he will so or-
ganize his life that in all things it will be inspired
by the spirit of atonement.

III Nocturn

The reading of the holy Gospel
according to St. John

At that time: The Jews, because it was the parasceve, that the bodies might not remain upon the
cross on the sabbath day, for that was a great sabbath day, besought Pilate that their legs might be
broken, and that they might be taken away. And
so forth.

Homily of St. Augustine, Bishop

But after they were come to Jesus, when they
saw that He was already dead, they did not break
His legs, but one of the soldiers with a spear opened
His side, and immediately there came out blood and
water. The Evangelist made use of a suggestive
word, in that he did not say: Pierced His side; or:

Wounded or anything else; but: Opened; that thereby in a sense the door of life might be thrown open, from whence the Sacraments of the Church have flowed forth, without which there is no entrance into the life which is the true life. That Blood was shed for the remission of sins. That water it is that makes up the health-giving cup, and supplies at the same time the bath of baptism and water for drinking.

This was announced beforehand when Noe was commanded to make a door in the side of the ark, through which the animals not destined to perish in the flood might enter, and by which the Church was foreshown. On account of this, the first woman was made from out of the side of the man while he slept, and she was called: Life; and: Mother of the living. Truly, it pointed to a great good, before the great evil of the transgression. Here the second Adam bowed His head and slept on the cross that a spouse might be formed for Him from that which flowed from His side as He slept.

O death, whereby the dead are raised anew to life! What is cleaner than this Blood? What more health-giving than this wound? And he that saw it, says he, hath given testimony, and his testimony is true; and he knoweth that he saith true that you also may believe. He said not: That you also may know; but: That you may believe. For he who has seen knows that he who has not seen may believe his testimony. For believing belongs more to the nature of faith, than seeing does.

He has given two testimonies from the Scriptures for each of the things which he has recorded as having been done. For because he had said: But after they were come to Jesus, when they saw that He was already dead, they did not break His legs, to this pertains the testimony, You shall not break a bone of Him, which was a precept given to those who were commanded to celebrate the Pasch by the sacrifice of a sheep in the Old Law, which went before as a shadow of the Passion of the Lord; whence: Christ our Pasch is sacrificed; of whom the Prophet Isaias also had predicted: He was led as a sheep to the slaughter. In like manner because he had subjoined: But one of the soldiers with a spear opened His side, to this pertains the other testimony: They shall look on Him whom they pierced; where it was foretold that Christ would come in the very Flesh in which He had been crucified.

IV SUNDAY AFTER PENTECOST

I Nocturn

From the first book of Kings, c. 17, 1 - 16

II Nocturn

Sermon of St. Augustine, Bishop

The children of Israel stood over against their adversaries for forty days. These forty days, because of the four seasons of the year and the four quarters of the globe, signify this present life, in which the Christian people ceases not to fight against Goliath and his army, that is, against the devil and his angels. Nevertheless, it would not have been able to conquer unless Christ, the true David, with His staff, that is, with the mystery of the Cross, had come down.

For before the coming of Christ, dearly beloved brethren, the devil was at large; but when Christ came, He did to him as it is said in the Gospel: No one can enter into the house of the strong and rifle his goods, unless he first bind the strong. Therefore, Christ came and bound the devil. But someone says: If he is bound, why has he still so great a power? It is true, dearly beloved brethren, that he does prevail to a great extent; but it is the lukewarm and the careless, and such as fear not God in truth, over whom he has such power.

For he is bound like a dog that is chained up, and he cannot bite anyone, except him who approaches with a dangerous carelessness. See now, brethren, how foolish a man who is bitten by a chained dog must be. Let not the pleasures and lusts of the world draw thee to him, and he will not venture to approach thee. He can bark, he can fawn, but can by no means bite, unless thou dost let him. For he does us hurt, not by violence, but by persuasion; neither does he extort consent from us, he only asks it.

David, then, came and found the people of the Jews fighting against the devil; and since there was no one who would venture to meet Goliath in single combat, he who typified Christ went forth to battle, took his staff in hand, and advanced against Goliath.   And what he then did was indeed a figure of that which was fulfilled in the Lord Jesus Christ. For Christ, the true David, when He went forth to fight against the spiritual Goliath that is the devil, went forth carrying His Cross.   Take note, brethren, where David struck Goliath; of a truth, in the forehead, whereon he had never made the sign of the cross.   For as the staff was a type of the cross, so also that stone with which he was struck prefigured Christ the Lord.

R. I took thee from the house of thy father, saith the Lord, and set thee to feed the flock of My people: * And I have been with thee wheresoever thou hast walked, establishing thy kingdom forever.   V. And I have made thy name great, like unto the name of the great ones that are on the earth: and I have given thee rest from all thy enemies.   And I have been.   Glory.   And I have been.

V SUNDAY AFTER PENTECOST

I Nocturn

From the second Book of Kings, c. 1, 1 - 15

II Nocturn

From the book of Morals of St. Gregory, Pope

Why was it that David, who rendered no evil to them that did evil to him, when Saul and Jonathan had fallen in battle, cursed the mountains of Gelboe, saying: Ye mountains of Gelboe, let neither dew, nor rain come upon you; neither be they fields of first-fruits: for there was cast away the shield of the valiant, the shield of Saul, as though he had not been anointed with oil?

Why was it that Jeremias, when his preaching was rendered fruitless by the obstinacy of his hearers, cursed and said: Cursed be the man that brought the tidings to my father, saying: A man-child is born to thee? What, then, had the mountains of Gelboe done amiss that, because Saul was dead, neither dew nor rain might fall upon them, and that every green thing springing there should wither away at the word of the prophet?

But since Gelboe means: Downward flow; and Saul, who had been anointed and was now dead, typifies for us the death of our Mediator; the mountains of Gelboe signify very aptly the proud hearts of the Jews who, while they let themselves (as it were) flow down in pursuit of the desires of this world, have taken part in the death of Christ, that is, the anointed: and because among them the anointed king dies the death of the body, the dew of grace falls upon them no more.

And it is well said of them, that they could not be fields of first-fruits. For truly, the proud minds of the Jews bore no early fruits; since, remaining for the most part in infidelity at the coming of the Redeemer, they would not follow the first beginnings of the Faith. For indeed, holy Church was enriched with her first-fruits by the multitude of the Gentiles, and just before the end of the world she will receive such Jews as she shall then find; and gathering together these last remnants, lay them up as the gleanings of the harvest.

R. Ye mountains of Gelboe, let neither dew nor rain come upon you, * For upon you have fallen the valiant ones of Israel. V. O all ye mountains, who are in His circle, may the Lord visit you: but let Him pass over Gelboe. For. Glory. For.

VI SUNDAY AFTER PENTECOST

I Nocturn

From the second Book of Kings, c. 12, 1 - 16

II Nocturn

From the Book of St. Ambrose, Bishop,
on the defence of David

In how many things does each one of us hourly
fail! Yet among us ordinary men not one thinks
himself bound to confess his sins. That king, great
and powerful, would not suffer the consciousness of
sin to remain with him even for the shortest space
of time; but, confessing almost immediately and
with the greatest grief, he declared his sin to the
Lord.

Whom will you find me now among the rich and
honorable who does not take it ill if, being guilty
of any fault, he is rebuked? But that man, renowned for his royal power, approved by so many
divine oracles, when he was rebuked by a private
man for having grievously sinned, did not rage
with indignation, but confessed his sin and groaned
with sorrow for his fault. And then this heartfelt
sorrow so touched the Lord that Nathan could say:
Because thou hast repented, the Lord hath taken
away thy sin. Therefore the promptness of the pardon clearly showed that the king's repentance was

sincere; for though his sin was very great all trace
of it was removed.

Other men, when rebuked by priests, aggravate
their sins by seeking to deny or excuse them; and
the correction, intended for their amendment,
serves only to make their fall greater. But the
Saints of the Lord, who strive to fight a good fight,
and to run the course of salvation, if, at times, they
chance, being men, to fall, more on account of the
weakness of nature than because they love sin, yet
they rise and run on more swiftly than before, the
shame of their fall urging them to return to the
fight with greater vigor; and so their fall, far from
having delayed them in their course, has supplied
them with fresh incentives to advance more quickly.

David sinned, a thing not rare among kings; but
he did penance, he wept, he groaned, as kings are
not wont to do.   He confessed his fault, he sought
for pardon, prostrate on the ground he wept bitterly over his misery, he fasted, he prayed, and pub-
lishing abroad his grief, he left a witness of his
confession to all posterity.   This king was not a-
shamed to confess, a thing which meaner men blush
to do.   Those who are subject to the laws dare to
deny their sins, and scorn to ask for the pardon that
a king asked, though bound by no laws of men.   In
that he sinned, he showed the weakness of his nature; in that he asked pardon, he showed himself
amenable to correction.   To fall is common to all

men, but his confession was his own. Therefore, to have fallen into sin came from the weakness of his nature; but to have effaced it came from his virtue.

R. Who is a great God like our God? * Thou art the God that dost wonders. V. Thou hast made known Thy power among the nations: with Thine arm Thou hast redeemed Thy people. Thou art. Glory. Thou art.

VII SUNDAY AFTER PENTECOST

I Nocturn

From the third book of Kings, c. 1, 1 - 8

II Nocturn

From a letter of St. Jerome, Priest, to Nepotianus

When David, who had once been a warlike man, was seventy years old, the chill of age crept over him, and he could no longer get warm. So they sought out for him in all the coasts of Israel a maiden, Abisag, a Sunamitess, that she might sleep with the king and warm his aged body. Who is this Sunamitess, wife and virgin, so hot as to warm the cold; so holy as not to provoke to lust him whom she has warmed?

Let Solomon the most wise describe the pleasures of his father, and the peaceful one tell of the warlike man's embraces: Get wisdom, get understanding. Forget not, and do not decline from the words of my mouth: neither forsake her, and she shall take hold of thee: love her, and she shall preserve thee. The beginning of wisdom, get wisdom, and with all thy possession get understanding; encompass her, and she shall exalt thee; honor her, and she shall embrace thee, that she may give to thy head a crown of graces. And with a crown of delights she shall protect thee.

In old age almost all the powers of the body suffer change, and while wisdom alone increases, all other activities begin to fail: fasting, watching, lying on the ground, that is to say, sleeping on a paved floor, wandering hither and thither, receiving strangers, defending the poor, vehemence and perseverance in prayer, visiting the sick, manual labor whereby to provide alms. And lest I unduly protract my discourse, all the activities in which the body has a share become less frequent when it is enfeebled.

I do not mean to say that wisdom, which often fails even in the old, is wanting in the young and in those of maturer age, least of all in such as have acquired knowledge by hard work and study, joined to holiness of life and constant prayer to the Lord Jesus; but this I do say, that the young have to endure so many struggles with the body between provocations to vice and natural sensations of pruriency, that their wisdom is like a fire smothered with green wood, which hinders it from blazing forth in all its brightness. Yet when old age comes upon such as have spent their youth in honorable occupations and have meditated on the law of the Lord day and night, they become more learned with age, more experienced, wiser as the years go by, and they gather most sweet fruit from their former diligence.

R. God heareth all things: He hath sent His angel, and taken me from guarding my father's sheep: * And He hath anointed me with the oil of His mercy. V. The Lord, who delivered me out of the mouth of the lion, and freed me from the paw of the wild beast. And. Glory. And.

VIII SUNDAY AFTER PENTECOST

I Nocturn

From the third book of Kings, c. 9, 1 - 14

II Nocturn

From the book of St. Augustine, Bishop,
on the City of God

Indeed, even in Solomon there appeared some image of the future event, in that he built a temple, and had that peace which his name implies (for indeed the name Solomon is the equivalent of the Latin *pacificus*, peaceful), and in the beginning of his reign he was worthy of all praise. But while, as a shadow of Him that should come, he foreshowed Christ our Lord, he did not likewise in his own person resemble Him.

Whence some things concerning him are so written as if they were prophesied of Christ Himself, while the holy Scripture, prophesying even by events, somehow delineates in him a figure of what was to happen. For besides the books of sacred history in which his reign is recorded, the seventy-first Psalm also bears his name in the title.

Therein so many things are said which cannot at all apply to him, but which apply to the Lord Christ with a very evident fitness, that it is quite apparent that in Solomon is shadowed forth a kind of figure, but in Christ the very truth is presented to us.

For it is known within what boundaries the kingdom of Solomon was enclosed; and yet in that Psalm, to say nothing of other things, we read: He shall rule from sea to sea, and from the river unto the ends of the earth; which we see fulfilled in Christ. In truth, He took the beginning of His reigning from the river where He was baptized by John; for when John pointed Him out, He began to be acknowledged by the disciples, who called Him not master only, but Lord.

R. I took thee from the house of thy father, saith the Lord, and set thee to feed the flock of My people: * And I have been with thee wheresoever thou hast walked, establishing thy kingdom forever. V. And I have made thy name great, like unto the name of the great ones that are on the earth: And I have given thee rest from all thy enemies. And I have. Glory. And I have.

IX SUNDAY AFTER PENTECOST

I Nocturn

From the fourth book of Kings, c. 1, 1 - 10

II Nocturn

Sermon of St. Augustine, Bishop

In the lessons which are read to us on these days, dearly beloved brethren, I have often warned you that we should not follow the letter which killeth, while neglecting the spirit which quickeneth. For thus does the Apostle speak: For the letter killeth, but the spirit quickeneth. If then we are content to understand the literal sense only, we receive little edification or none at all from these sacred readings.

For all the things which are read were a type and image of things to come. For in the Jews, they were foreshadowed; in us, by God's gift and grace, they are fulfilled. For the blessed Elias was a type of the Lord, the Savior. For as Elias suffered persecution from the Jews, so our Lord, the true Elias, was rejected and despised by those very Jews.

Elias left his own nation; and Christ abandoned the synagogue. Elias went out into the desert; and Christ came into the world. Elias was fed in the desert by ministering ravens; and Christ in the desert of this world is comforted by the faith of the Gentiles.

For those ravens which at the command of the Lord ministered to blessed Elias were a figure of the Gentile people. And therefore it is said of the Church of the Gentiles: I am black but beautiful, O ye daughters of Jerusalem. Whence is the Church black but beautiful? She is black by nature, beautiful by grace. Whence black? Behold I was conceived in iniquities, and in sins did my mother bring me forth. Whence beautiful? Thou shalt sprinkle me with hyssop and I shall be cleansed: Thou shalt wash me, and I shall be made whiter than snow.

R. Ye mountains of Gelboe, let neither dew nor rain come upon you, * For upon you have fallen the valiant ones of Israel. V. O all ye mountains who are in his circle, may the Lord visit you; but let him pass over Gelboe. For. Glory. For.

X SUNDAY AFTER PENTECOST

I Nocturn

From the fourth book of Kings, c. 9, 29 - 37;
c. 10, 1 - 7

II Nocturn

Sermon of St. John Chrysostom

Let us not think that we shall be held excused for our sins if at any time we have found partners in them, for on the contrary, our punishment will be increased. Seeing that the serpent was punished more than the woman, in like degree the woman was punished more than the man. And Jezabel suffered greater penalties than Achab, who stole the vineyard; for in truth, it was she who had planned the whole matter and had prepared the occasion for the king's fall. Therefore thou also, if thou hast been the occasion of another's fall, shalt suffer more grievously than those whom thou hast ruined. For to sin alone is less harmful than to lead others into sin.

And so, if at any time we should see others sinning, let us not only refrain from urging them on, but let us draw them away from the very pit of wickedness lest we suffer the penalty of another's sin. Moreover, let us continually call to mind that terrible tribunal, the flames of fire, the chains that can never be loosed, the utter darkness, the gnashing of teeth, and the venomous worms. But thou sayest: God is kind. Are then all these things mere words, and was not that rich man punished who despised Lazarus, and were not the foolish virgins repelled by the bridegroom? Then, those who feared not Christ, will they not depart into the fire which was prepared for the devil? Then he whose garments were unseemly for the feast, will he not be cast out, bound hand and foot? Will not he who exacted the hundred pence from his fellow-servant be delivered over to the torturers? That which was said of the adulterers that truly their worm shall not die and their fire shall not be extinguished, will it not be true?

But does God merely threaten these things? Assuredly, wilt thou say. But tell me, I beg, how thou darest to speak openly of so great a matter and to put forth thy own opinion? I, indeed, both from what God has said and from what He has done, shall be able to prove the contrary. So that, if you are not convinced of what is to happen in the future, at least believe through what has already come to pass. For indeed those things cannot be called mere threats and words which have actually happened and have been realized in fact.

Who, then, was it who inundated the whole world by bringing about the deluge and caused that grave disaster, the ruin of almost the whole of our race? Who, then, was it who rained those bolts and darts of fire upon the land of the Sodomites? Who drowned all the host of Egypt in the sea? Who consumed with fire the synagogue of Abiron? Who slew those seventy thousand in one moment of time with a pestilence because of David's sin? Was it not God who brought about all these things, and more, upon them?

R. And it came to pass that when the Lord would take Elias by a whirlwind into heaven, * Eliseus cried, saying: My father, my father, the chariot of Israel, and the driver thereof. V. And as they went on walking and talking together, behold a fiery chariot an fiery horses parted them both asunder and Elias went up by a whirlwind into heaven. Eliseus. Glory. Eliseus.

XI SUNDAY AFTER PENTECOST

I Nocturn
From the fourth Book of Kings, c. 20, 1 - 11
II Nocturn

From the exposition of St. Jerome, Priest on the Prophet Isaias

Lest the heart of Ezechias should be lifted up after his unbelievable triumphs and his victory whilst yet a captive, he was visited with bodily sickness and heard that he was about to die, that he might turn to the Lord and beg him not to carry out his sentence. Which indeed we also read in the prophet Jonas, and in the threats made against

David, which were spoken of with regard to the future, and did not come to pass, not because God changes His mind, but because He wishes to awaken men to the knowledge of themselves. For the Lord repenteth Himself of evil.

And Ezechias turned his face to the wall because he was not able to go to the temple. Perhaps to the wall of the temple, near which Solomon had built a palace; or, simply, to the wall, so as to hide his tears from those who stood near him. And hearing that he was about to die, he prayed, not for life and many years, but left it to the judgment of God to grant what He pleased.

For he knew how in that manner Solomon had pleased God because he did not ask for many more years of life; but being then about to go to God, he makes mention of his deeds, how he had walked before God in truth and with a perfect heart. Happy he whose conscience in time of affliction can remember good works. For: Blessed are the clean of heart; for they shall see God. And even as it is elsewhere written: Who will boast that he has a pure heart? Which is thus explained: by his perfection of heart is meant that he has destroyed the idols, opened the doors of the temple, broken in pieces the brazen serpent, and done the other things which are mentioned in the Scriptures.

And he wept with much weeping, because it seemed that the Lord's promise to David would be made void by his death. For at that time Ezechias had no children; for after his death, Manasses began to reign in Judea, being then twelve years old: from which it is clear, that Manasses was begotten after the third year of the new span of life granted to Ezechias. Therefore, Ezechias was all tears because he despaired of Christ being born of his seed. Others assert that very many holy men are terrified by death, on account of their uncertainty as regards the judgment and their ignorance of the sentence of God, as to what place will be allotted them.

R. The number of my sins is greater than that of the sands of the seashore, and my sins are multiplied: and I am not worthy to look up to the height of heaven because of the multitude of my iniquities: for I have provoked Thy wrath, * And done evil in Thy sight. V. For I acknowledge my iniquity, and my sin is continually before me, for against Thee only have I sinned. And done. Glory. And done.

I SUNDAY OF AUGUST

I Nocturn

From the Proverbs of Solomon, c. 1, 1 - 22

II Nocturn

From a Treatise of St. Ambrose, Bishop,
on Psalm 118

The prophet says that the beginning of wisdom is the fear of the Lord. What, then, is the beginning of wisdom, but to renounce the world? Because, to savour of the things of the world is foolishness. Therefore the Apostle says that the wisdom of this world is foolishness with God. But the fear of the Lord itself, unless it is according to knowledge, profits nothing, nay, it is hurtful to many.

The Jews indeed had a zeal for God; yet because it was not according to knowledge, this very zeal and fear led them into a greater offence against God. In that they circumcised their infant sons and kept the sabbath, they showed fear of God; but not understanding that the law was spiritual, they circumcised their bodies, and not their hearts.

And why do I speak of the Jews? There are some even among ourselves who have the fear of God, but not according to knowledge, laying down precepts too hard for human nature to bear. They fear God in that they seem to themselves to have regard for discipline and to enjoin the practice of virtue; but they lack knowledge, in that they have no compassion for the weakness of nature, nor do they consider whether a thing can be done or not. Let not, then, the fear of God be unreasonable. For indeed, true wisdom begins with the fear of God, neither is it spiritual wisdom without the fear of God; therefore this fear should never lack wisdom.

Holy fear is a good base for the word. For, just as any statue is set upon a base and thereby its beauty is enhanced, and since when a statue is set upon its base it is thereby made steady: so the word of God is better placed upon the base of holy fear, and is more strongly rooted in the breast of one who fears the Lord, that the word may not fall off from the heart of man, that birds may not come and carry it off, as from the heart of one who is careless and neglectful.

R. Give me, O Lord, wisdom that sitteth by Thy throne, and cast me not off from among Thy children: * For I am Thy servant, and the son of Thy handmaid. V. Send her from the throne of Thy greatness, that she may be with me, and may labor with me. For I am. Glory. For I am.

II SUNDAY OF AUGUST

I Nocturn

From the Book of Ecclesiastes, c. 1, 1 - 17

II Nocturn

Sermon of St. John Chrysostom

So long as Solomon's desires were set upon the things of this world, he looked upon them as of importance and worthy of admiration, and expended much care and labor upon them, building magnificent palaces, heaping up gold in plenty, gathering together choirs of singers and servants of every degree for the table and the kitchen, seeking pleasure for his soul in the beauty of gardens and shapely bodies, and in a word, giving himself up to the pursuits of enjoyment and recreation in every possible way.

But when he came to himself again, and from out that dark pit, as it were, was able once more to look upon the light of true wisdom, then he uttered that saying so high, so worthy of heaven: "Vanity of vanities, and all is vanity." And you also, if you will to do so, will give voice to this opinion, and even a more forcible one, concerning those ill-timed pleasures if for awhile you will lay aside your evil habits.

But although so diligent a pursuit of wisdom was not required in those former ages of Solomon's time, for the old law neither forbade these indulgences, nor held it folly to enjoy other superfluities, but yet, even in such circumstances, we can see how vile and full of deception these things are.

As for us, we are called to a higher life, and we must climb to a loftier summit, and be trained in a nobler school; and for what other reason, than that we are bidden to prepare for a life like that of the heavenly powers, the life of the soul, not of the body?

R. The fear of the Lord is the beginning of wisdom: * A good understanding have all they that do thereafter: His praise endureth forever and ever. V. Love is the keeping of His laws: for the fear of the Lord is the whole of wisdom. A good. Glory. A good.

III SUNDAY OF AUGUST

I Nocturn
From the Book of Wisdom, c. 1, 1 - 13

II Nocturn

From the Book of Offices of St. Ambrose, Bishop

Great is the glory of justice. She is made for others rather than for herself, she assists our fellowship and union, she holds the highest place that all things may be subject to her judgment, that she may give help to others, bestowing money upon them, not refusing to serve them, and taking upon herself the dangers of others. Who would not wish to hold this citadel of virtue, unless that former covetousness had weakened and distorted the strength of so great a virtue? For indeed, when we desire to increase our wealth, to amass money, to acquire lands and estates, to surpass others in riches, we put off the image of justice, and lose the charity which obliges us to do good to one another.

And how wide the field of justice is may be realized from this, that she takes no account of places, persons, or times, even as regards enemies; so that if a place or day of battle has been agreed upon with an enemy, it would be considered contrary to justice to change the place or begin before the time. For it concerns justice also whether an enemy is taken in battle by hard fighting, or surrenders himself, or is overcome by some chance.

If therefore justice is observed in war, how much more ought it to be observed in peace? The foundation of justice, therefore, is faith. For the hearts of the just meditate upon faith; and when the just man accuses himself, he bases his justice on faith. For then is his justice made manifest if his confession is sincere.

And accordingly, the Lord said by the mouth of Isaias: Behold, I lay a stone in the foundation of Sion; that is: Christ in the foundation of the Church. For the faith of all is Christ; but the Church is, as it were, a pattern of justice, the common law of all; she prays in common, works is common, in common she is tried. Lastly, he who denies himself to himself, he indeed is just, he indeed is worthy of Christ. And therefore did Paul make Christ the foundation, that we might place thereon the works of justice because faith is the foundation.

R. Remove far from me the wicked and deceitful word, O Lord: * Give me neither riches nor beggary, but give me only the necessaries of life. V. Two things I have asked of Thee, deny them not to me before I die. Give. Glory. Give.

IV SUNDAY OF AUGUST

I Nocturn

From the Book of Ecclesiasticus, c. 1, 1 - 16

II Nocturn

From the Book of Morals of St. Gregory, Pope

Some there are who are careless how they live their lives, and, untouched by remorse, they know not how to take good advice, for their heart is set upon passing things and things eternal are not understood, or, if understood, they are treated with disdain; and while they take no account of the heavenly goods which they have lost, they think, poor wretches, that they are happy in the possession of earthly goods. For in no wise do they raise their eyes to the light of truth, for which they were created; in no wise do they direct a longing gaze to the contemplation of the eternal fatherland; but, giving themselves up to those things to which they are inclined, they prefer the exile which is their lot to the fatherland, and rejoice in the darkness which they suffer as though it were the brightest light.

The minds of the elect, on the contrary, recognizing the nothingness of all that passes away, seek after the things for which they were created; and since nothing out side of God can satisfy them, their very faculty of thought, wearied in the effort of its search after God, finds rest in the hope and contemplation of its Creator and longs to be among the citizens above; and each one of them, while yet on earth and in the body, nevertheless, in mind soars above the world; each one bewails the weary exile he endures, and with incessant goads of love urges himself on to the fatherland above.

Therefore, when he sees with grief that what he has lost is eternal, he makes a good resolution to despise temporal things which pass away; and as he learns better how to carry out his purpose to forsake perishable things, so his grief increases that he cannot yet attain unto the things that endure. We must also note that they who act with haste are without compunction. For such as live without thought and let themselves drift at the mercy of events, do not weary their minds with anxious reflection.

But he who prudently settles on a plan of life

carefully takes account of himself, being circumspect in every action; first gently feeling it, as it were, with the foot of thought lest it unexpectedly turn against him; he takes thought lest fear should prevent him doing what ought to be done; lest haste should urge him to do what had better be deferred; lest, through the concupiscence of his nature, evil should get the better of him in open war; lest good should bring about his downfall by suggesting motives for vainglory.

R. Leave me not, O Lord, father and ruler of my life, lest I fall before my adversaries: * Lest my enemy rejoice over me. V. Take hold of arms and shield and rise up to help me. Lest my enemy. Glory. Lest my enemy.

V SUNDAY OF AUGUST

I Nocturn

From the Book of Ecclesiasticus, c. 5, 1 - 16

II Nocturn

Sermon of St. John Chrysostom

Delay thou not to be converted to the Lord, and put it not off from day to day; for thou knowest not what the morrow may bring forth. For delay is dangerous and to be dreaded; but safety is certain and sure if there is no delay. Therefore cultivate virtue; and thus, even if thou diest young thou wilt depart in safety; but if thou shouldst reach old age, thou wilt depart this life with much easiness and without trouble; and thou wilt have a twofold rejoicing, both because thou hast refrained from the evils of this life and because thou hast practiced virtue. Say not: The time will come when I shall be able to turn to God; for by these words God is greatly angered.

For why, since He Himself has promised thee life everlasting, wilt thou not labor in this present life which is short and fleeting; but behavest as slothfully and laxly as if the life thou seekest were shorter than this? Do not these daily convivialities, do not these banquets, do not these playhouses, do not these displays of wealth bear witness to the insatiable craving for wickedness? Consider well, that as often as thou hast gone sinning, so often hast thou damned thyself; for this is the nature of sin, that as soon as it is committed, the judge pronounces sentence.

Hast thou drunk to excess? Hast thou pampered thy belly? Hast thou been a robber? Do not go another step; turn thy steps in another direction; give thanks to God that He has not taken thee away in the midst of thy sins. Seek not to prolong the time wherein thou mayest do evil. Many who were living bad and vicious lives have perished suddenly and have gone to manifest damnation. Have a fear lest the same fate befall thee.

But to many, sayest thou, God has given time to

repent in extreme old age. What then? Will He also give it to thee? Perhaps He will, sayest thou. Perhaps? Does it often happen? Remember that it is of thy soul that thou art considering, then consider also the contrary and say: But what if He should not give me time? But, sayest thou, what if He does give it? May it be so, He does indeed give it sometimes; nevertheless, this is the safer and better way.

R. O Lord, Father and God of my life, do not abandon me to evil thoughts; give me not haughtiness of my eyes, and turn away from me all evil desires, O Lord; remove concupiscence from me, * And give me not over to a shameless and foolish mind, O Lord. V. O Lord, leave me not, lest my ignorances increase, and my offences be multiplied. And give. Glory. And give.

I SUNDAY IN SEPTEMBER

I Nocturn

From the Book of Job, c. 1, 1 - 11

II Nocturn

From the Book of Morals of St. Gregory, Pope

Sacred Scripture is held up to our mental vision as a kind of mirror that in it we may see our interior countenance. There indeed we learn both our deformity and our beauty; there we perceive how much ground we have gained; there, how far we are from proficiency. Moreover, it tells of the deeds of the saints and rouses the hearts of the weak to imitate them; and while on the one hand it commemorates their victories, on the other, it strengthens our weakness against the assaults of vice. So by its teaching the mind is rendered less dismayed amid combats in that it sees before it the triumphs of so many brave men.

Sometimes, indeed, it not only relates their virtues, but even takes note of their failures, that in the victory of brave men, we may see what we should lay hold of and imitate, and again, in their falls, learn what we ought to fear. For behold Job is described as ennobled by temptation; David, as overcome by it; that the virtue of the great might keep up our hope, we are uplifted to joy by the former, by the latter, we are kept down and made to fear. From the one source the hearer's mind is imbued with confidence springing from hope, and from the other, with humility arising from fear, with such effect that it may not swell with rash pride in that it is kept down by alarm, nor be so crushed by fear as to despair, in that it finds motive for confident hope in the example of virtue.

There was in the land of Hus a man named Job. We are told the dwelling place of the holy man in order that the merit of his righteousness may be brought out. For who does not know that Hus is in the land of the Gentiles? But the Gentile world, having no knowledge of its Creator, lived enchained in vice.

Therefore, let it be told where he dwelt that it may redound to his praise that he was good among the evil. For to be good amid good people calls for no great praise, whilst to be good among unrighteous men is praiseworthy. For as it is a graver fault not to be good when living with good men, so also is it highly praiseworthy to have lived righteously amidst the unrighteous.

R. My flesh is clothed with rottenness and the filth of dust, my skin is withered and drawn together; * Remember me, O Lord, for my life is but wind. V. My days have passed more swiftly than the web is cut by the weaver, and are consumed without any hope. Remember. Glory. Remember.

II SUNDAY IN SEPTEMBER

I Nocturn
From the Book of Job, c. 9, 1 - 17

II Nocturn
From the Book of Morals of St. Gregory, Pope

Indeed I know that it is so, and that man cannot be justified, compared with God. For man may be accredited with justice when not compared with God, but he loses that justice when compared with God. For whoever compares himself with God, deprives himself of the good which he has received. For he who attributes to himself the good which he has received fights against God with the very gifts of God. Whence, therefore, it is fitting that the humble should be exalted, and that the proud should be abased.

But because the holy man perceives that all the merit of our virtue is as vice when it is judged strictly by Him who judges the interior, rightly he subjoins: If he will contend with Him, he cannot answer Him one for a thousand.

In Holy Scripture the number of a thousand is commonly understood to express totality. Hence also the Psalmist says: Of the word which He commanded unto a thousand generations, when, notwithstanding, it is agreed that from the very beginning of the world until the coming of the Redeemer, not more than seventy-seven generations are reckoned by the Evangelists. Therefore, what is signified by the number of a thousand, save, until the bringing forth of the new offspring, the totality of the race foreseen? Likewise it is said by John: And they shall reign with Him a thousand years, because, indeed, the kingdom of Holy Church is established by being perfected in entireness.

For a unit ten times multiplied becomes ten; the number ten multiplied by itself is increased to an hundred; which again multiplied by ten becomes a thousand. Since we begin at one in order that we may come to a thousand, what in this place means the expression "one" but the beginning of good living? What is meant by the greatness of the number one thousand but the perfection of the same virtuous life? But to contend with God is for a man to assume to himself the credit of his own justice, and not to ascribe it to God. But let the holy man perceive that if he who has received the greatest gifts be uplifted by what he has received, he loses everything which he had possessed.

R. The fewness of my days shall be ended shortly; suffer me, Lord, that I may lament my sorrow a little, * Before I go to a land that is dark and covered with the mist of death. V. Thy hands have made me, O Lord, and fashioned me wholly round about; and dost Thou cast me down headlong of a sudden? Before. Glory. Before.

III SUNDAY IN SEPTEMBER

I Nocturn
From the Book of Tobias, c. 1, 1 - 15

II Nocturn
Sermon of St. Leo, Pope

I know, indeed, beloved, that very many of you are devout in your observance of all those practices which belong to the Christian Faith, so that such need not to be admonished by our exhortations. For what tradition has laid down and custom well es-

tablished is neither unknown to the learned nor neglected by the pious. But because it belongs to the
priestly office to have the general care of all the
children of the Church in those matters which are
profitable to both learned and simple, who are
equally dear to us, we exhort both alike that we
may celebrate the fast, of which the recurrence of
the seventh month reminds us, with lively faith, by
the discipline of soul and of body.

For the observance of temperance is therefore
specially assigned to the Ember seasons, in order
that, by the return of these selfsame in the course
of the year, we might learn how unceasingly we
need to be purified, and how, as long as we are
tossed about in the changes of this life, we need by
fasting and almsdeeds to be cleansed from the stain
of that sin which we have contracted by the frailty
of our flesh and our concupiscence.

Let us hunger a little, beloved, and take a little
from our habitual measure in order that we may
help the poor. Let the conscience of the generous
be made glad by the fruits of his liberality; and
whilst thou art giving joy, thou shalt receive thereby gladness. The love of thy neighbor is the love
of God, who declared that in the unity of this twofold charity lay all the fulfilment of the law and the
prophets. And that no man should doubt that what
he gives to man he offers to God, we have the saying of our Lord and Savior, when He spoke of feed-

ing and helping the poor: Whatever you have done to one of them you have done to Me.

Therefore, let us fast on the fourth and sixth ferias; and on Saturday let us celebrate the Vigils at the shrine of Blessed Peter the Apostle, by whose merits and prayers we believe that we shall be aided, so that we may please God by our fast and prayer.

R. It is time that I return to Him that sent Me, * But bless ye God and publish all His wonderful works. V. Give glory to Him in the sight of all that live, because He hath shown His mercy to you. But. Glory. But.

EMBER WEDNESDAY

The reading of the holy Gospel according to St. Mark

At that time: One of the multitude, answering, said to Jesus: Master I have brought Thee my son, having a dumb spirit. And so forth.

Homily of St. Bede the Venerable, Priest

According to Mark this demoniac, whom the Lord cured when He came down from the mountain, was deaf and dumb, but Matthew calls him a lunatic. He typifies those of whom it is written: The fool is fickle as the moon. Such never remain in the same state, but change now to one vice, now to another, their sins increasing and decreasing. They are dumb by not confessing the faith; in a measure deaf, in that they do not hear the word of truth. They foam at the mouth also when they are consumed with folly. For it is the mark of madmen and imbeciles and simpletons that they dribble at the mouth. They gnash their teeth when they are set on fire with fury; they pine away when they languish with the torpor of sloth; and live useless lives, never being strengthened by the practice of virtue.

But by this speech: And I spoke to Thy disciples to cast him out and they could not, he, by implication, accuses the Apostles; since a cure is sometimes rendered impossible, not owing to the powerlessness of them who cure, but owing to the defective faith of those who are to be cured: as witness the saying of the Lord: According to thy faith so be it done unto thee. And He, answering them, said: O incredulous generation, how long shall I be with you? How long shall I suffer you? Not that He was overcome with disgust, He who, meek and gentle as a lamb dumb before his shearer, did not open His mouth nor break out in words of anger; but as a physician who sees his patient disobey his orders, He says: How long shall I continue to visit thy house? how long shall I practice my art in vain, ordering thee to do one thing while thou dost another?

And He said to them: This kind can go out by nothing but by prayer and fasting. While He teaches His Apostles how the worst kind of devil must be cast out, He instructs all unto life, to the end that we may know that the most grievous trials, either from impure spirits or from men, must be overcome by fasts and prayers. And when the wrath of the Lord has been stirred, in order that He may requite us for our evil deeds, it may be appeased only by this remedy. But when we speak of fasting in general we mean not only abstinence from food, but likewise from all unlawful carnal pleasures, and also to restrain ourselves from all indulgence of our passions. Moreover, speaking generally of prayer, we mean not only those words by which we invoke the divine clemency, but likewise all those deeds which in faith we devoutly perform in the service of our Creator.

EMBER FRIDAY

The reading of the holy Gospel
according to St. Luke

At that time: One of the Pharisees desired Jesus to eat with him; and He went into the house of the Pharisee, and sat down to meat. And so forth.

Homily of St. Gregory, Pope

What is represented by the Pharisee, presuming upon his false righteousness, but the Jewish people;

what by the woman who was a sinner, coming and weeping at the feet of the Lord, but the Gentile world? She came with her alabaster box: She poured out her ointment: She stood behind at His feet: She washed them with her tears and wiped them with her hair, and ceased not to kiss those feet which she had so anointed and wiped. That woman stands also for us if, when we have sinned, we will return to the Lord with our whole heart and imitate her in the mourning of penance. And what is signified by the ointment but that odor of good report of which Paul says: In every place we are to God the good odor of Christ?

Therefore, if we shed abroad through the Church the good odor of good report by doing good works, what do we but pour our ointment upon the Lord's body? But the woman stood behind at the feet of Jesus; we stood opposite to the Lord's feet when, obstinate in sin, we resisted His ways. But if we be converted from our sins to true repentance, then we stand behind His feet for we follow in His footsteps against whom we once contended. The woman watered His feet with her tears, which indeed we do if we be moved with compassion towards the least of the members of our Lord: if we comfort His holy ones in tribulation, if we consider their sorrows as our own.

Hence we wipe the feet of the Lord with hair when out of charity we not only pity His saints, but also help them with our more abundant possessions, inasmuch as the hand shows itself more generous according as the mind is more moved by compassion. For he washes the feet of our Redeemer with his tears, but does not wipe them with his hair, who, however much he may sympathize with the sufferings of his neighbors, nevertheless, does not aid them with his superfluous goods. He weeps, but does not wipe the feet, who indeed gives words of pity, but fails to remove the source of the sufferings by ministering to his brethren what is lacking. The woman kissed the feet which she had wiped; which we also certainly do if we zealously love those whom we support by our liberality; so that the neediness of our neighbor is not irksome to us; nor his penury which we relieve burdensome to us; nor, whilst our hand ministers to his wants, does our heart slacken from compassion.

EMBER SATURDAY

The reading of the holy Gospel
according to St. Luke

At that time: Jesus spoke to the multitude this parable: A certain man had a fig tree planted in his vineyard, and he came seeking fruit on it, and found none. And so forth.

Homily of St. Gregory, Pope

Our Lord and Redeemer sometimes speaks through His Gospel by words only, sometimes by actions: sometimes one thing is taught by word and another by deed; but again, the same thing is taught both by word and by deed. Brethren, we have heard of two things from the Gospel: of an unfruitful fig tree and of a deformed woman, and to each of these is attached a religious significance. In the first He speaks by a parable; in the other, by a demonstration. But the barren tree and the afflicted woman stand for the same things, as do also the patience shown to the tree and the cure of the woman.

What does the fig tree represent but mankind? What does the crippled woman denote but that same human nature for which she stands? The fig tree is planted aright, the woman created sound; but having, of his own free will, fallen into sin, man keeps neither the fruit of good works nor the stature of right living. For, wilfully rushing into sin because he is unwilling to bear the fruit of obedience, he thereby loses his uprightness. That human nature, made in the likeness of God, when it loses its essential dignity, scorns to preserve what was planted aright or created sound. Three times the lord of the vineyard came to the fig tree, because God sought the human race, waiting for it and warning it, visiting it before the law, under the law, and under grace.

He came before the law in that, by the natural understanding, He made known how each, by his example, ought to act towards his neighbors. He came in the law, because He taught therein. After the law He came by grace, because by His presence He showed His love. Yet He complains that in three years He has found no fruit: because the minds of those perverse people, the inspired law of nature fails to correct; the precepts of the law, to instruct; and the miracles of the Incarnation, to convert. Who are represented by the cultivator of the vine but the ordained rulers who, while they preside over the Church, undoubtedly have care of the Lord's vineyard?

IV SUNDAY OF SEPTEMBER

I Nocturn

From the Book of Judith, c. 1, 1 - 12; c. 2, 1 - 3

II Nocturn

From the Book of St. Ambrose, Bishop, on Elias and Fasting

The mighty are forbidden to drink wine lest, when they have drunk, they forget wisdom. Indeed, those rulers who were eager to surrender themselves to Holofernes, the leader of the army of the king of the Assyrians, drank wine to excess. But the woman, Judith, drank not, fasting all the days of her widowhood except upon the solemn feast days. Thus armed, she went forth and foiled the whole army of the Assyrians. With the power of sober counsel she took away the head of Holofernes, preserved her own honor, and gained the victory.

For this woman, armed by fasting, entered the enemy's camp. Holofernes lay as one dead with wine, so that he could not feel the blow of the wound. Therefore, the fasting of one woman laid low the countless hosts of the Assyrians. Esther also became more beautiful by fasting, and the Lord increased His grace in reward of her abstinence. She delivered her whole people, that is to say, the whole Jewish nation, from a bitter persecution so as to make the king subject to her.

Therefore, she who fasted continuously for three days and washed her body with water was more pleasing and procured vengeance; but Aman, when he spoke boastfully at the royal banquet, paid the penalty of his drunkenness. Therefore, fasting is a sacrifice of reconciliation, and increase of strength, which by the growth of grace has made even women strong.

Fasting knows not fraud, knows not the lot of the extortioner; the table of those who fast does not lead to enjoyment, but the fast gives grace even to the guests. A feast is the more pleasing after hunger, while by constant repetition it becomes irksome, and if long continued, ceases to be valued. Fasting is the sauce of food. The meat is more welcome in proportion as the appetite is more keen.

R. We know no other God but the Lord, in whom

we hope: * He despiseth us not, neither doth He put away His salvation from our nation. V. Let us seek His mercy with tears, and humble our souls before Him. He. Glory. He.

V SUNDAY OF SEPTEMBER

I Nocturn

From the Book of Esther, c. 1, 1 - 9

II Nocturn

From the Book of Offices of S. Ambrose, Bishop

What did Queen Esther do? In order to deliver her nation from danger (which was a virtuous and noble object), did she not offer herself to die, and feared not the anger of the pitiless king? And this Persian king, though fierce and proud of heart, yet judged it fitting to show grace to the man who showed the plot that was made against him, to release a free people from slavery, to save them from death, and not to spare him who would have persuaded such an unworthy deed.

Finally, he delivered up to the gallows him whom he had placed second only to himself and had held as the greatest of all his friends, because he realized that he himself had been disgraced by his crafty counsels. For that worthy friendship which preserves virtue is certainly to be preferred to riches, honors or power; for such is wont to follow after justice, truly preferring nothing thereto. Such was the friendship of Jonathan who, because of his love, sought safety neither from the anger of his father nor from his personal danger. Such was that of Achimelech who, for the sake of the virtue of hospitality, chose to die himself rather than betray the fugitive.

Therefore, nothing is to be preferred before justice; but lest in considering friendship this should be omitted, Scripture also admonishes us. For there are many questions raised by philosophers: Whether for the sake of his friend a man should act against his country that he may obey the friend; Whether it behooves a man to break faith, while favoring and serving the interests of a friend.

And Scripture also says: As a club and a sword and an ironpointed arrow; so is he who bears false witness against his friend. But observe the word added: not the bearing witness against a friend is blamed, but false witness. For what if the cause of God or the need of the fatherland compels a man to testify against a friend? Ought friendship to outweigh the interests of religion; injustice to outweigh charity?

R. Remember me for good, O Lord God: * And set not aside the works of mercy which I wrought in the house of my God and in His sacred rites. V. Be mindful of me, O Lord my God. And. Glory. And.

I SUNDAY OF OCTOBER

I Nocturn

From the First Book of Machabees, c. 1, 1 - 16

II Nocturn

From the Book of the Offices of S. Ambrose, Bishop

Perhaps military glory holds some so enthralled that they think warlike valor the only bravery; and that I have digressed to these other subjects because we are lacking in military glory. How valiant was Josue the son of Nun, that in one battle he laid low five kings with their hosts! Then, when he made war upon the Gabaonites and feared lest the oncoming night might hinder the victory, with strong mind and faith he cried: Let the sun stand still; and it stood still until the victory was gained. Gedeon, with three hundred men achieved a triumph over a great and fierce enemy. The youth, Jonathan, showed great valor in battle.

What shall I say of the Machabees? But first I will speak concerning their ancestors, who, when they were prepared to fight for the temple of God and their rights, and by the crafty enemy had been attacked on the Sabbath day, preferred to expose to wounds their unarmed bodies rather than retaliate, lest they should violate the Sabbath. Therefore, joyfully they gave themselves up to death. But considering how, following this example, the whole people might perish, the Machabees avenged the slaughter of their innocent brethren when they themselves were drawn into battle, even though it was the Sabbath. Whence, afterwards, when the enraged king, Antiochus, waged war through his generals Lysias, Nicanor and Gorgias, he was so defeated that, together with the eastern and Assyrian forces, forty-eight thousand were struck down in the middle of the plain by three thousand.

Consider the valor of one soldier of the same Judas Machabeus. For Eleazar, having caught sight of the elephant arrayed in the royal harness towering above the rest, thought that the king was there, and rushing forward, dashed into the middle of the legion. He threw away his shield, and, killing a man with either hand until he reached the beast, going beneath it, he killed it by stabbing upwards with his sword. So the falling animal crushed Eleazar and he died.

What valor was in that soul! first that he did not fear death; then that, surrounded by hostile hosts, he let himself be carried away into the thick of the enemy that he might penetrate to the center of the army, and being the fiercer as he was contemptuous of death, casting away his shield, he fought his way with both hands to the huge bulk of the wounded beast, and going beneath it, went right under so that he might strike a more effective blow. Perishing with it rather than crushed in its fall, he was buried in his triumph.

R. Thine is power, Thine is the kingdom, O
Lord: Thou art above all nations: * Give peace
in our days, O Lord. V. O God, Creator of all
things, dreadful and strong, just and merciful. Give.
Glory. Give.

II SUNDAY OF OCTO0BER

I Nocturn

From the first Book of Machabees, c. 4, 36 - 51

II Nocturn

From the Book of St. Augustine, Bishop,
on the City of God

After the Jewish nation ceased to have prophets,
that is to say, at that time after the captivity in
Babylon when, having restored the temple, they
hoped for a better future, without doubt their state
became worse. For so, indeed, did that carnal people understand what was foretold by the prophet
Aggeus when he said: Great shall be the glory of
this last house, more than of the first. That this
was said concerning the new covenant, he showed
a little before, where, plainly promising Christ, he
says: And I will move all nations, and the Desired
of all nations shall come.

For by such chosen ones of the nations there is
built, through the new covenant, with living stones,
a house of God far more glorious than was that

temple which was built by Solomon the king, and restored after the captivity. For this reason, therefore, that nation had no prophets from that time; but it was afflicted with many calamities by kings of alien race, and by the Romans themselves, lest it might be thought that this prophecy of Aggeus had been fulfilled by that restoration of the temple.

For not long afterwards, Alexander came and subdued the land; when, although it was not laid waste because they dared not resist him, and thus, being very easily subdued, they received favorable terms; nevertheless, the glory of that house was not so great as it was under the free dominion of their own kings. Then Ptolemy, the son of Lagus, after the death of Alexander, carried them thence into Egypt as captives; his successor Ptolemy Philadelphus, most benevolently let them go; and through him it came about that we have the version of the Scriptures called the Septuagint.

Then they were crushed by wars, which are recounted in the books of the Machabees. After this they were taken captive by Ptolemy, king of Alexandria, who was called Epiphanes; then by Antiochus, king of Syria, who compelled them by many and most grievous sufferings to worship idols, and filled the temple itself with the sacrilegious superstitions of the Gentiles; yet their most vigorous leader, Judas, who is also called Machabeus, after he had defeated the generals of Antiochus, cleansed it from all that defilement of idolatry.

R. The nations are come together against us to destroy us, and we know not what we should do: * O Lord God, our eyes look to Thee that we may not perish. V. Thou knowest what they intend against us. How shall we be able to stand before their face unless Thou help us? O Lord God. Glory. O Lord God.

III SUNDAY OF OCTOBER

I Nocturn
From the first Book of Machabees, c. 9, 1 - 20

II Nocturn
From the Book of Offices of St. Ambrose, Bishop

Since courage is proved not only in success, but also in misfortune, let us consider the death of Judas Machabeus. For after having conquered Nicanor, the general of king Demetrius, Judas, fearless against a royal army of twenty thousand men, joined battle with eight hundred. And when these wished to surrender lest they should be crushed by superior numbers, he persuaded them to embrace a glorious death rather than a base flight. Let us not stain our glory, he said.

Thus, when they began the conflict and had fought from dawn till evening, when he attacked on the right wing where he perceived the strongest forces of the enemy, he easily checked them. But while he followed up the fugitives, he exposed himself to attack from behind; therefore, he found a death which was more glorious than a victory. Why should I instance further his brother, Jonathan, who, fighting with a small force against the royal armies, deserted by his men, and left with only two, yet repaired the fortunes of war, discomfited the enemy, and recalled his own deserters to associate them to his triumph?

You have warlike courage, which is of no ordinary nobility and dignity in that it prefers death to slavery or disgrace. But what shall I say of the sufferings of the martyrs? And lest we should digress further, the sons of the Machabees gained no less a triumph over the proud king Antiochus than did their own parents; as the latter overcame by arms so did the former without arms.

Unconquered, the band of seven youths stood surrounded by the royal legions; tortures failed, torturers desisted, but the martyrs did not flinch. One, stripped of the skin of his head, had changed his outward appearance, but increased his virtue; another, ordered to put forth his tongue that it might be cut out, answered: The Lord, who heard Moses when he was silent, hears not only those who speak. He heard the silent thoughts of his kindred more than the voices of all. Thou fearest the scourge of the tongue; fearest thou not the scourge of blood? For blood, too, hath its voice, which cries unto God as cried the blood of Abel.

R. Thine is power; thine is the kingdom, O Lord: Thou art above all nations: * Give peace in our days, O Lord. V. O God, Creator of all things, dreadful and strong, just and merciful. Give. Glory. Give.

IV SUNDAY OF OCTOBER

I Nocturn

From the second Book of Machabees, c. 1, 1 - 6

II Nocturn

From the Treatise of St. John Chrysostom
on the forty-third Psalm

We have heard, O God, with our ears: our fathers have declared to us the work thou hast wrought in their days. The Prophet utters this psalm indeed, but he speaks not in his own person, but in the person of the Machabees, relating and foretelling what events were to happen at that time. For such are the Prophets. They outrun all times, past, present, and future.

But in order that their details in the subject may be more intelligible, we must first state who were these Machabees, and what they suffered and what they did. For when Antiochus, surnamed Epiphanes, had invaded Judea and laid all waste and had forced many who dwelt there to depart from the laws of their fathers, those men remained unsullied by these temptations. And when a serious war broke out and they could do nothing to help themselves, they hid themselves as also did the Apostles. For they did not always rush openly into the midst of dangers, but sometimes withdrew both by flight and by concealing themselves.

But after a short respite, like eager animals leaping out of their caves and coming forth from their lairs, they swore that thenceforth they would no longer save only themselves, but also others whomever they could. And going out through the state and the whole country, they gathered together as many as they found who were still healthy and steadfast; and even many who were weary and had been led away, they persuaded to return to the law of their fathers.

For they told them that God was kind and merciful, and that He never withholds that salvation which is obtained by penance. And when they said this, they had a levy of the most valiant men. For they fought not for their wives, their children, and their handmaids, and because of the ruin and captivity of their fatherland; but for the law and state of their fathers. And God was their leader. Therefore, when they arrayed their battle line and were careless of their lives, they overwhelmed their adversaries, trusting not to arms, but considering that the cause of the war sufficed in place of all armor. Moreover, when they went forth to the conflict, they did not call forth lamentations nor sing battle songs, as some do; nor did they admit flute players as was done in other camps; but they invoked the aid of the most high God, that He might be with them and help them, and strengthen their hand, because that war which they waged was fought for His glory.

R. Open Thine eyes, O Lord, and behold our affliction; for the Gentiles have come round about us to punish us * But do Thou, O Lord, stretch forth Thine arm and deliver our souls. V. Punish them that afflict us and with pride do us wrong, and keep Thy portion. But. Glory. But.

I SUNDAY OF NOVEMBER

I Nocturn

From the Book of Ezechiel the Prophet, c. 1, 1 - 12

II Nocturn

From the Exposition of St. Gregory, Pope, on Ezechiel the Prophet

It is customary in prophetic speech that first the person, time, and place should be described, and afterwards the telling of the mystery of the prophecy should be begun. Because the prophet would show forth the truth more perfectly, he first fixes the literal story, as if it were the root, and then brings forth the fruit of the spirit by signs and allegories. Therefore Ezechiel tells us the period of his own life, saying: It came to pass in the thirtieth year, in the fourth month, on the fifth day of the month. And indicating the place, he adds: When I was in the midst of the captives, by the river Chobar the heavens were opened and I saw the visions of God. He also gives the historic period, saying also: On the fifth day of the month, the same was the fifth year of the captivity of king Joachim. That he may clearly describe himself, he also mentions his family, adding: And the word of the Lord came to Ezechiel the priest, the son of Buzi.

But the first question which occurs to us is why does the writer, who up to now has said nothing, begin thus: And it came to pass in the thirtieth year? For *and* is a conjunction, and we know that no speech can be joined by it unless there be a preceding phrase to which to join it. Since he has said nothing, why does he say: And it came to pass, when there is nothing to which the beginning may be joined? In this case we must consider that as we look to the letter, so the Prophets look to the spirit; and those things are present to them which we, owing to our ignorance, cannot see.

Whence it happens that in the mind of the Prophets, interior things are so united to exterior things that they are seen by them at one and the same time; and in them is accomplished together both the word which they hear within, and the word which they speak without. Therefore it is evident why he, who had said nothing, began saying: And it came to pass in the thirtieth year, for this speech spoken outwardly is joined to that which he had heard inwardly.

Hence he has continued the words produced in the inner vision, and begins saying: And it came to pass. For he has subjoined what he is beginning to say outwardly as though what he saw within were outwardly visible. But in his saying that in the thirtieth year he received the spirit of prophecy, there is something worthy of our consideration; namely, that the power to teach does not correspond with the use of reason until a certain age. Whence the Lord Himself in the twelfth year of His age, sitting amid the doctors in the temple, willed to be found, not teaching, but asking questions.

R. Upon thy walls, O Jerusalem I have appointed watchmen: * All the day and the night they shall not hold their peace to praise the name of the Lord. V. They shall proclaim My might unto the nations, and declare My glory unto the Gentiles. All the day. Glory. All the day.

II SUNDAY OF NOVEMBER

I Nocturn

From Ezechiel the Prophet, c. 21, 1 - 15

II Nocturn

From the Exposition of St. Jerome, Priest, on Ezechiel the Prophet

Because he had said previously: They say to me: doth he speak parables? and the people demanded plain speech; wherefore, what the Lord spoke by figure or parable and as others translate, proverb, He now speaks more plainly. The forest of Nageb and Darom and Theman represent Jerusalem and her temple, the holy of holies, and all the land of Judea. By the flame which will burn up the forest is to be understood the devastating sword, which has been unsheathed to destroy both the just and the wicked. For this is the green wood and the dry. Whence the Lord said: For if in the green wood they do these things, what shall be done in the dry?

At first he had said: Prophesy or let fall thy word to the South, towards the south wind and to the forest of the South. But because the people did not understand the sayings of the prophets, and this prophecy seemed hard to understand, the second time he explains more clearly that the forest of the south is Jerusalem; and all the barren trees to the roots of which the axe is laid are her inhabitants, and the fire is to be interpreted as the sword.

A third time He orders the prophet that when they are silent and do not ask him why he prophesies these things, he shall act in such a manner as to make them question him and shall answer the things which the Lord has spoken. Groan, He says, not in a weak voice nor with light sorrow, but in deep compunction, that thy wailing may come in bitterness of soul from thy innermost being.

And thou shalt do this before them that they may ask thee why thou dost consume thyself with so great sighing and what evil has come upon thee that thou shouldst mourn in such manner. And thou shalt answer them in My words: For this reason I weep and cannot hide my sorrow of heart, because what I have heard which is ever resounding in my ears will be fulfilled in deed. There is coming the threatening army of the fierce Babylonian, who shall come and invest Jerusalem. Then every heart shall melt with fear and every hand fall powerless; and terror shall so seize upon men's minds that none shall dare to resist.

R. We looked for peace and it came not; we sought good and behold trouble; we acknowledge, O Lord, our wickedness: * Forget us not for ever. V. We have sinned, we have done wickedly, we have acted unjustly, O Lord, against all Thy justices. Forget. Glory. Forget.

III SUNDAY OF NOVEMBER

I Nocturn

From the Book of Daniel the Prophet, c. 1, 1 - 15

II Nocturn

From the Book of St. Athanasius, Bishop, to Virgins

If any approach thee and say: Do not fast often lest thou become weakly, do not believe or listen to them, for through them the enemy is dissuading thee. Remember what is written, how that when the three children and Daniel and other youths had been led away captive by Nabuchodonoser, king of Babylon, it was ordered that they should eat the food and drink the wine from the royal table. Daniel and the three children did not wish to be defiled by eating from the king's table, but said to the eunuch who had charge of them: Give us of the seeds of the earth and we will eat: But the eunuch said: I fear the king who hath appointed you meat and drink; lest perchance your face shall appear to the king thinner than those of the other children who are fed from the royal table, and he will punish me.

And they said to him: Try thy servants ten days and let pulse be given us to eat. And he gave them pulse to eat and water to drink; and he brought them into the king's presence, and their faces appeared fairer than those of the other children who were fed from the king's table. Do you see what is the result of fasting? It cures diseases, it dries up the humors of the body; it drives away demons; it banishes evil thoughts; it makes the mind clearer; it purifies the heart; it sanctifies the body; and at length it places man before the throne of God.

And lest you should think that I say this rashly, you have the witness borne by our Savior in the Gospels. For when His disciples asked Him how they might cast out unclean spirits, the Lord answered: This kind can go out by nothing but by prayer and fasting. Therefore, whoever is vexed by an evil spirit, if he be mindful of this remedy and use it, I say that, fearing the power of fasting, the evil spirit will depart vanquished. For the devils are greatly pleased by surfeiting, drunkenness, and bodily indulgences.

In fasting is great strength, and by it are done great and marvelous things. How otherwise could men perform such wonders and work such miracles, so that by their means God granted health to the sick, but simply by means of spiritual exercises, humility of heart, and a good conversation? For fasting is the food of angels; and he who makes use of it is counted among the ranks of the angels.

R. The Lord hath sent His angel and hath shut up the mouth of the lions, * And they have not hurt me, forasmuch as before Him injustice hath not been found in me. V. God hath sent His mercy and His truth: He hath delivered my soul from the midst of the young lions. And they. Glory. And they.

IV SUNDAY OF NOVEMBER
I Nocturn
From the Book of Osee the Prophet, c. 1, 1 - 11
II Nocturn

From the Book of St. Augustine, Bishop,
on the City of God

The prophet Osee speaks so very profoundly that it is a laborious work to penetrate his meaning. But something must be taken therefrom and here set forth, according to our promise. And it shall be, says he, in the place where it was said to them: You are not my people; and they shall be called the sons of the living God. Even the Apostles understood this as a prophetic testimony of the calling of the people of the Gentiles which formerly did not belong to God.

And because this same people of the Gentiles is itself spiritually among the children of Abraham, and for that reason is rightly spoken of as Israel; therefore he continues and says: And the children of Juda, and the children of Israel shall be gathered together in one, and they shall appoint themselves one headship, and shall come up out of the land.

If we set ourselves to expound this further, we shall weaken the force of the prophetic eloquence. Let the reader but call to mind that corner-stone, and those two walls, the one of the Jews, the other of the Gentiles, and he will recognize them, the one under the name of the sons of Juda, the other under the name of sons of Israel, supporting themselves by one and the same headship and coming up out of the land..

But that those carnal Israelites who now refuse to believe in Christ shall believe, that is to say, their descendants shall (for it is evident that the former will pass by death to their own place), this same prophet testifies saying: For the children of Israel shall sit many days without prince, without altar, without sacrifice, without priesthood, without manifestations. Who can fail to see that such is the present state of the Jews?

R. Before the face of Thine anger, O God, the whole earth is troubled: * But Thou, O Lord, have mercy, and make not an end utterly. V. O Lord, our Lord: how admirable is Thy name! But Thou. Glory. But Thou.

V SUNDAY OF NOVEMBER

I Nocturn

From the Book of Micheas the Prophet, c. 1, 1 - 9

II Nocturn

Sermon of St. Basil the Great
on the Thirty-third Psalm

When the longing to sin comes upon thee, I wish thee to consider that dread and awful judgment-seat of Christ where, exalted upon a throne, the judge sits on high, but every creature shall stand, trembling before His glorious countenance. One by one we shall be led before Him to render an account of the deeds we have done in this life.

At once angels of terrible and hideous aspect will take their stand beside those who have wrought great evil in this life. These angels have fiery countenances and scorching breath, and show their evil will by their faces like to the night, because of their despair and hatred of mankind.

Think on that deep abyss, that impenetrable darkness, that fire which has the power of burning, yet lacks the brightness and light of fire. Think upon the worms breathing out venom, devouring the flesh, ever consuming, yet never satisfied, inflicting unbearable pain with their gnawing. Lastly, consider the most terrible of all torments, the everlasting confusion and hatred. Fear these things and let thy fear lead thee to bridle the lust of sin.

The prophet promised to teach this fear of the Lord; not simply to all, but to those who were willing to hear; not to those who have wandered afar off, but to those who run to Him, desiring their salvation. He does not promise to teach those who are strangers to the promises, but those who are reconciled and united with the Word Himself, by the baptism of the adoption of sons. Wherefore He says: Come, that is, approach to Me by good works as sons, for by the regeneration you are become children of the light; hear you who have the ears of your hearts opened: I will teach you the fear of the Lord: that is to say, of Him Whom we have just described in our discourse.

R. Before the face of Thine anger, O God, the whole earth is troubled: * But Thou, O Lord have mercy, and make not an end utterly. V. O Lord, our Lord: how admirable is Thy name! But Thou. Glory. But Thou.

Homilies And Gospels For
The Sundays After Pentecost

IV SUNDAY AFTER PENTECOST

III Nocturn

The reading of the holy Gospel
according to St. Luke

At that time: When the multitude pressed upon Jesus to hear the word of God, He stood by the lake of Genesareth. And so forth.

Homily of St. Ambrose, Bishop

Since the Lord bestowed health upon so many, no matter what their disease, neither time nor place could keep back the multitude of those who wished to be healed. Evening fell, and still they followed Him; He came to the borders of the lake, and still they pressed on; therefore the Lord went up into Peter's boat. This is the ship which, according to Matthew, is still tossing about in the sea, but according to Luke is filled with fishes. From this we may learn how in the beginning the Church was tossed about by storms, but afterwards was filled to overflowing.

The fish signify men swimming through the waters of this life. In the ship of Matthew Christ sleeps in the midst of His disciples, in the ship of Luke He gives commands; for He sleeps with the lukewarm, but watches with the perfect. This ship has nothing to fear, for she is steered by wisdom, she has no traitors on board, the wind of faith fills her sails. How could she be troubled when she is commanded by Him upon Whom the Church is stayed? Where there is little faith, there indeed is fear; but here is safety, for here is perfect love.

Even if the others are ordered to let down their nets, yet to Peter alone it is said: Launch out into the deep, that is, into the depths of doctrine. What is there so deep as to behold the depth of the divine riches, to know the Son of God and to take upon oneself to make profession of the divine generation? Though the human mind cannot by any effort of reason fully understand this mystery, yet it is grasped by a profound faith.

For though it is not given me to know in what manner He was born, yet I may not ignore the fact that He was born. I know not the order of this generation, but I acknowledge its source. We were not present when the Son of God was born of the Father, but we have heard the voice of the Father speaking to His Son. If we do not believe God, whom shall we believe? For we believe only what we have seen or heard; now sight is often deceived, but faith cometh by hearing.

R. God heareth all things: He hath sent His angel, and taken me from guarding my father's sheep: * And He hath anointed me with the oil of His mercy. V. The Lord, who delivered me out of the mouth of the lion, and freed me from the paw of the wild beast. And. Glory. And.

✠ Continuation of the holy Gospel according to St. Luke.—At that time: When the multitude pressed upon Jesus to hear the word of God, He stood by the lake of Genesareth. And He saw two ships standing by the lake; but the fisherman were gone out of them, and were washing their nets; and going up into one of the ships that was Simon's, He desired him to draw back a little from the land: and sitting, He taught the multitudes from the ship. Now when He had ceased to speak, He said to Simon: Launch out into the deep, and let down your nets for a draught. And Simon, answering, said to Him: Master, we have labored all the night, and have taken nothing, but at Thy word I will let down the net. And when they had done this, they enclosed a very great multitude of fishes; and their net broke; and they beckoned to their partners that were in the other ship, that they should come and help them; and they came, and filled both the ships so that they were almost sinking. Which when Simon Peter saw, he fell down at the feet of Jesus saying: Depart from me, for I am a sinful man, O Lord. For he was wholly astonished, and all that were with him, at the draught of fishes which they had taken; and so were also James and John the sons of Zebedee, who were Simon's partners. And Jesus saith to Simon: Fear not, from henceforth thou shalt catch men. And having brought their ships to land, leaving all things they followed Him.

LET US PRAY

Grant, we beseech Thee, O Lord, that for us the affairs of the world may be peacefully directed according to Thy plan; and Thy Church may be made joyful by a peaceful devotion. Through our Lord.

V SUNDAY AFTER PENTECOST

III Nocturn

The reading of the holy Gospel
according to St. Matthew

At that time: Jesus said to His disciples: Except your justice abound more than that of the Scribes and Pharisees, you shall not enter the kingdom of heaven. And so forth.

Homily of St. Augustine, Bishop

The righteousness of the Pharisees is that they shall not kill; the righteousness of those who are destined to enter into the kingdom of heaven is that they shall not be angry without cause. Not to kill, is therefore the least commandment; and whosoever shall break that, shall be called the least in the kingdom of heaven. But whosoever shall fulfil that commandment not to kill, will not necessarily be great and fit for the kingdom of heaven; but yet he has ascended to a certain degree; he will be made perfect, however, if he refrains from anger without cause; and if he shall do this, he will be much further removed from the guilt of murder.

And, therefore, He who teaches that we should not be angry does not destroy the law which forbids us to kill, but rather completes it; so that we preserve our innocence both outwardly when we do not kill, and in the heart when we refrain from anger. There are, then, degrees in these sins; so that, first of all, a man is angry and keeps that feeling unexpressed in his heart. But if now that emotion shall draw forth an exclamation of anger that does not have any definite meaning, which gives evidence of that feeling of the mind by the very fact of the outbreak wherewith he is assailed with whom one is angry; then indeed, this is more than if the rising anger were repressed by silence.

But if there is heard not merely an exclamation of anger, but also a definite word by which the person using it now indicates and signifies a distinct censure of him against whom it is directed, then, who is there that doubts that this is something more than if merely an exclamation of anger were to be uttered? Observe now also the three degrees of liability: to the judgment, to the council, and to the hell of fire. For in the judgment an opportunity is still given for defence.

But in the council, although there is wont to be a judgment, nevertheless, because the very fact of a distinction being made compels us to acknowledge that there is a certain difference in this passage, the pronouncing of the sentence seems to belong to the council; inasmuch as it is not now the case of the accused himself that is in question, whether he is to be condemned or not; but, it is a conferring with one another, on the part of those who are judging, as to what punishment he, who, it is clear, is to be condemned, ought to be condemned to suffer. But as to the hell of fire, it does not treat as a doubtful matter either the condemnation, like the judgment, or the punishment of him who is condemned, like the council; for in the hell of fire, both the condemnation and the punishment of him who is condemned are certain.

R. Prepare your hearts for the Lord and serve Him only: * And He will deliver you out of the hands of your enemies. V. Turn to the Lord with all your hearts, and put away the strange gods from among you. And. Glory. And.

✠ Continuation of the holy Gospel according to St. Matthew.—At that time: Jesus said to His disciples: Except your justice abound more than that of the Scribes and the Pharisees, you shall not enter into the kingdom of heaven. You have heard that it was said to them of old: Thou shalt not kill; and whosoever shall kill, shall be in danger of the judgment. But I say to you, that whosoever is angry with his brother, shall be in danger of the judgment; and whosoever shall say to his brother:

Raca, shall be in danger of the council; and whosoever shall say: Thou fool, shall be in danger of
hell fire.   If therefore thou offer thy gift at the
altar, and there thou remember that thy brother
hath anything against thee, leave there thy offering
before the altar, and go first to be reconciled to thy
brother; and then coming thou shalt offer thy gift.

LET US PRAY

O God, who hath prepared unseen blessings for
those who love Thee, pour forth into our hearts a
love for Thee, that loving Thee in all things and
above all things, we may obtain Thy promises,
which surpass all our desires.   Through our Lord.

VI SUNDAY AFTER PENTECOST

III Nocturn

The reading of the holy Gospel
according to St. Mark

At that time: When there was a great multitude
with Jesus and they had nothing to eat, calling His
disciples together, He saith to them: I have compassion on the multitude, for behold they have been
with Me now three days, and have nothing to eat.
And so forth.

Homily of St. Ambrose, Bishop

After that woman, who may be taken as a type of
the Church, had been cured of an issue of blood,
after the Apostles had been sent out to preach the

kingdom of God, the food of heavenly grace is bestowed. But consider to whom it is given. Not to the idle, not in the city, as, for example, in a synagogue, or to those accustomed to worldly dignity; but in desert places, to those seeking Christ.

For Christ receives the humble, and the Word of God speaks with them, not of worldly things, but of the kingdom of God. And if any have ulcers of bodily passions, to such He willingly grants His healing grace. This, then, was the order of events, that those whom He had healed of the pain of their wounds, He delivered from fasting by spiritual alms.

No one, therefore, receives the food of Christ, unless he be first healed; and those who are invited to the feast are healed by that very call. If a man were lame, he received the power to walk, so that he might come: if he were deprived of the light of his eyes, he could not enter the house of the Lord unless his sight were restored to him.

Everywhere, therefore, the order of the mystery is kept, that first healing is applied to wounds by the remission of sins, and afterwards the food of the holy table abounds; although this crowd is not yet refreshed with the stronger meat, nor are their hearts, fasting from solid food of faith, fed with the Body and Blood of Christ. I have fed you, He says, with milk, not meat; for as yet you were not able, nor even now are you able. The five loaves are like milk: but the more solid meat is the Body of Christ; the stronger drink is the Blood of the Lord.

R. The number of my sins is greater than that of the sands on the sea shore, and my sins are multiplied: and I am not worthy to look up to the height of heaven because of the multitude of my iniquities: for I have provoked Thy wrath, * And done evil in Thy sight. V. For I acknowledge my iniquity: and my sin is continually before me, for against Thee only have I sinned. And done. Glory. And done.

✠ Continuation of the holy Gospel according to St. Mark.—At that time: When there was a great multitude with Jesus, and they had nothing to eat, calling His disciples together, He saith to them: I have compassion on the multitude, for behold they have now been with Me three days, and have nothing to eat; and if I shall send them away fasting to their homes, they will faint in the way: for some of them came from afar off. And His disciples answered Him: From whence can any one fill them here with bread in the wilderness? And He asked them: How many loaves have ye? who said: Seven. And He commanded the people to sit down on the ground. And taking the seven loaves, giving thanks, He broke and gave to His disciples to set before the people. And they had a few little fishes, and He blessed them, and commanded them to be set before them. And they did eat, and were filled; and they took up that which was left of the fragments, seven baskets: and they that had eaten were about four thousand: and He sent them away.

LET US PRAY

O God all powerful, who art all good, implant in our hearts a love of Thy Name and increase within us the spirit of piety; and as Thou dost foster and care for the good that is within us, so mayest Thou also protect what Thou dost foster. Through our Lord.

VII SUNDAY AFTER PENTECOST

III Nocturn

The reading of the holy Gospel
according to St. Matthew

At that time: Jesus said to His disciples: Beware of false prophets, who come to you in the clothing of sheep, but inwardly are ravening wolves. And so forth.

Homily of St. Hilary, Bishop

The Lord warns us that we must measure the worth of fair words and seeming meekness by the fruit of works; so that we should look not so much to what a man says of himself, as to what he does; for many there are who hide the ravening of a wolf under sheep's clothing. As thorns, then, do not bear grapes, nor do thistles produce figs, and evil trees do not bring forth good fruit; so the Lord teaches, neither do evil men bring forth good works; therefore all men are to be known by their works.

Words alone will not win the kingdom of heaven, nor will he ever inherit it who says only: Lord, Lord. Of what use is it to say to the Lord: Lord? Would He not be the Lord unless we called Him so? And what has the naming of a name to do with holiness, when the way to the kingdom of heaven is to be found in obedience to the will of God, and not in calling on His name?

Many will say to Me in that day: Lord, Lord, have we not prophesied in Thy name? Christ here condemns also the deceitfulness of false prophets and the feigning of the hypocrites, who, seeing the power of their words in the teaching of doctrine, the putting to flight of devils, and in such like mighty works, take the glory to themselves. And hence they promise themselves the kingdom of heaven, not as an effect of the power of God upon all who have invoked it, but as something consequent on what they themselves say or do; since by reading they acquire knowledge of doctrine, and the very name of Christ troubles the devils.

Therefore that blessed eternity is to be merited by us, and we must do our part, in desiring what is good, in avoiding evil, in obeying the heavenly precepts with our whole heart, that by such services we may be approved by God. Let us do His will rather than boast of His power, repudiating and repelling those whose wicked deeds have turned them aside from the knowledge of themselves.

R. Saul slew his thousands, and David his ten thousands: * For the hand of the Lord was with him; he struck the Philistine and took away the reproach from Israel. V. Is not this David of whom they sang in chorus, saying: Saul slew his thousands and David his ten thousands For. Glory. For.

✠ Continuation of the holy Gospel according to St. Matthew.—At that time: Jesus said to His disciples: Beware of false prophets, who come to you in the clothing of sheep, but inwardly they are ravening wolves. By their fruits you shall know them. Do men gather grapes of thorns, or figs of thistles? Even so every good tree bringeth forth good fruit, and the evil tree bringeth forth evil fruit. A good tree cannot bring forth evil fruit, neither can an evil tree bring forth good fruit. Every tree that bringeth not forth good fruit shall be cut down and shall be cast into the fire. Wherefore by their fruits you shall know them. Not every one that saith to Me: Lord, Lord, shall enter into the kingdom of heaven; but he that doth the will of My Father who is in heaven, he shall enter into the kingdom of heaven.

LET US PRAY

O God, whose Providence doth not fail in its plans; we humbly beseech Thee to take away from us whatever is harmful and grant unto us whatever is good for us. Through our Lord.

VIII SUNDAY AFTER PENTECOST

III Nocturn

The reading of the holy Gospel according to St. Luke

At that time: Jesus spoke to His disciples this parable: There was a certain rich man who had a steward; and the same was accused unto him that he had wasted his goods. And so forth.

Homily of St. Jerome, Priest

If the dispenser of the riches of iniquity is praised by the mouth of his lord because by unjust means he has taken care to ensure compassion for himself, and if his lord, in spite of having suffered loss, praises the wisdom of his steward who has with prudence safeguarded his own interests, although at the expense of his master, how much more will Christ, who can suffer no loss and is disposed to mercy, commend His disciples if they have compassion on those who would believe in Him?

He ends His parable with these words: And I say to you: Make unto you friends of the mammon of iniquity. Mammon is a Syriac, not a Hebrew word, signifying ill-gotten gains. If, then, the wise use of such gains turns iniquity into righteousness, how much more will the divine word, wherein is no wickedness, which is entrusted to the Apostles, raise its stewards to heaven if they shall have dispensed it faithfully?

Therefore the Lord adds: He that is faithful in that which is least, that is, in carnal things, is faithful also in that which is greater, that is, in spiritual things. And he that is unjust in that which is little, so that he will not share with his brethren what God has created for the use of all, such a one will be unjust in dealing out spiritual riches, so that he will dispense the Lord's teaching, not according to need, but having respect of persons.

If, then, says the Lord, you have not been faithful in using material riches which pass away, who will trust you with the true and everlasting riches of divine doctrine? And if you have been unfaithful in those things which are another's (another's things are to be considered as things belonging to the world), who could trust you with those things which are yours (which, properly speaking, are to be considered as belonging to man).

R. Remember, O Lord, Thy covenant, and say to the destroying Angel: Hold now thy hand, * That the land be not laid waste, and that Thou destroy not every living soul. V. I am he that has sinned; I have done wickedly: these that are sheep, what have they done? I beseech Thee, O Lord, let Thine anger be turned from Thy people. That. Glory. That.

✠ Continuation of the holy Gospel according to St. Luke.—At that time: Jesus spoke to His disples this parable: There was a certain rich man who had a steward; and the same was accused unto him that he had wasted his goods; and he called him, and said to him: How is it that I hear this of thee? give an account of thy stewardship, for now thou canst be steward no longer. And the steward said within himself: What shall I do, because my lord taketh away from me the stewardship? To dig, I am not able; to beg, I am ashamed. I know what I will do, that when I shall be put out of the stewardship, they may receive me into their houses. Therefore, calling together every one of his lord's debtors, he said to the first: How much dost thou owe my lord? But he said: A hundred barrels of oil. And he said to him: Take thy bill, and sit down quickly and write fifty. Then he said to another: And how much dost thou owe? Who said: A hundred quarters of wheat. He said to him: Take thy bill, and write eighty. And the Lord commended the unjust steward, for as much as he had done wisely; for the children of this world are wiser in their generation than the children of light. And I say to you: Make unto you friends of the mammon of iniquity, that when you shall fail, they may receive you into everlasting dwellings.

LET US PRAY

Grant to us, we beseech Thee, O Lord, the spirit of always thinking and of doing what is right; that we, who cannot live without Thee, by Thy help may live according to Thy will. Through our Lord.

IX SUNDAY AFTER PENTECOST

III Nocturn

The reading of the holy Gospel according to St. Luke

At that time: When Jesus drew near to Jerusalem, seeing the city, He wept over it, saying: If thou also hadst known, and that in this thy day, the things that are to thy peace: but now they are hidden from thy eyes. And so forth.

Homily of St. Gregory, Pope

No one who has read the history of the destruction of Jerusalem by the Roman rulers Vespasian and Titus can be ignorant that this was the destruction over which the Lord wept as He described it. Truly these Roman rulers are referred to when it is said: For the days shall come upon thee and thy enemies shall cast a trench about thee.

The words which follow: They shall not leave in thee a stone upon a stone, are fulfilled in the change of site of the same city, which is now built outside the gate: in the place where the Lord was crucified, the original city having been altogether overthrown.

Upon whom and for what sin the punishment of this destruction was inflicted, we are told in the following words: Because thou hast not known the time of thy visitation. The Creator of men deigned to visit her through the mystery of His Incarnation, but she remembered not to fear and love Him. Hence also the prophet, rebuking the hardness of man's heart, calls upon the birds of heaven to bear witness against her, saying: The kite in the air hath known her time: the turtle and the swallow and the stork have the time of their coming: but my people have not known the judgment of the Lord.

The Redeemer wept over the ruin of the unfaithful city, while she herself as yet knew not that it was coming. Rightly does the Lord say to her as He weeps: If thou also hadst known, meaning, thou also wouldst weep, instead of rejoicing in ignorance of what is coming upon thee. Therefore He adds: And that in this thy day, the things that are to thy peace. For while she gave herself up to the pleasures of the flesh, not anticipating the evils that were to come, she had in her day the things which might have been for her peace.

R. O Lord, Thou hast heard the prayer of Thy servant, that I might build a temple unto Thy name: * Bless and sanctify this house forever, O God of Israel. V. O Lord, who keepest covenant with Thy servants that walk before Thee with all their heart. Bless. Glory. Bless.

✠ Continuation of the holy Gospel according to St. Luke.—At that time: When Jesus drew near to Jerusalem, seeing the city, He wept over it, saying: If thou also hadst known, and that in this thy day, the things that are to thy peace: but now they are hidden from thy eyes. For the days shall come upon thee, and thy enemies shall cast a trench about thee, and compass thee round, and straiten thee on every side; and beat thee flat to the ground, and thy children who are in thee; and they shall not leave a stone upon a stone because thou hast not known the time of thy visitation. And entering into the temple, He began to cast out them that sold therein, and them that bought, saying to them; It is written, My house is the house of prayer, but you have made it a den of thieves. And He was teaching daily in the temple.

LET US PRAY

In Thy mercy, O Lord, mayest Thou be ready to hear the prayers of Thy servants; and that Thou mayest grant unto us what we ask; make us ask for those things which are pleasing to Thee. Through our Lord.

X SUNDAY AFTER PENTECOST

III Nocturn

The reading of the holy Gospel
according to St. Luke

At that time: Jesus spoke this parable to some who trusted in themselves as just and despised others: Two men went up into the temple to pray: the one a Pharisee, and the other a publican. And so forth.

Homily of St. Augustine, Bishop

The Pharisee might at least have said: I am not as many men are. What is the meaning of: The rest of men, if not all men except himself? I, says he, am just; the rest are sinners. I am not as the rest of men, unjust, extortioners, adulterers. And lo, from thy neighbor the publican, thou takest occasion of greater pride: as, he says, this publican. I, he says, am alone; he is of the rest. Through my righteous deeds, he says, whereby I am not unjust, such as this man is.

I fast twice in a week, I give tithes of all that I possess. In his words seek for any one thing that he asked of God, and you will find nothing. He went up to pray: he did not wish to ask God for anything, but praised himself. This is but a small part of it, that he asked God for nothing, and praised himself; over and above this, he mocked the one who did pray.

But the publican stood afar off, and yet he indeed was near to God; the feelings of his heart kept him afar off, but his piety brought him close. But the publican stood afar off, yet the Lord considered him to be near by. For the Lord is high, and looketh on the low; but those that are high, as was this Pharisee, He knoweth afar off. The high, indeed, God knoweth afar off, but He does not pardon them.

Hear more of the humility of the publican. It is but a small matter that he stood afar off; he did not so much as lift up his eyes towards heaven; that he might be looked upon, he himself did not look; he did not dare to look upwards; his conscience pressed him down, but hope lifted him up. Listen once more: He struck his breast. He himself inflicted pains upon himself; wherefore the Lord spared him for his confession. He struck his breast, saying: O Lord, be merciful to me, a sinner. Behold who it is that prays. Why dost thou marvel that God should pardon when he acknowledges his own sin?

R. Hearken, O Lord, to the hymn and the prayer which Thy servant prayeth before Thee this day, that Thy eyes may be opened, and Thy ears attentive, * Upon this house day and night. V. Look down, O Lord, from Thy holy place, and from Thy dwelling in the height of heaven. Upon. Glory. Upon.

✠ Continuation of the holy Gospel according to St. Luke.—At that time: Jesus spoke this parable to some who trusted in themselves as just and despised others. Two men went up into the temple to pray; the one was a Pharisee, and the other a Publican. The Pharisee standing, prayed thus with himself: O God, I give Thee thanks that I am not as the rest of men, extortioners, unjust, adulterers; as also is this publican. I fast twice in the week; I give tithes of all that I possess. And the Publican, standing afar off, would not so much as lift up his eyes towards heaven, but struck his breast saying: O God, be merciful to me a sinner. I say to you, this man went down to his house justified rather than the other; because every one that exalteth himself shall be humbled, and he that humbleth himself shall be exalted.

LET US PRAY

O God, who dost manifest Thy great power by sparing and by having mercy on us, increase Thy mercy towards us and make those who hasten forward to Thy promises to be sharers in Thy heavenly blessings. Through our Lord.

XI SUNDAY AFTER PENTECOST

III Nocturn
The reading of the holy Gospel
according to St. Mark

At that time: Jesus going out to the coasts of Tyre, came by Sidon to the sea of Galilee, through the midst of the coasts of Decapolis. And so forth.

Homily of St. Gregory, Pope

Why, when He wished to heal the deaf and dumb man, did God, Creator of all, put His fingers into the man's ears and touch his tongue with spittle? What do the fingers of the Redeemer signify but the gifts of the Holy Ghost? And so elsewhere we read that when casting out a devil He said: If I by the finger of God cast out devils, doubtless the kingdom of God is come upon you. These words are given thus by another Evangelist: If I by the Spirit of God cast out devils, then is the kingdom of God come upon you. Comparing these passages, we see that the finger is called the Spirit.

For the Lord, then, to put His fingers into the deaf man's ears was, by the gift of the Holy Spirit, to enlighten his mind unto obedience. And why did He touch his tongue with spittle? We receive spittle from the Redeemer's mouth when we receive wisdom in speaking of the things of God. Saliva flows from the head into the mouth, and so when that wisdom which is Himself touches our tongue, forthwith it enables us to preach.

And looking up to heaven He groaned: not that He had any need to groan for (being God) He gave what (as man) He asked; but that He might teach us to sigh to Him whose throne is in heaven, that our ears be opened by the gift of the Holy Spirit, and our tongue loosed by the spittle of His mouth, that is, by the knowledge of the divine word, in order to preach to others.

Then the Lord said to him: Ephpheta, which is, Be thou opened: and immediately his ears were opened and the string of his tongue was loosed. Here it is to be noted that the words: Be thou opened, were addressed to deaf ears. But when the ears of a man's heart have been opened to obey, without doubt the string of his tongue is also loosed, that he may exhort others to do the good deeds which he himself has done. It is well added: and he spoke right. For he speaks rightly who first practices himself what he preaches to others.

R. Remember, O Lord, Thy covenant and say to the destroying angel: Hold now thy hand, * That the land be not laid waste, and that Thou destroy not every living soul. V. I am he that has sinned, I have done wickedly: these that are sheep, what have they done? I beseech Thee, O Lord, let Thine anger be turned away from Thy people. That. Glory. That.

✠ Continuation of the holy Gospel according to St. Mark.—At that time: Jesus going out to the coasts of Tyre, came by Sidon to the sea of Galilee, through the midst of the coasts of Decapolis. And they brought to Him one deaf and dumb, and they besought Him that He would lay His hand upon him. And taking him from the multitude apart, He put His fingers into his ears, and spitting, He touched his tongue; and looking up to heaven, He groaned and said to him: Ephpheta, that is, be thou opened: and immediately his ears were opened, and the string of his tongue was loosed, and he spoke right. And He charged them that they should tell no man, but the more He charged them so much the more a great deal did they publish it; and so much the more did they wonder, saying: He hath done all things well; He hath made both the deaf to hear, and the dumb to speak.

LET US PRAY

O almighty and eternal God, who in the greatness of Thy love dost exceed our merit and our desires; pour forth Thy mercy upon us, we beseech Thee, and pardon the sins which trouble our conscience and grant those petitions for which our prayers do not presume to ask. Through our Lord.

XII SUNDAY AFTER PENTECOST

III Nocturn

The reading of the holy Gospel according to St. Luke

At that time: Jesus said to His disciples: Blessed are the eyes which see the things that you see. For I say to you that many prophets and kings have desired to see the things that you see, and have not seen them. And so forth.

Homily of St. Bede the Venerable, Priest

Blessed are the eyes, not of the scribes and Pharisees, which saw only the Lord's visible form, but blessed are the eyes which are able to penetrate into hidden mysteries, of which it is said: Thou hast revealed them to little ones. Blessed are the eyes of the little ones to whom the Son has deigned to reveal both His Father and Himself. Abraham rejoiced that he might see Christ's day; he saw it and was glad.

Isaias, too, and Micheas and many other prophets saw the glory of the Lord, and therefore were called seers; but all these, beholding and hailing Him from afar, saw as through a glass darkly. But the Apostles, who had the Lord present with them, who sat at table with Him and learned from Him all that they had a mind to ask, had no need of being taught by angels or visions of any kind.

Now the many princes and kings of whom Luke speaks, Matthew more clearly calls prophets and just men. For just men are mighty kings who, refusing consent to the stirrings of temptation, do not give way, but know how to master them and keep them under control. And behold a certain lawyer stood up, tempting Him and saying: Master, what must I do to possess eternal life?

This lawyer, who to try the Lord questioned Him concerning eternal life, took occasion, as I think, of tempting Him through His own words: Rejoice that your names are written in heaven. In thus questioning Him, he proved how true was that confession the Lord had just made to His Father: Because Thou hast hidden these things from the wise and prudent and hast revealed them to little ones.

R. Leave me not, O Lord, father and ruler of my life, lest I fall before my adversaries: * Lest my enemy rejoice over me. V. Take hold of arms and shield and rise up to help me. Lest. Glory. Lest.

✠ Continuation of the holy Gospel according to St. Luke.—At that time: Jesus said to His disciples: Blessed are the eyes that see the things which you see. For I say to you, that many prophets and kings have desired to see the things that you see, and have not seen them; and to hear the things that you hear, and have not heard them. And behold a certain lawyer stood up, tempting Him, and saying: Master, what must I do to possess eternal life? But He said to him: What is written in the law? how readest thou? He answering said: Thou shalt love the Lord thy God with thy whole heart, and with thy whole soul, and with all thy strength, and with all thy mind; and thy neighbor as thyself. And He said to him: Thou hast answered rightly: this do, and thou shalt live. But he, willing to justify himself, said to Jesus: And who is my neighbor? And Jesus answered, saying: A certain man went down from Jerusalem to Jericho and fell among robbers, who also stripped him, and having wounded him went away leaving him half dead: and it chanced that a certain priest went down the same way, and seeing him, passed by. In like manner also a Levite, when he was near the place and saw him, passed by. But a certain Samaritan being on his journey, came near him, and seeing him, was moved with compassion, and going up to him, bound up his wounds, pouring in oil and wine; and setting him upon his own beast, brought him to an inn, and took care of him: and the next day he took out two pence and gave to the host, and said: Take care of him, and whatsoever thou shalt spend over and above, I, at my return will repay thee. Which of these three, in thy opinion, was neighbor to him that fell among robbers? But he said: He that showed mercy to him. And Jesus said to him: Go and do thou in like manner.

Let Us Pray

O almighty and merciful God, by whose grace Thy people are able to serve Thee in a true and praiseworthy manner; grant unto us, we beseech Thee, that without sin we may hasten to the rewards Thou hast promised. Through our Lord.

XIII SUNDAY AFTER PENTECOST

III Nocturn

The reading of the holy Gospel
according to St. Luke

At that time: As Jesus was going to Jerusalem He passed through the midst of Samaria and Galilee: and as He entered into a certain town, there met Him ten men that were lepers. And so forth.

Homily of St. Augustine, Bishop

As to the ten lepers whom the Lord cleansed, when He said: Go, show yourselves to the priest, it may be asked why He sent them to the priests, so that as they went they were made clean. Of all those to whom He granted bodily favors it is not said that He sent any to the priests except the lepers. It was from leprosy He had cleansed that other man to whom He said: Go, show thyself to the priest and offer sacrifice for thyself, as Moses commanded for a testimony to them.

We ask, then, of what was leprosy a type; since those who were delivered from it were said not to be healed but cleansed. Leprosy is rather a blemish which changes the color of the skin than a disease which destroys the health of the body or impairs its senses and members. Not unreasonably, then, we may understand by lepers those who, lacking the knowledge of the true faith, profess various erroneous doctrines. They do not hide their ignorance, but bring it forth into the light as though it were the highest wisdom and proclaim it in high sounding phrases.

Now, there is no false doctrine which does not contain some element of truth, and when, in any argument or discourse, there is both truth and falsehood, it may be compared to the mingling of different colors on the body of a leper, for the disease of leprosy causes unnatural stains and spots on men's bodies.

But let those lepers, so shunned by the Church that if possible she banishes them to a distance, cry out to Christ with a loud voice, as did the ten who stood afar off and lifted up their voice, saying: Jesus, Master, have mercy on us. The fact that they called Him master by which name I know not if any others had besought the Lord for bodily healing is enough, I think, to show that false doctrine was the leprosy from which the good Master made them clean.

R. Blessed is the people * whom the Lord God hath blessed, saying: Thou art the work of Mine hands, O Israel, thou art Mine inheritance. V. Blessed is the nation whose God is the Lord, the people whom He hath chosen for His own inheritance. Whom. Glory. Whom.

✠ Continuation of the holy Gospel according to St. Luke.—At that time: As Jesus was going to Jerusalem, He passed through the midst of Samaria and Galilee: and as He entered into a certain town, there met Him ten men that were lepers, who stood afar off, and lifted up their voice, saying: Jesus, Master, have mercy on us. Whom when He saw, He said: Go, show yourselves to the priests. And it came to pass, that, as they went, they were made clean. And one of them, when he saw that he was made clean, went back with a loud voice praising God: and he fell on his face before His feet, giving thanks; and this was a Samaritan. And Jesus answering said: Were not ten made clean? And where are the nine? There is no one found to return and give glory to God but this stranger. And He said to him: Arise, go thy way; for thy faith hath made thee whole.

LET US PRAY

O almighty and eternal God, grant unto us an increase of faith, hope, and charity; and that we may merit to obtain what Thou dost promise, make us love what Thou dost command. Through our Lord.

XIV SUNDAY AFTER PENTECOST

III Nocturn
The reading of the holy Gospel
according to St. Matthew

At that time: Jesus said to His disciples: No man can serve two masters. And so forth.

Homily of St. Augustine, Bishop

No man can serve two masters. These words are to be referred to this very intention, as He goes on to explain, saying: For either he will hate the one, and love the other; or he will sustain the one, and despise the other. Which words are to be carefully considered; for, who the two masters are, He forthwith shows, when He says: You cannot serve God and mammon.

Mammon is a word said to be used by the Hebrews for riches. The Punic name also corresponds; for gain is called mammon in Punic. But he who serves mammon in reality serves him who, as being set over those earthly things by reason of his perversity, is called by the Lord the prince of this world.

A man will therefore either hate the one and love the other, that is to say, God; or he will sustain the one and despise the other. For whosoever serves mammon will suffer under a hard and cruel master; for led captive by his own cupidity, he is under the power of the devil, though he loves him not. For who is there who loves the devil? But yet he submits to him.

Therefore, I say to you, says He, be not solicitous for your life, what you shall eat, nor for your body, what you shall put on. Lest perchance, although it is not now superfluities that are sought after, the heart should be made double by reason of its very necessities, and the aim should be forcibly deflected to seek after those things of our own when we are doing something as it were from compassion; that is, so that when we wish to appear to be consulting someone's interests, we are in that matter looking after our own advantage; and we do not seem to ourselves to be sinning for this reason, that it is not superfluities, but necessaries, which we wish to obtain.

R. Give me, O Lord, wisdom that sitteth by Thy throne, and cast me not off from among Thy children: * For I am Thy servant, and the son of Thy handmaid. V. Send her from the throne of thy greatness, that she may be with me and may labor with me. For. Glory. For.

✠ Continuation of the holy Gospel according to St. Matthew.—At that time: Jesus said to His disciples: No man can serve two masters; for either he will hate the one and love the other, or he will sustain the one and despise the other. You cannot serve God and mammon. Therefore I say to you be not solicitous for your life, what you shall eat, nor for your body, what you shall put on. Is not the life more than the meat, and the body more than the raiment? Behold the birds of the air; for they neither sow nor do they reap, nor gather into barns, and your heavenly Father feedeth them. Are you not of much more value than they? And which of you by taking thought, can add to his stature one cubit? And for raiment why are you solicitous? Consider the lilies of the field, how they grow; they labor not, neither do they spin; but I say to you, that not even Solomon in all his glory was arrayed as one of these. Now if God so clothe the grass of the field, which is today, and tomorrow is cast into the oven, how much more you, O ye of little faith! Be not solicitous therefore saying, what shall we eat, or what shall we drink, or wherewith shall we be clothed, for after all these things do the heathens seek. For your Father knoweth that you have need of all these things. Seek ye therefore first the Kingdom of God, and His justice: and all these things shall be added unto you.

LET US PRAY

Protect Thy Church, we beseech Thee, O Lord, with Thy constant care; and since our human weakness doth fail without Thy help, may Thy assisting grace restrain us from evil and guide us in the way of salvation. Through our Lord.

XV SUNDAY AFTER PENTECOST

III Nocturn

The reading of the holy Gospel
according to St. Luke

At that time: Jesus went into a city called Naim: and there went with Him His disciples, and a great multitude. And so forth.

Homily of St. Augustine, Bishop

When that young man was raised from the dead, the widowed mother rejoiced; and when, in a spiritual sense, men are restored to life, as happens daily, their mother the Church rejoices. That young man was dead in the body; but they are dead in the soul. His was a visible death, visibly lamented; theirs, an invisible death, neither enquired into, nor even perceived. He sought them out who knew them to be dead. He alone knew them to be dead who was able to recall them to life. For if He had not come to raise the dead, the Apostle would not have said: Rise, thou that sleepest, and arise from the dead, and Christ shall enlighten thee.

Now we find that three dead persons were raised to life by the Lord visibly, thousands invisibly. Nay, who knows how many dead He invisibly raised? For not all the things that He did are written down. John tells us this: Many other things Jesus did which, if they should be written, I think that the whole world would not be able to contain the books. So then, there were doubtless many others raised, but not without reason is mention made of three.

For our Lord Jesus Christ willed that those works that He performed on the body should also be understood spiritually. For He did not merely do miracles for the miracles' sake; but in order that the things which He did should inspire wonder in those who saw them, and convey the truth to those who understood. As he who sees letters in an excellently written manuscript and does not know how to read, praises indeed the hand of the scribe, admiring the beauty of the characters; but what those characters mean or signify he does not know; and by the sight of his eyes he is a praiser of the work, but in his mind he has no comprehension of it.

But another man both praises the craftsmanship, and grasps the meaning; such a one, I mean, who not only can see what is common to all, but who can also read; which is impossible for one who has not learned. So those who beheld Christ's miracles and understood not their signification, and what they in a manner conveyed to such as could understand, wondered merely at what was done; but others both wondered at the miracles wrought, and grasped their meaning. Such ought we to be in the school of Christ.

R. Leave me not, O Lord, father and ruler of my life, lest I fall before my adversaries: * Lest my enemy rejoice over me. V. Take hold of arms and shield and rise up to help me. Lest. Glory. Lest.

✠ Continuation of the holy Gospel according to St. Luke.—At that time: Jesus went into a city called Naim; and there went with Him His disciples, and a great multitude. And when He came nigh to the city, behold a dead man was carried out, the only son of his mother, and she was a widow, and much people of the city were with her. And when the Lord saw her, He had compassion on her and said to her: Weep not. And He came near and

touched the bier. And they that carried it stood
still. And He said: Young man, I say to thee, A-
rise; and he that was dead sat up, and began to
speak. And He delivered him to his mother. And
there came a fear on them all; and they glorified
God, saying: A great prophet is risen up amongst
us, and God hath visited His people.

LET US PRAY

May Thy constant mercy cleanse and strengthen
Thy Church; and since without Thy help she cannot
be safe, may Thy grace rule and guide her always.
Through our Lord.

XVI SUNDAY AFTER PENTECOST

III Nocturn

The reading of the holy Gospel
according to St. Luke

At that time: When Jesus went into the house
of one of the chief of the Pharisees on the sabbath
day to eat bread, they watched Him. And behold,
there was a certain man before Him that had the
dropsy. And so forth.

Homily of St. Ambrose, Bishop

Now is cured the man afflicted with dropsy in
whom an excessive bodily flux lowered his vitality
and so quenched his spiritual ardor. Then a lesson
is given in humility, when it is forbidden to sit in
the highest places at the marriage feast. But this

is done gently, that kindly persuasion may take the place of harsh compulsion, reason may further the effect of persuasion, and correction may amend the affliction.

The teaching on humility is closely followed by a lesson on kindliness which the Lord defines when He says that it is to be shown to the poor and feeble; for to show hospitality to those who can make some return is nothing but one form of avarice. Lastly, as pay is given to a soldier who has served in a campaign in place of riches he has given up, so the kingdom of heaven is gained only by one who cares nothing for lower pursuits and purchases not for himself earthly possessions, since the Lord says: Sell all that thou hast and follow Me.

Neither can he gain it who buys oxen, since Eliseus slew those he had and gave them to the people. Neither can he win it who marries a wife, for his mind is set on worldly things, not on the things of God. Not that marriage is to be blamed, but virginity is called the more honorable way, since the unmarried woman, and she who is a widow, thinketh on the things of the Lord, that she may be holy both in body and spirit.

But now, that we may return into favor with the married, as we have already done with the widows, we do not shrink from the opinion which is held by so many that only three classes of man are shut out from partaking in that great supper; namely, Gentiles, Jews, and heretics. And therefore the Apostle says that avarice is to be shunned, lest being hindered, as the Gentiles are, by wickedness, malice, uncleanness and covetousness, we are unable to enter into the kingdom of Christ. For no unclean or covetous person (which is a serving of idols) hath inheritance in the kingdom of Christ and of God.

R. Why have you detracted the words of truth? You dress up speeches only to rebuke and you endeavor to overthrow your friend: * However, finish what you have in mind. V. Judge what is just and you shall not find iniquity in my tongue. However. Glory. However.

✠ Continuation of the holy Gospel according to St. Luke.—At that time: When Jesus went into the house of one of the chief of the Pharisees on the sabbath day to eat bread, they watched Him. And behold, there was a certain man before Him that had dropsy: and Jesus answering, spoke to the lawyers and Pharisees, saying: Is it lawful to heal on the sabbath day? But they held their peace: but He, taking him, healed him and sent him away, And answering them, He said: Which of you shall have an ass or an ox fall into a pit, and will not immediately draw him out on the sabbath day? And they could not answer Him these things. And He spoke a parable also to them that were invited, marking how they chose the first seats at the table, saying to them: When thou art invited to a wedding, sit not down in the first place, lest perhaps one more honorable than thou be invited by him; and he that invited thee and him come and say to thee: Give this man place; and then thou begin with shame to take the lowest place. But when thou art invited, go, sit down in the lowest place, that when he who invited thee cometh, he may say to thee: Friend, go up higher: then thou shalt have glory before them that sit at table with thee: because every one that exalteth himself shall be humbled, and he that humbleth himself shall be exalted.

LET US PRAY

May Thy grace, we beseech Thee, O Lord, always precede and follow our actions, and may it make us always faithful in performing good works. Through our Lord.

XVII SUNDAY AFTER PENTECOST

III Nocturn
The reading of the holy Gospel
according to St. Matthew

At that time: The Pharisees came to Jesus, and one of them, a doctor of the law, asked Him, tempting Him; Master, which is the great commandment of the law? And so forth.

Homily of St. John Chrysostom

The Sadducees having been put to shame, the Pharisees again approach Jesus; and whereas they should rather have held their peace, they are eager for a contest. They put forward, therefore, a man well skilled in the law, not from any desire to learn from Jesus, but to test Him. Thus they inquire of Him as to which is the first commandment of the law. They put their question in this way because the first commandment being: Thou shalt love the Lord thy God, they think He will adduce reasons for amending this commandment by some addition, because He made Himself God.

What, then, does Christ do? To show that they have come to this pass because they are devoid of all charity and are consumed with envy, He says: Thou shalt love the Lord thy God; this is the first and the greatest commandment. And the second is like to this: Thou shalt love thy neighbor as thyself.

Why is the second like to this? Because the first leads to the second and is, in turn, confirmed by it. For every one that doth evil hateth the light, and cometh not to the light. And again: The fool hath said in his heart, There is no God. From which follows: They are corrupt and are become abominable in their ways. Again: The desire of money is the root of evils; which some coveting, have erred from the faith. And: He that loveth Me will keep My commandments—of which the first of all and the root of all is: Thou shalt love the Lord thy God, and thy neighbor as thyself.

If then, to love God is to love our neighbor—For if thou love Me, Peter, He says, feed My sheep—if the love of our neighbor leads us to keep the commandments, with good reason He says that on these two commandments depend all the law and the prophets. And as in the passage above, when questioned concerning the Resurrection, His answer comprised more than the question demanded; so here, when asked which was the first commandment, He gives them, unasked, the second, as little inferior to the first. Thus He covertly insinuates that the question is inspired by hatred: For charity envieth not.

R. Bless ye the God of Heaven, give glory to Him in the sight of all that live, * Because He hath shown His mercy to you. V. Bless ye Him and sing praises to Him: and publish all His wonderful words. Because. Glory. Because.

✠ Continuation of the holy Gospel according to St. Matthew.—At that time: The Pharisees came to Jesus, and one of them, a doctor of the law, asked Him, tempting Him: Master, which is the great commandment of the law? Jesus said to him: Thou shalt love the Lord thy God with thy whole heart, and with thy whole soul and with thy whole mind. This is the greatest and the first commandment. And the second is like to this:

Thou shalt love thy neighbor as thyself. On these two commandments dependeth the whole law and the prophets. And the Pharisees being gathered together, Jesus asked them, saying: What think you of Christ, whose son is He? They say to Him: David's. He saith to them: How then doth David, in spirit, call Him Lord, saying: The Lord said to my Lord: Sit on My right hand until I make Thy enemies Thy footstool? If David then call Him Lord, how is He his son? And no man was able to answer Him a word; neither durst any man, from that day forth, ask Him any more questions.

LET US PRAY

Grant Thy people, we beseech Thee, O Lord, to avoid all the sinful influences of the devil and with a pure mind to serve Thee, the only true God. Through our Lord.

XVIII SUNDAY AFTER PENTECOST

III Nocturn

The reading of the holy Gospel according to St. Matthew

At that time: Jesus entering into a ship passed over the water and came into His own city. And so forth.

Homily of St. Peter Chrysologus

Today's lesson clearly shows that Christ in His actions as man manifested the mysteries of God, and by means of visible things accomplished what was invisible. The Evangelist says: Entering into a boat, He passed over the water and came into His own city. Is not this He who, driving back the waves laid bare the depths of the sea that the people of Israel might cross over dry-shod, while the stricken water stood still on either side like mountains overhanging a pass?

Is not this He who restrained the eddying billows beneath Peter's feet that the path upon the waters might be firm enough to bear his steps? Why, then, did He deny Himself a like service from the sea, but sought the borrowed aid of a boat in crossing that narrow lake? For He entered into a boat and crossed over.

What wonder, my brethren! Christ came to take our human weakness upon Himself and to grant us His strength; He came to seek the things of men and to strive to give to men divine blessings; to receive insults and to bestow honors; to bear afflictions and to give back health. For a physician not subject to infirmity knows not how to heal others; he who suffers not with the sick cannot restore health.

If Christ, therefore, had continued in His almighty power, He would have had nothing in common with men. Unless He had accepted the conditions of a human body, He would have assumed the body in vain. The Lord and Creator of the universe, when for our sakes He had confined Himself within the narrow limits of the flesh, took to Himself a home, became a Jewish citizen, and Himself the parent of all parents, acknowledged a human parentage that He might draw to Himself by love, bind by tenderness, win by affection, conquer by kindness those whom tyranny had driven away, fear had scattered and the power of the devil had driven into exile.

R. O Lord, Ruler of the heavens and the earth, Creator of the waters, King of all creatures: * Hear the prayer of Thy servants. V. For the prayer of the humble and the meek hath always pleased Thee. Hear. Glory. Hear.

✠ Continuation of the holy Gospel according to St. Matthew.—At that time: Jesus entering into a boat, passed over the water and came into His own city. And behold, they brought Him one sick of the palsy lying in a bed; and Jesus seeing their faith, said to the man sick of the palsy: Be of good heart, son, thy sins are forgiven thee. And behold some of the Scribes said within themselves: He blasphemeth. And Jesus seeing their thoughts, said: Why do you think evil in your hearts? whether is it easier to say: Thy sins are forgiven thee; or to say: Arise and walk? But that you may know that the Son of man hath power on earth to forgive sins (then said He to the man sick of the palsy): Arise, take up thy bed, and go into thy

house.   And he arose, and went into his house.
And the multitude seeing it, feared, and glorified
God who had given such power to men.

LET US PRAY

We beseech Thee, O Lord, let our hearts be
guided by Thy merciful grace, for without Thy
help, we cannot please Thee.   Through our Lord.

XIX SUNDAY AFTER PENTECOST

III Nocturn

The reading of the holy Gospel
according to St. Matthew

At that time: Jesus spoke to the chief priests
and the Pharisees in parables, saying: The kingdom of heaven is likened to a king who made a
marriage for his son.   And so forth.

Homily of St. Gregory, Pope

I remember often having said that in the holy
Gospel the Church is commonly alluded to as the
kingdom of heaven, because this is the name given
to the assembly of the just.   Now, since the Lord
says by His prophet: Heaven is My throne; and
Solomon has: The throne of wisdom is the soul
of the righteous; and Paul also calls Christ the
power of God and the wisdom of God, we may certainly conclude that as God is wisdom, and the
souls of the just the seat of wisdom, while heaven
is called the throne of God, then heaven is in the

soul of the just. And hence the Psalmist, speaking of holy preachers, says: The heavens show forth the glory of God.

The kingdom of heaven, then, is the church of the just. For whereas the hearts of just men are set upon nothing earthly, but are ever sighing for the joys of heaven, the Lord already reigns in them as in heavenly places. And thus it is said: The kingdom of heaven is likened to a king who made a marriage for his son. It is well known to you, dearly beloved, who is this King, the father of a King; verily it is He to whom the Psalmist says: Give to the King Thy judgments, O God, and to the King's Son Thy justice.

Who made a marriage for his son. Then, indeed, did God the Father make a marriage for God His Son, when in the womb of the Virgin He joined Him to our nature, when He willed that He who was God before all time should be made man at the end of time. But because the marriage bond ordinarily unites two persons, God forbid we should entertain the belief that the Person of God and the person of the man Jesus Christ, our Redeemer, were thus united to form one Person.

We say truly that Christ's existence was the outcome of the union of two natures, and that in Him those two natures continued to exist; but that His existence resulted from the union of two persons, this we reject as an impious suggestion. It will then be clearer and safer to say that the Father made a marriage for His Son the King, when, by the mystery of the Incarnation, He espoused Him to holy Church. The womb of the Virgin Mary was His bride-chamber; and hence the Psalmist says: He hath set His tabernacle in the sun and He is as a bridegroom coming out of His bride-chamber.

R. Lord, Almighty King, all things are in Thy power and there is none that can resist Thy will * Deliver us for Thy name's sake. V. Hear our prayer and turn our mourning into joy. Deliver. Glory. Deliver.

✠ Continuation of the holy Gospel according to St. Matthew.—At that time: Jesus spoke to the chief priests and the Pharisees in parables, saying: The kingdom of heaven is likened to a king, who made a marriage for his son; and he sent his servants to call them that were invited to the marriage, and they would not come. Again he sent other servants, saying: Tell them that were invited: Behold, I have prepared my dinner; and my beeves and fatlings are killed, and all things are ready; come ye to the marriage; but they neglected, and went their ways, one to his farm, and another to his merchandise; and the rest laid hands on his servants, and having treated them contumeliously, put them to death. But when the king had heard of it, he was angry; and sending

his armies, he destroyed those murderers, and
burnt their city. Then he saith to his servants:
The marriage indeed is ready, but they that were invited were not worthy. Go ye therefore into the
highways, and as many as you shall find, call to
the marriage. And his servants, going forth into
the ways, gathered together all that they found,
both bad and good; and the marriage was filled
with guests. And the king went in to see the
guests; and he saw there a man who had not on a
wedding garment; and he saith to him: Friend,
how camest thou in hither, not having on a wedding garment? but he was silent. Then the king
said to the waiters: Bind his hands and feet, and
cast him into exterior darkness: there shall be
weeping and gnashing of teeth. For many are
called, but few are chosen.

LET US PRAY

O Almighty and merciful God, graciously protect
us from all danger; that ready in both body and
soul, we may with a free spirit seek to do Thy will.
Through our Lord.

XX SUNDAY AFTER PENTECOST

III Nocturn

The reading of the holy Gospel
according to St. John

At that time: There was a certain ruler whose
son was sick at Capharnaum. And so forth.

Homily of St. Gregory, Pope

The lesson from the holy Gospel, brethren, which you have just heard read, needs no explanation. However, lest we should seem to have passed over it in silence, we will say something thereon, more by way of exhortation than explanation. This alone seems to me to require explaining: why this man, who came to beg the cure of his son, should have been told: Unless you see signs and wonders, you believe not. For since he came to ask that his son might be healed, assuredly he did believe; unless he had believed Jesus to be the Savior, he would never have asked Him to save his son's life.

Why then were these words: Unless you see signs and wonders, you believe not; spoken to one who believed before he saw such things? But you must remember what it was he asked, and then you will plainly see that he was wanting in faith. For he begged Him to come down and heal his son: He sought the bodily presence of the Lord, who in spirit is never absent.

Therefore, his faith in Christ was wanting, for he thought that He could not heal unless He were actually present. If his faith had been perfect, without doubt he would have known that there is no place where God is not. Indeed his faith was greatly lacking, since he attributed the Lord's power to His mere bodily presence and not to His Sovereign Majesty.

And thus he was wanting in faith even while he asked for his son to be healed; for though he believed the Lord, to whom he had come, had power to work the cure, yet he supposed Him absent from his dying son. Then the Lord, thus asked to go, showed that He was not absent from the place to which He was invited; and He, by whose will all things were created, gave health by His word alone.

R. Be ye not afraid of the assault of the enemy. Remember in what manner our fathers were saved, * And now let us cry to heaven and our God will have mercy on us. V. Remember His marvellous works which He hath done to Pharao and his host in the Red Sea. And. Glory. And.

✠ Continuation of the holy Gospel according to St. John.—At that time: There was a certain ruler whose son was sick as Capharnaum. He, having heard that Jesus was come from Judea into Galilee, went to Him, and prayed Him to come down and heal his son; for he was at the point of death. Jesus therefore said to him: Unless you see signs and wonders, you believe not. The ruler saith to Him: Lord come down before my son die. Jesus saith to him: Go thy way; thy son liveth. The man believeth the word which Jesus said to him and went his way. And as he was going down, his servants met him, and they brought word, saying that his son lived. He asked, therefore, of them the hour the fever left him. And they said to him: Yesterday at the seventh hour the fever left him. The father therefore knew that it was at the same hour that Jesus said to him: Thy son liveth; and himself believed, and his whole house.

Let Us Pray

Grant, we beseech Thee, O Lord, pardon and peace to Thy faithful people, that cleansed from every sin, they may serve Thee with a peaceful mind. Through our Lord.

XXI SUNDAY AFTER PENTECOST

III Nocturn

The reading of the holy Gospel according to St. Matthew

At that time: Jesus spoke to His disciples this parable: The kingdom of heaven is likened to a king who would take an account of his servants. And so forth.

Homily of St. Jerome, Priest

It is the custom among the people of Syria, and especially of Palestine, to illustrate every discourse by a parable, that by simile and example they may impress truths upon their hearers in a way that instruction alone might not do. And thus the Lord by an allegory of a royal master and of his servant, who, owing him ten thousand talents, sought and obtained of his lord forgiveness of the debt, taught Peter that he in like manner should forgive his fellow-servants their lesser offences.

For if that lord and king so readily forgave his servant a debt of ten thousand talents, how much more ought they who are themselves servants to forgive lesser debts to their fellow-servants? To make this clearer let us give an example. If one of us were to commit adultery or murder or sacrilege, these greater crimes, typified by the ten thousand talents, would be forgiven us when we asked for pardon, if we ourselves forgave lesser offences.

But if we resolutely refuse to pardon an injury and keep up an endless quarrel because of an unkind word, is it not mere justice to send us back to prison, and according to the example we ourselves have set, to refuse us pardon for these our greater offences?

So also shall My heavenly Father do to you if you forgive not every one his brother from your hearts. A terrible sentence, if the judgment of God may be turned away and changed according to our own attitude of mind, so that He will not grant us pardon for great things unless we forgive our brethren in small things. Yet because anyone might say: I have nothing against him, he knows that God is his judge; what he chooses to do is no concern of mine, I have forgiven him; the Lord confirms His sentence and removes the possibility of any such feigned peace by saying: If you forgive not every one his brother from your hearts.

R. They blessed the Lord with hymns and thanksgiving: * The Lord Almighty who had done great things in Israel and given them the victory. V. They adorned the front of the temple with crowns of gold and dedicated the altar to the Lord. The Lord. Glory. The Lord.

✠ Continuation of the holy Gospel according to St. Matthew.—At that time: Jesus spoke to His disciples this parable: The kingdom of heaven is likened to a king who would take an account of his servants. And when he had begun to take the account, one was brought to him that owed him ten thousand talents; and as he had not wherewith to pay it, his lord commanded that he should be sold, and his wife and children, and all that he had, and payment to be made. But that servant falling down, besought him saying: Have patience with me, and I will pay thee all. And the lord of that servant, being moved with pity, let him go; and forgave him the debt. But when that servant was gone out, he found one of his fellow-servants that owed him a hundred pence: and laying hold of him, he throttled him, saying: Pay what thou owest. And his fellow-servant falling down besought him, saying: Have patience with me, and I will pay thee all. And he would not; but went and cast him into prison till he paid the debt. Now his fellow-servants, seeing what was done, were very much grieved; and they came and told their lord all that was done. Then this lord called him, and saith to him: Thou wicked servant, I forgave thee all the debt, because thou besoughtest me; shouldst not thou then have had compassion also on thy fellow-servant, even as I had compassion on thee? And his lord being angry, delivered him to the tortures until he paid all the debt. So also shall My heavenly Father do to you, if you forgive not every one his brother from your hearts.

LET US PRAY

O Lord, we beseech Thee, in Thy constant goodness protect Thy family; that under Thy protection it may be free from all danger and devoted to Thy name in performing good works. Through our Lord.

XXII SUNDAY AFTER PENTECOST
III Nocturn
The reading of the holy Gospel
according to St. Matthew

At that time: The Pharisees went and consulted among themselves, how to ensnare Jesus in His speech. And so forth.

Homily of St. Hilary, Bishop

The Pharisees, often refuted, could find nothing in Jesus' past conduct of which to accuse Him: for

no fault could be found with His deeds or words,
yet in their spite they tried to discover something
blameworthy in everything. He was inviting all
men to hope in the kingdom of heaven, calling
them away from worldly vices and the vain superstitions of religions invented by man.

And therefore, by the terms of the questions
proposed, they would test whether He would attack the evil power, or on the other hand, would
hold it lawful to give tribute to Caesar. But Jesus, knowing their inmost thoughts (for their is
nothing hidden in the hearts of men God does not
behold), bade them bring Him a penny, and asked
them whose was the image and inscription upon it.

The Pharisees answered that it was Caesar's.
He bade them therefore: Render unto Caesar the
things that are Caesar's, and unto God the things
that are God's. O wonderful answer! O perfect
fulfilment of the divine command! In ordaining
that what is Caesar's must be rendered to him, it
so adjusts the balance between contempt of the
world and offering insult to Caesar, as to deliver
souls entirely devoted to the service of God from
the cares and obligations of human affairs. For if
nothing at all of Caesar's remains with us, we shall
not be bound to render to him what is his.

But if, on the other hand, we retain possession
of things under his control, if we avail ourselves of
his authority and surrender ourselves as hirelings

to obtain an inheritance among strangers, we are bound in justice to render unto Caesar the things of Caesar, and to God what is His own; that is to say, our bodies, our souls, our wills. For God is their Author and Maker, and hence it is fitting we should yield them wholly to Him, to whom we owe both their origin and development.

R. The sun shone upon the shields of gold and the mountains glittered therewith: * And the strength of the nations is scattered. V. For the army was exceeding great and strong. And Judas and his army drew near for battle. And. Glory. And.

✠ Continuation of the holy Gospel according to St. Matthew.—At that time: The Pharisees went and consulted among themselves, how to ensnare Jesus in His speech. And they send to Him their disciples, with the Herodians, saying: Master, we know that Thou art a true speaker, and teachest the way of God in truth, neither carest Thou for any man, for Thou dost not regard the person of men. Tell us therefore, what dost Thou think? Is it lawful to give tribute to Caesar, or not? But Jesus knowing their wickedness, said: Why do you tempt Me, ye hypocrites? Show Me the coin of the tribute. And they offered Him a penny. And Jesus saith to them: Whose image and superscription is this? They say to Him: Caesar's. Then He saith to them: Render therefore to Cae-

sar the things that are Caesar's, and to God the
things that are God's.

LET US PRAY

O God, our refuge and our strength; hear the
devout prayers of Thy Church, Thou who art the
Author of goodness; and grant that what we ask
in faith we may surely obtain.   Through our Lord.

XXIII SUNDAY AFTER PENTECOST

III Nocturn

The reading of the holy Gospel
according to St. Matthew

At that time: As Jesus was speaking to the mul-
titudes, behold a certain ruler came up, and adored
Him, saying: Lord, my daughter is even now dead.
And so forth.

Homily of St. Jerome, Priest

The Lord worked His eighth miracle at the request of a certain ruler who asked Him to raise
his daughter to life, not wishing to be excluded
from the mystery of the true circumcision.   But a
woman troubled with an issue of blood presents
herself, and her cure occupies the eighth place; so
that the ruler's daughter is excluded from this
number and takes the ninth place, as it is said in
the Psalms: Ethiopia shall stretch out her hands
to God; and again: When the fulness of the Gentiles is come in, then all Israel shall be saved.

And behold a woman who was troubled with an issue of blood twelve years came behind Him and touched the hem of His garment. In the Gospel according to St. Luke it is written that the ruler's daughter was twelve years of age. Note, therefore, that this woman, who is a type of the Gentiles, had been ailing for the same time as the Jewish nation, typified by the ruler's daughter, had been living in the faith. For vice does not appear (in all its deformity) until it is compared with its opposite virtue.

This woman with the issue of blood came not to the Lord in a house or in a city, for according to the Law, such as she were not allowed in cities; but she came to Him in the way, as He walked; so that as He was going to find one person, He healed another. Whence the Apostle also said: To you it behooved us first to speak the word of God: but because you judge yourselves unworthy of eternal life, we turn to the Gentiles.

For she said within herself: If I shall touch the hem of His garment, I shall be healed. According to the law, whoever touched a menstruous woman or one having a flow of blood was unclean; however, she touched the Lord that she herself might be cured of the evil of the flow of blood. Be of good heart, daughter, thy faith hath made thee whole. For this reason, O daughter, because thy faith hath made thee whole. Nor did He say: Thy faith shall make thee whole; but, hath made thee whole; for in that which thou hast believed, thou art already made whole.

R. The nations are come together against us to destroy us, and we know not what we should do: * O Lord God, our eyes look to Thee that we may not perish. Thou knowest what they intend against us. V. How shall we be able to stand before their face unless Thou help us? O Lord. Glory. O Lord.

✠ Continuation of the holy Gospel according to St. Matthew.—At that time: When Jesus was speaking to the multitudes, behold a certain ruler came up and adored Him, saying: Lord, my daughter is even now dead; but come, lay Thy hand upon her, and she shall live. And Jesus, rising up, followed him, with His disciples. And behold a woman who was troubled with an issue of blood twelve years came behind Him, and touched the hem of His garment. For she said within herself: If I shall touch only His garment, I shall be healed. But Jesus turning and seeing her, said: Be of good heart, daughter, thy faith hath made thee whole. And the woman was made whole from that hour. And when Jesus was come into the house of the ruler and saw the minstrels and the multitude making a tumult, He said: Give place; for the girl is not dead, but sleepeth. And they laughed Him to scorn. And when the multitude was put forth, He went in and took her by the hand. And the maid arose. And the fame thereof went abroad into all that country.

LET US PRAY

O Lord, we beseech Thee, forgive the sins of Thy people, and in Thy goodness deliver us from the bonds of those sins we have committed by our weakness. Through our Lord.

XXIV SUNDAY AFTER PENTECOST

III Nocturn

The reading of the holy Gospel according to St. Matthew

At that time: Jesus said to His disciples: When you shall see the abomination of desolation which was spoken of by Daniel the prophet, standing in the holy place: he that readeth let him understand. And so forth.

Homily of St. Jerome, Priest

By this injunction we are warned to understand that there is something mysterious in what is said. In Daniel we read as follows: And in the half of the week the sacrifice and the oblations shall be taken away, and there shall be in the temple the abomination of desolation, even until the consummation of time, and a consummation shall be given to the desolation.

It is of this that the Apostle speaks when he says that the man of sin and the adversary is to be lifted up against all that is called God or that is worshipped; so that he dares to stand in the temple of God and to show himself as if he were God; whose coming, according to the working of Satan, shall destroy all who shall receive him and shall banish them from God.

This prophecy may be taken simply either of Antichrist or of the statue of Caesar which Pilate put in the temple, or of the equestrian statue of Hadrian which has stood even to the present day upon the very site of the holy of holies. In the Old Testament scriptures, abomination is a word used for idols and the word desolation is added because the idol was placed in a desolate and ruined temple.

By the abomination of desolation we may also understand every perverse doctrine, and when we see such doctrine standing in the holy place, that is, in the Church, and pretending that it is of God, we must flee from Judea to the mountains; that is, leaving the letter which kills, and Jewish depravity, we must draw near to the everlasting hills from whence God shines so wonderfully. We must be on a house-top and in a house where the fiery darts of the devil cannot reach us; neither must we come down to take anything out of the house of our old manner of life, nor seek the things that are behind; but rather we must sow in the field of the spiritual scriptures that we may gather fruit from them:

neither are we to take another coat, which was forbidden to the Apostles.

R. O Lord God, * Have mercy on the sinful nation, upon a people laden with iniquity. V. Be appeased concerning the transgression of Thy people. Have mercy. Glory. Have mercy.

✠ Continuation of the holy Gospel according to St. Matthew.—At that time: Jesus said to His disciples: When you shall see the abomination of desolation which was spoken of by Daniel the prophet, standing in the holy place; (he that readeth, let him understand): then they that are in Judea, let them flee to the mountains; and he that is on the house-top, let him not come down to take anything out of his house; and he that is in the field, let him not go back to take his coat. And woe to them that are with child and that give suck in those days. But pray that your flight be not in winter, or on the sabbath; for there shall be then great tribulation, such as hath not been found from the beginning of the world until now, neither shall be: and unless those days had been shortened, no flesh should be saved; but for the sake of the elect, those days shall be shortened. Then if any man shall say to you: Lo, here is Christ, or there; do not believe him; for there shall arise false Christs, and false prophets, and shall show great signs and wonders, insomuch as to deceive (if possible) even the elect.

Behold I have told it to you beforehand: if therefore they shall say to you: Behold He is in the desert, go ye not out; behold He is in the closets, believe it not. For as lightning cometh out of the east and appeareth even into the west, so shall also the coming of the Son of man be. Wheresoever the body shall be, there shall be the eagles also gathered together. And immediately after the tribulation of those days, the sun shall be darkened, and the moon shall not give her light, and the stars shall fall from heaven, and the powers of heaven shall be moved; And then shall appear the sign of the Son of man in heaven, and then shall all the tribes of the earth mourn; and they shall see the Son of man coming in the clouds of heaven with much power and majesty; and He shall send His angels with a trumpet and a great voice, and they shall gather together His elect from the four winds, from the farthest parts of the heavens to the utmost bounds of them. And from the fig-tree learn a parable: when the branch thereof is now tender and the leaves come forth, you know that summer is nigh. So you also, when you shall see all these things, know ye that it is nigh even at the doors. Amen I say to you that this generation shall not pass till all these things be done. Heaven and earth shall pass away, but My words shall not pass away.

Let Us Pray

Arouse, we beseech Thee, O Lord, the wills of Thy faithful people, that more zealously seeking the fruit of the divine grace, they may receive greater helps from Thy goodness. Through our Lord.

THE SANCTORAL CYCLE

November 30

ST. ANDREW THE APOSTLE

I Nocturn

*From the Epistle of the blessed Apostle Paul
to the Romans, c. 10, 4 - 21*

II Nocturn

Andrew, the Apostle, born at Bethsaida, a village of Galilee, was the brother of Peter and a disciple of John the Baptist, and having heard him say to Christ: Behold the Lamb of God; he followed Jesus and brought to Him his brother also. When afterwards he was fishing with his brother in the sea of Galilee, they were both called before any of the other Apostles by Christ the Lord, who, passing by, said to them: Come after Me, I will make you to be fishers of men. Without delay they left their nets and followed Him. After His passion and resurrection, Andrew went to spread the faith of Christ in European Scythia, which was the province assigned to him; then he travelled through Epirus and Thrace and by his teaching and miracles converted innumerable souls to Christ.

Afterwards, having reached Patræ in Achaia, he persuaded many in that city to embrace the truth of the Gospel. Finding that the Proconsul Aegeas resisted the preaching of the Gospel, he most freely upbraided him for that he, who desired to be con-

sidered as a judge of men, should be so far deceived
by devils as not to acknowledge Christ to be God,
the Judge of all. Then Aegeas, being angry, says:
Cease to boast of this Christ whom such words as
these kept not from being crucified by the Jews.
But finding that Andrew continued boldly preaching that Christ had offered Himself to be crucified
for the salvation of mankind, he interrupts him by
an impious speech and at length exhorts him to
look to his own interest and sacrifice to the gods.
Andrew answers: I offer up every day to almighty
God, who is one and true, not the flesh of oxen, not
the blood of goats, but the spotless Lamb upon the
altar; of whose flesh the whole multitude of the
faithful eat and the Lamb that is sacrificed remains whole and living.

Whereupon Aegeas, being exceedingly angry, orders him to be thrust into prison; but the people
would easily have freed Andrew had he not himself
calmed them, begging with most earnest entreaty
that they would not keep him from the long-de-
sired crown of martyrdom to which he was hastening. Not long after this he was brought before the
tribunal where he began to extol the mystery of
the Cross and rebuke Aegeas for his impiety.
Aegeas, no longer able to contain himself, ordered
him to be raised on a cross and so to die like Christ.

Andrew, having been brought to the place of execution, saw the cross at some distance and began

to cry out: O good cross, made beautiful by the
body of my Lord! so long desired, so anxiously
loved, so unceasingly sought after, and now at last
ready for my soul to enjoy; welcome me from a-
mong men and join me again to my Master; that
as by thee He redeemed me, so by thee also He may
take me unto Himself. He was therefore fastened
to the cross on which he hung alive two days,
preaching without ceasing the faith of Christ; after which he passed to Him, the likeness of whose
death he had so coveted. The priests and deacons
of Achaia, who wrote his passion, attest that all
the things which they have recorded were heard
and seen by them. His relics were first translated
to Constantinople in the reign of the emperor Constantine and afterwards to Amalfi. During the
pontificate of Pius II the head was taken to Rome
and placed in the Basilica of St. Peter.

R. The Lord, walking by the sea of Galilee, saw
Peter and Andrew casting their nets into the sea
and He called them saying: * Follow Me and I
will make you fishers of men. V. For they were
fishermen and He saith unto them. Follow Me.
Glory. Follow Me.

III Nocturn

The reading of the holy Gospel
according to St. Matthew

At that time: Jesus, walking by the sea of Galilee, saw two brethren, Simon who is called Peter, and Andrew his brother, casting a net into the sea. And so forth.

Homily of St. Gregory, Pope

You have heard, dearest brethren, how at one word of command Peter and Andrew left their nets and followed the Redeemer. They had as yet seen Him work no miracles; they had heard nothing from Him of the gain of an eternal reward; and yet at one word of the Lord's they forgot all that seemed to be theirs. How many miracles we see, how many scourges afflict us, how many threats fill our hearts with terror, and yet we spurn the call to follow Him?

He who calls us to conversion is already enthroned in heaven; He has bowed the necks of the Gentiles under the yoke of faith, He has laid low the glory of this world, and ruins on all sides announce the speedy approach of His judgment. And yet our proud mind will not of its own free will give up what every day we lose against our will.

What shall we say when we are called before His judgment seat, dearest brethren, since we cannot be turned from the love of this world by His commandments nor corrected by His stripes? But perhaps someone will say in his heart: What did these fishermen give up at the word of the Lord, for what they had was almost nothing?

But in such matters, dearest brethren, we ought to consider rather the state of mind than the material profit. He leaves much who keeps back nothing for himself; he leaves much who leaves all, however little it may be. We not only feel attachment to the things which we possess but we desire also the things we do not possess. Peter and Andrew left much for they gave up even the desire of possessing.

R. Holy Andrew prayed, looking up to heaven, and cried out with a loud voice, saying: Thou art my God whom I have seen; suffer me not to be taken down from hence by the impious judge: * For I know the virtue of the holy cross. V. Thou art Christ, my Master, whom I have known and loved, whom I have confessed: hear me now in this prayer. For I know. Glory. For I know.

✠ Continuation of the holy Gospel according to St. Matthew.—At that time: Jesus, walking by the sea of Galilee, saw two brethren, Simon, who is called Peter, and Andrew his brother, casting their nets into the sea (for they were fishermen). And He saith to them: Come ye after Me and I will make you to be fishers of men: and they immediately leaving their nets followed Him. And going on from thence, He saw other two brethren, James, the son of Zebedee, and John his brother, in a ship with Zebedee their father, mending their nets; and

He called them. And they forthwith left their nets and father and followed Him.

LET US PRAY

We humbly beseech Thy Majesty, O Lord, that as blessed Andrew was both a preacher and ruler for Thy Church, so may he also be for us a constant intercessor with Thee. Through our Lord.

December 8

THE IMMACULATE CONCEPTION OF THE BLESSED VIRGIN MARY

I Nocturn

From the book of Genesis, c. 3, 1 - 15

II Nocturn

Sermon of St. Jerome, Priest

The Angel, divinely inspired, declared the nature and the greatness of the blessed and glorious Virgin Mary when he said: Hail, full of grace; the Lord is with thee: blessed art thou among women. For surely it was fitting that to the Virgin should be given, as a pledge of such gifts, that she should be full of grace, she who gave glory to heaven and the Lord to the earth; she restored peace; to the Gentiles she gave faith; vice she brought to an end; life she harmonized and to the realm of conduct she brought discipline. And it is well said: Full; for

Thou art the glory of Jerusalem;

Thou art the Joy of Israel;

Thou art the honor of our people:
(Jud. 15, 10)

to others it is given only in part; while upon Mary
the whole fulness of grace was poured out at once.
Truly, full; for although we believe grace to have
been in the holy Fathers and Prophets, nevertheless
it was not full to that extent; but all the abundance
of grace which was in Christ came to Mary, although in a different manner.   And therefore he
says: Blessed art thou among women; that is, more
blessed than all women.   And thus the blessing of
Mary took away wholly whatever curse was put
upon Eve. Solomon says, as if in praise of her, in
the Canticles: Come, my dove, my spotless one. For
winter is now past, the rain is over and gone. And
then he says: Come from Libanus, come, thou shalt
be crowned.

Not unfittingly therefore is she bidden to come
from Libanus, for Libanus means a radiant whiteness. For she was dazzlingly white with her many
virtues and merits, and by the gifts of the Holy
Ghost she was cleansed whiter than snow; showing
in all things the simplicity of a dove; for all in her
was purity and simplicity, truth and grace; all mercy and justice which hath looked down from heav-
en: and for this reason was she immaculate because
corruption was not found in her. She encompassed
a man in her womb, as holy Jeremias testifies, and
she received Him from no other person. The Lord,
he says, has made a new thing upon the earth and
a woman shall encompass a man.

Truly a new thing and a novelty of power preeminent above all novelties, in that God (whom the world cannot bear nor man see and live), entered the hospice of her womb, as if unaware of her virginity; was so borne therein that the whole God was in her; and so came forth that (as Ezechiel prophesies), the door remained shut. So the same Canticle sings of her: A garden enclosed, a fountain sealed up, thy plants are a paradise. Truly a garden of delights in which were all manner of flowers and the perfume of virtues; so enclosed that neither violation nor corruption by any deceit were known. Therefore: a fountain sealed with the seal of the whole Trinity.

R. No defiled thing cometh unto her: * She is the brightness of eternal light and an unspotted mirror. V. For she is more beautiful than the sun and compared with light she is found brighter. * She is.

From the Acts of Pope Pius IX

The victory gained by the Virgin Mother of God in her Conception over the deadly enemy of the human race had been already wonderfully shown forth in the inspired word of God, in a venerable tradition, and in the mind of the Church throughout the ages in the striking agreement of thought between the bishops and the faithful and in noteworthy acts and constitutions of the Sovereign Pontiffs when Pope Pius IX, assenting to the prayers

of the whole Church, resolved solemnly to proclaim
it by his supreme and infallible decree. Therefore
on December 8, 1854, in the presence of an immense
concourse of Fathers, Cardinals and Bishops of the
holy Roman Church gathered together in the Vatican basilica from the remotest parts of the earth.
and with the applause of the whole world, he solemnly pronounced and defined: That the doctrine
which holds that the Blessed Virgin Mary was, at
the first instant of her Conception, by a singular
privilege of God preserved from all stain of original
sin has been revealed by God and is therefore to be
believed by the faithful with firmness and constancy.

R. By one man in whom all have sinned, sin entered into this world. * Fear not, Mary, for thou
hast found grace with God. V. The Lord hath delivered my soul from death and hath become my
protector against the enemy. Fear not. Glory.
Fear not.

III Nocturn

The reading of the holy Gospel
according to St. Luke

At that time: The angel Gabriel was sent from
God into a city of Galilee, called Nazareth, to a virgin espoused to a man whose name was Joseph, of
the house of David; and the virgin's name was
Mary. And so forth.

Homily of St. Germanus, Bishop

Hail, Mary, full of grace, holier than the Saints, loftier than the heavens, more glorious than the Cherubim, more honorable than the Seraphim, above all creatures more worthy of veneration. Hail, dove, thou who brings to us the fruit of the olive and announces a preserver and a harbor of safety from the spiritual deluge; whose wings, covered with silver, and the hinder parts of her back with the paleness of gold, shine with the brightness of the most holy and enlightening Spirit. Hail, O lovely human paradise of God, planted today in the East by His almighty and benevolent right hand, bringing forth the fragrant lily and the unfading rose for the cure of those who have drunk the poisonous and deadly bitterness of death to the soul in the West: O paradise, where blooms the tree of life for the knowledge of truth, bringing to those who taste it life everlasting.

Hail, O most holy building, spotless and pure palace of God, the most high king, adorned with the magnificence of God the King Himself, receiving all with hospitality and refreshing them with mystical delights; wherein is that couch of the mystical Spouse, not made with hands, gleaming with every beauty; in which the Word, wishing to recall the wandering human race, Himself espoused flesh that He might reconcile to His Father those who, of their own will, had banished themselves from

Him. Hail, mountain of God, fertile and shady, whereat was fed the rational Lamb who bore our sins and our infirmities: from that mountain rolled the stone, not cut by hand, crushing the altars of the idols, that was made the head of the corner, wonderful in our eyes. Hail, holy throne of God, divine sanctuary, house of glory, jewel most fair, chosen treasure-house and mercy-seat for the whole world, heaven showing forth the glory of God. Hail, vessel made of the purest gold, where lies the sweetest delightfulness of our souls, containing as it were Christ our manna.

O purest Virgin, worthy of all praise and reverence, sanctuary dedicated to God and raised above all human condition, virgin soil, unploughed field, flourishing vine, fountain pouring out waters, virgin who brings forth, mother who knows not man, hidden treasure of innocence and ornament of sanctity; by thy most acceptable prayers, strong with the authority of motherhood, to our Lord and God, Creator of all, thy Son who was born of thee without a father, steer that ship which is the Church, and bring it to a quiet harbor.

Invest priests with judgment and the most noble joy of a proved, spotless and sincere faith. Guide in prosperity and peace the sceptres of those orthodox princes who, rather than the splendor of purple and gold, pearls or precious stones, have thee as their diadem and robe and as a lasting glory to their kingdoms. Cast under their feet the faithless nations who have blasphemed thee and the God born of thee; strengthen their subject peoples that, according to the precept of God, they may persevere in the sweet service of obedience. Crown with the triumph of victory this thy city which has thee both as a tower and a foundation; and keep thou the house of God, surrounding it with strength, and preserve always the beauty of the temple; free those who praise thee from all dangers and anguish of mind; release all prisoners; console all strangers and those who have no roof or protection. Stretch out to the whole world thy helping hand, that in joy and exultation we may bring to a brilliant conclusion thy solemnities together with that feast which we have recently celebrated in Christ Jesus, King of the universe and our true God, to whom, together with the holy Father, the source of life, and the Spirit, co-eternal and consubstantial and co-reigning, be glory and power, now and always, forever and ever. Amen.

R. Magnify the Lord with me: * Because the mercy of the Lord is great towards me. V. The prince of this world has nothing in common with me. Because. Glory. Because.

✠ Continuation of the holy Gospel according to St. Luke.—At that time: The Angel Gabriel was sent from God into a city of Galilee, called Nazareth, to a virgin espoused to a man whose name was

Joseph, of the house of David: and the virgin's name was Mary. And the Angel being come in, said unto her: Hail, full of grace, the Lord is with thee: blessed art thou among women.

LET US PRAY

O God, who by the Immaculate Conception of the Virgin didst prepare a worthy dwelling for Thy Son, we beseech Thee, that as Thou didst preserve her from every stain through the foreseen merits of that same Son, Thou, by her intercession, wouldst grant us cleansed from sin to come to Thee. Through the same our Lord.

December 9

SECOND DAY WITHIN THE OCTAVE OF THE IMMACULATE CONCEPTION

From the Dogmatic Bull of Pope Pius IX

The ineffable God, whose ways are mercy and truth, whose will is omnipotence and whose wisdom reacheth from end to end mightily and ordereth all things agreeably, in that He foresaw from all eternity the unhappy ruin of the whole race of man through the sin of Adam; and moreover, since He had determined by a mystery hidden from all ages to accomplish the first work of His goodness in a sacred dispensation by the Incarnation of the Word; and this, in order that, against His own most merciful purpose, man, led away into sin by the guile of the devil, might not be brought to destruction;

and further that what He foresaw was to fall in the
first Adam might in the second Adam more happily be raised up again;—He, for all these reasons,
chose and ordained from the beginning and before
all ages a Mother for His only-begotten Son, that,
taking flesh from her, He might be born in the
blessed fulness of time. And upon her too He bestowed so great a love beyond all other creatures
that in her alone He delighted exceedingly with a
most affectionate will.

Wherefore He so wonderfully adorned her above
all Angels and Saints with abundance of all heavenly gifts drawn from the divine treasury, that always free from every stain of sin, wholly beautiful
and perfect, she might show forth a fulness of innocence and holiness than which, under God, no
greater can be imagined, and which, save God, no
one can attain to in thought. And indeed it was
most fitting that so venerable a mother should shine
forth as ever adorned with radiance of perfect holiness, and further, as being entirely free from the
stain of original sin, should achieve the fullest victory over the old serpent; for it was to her that
God the Father purposed to give His only Son, begotten equal with Himself from His own bosom,
whom He loves as Himself; and to give Him, moreover, in such a way that He should be by nature
the one common Son both of God the Father and of
the Virgin.

This, the august Virgin's original sinlessness, wholly befitting her admirable sanctity and her eminent dignity as Mother of God, the Catholic Church, which through the continual guidance of the Holy Ghost is the pillar and ground of truth, has never ceased to explain, declare, and cherish with ever-increasing clearness and glorious deeds, holding it for a doctrine divinely revealed, and contained in many ways in the deposit of revelation. This doctrine, which flourished from earliest times and was firmly rooted in the souls of the faithful and, by the care and efforts of holy bishops, wonderfully propagated through the Catholic world, was set forth by the Church herself in the clearest manner when she hesitated not to propose the Conception of the Virgin for the public worship and veneration of the faithful. By which striking fact she showed the Virgin's Conception to be singular, admirable, entirely apart from the origin of the rest of mankind, and a thing worthy of holy veneration, since the Church venerates merely the days of the death of the Saints.

December 10

THIRD DAY WITHIN THE OCTAVE
OF THE IMMACULATE CONCEPTION

From the Dogmatic Bull of Pope Pius IX

The Church has been accustomed both in ecclesiastical offices and in the most sacred liturgy to apply and transfer to the origin of the Virgin, which was indeed decreed at one and the same time with the Incarnation of the Divine Wisdom, the very words in which the divine Scriptures speak of uncreated Wisdom and set forth His eternal origin. And although the acceptance of all these passages by almost all the faithful shows with what care the Roman Church herself, the mother and mistress of all the churches, cultivated the doctrine of the Immaculate Conception of the Virgin, yet her manifest dealings in this respect are worthy of individual mention. For the dignity and authority of that Church are such as are due to her who is the center of Catholic truth and unity, in whom alone has religion been kept inviolate, and from whom it behooves all other churches to receive the tradition of faith. That Roman Church therefore had nothing so much at heart as that the Immaculate Conception of the Virgin, both as to doctrine and cult, should in the most eloquent manner be asserted, defended, promoted, and vindicated.

Wherefore our predecessors greatly rejoiced to institute in the Roman Church the feast of the Conception with a proper Office and a proper Mass, in which should be plainly asserted the prerogative of immunity from the hereditary stain. They rejoiced, moreover, to increase, enrich, honor, and promote by every means in their power the cult so instituted by the grant of indulgences as well as

of faculties bestowed on cities, provinces, and kingdoms to choose as their patron the Mother of God
under the title of the Immaculate Conception, by
privileges granted to approved sodalities, congre-
gations, and religious families founded in honor of
the Immaculate Conception, by praise bestowed
upon the piety of such as shall found monasteries,
hostels, altars, and churches under the title of the
Immaculate Conception, or again, who shall promise by vow vigorously to defend the doctrine of the
Conception of the Mother of God.

Moreover, they rejoiced above all things to decree that the feast of the Conception should be considered by the whole Church as a feast of the same
rank and class as that of the Nativity; that that
feast of the Conception should be celebrated by the
universal Church with an octave; that it should be
piously observed by all as a feast of obligation; and
that Mass should be solemnly celebrated every
year on the day of the Virgin's Conception in the
pontifical chapel of our patriarchal basilica of St.
Mary Major.   Furthermore, since it was their earnest desire to foster in the souls of the faithful an
ever-increasing devotion to the doctrine of the Immaculate Conception of the Mother of God and to
arouse within them piety and veneration for the
Virgin conceived without the stain of original sin,
they willingly and gladly granted permission to proclaim the Immaculate Conception of that Virgin

in the Litany of Loretto, and even in the very Preface of the Mass, that thus the law of faith might be confirmed by the law of prayer.

December 11

FOURTH DAY WITHIN THE OCTAVE OF THE IMMACULATE CONCEPTION

From the Dogmatic Bull of Pope Pius IX

Since it is clear that what pertains to worship is intimately bound up with its object and cannot remain sure and stable if the latter be uncertain and doubtful; therefore our predecessors, the Roman Pontiffs, furthering by all means in their power devotion to the Conception, strove earnestly to set forth and inculcate its object and doctrine. For they taught clearly and openly that the feast was of the Virgin's Conception, and they condemned as false and utterly foreign to the Church's mind the opinion of those who held and taught that what the Church venerated was not her Conception, but her sanctification.

Nor did they deal less severely with those who, to impugn the doctrine of the Virgin's Immaculate Conception, made an imaginary distinction between the first and second instant and moment of conception, and then allowed the celebration of the Conception, but not for the first instant and moment. Our predecessors, however, thought it their

duty zealously to defend and uphold the feast of
the Conception of the most blessed Virgin and that
the first moment of the Conception was the real object of the devotion.   Hence, in words clearly having the force of a decree, our predecessor, Alexander VII, declared the sincere mind of the Church,
saying: Plainly the ancient piety of the faithful of
Christ towards the most blessed Virgin Mary, His
Mother, held that her soul, in the first instant of
its creation and infusion into the body, was by a
special grace and privilege of God, through the
merits of her Son, Jesus Christ, Redeemer of mankind, preserved immune from the stain of original
sin; and in this sense the feast of her Conception
is in solemn rite held and celebrated.

It was this in particular that those our predecessors held as a sacred duty, namely, to preserve
whole and intact with all care, diligence and effort,
the doctrine of the Immaculate Conception of the
Mother of God.   For not only did they refuse to
allow this doctrine to be called in question or to be
censured by anyone, but going yet further than
this, they proclaimed in clear statements and on repeated occasions: That the doctrine by which we
profess the Immaculate Conception of the Virgin
is rightly to be held as fully in harmony with ecclesiastical worship; that it is ancient and almost
universal; that it is of such a nature as to be taken
under the fostering care and protection of the Ro-

man Church; and that it is altogether worthy to be celebrated in the sacred liturgy and with the most solemn invocations. Not content with this, in order that the doctrine of the Immaculate Conception of the Virgin might be maintained in its integrity, they strictly forbade the defence, either public or private, of any opinion contrary to this doctrine, smiting such adverse opinion, as it were, with repeated blows.

December 12

FIFTH DAY WITHIN THE OCTAVE OF THE IMMACULATE CONCEPTION

From the Dogmatic Bull of Pope Pius IX

It is known to all with what zeal the doctrine of the Immaculate Conception of the Virgin Mother of God has been handed down, proclaimed, and defended by the most prominent religious orders, the most famous schools of theology, and the doctors most eminent in the knowledge of sacred things. And likewise, all know how solicitous were the bishops in ecclesiastical assemblies openly and publicly to profess that the most holy Virgin Mary, Mother of God, was through the foreseen merits of Christ, the Lord and Redeemer, never subjected to original sin, but completely preserved from the original stain, and therefore redeemed in a more sublime manner. To these declarations indeed must be add-

ed one that is of greater weight and importance
than all, that declaration made by the Council of
Trent when, in issuing the dogmatic decree concerning original sin, it declared and defined in accordance with the testimony of the sacred Scriptures, the holy Fathers, and the approved Councils,
as follows: That all men are born tainted with
original sin; but at the same time declaring: That
it was not their intention to include in that decree
and within the scope of that broad definition the
blessed and immaculate Virgin Mary, Mother of
God. By this declaration the Fathers of Trent sufficiently indicated, time and circumstances being
considered, that the most blessed Virgin was free
from the original sin, and that nothing could be
justly cited from holy Scripture, from tradition, or
from the testimony of the Fathers, that in any way
opposes the Virgin's great privilege.

And indeed, this doctrine of the Immaculate Conception of the most blessed Virgin Mary, every day
more gloriously set forth, declared and confirmed
by the weightiest opinion, teaching, care, wisdom,
and knowledge of the Church; this doctrine, which
spread in a way that is truly wonderful throughout
all peoples and nations of the Catholic world; this
doctrine, it is clear, as the most authentic records
of antiquity in both the eastern and the western
Church bear testimony, has always been accepted
by the Church and stamped with the character of

revealed dogma. Moreover, the Fathers and writers of the Church, endowed with heavenly eloquence, have from the remotest times, in books dedicated to the explanation of the Scriptures, the defence of doctrine, and the instruction of the faithful, ever asserted and proclaimed in many wonderful ways the supreme sanctity and dignity of the Virgin, her freedom from all stain of sin, and her signal victory over the foul enemy of the human race.

Wherefore they quoted the words in which God at the beginning of the world foretold the remedy His mercy had prepared for the restoration of mankind; words in which He both repressed the boldness of the crafty serpent and wonderfully raised the hope of our race, saying: I will put enmities between thee and the woman, and thy seed and her seed. This divine utterance, they taught, pointed unmistakably to the merciful Redeemer of mankind, Christ Jesus, the only-begotten Son of God, while at the same time it foreshowed His Mother, the most blessed Virgin Mary, and in a signal manner expressed the enmity of both against the devil. Thus has Christ, the mediator between God and man, having assumed our human nature, blotted out the handwriting of the decree that was against us and nailed it in triumph to the cross; so the most holy Virgin, being strictly and indissolubly bound to Him, waged with Him and through Him an eternal warfare against the venomous serpent and, gaining a complete victory, crushed his head beneath her own spotless foot.

December 14

SEVENTH DAY WITHIN THE OCTAVE OF THE IMMACULATE CONCEPTION

From the Dogmatic Bull of Pope Pius IX

This exceptional and singular triumph of the Virgin, her surpassing innocence, purity, holiness, her integrity free of any spot, and the ineffable plenitude and extent of all heavenly graces, virtues and privileges; all these, the same Fathers saw not alone in that ark of Noe which, divinely established, quite safe and unharmed escaped the common shipwreck of the whole world; but also in that ladder which Jacob saw reaching from earth even to heaven, whose rungs the angels of God were ascending and descending, and at whose top the Lord Himself was resting; as likewise in that bush which in the holy place Moses saw entirely aflame and yet amidst the crackling tongues of fire not burnt nor suffering even the least damage, rather he beheld it thrive and blossom beautifully; as likewise in that impregnable tower from the face of the enemy, from which a thousand shields hang and all the armor of the strong; as likewise in that enclosed garden which knows not violation or corruption by any deceitful trickery; as likewise in that radiant city of God whose foundations are in the holy mounts; as likewise in that awesome temple of God which, bright with divine splendor, is full of the glory of God; and likewise in several other instances quite of the same kind in which the Fathers tell us that the exalted dignity of the Mother of God, her unstained innocence and sanctity, never marred by a birth-mark, were foretold.

To describe this same totality, as it were, of divine gifts and the original integrity of which Jesus was born, the same Fathers, using the writings of the Prophets, not otherwise have honored this august Virgin than as a pure dove, as the holy Jerusalem, as the exalted throne of God, as the ark and home of sanctification, which eternal Wisdom built for itself, as that Queen, flowing with delights and leaning upon her Beloved, who came forth from the mouth of the most High, entirely perfect, beautiful and altogether precious to God, and in no way ever stained by the birth-mark of the fall.

Inasmuch, then, as the very Fathers and Writers of the Church are wont wholeheartedly to reckon that the ever-blessed Virgin was called, in the name of and at the command of God Himself, full of grace by the angel Gabriel when he announced to her that sublimest dignity of being God's Mother; thus they teach that by this singular and solemn greeting, never elsewhere heard, it is shown that the Mother of God was the seat of all divine graces, adorned with all the *charismata* of the divine Spirit; rather, the treasury nearly infinite and unexhausted abyss of these same *charismata*; so that, never subject to the Cursed One, together with her Son a sharer of endless blessing, she merited to hear from Elizabeth, moved by the divine Spirit, that: Blessed art thou among women and blessed is the fruit of thy womb. To this (add) these same writers' opinion, not less splendid than concordant, that the ever-glorious Virgin, to whom He that is mighty hath done great things, has shone with such power of all heavenly gifts, with such fulness of grace, with such innocence, that, as it were, an ineffable miracle of God—rather, the crown of all miracles—she has been established the worthy Mother of God; approaching God Himself, as much as may be in consideration of her created nature, she has become more sublime than the eulogies alike of men and angels.

December 15
OCTAVE DAY OF THE IMMACULATE CONCEPTION

From the Dogmatic Bull of Pope Pius IX

From ancient times pontiffs, ecclesiastics, the regular Orders, emperors moreover and kings, have earnestly demanded that this Apostolic See define the Immaculate Conception of the most holy Mother of God as a dogma of Catholic faith. These requests have been repeated in our own times, and especially in the days of our predecessor Gregory XVI of happy memory, and have been presented to us also by bishops, secular clergy, and religious orders, by princes of the highest rank, and by the faithful in general.

Recognizing these things to our great joy and seriously considering them, as soon as the mysterious decree of Divine providence raised us, though unworthy, to the sublime chair of Peter and entrusted us with the government of the whole Church, we made it our duty, according to the tender devotion and veneration which from our youth we have professed towards the most holy Virgin Mary, to carry out all that the Church could desire, in order to add to the honor of the most Blessed Virgin and set her privilege in fuller light.

Now, therefore, trusting in God that the time has come for the definition of the Immaculate Conception of the most holy Virgin Mary, Mother of God, which the divine word, venerable tradition, the constant mind of the Church, the unanimous consent of Catholic bishops and the faithful, and the noteworthy acts and constitutions of our predecessors show forth and declare in a wonderful manner; having weighed all things most carefully, and after fervent and constant prayers to God, we have resolved without further delay to sanction and define, by our supreme jurisdiction, the Immaculate Conception of the Virgin; and thus to satisfy the pious de-

sires of the Catholic world, and our own devotion
to the most holy Virgin; and in her we shall honor
at the same time more and more her only Son, our
Lord Jesus Christ; for upon the Son redounds all
the honor and praise given to the Mother.

Thus, since we have never ceased to offer, in humility and fasting, both our private prayers, and
the public prayers of the Church to God the Father,
through His Son, that He would vouchsafe to guide
and strengthen our mind with the Holy Ghost;
since we have implored the assistance of the whole
court of heaven, and summoned to our aid with
groanings the Spirit, the Paraclete, and since He
has also inspired us in this sense; for the honor
and glory of thy holy and undivided Trinity, for
the beauty and adornment of the Virgin Mother of
God, for the exaltation of the Catholic faith and
the increase of the Christian religion, we declare,
proclaim, and define, by the authority of our Lord
Jesus Christ, of the blessed Apostles Peter and
Paul, and by our own authority: That the doctrine, which maintains that the most blessed Virgin Mary was, in the first instant of her conception,
by the singular grace and privilege of Almighty
God, through the merits of Christ Jesus, Savior of
mankind, preserved immune from all stain of original sin, is revealed by God, and as such is to be
constantly and firmly believed by all the faithful.
Wherefore if any, which God forbid, shall presume

to think in their hearts otherwise than we have defined, let those ones understand and know for certain that they are by their own judgment self-condemned, that they have made shipwreck of their faith, and have fallen away from the unity of the Church.

R. Magnify the Lord with me: * Because the mercy of the Lord is great towards me. V. The prince of this world has nothing in common with me. Because. Glory. Because.

III Nocturn

The reading of the holy Gospel according to St. Luke

At that time: The angel Gabriel was sent from God into a city of Galilee, called Nazareth, to a virgin espoused to a man whose name was Joseph, of the house of David, and the virgin's name was Mary. And so forth.

Homily of St. Epiphanius, Bishop

What shall I say, or what shall I declare, concerning this excellent and holy Virgin? For with the exception of God alone, she stands out as superior to all; more beautiful by nature than the Cherubim and Seraphim themselves, and all the angelic host. No tongue of earth or heaven or even that of Angels, can fittingly praise her. O blessed Virgin, pure dove and heavenly spouse, Mary, heaven, temple, throne of the divinity, who hast Christ the sun shining in heaven and on earth! Bright cloud which drew Christ down from heaven, the brilliant lightning that illumines the world.

Hail, full of grace, gate of the heavens, of whom the prophet spoke plainly and openly in the course of his oration in the Canticles, crying out: My sister, my spouse, is a garden enclosed, a garden enclosed, a fountain sealed up. The Virgin is a spotless lily, who bore Christ, the rose that cannot wither. O holy Mother of God, spotless ewe, that brought forth Christ the Lamb, the Word incarnate! O most holy Virgin, who hast filled the angelic hosts with wonder!

Marvelous is the miracle in heaven, a woman clothed with the sun, and bearing light in her arms; a marvelous miracle in heaven, the bedchamber of the Virgin having the Son of God; a marvelous miracle in heaven, the Lord of Angels has become the babe of a Virgin. Eve was accused by the Angels, but now they attend upon the glory of Mary, who raised up the fallen Eve, and sent to heaven Adam cast out of Paradise. She is the mediatrix between heaven and earth, who effected their union by nature.

The grace of the holy Virgin is immeasurable. Thus Gabriel first salutes her, saying: Hail, full of grace, thou art a glorious heaven. Hail, full of grace, Virgin adorned with many virtues. Hail, full of grace, thou art a golden vessel containing

the heavenly manna. Hail, full of grace, thou dost
satisfy the thirsty with the sweetness of an everlasting fountain. Hail, most holy Mother Immaculate, who hast given birth to Christ, who is before
thee. Hail, royal purple, which hath clothed the
King of heaven and earth. Hail, book unfathomable, that shows forth the Word and the Son of the
Father, to be read by the world.

R. My soul doth magnify the Lord; * Because
He that is mighty hath done great things to me,
and holy is His name. V. For behold from henceforth all generations shall call me blessed. Because.
Glory. Because.

✠ Continuation of the holy Gospel according to
St. Luke.—At that time: The Angel Gabriel was
sent from God into a city of Galilee, called Nazareth, to a virgin espoused to a man whose name
was Joseph, of the house of David: and the virgin's name was Mary. And the Angel being come
in, said unto her: Hail, full of grace, the Lord is
with thee: blessed art thou among women.

LET US PRAY

O God, who by the Immaculate Conception of the
Virgin Mary didst prepare a worthy dwelling for
Thy Son, we beseech Thee, that as Thou didst preserve her from every stain through the foreseen
merits of that same Son, Thou, by her intercession
wouldst grant us cleansed from sin to come to Thee.
Through our Lord.

December 21

ST. THOMAS APOSTLE

I Nocturn

From the First Epistle of St. Paul to the Corinthians, c. 4, 1 - 15

II Nocturn

Thomas the Apostle, also named Didymus, was a Galilean. After he had received the Holy Ghost, he travelled through many provinces, preaching the Gospel of Christ. He transmitted the precepts of the Christian faith and life to the Parthians, Medes, Persians, Hyrcanians, and Bactrians. He finally went to the Indies and instructed the inhabitants in the Christian religion. When, up to the last, by the holiness of his life and teaching and by the greatness of the miracles which he wrought, he had excited the admiration of all men and led them to the love of Jesus Christ, the king of that nation, a worshipper of idols, became furiously angry: by whose orders he was condemned to be pierced by javelins; and thus, at Calamia, the crown of martyrdom decorated the glory of his apostolate.

Sermon of St. Gregory, Pope

It is written: The spirit of the Lord hath adorned the heavens. For the ornaments of the heavens are the virtues of preachers. Which ornaments are thus enumerated by Paul in the words:

To one, by the Spirit, is given the word of wisdom; to another, the word of knowledge, according to the same Spirit; to another, faith in the same Spirit; to another, the grace of healing in one Spirit; to another, the working of miracles; to another, prophecy; to another, the discerning of spirits; to another, diverse kinds of tongues; to another, interpretation of speeches. But all these things one and the same Spirit worketh, dividing to everyone according as He will.

The heavens, therefore, have as many ornaments as preachers have virtues. Wherefore, it is also written: By the word of the Lord the heavens were established. For the Word of the Lord is the Son of the Father. But that we may know that these heavens, that is, the holy Apostles, at the same time display the work of the whole Trinity, there is added at once, in reference to the divinity of the Holy Ghost: And all the power of them by the spirit of His mouth. Therefore, the power of the heavens is taken from the Holy Ghost; for they would not have dared to withstand the powers of this world if the Holy Ghost had not confirmed them with His fortitude.

We know what these Doctors of the holy Church were before the coming of that Spirit, and we see how they were endowed with such fortitude after He had descended upon them. Indeed, this very shepherd of the Church, near whose holy remains

we are assembled, displayed such great weakness
and such great timidity, as we may learn if we ask
the servant-maid who kept the door. For he was
so stricken with terror at the mere voice of a woman, that in fear of death, he denied the Life.

R. I saw men standing together, clad in shining
garments; and the Angel of the Lord spoke to me,
saying: * These holy men became the friends of
God. V. I saw a mighty Angel of God, flying
through the midst of heaven, crying out with a loud
voice and saying. These. Glory. These.

III Nocturn

The reading of the holy Gospel
according to St. John

At that time: Thomas, one of the twelve, who is
called Didymus, was not with them when Jesus
came. And so forth.

Homily of St. Gregory, Pope

What, dearest brethren, do you notice in this passage? Do you think that it happened by chance
that this chosen disciple was absent at that time,
and afterwards coming, heard the news; and hearing, doubted; that doubting, he touched; and touching, he believed? This did not happen by chance,
but by divine dispensation. For the supernal clemency brought it about in a wonderful way, that that
doubting disciple, while touching the wounds in his

Master's flesh, should thereby heal the wounds of our unbelief.

The unbelief of Thomas has done more for our faith than the faith of the believing disciples. While he is brought back to faith by touching, our minds are set free from doubt and established in the faith. So the Lord indeed permitted after His Resurrection that His disciple should doubt, but He did not leave him in unbelief; just as before His Birth He wished Mary to have a spouse, who, however, never attained to the married state. The disciple who doubted and touched his risen Lord thus became a witness to the truth of the Resurrection just as the spouse of His mother was the guardian of her inviolate virginity.

Thomas touched, and cried out: My Lord, and my God. Jesus said to him; Because thou hast seen Me, thou hast believed. But since the Apostle Paul says: Now faith is the substance of things to be hoped for, the evidence of things which cannot appear. The things which appear are the object, not of faith, but of knowledge.

Why, then, is it said to Thomas, who saw and touched: Because thou hast seen Me, thou hast believed? But he saw one thing, and believed another. Indeed, mortal man cannot see the divinity. So Thomas saw a man and confessed Him to be God, saying: My Lord, and my God. He therefore believed through seeing; for, looking upon one who was truly man, he cried out that this was God whom he could not see. The words which follow are a cause of great joy to us: Blessed are they who have not seen and have believed. These words are meant especially for us who cherish in our minds Him whom we do not see in the flesh. They are meant for us; but only if we carry out our faith in works. For he truly believes who puts his faith into practice.

R. These are the conquerors and the friends of God, who, despising the orders of princes, merited an eternal reward: * Now they are crowned, and they receive the palm. V. These are they who have come out of great tribulation, and have washed their robes in the blood of the Lamb. Now. Glory. Now.

✠ Continuation of the holy Gospel according to St. John.—At that time: Thomas, one of the twelve, who is called Didymus, was not with them when Jesus came. The other disciples, therefore, said to him: We have seen the Lord. But he said to them: Except I shall see in His hands the print of the nails, and put my hand into His side, I will not believe. And after eight days, again His disciples were within, and Thomas with them. Jesus cometh, the doors being shut, and stood in the midst, and said: Peace be to you. Then He saith to Thomas: Put in thy finger hither, and see My hands, and bring hither thy hand and put it into My side; and

be not faithless but believing. Thomas answered
and said to Him: My Lord and my God. Jesus
saith to him: Because thou hast seen Me, Thomas,
thou hast believed: blessed are they that have not
seen and have believed.

LET US PRAY

Grant us, we beseech Thee, O Lord, to rejoice in
the solemn feast of blessed Thomas, Thy Apostle;
that we may be always assisted by his help and imitate his faith with sincere devotion. Through our
Lord.

January 15

St. Maurus, Abbot

I Nocturn

From the Book of Ecclesiasticus, c. 44, 1 - 15

II Nocturn

From the second book of the Dialogues
of St. Gregory, Pope

The holy man, St. Benedict, having returned to
Subiaco, long continued to shine by his virtue and
miracles, and assembled a great number of soli-
taries who consecrated themselves to the service
of God. So that with the aid of our Lord Jesus
Christ, he built twelve monasteries, placing in each
twelve Religious, with an Abbot to govern them.
He retained with himself only a few of his disciples, who, he thought, still needed his presence to
be better formed to perfection. It was at this
time that many persons in Rome, conspicuous for

their nobility and virtue, began to visit him and offer their children that he might mould them to piety, and teach them to live for God alone. Aequitius and Tertullus, who had the honor of being Roman Patricians, came to see the saint and confided to his care their two children; the former offered his son Maurus, and the latter, his son Placidus. Maurus was distinguished for spotless innocence of life, and merited, though young, to be chosen by his master to assist him in his functions. As to Placidus, being only a boy, he was subject to the weaknesses inseparable from tender age.

On another occasion, a certain Goth, a man of much simplicity, presented himself to Saint Benedict to become a monk, and the man of God most gladly received him among his disciples. One day the saint ordered a hook to be given him to cut some bush and thorns occupying a place intended for a garden. The place given him to clear was situated on the border of a lake, and as he worked with might and main, the iron slipped off the handle and flew into the lake whose water was so deep that there could be no hope of recovering the lost blade. The Goth seeing his iron lost, went, trembling with fear, to the monk, Maurus, and told him the loss the monastery sustained and underwent penance. Maurus made the matter known at once to Benedict, the servant of God, who, as soon as he had heard it, went to the shore. He took the handle from the Goth and immersed it a little in the water. Immediately the blade returned from the bottom of the lake and adjusted itself to the handle. The hook having been thus restored, Benedict returned it to the Goth, saying: "Take thy hook, go to work and trouble thyself no further."

The venerable Benedict being one day in his cell, the boy Placidus, one of his religious went out to fetch water from the lake, but when dipping his pitcher into the water, not taking sufficient heed, his body followed the vase and he fell into the lake. The waves immediately bore him out from the land as far as the usual flight of an arrow. The saint, who was in his cell, knew the sad accident at the very instant, and at once calling Maurus, his disciple, said to him: "Brother Maurus, run with all speed; the boy who went to fetch water fell into the lake and has been already carried off a long distance."

A thing wonderful and unheard of since that instance of the Apostle Peter! Maurus having asked and received the blessing, ran to the lake to execute the order of his Abbot. Thinking he was treading upon dry land, he advanced to the very place whither the waves had carried off the child, and laying hold of him by the hair, brought him back with great haste to the shore. Having reached the land, he began to reflect on what he did, and casting a look behind, saw that he had been running over the waves. He was astonished thereat and sore affrighted, seeing that he had performed what he could not dare to undertake if he was aware of what he was doing. Having returned to the monastery, he narrated the whole occurence to the Abbot. The venerable Benedict did not attribute this miracle to his own merit, but to the obedience of the disciple. Maurus, on the other hand, said he was only fulfilling a command, and could have no share in a miracle which he unconsciously performed. During this pious dispute, arising from the humility of the holy Abbot and his disciple, the boy rescued from peril presented himself as umpire, and put an end to the contest thus: "When I was being drawn out of the waves, I saw the Abbot's robe above my head, and it seemed to me that it was he who delivered me from the water." This is narrated by Pope St. Gregory. An ancient tradition says that the monk Maurus was sent into Gaul by the same holy Father. There, according to the same tradition, he founded a monastery at Glannofol; after having governed it for a long time, he died in the Lord in a good old age, renowned for his sanctity and miracles.

R. This man knew righteousness and saw great wonders, and made his prayer to the Most High: * And he is numbered among the Saints. V. This is he who despised the life of the world, and hath

attained to the heavenly kingdom. And. Glory.
And.

III Nocturn

The reading of the holy Gospel
according to St. Matthew

At that time: Peter making answer, said: Lord,
if it be Thou bid me come to Thee upon the waters.
And He said: Come. And so forth.

Homily of St. Jerome, Priest

In all places Peter is found to be a man of a
most ardent faith. When the Apostles were asked
whom men said Jesus was, he (Peter) confessed
Him to be the Son of God. He restrained Him in
His desire to push on to His Passion; and, although
by not wishing Him whom he had just before confessed to be the Son of God to die, he errs in perception, yet he does not err in affection. As the
first among the first, he ascends the mountain with
the Savior, and at the Passion he followed alone.
The sin of denial which had come upon him from
a sudden fear he suddenly washed away with bitter
tears. After the Passion, when they were fishing
in Lake Genesareth and the Lord stood on the shore,
while the others slowly advanced, Peter brooked no
delay, but girt with his coat instantly cast himself
into the waves.

With the same burning faith with which he always believed, he now, while the rest remain si-

lent, believes that he can now do, by the will of his
Master, that which the Master could do by His
very nature. "Bid me come to Thee upon the waters." Do Thou comand, and on the spot the waves
will become firm; let the body which of itself is
heavy become light. And Peter, going down out of
the boat, walked upon the waters to come to Jesus.
Let those who think that the Body of the Lord is
not a real body because, not being weighty, it easily passed over the unresisting waters, explain how
Peter, whom they will certainly not deny is a true
man, walked upon the waves.

But seeing the wind strong, he was afraid, and
when he began to sink, he cried out, saying, "Lord,
save me." The faith of his soul was ardent; nevertheless, human frailty was drawing him into the
deep. He was therefore abandoned to the temptation for a time that his faith might be increased
and that he might know that he was saved not by
merely asking, but by the power of the Lord. And
Jesus, immediately stretching forth His Hand,
took hold of him and said: "O thou of little faith,
why didst thou doubt?" If these words are addressed to the Apostle Peter, concerning whose
faith and ardor we have just spoken above, who
confidently besought the Savior, saying to Him,
"Lord if it be Thou, bid me come to Thee upon the
waters," what is to be said to us who have not even
the smallest portion of his little faith?

And they that were in the boat came and adored Him, saying: Indeed Thou art the Son of God. At this one event, when the tranquillity of the sea was restored, which after fierce storms usually happens gradually and by natural order, sailors and fishermen confess that the Lord is indeed the Son of God; and does Arius preach in the Church that He is a creature?

R. The Lord hath loved him, and hath adorned him: * He hath clothed him with a robe of glory. V. And hath crowned him at the gates of Paradise. He. Glory. He.

✠ Continuation of the holy Gospel according to St. Matthew.—At that time: Peter making answer, said: Lord, if it be Thou, bid me come to Thee upon the waters. And He said: Come. And Peter going down out of the boat, walked upon the water to come to Jesus. But seeing the wind strong, he was afraid: and when he began to sink, he cried out, saying: Lord, save me! And immediately Jesus stretching forth His hand took hold of him, and said to him: O thou of little faith, why didst thou doubt? And when they were come to the boat, the wind ceased. And they that were in the boat came and adored Him, saying: Indeed Thou art the Son of God.

LET US PRAY

O God, who to teach us obedience, didst make St. Maurus to walk dry-shod upon the waters; grant

that we may merit to follow the example of his virtues and share in his reward. Through our Lord.

January 21
ST. MEINRAD, MARTYR, AND PATRON
OF THE ABBEY

I Nocturn
From the Epistle of St. Paul
to the Romans, c. 8, 12 - 19 and 28 - 39

II Nocturn

Meinrad, born of noble parentage in Alemannia,
while yet a boy was sent by his father Bertholde,
count of Sulgovia, to the holy monastery at Auga,
and was entrusted to his relative Erlebald, a monk
of remarkable holiness. From that time on he
(Meinrad) held him as his model, so that when he
was twenty-five years old, as a priest—afterwards
becoming a monk also—he was to be far in advance
of those seeking the more perfect life. And after
his perfection in christian virtues had been publicly approved, especially those of chastity, humility
and obedience, he became spiritual director of the
school at Bollingen; in this place he soon began to
be tempted with a longing for a life of solitude.

And so in time, when the possibilities of a near-
by wood had been explored and the permission of
the Abbot obtained, taking along with him a Missal,
Breviary, the Rule of our Holy Father Benedict,

and small editions of Cassian, he retired to Mt. Etzel, rising above the Lake of Zurich; here, although he was severe in his fasts, vigils, and discipline of the body, he nevertheless spent seven delightful years in prayer and contemplation of things divine. And when the frequent concourse of men who were attracted by his holiness became overly burdensome, in order to forestall it and at the same time to enjoy seclusion, he betook himself to the vast solitude of a hidden glen, and lived the rest of his life in admirable sanctity.

Although at other times the devil tried him by recurring onslaughts, on one day, however, he attacked him while he was praying very recollectedly with a fury more violent than usual; besides the terrifying screams and uproar, he was enveloped by so great a number of spectres about him that the princes of darkness even cut out the very light of day. Meinrad in the midst of the horrors of the night and of the onrushing phantoms sought help from heaven and received it. For immediately an Angel of the Lord, vested in a most brilliant light, so forcefully dispersed the damned spirits that from that time on they never again dared to approach him. Another consolation from heaven also followed. A very little boy of seven years of very noble mein seemed to come to him from the chapel and pray with him and relate to him mysteries of which it was not given man to speak.

After twenty-six years had been passed by the holy man in this great wilderness, two evil fellows who had plotted against him ventured into the solitude and although received by him in a most hospitable manner and told of their purpose by him (for he had, indeed, during the Sacrifice which he had just offered shortly before in the Presence of the Most High, been admonished of the design of the assassins), they nevertheless wickedly and miserably strangled him after he had been brutally beaten, on the twenty-first of January, in the year of Redemption, 861. How pleasing this victim was to God, several miracles soon after proved. For the candle placed at the head of the Martyr was divinely lighted; the whole hermitage was pervaded with the sweetest odor; and the wicked men, betrayed by the nipping and pecking of ravens which the Saint had formerly fed, were burned alive head downward. Some years after a great monastery was erected over the Martyr's dwelling, which today is venerated over the whole world in his memory, and especially because the chapel of the Virgin Mother of God has been divinely consecrated, and moreover because of the graces and frequent miracles from this same Virgin.

R. The Saints of God feared not the stripes of the tormentors, dying for Christ's name: * That they might be heirs in the house of the Lord.

V. They gave their bodies to torment for God. That. Glory. That.

III Nocturn

The reading of the holy Gospel according to St. Matthew

At that time: Jesus said to His disciples: think not that I came to send peace upon earth: I came not to send peace, but the sword. And so forth.

Homily of St. Peter Chrysologus

Think ye that I came to send peace on the earth? Not so, I tell you, but separation. But what of that saying: Behold the Lamb of God? What of this other: As a sheep is led to the slaughter and as a lamb that is dumb in the presence of its shearer, so He did not open His Mouth? And of this one: Say to the daughter of Sion: Behold, thy King cometh to thee in meekness? Why is it that this Lamb strikes so harshly in His preaching? Why doth He grow so violent in word who in His Passion holds His peace with such patience, who in death submits in all humility?

And indeed, brethren, Christ entered into this world in all things meek and gentle: For He is sweetly born into our race; in the cradle He allows Himself to be lovingly fondled, being Himself even more affectionate; He shows Himself as a little boy and even relaxes on a human lap; being caressed on the neck of His Mother He returns the caress with the whole-hearted embrace of love; He always acts like a poor man; He always goes about as a solitary, because the poor man is always common (approachable); the solitary is accessible to all.

Now why is it that He scatters such fire in His words and that He enkindles and spreads abroad so great and such fiery doctrines? Water begets fire— thus one must think—a union (of things) so opposing. Water begets flame and the flame increases the water. What is this? How reconcile such discord? Herein is made known the action of the divine Husbandman; for absolutely everything springs forth by His heat and by His moisture is nourished.

Whence God, the Origin of all, by the mingling together of fire and water begets us and nourishes us, for whom He longs, wishes, seeks, and desires with such ardent affection. Think you, He said, that I came to send peace on earth? No. Why? Because heavenly union is in this earthly separation. No one can be connected to the earth and joined to heaven. Precious, therefore, and dear is this earthly separation which so separates us from earthly things that it makes us participate in those that are divine.

R. Thou hast crowned him * With glory and honor, O Lord. V. And hast set him over the works of Thy hands. With. Glory. With.

✠ Continuation of the holy Gospel according to St. Matthew.—At that time: Jesus said to His disciples: Do not think that I came to send peace upon the earth: I came not to send peace, but the sword. For I came to set a man at variance against his father, and the daughter against her mother, and the daughter-in-law against her mother-in-law. And a man's enemies shall be they of his own household. He that loveth father or mother more than Me is not worthy of Me; and he that loveth son or daughter more than Me is not worthy of Me. And he that taketh not up his cross and followeth Me is not worthy of Me. He that findeth his life shall lose it: and he that shall lose his life for Me shall find it. He that receiveth you receiveth Me; and he that receiveth Me receiveth Him that sent Me. He that receiveth a prophet in the name of a prophet shall receive the reward of a prophet: and he that receiveth a just man in the name of a just man shall receive the reward of a just man. And whosoever shall give to drink to one of these little ones a cup of cold water only in the name of a disciple, amen I say to you, he shall not lose his reward.

Let Us Pray

O almighty and eternal God, who art ever wonderful in the merits of St. Meinrad, Thy Martyr, we beseech Thee, that as Thou hast granted him the eminent glory of martyrdom, thus also wouldst

Thou grant us Thy mercy through his prayers. Through our Lord.

January 22

II DAY IN THE OCTAVE OF ST. MEINRAD
Sermon of St. Ambrose

Although such a great witness of Christ, rich in his praise, richer in his blood, richer in his cruel wound, and more resplendent in his stained robe, may be thought to be withdrawn (from us) by the honor of his burial place, he belongs to us all through the communion of prayer. What is poured out in merits is not confined to bounds! You have, in every place, invoked the Martyr; in every place has He who is honored in the Martyr, heard you. Through the mediation of him, who examines your prayers and distributes his blessings, the presence of the powerful advocate is made so much the more intimate as the faith of you who call upon him shall be devoted. For the prayer which is enhanced by acts of chastity, justice, and charity passes beyond the world, penetrates into Paradise, soars up even into the every sight of the Supreme Majesty, borne by an Angel.

Since these things are so, let us honor the blessed Martyrs, the Princes of our Faith, the Mediators for the world, the Heralds of the Kingdom, Co-heirs of God. Perhaps you will say to me: Why do you honor the things of the flesh already dissolved and consumed, for which God has now no care? Indeed, whence is that, dearly beloved, which Truth Itself speaks by the Prophet? He says: Precious in the sight of the Lord is the death of His saints. And again: But to me Thy friends, O God, are made exceedingly honorable. We are to honor the servants of God; how much more God's Saints! Of them it is declared in another passage: The Lord keepeth their bones, not one of them shall be broken.

And so I honor in the flesh of the Martyr the wounds received in the name of Christ; I honor the memory of him, living through the enduring of his virtue. I honor the ashes made sacred by praise for their Lord; I honor in these ashes the seed of eternity; I honor the body which has shown me how to love my Lord, which has taught me not to fear death for my Lord's sake. Why should not the faithful honor that body which even the demons reverence? that body which they (the demons) have tormented with suffering, but now glorify in its sepulchre? Therefore do I honor the body which Christ has glorified by the sword, which shall reign with Christ in heaven.

January 23

III DAY IN THE OCTAVE OF ST. MEINRAD

Sermon of St. Augustine, Bishop

May the Holy Ghost teach us at this time what we should say; for we are about to say something in praise of Saint Meinrad, the ever-glorious mar-

tyr, whose birthday, as you know, we keep today.
And these, that is the birthdays, the Church cele-
brates in such wise that she calls the dear death of
the martyrs, birthdays. What is this, brethren?
When he was born, we know not; but because today he suffered, today we keep his birthday. Yet
that former day, even though we knew it, we would
not keep it. For on that day he contracted original
sin; but on this, he overcame every sin.

For us the passion of the most blessed martyr,
Meinrad, has made this day a feast; the fame of
his victory has brought us, his devoted clients, to
this place. Now the celebration of the martyr's
solemnities should be an imitation of their virtues.
It is easy to celebrate a feast in a martyr's honor;
it is a great thing to imitate the faith and suffering
of a martyr. In such wise let us keep this latter
that we may expect the former; thus let us celebrate the latter that we may the more effectively
prize the other. Why do we sing the praises of a
martyr's faith? Because he battled even to death
for the truth and therefore he conquered. The al-
luring world he spurned; to the raging world, he
yielded not; therefore, a victor he approaches God.
In this world errors and terrors abound. Our
blessed martyr evercame the errors with wisdom,
the terrors with suffering.

Spurn the world, therefore, Christians, spurn,
spurn the world. The martyrs spurned it, the apos-

tles spurned it. Blessed Meinrad, whose memory
we keep today, spurned it. Do you wish to be rich?
honored? healthy? All these he in whose memory
you have come together has spurned. Surely, if he
had not spurned these things, you would not so
honor him. Why do I find you a lover of those
things whose scorner you venerate? Without doubt
if he had loved them you would not venerate him.
Do not love them; for he has not entered and closed
the door against you. Do you also spurn them and
enter after him.

January 24
IV DAY IN THE OCTAVE OF ST. MEINRAD
Sermon of St. Peter Chrysologus

Because today we gather with God on the birthday of the Martyr, St. Meinrad, when he triumphed
in glorious battle over the devil and left us the
wonderful example of his virtues, it is therefore
fitting that we rejoice and be glad. So when you
hear of the birthday of the Saints, dearly beloved,
do not think that that day is spoken of when men
are born on earth in the flesh; but the day when
they are born from the earth into heaven; from
toil to rest; from trials to peace; from hardships
to delights; not passing, but constant, stable, and
eternal; from the vanities of the world to a crown
and glory. Such birthdays are worthily celebrated
for the Martyrs.

Thus, dearly beloved, when a feast of this kind is held, do not reckon that martyr's birthdays are to be celebrated solely with luncheons and more lavish banquets; rather, what you honor on the commemoration of a martyr is proposed to you for imitation. Hence, look on, dearly beloved, the spirit of the people standing about. For once on this day a mob of wicked men looked on while St. Meinrad, by the tyrant's command, was being flogged; they were crowds of evil men, groups of spectators; now, a multitude of the faithful, set on praising him, has gathered together; then there was a mob of savages, now a crowd of rejoicers; then a mob of despairing men, now a crowd of men who hope.

For this reason, then, the birthdays of the martyrs are celebrated with joy each year; so that what happened but once might forever remain in the memory of the faithful. The act was performed, dearly beloved, that you might not say you did not know; it is celebrated yearly lest you should say: I forgot. So spur yourselves on to imitate these things, dearly beloved; yearn for the grace of generous love; beg that that might be granted to you which he merited to obtain.

January 25

CONVERSION OF ST PAUL

I Nocturn

From the Acts of the Apostles, c. 9, 1-16

II Nocturn

Sermon of St. Augustine, Bishop

Today we read in the Acts of the Apostles how Paul the Apostle was changed from a persecutor of the Christians to a herald of Christ. Christ struck down the persecutor that He might make him a doctor of the Church. He wounded him, and healed him; He slew him, and raised him to life; the lamb was slain by the wolves, and made the wolves to be lambs. For so that which happened to Paul was foretold in that very distinct prophecy when the Patriarch Jacob blessed his sons (laying hands on the present, looking into the future).

For Paul, as he himself says, was of the tribe of Benjamin. And when Jacob, blessing his sons, came to bless Benjamin, he said of him: Benjamin, a ravenous wolf. What then? Will he always be a ravenous wolf? God forbid; but he who in the morning seizes the prey, in the evening divides the food. This was fulfilled in the Apostle Paul, because it was foretold of him.

Now, if you please, let us hear how he seized the prey in the morning, and divided the food in the evening. Morning and evening for him signify, so to speak, earlier and later. So therefore we take it: earlier he seizes, later he divides the food. Consider this seizer of prey: Saul, it is said, having received letters from the chief priests, went forth, that wheresoever he might find the Christians, he might seize them and lead them without fail to the priests for punishment.

He went breathing and gasping out slaughter, that is, seizing in the morning. For when Stephen, the first Martyr, was stoned for the name of Christ, Saul was undoubtedly present; and in such a manner was he present with the stoners that it did not content him merely to cast stones with his own hands. For it was as if he made use of all their hands when he himself took care of the garments for all the stoners; venting his rage more completely by helping them all than if he had merely stoned him with his own hands. We have heard, he shall seize in the morning; let us see how he divides the food in the evening. He was struck down by the voice of Christ from heaven, and, receiving from above a prohibition of further raging, he fell on his face, first to be prostrated, then to be raised up; first to be wounded, then to be healed.

R. Thou are a vessel of election, O holy Apostle Paul, a preacher of the truth to the whole world: * Through whom all nations have known the grace of God. V. Intercede for us with God, who chose thee. Through. Glory. Through.

III Nocturn

The reading of the holy Gospel according to St. Matthew

At that time: Peter said to Jesus: Behold we have left all things, and have followed Thee: what, therefore, shall we have? And so forth.

Homily of St. Bede the Venerable, Priest

That man is perfect who, going, sells all that he has and gives to the poor, and follows Christ; for he shall have an enduring treasure in heaven. And rightly did Jesus say to such ones, when Peter questioned Him: Amen, I say to you, that you who have followed Me in the regeneration, when the Son of man shall sit on the seat of His majesty, you also shall sit on twelve seats, judging the twelve tribes of Israel.

He taught those who labor for His name's sake in this life to expect their reward in another, that is, in the regeneration; namely, when we, who were born as mortals into this uncertain life, shall be re-born, after the resurrection, unto life everlasting. And certainly it is a just recompense that they who here below despised the height of earthly glory for Christ's sake and who could in no wise be dissuaded from following His footsteps, should be in another place singularly glorified by Christ and take their seats with Him.

But let no one think that only the twelve Apostles —for Matthias was chosen in the place of Judas, who walked astray—are then to be judges, or that only the twelve tribes of Israel are to be judged; for then the tribe of Levi, which is the

thirteenth, would escape judgment. Paul also, who
is the thirteenth Apostle, will he be deprived of all
part in the judgment, when he himself says: Know
you not that we shall judge angels, how much more
things of this world?

For we must understand that all who, like the
Apostles, have left all things and followed Christ
will come with Him as judges, even as the whole
human race is to be judged. For since the number
twelve is often used in Scripture to signify universality, the twelve thrones of the Apostles imply
the whole body of judges; and the whole multitude
of the judged is implied by the twelve tribes of
Israel.

R. O holy Apostle Paul, preacher of the truth
and teacher of the Gentiles, * Intercede for us to
God who chose thee, that we may be made worthy
of the grace of God. V. Thou art a vessel of election, O holy Apostle Paul, a preacher of the truth.
Intercede. Glory. Intercede.

✠ Continuation of the holy Gospel according to
St. Matthew.—At that time: Peter said to Jesus:
Behold we have left all things and have followed
Thee: what, therefore, shall we have? And Jesus
said to them: Amen, I say to you, that you who have
followed Me in the regeneration, when the Son of
man shall sit on the seat of His majesty, you also
shall sit on twelve seats, judging the twelve tribes
of Israel. And every one that hath left house, or

brethren, or sisters, or father, or mother, or wife, or children, or lands, for My name's sake, shall receive a hundredfold and shall possess life everlasting.

LET US PRAY

O God, who hast instructed the whole world by the preaching of blessed Paul the Apostle, grant us, we beseech Thee, that we who honor the memory of his conversion may come to Thee through his example. Through our Lord.

January 26

VI DAY IN THE OCTAVE OF ST. MEINRAD

Sermon of St. Bernard

"Precious in the sight of the Lord is the death of His saints." "Let the sinner hear and be angry, let him gnash his teeth and pine away." "He has been caught in his own craftiness, he has fallen into the pit he made, he has entangled himself in the snare which he hath set for us." For it was by the envy of the devil that death came into the world; and now, behold: precious in the sight of the Lord is the death of His saints. For it was not otherwise than by his bodily death—which is thy handiwork—that the holy Martyr whose festival we are keeping today triumphed. He made virtue out of necessity, he changed what was the penalty of sin into a title to eternal glory; he proved himself faithful in a little thing in order that he might be found worthy to be placed over many things.

Therefore, he proved himself faithful to the
Benefactor, to whom he owed everything, by despising everything for His love, and by counting all
things to be but loss and esteeming them as dung
that he might gain Christ. But perhaps the enemy
is not satisfied even yet, and begins to murmur
saying: "Skin for skin and all that a man hath he
will give for his life." What then? Deemest thou
that when there is question of sacrificing his bodily
life he will be found unfaithful to the Lord from
whom he received it, so as to prefer his own life
to Him? Behold he is in thy hand. Command thy
satellites to rush upon him and to reduce him to
such straits that he shall be under the necessity of
either renouncing his allegiance to the Lord or of
losing his corporal life. Devise various and cruel
kinds of torture; but remember that thou art only
fashioning crowns for our Martyr.

He shall be crowned, consequently, because he
has lawfully striven, because he has faithfully conquered, because neither the pleasures of this world
nor the fear of death could separate him from the
charity of Christ. What say we to this, brethren?
We felicitate the martyr on his triumph, but the
thought of his glory ought to cover us with confusion. For the blessed Meinrad was a man passible
like unto us, encompassed with infirmity like unto
us, and like unto us attached to his body by the
bonds of natural affection. Therefore, if he thus

glorified Christ in his body and took the chalice of salvation, what have we rendered to the Lord for all the things that He hath rendered to us?

January 28
OCTAVE DAY OF ST. MEINRAD
Sermon of St. Augustine, Bishop

Men who are ill patiently allow themselves to be cut by the surgeons, to be cauterized, and to be annoyed by different compounds of bitters, so that finally they may be restored to temporal healthfulness; how much better has this blessed man perseveringly suffered all the bitterness of temporal torments that he might be crowned with mercy and compassion, and that his desire might be satiated with riches? In the wine-press, therefore, he wished to be trodden upon so that as a ripened grape he might change into wine and give the wine of pomegranates to his Beloved to drink—as inebriated religious minds know how to tread manfully and to strive with unflinching eyes for things eternal.

Therefore, he, who in the beginning of his life has despised worldly riches, who has likewise tamed the lusts of the body, who in the carrying on of his warfare has suffered many injuries, by keeping nothing back for himself in the consummation of the sacrifice, has offered himself as a holocaust, drinking of that precious chalice which he had seen first placed before him by his Host while sitting at the great table of sacred reading. His death, however, much as it may appear despicable in the eyes of the reprobate, is nevertheless precious in the eyes of Him who is wonderful in His Saints.

For He, in the first place, has called His soldier; He has Himself justified him; He has made him great, He has granted him to fight; He has granted him to conquer. Far different is this warfare from the warfare in the world in which they are reckoned as victors who achieved what they wrongly desire, who are made glad when they shall have committed evil, and exult in their most infamous acts.

However, in a Christian's martyrdom the penalty is manifest, the victory hidden, according to which the Psalmist cries out in the person of the martyrs: "O grant us help from trouble: for vain is the help of man"—as if they would declare: "Our victory, our glory is within; and it is not without. On the outside we are despised; within, beloved!"

February 2

PURIFICATION OF THE BLESSED VIRGIN

I Nocturn

From the Book of Exodus, c. 13, 1 - 3, 11 - 13, and from the Book of Leviticus, c. 12, 1 - 8

II Nocturn
Sermon of St. Augustine, Bishop

Thus it was said of old: Mother Sion says: And a Man is made man in her; and the Highest Himself hath founded her. O almighty power of a newborn child! O magnificence coming down from heaven to earth! He is still being carried in the womb, and is saluted by John the Baptist from the womb of his mother; is presented in the temple, and is recognized by Simeon, an old man, famous and full of years, proved and crowned.

First he recognized, then he adored, then he said: Now Thou dost dismiss Thy servant O Lord, in peace, because my eyes have seen Thy salvation. He delayed his going from the world that he might see born, Him by whom the world was made. The old man knew the Child, and in the Child became a child. He, who was filled with devotion, found himself renewed in old age. Simeon, the old man, bore Christ, the child; but Christ ruled the old age of Simeon.

It had been said to him by the Lord that he should not taste death before he had seen the Christ of the Lord born. Christ was born; and in the old age of the world the desire of the old man was fulfilled. He who found a world broken with age, came to an aged man. Indeed, he did not wish to stay longer in this world, and in this world he desired to see Christ, singing and saying with the

Prophet: Show us, O Lord, Thy mercy, and grant us Thy salvation.

And lastly, that thus you should know that it was a joy to him, in conclusion he says: Now Thou dost dismiss Thy servant in peace: for mine eyes have seen Thy Salvation. The prophets sang that the Creator of heaven and earth should eventually be on earth with men; the angel announced that the Creator of spirit and flesh should come in the flesh; John from the womb saluted the Savior in the womb; Simeon the old man recognized God the Child.

R. Simeon received an answer from the Holy Ghost that he should not see death before he had seen the Christ of the Lord: * And he blessed God and said: Now Thou dost dismiss Thy servant, O Lord, in peace, because my eyes have seen Thy Salvation. V. When His parents brought in the child Jesus to do for Him according to the custom of the law, he took Him into his arms. And. Glory. And.

III Nocturn

The reading of the holy Gospel according to St. Luke

At that time: After the days of Mary's purification, according to the law of Moses, were accomplished, they carried Jesus to Jerusalem to present Him to the Lord, as it is written in the law of the Lord. And so forth.

Homily of St. Ambrose, Bishop

And behold there was a man in Jerusalem named Simeon, and this man was just and devout, waiting for the consolation of Israel. Not only do the Angels, prophets, and shepherds give testimony to the Birth of the Lord, but the ancients and the just ones also. All ages and both sexes, and even miraculous happenings, build up our faith.

A Virgin conceives; a barren woman gives birth; a dumb man speaks; Elizabeth prophesies; the wise man adores; the child shut up in the womb leaps; the widow confesses; the just man awaits. And rightly was he, who sought not his own, but the people's welfare, called just, desiring himself to be freed from the chains of bodily weakness, but waiting to see the Promised One; for he knew that the eyes which should see Him would be blessed.

He also took Him into his arms and blessed God, and said: Now Thou dost dismiss Thy servant, O Lord, in peace, according to Thy word. See the just man, shut in as in a prison by the weight of the body, desire to die, that he might begin anew with Christ. For to die and to be with Christ is a thing by far the better. But let him who wishes to be dismissed come into the temple; let him come to Jerusalem; let him await the Christ of the Lord, and let him receive in his hands the Word of God, let him lay hold of Him with his works, as if

with the arms of his faith; then will he be dismissed as one who shall not see death, for he will
have seen the Life.

You see that abundant grace was poured out on
all at the Birth of the Lord; and that prophecy was
denied, not to the just, but to the unbelieving. Behold Simeon prophesied that the Lord Jesus Christ
had come for the fall and for the resurrection of
many, that he might discern the merits of the just
and of the unjust, and might decree as a true and
just Judge reward or punishment according to our
deeds.

R. The old man bore the Child, but the Child
was the old man's King: * Whom a virgin conceived, a virgin brought forth, a virgin she remained, and adored Him whom she had brought
forth. V. Simeon taking the Child in his arms,
gave thanks and blessed the Lord. Whom. Glory.
Whom.

✠ Continuation of the holy Gospel according to
St. Luke.—At that time: After the days of Mary's
purification, according to the law of Moses, were
accomplished, they carried Jesus to Jerusalem, to
present Him to the Lord; as it is written in the law
of the Lord: Every male opening the womb shall
be called holy to the Lord; and to offer a sacrifice,
according as it is written in the law of the Lord,
a pair of turtle doves, or two young pigeons. And
behold there was a man in Jerusalem named Si-

meon, and this man was just and devout, waiting for the consolation of Israel, and the Holy Ghost was in him: and he had received an answer from the Holy Ghost, that he should not see death before he had seen the Christ of the Lord. And he came by the Spirit into the temple. And when His parents brought in the Child Jesus, to do for Him according to the custom of the law, he also took Him into his arms, and blessed God, and said: Now Thou dost dismiss Thy servant, O Lord, according to Thy word in peace; because my eyes have seen Thy salvation, which Thou hast prepared before the face of all peoples; a light to the revelation of the Gentiles, and the glory of Thy people Israel.

Let Us Pray

O almighty and eternal God, we suppliantly beseech Thy Majesty that as Thy only begotten Son was on this day in the substance of the flesh offered in the temple, Thou wouldst grant us to be offered to Thee with purified souls. Through the same our Lord.

February 10

ST. SCHOLASTICA, VIRGIN

I Nocturn

From the Canticle of Canticles, c. 2, 1-5; c. 8, 1-7

II Nocturn

From the second Book of the Dialogues
of St. Gregory, Pope

Scholastica was the sister of the venerable father Benedict. She had been consecrated to almighty God from her very infancy, and was accustomed to visit her brother once a year. The man of God came down to meet her at a house belonging to the monastery, not far from the gate. It was the day for the usual visit, and her venerable brother came down to her with some of his brethren. The whole day was spent in the praises of God and holy conversation; and at nightfall they took their repast together. Whilst they were at table and it grew late, as they conferred with each other on sacred things, the holy woman thus spoke to her brother: I beseech thee, stay the night with me, and let us talk till morning on the joys of heaven. He replied: What is this thou sayest, O sister? On no account may I remain out of the monastery. The evening was so fair, that not a cloud could be seen in the sky.

When, therefore, the holy woman heard her brother's refusal, she clasped her hands together and, resting them on the table, she hid her face in them and prayed to the almighty God. As soon as she raised her head from the table, there came down so great a storm of thunder and lightning and torrents of rain, that neither the venerable Benedict nor the brethren who were with him could set foot outside the place where they were sitting. Indeed, the holy woman, bowing her head in her hands, had shed a torrent of tears on the table; and as she wept, the clear sky produced rain. Almost immediately after the prayer the rain fell in torrents; such was the accord between the prayer and the storm that, when she raised her head from the table, the thunder came; since it was in one and the same instant that she raised her head, and that the rain fell.

Then the man of God, seeing it was impossible to reach the monastery in lightning and thunder and torrential rain, was sad, and said complainingly: Almighty God forgive thee, sister; what hast thou done? But she replied: I asked thee a favor, and thou wouldst not hear me; I asked it of my God, and he heard me: go now if thou canst; send me away and go back to the monastery. But it was not in his power to leave the shelter; so that he who would not have stayed willingly had to stay unwillingly. And so it came about that they passed the whole night without sleep, entertaining each other with discussions about the mysteries of the spiritual life.

On the morrow the holy woman returned to her own cell, and the man of God to the monastery. When lo! three days after, he was in his cell; and raising his eyes, he saw the soul of his sister going up to heaven in the shape of a dove. Full of joy at her being thus glorified, he thanked almighty God in hymns of praise, and told the brethren of

her death. He straightway bade them go and bring
the body to the monastery, and he had it buried in
the tomb he had prepared for himself. Thus it
was that as they had ever been one soul in God,
their bodies were united in the same grave.

R. After her shall virgins be brought to the
King; her neighbors * shall be brought to thee with
gladness and rejoicing. V. With thy comeliness
and thy beauty set out proceed prosperously and
reign. Shall. Glory. Shall.

III Nocturn

The reading of the holy Gospel
according to St. Matthew

At that time: Jesus spoke to His disciples this
parable: The kingdom of heaven shall be like to
ten virgins, who taking their lamps went out to
meet the bridegroom and the bride. And so forth.

Homily of St. Hilary, Bishop

Our Lord and God in the body is the bridegroom
and the bride. For as the spirit (the bridegroom)
is to the flesh, so the flesh is the bride of the spirit.
At length at the sounding of the trumpet the virgins went forth to meet the bridegroom alone; for
now the two were one, because the lowliness of the
body had been drawn beyond itself into spiritual
glory. By our first progress, by the duties of this
life, we are prepared to hasten to the resurrection
from the dead. The lamps are the light of shining

souls, made brilliant by the Sacrament of Baptism. The oil is the fruit of good works. The human bodies are the vessels, in the interior of which the treasure of a good conscience lies hidden. The sellers are those who, being in need of the mercy of the faithful, of themselves give ample return for the help which they seek, namely, the relief of their necessity, by holding up their knowledge of our good works. This is the plentiful fuel for the unfailing light which, by the fruits of mercy, is purchased and stored up.

The wedding itself is the assumption of immortality and the union in a new state between corruption and incorruption. The delay of the bridegroom is the time of penance. The sleep of those awaiting the bridegroom is the repose of those who believe; and in the time of penance this sleep is the temporary death of all. The cry in the middle of the night when all are unaware is the voice of the trumpet preceding the coming of the Lord and rousing all to go forth to meet the bridegroom. The taking up of the lamps signifies the return of the souls into the bodies, and the light of the lamps, which is contained in the vessels of the bodies, is the consciousness of good works shining forth.

Those who will have in the body taken advantage of the opportune time for working and have prepared to go forth immediately at the coming of the bridegroom are the prudent virgins. The foolish ones are they who, careless and negligent, cared only for the things of the present, and, unmindful of the Lord's promises, have not concerned themselves with any hope of the resurrection. And now, because they could not go out to meet the bridegroom with unlighted lamps, they besought those who were prudent to lend them oil. But these answered that they could not give any, lest perhaps there would not be enough for all. By this is signified that no one is to be helped by the works and merits of others, since it is necessary that each one buy oil for his own lamp. The wise exhorted the foolish to return and buy oil, in order that, although late in observing the precepts of God, they might, with lamps lighted, perhaps be made worthy for the coming of the bridegroom.

Whilst the foolish were thus delayed, the bridegroom came; and the wise ones, who were encircled by the carefully prepared light of their lamps, entered with him to the wedding feast; that is, they at once entered into heavenly glory at the coming of the majesty of the Lord. And because there is now no time for penance, the foolish hasten and ask that the door be opened to them. To whom the bridegroom makes answer that he does not know them. These were not at the ceremony of the Lord's coming, neither had they hastened at the sound of the trumpet warning them, neither had they joined the company of those entering with the bridegroom, but by delaying had wasted their time and so were unworthy of entering into the wedding feast.

R. This is a wise virgin whom the Lord found watching, who, when she took her lamp, brought oil with her: * And when the Lord came, she went in with Him to the marriage. V. At midnight there was a cry made: Behold the Bridegroom cometh, go ye forth to meet Him. And. Glory. And.

✠ Continuation of the holy Gospel according to St. Matthew.—At that time: Jesus spoke to His disciples this parable: The kingdom of heaven shall be like to ten virgins, who taking their lamps went out to meet the bridegroom and the bride. And five of them were foolish, and five wise: But the five foolish, having taken their lamps, did not take oil with them: but the wise took oil in their vessels with the lamps. And the bridegroom tarrying they all slumbered and slept. And at midnight there was a cry made: Behold the bridegroom cometh, go ye forth to meet him. Then all those virgins arose and trimmed their lamps. And the foolish said to the wise: Give us of your oil, for our lamps are gone out. The wise answered, saying: Lest perhaps there be not enough for us and for you, go ye rather to them that sell, and buy for yourselves. Now whilst they went to buy, the bridegroom came: and they that were ready went in with him to the marriage, and the door was shut.

But at last came also the other virgins, saying:
Lord, Lord, open to us. But he answering, said:
Amen I say to you, I know you not. Watch ye
therefore, because you know not the day nor the
hour.

LET US PRAY

O God, who to show us the path of innocence
didst cause the soul of Thy blessed virgin Scholastica to enter heaven in the likeness of a dove;
grant us by her merits and prayers to live so in-
nocently, that we may merit to attain the eternal
joys. Through our Lord.

February 22
ST. PETER'S CHAIR
I Nocturn

From the first Epistle of blessed Peter the Apostle
c. 1, 1-12

II Nocturn
Sermon of St. Leo, Pope

When the twelve Apostles, after receiving the
gift of all tongues from the Holy Ghost, divided the
regions of the earth among themselves for the
preaching of the Gospel to the world, blessed Peter,
prince of the apostolic order, received as his share
the citadel of the Roman empire, that the light of
truth, revealed for the salvation of all nations,
might penetrate more easily to the whole body by
streaming forth from the head.

For what race of men is there which you would not find represented in this city? Or what nations would ignore what Rome had learned? Here were to be refuted the theories of philosophers, here dissolved the vanities of earthly wisdom, here overthrown the worship of devils, here destroyed the impiety of every sacrilege; here, where superstitious zeal had collected all the error and vanity of the world.

Therefore, to this city, O most blessed Peter, thou dost not fear to come, and while thy companion in glory, the Apostle Paul, is still occupied with the government of other churches, thou dost enter this forest of savage beasts, this deep and turbulent ocean, with more boldness than when thou didst walk upon the water.

Thou hast already instructed the people of the circumcision who accepted the faith; thou hadst founded the church of Antioch, where the dignity of the Christian name first arose; thou hadst filled Pontus, Galatia, Cappadocia, Asia and Bithynia with the laws of the Gospel preaching; and then, not doubting the success of thy work nor ignorant of thy burden of years, thou didst carry the trophy of the cross of Christ into the citadel of Rome, where divine predestination had prepared for thee the honor of power and a glorious martyrdom.

R. Peter, lovest thou Me? Lord, Thou knowest that I love Thee. * Feed My sheep. V. Simon, son

of John, lovest thou Me more than these? Lord,
Thou knowest that I love Thee. Feed. Glory. Feed.

III Nocturn

The reading of the holy Gospel
according to St. Matthew

At that time: Jesus came into the quarters of
Caesarea Philippi, and He asked His disciples, say-
ing: Whom do men say that the Son of man is?
And so forth.

Homily of St. Hilary, Bishop

The Lord asked His disciples whom did men say
that He was: and He used the words, the Son of
man. For we must so confess Him as to remember
that He is both Son of God, and Son of man: the
one without the other could give us no hope of salvation. When He had thus elicited the various
opinions of Him by men, He asked what they themselves thought. Peter answered: Thou art Christ,
the Son of the living God.

But Peter had duly weighed the terms of the
question. For the Lord had said: Whom do men
say that I, the Son of man, am? Bodily sight
certainly showed Him to be the Son of man. But
when He added: Whom do they say that I am, He
meant that there was more in Him than was perceived by the senses; for He was indeed the Son of
man. What opinion of Himself, then, did He seek?
We do not believe it was that which He Himself

said of Himself; but it was a hidden thing which
He sought, which the faith of those that believe in
Him should embrace.

Peter's confession received a worthy reward, for
he saw the Son of God in a man. Blessed is he who
was praised for having gazed at and seen what
human eyes could not see; he did not contemplate
what was of flesh and blood, but saw the Son of God
by the revelation of the heavenly Father; and he
was judged worthy to be the first to recognize the
divine in Christ.

O how happily was the Church founded in the
giving of his new name, how worthy to be built on
is Her rock, which was to destroy the infernal laws
and the gates of hell and all the barriers of death!
O blessed is the door-keeper of heaven, to whose
judgment the keys of the eternal entrance are entrusted, whose sentence on earth is already ratified
in heaven! So that what he binds or looses on
earth, the same decision shall be ratified in heaven.

R. Jesus said to His disciples: Whom do men
say that the Son of man is? Peter answered and
said: Thou are Christ, the Son of the living God. *
And I say to thee that thou art Peter, and upon
this rock I will build My Church. V. Blessed art
thou, Simon Bar-Jona, because flesh and blood hath
not revealed it to thee, but My Father who is in
heaven. And I say. Glory. And I say.

✠ Continuation of the holy Gospel according to St. Matthew.—At that time: Jesus came into the quarters of Caesarea Philippi, and He asked His disciples, saying: Whom do men say that the Son of man is? But they said: Some, John the Baptist, and other some, Elias, and others, Jeremias, or one of the prophets. Jesus saith to them: But whom do you say that I am? Simon Peter answered, and said: Thou art Christ, the Son of the living God. And Jesus answering, said to him: Blessed art thou, Simon Bar-Jona, because flesh and blood hath not revealed it to thee, but My Father who is in heaven; and I say to thee: That thou art Peter, and upon this rock I will build My Church, and the gates of hell shall not prevail against it; and whatsoever thou shalt bind upon earth, it shall be bound also in heaven; and whatsoever thou shalt loose on earth, it shall be loosed also in heaven.

LET US PRAY

O God, who didst give the keys of the heavenly kingdom and the priestly power of binding and loosing to blessed Peter Thy Apostle, grant by the power of his intercession that we may be freed from the bonds of our sins; who livest and reignest with God the Father.

February 24
(*In Leap Year, February 25*)
ST. MATTHIAS, APOSTLE

I Nocturn

From the Acts of the Apostles, c. 1, 15-26

II Nocturn

From the Commentary of St. Augustine,
Bishop, on Psalm 86.

The foundations thereof are in the holy mountains: the Lord loveth the gates of Sion. Why are the Apostles and Prophets called foundations? Because their authority bears up our weakness. Why are they called gates? Because through them we enter the kingdom of God. For they preach to us; and, when we enter through them, we enter through Christ; for He is the gate. And whereas it is written that Jerusalem has twelve gates, Christ is the one gate and Christ is also the twelve gates, for He is in the twelve gates; and therefore the number of Apostles was twelve.

There is a great mystery in the signification of this number twelve. You shall sit, says our Lord, upon twelve thrones, judging the twelve tribes of Israel. But if there are twelve thrones there, there is no throne for Paul, the thirteenth Apostle, to take his seat and judge; and yet he said that he was to judge not only men, but also angels. Which angels, unless the fallen angels? Know you not, he says, that we shall judge angels? The multitude might answer him: Why dost thou boast that thou art about to judge? Where is thy throne? The Lord said that there were to be twelve thrones for the twelve Apostles. One—Judas—fell indeed, but holy Matthias was appointed in his place; and so the number of twelve thrones was filled up. First find the place where thou shalt sit, and then threaten that thou wilt judge.

Let us therefore consider what these twelve thrones mean. The mysterious term signifies a sort of universality; for the Church was to spread through all the earth, whence this edifice is styled a building-together unto Christ. And therefore there are twelve thrones, since mankind is to come from all quarters to be judged; and in like manner there are twelve gates to the heavenly city, because mankind will come from all quarters to enter it.

So, not only the Twelve and the Apostle Paul, but all who are to judge, will have part in these twelve thrones, according to this notion of universality; even as all who enter must enter by one or other of the twelve gates. For the four quarters of the earth, East, West, North, and South are constantly mentioned in the Scriptures. From these four winds, as the Lord declares in the Gospel, He will gather His elect from the four winds. Therefore, from all those four winds is the Church called. But how is it to be called? On every side it is called in the name of the Trinity. Not otherwise is it called than by baptism in the name of the Father, and of the Son, and of the Holy Ghost. Therefore, four being taken thrice, the number twelve is found.

R. These are they who, living in the flesh, planted the Church in their blood: * They drank the chalice of the Lord, and became the friends of God. V. Their sound hath gone forth into all the earth, and their words unto the ends of the world. They drank. Glory. They drank.

III Nocturn

The reading of the holy Gospel
according to St. Matthew

At that time: Jesus answered and said: I confess to Thee, O Father, Lord of heaven and earth, because Thou hast hid these things from the wise and prudent, and hast revealed them to little ones. And so forth.

Homily of St. Augustine, Bishop

Come to Me, all you that labor. And why do we all labor if it be not because we are mortal men, frail and weak, bearing earthen vessels which straiten one another? Yet, when the vessel of the flesh is straitened, let the open expanse of charity spread abroad. Why then does He say, Come to Me, all you that labor, unless it means that you shall not labor? It is indeed clear that such is His promise; for since He calls those that labor, they will per-

chance ask to what reward they are called. And I
will refresh you, He says.

Take up My yoke upon you, and learn of Me;
not how to make the world; not to create all things
visible and invisible; not how to work wonders in
this world and raise the dead; but: because I am
meek and humble of heart. Dost thou desire to be
great? Begin first by being the least. Dost thou
think to raise a mighty building of great height?
Think first of the lowness of the foundation.

And however great a mass of building anyone
may wish and design to erect, the higher he in-
tends to raise it, the deeper he digs his foundation.
And as the structure is built up, it rises heaven-
ward: but he that digs the foundation, must dig
down very low. The building therefore must be
built in the ground before it rises on high, and the
roof is erected only after a lowly beginning.

What is the roof of the building which we are
raising? How high will its peak reach? I answer
you at once: Even to the very sight of God. You
see how high, how great a thing it is to behold God.
He who desires it, will understand both what I say
and what he hears. The sight of God, the true God,
the God most High, is promised to us. This indeed
is good, to see Him who seeth. For they who worship false gods can easily see them; but they see
idols, who have eyes and see not. But unto us is

promised the vision of the living and the seeing God.

R. Blessed are ye when men shall revile and persecute you, and speak all that is evil against you, untruly, for My sake: * Be glad and rejoice, for your reward is very great in heaven. V. When men shall hate you, and when they shall separate you and shall reproach you, and cast out your name as evil, for the Son of man's sake. Be glad. Glory. Be glad.

✠ Continuation of the holy Gospel according to St. Matthew.—At that time: Jesus answered, and said: I praise Thee, O Father, Lord of heaven and earth, because Thou hast hid these things from the wise and prudent, and hast revealed them to little ones. Yea, Father; for so it hath seemed good in Thy sight. All things are delivered to Me by My Father; and no one knoweth the Son, but the Father; neither doth anyone know the Father, but the Son, and he to whom it shall please the Son to reveal Him. Come to Me, all you that labor, and are burdened; and I will refresh you. Take up My yoke upon you, and learn of Me, because I am meek and humble of heart; and you shall find rest to your souls: for My yoke is sweet, and My burden light.

Let Us Pray

O God, who didst join blessed Matthias to the company of Thy Apostles, grant, we beseech Thee,

that by his intercession we may always experience
Thy loving kindness towards us.   Through our
Lord.

March 12
ST. GREGORY THE GREAT
I Nocturn
From the Book of Ecclesiasticus, c. 39, 1-14
II Nocturn

Gregory the Great, a Roman, son of the senator
Gordian, as a youth applied himself to philosophy;
and having discharged the pretorian office, after
his father's death, he built six monasteries in Sicily,
and a seventh, under the title of St. Andrew, in
his own house in Rome, near the basilica of SS.
John and Paul, at the hill of Scaurus where, with
his teachers Hilarion and Maximian, he embraced
the monastic life, and was later Abbot.   Shortly
afterwards, he was created Cardinal deacon, and
was sent to Constantinople as legate from Pope Pelagius to the emperor Tiberius Constantine; before
whom he achieved such a memorable victory over
the patriarch Eutychius, who had written against
the real and physical resurrection of the body, that
the emperor threw his book into the fire. Wherefore, when Eutychius fell ill not long after, at the
approach of death he took hold of the skin of his
hand and said in the presence of several persons:
I acknowledge that we shall all rise in the flesh.

Returning to Rome, Pelagius having been carried

off by the plague, he was unanimously elected sovereign Pontiff. He refused the honor as long as possible; for he disguised himself and hid in a cave; but he was discovered by the sign of a pillar of fire, and was consecrated at St. Peter's. As Pontiff, he left many examples of learning and holiness to his successors. Every day he admitted pilgrims to his table; among whom he received, not merely an Angel, but the Lord of Angels, in the garb of a pilgrim. He charitably provided for the poor both in and out of Rome, and kept a list of them. He re-established the Catholic faith in several places where it had become weak; for he put down the Donatists in Africa, the Arians in Spain, and drove the Agnoetæ out of Alexandria. He refused to give the pallium to Syagrius, bishop of Autun, unless he would expel the neophyte heretics from Gaul. He also induced the Goths to abandon the Arian heresy.

He sent Augustine and other monks into Britain, and, by these learned and saintly men, converted that island to the faith of Jesus Christ; so that Bede the priest truly calls him the Apostle of England. He checked the haughty pretensions of John, Patriarch of Constantinople, who had arrogated to himself the title of ecumenical bishop of the Church. He persuaded the emperor Maurice to revoke the decree whereby he had forbidden soldiers to become monks. He enriched the Church with most holy practices and laws. In a synod he called together at St. Peter's, he passed several decrees; among them, that in the Mass, the Kyrie eleison should be said nine times; that the Alleluia should be said, except during the interval between Septuagesima and Easter; that there should be inserted in the Canon: *Diesque nostros in tua pace disponas* (and mayest thou dispose our days in Thy peace). He augmented the Litanies, the Stations, and the ecclesiastical office.

He wished that the four Councils of Nice, Constantinople, Ephesus, and Chalcedon be honored like the four Gospels. He allowed the bishops of Sicily, who, according to an ancient custom of their churches, used to visit Rome every three years, to make that visit every fifth year. He wrote many books; Peter the Deacon testifies that he frequently saw the Holy Ghost resting on the head of the Pontiff in the form of a dove whilst he was dictating. It is a matter of wonder that with his incessant sickness and ill-health he could have said, done, written, and decreed as he did. At length, after performing many miracles, he was called to his reward in heaven, after being Pope thirteen years, six months, and ten days, on March 12, which the Greeks also observe as a great feast on account of this Pontiff's extraordinary learning and virtue. His body was buried in the Basilica of St. Peter, near the Secretarium.

R. This is he who worked great wonders before God, and all the earth is filled with his teaching: * May he intercede for the sins of all peoples. V. This is he who despised the life of the world and attained to the heavenly kingdom. May. Glory. May.

III Nocturn

The reading of the holy Gospel
according to St. Matthew

At that time: Jesus said to His disciples: You are the salt of the earth. But if the salt lose its savor, wherewith shall it be salted? And so forth.

Homily of St. Gregory, Pope

We should remark, that he who is not able in one and the same exhortation to admonish all at once, must strive according to his ability to instruct each one in private by means of personal exhortation. For we ought always to bear in mind those words spoken to the holy Apostles, and through the Apostles, to us: You are the salt of the earth. If therefore we are salt, we ought to season the minds of the faithful.

You, then, who are shepherds, remember it is God's animals you are feeding; actually those animals of which the Psalmist says to God: In it shall thy animals dwell. Moreover, we often see a block of salt set before cattle, that, through licking the salt, they may grow into better condition. Now the

priest among his people should be like a block of
salt among cattle. For a priest must weigh well
what he saith to each, and the counsels he gives
to each; so that whosoever comes in contact with
a priest may, as though touching salt, be seasoned
with the savor of eternal life.

For we are not the salt of the earth unless we
season the hearts of our hearers; that seasoning,
however, one verily bestows upon his neighbor when
he withholds not the word of exhortation. But only
then do we rightly preach good ways to others when
we show forth our admonitions by deeds and example. My dearly beloved brethren, God, so I
think, tolerates no harm greater than that which is
done by priests when He sees those whom He has
appointed for the correction of others give themselves up to wickedness; when we priests, who
ought to crush sins, sin ourselves. We do not seek
after the welfare of souls when we daily devote
ourselves to our own pursuits, when we unlawfully
desire earthly things, when we eagerly receive the
glory of men. And for the very reason that we are
placed over others, we have the greater opportunity
to do what we please. We turn the sacred ministry
which we have taken upon ourselves into a means
of furthering our ambition. We give up the cause
of God and devote ourselves to worldly affairs. We
receive a position in sacred matters, but we are
involved in earthly entanglements.

R. The Lord hath sworn and He will not repent:
* Thou are a priest forever according to the order
of Melchisedech. V. The Lord said to my Lord,
sit Thou at My right hand. Thou art. Glory. Thou
art.

✠ Continuation of the holy Gospel according to
St. Matthew: At that time: Jesus said to His disciples: You are the salt of the earth. But if the
salt lose its savor, wherewith shall it be salted?
It is good for nothing anymore but to be cast out,
and to be trodden on by men. You are the light
of the world. A city seated on a mountain cannot
be hid. Neither do men light a candle and put it
under a bushel, but upon a candlestick, that it may
shine to all that are in the house. So let your light
shine before men that they may see your good
works, and glorify your Father, who is in heaven.
Do not think that I am come to destroy the law or
the prophets: I am not come to destroy, but to fulfill. For amen, I say unto you, till heaven and
earth pass, one jot or one tittle shall not pass of the
law, till all be fulfilled. He, therefore, that shall
break one of these least commandments and shall so
teach men, shall be called the least in the kingdom
of heaven; but he that shall do and teach, he shall
be called great in the kingdom of heaven.

LET US PRAY

O God, who didst give the reward of eternal
happiness to the soul of Thy servant Gregory;

mercifully grant, that we who are burdened by the weight of our sins, may be raised up by his prayers. Through our Lord.

March 19
ST. JOSEPH, SPOUSE OF THE BLESSED VIRGIN MARY, CONFESSOR

I Nocturn
From the Book of Genesis, c. 39, 1-5; c. 41, 37-44

II Nocturn
Sermon of St. Bernard, Abbot

Who and what manner of man this blessed Joseph was, you may imagine from the name by which, a dispensation being allowed, he deserved to be so honored as to be believed and to be called the father of God. You may conjecture it from his very name, which, being interpreted, means *Increase*. At the same time remember that great man, the former Patriarch, who was sold into Egypt; and know that Joseph not only inherited the latter's name, but also attained to his chastity and equalled his grace and innocence.

If, then, that Joseph, sold by fraternal envy and carried into Egypt, foreshadowed the selling of Christ; this Joseph, flying from the envy of Herod, carried Christ into Egypt. The former, keeping faith with his Lord, would have no intercourse with the lady; the latter, recognizing his Lady, the Mother of his Lord, to be a virgin, and being himself chaste, guarded her faithfully.

To the former was given discernment in the mysteries of dreams; to the latter it was given to know and to share in the heavenly mysteries. The former laid up wheat, not for himself, but for all the people; the latter received the living Bread from heaven to guard it, for himself and for the whole world.

There is no doubt that that Jospeh, to whom the Mother of the Savior was espoused, was a good and faithful man. A faithful and prudent servant, I say, whom the Lord gave as a consolation to His Mother, as the guardian of His own Body, and finally, as the only and most faithful helper upon earth in the great plan of His Incarnation.

R. Arise, and take the Child and His Mother, and fly into Egypt; * And be there until I shall tell thee. V. That it might be fulfilled which the Lord spoke by the prophet saying: Out of Egypt have I called My Son. And. Glory. And.

III Nocturn

The reading of the holy Gospel
according to St. Matthew

When Mary the Mother of Jesus was espoused to Joseph, before they came together, she was found with Child of the Holy Ghost. And so forth.

Homily of St. Jerome, Priest

Why is He conceived, not by a simple virgin, but by an espoused woman? In the first place, that the origin of Mary might be manifested by means of the genealogy of Joseph. Secondly, that Mary might not be stoned by the Jews as an adulteress. Thirdly, that she might have a guardian during the flight into Egypt. Ignatius the Martyr adds a fourth reason why He was conceived by an espoused woman: Namely, that His Birth might be concealed from the devil, who thought Him to have been born of a wife, not of a virgin.

Before they came together, she was found with Child of the Holy Ghost. Not by another was she discovered, but by Joseph, who had the privilege of a husband to know all things concerning his future wife. But because it is said "Before they came together," it does not follow that afterwards they did come together. Scripture, indeed, shows that this did not happen.

Whereupon Joseph her husband, being a just man and not willing publicly to expose her, was minded to put her away privately. If one be joined to an adulteress, they are made, as it were, one body; and in the law there is a precept whereby not only the accused, but those who are accomplices in the crime as well, are guilty of sin. How, then, is Joseph represented as a just man whilst concealing the crime of his wife? But this is a testimony in Mary's favor, that Joseph, aware of her chastity and filled with awe at what had come to pass, kept silence about the mystery he did not understand.

Joseph, son of David, fear not to take unto thee Mary thy wife. Above we stated that spouses are called wives; which fact the Book against Helvidius explains more fully. Now, by way of approval the angel speaks to him during sleep, to sanction the appropriateness of his silence. It is likewise to be noted that Joseph is called the son of David in order that Mary might be shown to be of the offspring of David.

R. Joseph went up from Galilee out of the city of Nazareth into Judea, to the city of David, which is called Bethlehem: * Because he was of the house and family of David. V. To be enrolled with Mary his espoused wife. Because. Glory. Because.

✠ Continuation of the holy Gospel according to St. Matthew.—When Mary, the mother of Jesus, was espoused to Joseph, before they came together, she was found with Child, of the Holy Ghost. Whereupon Joseph her husband, being a just man and not willing publicly to expose her, was minded to put her away privately. But while he thought on these things, behold the Angel of the Lord appeared to him in his sleep, saying: Joseph, son of David, fear not to take unto thee Mary thy wife, for that which is conceived in her is of the Holy Ghost. And she shall bring forth a Son: and thou shalt call His name Jesus. For He shall save His people from their sins.

O Holy Father
Saint Benedict,
intercede for us
thy
children.

LET US PRAY

May we be assisted by the merits of the Spouse of Thy most holy Mother, we beseech Thee, O Lord, that we may obtain by his intercession what we could not obtain by ourselves alone; who livest and reignest with God the Father.

March 21
OUR MOST HOLY FATHER ST. BENEDICT
I Nocturn
From the Book of Ecclesiasticus, c. 44, 1 - 15
II Nocturn

Benedict was born of a noble family at Nursia and received a liberal education at Rome; he withdrew to a place called Subiaco and there hid himself in a very deep cave that he might give himself entirely to Jesus Christ; he passed three years in that retirement, unknown to all save to a monk, by name Romanus, who supplied him with the necessaries of life. The devil having one day excited him to a violent temptation of impurity, he rolled himself amidst bramble-bushes for so long a time that, his body being lacerated, he extinguished the desire of carnal pleasure by the pain.

The fame of his sanctity, however, became known outside his hiding-place, and certain monks put themselves under his guidance; but the looseness of their lives was such that they could not endure his reproofs, and they resolved to put poison in his drink. He made the sign of the cross over the proffered cup, whereupon it broke, and he, leaving that monastery, returned to solitude. But when many disciples daily came to him, he built twelve monasteries and drew up most holy rules for them.

He afterwards went to Monte Cassino where he destroyed an image of Apollo, who was still worshipped there, overturned the altar, and burnt the groves; and there he built the chapel of St. Martin and the small temple of St. John and instilled Christian precepts into the townsmen and other inhabitants. Day by day Benedict advanced in the grace of God, and he also foretold, in a spirit of prophecy, what was to come. Totila, king of the Goths, hearing of this and anxious to find out if it were so, sent his sword-bearer, with the royal insignia and attendants, before him, to pretend that he was the king. When Benedict saw him, he said: Put off, my son, put off this dress; for it is not thine. But he foretold to Totila that he would reach Rome, cross the sea, and die after nine years.

Several months before he departed from this life, he foretold to his disciples the day on which he would die; and he ordered them to open the sepulchre, wherein he wished his body to be buried, six days before he should be carried to it. On the sixth day he desired to be carried to the church; and there, having received the Eucharist, with his eyes raised in prayer towards heaven and held up by his disciples, he breathed forth his soul. Two monks saw it ascending to heaven, adorned with a most precious robe, surrounded by shining lamps, and they heard a man of illustrious and venerable aspect, standing over his head, and speaking thus: This is the way whereby Benedict, the beloved of the Lord, ascends to heaven.

R. This is he who wrought great things before God, and praised the Lord with his whole heart: * May he intercede for the sins of all men. V. Behold a man without reproach, a true worshipper of God, keeping himself from every evil deed, and ever abiding in innocence. May. Glory. May.

III Nocturn

The reading of the holy Gospel
according to St. Matthew

At that time: Peter said to Jesus: Behold we have left all things, and have followed Thee. What, therefore, shall we have? And so forth.

Homily of St. Peter Damian, Bishop

Behold, we have left all things, and have followed Thee. A solemn word, a great promise, a holy deed worthy of benediction—to leave all things and to follow Christ. These are the words exhorting voluntary poverty that have given birth to monasteries, that have filled cloisters with monks, that have peopled the forests with anchorites. It is of them the Church sings: For the sake of the words of Thy lips I have kept hard ways—words promising rest for labor, riches for poverty, reward for tribulation. Indeed, it is a great thing to leave all things, but it is greater to follow Christ. This is the work, this is the labor, yea, this is the very summit of man's sanctification. Unless we abandon all, it is impossible for us to follow Christ, who "rejoices as a giant to run His course"; one who is weighed down cannot follow Him.

Behold, he says, we have left all things—not only the goods of this world, but also the desires of our souls; for that man has not abandoned all things who retains himself; yea, it profits him nothing to have left all things if he has not left himself, since no burden weighs more heavily on a man than the man himself. What tyrant is more cruel, what power more violent to a man than his own will? Then he continues: What, therefore, shall we have? Peter has already left all, and not only does he follow Christ now, but he has done so for a long time; and now for the first time does he ask what he will receive. What does this mean, Peter? Have you not promised obedience at the hearing of the ear, not in the form of a contract? Yet, hearken to what the Lord God speaks, and consider the hope we ought to have amidst this world's vicissitudes. You shall be seated, says the Lord, who is Truth. O august session, delightful rest, consummate bliss.

But lest long expectation turn away the sweetness of this great promise, He soothes the perturbation of our mind with a more sweet word. For He knows our frame—that our littleness would brook no delays; therefore, in His benignity He brushes aside also this thought and accedes to us even in this regard, saying: And everyone that hath left house, or father, or mother, or brother, or wife, or fields, or children for My name's sake shall receive a hundredfold and shall possess life everlasting. Indeed the mouth of them is stopped that speak wicked things. And now let all them be confounded that do unjust things without cause. We have a promise both for this present life and for that which is to come, the former being evidently that of the hundredfold, as may be deduced from that which follows: and he shall possess eternal life.

Therefore, they who have not yet received the hundredfold should scrutinize their hearts and carefully examine all the works of their hands; without a doubt, they will find some nook and corner strange to the Savior. But what is this hundredfold except the visitations, the consolations, the firstfruits of the Spirit who is sweeter than honey; what is it but the testimony of our conscience; what but the joyous and most delightful expectation of the just, the remembrance of the abundance of God's sweetness, yea, the superabundance of His sweetness, concerning which it is not necessary to speak to those who have experienced it; and as for those who have not experienced it, who can describe such things in words? Now to whom can this whole passage of the Gospel lesson be so fittingly applied as to our Father and Guide, Saint Benedict? From early youth he abandoned the world with its allurements, and pursued Christ with the most rapid strides, never faltering in his course until he had reached Him.

R. The Lord hath loved him and hath adorned him; He hath clothed him with a robe of glory, * And hath crowned him at the gates of paradise. V. The Lord hath put on him the breastplate of faith, and hath adorned him. And. Glory. And.

✠ Continuation of the holy Gospel according to Matthew.—At that time: Peter said to Jesus: Behold we have left all things and have followed Thee: what, therefore, shall we have? And Jesus said to them: Amen I say to you, that you who have followed Me in the regeneration, when the Son of man shall sit on the seat of His majesty, you also shall sit on twelve seats, judging the twelve tribes of Israel. And every one that hath left house, or brethren, or sisters, or father, or mother, or wife, or children, or lands, for My name's sake, shall receive a hundredfold and shall possess life everlasting.

LET US PRAY

O Almighty and eternal God, who on this day, having freed Thy most holy confessor Benedict from the prison of the body, didst raise him up to heaven, grant, we beseech Thee, to Thy servants celebrating this feast, the remission of all their sins; that they who with joyful hearts rejoice at his glory may, by his intercession with Thee, share also in his merits. Through our Lord.

March 25

ANNUNCIATION OF THE BLESSED VIRGIN MARY

I Nocturn

From Isaias the Prophet, c. 7, 10 - 15; c. 11, 1 - 5; c. 35, 1-7

II Nocturn

Sermon of St. Leo, Pope

The omnipotent and merciful God, whose nature is goodness, whose will is power, whose work is mercy, at the very beginning of the world—as soon as the devil's malice had destroyed us with the poison of his envy—pre-ordained the remedies of His love which were intended to restore mortals, announcing to the serpent the future seed of a woman which would crush by its strength the pride of his venomous head; that is, that Christ would come in the flesh; signifying Him who as God and man, born of a Virgin, would condemn by His stainless Birth the seducer of the human race.

The devil rejoiced that he had so deceived man by his artifices as to make him lose the gifts of God, that he had stripped him of the privilege of immortality, had brought him under the hard sentence of death, and that he himself had found some sort of solace in his unhappiness, in that he had found a comrade in guilt. He thought also to bring it to pass that God by a justly-earned severity should change His feelings towards man whom He had created in such honor. There was need, beloved brethren, that God, who is unchangeable, whose will and loving-kindness are inseparable, should fulfil His original purpose of goodness by a mysterious dispensation, so that man, driven into crime by the wicked cunning of the devil, should not perish and frustrate the plan of God.

As the time approached, beloved, which had been ordained for the redemption of man, our Lord Jesus Christ entered these depths, coming down from His heavenly throne, yet departing not from the Father's glory, born in a new order, begotten by a new birth; in a new order, for, invisible in His own, He has become visible in ours; incomprehensible, He willed to be understood; abiding before time, He began to exist in time; Lord of all, the dignity of His majesty having been overshadowed, He took on the form of a servant; as God unable to suffer, He did not disdain to be man subject to suffering; and immortal, He did not disdain to submit to the laws of death.

For, while many things would wondrously be of service to Him in restoring mankind, the true and efficacious mercy of God chose this way of helping above all, by which, to destroy the devil's work, He would use, not the might of dominion, but the reckoning of justice. For not without reason was the pride of the old enemy asserting a tyrannical rule over all men; nor was he oppressing with an undue sway those whom of their own choice he had enticed from God's commandments to the service of his own will. So then he would not justly lose the original slavery of the surrendered race unless he should be overcome by the race he had subdued.

R. Behold a Virgin shall conceive and bear a Son, saith the Lord: * And His name shall be called Wonderful, God, the Mighty One. V. He shall sit upon the throne of David, and upon His kingdom forever. And His name. Glory. And His name.

III Nocturn
The reading of the holy Gospel
according to St. Luke

At that time: The Angel Gabriel was sent from God into a city of Galilee called Nazareth, to a Virgin espoused to a man whose name was Joseph, of the house of David, and the Virgin's name was Mary. And so forth.

Homily of St. Ambrose, Bishop

Divine mysteries are indeed hidden, and according to the saying of the prophets, it is not easy for any man to know the council of God. Nevertheless,

from the other deeds and precepts of our Lord and
Savior we are able to understand that this was also
more in keeping with the divine plan, that she who
was espoused to a husband should be chosen to
give birth to the Lord. But why did she not become pregnant before her espousal? Perhaps lest
it be said that she had conceived in adultery.

And the Scripture clearly demonstrates that she
would be both espoused and a virgin: a virgin,
that it might be clear that she was free from intercourse with man; espoused, lest she be seared by
the infamy of violated virginity, to which desecra-
tion the fact of the pregnant womb would seem to
point. For the Lord preferred that some should
be in doubt rather about the manner of His Birth
than about the purity of His Mother. For He
knew the delicate reserve of the Virgin and the
elusive fame of modesty, and He did not think that
faith in His Birth ought to be built up by injuries
to His Mother.

And the angel went in to her. Learn to know the
virgin in her actions, in her modesty, know her in
the word spoken, know her in the mystery. It is
the nature of virgins to tremble at and to fear
every approach of man, to dread all conversation
with man. Let women learn to imitate this example
of modesty. Alone in her room, she, whom no man
ever gazed at, and whom an Angel alone discovered,
alone—without companion or witness by whose dis-

course she might be distracted—she was saluted by an angel.

For the mystery of so great a message must be proposed not by the mouth of man, but by that of an angel. Today for the first time is heard: The Holy Spirit will overshadow thee; and it is heard and believed. And then she says: Behold the handmaid of the Lord; be it done unto me according to thy word. See the humility, behold the devotion! She who is chosen to be the Mother of the Lord calls herself His Handmaid; she is not forthwith elated by the promise.

R. Rejoice, O Virgin Mary, thou alone hast trampled down all heresies because thou didst believe the Archangel Gabriel's words: * When thou, a virgin, didst give birth to God and man, and after childbirth didst remain ever a virgin. V. Blessed art thou who didst believe: for those things have come to pass which were told thee from the Lord. When. Glory. When.

✠ Continuation of the holy Gospel according to Luke.—At that time: The angel Gabriel was sent from God into a city of Galilee, called Nazareth, to a virgin espoused to a man whose name was Joseph, of the house of David: and the virgin's name was Mary. And the angel being come in, said unto her: Hail, full of grace, the Lord is with thee: blessed are thou among women. Who having heard, was troubled at his saying and thought within herself what manner of salutation this might be. And the angel said to her: Fear not, Mary, for thou hast found grace with God. Behold thou shalt conceive in thy womb and shalt bring forth a Son and thou shalt call His name Jesus. He shall be called the Son of the Most High, and the Lord God shall give unto Him the throne of David His father: and He shall reign in the house of Jacob forever, and of His kingdom there shall be no end. And Mary said to the angel: How shall this be done, because I know not man? And the angel answering, said to her: The Holy Ghost shall come upon thee and the power of the Most High shall overshadow thee. And therefore also the Holy which shall be born of thee shall be called the Son of God. And behold thy cousin Elizabeth, she also hath conceived a son in her old age; and this is the sixth month with her that is called barren; because no word shall be impossible with God. And Mary said: Behold the handmaid of the Lord, be it done unto me according to thy word.

Let Us Pray

O God, who hast willed that Thy Word should become Man in the womb of the Virgin Mary at the message of an Angel; grant to us Thy servants that we who believe she is truly the Mother of God, may be assisted by her intercession with Thee. Through the same Lord.

April 25
ST. MARK THE EVANGELIST

I Nocturn

From the Book of Ezechiel the Prophet, c. 1, 1 - 13

II Nocturn

From the Book of St. Jerome, Priest, on
Ecclesiastical Writers

Mark, the disciple and interpreter of Peter, according to what he had heard Peter announce, wrote a short Gospel at the request of the brethren at Rome. Which, when Peter had heard, he approved, and commanded it to be read in the Church by his authority. Then, taking the Gospel which he himself had produced, he went to Egypt, where he was the first to preach Christ at Alexandria, and there established the church with such learning and austerity of life that he compelled all the followers of Christ to imitate him.

Then, Philo, the most learned of the Jews, seeing the first Church of Alexandria still under Jewish influence, wrote a book concerning its usages, as it were, in praise of his own nation. And as Luke relates that at Jerusalem the faithful had all things in common; so Philo records what he himself had seen done at Alexandria under the teaching of Mark. He died in the eighth year of the reign of Nero and was buried at Alexandria, being succeeded by Arianus.

From the Commentary of St. Gregory, Pope,
on the Prophet Ezechiel

The prophet gives a minute description of the
four holy living creatures, which he foresaw in the
spirit as being to come when he says: Every one
had four faces, and every one, four wings. What
is signified by face, if it be not celebrity; or by
wings, unless it be the power of flight? For it is
by the face that a man is recognized; but by their
wings the bodies of birds are raised in the air.
Thus the face pertains to faith, the wings to contemplation. For in our faith we are known to almighty God, as He says of His sheep: I am the
good shepherd; and I know Mine, and Mine know
Me. And again He says: I know whom I have
chosen.

For by contemplation we are raised above ourselves, as it were, to heaven. Every one, then,
had four faces: for if thou inquirest what Matthew held concerning the Incarnation of the Lord:
he assuredly held the same doctrine as Mark, Luke
and John. If thou askest what John held; it was
undoubtedly that which was held by Luke, Mark,
and Matthew. If thou askest what Mark held: it
was the same as that of Matthew, John, and Luke.
If thou askest what Luke held; it was the same as
that of John, Matthew and Mark.

R. With great power the Apostles gave * Testimony of the Resurrection of Jesus Christ our Lord,

alleluia, alleluia. V. They were indeed filled with
the Holy Ghost, and they spoke the word of God
with boldness. Testimony. Glory. Testimony.

III Nocturn

The reading of the holy Gospel
according to St. Luke

At that time: The Lord appointed also other
seventy-two: and He sent them two and two before
His face into every city and place whither He Himself was to come. And so forth.

Homily of St. Gregory, Pope

Our Lord and Savior, dearest brethren, admonishes us at one time by His words, but at another
time by His works. For His very deeds are precepts: for though He utters no word, He shows
us clearly what we ought to do. Behold, He sends
His disciples forth to preach, two by two; for the
precepts of charity are two, namely, the love of
God, and the love of our neighbor; for love cannot
be said to exist at all unless there be two parties.

No one can properly be said to have charity towards himself; for the name of charity can be applied only to love which tends outward to another.
Behold, the Lord sends forth His disciples to preach,
two by two; and in so doing, teaches us without
any need of words that he who has not charity towards his neighbor, ought by no means to undertake the office of preaching.

It is rightly said that He sent them before His face into every city and place whither He Himself was to come. For the Lord follows His preachers. First comes preaching, afterwards the Lord comes to the dwelling-place of our soul; the words of exhortation go before, and by them truth is taken into the mind.

Hence Isaias says to the same preachers: Prepare ye the way of the Lord, make straight the paths of our God. Hence the Psalmist cries to his children: Make a way for Him who ascendeth upon the west. The Lord does indeed ascend upon the west; for whereas He set, as it were in His Passion, on the other hand He rose with greater glory in His Resurrection. He ascends upon the west evidently in that, by rising from the dead, He tramples upon the death which He had suffered. So we make a way for Him who ascends upon the west when we set forth His glory before the eyes of your minds, in order that He, following after us, may enlighten you by the presence of His love.

R. I am the true vine, and you the branches: * He that abideth in Me and I in him, the same beareth much fruit, alleluia, alleluia. V. As the Father hath loved Me, I also have loved you. He. Glory. He.

✠ Continuation of the holy Gospel according to St. Luke.—At that time: The Lord appointed also other seventy-two; and He sent them two and two before His face into every city and place whither He Himself was to come. And He said to them: The harvest indeed is great, but the laborers are few: pray ye therefore the Lord of the harvest that He send laborers into His harvest. Go, behold I send you as lambs among wolves. Carry neither purse, nor scrip, nor shoes, and salute no man by the way. Into whatever house you enter, first say: Peace be to this house; and if the son of peace be there, your peace shall rest upon it; but if not, it shall return to you. And in the same house remain, eating and drinking such things as they have: for the laborer is worthy of his hire. Remove not from house to house. And into what city soever you enter, and they receive you, eat such things as are set before you, and heal the sick that are therein; and say to them: The kingdom of God is come nigh unto you.

Let Us Pray

O Lord, who didst elevate blessed Mark Thy Evangelist to the dignity of preacher of the Gospel, grant, we beseech Thee, that we may always profit by his knowledge and be protected by his prayers. Through our Lord.

Wednesday of the III Week after Easter
SOLEMNITY OF ST. JOSEPH
SPOUSE OF THE BLESSED VIRGIN MARY
CONFESSOR AND PATRON OF THE UNIVERSAL CHURCH

I Nocturn

From the Book of Genesis, c. 39, 1 - 6; c.41, 37 - 49

II Nocturn

Sermon of St. Bernardine of Siena

It is a general rule of all special favors conferred upon any rational creature, that whenever divine grace chooses anyone for some particular grace or for some high station, it likewise bestows on the person so chosen all the gifts necessary for that high station, and furnishes them abundantly. This was verified in a marked degree in St. Joseph, the supposed father of our Lord Jesus Christ, and the true spouse of the Queen of the world and Mistress of the Angels, who was chosen by the eternal Father as the faithful tutor and guardian of His greatest treasures that is to say, of His own Son, and of Joseph's Spouse; which duty he most faithfully discharged. Wherefore the Lord says: Good and faithful servant, enter thou into the joy of Thy Lord.

If thou considerest him in connection with the whole Church of Christ, is he not that specially chosen man by whom and under whom Christ was becomingly and honestly brought into the world? If then the whole of Holy Church is indebted to

the Virgin Mother, because through Mary She was
made worthy to receive Christ; so also next to
Mary it is to Joseph She owes special thanks and
respect. He is indeed the key of the Old Testament in whom the worthiness of patriarchs and
prophets obtains the promised fruit. For he alone
possessed in the flesh what the divine goodness had
given them in promise. Justly, then, we recognize
a type of him in the person of the patriarch Joseph,
who laid up a store of wheat for the people. But
the second Joseph far exceeds the first, since he did
not merely provide bread for the bodily sustenance
of the Egyptians, but with the greatest dexterity
provided for all the elect the heavenly Bread, which
feeds the soul unto life everlasting.

Indeed, there can be no doubt that Christ treated
Joseph in heaven with the same familiarity, esteem,
and high honor which He paid him, as a son to his
father, whilst He walked among men; nay rather,
that He fulfilled and perfected these habits. Hence
it may reasonably be inferred that there was a
special significance in the words uttered by the
Lord: Enter thou into the joy of Thy Lord.
Whence the joy of being happy forever enters into
the heart of man, but the Lord preferred to say to
him: Enter thou into joy; that He might mystical-
ly intimate to him that joy which should not only
be within him, but everywhere around him, ab-

sorbing his whole being, and, as it were, swallowing him up in an abyss of infinite joy.

Therefore, O blessed Joseph, remember us, and by the voice of thy prayer intercede with Him who was deemed to be thy Son; yea, obtain for us favor with the most blessed Virgin, thy Spouse, and the Mother of Him, who, with the Father and the Holy Ghost, liveth and reigneth world without end. Amen.

R. Thou hast given me the protection of thy salvation, and thy right hand hath held me up: * Thou art my protection, the horn of my salvation and my support, alleluia. V. I am thy protector, and thy reward is exceedingly great. Thou art. Glory. Thou art.

III Nocturn
The reading of the holy Gospel
according to St. Luke

At that time: It came to pass that when all the people were baptized, Jesus also being baptized and praying, heaven was opened. And so forth.

Homily of St. Augustine, Bishop

It is evident that the words which he used: Being, as it was supposed, the son of Joseph; were used on account of those who thought He was begotten by Joseph as other men are begotten. But if any are troubled because Matthew gives one line of ancestors, descending from David to Joseph, and Luke another, ascending from Joseph to David, it

is easy when they consider that Joseph could have
had two fathers: one by whom he was begotten,
the other by whom he was adopted. Of old, adoption was customary among that people of God that
they might have sons, though not begotten by them.
Hence, Luke in his Gospel is understood to have
taken as the father of Joseph, not him by whom
Joseph was begotten, but him by whom Joseph was
adopted; and it is the ancestors of this adoptive
father who are recounted in an upward direction,
until they reach to David.

But since it is necessary—as both Evengelists,
namely Matthew and Luke, tell the truth—that one
of them should show the origin of that father who
begot Joseph; the other, the origin of him who
adopted him; which Evangelist do we think more
probably shows the origin of the father who
adopted Joseph than the one who would not say
that Joseph was "begotten" by that man whose son
the Evangelist says he was? Matthew, by saying:
Abraham begot Isaac, Isaac begot Jacob, and so continuing with the word: begot; until at last he says:
Jacob begot Joseph: shows well enough that he
was tracing the natural genealogy to that father
by whom Joseph was not adopted, but begotten.

Although even if Luke had said that Joseph was
begotten by Heli, it should not upset our interpretation so as to think anything else than that by

one Evangelist is mentioned the natural father, and by the other the one who adopted Joseph.

And it is not absurd to say of the son whom a man has adopted that he is begotten by him, not in the flesh, but by charity. For even we, to whom God gave the power to be made His sons, are not begotten of His nature and substance, as His only Son, but are only adopted in love.

R. Arise, and take the Child and His Mother, and fly into Egypt: * And be there until I shall tell thee, alleluia. V. That it might be fulfilled which the Lord spoke by the prophet, saying: Out of Egypt have I called My Son. And be. Glory. And be.

✠ Continuation of the holy Gospel according to St. Luke.—At that time: It came to pass that when all the people were baptized, Jesus also being baptized and praying, heaven was opened; and the Holy Ghost descended in a bodily shape as a dove upon Him: and a voice came from heaven: Thou art My beloved Son, in Thee I am well pleased. And Jesus Himself was beginning about the age of thirty years: being (as it was supposed) the son of Joseph.

LET US PRAY

O God, who in Thy wonderful providence didst choose blessed Joseph to be the spouse of Thy most holy Mother; grant, we beseech Thee, that we may merit to have him as our intercessor in heaven, whom we venerate as our protector on earth; Who livest and reignest with God the Father.

THURSDAY
Sermon of St. Bernardine of Siena

Since the marriage between Mary and Joseph was a real marriage contracted by divine inspiration, and since marriage involves so close a union of souls that the bridegroom and the bride are said to be one person, which may be called, as it were, the perfection of unity, how can any discerning person think that the Holy Ghost would unite in such a union the soul of such a Virgin to any soul that did not closely resemble her in the works of virtue? Therefore I believe that this man, St. Joseph, was adorned with the most pure virginity, the most profound humility, the most ardent love and charity towards God, and the loftiest contemplation. And since the Virign knew that he was given her by the Holy Ghost to be her spouse and the faithful guardian of her virginity, and to share besides in affectionate love and indulgent care towards the most divine Son of God, therefore I believe that she loved St. Joseph sincerely with all the affection of her heart.

Joseph had the most ardent love for Christ. Who, I pray, would deny that Christ, whether as a child or a grown man, would most deeply inspire His own ineffable sentiments and joys in one who held Him in his arms and conversed with Him, and this together with the exterior grace of the filial gaze, speech, and embrace of Christ? O how sweet were the kisses he received from Him! O how sweet to hear the Little One lisp the name of father and how delightful to feel His gentle embrace! Think again, when the little Jesus was growing big and was wearied with much walking on the journeys they made, how Joseph, full of compassion, made Him rest in his bosom; for he bore towards Him all the fulness of an adoptive love, as to a most dear son given to him by the Holy Ghost in his Virgin bride.

So the most prudent Mother, who knew his affection, says to her Son, Jesus, when she found Him in the temple: Son, why hast Thou done so to us? Behold Thy father and I have sought Thee sorrowing. In order to understand this, we must note that Christ contains in Himself two savors: sweetness and sorrow; and since the most holy Joseph was in a wonderful manner a partaker of these two savors, therefore the blessed Virgin calls him in a special sense the father of Christ. This is the only place where we read that she called St. Joseph the father of Jesus: because the sorrow which he felt at the loss of Jesus showed the fatherly affection he bore Him. For if according to human laws which are approved by God a man can adopt as his son the child of another family, how much more truly ought the Son of God, given to this Joseph in his most holy Spouse in the wonderful mystery of a virginal marriage, to be called his son; and it is also to be believed that in him there was the savor of paternal love and sorrow towards the beloved Jesus.

FRIDAY

Sermon of St. John Chrysostom

It was usual in ancient times for betrothed brides to dwell in the houses of their bridegrooms; so Mary dwelt with her Spouse. Why, then, did it happen that this Virgin did not conceive before she was espoused? In order that the mystery might be hid in the meantime, and that the Virgin might escape all danger of evil suspicion. For if he, who had the best right to be excited by jealousy, is seen not merely to refrain from sending away his Spouse or branding her with infamy, but to receive her as his own and cherish her, after she conceived, it is indeed evident that he would never have kept her in his house or ministered to all her needs if he had not clearly known that she had conceived by the operation of the Holy Ghost.

Joseph being a just man, and not willing publicly to expose her, was minded to put her away privately. After he said that she was with child of the Holy Ghost and without sexual intercourse, the Evangelist brings testimony from another source to confirm his statement. For lest anyone should say: And how can this be proved? Who saw it?

Who ever heard of any such thing having happened? And lest you might think that a disciple had invented this tale to please his master, the Evangelist brings forward Joseph, confirming the story by all he has done and suffered, as if to say: If you will not believe me and you hold my testimony in suspicion, at least believe the husband.

He says: Then Joseph her husband, being a just man. To be just means here to have every virtue in perfection. Being therefore a just man, that is, a worthy and good man, he was minded to put her away privately. On that account indeed the Evangelist hath said what happened to this just man before he knew the secret, lest thou shouldst have doubts concerning what happened after he knew the secret. And certainly, if Mary had been such as suspicion would make her out to be, she would have deserved not merely to be denounced, but to be punished by the authority of the law; but Joseph was not merely unwilling to condemn her, but even to denounce her. Thou hast seen, for instance, a man full of sublime philosophy, and free from the slavery of suspicion. But how could one speak merely of suspicion, when the very swelling of her body seemed to prove the fact? But nevertheless, this man was so pure and free from that kind of jealousy, that he would not cause the Virgin even the slightest grief; and although he lived under the law, his philosophy was above the law;

for indeed, as grace was already approaching, it was fitting to call forth examples of a much more sublime teaching.

SATURDAY
Sermon of St. John Chrysostom

Joseph, son of David, fear not to take unto thee Mary thy wife. But what is: to take? Undoubtedly, to maintain in his own house; for he had already sent her away in his mind; but her whom you sent away (the Angel says), maintain; she whom God, not her parents, joins to thee; whom He joins, indeed, not in the solemn contract of marriage, but in the fellowship of a common dwelling; and He joins her to thee through the ministry of my words. Just as Christ Himself later entrusted her to the care of His disciple, so now the Angel gives her to her spouse; in such manner that she may have the consolation of his company without conjugal rights. By this means her confinement would be explained in a worthier and more honorable way, and suspicion would be allayed. Not only, says the Angel, was she not dishonored by an unlawful embrace, but even is fruitful in a manner above nature and custom. Therefore, do not grieve at the happy confinement of thy Bride, but break forth into greater joy; for that which is born of her is of the Holy Ghost.

She shall bring forth a Son, and thou shalt call His name Jesus; for thou must not think that because it is from the Holy Ghost the ministry of this great dispensation is a thing apart from thee. For although thou hast no part in His generation (since the Virgin remained undefiled), yet do I readily grant thee this, that is, whatever are the rights of a father and in no way obscure the dignity of the Virgin; thou shalt certainly give the newborn His name; thou shalt be the first to call Him by His name. For although He who is born is not thy Son, thou shalt, however, show Him the care and solicitude of a parent; and therefore I unite thee to Him by this immediate giving of the name. Then, lest anyone might think from this that Joseph was the father of Christ, the Angel says: She shall bear a Son. He does not say: She shall bear thee a Son; but puts it in an undetermined and indefinite way. She did not bear Christ to Joseph, but absolutely to the whole world.

Therefore, the Evangelist relates that the angel brought His name from heaven, that by this means also he might show how wonderful was the Birth of Him who taught His name to Joseph by an Angel sent from God. For this name, which indeed contains a thousand treasures of good, was not given without meaning. Therefore the Angel himself interprets it, consoling the mourner with good hopes; and thus also he invites him to believe his words. For we are easily summoned to that which is pleasant and give prompt credence to good tid-

ings. The Angel said: He shall save His people
from their sins. This also shows the novelty of the
gift. He announces that His people are to be
saved, not indeed from visible war nor from the
swords of barbarians, but from what is far greater
than these: from their own sins; and no mere
man could ever accomplish this.

MONDAY
Sermon of St. Bernard, Abbot

Mary was espoused to Joseph, or rather (as the
Evangelist puts it), to a man whose name was
Joseph. He is called a man, (*vir*) not because he
was a husband, but because he was a man of virtue;
or again, since according to another Evangelist, he
is not called merely "man," but "her man," he is
rightly called what he necessarily was supposed to
be. He had to be called her man, because it was
necessary that he should be thought so. In like
manner he was found worthy, not indeed to be the
father of the Savior, but to be called so, that men
might think him to be so, as the Evangelist himself says: And Jesus Himself was beginning about
the age of thirty years, being, as it was supposed,
the son of Joseph.

There is no doubt that this Joseph to whom the
Mother of the Savior was espoused was a good
and faithful man. A faithful and prudent servant,
I say, whom the Lord appointed to be the consolation of His Mother, the tutor of His own Person,

and the one faithful coadjutor on earth of His great counsel. Add to this that he is said to have been of the house of David. For truly of the house of David, this Joseph was a true son of a race of kings, noble in descent, more noble in mind. A true son of David, no degenerate descendant of his father David; truly, I say, a son of David, not so much according to the flesh as in faith, holiness, and devotion, whom, like another David, the Lord found to be a man after His own heart; to whom He safely entrusted the most holy and hidden secret of His heart; to whom, like another David, he showed the secret and hidden things of His wisdom, and granted that He should not be ignorant of a mystery which was known to none of the princes of this world.

Lastly, there was given to him what many kings and prophets desired to see, and saw not; desired to hear, and heard not; he was allowed not merely to hear and see, but also to carry, lead, embrace, kiss, nourish and protect. We must believe that Mary too, like Joseph, was descended from the house of David; otherwise she would not have been espoused to a man of the house of David if she had not herself been of the house of David. Both, therefore, were of the house of David; but in one the truth, which the Lord had sworn to David, was fulfilled; while the other knew and bore witness to the fulfilment of the promise.

TUESDAY

Sermon of St. Bernard, Abbot

It is written: Joseph, her husband, being a just man and not willing publicly to expose her, was minded to put her away privately. Being a just man, he was rightly unwilling to expose her; for as he would not have been a just man if he had connived at known guilt, he would have been even less just if he had condemned proved innocence. Being a just man, therefore, and not willing to expose her, he was minded to put her away privately. Why did he wish to put her away? On this point, hear, not my opinion, but that of the Fathers. Joseph wished to put her away for the same reason that made Peter seek to put away the Lord when he said: Depart from me, O Lord, for I am a sinful man; just as the centurion also sought to keep Him away from his house when he said: Lord, I am not worthy that Thou shouldst enter under my roof.

In like manner Joseph held himself to be sinful and unworthy, and thought he ought no longer to enjoy the familiar companionship of her whose marvelous dignity filled him with awe. He saw and trembled at the unmistakable signs of the divine presence; and, since he could not fathom the mystery, he was minded to put her away. Peter trembled at the greatness of the Divine power; the centurion trembled at the presence of the Divine Majesty; Joseph too, being but a man, was filled with awe at the novelty of this mystery. Dost thou wonder that Joseph judged himself unworthy of the companionship of this pregnant Virgin, when thou hearest that St. Elizabeth too was filled with reverence and trembling at her presence? For she said: Whence is this to me, that the Mother of my Lord should come to me?

And so Joseph was minded to put her away. But why privately, and not publicly? Lest perhaps inquiry should be made about this divorce, and he would be asked for reasons. What should a just man reply to a stiffnecked people, an unbelieving and an argumentative people? If he were to say what he thought and had proved of her purity, would not the cruel and incredulous Jews have soon laughed at him and stoned her? How would they have believed in the Truth lying silent in her womb when they afterwards despised Him preaching in the Temple? What would they have done to Him before His appearance in the flesh when afterwards they laid impious hands on Him in spite of His wonderful miracles? The just man, therefore, was right in wishing to put her away privately, lest he should be thought to lie or to defame an innocent woman.

OCTAVE DAY OF ST. JOSEPH

I Nocturn

From the Book of Genesis, c. 39, 1 - 6; c. 41, 37 - 49

II Nocturn

Sermon of St. Augustine, Bishop

The Angel did not speak falsely when he said to Joseph: Fear not to take unto thee Mary thy wife. She is called wife because of the confidence established at the time of her espousal, although he had not known her carnally, nor was he ever to do so; and the name of wife was not lost nor rendered untrue because there had not been any carnal intercourse, and would not be any in the future. She was, in fact, a Virgin; and therefore she was a holier and a more wonderful source of joy to her husband just because she became a mother without a man's intervention; like to him in faith, unlike him as regards her offspring. On account of this faithful union both of them merited the name of Christ's parents; and not only is she called His mother, but he also is called His father, as being the husband of His mother, not according to the flesh, but according to the spirit. But whether he was a father only in spirit, and she a mother also according to the flesh, yet both were the parents of His humility, not of His glory; of His infirmity, not of His divinity.

For neither does the Gospel lie where one reads: and His father and mother were wondering at those

things which were spoken concerning Him. And
in another place: His parents went every year to
Jerusalem. And a little further on: And His
mother said to Him: Son, why hast Thou done so
to us? Behold Thy father and I have sought Thee
sorrowing. But He, that He might show them that
He had a Father apart from them, who begot Him
without a mother, answered them: How is it that
you sought Me? Did you not know that I must be
about My Father's business?

And, as a set-off to this, lest anyone might think
that by these words He denied His parents, the
Evangelist immediately adds: And they understood
not the word that He spoke to them. And He went
down with them, and came to Nazareth and was
subject to them. To whom was He subject, but to
His parents? And who was thus subject, but Jesus
Christ, who, being in the form of God, thought it
not robbery to be equal with God?

Why, therefore, was He subject to them who
were so far below the form of God, unless that
He emptied Himself, taking the form of a servant,
of which form they were the parents? But truly,
both of them would not have been the parents even
of this form of a servant unless they had been
respectively husband and wife, although without
any carnal intercourse. And hence, when the ancestors of Christ are recounted in direct line of
succession, the series of generations was preferably

to be traced down to Joseph (as has been done), lest in that connection a slur should be cast upon the male sex, admittedly the stronger; while at the same time the truth did not suffer, for both Joseph and Mary were of the seed of David, from which it was prophesied that Christ should come. So all the good things of marriage are found in these parents of Christ: offspring, fidelity, sacrament. The offspring, we know, was the Lord Jesus Himself; their fidelity is proved because there was no adultery; the sacrament, because there was no divorce.

III Nocturn

The reading of the Holy Gospel
according to St. Luke

At that time: It came to pass that when all the people were baptized, Jesus also being baptized and praying, heaven was opened. And so forth.

Homily of St. Augustine, Bishop

Today is, as it were, a second birthday of the Savior. For we know that He was born with the same signs and wonders, but now there is a greater mystery in His baptism. For God says: This is My beloved Son, in whom I am well pleased. This second birth is indeed more glorious than the first. For then, He was born in silence and without witnesses; now the Lord is baptized with a proclamation of His Divinity. Then Joseph, who was thought to be His father, excused himself; now

His true Father, who was not believed to be so, introduces Himself. Then, the Mother was enduring suspicion, because no father was acknowledged; now she that bore Him is honored, because the Divinity makes Him known as His Son.

I say that the second birth was more glorious than the first. For now, the God of majesty records Himself as His Father; then, the workman, Joseph, was so accounted. And although in both cases it was the Holy Ghost through whom the Lord was born and baptized, yet the Father, whose voice was heard from heaven, is greater than the father who labored on earth.

Therefore, on earth Joseph the carpenter was thought to be the father of the Lord and Savior. But God, the true Father of our Lord Jesus Christ, is not excluded from this trade, for He too is a carpenter. For He is the artificer who hath wrought the fabric of this world with not merely wonderful, but with ineffable power.

Like a wise architect He hath erected the heavens on high; He hath laid the foundations of the earth; He hath constrained the sea within its beaches. He is the Artificer who, in due measure, lowers the pinnacles of pride and brings to the surface the bedrock of humility. He is the artificer who cuts off the unnecessary material in our behavior and preserves whatever is useful. He is the artificer whose axe, as John the Baptist warns us, is laid to the root of our tree, so that every tree which departs from the rule of just discretion may be torn up by the roots and consigned to the flames; but that which is according to the measure of truth may be trimmed in the heavenly workshop.

May 1

SS. PHILIP AND JAMES, APOSTLES

I Nocturn

From the Catholic Epistle of St. James the Apostle, c. 1, 1 - 16

II Nocturn

Philip was born at Bethsaida, and was one of the twelve Apostles that were first called by Christ the Lord. It was by Philip that Nathanael, when he had learned that the Messias who was promised in the law had come, was led to the Lord. How familiarly Christ treated Philip is well shown by the fact that certain Gentiles, when they wished to see the Savior, went to Philip; and when the Lord wished to feed the great multitude in the desert, He spoke to Philip thus: Whence shall we buy bread that these may eat? Philip, after having received the Holy Ghost, when Scythia fell to him wherein to preach the Gospel, converted almost its entire population to the Christian faith. Finally, when he reached Hierapolis in Phrygia, he was crucified for the name of Christ, and stoned to death on May 1. The Christians buried his body in that place; but it was afterwards taken to Rome, and, together with the body of the Apostle St. James, was placed in the Basilica of the Twelve Apostles.

James, the brother of the Lord, surnamed the Just, from his childhood never drank wine or strong drink, abstained from flesh-meat, and never cut his hair, or used ointments or the bath. He was the only one permitted to enter the Holy of holies. His garments were of linen. So assiduous was he in prayer that his knees were covered with a hard skin which resembled the hide of a camel in toughness. After Christ's ascension, the Apostles made him bishop of Jerusalem; and it was to him that the Prince of the Apostles sent the news of his being delivered out of prison by an Angel.

A dispute having arisen in the council of Jerusalem concerning the law and circumcision, James followed the opinion of Peter, and, in a speech which he made to the brethren, approved the calling of the Gentiles, and said that the absent brethren were to be told by letter not to impose the yoke of the Mosaic Law upon the Gentiles. It is of him the Apostle speaks to the Galatians: But other of the Apostles I saw none, saving James the brother of the Lord.

Such was James' holy life that people used to strive with each other in their desire to touch the hem of his garment. At the age of ninety-six years, of which he had spent thirty governing the Church of Jerusalem in the most saintly manner, as he was preaching with great courage Christ, the Son of God, he was first attacked with stones; after which he was taken to the highest part of the Temple and cast headlong down. His legs were broken by the fall; and as he was lying half-dead uopn the ground, he raised his hands to heaven and prayed to God for their salvation in these words: Forgive them, O Lord, for they know not what they do. Whilst thus praying, he received a heavy blow on the head from a fuller's club and gave up his soul to God, in the seventh year of Nero's reign. He was buried near the Temple from which he had been thrown down. He wrote one of the seven Catholic Epistles.

R. Your sorrow, alleluia, * Shall be turned into joy, alleluia, alleluia. V. The world shall rejoice, but you shall be made sorrowful, but your sorrow. Shall. Glory. Shall.

III Nocturn
The reading of the holy Gospel
according to St. John

At that time: Jesus said to His disciples: Let not your heart be troubled. You believe in God, believe also in Me. In My Father's house there are many mansions. And so forth.

Homily of St. Augustine, Bishop

A greater attention to God, brethren, must be aroused in us, that we may take in with our minds the words of the holy Gospel which have just now sounded in our ears. For the Lord Jesus said: Let not your heart be troubled. You believe in God, believe also in Me. Lest they, as men, should fear death and so be troubled, He consoles them, testifying that He also is God.

You believe in God, He says, believe also in Me. For it follows that if you believe in God, you ought also to believe in Me; which would not follow if Christ were not God.

You believe in God, believe also in Him with whom it is natural, not a robbery, to be equal with God; for He emptied Himself, not, however, relinquishing the form of God, but taking the form of a servant. You fear death for this form of a servant; let not your heart be troubled. The form of God will raise it up.

But what is the meaning of this that follows: In My Father's house there are many mansions. unless it was that they also feared for themselves? Therefore they should have heard: Let not your heart be troubled. For which of them would not fear when it was said to Peter, the readiest and most confident of all: The cock shall not crow before you deny Me thrice?

At the thought that they might fall away from Him, they were justly troubled; but when they heard: In My Father's house there are many mansions; if not, I would have told you, for I go to prepare a place for you; they were relieved of their anxiety, being certain and confident that after the danger of temptation they would remain in the presence of God with Christ. For although one is stronger than another, one wiser than another, one more righteous than another, one holier than another, in My Father's house there are many mansions. Not one of them shall be estranged from that house, where each will receive a mansion according to his merits.

R. I am the true Vine, and you the branches: * He that abideth in Me, and I in him, the same beareth much fruit, alleluia, alleluia. V. As the Father hath loved Me, I also have loved you. He that abideth. Glory. He that abideth.

✠ Continuation of the holy Gospel according to St. John.—At that time: Jesus said to His disciples: Let not your heart be troubled; you believe in God, believe also in Me. In My Father's house there are many mansions. If not, I would have told you; for I go to prepare a place for you. And if I shall go and prepare a place for you, I will come again and will take you to Myself, that where I am you also may be. And whither I go you know and the way you know. Thomas saith to Him: Lord, we know not whither Thou goest; and how can we know the way? Jesus saith to him: I am the way, the truth, and the life. No man cometh to the Father but by Me. If you had known Me, you would without doubt have known My Father also: and from henceforth you shall know Him: and you have seen Him. Philip saith to Him: Lord, show us the Father, and it is enough for us. Jesus saith to him: So long a time have I been with you, and have you not known Me? Philip, he that seeth Me, seeth the Father also. How sayest thou, Show us the Father? Do you not believe that I am in the Father, and the Father in Me? The words that I speak to you, I speak not of Myself. But the Father who abideth in Me, He doeth the works. Believe you not that I am in the Father, and the Father in Me? Otherwise, believe for the very works' sake. Amen, amen, I say to you, he that believeth in Me, the works that I do, he also shall do; and greater than these shall he do; because I go to the Father, and whatsoever you shall ask the Father in My name, that will I do.

LET US PRAY

O God, who dost gladden us by the annual celebration of the feast of Thy Apostles Philip and James; grant, we beseech Thee, that as we rejoice in their merits, we may be instructed by their example. Through our Lord.

May 3
FINDING OF THE HOLY CROSS
I Nocturn
*From the Epistle of St. Paul the Apostle to the
Galatians, c. 3, 10 - 14; to the Philippians, c. 2,
5 - 11; to the Colossians, c. 2, 9 - 15*

II Nocturn

After the great victory which the emperor Constantine gained over Maxentius having received from God the sign of the Lord's Cross, Helena, the mother of Constantine, at the suggestion of a dream came to Jerusalem eagerly searching for the Cross; there she ordered to be overthrown the marble statue of Venus, which had been set up by the Gentiles on the site of the Cross about a hundred and eighty years before, to destroy the memory of the Passion of Christ the Lord. She did likewise at the manger of the Savior, and at the place of the Resurrection, removing from the former an idol of Adonis, and from the latter an idol of Jupiter.

The site of the Cross having been thus cleansed, three crosses which had been deeply buried were dug up, and near them was also found the inscription of the Lord's Cross; though it was not clear to which of the three it had been attached, this doubt was removed by a miracle. For, after having prayed to God, Macarius, bishop of Jerusalem, applied each of the crosses to a woman who was afflicted with a dangerous malady; the first two produced no result; the third Cross was then applied, and the woman was instantly restored to health.

Helena, having found the saving Cross, built there a very splendid church in which she left a portion of the Cross, enclosed in a silver case; another part she took to her son, Constantine, and it was placed in the church called Holy-Cross-in-Jerusalem, built on the site of the Sessorian palace.

She also took to her son the nails wherewith the most holy Body of Jesus Christ had been fastened. Constantine passed a law that from that time forward, a cross should never be used as an instrument of punishment; and thus, what hitherto had been an object of reproach and derision, became one of veneration and glory.

R. It behoveth us to glory in the Cross of our Lord Jesus Christ, in whom is our salvation, life and resurrection: * By whom we have been saved and delivered, alleluia. V. We adore Thy Cross, O Lord, and we remember Thy glorious Passion. By whom. Glory. By whom.

III Nocturn
The reading of the holy Gospel
according to St. John

At that time: There was a man of the Pharisees named Nicodemus, a ruler of the Jews. This man came to Jesus by night and said to Him: Rabbi, we know that Thou art come a teacher from God. And so forth.

Homily of St. Augustine, Bishop

Nicodemus was one of those who believed in the name of Jesus, seeing the signs and wonders that He did, For it is said above: When He was at Jerusalem, at the Pasch, upon the festival day, many believed in His name. Why did they believe in His name? It goes on to say: Seeing His signs and wonders which He did.

And what does it say to Nicodemus? There was a ruler of the Jews named Nicodemus. This man came to Jesus by night and said to Him: Rabbi, we know that Thou art come a teacher from God. And therefore he had believed in His name. And why had he believed? It goes on: For no man can do these signs which Thou dost, unless God be with him.

If therefore Nicodemus was one of the many who had believed in His name, let us seek to find in Nicodemus why Jesus would not trust Himself to them. Jesus answered and said to him: Amen, amen, I say to thee, unless a man be born again, he cannot see the kingdom of God. Hence Jesus entrusts Himself to those who have been born again. Behold, they had believed in Him, but Jesus did not entrust Himself to them. Such are all catechumens: they themselves believe in the name of Christ, but Jesus does not entrust Himself to them.

Mark well, and understand, beloved. If we say to a catechumen: Do you believe in Christ? he answers: I believe; and signs himself with the Cross of Christ. He carries it upon his forehead and is not ashamed of the Cross of the Lord. Behold, he believes in His name. Let us ask him: Do you eat the Flesh of the Son of Man and do you drink the Blood of the Son of Man? He does not understand what we say, for Jesus has not entrusted Himself to him.

R. O sweet the wood, sweet the nails, sweet the burden they sustain: * That wood alone was worthy to bear the ransom of this world, alleluia. V. This sign of the Cross will be in the heavens when the Lord shall come to judge. That wood. Glory. That wood.

✠ Continuation of the holy Gospel according to St. John.—At that time: There was a man of the Pharisees, named Nicodemus, a ruler of the Jews. This man came to Jesus by night; and said to Him: Rabbi, we know that Thou art come a teacher from God: for no man can do these signs which Thou dost, unless God be with him. Jesus answered, and said to him: Amen, amen I say to you, unless a man be born again, he cannot see the kingdom of God. Nicodemus saith to Him: How can a man be born again when he is old? Can he enter a second time into his mother's womb, and be born again? Jesus answered: Amen, amen I say to thee, unless a man be born again of water and the Holy Ghost, he cannot enter the kingdom of God. That which is born of the flesh, is flesh; and that which is born of the spirit, is spirit. Wonder not that I said to thee: you must be born again. The Spirit breatheth where He will; and thou hearest His voice, but thou knowest not whence He cometh, nor whither He goeth; so is every one that is born of the Spirit. Nicodemus answered, and said to Him: How can these things be done? Jesus answered, and said to him: Art thou a master in Israel, and knowest not these things? Amen, amen, I say to thee, that we speak what we know, and we testify what we have seen, and you receive not our testimony. If I have spoken to you earthly things, and you believe not; how will you believe if I shall speak to you heavenly things? And no man hath ascended into heaven, but He that descended from heaven, the Son of Man who is in heaven. And as Moses lifted up the serpent in the desert, so must the Son of Man be lifted up; that whosoever believeth in Him may not perish, but may have life everlasting.

LET US PRAY

O God, who in the wonderful finding of Thy saving Cross hath renewed the miracles of Thy Passion, grant that by the price of this life-giving wood we may obtain the right to eternal life; Who livest and reignest with God the Father.

May 6

ST. JOHN, APOSTLE, BEFORE THE LATIN GATE

I Nocturn

*From the first Epistle of St. John the Apostle,
c. 1, 1 - 10; c. 2, 1 - 6*

II Nocturn

From the Book of St. Jerome, Priest, against
Jovinian

John the Apostle, one of the disciples of the Lord,
who is said to have been the youngest of the Apostles, and whom the faith of Christ had found as
a virgin, remained a virgin; and therefore he is
the more loved by the Lord, and reclines upon the
breast of Jesus. So too, when Peter, who had a
wife, dared not ask the Lord a question, he begged
John to ask; and after the Resurrection, when
Mary Magdalen proclaimed that the Lord had
risen from the dead, both ran to the sepulchre, but
John arrived first. Again when they were in the
boat fishing in the lake of Genesareth, and Jesus
stood on the shore, the Apostles knew not whom
they saw; only John, the virgin, recognized his
Virgin Master and said to Peter: It is the Lord.

John was not only an Apostle, but an Evangelist
and a Prophet as well; he was an Apostle, because he wrote to the churches as a teacher; an
Evangelist, because he composed a book of the Gospel, which no other of the twelve Apostles but

Matthew had done; a Prophet, because in the isle of Patmos, whither he had been banished by the emperor Domitian on account of his bearing witness to the Lord, he saw the Apocalypse, containing unfathomable mysteries of future events.

Tertullian relates moreover that at Rome he was cast into a cauldron of boiling oil, but came out healthier and more vigorous than when he was cast in. But his Gospel too is very different from the others. Matthew begins, as if writing of a man: The book of the generation of Jesus Christ, the son of David, the son of Abraham; Luke, with the priesthood of Zachary; Mark, with the prophecies of Malachias and Isaias.

The first has the appearance of a man, because of the genealogy; the second, that of an ox, because of the priesthood; the third, that of a lion, because of the voice of one crying in the desert: Prepare ye the way of the Lord, make straight His paths. But our John, like an eagle, flies aloft and attains to the Father Himself, saying: In the beginning was the Word, and the Word was with God, and the Word was God.

R. You have not chosen Me: but I have chosen you, and have appointed you * That you should go and should bring forth fruit, and your fruit should remain, alleluia, alleluia. V. As the Father hath sent Me, I also send you. That you. Glory. That you.

III Nocturn
The reading of the holy Gospel
according to St. Matthew

At that time: There came to Jesus the mother of the sons of Zebedee with her sons, adoring and asking something of Him. And so forth.

Homily of St. Jerome, Priest

From where did the mother of the sons of Zebedee get her idea of a kingdom, when the Lord had said: The Son of Man shall be betrayed to the chief priests and the scribes, and they shall condemn Him to death, and shall deliver Him to the Gentiles to be mocked and scourged and crucified; and when He had announced to the frightened disciples the ignominy of His Passion, she asks for the glory of a triumph? For this reason, as I think, because at the end the Lord said: And the third day He shall rise again. The woman thought that immediately after His Resurrection He would reign, and that that which is promised for the second coming, was to be fulfilled in the first; and with feminine greed, she desired the present glory, forgetful of the future.

The question, "What do you wish," which the Lord asked the woman who petitioned Him, and the answer that He made does not come from ignorance, but rather is said of His own person which would be beaten and crucified. The same is true in the case of the woman with the issue of blood: "Who has touched Me?" And of Lazarus: "Where have you laid him?" Also of the Old Testament: "Adam, where art thou," and, "I shall go down and see if they have done according to the cry which has come to Me, that I may know that it is so." The mother of the sons of Zebedee asked something from feminine fickleness and motherly affection, not knowing what she asked. It is no wonder that she should be accused of a lack of knowledge when even of Peter it is said that he did not know what he said when he wished to build three tabernacles on Mount Tabor.

It was the mother who asked, but it was to the disciples that the Lord gave answer, knowing that her prayers were prompted by the desire of her sons. Can you drink of the chalice that I shall drink? In holy Scripture we understand the chalice to mean the Passion, according to the words: Father, if it be possible, let this chalice pass from Me: and in the Psalm: What shall I render to the Lord, for all the things that He hath rendered to me? I will take the chalice of salvation, and I will call upon the name of the Lord. And at once He shows what this chalice is, saying: Precious in the sight of the Lord is the death of His saints.

It may be asked in what way the sons of Zebedee, namely, James and John, drank the chalice of martyrdom; since the Scripture says that the Apostle

James was beheaded by Herod, and that John died a natural death. But if we read ecclesiastical history, in which it says that he (John), on account of his bearing witness, was plunged into a vessel of boiling oil, and thence went to receive his crown as an athlete of Christ, being at once banished to the island of Patmos, we shall see that martyrdom was not absent from his mind, and that John drank the same cup of martyrdom which the Three Children drank of in the fiery furnace, though the persecutor did not in either case shed blood.

R. When ye stand before kings and governors, take no thought how or what you shall speak: * For it shall be given you in that hour what ye shall speak. V. For it is not you that speak; but the Spirit of your Father that speaketh in you. For. Glory. For.

✠ Continuation of the holy Gospel according to St. Matthew.—At that time: The mother of the sons of Zebedee came to Jesus with her sons, adoring, and asking something of Him. Who said to her: What wilt thou? She saith to Him: Say that these my two sons may sit, the one on Thy right hand, and the other on Thy left, in Thy kingdom. And Jesus answering said: You know not what you ask, can you drink the chalice that I shall drink? They say to Him: We can. He saith to them: My chalice indeed you shall drink; but to sit on My right or left hand is not Mine to give to you, but to them for whom it is prepared by My Father.

LET US PRAY

O God, who dost behold that we are everywhere troubled by all our sins, grant, we beseech Thee, that the glorious intercession of blessed John, Thy Apostle and Evangelist, may protect us. Through our Lord.

May 13
FEAST OF THE HOLY RELICS
I Nocturn

From the Apocalypse of blessed John the Apostle, c. 6, 9 - 11; c. 7, 14 - 17; c. 12, 9 - 12; c. 14, 9 - 12

II Nocturn
Sermon of St. Bernard, Abbot

Although the Saints do not need our honor, nor is anything excellent given them by it, it is clearly for our own interest more than for their benefit that we venerate their memory. Do you wish to know how much it is for our benefit? By this recollection I find myself inflamed most vehemently by a threefold desire. The first desire that the memory of the Saints either arouses or increases in us is to enjoy their most enviable companionship, to merit brotherhood with them, to live in common with those blessed spirits, and finally to enjoy the communion of the Saints.

The recollection of each one, whether he be only as a faint glimmer or as the most brightly burning

torch, makes the hearts of devoted friends to burn
and thirst not only to see, but also to embrace them,
so that many count themselves already among their
number—either among all at once, or among this or
that particular class—with hearts all afire with
vehement longing. We ought to long not only for
the society of the Saints, but also for their happiness; let us seek, too, their glory with a most
fervent desire. This second desire which burns in
us from the commemoration of the Saints is that
Christ may so appear to us during our life as He
does to them, and that we also may dwell with Him
in glory.

Indeed, if we are allowed to hope for such glory
and aspire to such happiness, we should also desire
the intercession of the Saints, so that what is impossible for us may be obtained through their intercession. Have mercy on me, have mercy on me, at
least you, my friends. You, O Saints, know our
dangers, ignorances, the attacks of the enemy, our
violent impulses, our frailty. I speak to you who
fought in the same temptations, who overcame in
the same conflicts, who evaded the same snares, who
have learned compassion from those things which
you yourselves have suffered. With greater confidence I take refuge to you. I have you as companions in humanity, so it also behooves you to
show a special and more familiar mercy to bone of
your bone and flesh of your flesh.

Passing from this world to the Father, the saints have left us a pledge. Their bodies are indeed buried in peace amongst us, but their names shall live forever; that is, their glory is never buried. Far be from us, O holy souls, far be from us that cruelty of the chief butler of Pharao, who, when restored to his former position in Egypt, presently forgot holy Joseph, who lay bound in prison. For the Egyptians were not members of one head, nor had the unfaithful part with the faithful, that is, Egypt with Israel, any more than does darkness with light. For Egypt means darkness; Israel means the living God; and therefore where Israel was, there was light. But our union with the Saints is such that while we rejoice with them, they suffer with us; while we, by devout meditation, reign with them, they, by their devoted intercession, fight with us and for us.

R. Let the just rejoice in the Lord and let them hope in Him, and they shall be praised. * All ye right of heart rejoice in the Lord and exult. V. And ye shall be glorified, alleluia, alleluia. All. Glory. All.

III Nocturn
The reading of the holy Gospel
according to St. Luke

At that time: Jesus, coming down from the mountain, stood in a plain place, and the company of His disciples, and a very great multitude of people from all Judea and Jerusalem and the sea coast both of Tyre and Sidon. And so forth.

Homily of St. Ambrose, Bishop

Observe the order of things. You should be poor in spirit; for humility of spirit is richness in virtue. Unless you become poor, you cannot be meek. He who is meek can mourn for the present. He who mourns in his lower self can desire better things. He who seeks higher things deprives himself of the lower, in order to be helped by the higher. He who shows mercy cleanses his own heart. For what is the cleansing of the heart except the ridding it of the filth of death? For alms free the soul from death; yet the perfection of charity is patience. He who suffers persecution and is tried by adversities is strengthened for the final combat, so that, having fought manfully, he may be crowned.

Some wish that there should be degrees of virtue by which we may ascend from the lowest to the highest. In short, as the growth in virtue, so also the growth in recompense; for to be a child of God is more than to possess the earth and to merit consolation. But because the kingdom of heaven is both the first as well as the last recompense, shall the recompense for those who are just beginning be equal to those who are perfect?

You have the first kingdom when the Saints are met by Christ in the clouds on the last day. Many of those sleeping will rise, some unto life everlasting, others to perdition. The first kingdom of heaven is set before the Saints after the dissolution of the body; the second kingdom is after the resurrection; namely, to be with Christ. When you have entered into the kingdom of heaven, your reward is lastingly fixed. And although the kingdom is only one, the rewards are different in the kingdom of heaven.

After the resurrection, being freed from death, you will begin to possess your land. He to whom it is said: "Thou art earth and into earth thou shalt return," shall not possess his land; he who does not receive the fruit cannot be a possessor. Therefore, freed by the cross of the Lord, if then you will be found under the Lord's yoke, you shall reap consolation in that possession. Delight follows consolation, divine mercy follows delight. Him upon whom the Lord has mercy, He also calls; he who is called sees Him who calls; he who sees God, is assumed into the law of divine generation; then, finally, as a son of God, he will be delighted by the celestial riches of the Kingdom.

R. Rejoice, ye just, in the Lord, alleluia. * Jubilation is becoming for the just, alleluia. V. Sing to Him a new canticle, sing to Him psalms in a loud voice. Jubilation. Glory. Jubilation.

✠ Continuation of the holy Gospel according to St. Luke.—At that time: Jesus, coming down from the mountain, stood in a plain place, and the company of His disciples, and a very great multitude of people from all Judea and Jerusalem, and the sea coast both of Tyre and Sidon, who were come to hear Him, and to be healed on their diseases. And they that were troubled with unclean spirits were cured. And all the multitude sought to touch Him, for virtue went out from Him, and healed all. And He, lifting up His eyes on His disciples, said: Blessed are ye poor, for yours is the kingdom of heaven. Blessed are ye that hunger now: for you shall be filled. Blessed are ye that weep now; for you shall laugh. Blessed shall ye be when men shall hate you, and when they shall separate you, and shall reproach you, and cast out your name as evil, for the Son of man's sake. Be glad in that day and rejoice; for behold, your reward is great in heaven.

LET US PRAY

O God, who has willed to enrich this most holy Church with so many Relics of the Saints; increase our faith in the resurrection, and make us to be partakers of that immortal glory whose pledge we honor in these holy Relics. Through our Lord.

June 11
ST. BARNABAS, APOSTLE
I Nocturn
From the Acts of the Apostles, c. 13, 43 - 52;
c. 14, 1 - 3
II Nocturn

Barnabas, a Levite, a Cyprian born, who was also called Joseph, was appointed with Paul an Apostle of the Gentiles to preach the Gospel of Jesus Christ. Barnabas, having sold the land which he possessed, brought the money received by the sale to the Apostles. And having been sent to Antioch to preach, when he had ascertained that many people there had been converted to the faith of Christ the Lord, he was unbelievingly overjoyed, and he exhorted them that they might continue in the way of Christ. Which exhortation profited much, for by them all he was held to be a good man and filled with the Holy Ghost.

He went thence to Tarsus to seek Paul, and came with him to Antioch. In the church of that city they tarried for a year, and gave the commandments of the Christian faith and life to those men; and here also it was that the worshippers of Jesus Christ were first called Christians. Moreover, the disciples of Paul and Barnabas supported by their own resources the Christians that were in Judea, sending the money thither by Paul and Barnabas. Having performed this work of charity, taking with them John, who was surnamed Mark, they returned to Antioch.

And while Paul and Barnabas were zealously serving the Lord in the Church of Antioch, fasting and praying with the other prophets and doctors, the Holy Ghost said: Separate me Saul and Barnabas for the work whereunto I have taken them. Then they fasting and praying, and imposing their hands upon them, sent them away. Therefore they went to Seleucia, and thence to Cyprus; and besides this, they passed through many cities and countries, preaching the Gospel with the greatest profit to their hearers.

Finally Barnabas separated from Paul, and together with John, who was surnamed Mark, sailed to Cyprus; and there, about the seventh year of the reign of Nero, on June 11, he joined the martyr's crown to the dignity of the apostolic office. In the reign of the Emperor Zeno, his body was discovered in the island of Cyprus; on his breast lay the Gospel of Matthew, copied by the hand of Barnabas.

R. Take up My yoke upon you, saith the Lord, and learn of Me, because I am meek and humble of heart: * For My yoke is sweet and my burden light. V. And you shall find rest for your souls. For My yoke. Glory. For My yoke.

III Nocturn
The reading of the holy Gospel
according to St. Matthew

At that time: Jesus said to His disciples: Behold I send you as sheep in the midst of wolves. And so forth.

Homily of St. John Chrysostom

When the Lord had dispelled all anxiety from the hearts of His disciples and had furnished them with weapons by a display of miracles, having withdrawn them from all earthly concerns and freed them from all solicitude for worldly affairs, and finally had made them strong as iron, and even as steel, then at length He foretells to them their future adversities.

For many advantages were to follow from this prediction of future events. First, that they might learn the power of His foreknowledge. And then, that no one might suspect that such great evils came from the Master's lack of power. Furthermore, lest those who were to suffer these things should be troubled by a sudden and unexpected turn of events. Finally, that they would not be too greatly distressed on hearing of these things at the very time of His Passion.

And now, that they may understand that this is a new kind of warfare and an unaccustomed manner of fighting, when He sends them forth unarmed, clad in only one garment, without shoes or staff or girdle or wallet, and commands them to receive nourishment from anyone who will receive them, He does not make an end of His discourse here, but giving evidence of His inexplicable power, He says: And in so going, show forth nevertheless the meekness of sheep although you are about to go to the wolves, and not simply unto wolves but even into the midst of wolves (and neither is it only the meekness of sheep that He bids them have, but also the simplicity of the dove); for thus shall I best show My power when the wolves shall be overcome by the sheep; and although they may be in the midst of wolves and mangled by countless bites, not only will they not be devoured, but will even change the nature of the wolves into their own.

Assuredly, it is a greater and a more wonderful thing to effect a change in the mind of enemies and to bring them to another way of thinking than to kill them; especially when they were only twelve, and the whole world was full of wolves. Let us, then, be ashamed of ourselves who act so very differently, and rush upon our enemies like wolves. For as long as we are sheep, we overcome; even if a thousand wolves surround us, we overcome, and are the conquerors. But if we are wolves, we are conquered; for then the aid of the shepherd departs from us, for He feeds the sheep, not the wolves.

R.   These are they who, living in the flesh, planted the Church in their blood: * They drank the
chalice of the Lord, and became the friends of God.
V. Their voice hath gone forth into all the earth,
and their words unto the ends of the world. They
drank. Glory. They drank.

✠ Continuation of the holy Gospel according to
St. Matthew.—At that time: Jesus said to His
disciples: Behold I send you as sheep in the midst
of wolves. Be ye therefore wise as serpents, and
simple as doves. But beware of all men: for they
will deliver you up in councils, and they will scourge
you in their synagogues. And you shall be brought
before governors and before kings, for My sake,
for a testimony to them and to the Gentiles. But
when they shall deliver you up, take no thought
how, or what, to speak; for it shall be given you
in that hour what to speak: for it is not you that
speak, but the Spirit of your Father that speaketh
in you. The brother also shall deliver up the brother
to death, and the father the son; and the children
shall rise up against the parents, and shall put them
to death; and you shall be hated by all men for My
name's sake: but he that shall persevere to the
end, he shall be saved.

LET US PRAY

O God, who dost make us glad by the merits and
intercession of blessed Barnabas, Thy Apostle;
mercifully grant that we who ask Thy favors

through his intercession may receive them by the gift of Thy grace. Through our Lord.

June 23
VIGIL OF ST. JOHN THE BAPTIST
The reading of the holy Gospel
according to St. Luke

There was, in the days of Herod the king of Judea, a certain priest named Zachary, of the course of Abia: and his wife was of the daughters of Aaron, and her name was Elizabeth. And so forth.

Homily of St. Ambrose, Bishop

Divine Scripture teaches us that we ought to praise the lives not only of those who are publicly honored, but also the lives of their parents; in order that, as it were, the transmitted heritage of spotless purity may stand out in those whom we wish to praise. For what other intention had the holy Evangelist in this place but to glorify St. John the Baptist in his parents as well as in his miracles, his manner of life, his gifts, and his sufferings? So also is praised Anna, the mother of holy Samuel; so did Isaac receive from his parents that nobility of goodness which he bequeathed to his descendants. Therefore, the priest Zachary was not only a priest, but even of the course of Abia, that is, of a house distinguished among the noble families.

And his wife, he says, was of the daughters of Aaron. Therefore the nobility of St. John was inherited not only from his parents, but also from ancestors not distinguished by worldly power, but by a venerable religious succession. For it behoved the forerunner of Christ to have such forefathers, that it might be evident that the preaching of faith in the coming of the Lord was not a gift suddenly received, but one inherited from his ancestors, and implanted in him by the very law of nature. And they were, he says, both just before God, walking in all the commandments and justifications of the Lord without blame. What do they make of this who, to show some excuse for their own sins, think that man cannot live without sinning often, and make use of the verse which is written in Job: No man is pure from sin even though his life on earth be but for one day?

We must answer such persons first by asking what they mean by a man without sin, whether he is a man who has never sinned, or one who has ceased to sin. For if by a man without sin they mean one who has never sinned, I myself agree. For all have sinned, and lack the glory of God. But if they deny that he who has amended his old fault and has changed his way of life in order to refrain from sin cannot keep from sins, I cannot agree with their opinion, since we read that: The Lord so loved the Church that He might present it to

Himself a glorious one, not having spot or wrinkle or any such thing, but that it should be holy and without blemish.

June 24
NATIVITY OF ST. JOHN THE BAPTIST
I Nocturn
From the Book of Jeremias the Prophet, c. 1, 1 - 10 and 17 - 19
II Nocturn
Sermon of St. Maximus, Bishop

The natural birth of the venerable John the Baptist, dearest brethren, made sacred the festival of this day; on this account, he was sent into this world by a heavenly dispensation not only that he himself might be exalted in the glory of a prophet, but also that the praises due all the prophets might be confirmed in him. We do not undeservedly venerate with especial honor him who by a certain, singular favor was the last to foretell the Savior of the world for this purpose, that he should be the first to point Him out to us.

For he alone of the prophets merited to see with his own eyes our Lord Jesus Christ, and to announce His presence whom the rest foreknew would come after a long time. He is the one whom Isaias, through the inspiration of God, proclaimed in prophecy, saying: the voice of one crying in the wilderness: Prepare ye the way of the Lord. How fittingly, dearly beloved brethren, was John announced beforehand as a voice, since he was to be sent as herald and witness of the celestial Word.

He is the one whose birth and name and merit were foretold by the Angel Gabriel. He is the one who in the judgment of a heavenly declaration is placed above all mortal men, our Lord Himself stating: There hath not risen among them that are born of women a greater than John the Baptist. How beautifully is it said: among them that are born of women there is none greater, for He who was born of the Virgin was in every way greater than John.

Having reflected on these things, consider, beloved, what great respect, what great devotion, we should tender this man who, in order that he might be honored, was foretold by the Holy Spirit, promised by an Angel, praised by God, and sanctified by the undying glory of a holy death! For it was befitting that a wonderful life should follow his mystical birth, and that a death consecrated to God should close his holy and perfect life. Consequently, brethren, does the Church of Christ over the whole world most correctly celebrate today with the greatest joy the first moments of the life of him who, as a most faithful witness, revealed to the insensible world that eternal joys were come to mortal men.

R. The Angel of the Lord came down to Zachary, saying: Thou shalt receive a son in thine old age: * And his name shall be John the Baptist.

V. This child is great before the Lord: for his hand is with him. And his name. Glory. And his name.

III Nocturn

The reading of the holy Gospel
according to St. Luke

Elizabeth's full time of being delivered was come, and she brought forth a son. And her neighbors and kinsfolk heard that the Lord had shown His great mercy towards her and they congratulated with her. And so forth.

Homily of St. Ambrose, Bishop

Elizabeth brought forth a son, and her neighbors rejoiced with her. The birth of Saints brings joy to very many, for it is a benefit to all; for justice is a virtue for all. And therefore, in the birth of a just man, a token of his future life is foreshown, and the grace of the virtue to come is expressed by the prophetic joy of the neighbors. It is fitting that there should be mention of the time when the Prophet was in the womb, lest the presence of Mary should not be remembered; but nothing is told of the time of his childhood, for he knew not the disabilities of childhood.

And therefore we read nothing of him in the Gospel except his birth, his announcement, the leaping in the womb, and the voice in the wilderness. For he did not experience the helplessness of childhood, he who, supernaturally outstripping his age,

began from the measure of the age of the fulness
of Christ when still lying in his mother's womb.
It is strange how the holy Evangelist thought it
necessary to tell us that many thought that the
child should be called by his father's name of
Zachary, in order that thou mightest notice that the
mother would not have the name of any kinsman,
but only that given by the Holy Ghost, which the
Angel had previously announced to Zachary.

And indeed, the latter, being dumb, could not
tell his wife the name of their son; but Elizabeth
learned by prophecy what she had not learned from
her husband. John, he says, is his name; that is,
it is not for us to give a name to him who has
already received a name from God. He has his
name, which we know, but we did not choose it.

To receive a name from God is one of the rewards
of the Saints. Thus Jacob was called Israel, because he saw God. Our Lord Jesus was named before He was born; but not an Angel, but His Father gave Him His name. Thou seest that Angels
announce what they have heard, not what they have
taken upon themselves. Do not marvel that the
woman pronounced a name she had not heard, since
the Holy Ghost, who had commanded the Angel, revealed it to her.

R.   The Angel Gabriel appeared to Zachary, saying: A son shall be born to thee, and his name
shall be called John: * And many shall rejoice on

his birthday. V. For he shall be great before the Lord, and he shall drink no wine nor strong drink. And many. Glory. And many.

✠ Continuation of the holy Gospel according to St. Luke.—Elizabeth's full time of being delivered was come, and she brought forth a son. And her neighbors and kinsfolk heard that the Lord had shown His great mercy towards her, and they congratulated with her. And it came to pass that on the eighth day they came to circumcise the child, and they called him by his father's name, Zachary. And his mother answering, said: not so, but he shall be called John. And they said to her: There is none of thy kindred that is called by that name. And they made signs to his father, how he would have him called. And demanding a writing table, he wrote, saying: John is his name. And they all wondered. And immediately his mouth was opened, and his tongue loosed, and he spoke, blessing God. And fear came upon all their neighbors: and all these things were noised abroad over all the hill country of Judea: and they that had heard them, laid them up in their heart, saying: What a one, think ye, shall this child be? For the hand of the Lord was with him. And Zachary his father was filled with the Holy Ghost: and he prophesied, saying: Blessed be the Lord God of Israel because He hath visited, and wrought the redemption of His people.

LET US PRAY

O God, who hath made this present day glorious for us by the birth of blessed John; grant to Thy people the grace of spiritual joys and guide the minds of all the faithful in the way of eternal salvation. Through our Lord.

June 29
SS. PETER AND PAUL, APOSTLES
I Nocturn
From the Acts of the Apostles, c. 3, 1 - 16
II Nocturn
Sermon of St. Leo, Pope

Dearly beloved, the whole world indeed shares in all holy feasts, and the devotion of a common faith demands that whatever has been performed for the salvation of all should be called to mind and celebrated with universal rejoicings. Nevertheless, the feast of this day must be reverenced with a special and peculiar joy in our City, over and above that veneration which it deserves from the whole world; so that, where the departure of the most famous of the Apostles gloriously took place, there, on the anniversary of their martyrdom, let there be the greatest gladness. For these are the men through whom the Gospel of Christ has shone upon thee, O Rome; and thou, who wert the teacher of error, hast become the learner of truth.

These are thy fathers and thy true shepherds, who, to place thee in the kingdom of heaven, founded thee far more happily and in a much better way, than did those by whose effort the first foundations of thy ramparts were laid; from which he who gave thee thy name defiled thee by the slaughter of his brother. These are they who raised thee to this glory, that thou hast become a holy race, a chosen people, a priestly and royal city, made the ruler of the world through the sacred Chair of blessed Peter; that thou shouldst rule a wider realm by a divine religion than by an earthly lordship.

For although, enlarged by many victories, thou didst extend thy imperial sway over land and sea; yet warlike toil hath subdued less to thee than that which Christian peace hath subjected. For it was most agreeable with the divine plan that many kingdoms should be united under one rule, that the world-wide preaching should have a speedy way through nations who were ruled from one city.

But this city knew not Him who was the author of her power, and while she ruled almost all nations, she preserved the errors of all nations; and because she rejected no false worship, she seemed in her own eyes to be most religious. Hence, the more firmly she was held in bondage by the devil, the greater miracle was her liberation through Christ.

R. Thou art the shepherd of the sheep, O Prince of the Apostles; to thee did God entrust all the kingdoms of the world: * And therefore to thee were given the keys of the kingdom of heaven.

V. Whatsoever thou shalt bind on earth, it shall be bound also in heaven; and whatsoever thou shalt loose on earth, it shall be loosed also in heaven. And. Glory. And.

III Nocturn

The reading of the holy Gospel
according to St. Matthew

At that time: Jesus came into the quarters of Cesarea Philippi, and He asked His disciples, saying: Whom do men say that the Son of man is? And so forth.

Homily of St. Jerome, Priest

He fitly asks: Whom do men say that the Son of man is? Because those who speak of the Son of man, are men; but those who discern his Divinity are not called men, but gods. But they said: Some, John the Baptist; and other some, Elias. I wonder that some commentators seek the causes of each of these mistakes, and prolong an interminable discussion as to why some men should have thought our Lord Jesus Christ to be John, others Elias, others Jeremias, or one of the prophets, since they could make the same mistake concerning Elias and Jeremias as Herod did concerning John, when he said: John, whom I beheaded, he himself is risen from the dead, and mighty works show forth themselves in him.

But whom do you say that I am? Notice, careful reader, that judging from what follows and from the wording of the speech, the Apostles are by no means called men, but gods. For when He had said: Whom do men say that the Son of man is? He continues: But whom do you say that I am? They, because they are men, hold a human opinion; you, who are gods, whom do you think I am?

Peter, in the name of all the Apostles, proclaims: Thou art Christ, the Son of the living God. He says: The living God; to distinguish Him from those deities which are considered gods, but are dead. And Jesus answering, said to him: Blessed art thou, Simon Bar-Jona. He Himself bears testimony to His Apostle in His turn. Peter had said: Thou art the Christ, the Son of the living God; his true confession receives its reward: Blessed art thou, Simon Bar-Jona. Why? Because flesh and blood hath not revealed it to thee, but it hath been revealed by the Father.

What flesh and blood could not reveal, was revealed by the grace of the Holy Ghost. Therefore, his name is decided by his confession, because he received a revelation from the Holy Ghost, whose son he is called, since Bar-Jona, in our language, means son of a dove.

R. I have prayed for thee, Peter, that thy faith fail not: * And thou being once converted, confirm thy brethren. V. Flesh and blood hath not revealed it to thee, but My Father, who is in heaven. And. Glory. And.

✠ Continuation of the holy Gospel according to St. Matthew.—At that time: Jesus came into the quarters of Cesarea Philippi, and He asked His disciples, saying: Whom do men say that the Son of man is? But they said: Some, John the Baptist, and other some Elias, and others Jeremias or one of the prophets. Jesus saith to them: But whom do you say that I am? Simon Peter answered, and said: Thou art Christ, the Son of the living God. And Jesus answering, said to him: Blessed art thou, Simon Bar-Jona, because flesh and blood hath not revealed it to thee, by My Father who is in heaven: and I say to thee, that thou art Peter, and upon this rock I will build My Church, and the gates of hell shall not prevail against it: and I will give to thee the keys of the kingdom of heaven; and whatsoever thou shalt bind upon earth, it shall be bound also in heaven; and whatsoever thou shalt loose upon earth, it shall be loosed also in heaven.

LET US PRAY

O God, who hast consecrated this day by the martyrdom of Thine Apostles Peter and Paul; grant to Thy Church to follow their commands in all things through whom She received the beginning of her religion. Through our Lord.

June 30
COMMEMORATION OF ST. PAUL
THE APOSTLE
I Nocturn
From the Acts of the Apostles, c. 13, 1 - 13
II Nocturn

From the Book of St. Augustine, Bishop, on grace
and free-will.

The Apostle Paul, of whom we undoubtedly find,
that far from having any good deserts of his own,
he had on the other hand many evil ones, obtained
the grace of God, who renders good for evil; let us
see what he says, when his martyrdom was approaching, in his letter to Timothy: For I am
even now ready to be sacrificed, he says, and the
time of my dissolution is at hand. I have fought
a good fight, I have finished my course, I have kept
the faith. Now especially he makes mention of
these, his good works, that a crown might follow
upon his good merits, as grace had followed upon
his demerits.

Notice what thereupon follows: There is laid
up for me, he says, a crown of justice, which the
Lord, the just judge, will render to me in that day.
To whom should the just judge render a crown, if
the merciful Father had not first given grace? And
how could it be a crown of justice, unless the grace
which justifies the ungodly had gone before it?

How could it be rendered as his due, unless the same grace had first been freely bestowed?

Accordingly, let us consider those very merits of the Apostle Paul, for which he looked to receive a crown from the just judge; and let us see if these merits of his were really his own, that is, derived by him from himself, or whether they were the gifts of God. He says: I have fought a good fight, I have finished my course, I have kept the faith. In the first place, those good works were nothing if they had not been preceded by good thoughts. Observe, therefore, what he tells us about those very thoughts; for writing to the Corinthians, he says: Not that we are sufficient to think anything of ourselves, as of ourselves; but our sufficiency is from God. Now let us examine this in detail.

He says: I have fought a good fight. I ask, by what power he fought; whether by a power which he possessed of himself, or by a power given to him from above? It is impossible to suppose that so great a teacher should not have known the law of God, whose voice speaks in Deuteronomy: Lest thou say in thy heart: My own might and the strength of my own hands have achieved this great strength for me: But remember the Lord thy God, that He giveth thee strength to do great things. But of what use is a good fight unless it is followed by a victory? And who gives the victory, save He, of whom Paul himself says: Thanks be to God, who giveth us the victory through our Lord Jesus Christ.

R. By the grace of God I am what I am: * And His grace in me hath not been void, but remaineth always with me. V. He who wrought in Peter to the Apostleship wrought in me also among the Gentiles. And His grace. Glory. And His grace.

III Nocturn
The reading of the holy Gospel
according to St. Matthew

At that time: Jesus said to His disciples: Behold I send you as sheep in the midst of wolves. And so forth.

Homily of St. John Chrysostom

He seems to say this: Fear not if, when I send you among wolves, I bid you to be as sheep and as doves. For although I am also able to order it otherwise, and not to allow you to suffer anything grievous, nor to be as sheep at the mercy of wolves, but to make you more terrible than prowling lions; nevertheless, it is expedient that it be thus ordered; and this shall make you more renowned, and shall show forth my power. For so, afterwards, He said to Paul: My grace is sufficient for thee; for power is made perfect in infirmity. Therefore, I Myself have made you such as you are.

But let us examine what wisdom He requires: that of the serpent, assuredly. For just as the serpent draws his whole body along, and cares very little if this body itself must be cut, so long as he keeps his head uninjured; so also in like manner thou shouldst not mind losing all else except the faith: either riches, or thy body, or if needs be, to lay down thy very life. For faith is the head and the root; if that be preserved, even though thou shouldst lose all else, yet thou shalt recover it all with greater glory.

Therefore He does not order us to be simple only, or prudent only; but He unites both in one, that they may be converted into strength. If thou desirest to see whether these things really happened, read the book of the Acts of the Apostles; thou wilt learn indeed how often the Jewish people rose up against the Apostles and gnashed their teeth, and the latter, imitating the simplicity of the dove and answering with becoming mildness, overcame their wrath, allayed their fury, and repelled their onslaught.

For, when these Jews said: Commanding, did we not command you that you should not teach in his name? although the Apostles could have worked innumerable miracles, yet they neither said nor did anything drastic, but, answering with the greatest mildness, they said: If it be just to hear you rather than God, judge ye. Thou hast perceived the simplicity of the dove, now see the wisdom of the serpent: For we cannot, they say, but speak the things which we have heard and seen.

R. Thou art a vessel of election, O holy Apostle Paul, a preacher of truth to the whole world, * Through whom the Gentiles have known the grace of God. V. Intercede for us with God, who chose thee. Through whom. Glory. Through whom.

✠ Continuation of the holy Gospel according to St. Matthew—At that time: Jesus said to His disciples: Behold I send you as sheep in the midst of wolves. Be ye therefore wise as serpents, and simple as doves. But beware of men: For they will deliver you up in councils, and they will scourge you in the synagogues. And you shall be brought before governors and before kings, for My sake, for a testimony to them and to the Gentiles. But when they shall deliver you up, take no thought how, or what to speak, for it shall be given you in that hour what to speak: for it is not you that speak, but the Spirit of your Father that speaketh in you. The brother also shall deliver up the brother to death, and the father the son; and the children shall rise up against the parents, and shall put them to death; and you shall be hated by all men for My name's sake: but he that shall persevere to the end, he shall be saved.

LET US PRAY

O God, who hast instructed the whole world by the preaching of blessed Paul the Apostle; grant us, we beseech Thee, that we who honor his heavenly birthday, may experience the effects of his intercession with Thee. Through our Lord.

FEAST OF THE MOST PRECIOUS BLOOD

I Nocturn

From the Epistle of blessed Paul the Apostle to the Hebrews, c. 9, 11 - 22 and c. 10, 19 - 24

II Nocturn

Sermon of St. John Chrysostom

Wouldst thou hear of the power of the Blood of Christ? Let us return to the figure thereof; let us recall the former type, and relate the ancient Scripture. In Egypt, at midnight, God threatened the Egyptians with the tenth plague, by which their first-born should perish, because they kept in captivity His first-born people. But, lest the beloved people of the Jews should share their danger, because they were all in the same place, He found in His wisdom a remedy. Behold, then, a wonderful figure, that thou mayest learn His power in truth. The wrath of the divine indignation was awaited, and the angel of death circled over every home. Therefore, what did Moses do? Kill a yearling, lamb, he says, and sprinkle the doors with its blood. What sayest thou, O Moses? Is the blood of a sheep likely to deliver a reasoning man? Certainly, he says, not by what that blood is in itself, but because by it there is displayed a figure of the Blood of the Lord.

For as the statues of rulers, which are without reason or speech, have sometimes been wont to help men who fled to them, though these latter had soul and reason, not because the images were made of bronze, but because they reproduced the likeness of the ruler; so also this blood, which was irrational, delivered human beings who had souls, not because it was blood, but because it showed forth the coming of that other Blood. And then the destroying Angel, when he saw the sprinkled doorposts and thresholds, passed over and did not dare to enter. But now if the enemy see not the typifying blood sprinkled on the lintels, but the Blood of the truth of Christ shining on the lips of the faithful, made holy as the gates of a temple, much more so does he withdraw himself. For if the Angel forebore before the type, how much more shall the enemy tremble if he should perceive the reality itself.

Wouldst thou wish to search further into the might of this Blood? I do wish that thou mayest observe whence it takes its source, and from what fountain it flows. First, it comes from the Cross itself; its source was the side of the Lord. For, says the Evangelist, when Jesus was dead and still hanging on the Cross, a soldier approached, struck His side with a lance, and thence flowed water and Blood; the one is a figure of Baptism, the other of the Sacrament. Therefore he does not say: There went forth Blood and water; but: There went forth first water and then Blood; for we are first washed in Baptism, and afterwards made holy by the Sacrament. The soldier opened His side and laid open the wall of that holy temple; and so I have found that most noble treasure, and I rejoice to discover the glittering riches. And so was it done concerning that lamb: the Jews killed a sheep, from which I have learned the value of the Sacrament. From His side flowed Blood and water. I would not, O hearer, that thou shouldst pass over the hidden meaning of such great mysteries; for I have yet a mystic and mysterious discourse to deliver. I have said that that water and Blood showed forth symbolically Baptism and the Sacraments. For from these holy Church was founded by the laver of regeneration and the renovation of the Holy Ghost. Through Baptism, I say, and through the Sacraments, which seem to have issued from His side.

Therefore, from His side Christ built the Church, just as from Adam's side, Eve, his wife, was brought forth. For because of this Paul also testifies, saying: We are members of His body and of His bones; meaning thereby, doubtless, His side.

For as God caused the woman to be created from the side of Adam, so also Christ from His own side gave us water and Blood, whence He formed His Church.—Moreover, when the 19th centenary of the redemption of the human race occured, the Supreme Pontiff, Pius XI, to recall to the minds of all so ineffable a benefit, wished it to be celebrated before all by a solemn and sacred jubilee; in order that the fruits of the Precious Blood of Christ, the immaculate Lamb, by which we have been redeemed, might abound more abundantly in men, and that its memory might be more vividly recommended to men, the same Supreme Pontiff raised the feast of the Most Precious Blood of our Lord Jesus Christ to the rank of a double of the first class, and ordered it to be observed annually by the universal Church.

R. God commendeth His charity towards us: * Because, when as yet we were sinners, in due time Christ died for us. V. Much more, therefore, being now justified by His Blood, shall we be saved from wrath through Him. Because. Glory. Because.

III Nocturn
The reading of the holy Gospel
according to St. John

At that time: When Jesus had taken the vinegar He said: It is consummated. And bowing His head, He gave up the ghost. And so forth.

Homily of St. Augustine, Bishop

A suggestive word was made use of by the Evangelist in not saying: He pierced His side; or: He wounded: or anything like that, but: He opened, that therein might, as it were, be thrown open the door of life, whence have flowed forth the sacraments of the Church, without which there is no entrance into life that is truly life. The Blood that was shed was shed for the remission of sins. That water it is that makes up the health-giving cup, and supplies at the same time the bath (of baptism), and a (saving) draught. This was announced beforehand, when Noe was commanded to make a door in the side of the ark, through which the animals not destined to perish in the flood might enter, and by which the Church was prefigured. Because of this, the first woman was made from the side of the man while he slept, and she was called Life and Mother of the living. For the name signified a great good, before the great evil of her sin. This second Adam bowed His head and fell asleep on the cross, in order that thence a Spouse might be formed for Him from that which flowed from His side as He slept. O death, by which the dead live again! What is purer than this Blood? What more health-giving than this wound?

Men were held in bondage under the devil and served the demons; but they have been redeemed from captivity. For they could sell themselves, but they could not redeem themselves. The Redeemer came, and paid the price. He shed His Blood, and bought the world. Do you ask what He bought? See what He gave, and you will find out what He bought. The Blood of Christ is the price. What is it worth? What, but the whole world? What, but all nations? Very ungrateful for their price, or very proud, are they who say that the price is of such small worth as to buy only the Africans; or that they are so great that it was given for them alone. Therefore let them not rejoice or be proud. What He gave, He gave for the whole world.

He had His Blood, by which He could redeem us; and to this end He took blood, that He might shed it in order to redeem us. If thou wishest it, the Blood of thy Lord was given for thee; if thou dost not wish it, it was not given for thee. For perchance thou sayest: My God had Blood with which He redeemed me, but now since He has suffered, He has given it all; what hath remained to Him, that He may also give for me?

This is a great thing, because He gave once, and He gave for all. The Blood of Christ is salvation to him who wishes it, punishment to him who wishes it not. Why, therefore, dost thou hesitate to be set free from the second death, thou who dost not wish to die? By this thou art set free, if thou art willing to take up thy cross, and follow the

Lord; for He took up His cross and sought His servant.

R. God hath predestined us unto the adoption of sons through Jesus Christ, * In whom we have redemption through His Blood. V. The remission of sins according to the riches of His grace, which hath superabounded in us. In whom. Glory. In whom.

✠ Continuation of the holy Gospel according to St. John.—At that time: Jesus, when He had taken the vinegar, said: It is consummated. And bowing His head, He gave up the ghost. Then the Jews (because it was the Parasceve), that the bodies might not remain upon the cross on the sabbath day (for that was a great sabbath day), besought Pilate that their legs might be broken and that they might be taken away. The soldiers, therefore, came; and they broke the legs of the first and of the other that was crucified with Him. But after they were come to Jesus, when they saw that He was already dead, they did not break His legs, but one of the soldiers with a spear opened His side, and immediately there came out blood and water. And he that saw it hath given testimony, and his testimony is true.

LET US PRAY

O almighty and eternal God, who hath appointed Thy only begotten Son to be the Redeemer of the world and wast willing to be appeased by His

Blood, grant, we beseech Thee, so to reverence with solemn devotion the price of our salvation, and by its power to be preserved from the evils of the present life that we may rejoice in its eternal fruit in heaven. Through the same our Lord.

July 2

VISITATION OF THE BLESSED VIRGIN

I Nocturn

From the Canticle of Canticles, c. 2, 1 - 17

II Nocturn

Sermon of St. John Chrysostom

When the Redeemer of our race had come to us, He went forthwith to His friend John, while he was still in his mother's womb. When John in the one womb perceived Him in the other, shaking the barriers of nature, he cried out: I see the Lord, who has set the barriers of nature, and I do not wait for the due season of my birth. That period of nine months is not needful for me; for He who is eternal is in me. I will go forth from this gloomy tabernacle; I will proclaim my manifold knowledge of marvelous things. I am a sign: I will show forth the coming of Christ. I am a trumpet: and I will make known the dispensation of the Son of God in the flesh. I will sound the trumpet: I will bless my father's tongue, and loose it, so that it may speak. I will sound the trumpet: and I will quicken my mother's womb.

Thou seest, O beloved, how new and wonderful is this mystery. He is not yet born, and he speaks by leapings; he does not yet appear, and he utters threats; he may not yet cry out, and by his acts he is heard; he does not yet draw the breath of life, and he preaches God; he does not yet behold the light, and he points out the Sun; he is not yet brought forth, and he hastens to be the forerunner. For, in the presence of the Lord, he cannot bear to be restrained; he cannot endure to await the time ordained by nature; but he strives to break free from the imprisoning womb, and is eager to herald the coming Savior. He approaches, he says, who loosens the bonds; and why do I sit in bonds, and why am I forced to remain here? The Word comes, that He may establish all things; and do I still remain imprisoned? I will go forth, I will run before Him, and will proclaim to all: Behold the Lamb of God, who taketh away the sins of the world.

But tell us, O John, how thou didst see and hear when thou wast still enclosed in the darkness of thy mother's womb? How didst thou behold these divine things? How didst thou leap and exult? A great mystery, says he, is accomplished here, and an act far beyond human understanding. Rightly do I do a new thing in nature, because of Him who will do new things which are above nature.

Even though I am yet in the womb, I see; for I see the Sun of justice being carried in a womb. With my ears I perceive, for I am born to be the voice of the great Word. I cry aloud, for I contemplate the only begotten Son of the Father clothed in flesh. I exult, for I see the Producer of all things take the form of a man. I leap, for I think of the Redeemer of the world incarnate. I run before His coming, and, as it were, by my confession I go before Him to you.

R. Blessed art thou because thou hast believed, for those things shall be fulfilled in thee which were spoken to thee by the Lord. And Mary said: * My soul doth magnify the Lord. V. Come, and listen, and I will relate what great things God hath done for my soul. My soul. Glory. My soul.

III Nocturn
The reading of the holy Gospel according to St. Luke

At that time: Mary, rising up, went into the hill country with haste into a city of Juda. And she entered into the house of Zachary, and saluted Elizabeth. And so forth.

Homily of St. Ambrose, Bishop

We must observe that the greater comes to the lesser in order to help the lesser: Mary to Elizabeth, Christ to John. And again afterwards, that He might sanctify the baptism of John, the Lord came to be baptized. And quickly were the bless-

ings of Mary's coming and the divine presence made
manifest. Notice the distinction, and how fitting is
every word. Elizabeth first heard the voice; but
John first felt the grace.

She heard by natural means, he leaped by reason
of the mystery. She perceived the coming of Mary,
he, that of the Lord. Mary and Elizabeth speak
words of grace, but their children work within, and
enter upon the mystery of piety as their mothers
meet each other; and by a double miracle the
mothers prophesy by the spirit of their little ones.
The babe leaped, the mother was filled. The mother
was not filled before the son; but when the son
had been filled with the Holy Ghost, he filled his
mother also.

And whence is this to me, that the Mother of
my Lord should come to me? That is: How has
so great a good happened to me, as that the Mother
of my Lord should come to me? I perceive the
miracle, I recognize the mystery: the Mother of
the Lord, pregnant with the Word, is full of God.
And Mary abode with her about three months, and
she returned to her own house. The point is well
made that holy Mary both showed this attention,
and kept the mystic number.

For she stayed a long time, not only for the sake
of friendship, but also for the advantage of the
great prophet. For, if at her first entrance so great
a result was seen as that at the salutation of Mary

the infant should leap in the womb, and the mother of the infant should be filled with the Holy Ghost, what great benefit must we not think was bestowed upon him by the presence of holy Mary for so long a time? Therefore was the Prophet anointed, and like a good athlete exercised in his mother's womb; for his courage was being prepared for a most arduous struggle.

R. Truly happy art thou, O holy Virgin Mary, and worthy of all praise: * For from thee hath dawned the Sun of justice, Christ our God. V. Pray for the people, plead for the clergy, intercede for all devout women; may all feel thy aid who celebrate thy holy Visitation. For. Glory. For.

✠ Continuation of the holy Gospel according to St. Luke.—At that time: Mary, rising up, went into the hill country with haste into a city of Juda. And she entered into the house of Zachary, and saluted Elizabeth. And it came to pass that when Elizabeth heard the salutation of Mary, the infant leaped in her womb. And Elizabeth was filled with the Holy Ghost; and she cried out with a loud voice, and said: Blessed art thou among women, and blessed is the fruit of thy womb. And whence is this to me, that the Mother of my Lord should come to me? For behold, as soon as the voice of thy salutation sounded in my ears, the infant in my womb leaped for joy. And blessed art thou who hast believed, because those things shall be accomplished that were spoken to thee by the Lord. And Mary said: My soul doth magnify the Lord: and my spirit hath rejoiced in God my Savior.

LET US PRAY

Grant to Thy servants, we beseech Thee, O Lord, the gift of heavenly grace; that as the birth of the Blessed Virgin was the beginning of our salvation, the solemn feast of her Visitation may give us an increase of peace. Through our Lord.

July 3

V DAY WITHIN THE OCTAVE OF SS. PETER AND PAUL

From a Sermon of St. Leo

Precious in the sight of the Lord is the death of His Saints; nor can the religion established through the mystery of the Cross of Christ be destroyed by any form of cruelty. The Church is not diminished by persecutions; rather, it is increased, and the Lord's field is always clothed with a richer harvest when the grains which die singly spring forth in multiple number. Wherefore, thousands of blessed Martyrs, who, emulous of the triumphs of the Apostles, have encompassed our City with people clothed in purple and shining far and wide, and have crowned her with one diadem, as it were, from the glory of the many gems fashioned together, proclaim into what a great plant these two wonderful shoots have grown.

Indeed, dearly beloved, in the commemoration of all the saints we should all be gladdened at their protection divinely arranged for us as an example to our patience and as a confirmation of our faith, but we should deservedly glory in a more special manner in the excellence of our Fathers (Peter and Paul), whom God's grace has raised up to such a height among all the Church's members that it has set them as the light of twin eyes in the Body whose Head is Christ. With regard to their merits and virtues which surpass all possibility of speech, we ought to recognize nothing different, nothing separate, because their election makes them like, their labor makes them similar, and their end makes them equal.

But as even we ourselves have experienced and our elders have proved, we believe and trust that among all the toils of this life we are always to be helped by the mercy of God through the prayers of special patrons, so that the more we are weighed down by our own sins, so the more are we lifted up through the merits of the Apostles; through our Lord Jesus Christ, to whom there is the same power together with the Father and the Holy Ghost, the one Divinity, forever and ever. Amen!

July 4
VI DAY WITHIN THE OCTAVE OF
SS. PETER AND PAUL

From the Commentary of St. John Chrysostom on
the Epistle to the Romans

Since the Apostle Paul prays that we may have
the grace of our Lord Jesus Christ, the mother of
all good things, it remains for us to show ourselves
worthy of such a protection, in order that not only
in this life we may hear the voice of Paul, but,
when we shall have eventually passed out of this
world, may deserve to see the athlete of Christ.
Yea, if we listen to him here, we shall by all means
see him there, although not standing nigh; yet we
shall see him near that shining regal throne, where
the Cherubim glorify God, where the Seraphim are
flying. There we shall see Paul with Peter, the
prince and leader of the choir of Saints, and we
shall delight in their brotherly love.

For if, when he was here, he so loved men that,
although he wished to be dissolved and to be with
Christ, he yet chose to remain on earth; much
more there does he show his most burning charity.
And because of this I love Rome, although I could
praise her on other grounds, namely, her greatness,
her antiquity, her beauty, her population, her empire, her riches, her warlike prowess. But I pass
over all these and hail her as blessed for this
reason, that during his life Paul felt so kindly dis-

posed towards her people, so loved them, discoursed in person there, and at last ended his life among them. They possess his holy body. And by this alone that city has become more renowned than by any other distinctions; and just as a great and strong body has two shining eyes, so are to Rome the bodies of these Saints.

The sky is not as resplendent when the sun sheds its beams as is the city of the Romans sending forth these two shining rays all over the earth. Hence shall Paul, hence shall Peter be caught up. Consider and tremble at such a sight as Rome shall see; namely, Paul with Peter rising suddenly from the tomb, to be borne on high to meet the Lord. What a rose will Rome offer to Christ! With what twin crowns is that city adorned! With what golden chains is she girt! What fountains she has! Wherefore I marvel at this city, not because of her wealth of gold, not for any other beauty whatsoever that she possesseth, but because of those pillars of the Church. Who will now allow me to embrace the body of Paul, to cling to his tomb, to see the dust of that body which filled up those things that are wanting of the sufferings of Christ, which bore the marks of the Lord Jesus, everywhere sowing the preaching of the Gospel?

July 5

VII DAY WITHIN THE OCTAVE OF
SS. PETER AND PAUL

Sermon of St. Maximus

Since all the most blessed Apostles obtain a like
reward of sanctity with the Lord, I do not know
by what consideration Peter and Paul, nevertheless, appear to excel the others in a certain
peculiar virtue of faith; which fact, indeed, we can
prove from the judgment of our Lord Himself.
For to Peter, as to a good steward, He gave the key
to the heavenly kingdom; on Paul, as an apt
teacher, He enjoins the instruction of the institution of the Church; so that, namely, those whom
the latter instructs unto salvation, the former receives into their reward; and to the souls of those
whose hearts Paul enlightens by the teaching of
words, Peter opens the realm of heaven. In a way
Paul, too, received the key of knowledge from
Christ. For that must be called a key by which the
hard hearts of sinners are unbolted to belief, the
secrets of the minds are revealed, and whatever is
kept inclosed within is brought forth plainly by a
reasonable manifestation. That is a key, I say,
which, on the one hand, opens the conscience to the
confession of its sin, and, on the other, makes fast
unto eternity the grace of the saving mystery.

Consequently, both men received keys from their
Lord: the latter (Paul) the key of knowledge, the

former (Peter) the key of power; the former bestows the riches of an immortal life, the latter grants the treasures of knowledge. For there are treasures of knowledge, as it is written: "In whom are hidden all the treasures of wisdom and knowledge." Hence blessed Peter and Paul stand out above all the Apostles and supersede them by a certain peculiar prerogative. But between these two it is uncertain who is to be placed before the other. For I think that they are equal in merits because they were equal in their suffering, and also that they, whom we see to have obtained the glory of martyrdom together, lived in a like devotion to their faith; for we are not of the opinion that it came about without cause that on the same day, in the same place, they suffered the condemnation of the same tyrant.

They suffered on the same day in order that they might go to Christ together; in the same place lest Rome be deprived of one of them; under the same persecutor so that an equal torture should afflict them both. Accordingly, I believe, the day was ordained for their merit; the place for their glory; the persecutor for their virtue. Yet, where did they finally suffer martyrdom? In that city of Rome which stands as the prince and head of nations, so that, namely, there where the source of superstition was, the source of sanctity should repose; and where the rulers of the nations dwelt, there the princes of the Church should remain. Of what merit blessed Peter and Paul might be we can comprehend from this, that while our Lord glorified the region of the Orient by His own Passion, He deigned to illuminate the land of the Occident (lest it should be of lesser account) by the blood of the Apostles instead of His own, and though His Passion merited for us salvation, nevertheless, He held forth their martyrdom as an example.

July 6
OCTAVE DAY OF SS. PETER AND PAUL
I Nocturn
From the first Epistle of blessed Paul the Apostle to the Corinthians, c. 4, 1 - 15
II Nocturn
Sermon of St. John Chrysostom

What sort of thanks shall we render to you, O blessed Apostles, who have labored so much for us? I remember thee, Peter, and I am amazed; I think of thee, Paul, and my mind is overwhelmed, and I am dissolved in tears. For I know not what to say or what to speak as I contemplate your sufferings. How many prisons have you hallowed! How many chains have you adorned! How many torments have you borne! How many revilings have you endured! How have you carried Christ! How have you rejoiced the churches by your preaching! Your tongues were blessed instruments; for the sake of the Church your limbs were sprinkled with blood.

In all things you have been made like unto Christ. Your sound is gone forth into all the earth, and your words unto the ends of the world. Thou rejoicest, O Peter, to whom it was granted to delight in the wood of the Cross of Christ. And to bear a certain likeness to the Master, thou didst will to be crucified, not indeed with head erect, as was Christ the Lord, but with head towards the earth, as one who travelled from earth to heaven.

Blessed are the nails which pierced thy holy limbs. In sure confidence thou didst resign thy soul into the hands of the Lord, thou, the most faithful of all the Apostles, who didst love the Lord with a most fervent spirit, and didst serve faithfully both Him and His Spouse, the Church. Thou also rejoicest, O blessed Paul, whose head was cut off by the sword, whose virtues no words can express.

What sort of sword severed thy holy neck? An instrument of the Lord, I say, at which heaven wonders and which the earth reveres. What kind of spot absorbed thy blood, which appeared like drops of milk upon the tunic of him who struck thee, and which made that barbarian's soul, together with his comrades, gentle and faithful above measure? Would that I might have that sword as a crown and the nails of Peter set as gems in the diadem.

III Nocturn
The reading of the holy Gospel
according to St. Matthew

At that time: Jesus obliged His disciples to go up into the boat and to go before Him over the water, till He dismissed the people. And so forth.

Homily of St. Jerome, Priest

The Lord commanded the disciples to sail across the water, and obliged them to go up into the boat. By this manner of speaking, it is shown that they were unwilling to leave the Lord, since their love of their Teacher made them desire not to be separated from Him for a moment. And having dismissed the multitude, He went up into a mountain alone to pray. If the disciples Peter, James and John, who had seen the glory of the Transfiguration, had been with Him, perhaps they would have gone up with Him into the mountain; but the crowd could not follow to those heights, and so He taught them by the sea and fed them in the wilderness.

And that He went up alone to pray refers not to Him who with five loaves fed five thousand men, besides women and children, but to Him who, when He heard of the death of John, withdrew into a desert place; not that we would separate the person of the Lord, but that His works may be distinguished according as they were done as God or as man.

But the boat in the midst of the sea was tossed with the waves. Rightly were the Apostles slow and unwilling to leave the Lord, lest in His absence they should suffer shipwreck. Then, while the Lord remained on the mountain-top, suddenly a contrary wind arose, the sea raged, and the Apostles were in danger; shipwreck was imminent, until Jesus came.

And in the fourth watch of the night He came to them walking upon the sea. Military guards and watches are divided into periods of three hours each. Therefore, when he says that the Lord came to them at the fourth watch of the night, it shows that they had been in danger all night; and it was at the close of the night, as it will be at the end of the world, that He will bring help to His own.

July 11
SOLEMNITY OF OUR HOLY FATHER
ST. BENEDICT

I Nocturn
From the Book of Ecclesiasticus, c. 45, 1 - 6; c. 47, 9 - 12; c. 48, 1, 5 - 7, 10, and 13 - 15

II Nocturn
Sermon of St. Bernard, Abbot

The most sweet name of our glorious Father, Benedict, ought to be embraced and honored by

you with every sign of joy because he is your
Leader, he is your Master and Lawgiver. Let his
sanctity, his piety, his justice, refresh you. The
blessed Benedict was a great and fruitful tree, like
a tree which is planted near the running waters.
He was so planted near the running waters that he
brought forth his fruit in due season. To his fruit
belong the three things whereof I have made mention above: his sanctity, his justice, his piety.
Miracles prove his sanctity; his teaching, his piety;
his life, his justice.

But why am I to propose his miracles to you? In
order that you may want to perform miracles? By
no means! But that you may lean on his miracles
for support; in other words, that you may be confident and glad because you have merited such a
great Protector. For most certainly he who was so
great and powerful on earth is very powerful in
heaven, being exalted to a greatness of glory cor-
responding to the magnitude of his grace. For, in
truth, the branches are known to shoot forth according to the size of the roots, and with as many
roots as the tree is supported, with so many branches, as they say, is it adorned. Thus, then, though
we may not have the power to perform miracles,
the miracles of our Patron should be a great consolation to us.

His teaching, too, instructs us and guides our
steps to the path of peace. Further, the justice of

his life in every way strengthens and vivifies us, so that we are so much the more enkindled to do the things he has taught us as we are assured that he has not taught us otherwise than he acted. The example of his work is, indeed, a living and effective sermon, making what is said very pleasing to hear in that it shows that what is urged can be done. Consequently, after this manner his sanctity consoles us; his piety enlightens us; his justice strengthens us. Of what great piety was he that he not only benefitted those present to him, but was also solicitous for those to come? Not only for those who then were, did this tree produce its fruit, but even today its fruit multiplies and remains.

Surely beloved of God and men is he whose presence was not only then in benediction (as many are beloved of God alone because they are now known to God alone), but his memory, too, is even now in benediction. For even until this day, as a threefold confession of his love for his Lord, he feeds the flock of the Lord with this threefold fruit. He feeds it by his life; he feeds it by his teaching; he feeds it through his intercession. Being unceasingly aided by him, do you also, dearest brethren, bear fruit, because for this have you been appointed: that you should go and bring forth fruit.

R.   This is he who wrought great things before God, and praised the Lord with his whole heart: * May he intercede for the sins of all men. V. Behold a man without reproach, a true worshipper of God, keeping himself from every evil deed and ever abiding in innocence. May he. Glory. May he.

III Nocturn
The reading of the holy Gospel according to St. Matthew

At that time: Peter said to Jesus: Behold, we have left all things and have followed Thee; what, therefore, shall we have? And so forth.

Homily of St. Bede the Venerable, Priest

In the final judgment there will be two classes of the elect: the one judging with the Lord (and of these He speaks in this place), who have left all things and followed Him; the other to be judged by the Lord, who indeed have not wholly left all things, but who, nevertheless, took care to bestow alms daily on Christ's poor ones out of the goods which they possessed. Wherefore, these will hear in the judgment: Come, ye blessed of My Father, possess you the kingdom prepared for you from the foundation of the world.   For I was hungry and you gave Me to eat; I was thirsty and you gave Me to drink, and the other things which the Lord enumerates in the preceding lines of this lesson, when a certain leader had asked what good he must do in order to possess life everlasting. If thou wilt enter into life, He said, keep the commandments. Therefore he who keeps the commandments of the Lord entereth into life everlasting; but he who also follows the counsels of the Lord shall not only attain life himself, but shall also judge with the Lord the life of others.

But, as the Lord testifies, we find that there will be two classes of the reprobate also: the first of these will comprise those who, having been initiated into the mysteries of the faith, spurn to do the works of faith; of these it is said in the judgment: Depart from Me, ye cursed, into everlasting fire, which was prepared for the devil and his angels. For I was hungry and you gave Me not to eat. The other class will comprise those who either never receive the faith and the mysteries of Christ or who, having once received them, wholly forsake them by apostasy; concerning whom He says: But he that doth not believe is already judged, because he believeth not in the name of the only begotten Son of God.

But now, after having for a brief moment recounted these things with fear and trembling, let us turn our attention rather to the more joyful promises of our Lord and Savior. Let us see what is the recompence of such great piety: to His followers He promises not only the reward of eternal life, but also extraordinary gifts in this present life. And everyone, He says, that hath left house, or brethren, or sisters, or father, or mother, or wife, or children, or lands for My name's sake, shall receive a hundredfold, and shall possess life everlasting.

The more one who shall have renounced earthly desires or possessions to become a disciple of Christ shall advance in His love, the more persons will he find who rejoice to receive him with heartfelt affection as one of their own, and to sustain him with their own goods; being companions in his profession and life, these make it their delight to receive him who has made himself poor for Christ's sake into their homes and lands, and to cherish him with a more devoted love than ever did a wife, a parent, a brother, or son according to the flesh.

R. This man did all things which God hath told him, and He said to him: Enter thou into My rest: * For thee I have seen the righteous before Me among all nations. V. This is he who despised the life of the world and attained to the kingdom of heaven. For. Glory. For.

✠ Continuation of the holy Gospel according to St. Matthew: At that time: Peter said to Jesus: Behold, we have left all things and have followed Thee: what, therefore, shall we have? And Jesus said to them: Amen, I say to you, that you who have followed Me in the regeneration, when the Son of man shall sit on the seat of His majesty, you also shall sit on twelve seats, judging the twelve tribes of Israel. And everyone that hath left house, or brethren, or sisters, or father, or mother, or wife, or children, or lands, for My name's sake, shall receive a hundredfold and shall possess life everlasting.

LET US PRAY

O God, who hath deigned to fill Thy blessed Confessor Benedict with the spirit of all the just, grant to us his children who celebrate his feast, that being filled with his spirit, we may faithfully fulfil what by Thy inspiration we have promised. Through our Lord.

July 13
III DAY WITHIN THE OCTAVE OF THE SOLEMNITY OF ST. BENEDICT

From the second Book of the Dialogues of St. Gregory, Pope

There was a man most venerable for the holiness of his life, named Benedict, and whom this appellation suited exceedingly well; for he was *blessed* of God and abundantly endued with His graces. From his earliest youth he possessed the heart and wisdom of old age. For even then, more sedate in his manners than is usual at that period of life, he followed not the allurements of sensuality, did not give way to pleasure, and permitted himself no worldly enjoyment. While yet in this land of exile, he despised the world with all its empty show and deceitful riches, although he had every opportunity of enjoying them as much as can be in this life; and he viewed them as a withered and barren tree from which no fruit may be expected. Being of a very respectable family in the vicinity of Nursia, his parents sent him to Rome to receive a liberal education. But seeing that many of those who studied there allowed themselves to be swept down by the flood of vice, and although it was his first entrance into the world, he resolved to fly from it, lest, becoming infected with its false maxims, he might be cast headlong into the abyss of sin. Taking no pains, then, to acquire learning, he left his father's house and estate, and, aspiring only to please God, he proceeded to seek one who had the power to invest him with the religious habit. He withdrew, therefore, *knowingly ignorant*, and *wisely unlearned*.

Having given up his studies, Benedict retired into a desert. He was accompanied only by his nurse who loved him tenderly. When he reached a place called Enfide, he met many respectable persons who, through charity, engaged him to converse with them awhile and stop in the church of St. Peter. His nurse, in the meantime, borrowed a sieve from some women of the neighborhood to clean wheat, and, when finished, carelessly laid it on a table where it was accidently broken, completely split in two. The woman, having come back to the table, was grieved to find the sieve, which was only lent to her, broken, and in her sorrow shed abundant tears. The pious and tender-hearted Benedict, beholding her thus weeping, was moved to compassion, and to console her took the two pieces of the sieve aside. There he prayed to God with fervent tears and his petition was granted; for no sooner had he risen from the ground than he found the sieve so perfectly sound that there remained not the slightest trace of its having been broken. He came immediately to his nurse, and, restoring the article which he had taken away broken, gently soothed her pain.

This fact became known to all the inhabitants and filled them with surprise. They hung up the sieve at the entrance of their church to make known to those then living and to posterity the progress the youthful Benedict had made in grace and virtue when he commenced to walk the narrow path of perfection. This sieve was thus exhibited to the eyes of all for many years, and remained above the entrance of the church until the invasion of the Lombards.

July 15
V DAY WITHIN THE OCTAVE OF THE SOLEMNITY OF ST. BENEDICT
From the second Book of the Dialogues of
St. Gregory, Pope

The province of Campania (where Monte Cassino is situated) was afflicted with famine, and all the inhabitants found themselves reduced to a great scarcity of provisions. Consequently, flour failed in Benedict's monastery. Most of the loaves had been consumed, and the monks had only five remaining for the next repast. The venerable father seeing them sad and grieved, reproved them gently for their weakness and want of confidence in God, and at the same time consoled them, saying: "Why do you afflict yourselves because you are in want of bread? There is but little of it today; tomorrow you shall have it in abundance." In fact, they found on the following day before the gate of the monastery two hundred bushels of wheat in sacks; and up to the present no one has known by whose agency Almighty God sent them to the holy Abbot. The monks, seeing themselves relieved in so wonderful a manner, gave thanks to God, and learned thereby to have more confidence in His bounty and to expect plenty even in the time of the greatest scarcity.

At another time when Campania was afflicted with a great famine, the man of God distributed all the provisions of the monastery to the poor. There remained almost nothing in the cellar but a little oil in a small glass bottle. There came, however, a deacon, named Agapitus, who earnestly asked for a little oil. The saint, who had resolved to give all he had on earth to receive it again in heaven, ordered the little that remained to be given him.

The religious who was then procurator heard the order, but delayed to execute it; and the saint inquiring shortly after if he had done what was told him, the procurator replied that he had not, for if he gave the oil none would remain for his brethren. Then the saint, greatly displeased, commanded other disciples to go and take the vessel containing the oil and throw it out the window, so that no one might be able to say disobedience had preserved anything to the monastery. And so was it done. There was beneath the window a very steep precipice, at the bottom of which were only pointed fragments of rocks.

Nevertheless, the glass vessel, falling on these rough stones, remained as safe and sound as if it had not been cast forth, and as if it could not be broken, nor the oil spilled. When this was told the saint, he gave orders to go and pick up the vessel and give it as it was to the person who had requested the oil. Then, having assembled the brethren, he reproved the disobedient monk for his pride and want of faith. The saint, having thus reprimanded the procurator, betook himself to prayer with the brethren. In the very place in which he was praying with his disciples there was a barrel in which there was no more oil, but, nevertheless, had the lid on. Benedict persevering in prayer, the lid began to rise, forced upwards by the abundance of oil in the barrel, and finally was

displaced altogether. The oil overflowed the brim,
innundating the pavement. The servant of God,
seeing it spreading, ended prayer, and the oil ceased
to increase and overflow on the pavement.

July 16
FEAST OF THE BLESSED VIRGIN MARY OF EINSIEDELN

I Nocturn
From the Canticle of Canticles, c. 1, 1 - 16
II Nocturn

Sermon of St. Bernard, Abbot

The Lord has effected something new on the
earth that a woman should encompass a man, who
is no other than Christ, of whom it is said: Behold the Man, the Orient is His name. God has
accomplished also a new thing in heaven that a
woman should appear clothed with the sun. She
both crowned Him and merited to be crowned in
turn by Him. Go forth, daughters of Sion, and see
king Solomon in the diadem with which his mother
hath crowned him. But of this elsewhere. Meanwhile, rather go in and see the Queen in the diadem
with which her Son has crowned her. And on her
head, it says, a crown of twelve stars.

Indeed worthy to be crowned by stars is that
head which, shining far more brilliantly than they,
rather enhances them than is adorned by them.
For why do the stars crown her whom the sun

clothes? As on a day of spring the roses and the
lilies of the valley surrounded her. Yea, more!
the left hand of the Spouse is under her head and
His right hand already embraces her. Who can appreciate those gems? Who can name the stars of
which the royal diadem of Mary is composed?

What, then, shines as a star in the generation of
Mary? Surely the fact that she is begotten of
royal ancestors, of the seed of Abraham, of the
root of David. If this seems insignificant, add that
which was divinely given to her at her birth on
account of the singular privilege of her sanctity;
that long before she had been promised from heaven
to these same Fathers; that she was prefigured by
mystical miracles and foretold by prophetic declarations. For the priestly rod, when it flourished without a root, the fleece of Gedeon, when it was moist
in the midst of the dry ground, the eastern gate in
the vision of Ezechiel, which was never opened to
anyone, all prefigured her. Finally, she was promised especially by Isaias, now as the rod that was to
spring up from the root of Jesse, again more evidently as the Virgin who was to bear a Child.

Rightly is it written that this great sign appeared in the sky, since it is known to have been
promised from heaven so long before. The Lord
said: He Himself will give you a sign. Behold a
Virgin shall conceive. Indeed He gave a great sign
because He also who gave it is great. Whose eyes,

then, does not the brightness of this prerogative vehemently dazzle? Already in the fact that she was greeted so reverently and respectfully by the Archangel that he seemed to see her already exalted on a royal throne above all the regions of the heavenly spirits, and in the fact that he, who was heretofore accustomed to be venerated by all men alike, was now, being a little less than she, about to venerate the woman, the most excellent merit and singular grace of our Virgin is commended to us.

R. Who is she that cometh forth as the sun and as beautiful as Jerusalem? * The daughters of Sion saw her and declared her blessed, and the queens praised her. V. And round about her, as in spring time, were flowers of roses and lilies of the valley. The daughters. Glory. The daughters.

III Nocturn
The reading of the holy Gospel
according to St. Luke

At that time: As Jesus spoke these things to the multitude, a certain woman from the crowd, lifting up her voice, said to Him: Blessed is the womb that bore Thee. And so forth.

Homily of St. Irenaeus, Bishop and Martyr

Just as the first-formed man, Adam, received his substance from untilled and as yet virgin soil (for God had not yet sent rain nor had man yet tilled the land) and was formed by the hand of God, that is, by the Word of God,—for all things were made by Him—and just as the Lord took slime of the earth and formed man, so did the Word Himself, recapitulating Adam in Himself and taking His own existence from Mary still a virgin, becomingly receive a birth like unto Adam's. Now if the first man was indeed taken from the earth and formed by the Word of God, it was necessary that this same Word, making a recapitulation in Himself of Adam, should have an analogous generation. Why, then, did not God again take the slime of the earth rather than effect this formation from Mary? It was that no new formation should come into being, nor any other which should have to be saved, but that the very same formation (which first had been created) should be recapitulated, thus preserving the analogy.

They err, therefore, who say that He received nothing from the Virgin, since, in order to cast away the inheritance of the flesh, they reject also the analogy (between Christ and Adam). But this is to say both that He appeared putatively as man while He was not man, and also that He was made man though taking nothing from man. For if He did not take the substance of flesh from man, then He was not made man, nor was He the Son of man. But the Apostle Paul in his epistle to the Galatians unmistakably asserts: God sent His Son, made of a woman.

And again in his letter to the Romans he says: Concerning His Son, who was made to Him of the seed of David, according to the flesh, who was predestinated the Son of God in power, according to the Spirit of sanctification, by the Resurrection of our Lord Jesus Christ from the dead.

Otherwise His descent into Mary has been in vain. For why did He descend into her if He were to take nothing from her? Or, if He had taken nothing from Mary, He would never have received that food by which the body is nourished, nor would His Body have hungered forty days seeking nourishment.

R. All generations shall call me blessed, * Because the Lord who is mighty hath done great things to me, and holy is His name. V. And His mercy is from generation unto generations to them that fear Him. Because. Glory. Because.

✠ Continuation of the holy Gospel according to St. Luke.—At that time: As Jesus spoke these things to the multitude, a certain woman from the crowd, lifting up her voice, said to Him: Blessed is the womb that bore Thee, and the paps that gave Thee suck. But He said: Yea, rather blessed are they who hear the word of God and keep it.

LET US PRAY

Grant us Thy servants, we beseech Thee, O Lord, to enjoy continual health of both soul and body, and, by the glorious intercession of the Blessed

Mary ever Virgin, to be delivered from the sorrows of this present life and to enjoy eternal happiness. Through our Lord.

July 17
II DAY WITHIN THE OCTAVE OF THE BLESSED VIRGIN

Sermon of St. Augustine, Bishop

Mary exults and is in joyful wonder that she is a mother; she rejoices that she has given birth through the Holy Spirit; nor is she terrified because she, though unwedded, gives birth, but she wonders with joy that she should have begotten a child. O woman blessed among women! who hast certainly not known man and yet hast enclosed a Man within her womb! Mary encloses a Man by giving faith to the angel because Eve destroyed man by consenting to the serpent. O happy obedience! O wonderful grace! whereby, when she humbly believed, she incorporated within herself the Maker of heaven. Through this did she merit the glory which she afterwards increased: "Behold," she says, "from henceforth all generations shall call me blessed."

O Blessed Mary, who can worthily render thanks and praise to you who, by your singular assent, sustained the fallen world? What praises may the frailty of the human race, which has found the way to its recovery in thy action alone, render to thee?

Accept, then, our thanks, however poor, however unequal to thy merits; and when you have received our supplications, excuse our faults by your prayers. Admit our prayers into the sanctuary of thy hearing, and obtain for us the means of our reconciliation!

Through thee, may that be without blame which we have done through thee; may that be easily obtained which we plead for with a confident mind. Accept what we offer; give what we ask; pardon what we fear, because thou art the only hope of sinners. Through thee we hope for forgiveness of sins, and in thee, O most blessed one, is the expectation of our rewards. Holy Mary, help the unfortunate, aid the pusillanimous, cherish the weak, pray for the people, plead for the clergy, intercede for the women vowed to God! May all experience thy aid who celebrate thy holy feast.

THE SAME DAY
VII Day within the Octave of the Solemnity of
St. Benedict
From the second Book of the Dialogues of
St. Gregory

On one occasion, the saint having gone to the fields to work with his brethren, a peasant whose son had been carried off by death came to the monastery, holding in his arms the body of his son and manifesting extreme grief at his loss. Inquiring for Father Benedict, and having been told he was in the field with the brethren, he laid down the body of his son before the gate of the monastery and, altogether discomposed and overcome with grief, ran with great speed to find the venerable father. Just at that moment the man of God was coming home from work in the company of his monks. As soon as the bereaved peasant saw him, he began to cry out: "Restore my son, restore my son!"

At these words Benedict stopped short and said: "Have I taken away your son?" "He is dead," replied the peasant, "come and restore him to life." The servant of God, listening to this demand, was greatly troubled and said: "Retire, brethren; it is not for us, but for the holy Apostles, to work miracles. Why do you lay upon us burdens which we are unable to bear?" But the man, overcome by the violence of grief, persisted in his demand, and swore that he would not leave him until he had restored his son.

"Where is your son?" asked the saint. "His body lies near the monastery gate," replied the peasant. The man of God, having arrived there with his brethren, went on his knees, stooped down over the body of the child, and, raising himself again, extended his hands towards heaven and said: "O Lord, look not on my sins, but on this man's faith, who implores that his son be restored to life. Replace in this little body the soul Thou hast thence withdrawn!" His prayer was hardly ended when the boy's whole body trembled as the soul returned; a thing noticed by all present, for they clearly saw the boy started in an extraordinary and wonderful manner. Then the saint took him by the hand and, presenting him to his father, restored him full of life and health.

July 18
OCTAVE DAY OF THE SOLEMNITY OF OUR HOLY FATHER, ST. BENEDICT
I Nocturn
From the third Book of Kings, c. 17, 2 - 24
II Nocturn
Sermon of St. Odo, Abbot

Wherever Holy Church is spread, through tribes, through nations, through tongues, the praise of Benedict is popular. For if in the multitude of people is the dignity of the king, as Solomon says, how great do we suppose is the dignity of this king, whom such a numerous host of monks follow? What king or emperor ever ruled in so many parts of the world, or drew out from such differing nations such great legions as this king indeed has enlisted as voluntarily sworn members of either sex and every age in Christ's militia?

Looking upon him as present, and marching after the banner of his corps, they crush the battalions of the devil. For these, that saying of the prophet is appropriated: Thy eyes shall see thy teacher.

There is a strong opinion that each of the saints shall arise at the regeneration in the company of those whom he has gained for the Lord. Therefore, when all the followers of his rule are brought together in a body, what a token of his apostolic work shall that numerous army then render to Benedict? And with what joy shall he who shall be able to join himself to these cohorts then leap about!

At this time let all men, whether associated by place or by affection, direct the vision of their hearts to him; for he is become all things to all men. Children first have in him, as a boy, a model which they may follow in order that, since they have been offered to God after the example of Isaac, they may take care to fill their early life with leaven. And so continuing, let their every advance in age be perfected in understanding so that they do not fall away from the paternal love of their guardian; lest, perchance, if they should fall from a higher position, they be the more seriously injured. But even we who have sinned should by no means fail in our hope for mercy, because he (Benedict), while living, raised the dead to life after their burial, mended that which was broken, and healed that which was despaired of.

And although we have not done His Will, let us, nevertheless, invoke the Lord; and let our eyes be upon His hands until He lift them above us and have mercy on us. May Benedict ever be with us in our heart, on our lips, and in our actions, that there may ever be virtue, that there may ever be praise of discipline; so that, imitating that admonition of the Apostle, we may attain to what we have seen in him, what we have heard from him, and what we have heard of him, in order that the God of Peace may be with us through him forever and ever. Amen!

III Nocturn
The reading of the holy Gospel according to St. Matthew

At that time: Peter said to Jesus: Behold, we have left all things and have followed Thee. What, therefore, shall we have? And so forth.

Homily of St. Bernard, Abbot

I think that the words of this lesson are those with which the Church cries from the ends of the earth to her Immortal Spouse: For the sake of the words of Thy lips I have kept hard ways. These are the words indeed which urge a contempt of the world on the whole world and voluntary poverty on men. These are the words which fill the cloisters with monks and the deserts with anchorites. These, I say, are the words which despoil Egypt and snatch away all her choicest vessels. This is a living and efficacious word, converting souls by the happy desire for sanctity and the faithful promise of the truth.

For both the world and its concupiscence pass away, and so it is more profitable to leave these things than to be left by them. Behold, he says, we have left all things and have followed Thee; surely, because he hath rejoiced as a giant to run his course, nor could you, being overburdened, overtake him as he ran. Yet, it is not a useless compensation to have left all things for Him who is above all things; for, to be sure, all things are given together with Him, and when you shall have taken hold of Him, He Himself shall be all things to all men who have left all for Him. Truly do I say all things; not possessions only, but desires also, and these especially.

Peter, casting his care upon the Lord and placing his own worry on Him, confident that He would care for him, left all things and followed the Lord, not even asking about a reward until, because the Savior was talking about the danger of riches, he took the occasion of inquiring: What, therefore, shall we have? And Jesus said to him: Amen, I say to you. A word of avowal is prefaced; you will recognize that it is a great thing which follows. In the regeneration you also shall sit. You shall go with Him, He declares, whom you follow, so that when He shall sit (in judgment), you, too, shall sit with Him. O what an enthronement! Who will give me to express in fitting words what I conceive in the affection of my heart concerning this enthronement? Yea, more, who will give me to share the undisturbed repose of this sitting which I desire, for which I long, after which I seek?

For behold, as I have declared, nothing is at rest within me, but all things are in motion; everything is unsettled; all things are disturbed. In short, where the flesh still lusts against the spirit, and the spirit against the flesh, what should indeed appear to be at rest in man? Already, to be sure, the Son of man sits on His throne of majesty; for now that He has ascended into heaven, He sits at the right hand of God. But it was said: when He shall sit; that is, when He shall appear sitting, as the Apostle says: When Christ, who is your life, shall appear, then you also shall appear with Him in glory. What could be more glorious? Let the sons of pride judge now and pass sentence beforehand; let them sit with their king who has chosen the sides of the North for himself. We shall pass beyond, and lo! they shall not be there.

July 19
IV DAY WITHIN THE OCTAVE OF THE BLESSED VIRGIN
Sermon of St. John Chrysostom

The Son of God did not choose for His Mother a rich or wealthy woman, but that blessed Virgin, whose soul was adorned with virtues. For it was because the blessed Mary had observed chastity in a way that was above all human nature that she conceived Christ the Lord in her womb. Let us then fly to this most holy Virgin and Mother of God and avail ourselves of her patronage. Therefore, let all of you who are virgins flee to the Mother of the Lord; for she, by her patronage, will guard in you that beautiful, precious, and incorruptible possession.

The blessed Mary, ever a Virgin, dearest brethren, was in truth a great wonder. For what greater or more wonderful one has ever at any time been discovered or can at any time be discovered? She alone is greater far than heaven and earth. Who is holier than she? Not the Prophets, not the Apostles, not the Martyrs, not the Patriarchs, not the Angels, not the Thrones, not the Dominations, not the Seraphim, not the Cherubim; in truth, no creature whatever, whether visible or invisible, is to be found greater or more excellent than she. She is at once the handmaid of God and His Mother; at once a Virgin and a parent.

She is the Mother of Him who was begotten of the Father before the beginning of all things; whom Angels and men acknowledge to be the Lord of all things. Wouldst thou know how much greater is this Virgin than any of the heavenly Powers? They stand in His presence with fear and trembling and veiled faces; she offers human nature to Him whom she brought forth. Through her we obtain the forgiveness of our sins. Hail, then, O

Mother, heaven, maiden, virgin, throne, ornament, glory, and foundation of our Church; pray without ceasing for us to Jesus, thy Son and our Lord, that through thee we may find mercy in the day of judgment and may be able to obtain those good things which are prepared for those who love God, through the grace and loving-kindness of Jesus Christ our Lord: to whom, with the Father and the Holy Ghost, be glory and honor and dominion, now and forever, world without end. Amen.

July 20

V DAY WITHIN THE OCTAVE OF THE BLESSED VIRGIN

From the Book of St. Epiphanius, Bishop, against Heresies

The blessed Mother of God, Mary, was prefigured by Eve, who in a mysterious way was given to be called mother of the living. For she (Eve) was called mother of the living even after she heard after her transgression: Thou art earth, and unto earth thou shalt return. It is truly an odd thing that after her transgression she kept this great title. And indeed, as to what pertains to sensible matter, the birth of all mankind on earth was brought about through Eve; but He who was the Life was truly born into the world through Mary, so that Mary gave birth to a living man and so became the Mother of the living. In a mystical way, then, Mary was named Mother of the living.

To Eve it was given to clothe the sensible body, because of the sensible nakedness; while to Mary it was given by God to bring forth for us the Lamb and His sheep (the Church), and that by the glory of this Lamb and His sheep there might be made for us, as it were, from His fleece, in His wisdom and by His power, a garment of incorruptibility. Eve, in truth, became the cause of death for men; for by her, death came into the world. But Mary, through whom the Life was born to us, was made the cause of life; through her the Son of God came into the world, and where sin abounded, grace did more abound; and whence death was brought in, thence life also proceeded, so that death might be converted into life, and He who became Life for us through the woman might exclude the death brought in through a woman. And because Eve, in the one instance, transgressed by her disobedience while still a virgin, in the other, when His coming in the flesh was announced from heaven, obedience to grace and life eternal was brought about through a Virgin also.

Through Mary is achieved, if I may so speak, what was written concerning the Church: A man shall leave father and mother and shall cleave to his wife; and they shall be two in one flesh. The Holy Apostle declares: This is a great sacrament; but I speak in Christ and in the Church. And note the Scripture's accurate term of expression, in that, on the one hand, it says with regard to Adam, He *formed* him, while it does not say that Eve was formed, but that she was *built*. It states: He took one of his ribs, and built it for him into a woman. By which it may be shown that the Lord, too, formed a body for Himself from Mary, while from His own rib was built the Church, in that His side was pierced and opened, and the mysteries of the blood and water were made the price of redemption.

July 21
VI DAY WITHIN THE OCTAVE OF THE BLESSED VIRGIN
Sermon of St. Cyril, Bishop of Alexandria

I see a joyful congregation of all the saints who have come together with ready hearts, called by the holy Mother of God, Mary ever a Virgin. Praise and glory be to Thee, O Holy Trinity, which has called all of us to this celebration. Praise also to thee, O holy Mother of God. For thou art the precious pearl of the whole earth; thou art an inextinguishable lamp, the crown of virginity, the scepter of the true faith, the indestructible temple containing Him who can be nowhere contained; Mother and Virgin; through whom He who comes in the name of the Lord is called blessed in the holy Gospels.

Through thee the Trinity is sanctified, through thee the holy Cross is celebrated and venerated in the whole world. Through thee heaven rejoices, the angels and archangels exult, the demons flee, and man himself is called back to heaven. Through thee every creature held in the error of idolatry has been turned to the knowledge of the truth, faithful men have come to holy Baptism, and throughout the whole earth churches have been built.

Helped by thee, the nations come to penance. What more? Through thee the only begotten Son of God, the true Light, has shone upon those sitting in darkness and in the shadow of death. Through thee the prophets prophesied; through thee the apostles preached salvation to the Gentiles. For who is able to unfurl the banners of thy praises, O Mary, Mother and Virgin? Let us honor her, dearly beloved, adoring her Son, the Immaculate Spouse of the Church, to whom be honor and glory forever and ever. Amen.

July 23
OCTAVE DAY OF THE BLESSED VIRGIN MARY OF EINSIEDELN

I Nocturn
From the Canticle of Canticles, c. 1, 1 - 16

II Nocturn
From the Exposition of St. Gregory, Pope, on the Books of Kings

There was a certain man of Ramathaimsophim, of Mount Ephraim. The most blessed and ever

Virgin Mary, Mother of God, can be signified by the name of this mountain. For she was truly a mountain, transcending by the dignity of her calling all the perfection of every other chosen creature.

Is not this mountain, Mary, sublime who, in order to come to the conception of the Eternal Word, elevated the height of her good actions above all the choirs of angels, even to the throne of the Godhead? Isaias, speaking in prophecy of the exceedingly excellent dignity of this mountain, said: And in the last days the mountain of the house of the Lord shall be prepared on the top of mountains. Truly the mountain was on the top of mountains, for the loftiness of Mary showed forth above all the saints.

From the Epistle of St. Leo, Pope, to Pulcheria Augusta

None of the types (of the Old Testament) paid the price of our reconciliation, determined before all ages: because the Holy Spirit had not as yet come upon the Virgin, nor had the power of the Most High overshadowed her, in order that, within her inviolate womb, Wisdom building a house for Himself, the Word might be made flesh, and, the form of God and the form of the servant uniting in one Person, the Creator of time might be born in time, and He by whom all things were made, might

Himself be begotten in the midst of all things. For unless the new Man, made unto the likeness of our flesh of sin, had taken on Himself our old nature, and, being consubstantial with the Father, had deigned to be consubstantial with His Mother, and as the only man free from sin had united our nature to Himself, human bondage would have wholly been kept beneath the yoke of the devil.

From the Exposition of St. Basil, Bishop, on Isaias the Prophet

He (Isaias) says: I went to the prophetess, and she conceived, and bore a Son. That Mary was the Prophetess to whom Isaias went by the inspiration of the Spirit, no one who is mindful of the words which Mary, inspired by a prophetic spirit, spoke will deny. And what did she speak? My soul doth magnify the Lord: And my spirit hath rejoiced in God my Savior. Because He hath regarded the humility of His handmaid: for behold, from henceforth all generations shall call me blessed. Now if you will but apply your mind to all these, her words, you will certainly not through ill-will deny that she was a prophetess, that the Spirit of the Lord came upon her, and that the power of the Most High overshadowed her.

III Nocturn

Homily on the Gospel as on the day of the Feast
Page 737

July 24

VIGIL OF ST. JAMES, APOSTLE

The reading of the holy Gospel
according to St. John

At that time: Jesus said to His disciples: This is My commandment, that you love one another as I have loved you. And so forth.

Homily of St. Gregory, Pope

Since all holy Scripture is full of the commandments of the Lord, why did He speak of love as though it were the only commandment, saying: This is My commandment, that you love one another? The reason is that all the commandments have love for their object, and all are, in fact, one commandment. For charity is the only basis of all that is commanded. The branches of a tree, though they are many, spring from one root; in like manner many virtues spring from one, charity. And unless it abide in the root of charity, the branch of good works will have no life in it.

The commandments of the Lord are many, and yet one: many in the diversity of their working, one in the root of love. But how we are to hold fast to this love He recommends to our notice in many passages of His Scriptures, when He bids us love our friends in Him, and our enemies for His sake. For he who loves his friend in God and his enemy for God's sake has true charity. For there are some who love their neighbor, but with a love based on nature and kinship; such a love is not indeed forbidden by holy Scripture, but it is one thing to love according to the impulse of nature, and quite another to love as we ought, in obedience to the Lord's commandment of love.

These (who love their neighbor according to nature) love him indeed, but do not attain to those sublime rewards of charity; for their love is inspired not spiritually, but carnally. Therefore, when the Lord said: This is My commandment, that you love one another; He added straightway: As I have loved you. As though to say openly: Love with the aim which I had in loving you. And in this matter, dearest brethren, we must prudently take note how, when the old enemy draws our hearts to the love of temporal things, he stirs up a weaker brother against us, to take from us those very things which we love.

July 25
ST. JAMES, APOSTLE
I Nocturn
From the first Epistle of blessed Paul the Apostle to the Corinthians, c. 4, 1 - 15
II Nocturn

James, the son of Zebedee, the brother of John the Apostle, was a Galilean and one of the first Apostles to be called, and together with his brother, leaving his father and his nets, he followed the

Lord; both of them were called Boanerges, that is, sons of thunder, by Jesus Himself. He was one of the three Apostles whom the Savior loved the most and whom He willed to be witnesses of His transfiguration, and also to be at hand at the miracle by which He raised from the dead the daughter of the ruler of the synagogue, and to be present when He retired to the Mount of Olives to pray to His Father, before He was taken prisoner by the Jews.

After the ascension of Jesus Christ into heaven, James preached His divinity in Judea and Samaria, and led many to the Christian faith. Thereafter he set out for Spain and there converted many to Christ, in the number of whom seven were afterwards made bishops by blessed Peter and were the first to be sent into Spain.

Thence James returned to Jerusalem, and instructed among others Hermogenes, the magician, in the truths of faith; Herod Agrippa, who had been raised to the kingship under the emperor Claudius, wishing to curry favor with the Jews, condemned James to death for openly proclaiming Jesus Christ to be God. When the man who had brought him to the tribunal saw the courage with which he went to martyrdom, he forthwith declared that he, too, was a Christian.

As they were being hurried to the execution, this man implored forgiveness from James; and James kissed him, saying: Peace be with you. Therefore both of them were beheaded shortly after James had cured a paralytic. His body was afterwards translated to Compostella, where it is honored with the highest veneration, pilgrims flocking thither from every part of the world out of devotion or to pay their vows. The commemoration of his feast is celebrated by the Church today, which is the day of his translation, but it was near the feast of the Pasch that he, the first of the Apostles to shed his blood, gave witness to Jesus Christ at Jerusalem.

R. I saw men standing together, clad in shining garments; and the Angel of the Lord spoke to me, saying: * These holy men became the friends of God. V. I saw a mighty Angel of God, flying through the midst of heaven, crying out with a loud voice and saying. These. Glory. These.

III Nocturn

The reading of the holy Gospel according to St. Matthew

At that time: There came to Jesus the mother of the sons of Zebedee with her sons, adoring and asking something of Him. And so forth.

Homily of St. John Chrysostom

Let no man be troubled if we say that the Apostles were yet so imperfect; for the mystery of the cross was not yet accomplished, the grace of the Spirit had not yet been poured into their hearts.

If thou wouldst learn their strength, consider what they were after the grace of the Spirit had been given to them, and thou wilt see that they had overcome every perverse desire. For this cause only is their imperfection made known, that thou mayest see clearly how they were forthwith changed by grace.

Therefore we perceive that they asked no spiritual favor, nor were they thinking in the least of the heavenly kingdom. Nevertheless, let us see how they came, and what they asked. We desire, they say, that whatsoever we shall ask, Thou wouldst do it for us. To which Christ answered: What do you wish? surely not because He did not know, but in order to compel them to answer, and to uncover the ulcer, that He might apply the remedy. But they were abashed and ashamed, since they had come from a human motive, and, taking Christ apart from the other disciples, they asked Him. For they had gone forward, he says, lest they might be seen by the others; and thus at length they told Him what they wished.

But, as I conjecture, since they heard that the disciples would be seated upon twelve thrones, they wished to obtain the first place in this assembly, for they knew that they were indeed preferred before the others; but fearing that Peter might be placed before them, they ventured to say: Say that one may sit at the right hand, the other at the left.

And they insisted, saying: Say. Therefore what did He answer? That He might point out that they were seeking nothing of a spiritual nature and that they did not even know what they were asking, for they would not have dared to ask if they had known, He says: You know not what you ask; you know not how great and marvelous a thing this is, surpassing even the highest virtues.

And He added: Can you drink of the chalice that I shall drink, and be baptized with the baptism wherewith I am baptized? Weigh carefully how He turns them away at once from this subject, and speaks to them of quite other matters. For you, He says, are concerned about sharing honors and crowns with Me; but I speak of the struggle and of the sweat. This is not the time for rewards, nor shall that glory of Mine appear soon; but this is the time of bloodshed and of perils. But observe in what manner, by His questioning, He both exhorts and draws them to Himself. For He did not say: Can you suffer death, can you shed your blood? But: In what manner are you able to drink this chalice? Then He says, inviting them: Which I shall drink; that He may render them the more ready to share that travail with Him.

R. Behold I send you as sheep in the midst of wolves, saith the Lord: * Be ye therefore wise as serpents and simple as doves. V. Whilst you have the light, believe in the light, that you may be the children of light. Be ye. Glory. Be ye.

✠ Continuation of the holy Gospel according to St. Matthew:—At that time: The mother of the sons of Zebedee came to Jesus with her sons, worshipping, and asking something of Him. Who said to her: What wilt thou? She saith to Him: Say that these my two sons may sit, the one on Thy right hand, and the other on Thy left, in Thy kingdom. And Jesus answering, said: You know not what you ask; can you drink the chalice that I shall drink? They say to Him: We can. He saith to them: My chalice indeed you shall drink: but to sit on My right or left hand is not Mine to give to you, but to them for whom it is prepared by My Father.

LET US PRAY

Be thou, O Lord, the sanctifier and guardian of Thy people that strengthened by the protection of Thy Apostle James, they may please Thee by their manner of life and serve Thee with a peaceful soul. Through our Lord.

July 26
SS. JOACHIM AND ANNE, PARENTS OF THE BLESSED VIRGIN MARY
I Nocturn
From Jeremias the Prophet, c. 33, 12 - 17 and 19 - 26

II Nocturn
Sermon of St. John Damascene

Joachim and Anne were the parents of the most blessed Virgin. While Joachim was being led by the Lord God as a sheep, he was in need of none of those things which are the best. But let no one think that I call best those things which are pleasing to most men and for which the mind of greedier men is accustomed to yearn, yet which are neither lasting in their nature nor know how to make a better man of him by whom they are held, even though they come to him in a certain abundance. Such are found to be the desires of this world which truly cannot possess a firm and stable power, but rapidly fall away, and as a rule, almost in the same hour in which they are gained, they will also be wiped away.

May these things be far from us! It is in no way proper that we be moved by them, nor is such the lot of those who fear the Lord. On the other hand, those things are really blessings which are sought after and greatly loved by men of sound judgment, which last forever, and, at the same time, please the Divine Majesty and produce a seasonable fruit for their possessors. Blessings of this type, I say, are the virtues which will give forth their fruit in due time; that is, in the world to come, will bestow eternal life on all who cultivate them here and direct their labors to them to the best of their ability. Toil, of course, comes first; eternal happiness shall follow.

Joachim was accustomed to nourish his thoughts interiorly in a place of pasture; that is, he dwelt in contemplation of the Sacred Words. He revived his soul on the water of refreshment of divine grace, and by this manner of comporting himself, wholly turning his mind away from things unlawful, he directed it on the paths of virtue. Truly, Anne was united with him as consort, no less by the bond of character than by marriage.

Joachim, then, joined himself in marriage to this venerable woman, Anne, who was worthy of the highest praise. But even as that former Anne, when she labored under the affliction of sterility, by prayer and by promise became the mother of Samuel; in the same manner also this Anne, through prayer and the divine promise, received from God the Mother of God. Wherefore, suffering no loss of dignity in the honor of motherhood, Anne will give place to none of those illustrious women. And thus grace (for this is the meaning of the name Anne) brings forth the Lady (which is the meaning of the name Mary). And truly indeed was she made the Mistress of all things created, since she became the Mother of the Creator.

R. O happy Joachim, who didst beget the child who was to bear the Redeemer of the world: * Rejoice, and intercede for us to the Queen of heaven.

V. O happy Father of a happier daughter, who brought forth the only begotten Son of God, made incarnate of her own flesh. Rejoice. Glory. Rejoice.

III Nocturn
The reading of the holy Gospel
according to St. Matthew

The Book of the generation of Jesus Christ, the Son of David, the Son of Abraham. Abraham begot Isaac; and Isaac begot Jacob. And so forth.

Homily of St. Leo, Pope

Most dearly deloved, the divine goodness has always cared for the human race in diverse ways and in many measures, and has benignly imparted to all past ages the very numerous gifts of His providence; but He has surpassed all the abundance of His wonted kindness in these recent times when, in Christ, Mercy itself came down to sinners, the Truth to the erring, and Life itself to the dead. For as that Word, coequal and coeternal with the Father in the unity of His Godhead, took on Himself the nature of our lowliness, so was that same God, begotten of God, born also as man from man.

Indeed this was promised from the foundation of the world and had been repeatedly foretold by many typifying signs and words; but how many men would these figures and hidden mysteries have saved had not Christ fulfilled their long-foretold and mysterious predictions! And what was then profitable to a few believers, now, by its fulfillment, benefits innumerable faithful. Hence we are not now led to believe by signs and representations, but, having been strengthened by the narrative of the Gospel, we adore that which we believe has happened; being inspired with the consideration of these prophetic instruments (the prophecies and types), we can in no wise consider doubtful what we know was foretold by such great prophecies.

From this follows what our Lord said to Abraham: In thy seed shall all the nations be blessed. Therefore also David in prophetic vision sings of the promise of God with the words: The Lord has sworn to David the truth and He will not bring it to nought. Of the fruit of thy womb I will set upon thy throne. So also the Lord said by Isaias: Behold, a Virgin shall conceive in her womb and bear a Son, and His name shall be called Emmanuel; which is interpreted, *God with us*. And again: There will come forth a rod out of the root of Jesse and a flower shall rise up from his root. In this rod, without any doubt, is foretold the blessed Virgin Mary who was born from the family of Jesse and David, and was made a Mother by the Holy Ghost; she brought forth the new Flower of human flesh in a maternal womb it is true, but by a virginal birth.

Let the just, therefore, rejoice in the Lord and their hearts in the praise of God, and let the sons of men praise His wonderful works; for especially in this work of God (the Incarnation) does our lowliness begin to understand how much her Creator has prized her. God gave much with the origin of mankind in that He made us according to His own image, but far more has He given for our restoration since the very Lord of all adapted Himself to the form of a slave. Although whatever the Creator has given to the creature comes from one and the same mercy, yet it is less wonderful for man to ascend to God than for God to descend to man.

R. To the righteous a light is risen up in darkness; * The Lord is merciful and compassionate and just. V. He hath made straight the way of the just and hath prepared the path of the Saints. The Lord. Glory. The Lord.

✠ Beginning of the holy Gospel according to St. Matthew.—The book of the generation of Jesus Christ, the Son of David, the Son of Abraham. Abraham begot Isaac; and Isaac begot Jacob; and Jacob begot Judas and his brethren; and Judas begot Phares and Zara of Thamar; and Phares begot Esron; and Esron begot Aram; and Aram begot Aminadab; and Aminadab begot Naasson; and Naasson begot Salmon; and Salmon begot Booz of Rahab; and Booz begot Obed of Ruth; and Obed begot Jesse; and Jesse begot David the King. And David the King begot Solomon of her who had been the wife of Urias; and Solomon begot Ro-

boam; and Roboam begot Abia; and Abia begot
Asa; and Asa begot Josaphat; and Josaphat begot Joram; and Joram begot Ozias; and Ozias
begot Joatham; and Joatham begot Achaz; and
Achaz begot Ezechias; and Ezechias begot Manasses; and Manasses begot Amon; and Amon begot
Josias; and Josias begot Jechonias and his brethren
in the transmigration of Babylon. And after the
transmigration of Babylon, Jechonias begot Salathiel; Salathiel begot Zorobabel; and Zorobabel
begot Abiud; and Abiud begot Eliacim; and
Eliacim begot Azor; and Azor begot Sadoc; and
Sadoc begot Achim; and Achim begot Eliud; and
Eliud begot Eleazar; and Eleazar begot Mathan;
and Mathan begot Jacob; and Jacob begot Joseph,
the husband of Mary, of whom was born Jesus,
who is called Christ.

LET US PRAY

O God, who didst choose holy Joachim and Anne
as the parents of the glorious Mother of Thy only
begotten Son; grant that by their prayers we may
ever praise Thy loving kindness in the company of
Thy elect. Through the same our Lord.

August 1
ST. PETER'S CHAINS
I Nocturn

From the Acts of the Apostles, c. 12, 1 - 11

II Nocturn

In the reign of the younger Theodosius, when his wife, Eudocia, had come to Jerusalem to fulfil a vow, she was there honored with many gifts. Notable above all the rest was the gift which she received of an iron chain, adorned with gold and precious stones, which they affirmed to be that very one whereby the Apostle Peter had been bound by Herod.

Eudocia piously venerated this chain, and thereafter sent it to Rome to her daughter Eudoxia, who carried it to the supreme Pontiff. And he in his turn showed her another chain by which the same Apostle had been bound when Nero was emperor. Therefore, when the Pontiff placed the Roman chain together with that which she had brought from Jerusalem, it happened that they fitted together in such a manner that they seemed no longer two chains, but a single one, made by the same workman.

On account of this miracle, the holy chains began to be held in so great honor that a church with the title of Eudoxia on the Esquiline was dedicated under the name of St. Peter-in-Chains, and the memory of its dedication was celebrated by a feast on August 1. From that time, the honor which was wont to be given on this day to the profane festivities of the heathens began to be given to Peter's chains, and the mere touch of them healed the sick and put the demons to flight.

Thus, in the year of man's salvation 969, a certain count of the household of the emperor Otto was possessed by an unclean spirit, so that he tore himself with his own teeth. Wherefore, by command of the emperor, he was taken to the Pontiff John, who touched the count's neck with the holy chain, and the wicked spirit, breaking forth, left the man free; and thereafter the devotion to the holy chains was spread throughout the City.

R. Arise, Peter, and cast thy garment about thee, and receive strength for the salvation of the Gentiles: * For the chains have fallen off from thy hands. V. An Angel of the Lord stood by him, and a light shone in the prison cell, and he, striking Peter on the side, raised him up, saying: Arise quickly. For. Glory. For.

III Nocturn

The reading of the holy Gospel
according to St. Matthew

At that time: Jesus came into the quarters of Cesarea Philippi, and He asked His disciples, saying: Whom do men say that the Son of man is? And so forth.

Homily of St. Augustine, Bishop

Peter alone among the Apostles was accounted worthy to hear: Amen I say to thee, that thou art

Peter, and upon this rock I will build My Church. Worthy indeed was he to be the foundation-stone, the supporting pillar, the key to the kingdom, in building up the peoples into the house of God.

Concerning this, the divine word says: And they laid their sick, that when Peter passed by, his shadow at least might overshadow them. If at that time the shadow of his body could give aid, how much more now can the fulness of his power? If a mere breath of air from him, as he passed by, was of such benefit to suppliants, how much more his favor now that he remains steadfast?

With good reason is the iron of those penal chains held throughout all the Churches of Christ to be more precious than gold. If the shadow of him who visited was so potent to cure, how much more the chains of him who binds? If even the mere appearance of an empty image could have the force of healing in it, how much more healthfulness ought the chains wherewith he suffered, whose iron weight had pressed upon his sacred members, deserve to draw forth from his body?

If he was so mighty to help his suppliants before his martyrdom, how much more must he avail after his triumph? Happy those bonds which by touching the Apostle rendered him a Martyr, and thus from manacles and fetters themselves were changed into a crown! Happy chains which brought their prisoner even unto the cross of Christ, not so much for condemnation as for consecration!

R. Thou art Peter, and upon this rock I will build My Church, and the gates of hell shall not prevail against it: * And to thee I will give the keys of the kingdom of heaven. V. Whatsoever thou shalt bind on earth, it shall be bound also in heaven; and whatsoever thou shalt loose on earth, it shall be loosed also in heaven. And to thee. Glory. And to thee.

✠ Continuation of the holy Gospel according to St. Matthew.—At that time: Jesus came into the quarters of Cesarea Philippi, and He asked His disciples, saying: Whom do men say that the Son of man is? But they said: Some, John the Baptist, and other some Elias, and others Jeremias, or one of the prophets. Jesus saith to them: But whom do you say that I am? Simon Peter answered, and said: Thou art Christ, the Son of the living God. And Jesus, answering, said to him: Blessed art thou, Simon Bar-Jona, because flesh and blood hath not revealed it to thee, but My Father who is in heaven: and I say to thee, that thou art Peter, and upon this rock I will build My Church, and the gates of hell shall not prevail against it; and I will give thee the keys of the kingdom of heaven; and whatsoever thou shalt bind upon earth, it shall be bound also in heaven; and whatsoever thou shalt loose on earth, it shall be loosed also in heaven.

Let Us Pray

O God, who didst free St. Peter from his chains and bring him forth from the prison unharmed, we beseech Thee, break the bonds of our sins and mercifully protect us from all evil. Through our Lord.

August 5
DEDICATION OF ST. MARY MAJOR
I Nocturn

From the Proverbs of Solomon, c. 8, 12 - 25 and 34 - 36; c. 9, 1 - 5

II Nocturn

When Liberius was supreme Pontiff, a certain John, a Roman patrician, and his wife, of equally noble race, since they had had no children whom they might leave as heirs to their estates, devoted their inheritance to the most holy Virgin Mother of God, continually begging of her with the most earnest prayers that she would make known to them, by some means, in what pious work in particular she wished them to expend the money. The Blessed Virgin Mary graciously heard their heartfelt prayers and vows and acknowledged them by a miracle.

Therefore on August 5, at which date the most intense heats usually occur in the City, a part of the Esquiline hill was covered with snow during the night. That same night, the Mother of God urged John and his wife separately, in their dreams, to build upon that spot which they should

see was sprinkled with snow a church which should
be dedicated to the name of the Virgin Mary; for
it was in this manner that she wished to become
their heiress. John related this to Pope Liberius,
who declared that the same thing had happened to
himself in a dream.

He went, therefore, with a solemn procession of
priests and people to the snow-clad hill, and marked
out the plan of a church on that site, which was
built with the money of John and his wife; it was
afterwards restored by Sixtus III. At first it was
called by various names: the Liberian basilica, St.
Mary at the Crib.

But since there were already many churches in the
City with the name of the holy Virgin Mary, and as
this basilica surpassed all the other basilicas named
after her, both by the strangeness of that miracle
and by its own grandeur, in order that its super-
eminence might likewise be indicated in its title,
it was called the church of St. Mary Major. A
commemoration of this dedication is celebrated by
a yearly feast that is named after the snow which
on this day so miraculously fell.

R. O holy and spotless virginity, how to proclaim thy praises, I know not: * For thou hast
borne in thy bosom Him whom the heavens cannot
contain. V. Blessed art thou among women, and
blessed is the fruit of thy womb. For. Glory. For.

III Nocturn
The reading of the holy Gospel
according to St. Luke

At that time: As Jesus was speaking to the multitudes, a certain woman from the crowd, lifting up her voice, said to Him: Blessed is the womb that bore Thee. And so forth.

Homily of St. Bede the Venerable, Priest

It is clear that this was a woman of great faith and devotion, for while the scribes and Pharisees were both tempting and blaspheming the Lord, she alone above all the rest so truly understood His Incarnation and so boldly confessed it that she confounded at once both the falsehoods of the great men there present and the faithlessness of the heretics who were yet to come. For the Jews of that time, blaspheming the work of the Holy Ghost, denied that He was the true Son of God, consubstantial with the Father. And in like manner, the heretics of a later day, denying that by the power and operation of the Holy Ghost, Mary, ever a Virgin, did verily give of her own flesh and blood in bringing forth the human Body of the only begotten of God, have maintained that He ought not to be acknowledged as the true Son of man, consubstantial with His Mother.

But if the flesh of the Word of God, born according to the flesh, had no connection with the flesh of His Virgin Mother, without reason do we call blessed the womb that bore Him and the paps that gave Him suck. But the Apostle says: For God sent His Son, made of a woman, made under the law. Neither are we to listen to them who would read the passage thus: Born of a woman, made under the law; but: made of a woman; for being conceived in the womb of a Virgin, He took not flesh from nothing, nor from elsewhere, but He partook of His Mother's flesh. Otherwise He could not truly have been called the Son of man, since He would have had no origin from mankind.

Let us, therefore, in condemnation of the doctrine of Eutyches, lift up our voices together with the Catholic Church, whereof this woman is a figure; and let us lift up our minds from the midst of the multitude, saying to the Savior: Blessed is the womb that bore Thee, and the paps that gave Thee suck. Yea, blessed indeed is that parent whereof a certain one has said: She has given birth to the King who rules over heaven and earth forever.

Yea, rather blessed are they who hear the word of God and keep it. The Savior graciously gives His approval to the woman's testimony, saying that not she alone was blessed who merited to give birth to the Word of God according to the flesh, but all they also who, by hearing the same Word and conceiving in faith according to the spirit, strive by good works to bring it forth and, as it were, nourish it either in their own hearts or in those of their neighbors. For the Mother of God was blessed indeed, in that she ever keeps that same Word in her love throughout eternity.

R. Rejoice with me all ye that love the Lord: for while I was a little one, I pleased the Most High, * And from my womb I have brought forth God and man. V. All generations shall call me blessed, because God hath regarded His lowly handmaid. And from. Glory. And from.

✠ Continuation of the holy Gospel according to St. Luke.—At that time: As Jesus was speaking to the multitudes, a certain woman from the crowd, lifting up her voice, said to Him: Blessed is the womb that bore Thee and the paps that gave Thee suck. But He said: Yea, rather blessed are they who hear the word of God and keep it.

LET US PRAY

Grant us Thy servants, we beseech Thee, O Lord, to enjoy continual health of both soul and body, and by the glorious intercession of the Blessed Mary ever Virgin to be delivered from the sorrows of this present life and to enjoy eternal happiness. Through our Lord.

August 6
THE TRANSFIGURATION OF OUR LORD
I Nocturn

From the second Epistle of blessed Peter the Apostle, c. 1, 10 - 21

II Nocturn
Sermon of St. Leo, Pope

The Lord displays His glory before chosen witnesses, and makes illustrious that bodily shape which He shared with others with such splendor that His countenance shone like the sun and His garments were white as snow. In this transfiguration the chief object was to remove the scandal of the cross from the hearts of the disciples and to prevent their faith being disturbed at the humiliation of His voluntary Passion by revealing the excellence of His hidden dignity.

But with no less foresight was laid the foundation of the hope of holy Church that the whole body of Christ might realize with what a change it was to be endowed, and that the members might promise themselves a share in that honor which had shone forth in their Head. But to confirm the Apostles and to lead them on to all knowledge, still further instruction was conveyed by that miracle. For Moses and Elias, that is, the law and the prophets, appeared talking with the Lord, so that in the presence of these five men might most truly be fulfilled what was said: In two or three witnesses every word stands.

What is more stable, what more steadfast, than the word, in the proclamation of which the trumpet of the old and of the new Testament sounds forth, and the records of ancient witnesses agree with the

teaching of the Gospel? For the pages of both
Covenants corroborate each other; and He whom
under the veil of mysteries the types that went
before had promised is displayed clearly and manifestly by the splendor of His present glory.

The Apostle Peter, therefore, being stirred by
the revelation of these mysteries, despising things
worldly and scorning things earthly, was carried
away by a certain ecstasy of mind to the desire of
things eternal; and, being filled with rapture at
the whole vision, longed to make his abode with
Jesus in the place where he was gladdened by the
sight of His glory. Whence also he says: Lord,
it is good for us to be here; if Thou wilt, let us
make here three tabernacles, one for Thee, one for
Moses, and one for Elias. But to this proposal the
Lord made no reply, signifying that what he asked
was not indeed wicked, but irregular; since the
world could not be saved except by Christ's death,
by the Lord's example in this the faithful were
called upon to believe that, although there ought not
to be any doubt about the promises of happiness,
yet we should understand that amidst the trials of
this life we must ask for power to endure rather
than for glory.

R. Behold what manner of charity God the Father hath bestwed upon us, * That we should be
called and should be the sons of God. V. For we
know that, when He shall appear, we shall be like

to Him, because we shall see Him as He is. That
we. Glory. That we.

III Nocturn

The reading of the holy Gospel
according to St. Matthew

At that time: Jesus took Peter and James and
John his brother, and bringeth them up into a high
mountain apart: and He was transfigured before
them. And so forth.

Homily of St. John Chrysostom

Since the Lord had spoken much of perils, much
of His own Passion, much of the death and of the
slaughter of His disciples, and had laid upon them
very many hard and difficult commandments; and
these, indeed, were of this present life and even
now impending, while the good things were but in
hope and expectation: as, for example, that they
would save their life if they should lose it; that
He would come in the glory of His Father, and
would render rewards; therefore, to assure them
by their own eyes and to show them what manner
of glory it is wherewith He is to come, He manifested and unveiled it as far as they could bear it in
this present life, lest they, and especially Peter,
should grieve over their own death or over that of
the Lord.

And see what He does when He had discoursed of
the kingdom and of hell. For of these He spoke
when He said: He that findeth his life shall lose

it; and whosoever shall lose his life for My sake shall find it; and when He said: He will render to every man according to his works; in these words he indicated both heaven and hell.

Therefore, since He had discoursed of both, He grants that heaven indeed may be perceived by their eyes, but hell by no means; for that might have been necessary if they had been more ignorant and foolish, but since they were upright and clear-sighted men, it was enough for them to be strengthened by a sight of the better things. This also was much more seemly for Him. Yet He did not altogether pass over the other, but sometimes He set the horrors of hell, as it were, before their very eyes, as He did in the parable of Lazarus and when He called to mind him who exacted the hundred pence.

But mark well Matthew's wisdom in not concealing the names of those who were preferred. John also does this often, recording the special praises of Peter with great truthfulness and care. For in this companionship of the Apostles there was no envy, nor did vainglory find place. He therefore took the leaders of the Apostles apart. Wherefore did He take these only? Because they were evidently superior to the rest. And why did He not do this straightway, and not until after six days? Evidently, to spare the natural feelings of the other disciples; and for the same reason He omits the names of those who are to go up.

R. God hath called us by His holy calling, according to His own grace which is now made manifest * By the illumination of our Savior Jesus Christ. V. Who destroyed death and brought to light life in incorruption. By the illumination. Glory. By the illumination.

✠ Continuation of the holy Gospel according to St. Matthew.—At that time: Jesus took Peter and James and John his brother, and bringeth them up into a high mountain apart: and He was transfigured before them. And His face did shine as the sun, and His garments became white as snow. And behold, there appeared to them Moses and Elias talking with Him. And Peter answering, said to Jesus: Lord, it is good for us to be here: if Thou wilt, let us make here three tabernacles, one for Thee, and one for Moses, and one for Elias. And as he was yet speaking, behold a bright cloud overshadowed them; and lo, a voice out of the cloud saying: This is My beloved Son in whom I am well pleased; hear ye Him. And the disciples hearing, fell upon their face, and were very much afraid: and Jesus came and touched them, and said to them: Arise, and fear not. And they, lifting up their eyes, saw no one, but only Jesus. And as they came down from the mountain, Jesus charged them, saying: Tell the vision to no man till the Son of man be risen from the dead.

LET US PRAY

O God, who in the glorious Transfiguration of Thy only begotten Son hast confirmed the mysteries of our faith by the testimony of the fathers, and by the voice coming from the bright cloud hast wonderfully foreshown the perfect adoption of sons: mercifully grant us to be made co-heirs of this same King of glory and partakers of the same glory. Through the same our Lord.

August 9
VIGIL OF ST. LAWRENCE

The reading of the holy Gospel
according to St. Matthew

At that time: Jesus said to His disciples: If any man will come after Me, let him deny himself, and take up his cross and follow Me. And so forth.

Homily of St. Gregory, Pope

Since our Lord and Redeemer came into the world the new man, he gave to the world new commandments. For He set His new life over against our old life, which is bred in sin. It was the old life, the way of the carnal man, if he could not keep his own goods, to seize those of his neighbor if he could, or covet them if he could not. But the heavenly Physician applies remedial drugs to each and all the diseases of sin.

For just as in the art of medicine hot things are cured by cold, and cold things by hot, so our Lord has set a remedy against sins by enjoining continence on the unchaste, generosity on the avaricius, meekness on the wrathful, and humility on the proud.   And so, when He gave new commandments to those who followed Him, He said: Unless a man renounce all that he possesseth, he cannot be My disciple;   as if to say openly: You who in your old life coveted the goods of other men must, in the fervor of your new life, give away what is your own.

Let us hear what He says in this place: If any man will come after Me, let him deny himself. There He says that we must give up what is ours; here He says that we must give up ourselves.   Perhaps it is not very hard for a man to leave his possessions;   but it is very much harder to leave himself.   It is a little thing to give up what we have; but a great thing to give up what we are.

August 10

ST. LAWRENCE, MARTYR

I Nocturn

From the Book of Ecclesiasticus, c. 51, 1 - 17

II Nocturn

Sermon of St. Leo, Pope

When the heathen rulers raged furiously against certain chosen members of Christ, and especially sought out those in priestly orders, the wicked persecutor raved with anger against the Levite Lawrence, who was foremost, not only in administering the sacraments, but also in dispensing the Church's substance, and by the seizure of one man he promised himself a double booty; for if he could induce him to betray his sacred treasure, he might also make him an apostate from the true religion.

Therefore this man, thirsting for riches, hating the truth, is thus furnished with a twofold stimulus: his avarice prompts him to steal the gold; his wickedness, to rob Christ. He summons the unsullied minister of the sanctuary to bring before him the Church's wealth for which he so eagerly longs. The most chaste Levite, to show him where he had laid up his treasures, presented to him a very numerous flock of the devout poor, in whose food and clothing he had invested those resources so that they could never be lost, for the treasures were as entirely safe as they were admirably spent.

Thus frustrated, the robber loudly complains, and, burning with hatred of a religion which had appointed such a use for wealth, he attempts to steal from him in whose hands he had found no money a higher treasure, namely, that possession which made him rich in holiness. He commands Lawrence to renounce Christ, and prepares cruel torments to overcome that most immoveable firm-

ness of the Levite's soul; and as the first applica-
tion of torture avails nothing, others more severe
follow. He orders his torn limbs, cut by so many
stripes, to be roasted over a fire placed beneath
him; so that by turning his body over from one
side to the other on the gridiron, which already had
the power of burning him by reason of the slow
fire, the agony might be sharper and the suffering
might last longer.

O raging cruelty, thou gainest nothing, thou
profitest nothing. That which can die is withdrawn
from thy torments, and when Lawrence has departed to heaven, thou hast failed with thy flames. The
love of Christ could not be conquered by flames;
and the fire which scorched without was not as
hot as that which burned within. Thou didst rage,
O persecutor, against the Martyr; thou didst rage,
yet thou didst but augment his palm whilst thou
wert increasing his torments. For what did thy
ingenuity discover that did not minister to the
glory of the victor, when the very instruments of
his torture turned to the honor of his triumph?
Therefore, dearly beloved, let us rejoice with spiritual joy, and in the most blessed end of this illustrious man let us glory in the Lord, who is wonderful in His Saints, and has given them to us
both as a help and an example; and has thus made
known His glory through the whole world, that
from the rising of the sun even unto the going down

thereof, amid the gleaming splendor of levitical lights, as Jerusalem is made glorious by Stephen, so Rome is made illustrious by Lawrence.

R. Blessed Lawrence cried out and said: I worship my God and Him only do I serve: * And therefore I am not afraid of your torments. V. Night hath no darkness for me, but all things become visible in the light. And therefore. Glory. And therefore.

III Nocturn
The reading of the holy Gospel
according to St. John

At that time: Jesus said to His disciples: Amen, amen I say to you, unless the grain of wheat falling into the ground die, itself remaineth alone. And so forth.

Homily of St. Augustine, Bishop

The Lord Jesus was Himself that grain which should die and be multiplied; die by the unbelief of the Jews, be multiplied by the faith of the Gentiles. But now, encouraging us to follow in the footsteps of His Passion, He says: He that loveth his life shall lose it. This may be understood in two ways. Firstly, he that loveth, shall lose; that is, if thou lovest, thou shalt lose. If thou desirest to possess life in Christ, fear not death for the sake of Christ.

Secondly, in another way: he that loveth his life, shall lose it; love not, lest thou lose; love it not in this life lest thou lose it in life everlasting. But what I have said last seems better to correspond with the meaning of the Gospel: for there follows: And he that hateth his life in this world keepeth it unto life eternal. Therefore, in what was said above: He that loveth; there is to be understood: In this world; he of course shall lose it. But he that hateth (that is, in this world) is he that shall keep it unto life eternal.

A great and wonderful saying, that in proportion as a man loveth his life, it perisheth; and as he hateth, so it abideth. If thou hast loved it ill, then hast thou hated it; if thou hast hated it well, then thou hast loved it. Happy are they who, hating their life, keep it, lest, by loving it, they should lose it. But take heed lest there steal upon thee a desire for self-destruction, understanding this in the sense that it is thy duty to hate thy life in this world.

For on such grounds certain wrong-minded and perverted men, who, with regard to themselves, are murderers of a specially cruel and impious character, give themselves to the flames, suffocate themselves in the waters, dash themselves to pieces by casting themselves headlong, and so perish. Christ did not teach thus; for He, when the devil suggested to Him that He should cast Himself headlong, answered: Return whence thou hast come, Satan, for it is written: Thou shalt not tempt the Lord thy God. And He said to Peter, signifying

by what death he should glorify God: When thou
wast younger, thou didst gird thyself, and didst
walk where thou wouldst; but when thou shalt be
old, another shall gird thee, and lead thee whither
thou wouldst not. In which passage He made it
sufficiently plain that he who follows in the footsteps of Christ must not be slain by himself, but
by another.

R. Leave me not, O holy father, for I have already distributed thy treasures. * I do not leave
thee, my son, nor forsake thee: but sterner struggles for Christ's faith await thee. V. We, as old
men, are given an easier race to run, but for those
in youth there is kept a more glorious triumph
over the tyrant; in three days' time thou, the
levite, wilt follow after me, the priest. I do not.
Glory. I do not.

✠ Continuation of the holy Gospel according to
St. John.—At that time: Jesus said to His disciples: Amen, amen I say to you, unless the grain
of wheat falling into the ground die, itself remaineth alone; but if it die, it bringeth forth much
fruit. He that loveth his life shall lose it; and he
that hateth his life in this world keepeth it unto
life eternal. If any man minister to Me, let him
follow Me; and where I am, there also shall My
minister be. If any man minister to Me, him will
My Father honor.

LET US PRAY

Grant us, we beseech Thee, almighty God, to extinguish the flames of our vices, Thou who didst grant blessed Lawrence the grace to conquer the fire of his executioners. Through our Lord.

August 14

VIGIL OF THE ASSUMPTION OF THE BLESSED VIRGIN MARY

The reading of the holy Gospel
according to St. Luke

At that time: As Jesus was speaking to the multitudes, a certain woman from the crowd, lifting up her voice, said to Him. Blessed is the womb that bore Thee. And so forth.

Homily of St. John Chrysostom

When you heard that woman saying: Blessed is the womb that bore Thee, and the paps that gave Thee suck; and then the Lord replying: Yea, rather blessed are they who hear the word of God and keep it; think not that He made this observation as slighting His Mother, but as wishing to show that it would profit her nothing to be called His Mother unless she excelled in goodness and faith. Now if a mother's love would avail Mary nothing without virtue, much less will it avail us to be a good father, brother, mother, or son, unless we are good in ourselves.

For indeed, salvation for anyone, apart from the divine grace, is to be hoped for in nothing else but his own virtues. For if her kinship in itself could have profited Mary, it would also have profited the Jews, for Christ was their kinsman according to the flesh; it would have profited the city in which He was born; it would have profited His brethren. Yet as long as His brethren cared only for their own interests, their relationship to Christ profited them nothing, but they were condemned with the rest of the world.

Then only did they begin to be worthy of admiration when they shone by their own virtue. His native land, indeed, having gained nothing from its connection with Him, fell and was burned by fire; His fellow-citizens were put to death and perished miserably; His kindred according to the flesh gained nothing towards their salvation as they lacked the protection of virtue. But of them all, the Apostles became the most renowned, since by obedience they joined themselves to Him in a right and desirable friendship and companionship. From this we learn that we have always need of faith and a life shining with virtues, since this alone will have power to save us.

August 15
ASSUMPTION OF THE BLESSED VIRGIN MARY
I Nocturn

From the Canticle of Canticles, c. 1, 1 - 16

II Nocturn

Sermon of St. John Damascene

This day the holy and animated ark of the living God, she who conceived in her womb her Creator, rests in the temple of the Lord which was not made with hands. Her ancestor David leaps, and with him the Angels lead the dance, the Archangels make celebration, the Virtues ascribe glory, the Principalities exult, the Powers rejoice together. the Dominations are joyful, the Thrones keep holiday, the Cherubim utter praise, the Seraphim proclaim her glory.

This day the Eden of the new Adam receives the living Paradise, wherein the condemnation was made void, wherein the tree of life was planted, wherein our nakedness was covered. This day the spotless Virgin, who was defiled with no earthly sensuality but trained to thoughts of heaven, returned not to dust, but, being herself a living heaven, took her place in the heavenly mansions.

For from her the true life had flowed for all men, and how should she taste of death? But she yielded to the law laid down by Him whom she had brought forth, and as a daughter of the old Adam, she underwent the old sentence (which even her Son, who is Life itself, had not refused); but, as the Mother of the living God, she was worthily taken up to Himself. Eve, who had given consent to the proposal of the serpent, was condemned to the pains of travail and sentenced to death, and found her place in the innermost regions of the lower world.

But this truly blessed one, who inclined her ears to the word of God and was filled by the action of the Holy Ghost, who, as soon as she heard the spiritual salutation of the Archangel, knowing nothing of sensual pleasure or intercourse with man, conceived the Son of God, brought Him forth without any pain, and consecrated herself wholly to God, how should she fall a prey to death? How should the dead receive her? How should corruption attack that body into which the Life was received? For her there was prepared a straight, smooth, and easy way to heaven. For if Christ, the Life and the Truth, says: Where I am, there also shall My servant be, how much more shall not His Mother be with Him?

R. Who is she that cometh forth as the sun, and as beautiful as Jerusalem? * The daughters of Sion saw her and declared her blessed, and the queens praised her. V. And round about her, as in spring time, were flowers of roses and lilies of the valley. The daughters. Glory. The daughters.

III Nocturn
The reading of the holy Gospel
according to St. Luke

At that time: Jesus entered into a certain town, and a certain woman named Martha received Him into her house. And so forth.

Homily of St. Augustine, Bishop

When the holy Gospel was being read, we heard that the Lord was received by a religious woman into her house, and her name was Martha. And while she was occupied in the care of serving, her sister, Mary, was sitting at the Lord's feet and hearing His word. The one was busy, the other was doing nothing; one was spending herself, the other was being enriched.

Yet Martha, exceedingly busy as she was in that occupation and toil of serving, appealed to the Lord and complained of her sister that she did not help her in her labor. But the Lord answered Martha for Mary, and He who had been appealed to as her judge became her advocate. Martha, He saith, thou art occupied about many things when one thing is necessary; Mary hath chosen the better part which shall not be taken away from her.

For we have heard both the appeal of the appellant and the sentence of the judge. Which sentence answered the appellant and defended the other's cause, for Mary was intent on the sweetness of the Lord's word. Martha was intent on how she might feed the Lord; Mary, on how she might be fed by the Lord. By Martha a feast was being prepared for the Lord, in whose feast Mary was even now delighting herself.

As Mary, then, was listening with delight to His most sweet word and feasting thereon with most earnest affection, why do we think that she, when the Lord was appealed to by her sister, feared lest He should say to her: Arise and help thy sister? For she was held by a wondrous sweetness; a sweetness of the mind which is doubtless greater than that of the body. She was excused, she sat in greater confidence. But how was she excused? Let us consider, examine, and search into it as far as we can that we also may be fed.

R. Truly happy art thou, O holy Virgin Mary, and worthy of all praise: * For from thee hath dawned the Sun of justice, Christ, our God. V. Pray for the people, plead for the clergy, intercede for all women vowed to God: may all experience thy help who celebrate thy holy festival. For from thee. Glory. For from thee.

✠ Continuation of the holy Gospel according to St. Luke.—At that time: Jesus entered into a certain town, and a certain woman named Martha received Him into her house: and she had a sister called Mary who, sitting also at the Lord's feet, heard His word. But Martha was busy about much serving: who stood and said: Lord, hast Thou no care that my sister hath left me alone to serve? Speak to her therefore, that she help me. And the Lord, answering, said to her: Martha, Martha, thou art careful and art troubled about many things: but one thing is necessary, Mary hath chosen the best part, which shall not be taken away from her.

LET US PRAY

Forgive, O Lord, we beseech Thee, the sins of Thy people; that we who are unable to please Thee by our own actions may be saved by the prayers of the Mother of Thy Son, our Lord, who liveth and reigneth with Thee.

August 16

II DAY WITHIN THE OCTAVE OF THE ASSUMPTION

From a Sermon of St. John Damascene

We, who worship God, God, I say, not created out of nothingness, but an Eternal Being from an Eternal Being and superior to every cause, reason, and consideration both of time and of nature, honor and venerate the Mother of God. Not that we hold that His Divinity took its origin from her (for indeed the generation of God is independent of time and is equally eternal with the Father), but we profess a second nativity, through a voluntary assumption of flesh, the cause of which we both know and praise. For because of us and for the sake of our salvation, He, who has been incorporeal from all eternity, is made flesh that He might bring salvation to a like creature through a like nature; and having assumed flesh without the cooperation of man, He is begotten from this holy Virgin, yet remaining wholly God and made wholly man: wholly God together with His flesh and wholly man with His Divinity. In this way we recognize that Virgin as the Mother of God and thus do we celebrate her falling asleep.

Let us who have been enriched by the Incarnate God praise today with holy canticles this, His Mother, and let us honor her by our nightly vigils, that we may be and may be called the people of Christ. We delight her by purity of soul and body; her, I say, who is truly pure and surpassing all, after God, in purity. Similar people are accustomed to rejoice over similar things. Let us then venerate and imitate her by mercy and sympathy towards the needy. For if God is honored by nothing so much as by mercy, who will deny that His Mother also rejoices over this same virtue?

She has appropriated for our use an ineffable abyss of divine love. Through her, that long war which was waged with our Creator has been brought to an end; through her, reconciliation with Him has been established for us, and peace and favor have been given us; wherefore the Angels sing praises together with men, and we, who before were despised, have been made sons of God. We have gathered a grape from that vine: from her we have extracted the germ of immortality. She has acquired all good things for us. In her, God has been made man, and man, God. And what is more admirable than this? What more blessed?

August 17

III DAY WITHIN THE OCTAVE OF THE ASSUMPTION

From a Sermon of St. John Damascene

Let us rejoice over the ark of the Lord with our whole heart and the walls of Jericho, the hostile fortifications, I say, of the powers opposing us, will fall. Let us rejoice in spirit with David, for the ark of the Lord today has rested. Let us cry with Gabriel, who holds the first place among the Angels: Hail, full of grace, the Lord is with thee. Hail, inexhaustible sea of joy; hail, only comfort in troubles; hail, remedy of all the sorrows of the heart. Hail, holy Virgin, through whom death has indeed been cast out and life brought in!

But, O thou holiest of holy sepulchres, except the sepulchre of the Lord which gave the beginning of life, which was the fount of the Resurrection (for I speak to thee as to an animate being), where is the gold which the hands of the Apostles placed in thee? Where are the riches which cannot be consumed? Where is that precious treasure which has received life? Where is the new volume in which the Word of God has been ineffably inscribed without a hand? Where is the abyss of grace? Where, the sea of cures? Where is that desirable body of the Virgin Mother of God?

Why do you seek in the tomb her who has been translated to the heavenly tabernacles? Why do you demand of me the reason of her custody? I am not able to resist the divine commands. That most holy body, which has imparted holiness to me also and has filled me with the fragrance of a most precious ointment and made me a divine temple, leaving behind its linen coverings, has been snatched up on high, accompanied by the Angels, Archangels, and all the heavenly powers. Now the Angels surround me; now divine grace dwells in me. I have become medicine to those who are ill; a perennial fount of cures; a remedy against the demons; a city of refuge to all who flee to me.

August 18
IV DAY WITHIN THE OCTAVE OF THE ASSUMPTION

From the Sermon of St. John Damascene
An ancient tradition has been handed down to us, that at the time of the glorious falling-asleep of the blessed Virgin, all the holy Apostles, who were wandering throughout the world preaching salvation to the Gentiles, were caught up aloft in the

twinkling of an eye and met together in Jerusalem.
And when they were all there, a vision of Angels
appeared to them and the chant of the heavenly
powers was heard; and so with divine glory she
gave up her holy soul into the hands of God. But
her body, which bore God in so ineffable a manner,
being lifted up amid the hymns of Angels and
Apostles, was laid in a tomb in Gethsemane. There
for three whole days the angelic song was heard.

But after three days the chant of the Angels
ceased, and the Apostles who were present opened
the tomb (for Thomas, the only one who had been
absent, came after the third day and wished to venerate the body that had borne God); but they
could by no means find her sacred body in any part
of it. But when they found only those garments in
which she had been buried and were filled with the
indescribable fragrance which emanated from them,
they closed the tomb. Amazed at this wonderful
mystery, they could only think that He, who had
been pleased to take flesh from the Virgin Mary, to
be made man, and to be born, though He was God
the Word and Lord of glory, who had preserved
her virginity without stain after childbirth, should
also have been pleased to honor her pure body after
her death, keeping it incorrupt, and translating it
to heaven before the general resurrection.

At this time there were present with the Apostles
the most holy Timothy, first bishop of Ephesus, and

Dionysius the Aereopagite, as he himself declares in the letters he wrote to the aforesaid Timothy about the blessed Hierotheus, who was also present. He speaks thus: For even when we also, as you know, and many of our holy brethren among those divinely inspired rulers of the Church had assembled for the purpose of viewing the body which gave the beginning of life and conceived God (and there were present both James, the brother of the Lord, and Peter, the first and most celebrated chief of theologians), and having beheld the sacred body, it pleased us all, according as each one was able, to celebrate with hymns the infinite goodness of the divine power.

August 19

V DAY WITHIN THE OCTAVE OF THE ASSUMPTION

Sermon of St. Bernard, Abbot

No doubt the glorious virgin, ascending today above the heavens, added an immense increase to the joys of the heavenly citizens. For this is she whose word of salutation makes even those whom the maternal womb still incloses exult in joy. But if the soul of a child not yet born was melted when Mary spoke, what do we think was that rejoicing of the heavenly citizens when they merited not only to hear her voice, but to see her face, and to enjoy her blessed presence?

But who can imagine how much the glorious Queen of heaven advanced today and by how great affection of devotion the whole multitude of the heavenly legions, by whose chants she was led to the throne of glory, profited by her coming; by how placid a countenance, by how serene a face, by what divine embraces she was received by her Son and raised above every creature with that honor of which such a Mother was worthy, with that glory which so well befitted her Son?

Happy indeed the kisses impressed by the lips of the suckling whom the Mother embraced on her virginal bosom. But shall we not think those yet happier which she received today in joyful salutation from the mouth of Him sitting on the right hand of the Father, when she ascended to the throne of glory, singing the nuptial song and saying: Let Him kiss me with the kiss of His mouth? Who will describe the generation of Christ and the assumption of Mary? For the more she has received grace above others on earth, so much the more singular glory does she obtain in heaven.

August 21
VII DAY WITHIN THE OCTAVE OF THE ASSUMPTION
Sermon of St. Bernard, Abbot

It is the time for all flesh to speak when the Mother of the Incarnate Word is taken up into heaven, nor ought human mortality cease to give praise since the nature alone of man is exalted in the Virgin above the immortal spirits. But neither does our devotion allow us to be silent, nor can our sterile thought conceive, nor our unlearned speach give forth, anything worthy concerning her glory. Hence it is that those princes of the heavenly court in the consideration of such an unheard-of thing cry out with admiration: Who is she who ascends from the desert abounding with delights?

As though they said more manifestly: How great is she, or whence is she, ascending indeed from the desert, so abounding in delights? For delights are not found equal in us whom the impetus of the river rejoices in the City of the Lord, who are given to drink by the countenance of Thy glory from the torrent of pleasure. Who is she who ascends from under the sun, where there is nothing but suffering and sadness and affliction of spirit, abounding in spiritual delights? Why should I not call delights the glory of virginity with the gift of fecundity, the ensign of humility distilling the honeycomb of charity, the bowels of mercy, the plenitude of grace, the prerogative of a singular glory?

Ascending, therefore, from the desert, the Queen of the world, as the Church sings, was made beautiful even to the holy angels and sweet in her delights. But let them cease to wonder at the delights of this desert, for the Lord hath given goodness and our earth hath yielded its fruit. Why do they wonder that Mary ascends from the desert of the earth abounding with delights? Let them wonder rather at Christ, being poor, descending from the plenitude of the heavenly kingdom, for it seems by far a greater miracle that the Son of God deigned to be made a little less than the angels than that the Mother of God should be exalted above the angels. Indeed, His humiliation has been made our exaltation; His miseries are the delights of the world. Finally, being rich, He was made poor on account of us, that He might enrich us by His poverty.

August 22
OCTAVE OF THE ASSUMPTION OF THE BLESSED VIRGIN MARY

I Nocturn
From the Canticle of Canticles, c. 8, 5 - 14
II Nocturn
Sermon of St. Bernard, Abbot

There is indeed nothing which delights me more, but there is nothing that terrifies me more, than to have to speak of the glory of the Virgin Mary. For behold, if I should praise virginity in her, there are many virgins after her time who seem to present themselves to me. If I should proclaim her humility, some will be found, few though they be, who have learned of her Son to become meek and humble of heart. If I should desire to extol the multitude of her mercies, there are some men who are merciful, and also women.

There is one thing in which no one has ever been or ever shall be, in the least degree, like unto her, as she has the joy of a mother together with the honor of virginity. This is the privilege of Mary which will not be given to any other; it is unique, but it will also remain forever unexplainable. And what it is words can never tell. Nevertheless, if thou considerest carefully, thou wilt find that not this grace only was absolutely peculiar to Mary, but others also, which might seem to be also possessed by others. For, can the purity even of the Angels venture to be compared with that virginity which was worthy to become the shrine of the Holy Ghost and the abode of the Son of God?

Again, how great and how precious was the virtue of humility in so great a purity, in so great an innocence, in a conscience absolutely without stain, in one who was indeed filled full of so great a grace? O blessed one, whence came thy humility, and such great humility? Worthy indeed wert thou that the Lord should look upon thee, that the King should desire thy beauty, that He should be drawn from His eternal rest in the bosom of the Father by thy sweet perfume.

O blessed Virgin, behold, with such prayers as we were able we have now conducted thee on thy way as thou goest up to the Son, and we have followed thee, at least from afar. In thy loving-kindness, make known to the world what grace thou hast found with God, by obtaining, through thy holy prayers, pardon for the guilty, healing for the sick, courage for the faint-hearted, comfort for the afflicted, help and deliverance for those in danger. And on this solemn festival, this day of joy, may Jesus Christ, thy Son, our Lord, bestow the gifts of His grace through thee, O merciful Queen, upon thy servants praising and invoking the most sweet name of Mary; for He is over all, God, blessed forever. Amen.

R. Like a cedar of Libanus I was exalted, and as a cypress tree on Mount Sion: like the best myrrh * I yielded a sweet odor. V. And like cinnamon and aromatical balm. I yielded. Glory. I yielded.

III Nocturn
The reading of the holy Gospel according to St. Luke

At that time: Jesus entered into a certain town, and a certain woman, named Martha, received Him into her house. And so forth.

Homily of St. Bernard, Abbot

Why do we speak of Him having entered into a town? He entered even into the most narrow lodging of a virginal womb. And then a certain woman received Him into her house. Happy was that woman whose house was found clean indeed for the Savior's entrance, but by no means empty! For who could say she was empty whom an Angel hails as full of grace?

And not only this; but he also declares that the Holy Ghost was about to come upon her. Why do you think He would come, unless to fill her to overflowing? Why, unless that she, who was already full of the Spirit when He came, should, when He came upon her, brim over and overflow upon us? Let the Savior then enter into the house; let Him often resort to the home cleansed by the repentant Lazarus, adorned by Martha, and filled by Mary, who gave herself to inward contemplation.

But perhaps some curious person will want to know why, in the lesson just read from the Gospel, absolutely no mention is made of Lazarus. Truly, I think, to avoid anything which did not fit in with the proposed similitude. For the Holy Ghost, wishing that this passage should be taken to signify the virginal dwelling, kept silence, as was fitting, about repentance, since this usually implies evil. For let it not be said that this house ever had any defilement within for which the broom of Lazarus was required.

Let it surprise no one that the woman receiving the Lord is called not Mary, but Martha, when in this one and highest Mary both the service of Martha and the inactivity, but not idleness, of

Mary is found. Indeed, all the glory of the King's daughter is within; nevertheless, she is clothed about with variety in golden fringes. She is not of the number of the foolish virgins: this virgin is prudent; she has a lamp; but she carries oil in her vessel.

R. Thou art blessed, O Virgin Mary, who didst bear the Lord, the Creator of the world: * Thou didst bring forth Him who made thee, and thou remainest a Virgin forever. V. Hail, Mary, full of grace; the Lord is with thee. Thou didst. Glory. Thou didst.

Gospel and Prayer as on the Feast, page 794

August 23
VIGIL OF ST. BARTHOLOMEW, APOSTLE
Lessons from the Homily on the Gospel as on the vigil of St. James, page 755

August 24
ST. BARTHOLOMEW, APOSTLE
I Nocturn
From the first Epistle of Blessed Paul the Apostle to the Corinthians, c. 4, 1 - 15
II Nocturn

Bartholomew the Apostle, a Galilean, when he went into the nearer parts of India (which had fallen to him in the apportionment of the world for the preaching of the Gospel of Jesus Christ), preached to those peoples the coming of the Lord Jesus according to the Gospel of St. Matthew.

But, after converting many souls to Jesus Christ in that province and undergoing much labor and suffering, he went into Greater Armenia. There he converted to the Christian faith the king Polymius and his queen, and likewise twelve cities.

This excited great hatred against him on the part of the priests of that nation. For they constantly inflamed Astyages, brother of Polymius the king, against the Apostle to such a degree that he commanded Bartholomew to be flayed alive in a most cruel manner and to be beheaded, in which martyrdom he gave up his soul to God.

His body was buried at Albanopolis, the city of Greater Armenia where he suffered. It was afterwards taken away to the island of Lipari, and thence translated to Benevento. Finally it was carried to Rome by the emperor Otto III, and laid in the church dedicated to God by the name of Bartholomew, on the island in the Tiber.

R. When ye stand before kings and governors, take no thought how or what ye shall speak: * For it shall be given you in that hour what ye shall speak. V. For it is not you that speak; but the Spirit of your Father that speaketh in you. For it shall. Glory. For it shall.

III Nocturn
The reading of the holy Gospel
according to St. Luke

At that time: Jesus went out into a mountain to pray, and He passed the whole night in the prayer of God. And when day was come, He called unto Him His disciples. And so forth.

Homily of St. Ambrose, Bishop

All the great, all the high-souled go up into the mountain. For it is not to every man that the prophet says: Get thee up on a high mountain, thou that bringest good tidings to Sion; lift up thy voice with strength, thou that bringest good tidings to Jerusalem. Not by corporeal footsteps, but by nobler deeds, get thee up into this mountain and follow Christ that thou mayest thyself be a mountain: For the mountains are round about Him. Wherefore in the Gospel thou shalt find that only the disciples went up into the mountain with the Lord.

The Lord prays, therefore, not to beg anything for Himself, but to entreat for me. For, although the Father has placed all things in the power of the Son, yet the Son, that He may fulfil all that belongs to man, thinks it fitting to beseech the Father for us, because He is our advocate. And He passed, it says, the whole night in the prayer of God. A pattern is given thee, O Christian, an example is furnished thee which thou shouldst follow.

For what doth it behove thee to do for thy salvation when, for thy sake, Christ passed the whole night in prayer? What is it fitting for thee to do when thou willest to begin some good work when Christ, when He was about to send forth His Apostles, first prayed, and prayed alone? Neither, if I am not mistaken, do we ever find in any other place that He prayed with His Apostles; in every case He prayed alone. For human desires cannot grasp the counsel of God, nor can any man, even a spiritual man, partake of Christ.

He called unto Him, it says, His disciples, and He chose twelve of them, whom He appointed to spread abroad the aid of human salvation throughout the world, as sowers of the seed of faith. At the same time, ponder on the heavenly wisdom: He did not choose any wise men, nor noble, but fishermen and publicans, whom He had taught, that He might not seem to have drawn men to His grace by wisdom, or to have redeemed them by riches, or to have attracted them by the authority of power and rank; that so the power of the truth, not the attraction of argument, might prevail.

R. Take up My yoke upon you, saith the Lord, and learn of Me, because I am meek and humble of heart: * For My yoke is sweet and My burden light. V. And you shall find rest to your souls. For My yoke. Glory. For My yoke.

✠ Continuation of the holy Gospel according to St. Luke.—At that time: Jesus went out into a mountain to pray, and He passed the whole night in the prayer of God. And when day was come, He called unto Him His disciples; and He chose twelve of them (whom also He named Apostles), Simon whom He surnamed Peter, and Andrew his brother, James and John, Philip and Bartholomew, Matthew and Thomas, James the son of Alpheus, and Simon who is called Zelotes, and Jude the brother of James, and Judas Iscariot, who was the traitor. And coming down with them, He stood in a plain place, and the company of His disciples, and a very great multitude of people from all Judea and Jerusalem, and the sea-coast both of Tyre and Sidon, who were come to hear Him and to be healed of their diseases. And they that were troubled with unclean spirits were cured. And all the multitude sought to touch Him, for virtue went out from Him and healed all.

LET US PRAY

O almighty and eternal God, who hast given us the holy and spiritual joy of this day on the feast of Thy blessed Apostle Bartholomew, grant, we beseech Thee, that Thy Church may love what he believed and preach what he taught. Through our Lord.

September 8
NATIVITY OF THE BLESSED VIRGIN MARY
I Nocturn
From the Canticles of Canticles, c. 1, 1 - 16
II Nocturn
Sermon of St. Augustine, Bishop

Dearly beloved, the day of the blessed and ever venerable Virgin Mary, so long desired, is here; therefore let our land rejoice with the greatest exultation and be illuminated by the birth of such a Virgin. For this indeed is the flower of the field, from whom sprang the precious lily of the valley; by whose birth the nature drawn from our first parents is changed, and their sin blotted out.

That unhappy curse of Eve, wherein it is said: in sorrow shalt thou bring forth children, is, in the case of Mary, taken away: for she brought forth the Lord in joy. For Eve mourned; this one rejoiced: Eve carried tears in her womb; Mary, joy; because the former brought forth the sinner; the latter, the innocent one. The mother of our race brought punishment into the world; the Mother of our Lord brought salvation into the world.

Eve was the authoress of sin; Mary, the authoress of merit. Eve hindered by killing; Mary helped by giving life. The former smote; the latter healed. For disobedience is replaced by obedience; fidelity atones for infidelity. Now let Mary play upon instruments, and let the timbrels resound between the active fingers of the young mother. Let the choirs sing together with joy, and let their sweet songs be mingled with the alternating strains.

Hear then, how our timbrel-player sang; for she says: My soul doth magnify the Lord; and my spirit hath rejoiced in God my Savior. Because He hath regarded the humility of His handmaid: for behold, from henceforth all generations shall call me blessed. Because He that is mighty hath done great things to me. Therefore the miraculous new birth conquered the prevailing error; and the song of Mary put an end to the lamentation of Eve.

R. Thy birth, O Virgin Mother of God, brought tidings of joy to the whole world: * For from thee rose the Sun of Justice, Christ our God: who has taken away the curse and given a blessing: and counfounding death, has given us everlasting life. V. Blessed art thou amongst women, and blessed is the fruit of thy womb. For from thee. Glory. For from thee.

III Nocturn

The reading of the Holy Gospel
according to St. Matthew

The book of the generation of Jesus Christ, the son of David, the son of Abraham. Abraham begot Isaac. And Isaac begot Jacob. And so forth.

Homily of St. Jerome, Priest

We read in Isaias: Who shall declare His generation? Let us not think that the Evangelist contradicts the Prophet because the one begins to declare what the other had said to be impossible: since the one speaks of the generation of the Divinity, the other of the Incarnation. And he begins with carnal things, that, through the manhood, we may learn to know the Godhead.

The son of David, the son of Abraham. The order is inverted, but necessarily changed. For if he had put Abraham first, and then David, he would have had to return again to Abraham in order to trace the series of generations.

And so, omitting the others, he calls Him the son of these, because to these alone was made the promise of Christ. To Abraham He says: In thy seed (which is Christ) shall all the nations of the earth be blessed. To David: Of the fruit of thy womb I will set upon thy throne.

And Judas begot Phares and Zara of Thamar. It is to be noted that in the Savior's genealogy, not one of the saintly women is mentioned, but those only whom Scripture reproves; because He who had come for the sake of sinners, was to be born of sinners, to blot out the sins of all. And likewise in subsequent verses mention is made of Ruth the Moabitess, and Bethsabee, the wife of Urias.

R. Truly happy art thou, O holy Virgin Mary, and worthy of all praise, * For from thee hath dawned the Sun of Justice, Christ our God. V. Pray for the people, plead for the clergy, intercede for all devout women; may all feel thy aid who celebrate thy holy Birthday. For from thee. Glory. For from thee.

✠ Beginning of the holy Gospel according to St. Matthew.—The book of the generation of Jesus Christ, the Son of David, the Son of Abraham. Abraham begot Isaac; and Isaac begot Jacob; and Jacob begot Judas, and his brethren; and Judas begot Phares and Zara of Thamar; and Phares begot Esron; and Esron begot Aram; and Aram begot Aminadab; and Aminadab begot Naasson; and Naasson begot Salmon; and Salmon begot Booz of Rahab; and Booz begot Obed of Ruth; and Obed begot Jesse; and Jesse begot David the King. And David the king begot Solomon, of her who had been the wife of Urias; and Solomon begot Roboam; and Roboam begot Abia; and Abia begot Asa; and Asa begot Josaphat; and Josaphat begot Joram; and Joram begot Ozias; and Ozias begot Joatham; and Joatham begot Achaz; and Achaz begot Ezechias; and Ezechias begot Manasses; and Manasses begot Amon; and Amon begot Josias; and Josias begot Jechonias and his brethren in the transmigration of Babylon. And after the transmigration of

Babylon, Jechonias begot Salathiel; Salathiel begot Zorobabel; and Zorobabel begot Abiud; and Abiud begot Eliacim; and Eliacim begot Azor; and Azor begot Sadoc; and Sadoc begot Achim; and Achim begot Eliud; and Eliud begot Eleazar; and Eleazar begot Mathan; and Mathan begot Jacob; and Jacob begot Joseph, the husband of Mary, of whom was born Jesus, who is called Christ.

LET US PRAY

Grant to Thy servants, we beseech Thee, O Lord, the gift of heavenly grace; that as the birth of the Blessed Virgin was the beginning of our salvation, so the solemnity of her birth may give us an increase of peace. Through our Lord.

September 12
THE MOST HOLY NAME OF MARY

I Nocturn

From the Proverbs of Solomon, c. 8, 12 - 25 and 34 - 36; c. 9, 1 - 5

II Nocturn

Sermon of St. Bernard, Abbot

And the Virgin's name, he says, was Mary. Let us speak for a little of this name, which is said to mean star of the sea, and is so well and suitably applied to the Virgin Mother. Indeed most aptly is she compared to a star, for as a star sheds its beams without any decay on its part, so the Virgin brought forth her Son without damage to her virginity. Neither does the beam lessen the brightness of the star, nor the Son the inviolateness of the Virgin.

She is then that famous star which rose out of Jacob, whose rays light up the whole world, whose brilliance both gleams in heaven and penetrates hell; flooding also the earth with light and warming minds rather than bodies, it fosters virtues and melts away sins. She, I say, is that bright and splendid star, lifted of necessity above this vast and boundless sea, glittering with merits, enlightening by her example.

Whosoever thou art, if thou findest thyself being tossed in the storms and tempests of this world's flood rather than walking upon dry land, do not take thine eyes from the brightness of this star if thou dost not wish to be overwhelmed by the storm. If the winds of temptation arise, if thou runnest upon the rocks of tribulation, look to the star, call upon Mary. If thou art thrown upon the waves of pride or ambition, detraction or jealousy, look to the star, call upon Mary. If anger or avarice or temptations of the flesh agitate the ship of thy mind, look upon Mary. If troubled by the enormity of thy crimes, confused by the blackness of thy conscience, and terrified by the horror of judgment, thou beginnest to be swallowed up in the bottomless pit of sorrow or the abyss of desperation, think upon Mary.

In dangers, in difficulties, in things doubtful, think upon Mary, call upon Mary. Let not her name depart out of thy mouth nor from thy heart. And that thou mayest obtain the help of her prayers, do not abandon the example of her conduct. Following her, thou dost not stray; praying to her, thou dost not despair; thinking of her, thou dost not err; supported by her, thou dost not fall; protected by her, thou dost not fear; led by her, thou dost not tire; if she is favorable, thou succeedest; and so thou dost experience in thyself with what justice it is said: And the Virgin's name was Mary.—On account of a signal victory gained at Vienna in Austria, obtained through the protection of that Virgin Mary over the most inhuman tyranny of the Turks who were trampling upon the necks of the Christian people, the Roman Pontiff, Innocent XI, ordered that this truly venerable name, already for some time honored by a special cult in some parts of the Christian world, should be celebrated every year throughout the universal Church as a perpetual memorial of that great deliverance.

R. Thou art blessed, O Virgin Mary, who didst bear the Lord, Creator of the world: * Thou didst bring forth Him who made thee, and thou remainest a Virgin forever. V. Hail, Mary, full of grace: the Lord is with thee. Thou didst. Glory. Thou didst.

III Nocturn

The reading of the holy Gospel
according to St. Luke

At that time: The Angel Gabriel was sent from
God into a city of Galilee called Nazareth, to a
Virgin espoused to a man whose name was Joseph,
of the house of David; and the Virgin's name was
Mary. And so forth.

Homily of St. Peter Chrysologus

Today, dearly beloved brethren, you have heard
how the Angel treated with the woman on the regeneration of man. You have heard them dis-
cussing how man might return to life by the same
road by which he fell into death. The Angel treat-
eth of salvation with Mary because an angel had
treated of ruin with Eve. You have heard how the
Angel with wonderful art made a temple of divine
majesty out of the slime of our flesh. You have
heard how God is placed on earth and man in
heaven by this incomprehensible mystery. You
have heard that God is united in one body with
man in an unheard-of way. You have heard that
the natural frailty of our flesh is strengthened by
angelic exhortation to bear the full glory of the
divinity.

And lastly, lest in Mary the fine sand of our
human nature should succumb beneath the great
weight of the heavenly building, and lest in the

Virgin the slender branch that was to carry the fruit of the whole human race should break, the voice of the Angel, in order to dispel her fear, proceeds at once to say: Fear not, Mary.

The dignity of the Virgin is told, before the cause of it, by her name; for the Hebrew word *Mary* means in Latin, *Lady*. Therefore the Angel calls her Lady that the timidity of the servile state may depart from the Mother of the Ruler; from her whom the power of her Offspring created and brought to pass that she should be born and called Lady. Fear not, Mary, for thou hast found grace. True it is, for he who finds grace knows not fear: Thou hast found grace.

Blessed is she who alone among mankind before all deserved to hear: Thou hast found grace. And how much? As much as he had said before, full. And indeed full, that drenches and soaks, as a plentiful shower, the whole creature: For thou hast found grace with God. When he says this, the Angel himself marvels that even a woman should merit eternal life or that all men should merit it through a woman; the Angel is amazed that the whole Godhead, to whom all creation is small, should enter the narrow womb of a Virgin. Thus it is that the Angel tarries; thus it is that he calls her a virgin as she deserved, and hails her full of grace; hardly, even after long hesitation, so putting it that it could be understood.

R. All generations shall call me blessed, * Because the Lord who is mighty hath done great things to me, and holy is His name. V. And His mercy is from generation unto generations to them that fear Him. Because. Glory. Because.

✠ Continuation of the holy Gospel according to St. Luke.—At that time: the Angel Gabriel was sent from God into a city of Galilee, called Nazareth, to a Virgin espoused to a man whose name was Joseph, of the house of David: and the Virgin's name was Mary. And the Angel being come in, said unto her: Hail, full of grace, the Lord is with thee: blessed art thou among women. Who, having heard, was troubled at his saying and thought with herself what manner of salutation this should be. And the Angel said to her: Fear not, Mary, for thou hast found grace with God. Behold, thou shalt conceive in thy womb and shalt bring forth a Son and thou shalt call His name Jesus. He shall be great and shall be called the Son of the Most High, and the Lord God shall give unto Him the throne of David His father: and He shall reign in the house of Jacob forever, and of His kingdom there shall be no end. And Mary said to the Angel: How shall this be done, because I know not man? And the Angel answering, said to her: The Holy Ghost shall come upon thee and the power of the Most High shall overshadow thee. And therefore also the Holy which shall be born of thee shall be called the Son of God. And behold thy cousin Elizabeth, she also hath conceived a son in her old age: and this is the sixth month with her that is called barren: because no word shall be impossible with God. And Mary said: Behold the handmaid of the Lord, be it done to me according to thy word.

LET US PRAY

Grant, we beseech Thee, O almighty God, that Thy faithful may always rejoice under the protection of the most holy name of the Virgin Mary, and by her loving intercession to be freed from all evils on earth and merit to come to the eternal joys in heaven. Through our Lord.

September 14
EXALTATION OF THE HOLY CROSS
I Nocturn

From the Book of Numbers, c. 21, 1 - 9

II Nocturn

About the end of the reign of the emperor Phocas, Chosroes, king of the Persians, invaded Egypt and Africa and took Jerusalem; and after massacring there many thousands of Christians, he carried away into Persia the Cross of Christ the Lord which Helena had set up upon Mount Calvary. Accordingly, Heraclius, who succeeded Phocas, embarrassed by many troubles and calamities of war, sued for peace; but he was unable to obtain it, even upon unjust terms, so elated was Chosroes by his victories. In this most perilous situation he applied himself to constant prayer and fasting, and earnestly implored God's assistance. Admonished by Him to raise an army, he engaged the enemy in close combat, and overcame three of Chosroes' generals with their three armies.

Subdued by these defeats, Chosroes took to flight, and, when about to cross the Tigris, named his son Medarses his associate in the kingdom. But his eldest son, Siroes, bitterly resenting this slight, plotted the murder both of his father and brother, which he carried out soon after they had returned from their flight, and obtained the kingdom from Heraclius on certain conditions, the first of which was that he should restore the Cross of Christ the Lord.

Thus, fourteen years after it had fallen into the hands of the Persians, the Cross was recovered. On his return to Jerusalem, Heraclius with great pomp bore it back on his own shoulders to that mount whither the Savior had carried it. This event was signalized by a remarkable miracle. For Heraclius, adorned as he was with gold and precious stones, was forced to stand still at the gate which led to Mount Calvary. The more he endeavored to advance, the more he seemed fixed to the spot.

Heraclius himself and all the people were astounded; but Zacharias, the bishop of Jerusalem, said: Consider, O emperor, how little thou imitatest the poverty and humility of Jesus Christ by carrying the Cross in triumphal robes. Heraclius thereupon laid aside his magnificent apparel, removed his shoes, and put on a mean garment, and so easily completed the rest of the way and replaced the Cross in the same place on Calvary from whence it had been carried off by the Persians. From this event, the feast of the Exaltation of the Holy Cross, which was celebrated yearly on this day, began to gain fresh luster in memory of the Cross being replaced by Heraclius on the spot where it had first been set up for the Savior.

R. It behoveth us to glory in the Cross of our Lord Jesus Christ, in whom is our salvation, life, and resurrection: * By whom we have been saved and delivered. V. We adore Thy Cross, O Lord, and we remember Thy glorious Passion. By whom. Glory. By whom.

III Nocturn
The reading of the holy Gospel
according to St. John

At that time: Jesus said to the multitudes of the Jews: Now is the judgment of the world; now shall the prince of this world be cast out. And so forth.

Homily of St. Leo, Pope
When Christ is lifted up on the Cross, dearly beloved, let not the mind's eye see merely that which

was seen by the eyes of the unjust, of whom it was said by Moses: And thy life shall be, as it were, hanging before thee, thou shalt fear night and day, neither shalt thou trust thy life. For they could imagine nothing in the crucified Lord but their own crime, being fearful not with that fear which justifies true faith, but with the fear that torments a bad conscience.

But let our understanding, enlightened by the spirit of truth, receive with a pure and open heart the glory of the Cross that irradiates heaven and earth, and let it see with interior vision what is meant when the Lord, speaking of His approaching Passion, said: Now is the judgment of the world, now shall the prince of this world be cast out. And I, if I be lifted up from the earth, will draw all things to Myself. O how wonderful is the power of the Cross! O unutterable glory of the Passion, wherein is the judgment-seat of the world, and the power of the Crucified! For Thou hast drawn all things unto Thyself, O Lord, and when all the day long Thou didst spread forth Thy hands to a people that believed not and contradicted Thee, the whole world perceived that Thy majesty was to be acknowledged.

Thou hast drawn all things unto Thyself, O Lord, when, in detestation of the Jews' crime, all the elements proclaimed the same opinion; when the light of heaven was obscured, and the day turned into night, the earth, too, was shaken with unwonted tremors, and creatures refused their service to the wicked. Thou hast drawn all things unto Thyself, O Lord, for the veil of the temple being rent, the Holy of Holies was separated from the unworthy priests, that shadow might be changed into truth, prophecy into manifestation, and the law into the Gospel.

Thou hast drawn all things unto Thyself, O Lord, so that what in one Jewish temple was hidden by the shadowy symbols should everywhere be celebrated by the devotion of all nations in a full and open sacrament. For now the order of Levites is more honorable, the dignity of the elders is greater, and the anointing of the priests is more holy: because Thy Cross is the fountain of all blessing and the cause of all grace; through which is given to those who believe strength for weakness, glory for blame, life for death. Now also, the varieties of fleshly sacrifices being at an end, the single oblation of Thy Body and Blood fulfils all these various types of sacrifices; for Thou art the true Lamb of God, who takest away the sins of the world; and so in Thyself Thou dost perfect all mysteries, that as there is one sacrifice in place of many victims, so there is one kingdom for every race.

R. As Moses lifted up the serpent in the desert, so must the Son of man be lifted up: * That whosoever believeth in Him may not perish, but may

have life everlasting. V. For God did not send His
Son into the world to judge the world, but that the
world might be saved by Him. That. Glory. That.

✠ Continuation of the holy Gospel according to
St. John.—At that time: Jesus said to the multitudes of the Jews: Now is the judgment of the
world; now shall the prince of this world be cast
out. And I, if I be lifted up from the earth, will
draw all things to Myself. (Now this He said, signifying what death He should die.) The multitude
answered Him: We have heard out of the law that
Christ abideth forever, and how sayest Thou: The
Son of man must be lifted up? Who is the Son of
man? Jesus therefore said to them: Yet a little
while the light is among you. Walk whilst you
have the light that the darkness overtake you not.
And he that walketh in darkness knoweth not
whither he goeth. Whilst you have the light, believe in the light, that you may be the children of
light.

LET US PRAY

O God, who on this day dost gladden us by the
annual feast of the Exaltation of the Holy Cross,
grant, we beseech Thee, that we who understand its
mystery upon this earth may merit the reward of
its redemption in heaven. Through the same Lord.

September 15
SEVEN DOLORS OF THE BLESSED VIRGIN MARY
I Nocturn
From Jeremias the Prophet, Lam., c. 1, 2 and 20 - 21; c. 2, 13 and 15 - 18
II Nocturn
Sermon of St. Bernard, Abbot

The martyrdom of the Virgin is set before us both in the prophecy of Simeon and in the story of the Lord's Passion. The holy old man said of the Child Jesus: Behold this Child is set for a sign which shall be contradicted; and to Mary he said: And thine own soul a sword shall pierce. Yea, truly, O blessed Mother, it pierced thy soul, for only by passing through thy soul could it penetrate the Body of thy Son. And when this Jesus of thine had given up the ghost, and the cruel spear which opened His side could not touch His Soul anymore, it pierced through thine. His Soul was certainly no longer there, but thine could not be torn thence.

The sword of sorrow did indeed pierce through thy soul, so that we may truly call thee more than a martyr in whom the love which made thee suffer with thy Son far exceeded any bodily pain. Yea, was not that word of His more piercing than any sword, reaching as it did unto the division of the soul and the spirit: Woman, behold thy Son? O what an exchange! Thou art given John for Jesus, the servant for the Lord, the disciple for the Master, the son of Zebedee for the Son of God, a mere man for very God. O how sharply must the sound of those words have pierced thy most loving soul, when only at the memory of them our stony, iron hearts are wrung with sorrow?

Wonder not, my brethren, that Mary should be called a martyr in spirit. He, indeed, may marvel who does not recall what Paul says, in mentioning among the greater sins of the Gentiles, that they were without affection. Such want of affection was far from Mary's heart; let it also be far from her servants.

But perchance someone may say: But did she not know beforehand that He was to die? Without the least doubt she knew it. Did she not hope that He would rise again? Yea, faithfully, she hoped it. Yet did she still mourn over Him as crucified? Yea, bitterly. But who art thou, my brother, and whence is this wisdom of thine, to marvel less that the Son of Mary suffered than that Mary suffered with Him? He could die in the body, and could she not die with Him in her heart? His death was wrought by a love greater than which had no man; hers by a love such as had none save she.

R. Jesus, bearing His own cross, went forth. * And there followed Him a company of women who bewailed and lamented Him. V. Daughters of Jerusalem, weep for yourselves and for your children. And there followed. Glory. And there followed.

III Nocturn
The reading of the Holy Gospel
according to St. John

At that time: There stood by the cross of Jesus, His mother, and His mother's sister, Mary of Cleophas, and Mary Magdalene. And so forth.

Homily of St. Ambrose, Bishop

Now there stood by the cross the Mother; she stood undaunted, the men fleeing away. See whether the Mother of Jesus, who did not lose her courage, lost her modesty.

She gazed with loving eyes upon the wounds of her Son, by which she knew all would be redeemed. This Mother, who did not fear the executioner, looked on no mean sight. The Son hung upon a Cross, the Mother offered herself to the persecutors.

Mary, the Mother of the Lord, stood before the cross of the Son. St. John the Evangelist alone taught me this. The others wrote that during the Passion of the Lord the world shook, the sky was shrouded in darkness, the sun disappeared, the thief was admitted into Paradise, but only after a devout confession.

John taught that which the others did not teach, how, hanging on the cross, He called her Mother. That the Conqueror of torments exhibited the duties of filial piety to the Mother is thought of more moment than that He gave the kingdom of heaven. Now if the forgiveness of the thief was a pious act, it was an act even more abounding in piety that the Son should honor the Mother with so much affection.

R. What were thy feelings, O Mother of sorrows, * When Joseph wrapped thy Son in linen and laid Him in the sepulchre? V. Attend and see if there be any sorrow like to my sorrow. When. Glory. When.

✠ Continuation of the holy Gospel according to St. John.—At that time: There stood by the cross of Jesus, His mother, and His mother's sister, Mary of Cleophas, and Mary Magdalen. When Jesus, therefore, had seen His Mother and the disciple standing whom He loved, He saith to His mother: Woman, behold thy son. After that He saith to the disciple: Behold thy Mother. And from that hour the disciple took her to his own.

LET US PRAY

O God, in whose Passion, according to the prophecy of Simeon, the sword of sorrow pierced the most tender soul of the glorious Virgin Mother Mary, mercifully grant that we who devoutly venerate her sorrows may receive the blessed fruits of Thy Passion; who livest and reignest with God the Father.

September 20
VIGIL OF ST. MATTHEW, APOSTLE
The reading of the holy Gospel
according to St. Luke

At that time: Jesus saw a publican named Levi sitting at the receipt of custom, and He said to him: Follow Me. And so forth.

Homily of St. Ambrose, Bishop

This call to a publican whom He orders to follow Him, not with bodily footsteps, but with his soul's love, is mystical. And so he, who once made greedy gains from merchandise and profit from the labors and dangers of seamen, he who took the goods of others, at the call of a mere word gives up his own; and leaving that vile seat, he follows after the Lord with every footstep of his soul. He also displays the preparations for a great feast; for he who receives Christ within his spiritual dwelling is fed with the highest delights of exceedingly great joy.

Thus the Lord willingly enters and reclines in the affection of the one who believes. But the envy of the wicked is again stirred up and an image of future punishment is prefigured. For while the faithful are feasting and reclining in that kingdom of heaven, the wicked will be tortured by fasting. At the same time it is shown how great is the distance between those zealous for the law and those zealous for grace, because those who follow the law will suffer the eternal hunger of fasting of mind; those, however, who have received the word into the interior of their soul, refreshed by abundance of heavenly food and drink, can neither hunger nor thirst.

And therefore those who fasted in their minds murmured, saying: Why doth He eat and drink with publicans and sinners? This is the voice of the serpent. For the serpent first spoke this word, saying to Eve: Why hath God commanded you, that you should not eat of every tree? Therefore they who say: Why doth He eat and drink with publicans and sinners? spread abroad the venom of their father. Whence the Lord, having Himself eaten with sinners, does not forbid us to attend banquets even with the Gentiles, saying: They who are in health need not a physician, but they who are sick.

September 21
ST. MATTHEW, APOSTLE AND EVANGELIST
I Nocturn
From the Book of Ezechiel the Prophet, c. 1, 1 - 13
II Nocturn

Matthew, also named Levi, the Apostle and Evangelist, was sitting at the receipt of custom at Capharnaum when called by Christ, whom he immediately followed, and then made a feast for Him and the other disciples. After the Resurrection of

Christ, and before setting out for the province which it was his lot to evangelize, while he was yet in Judea, he wrote the Gospel of Jesus Christ in Hebrew, for the sake of those of the circumcision who were believers. Soon after, he went into Ethiopia where he preached the Gospel and confirmed his preaching by many miracles.

One of the greatest of these miracles was his raising to life the king's daughter, whereby he converted her father the king, his wife, and the whole country to the faith of Christ. After the king's death his daughter Iphigenia was demanded in marriage by his successor, Hirtacus; who, finding that through Matthew's exhortation she had vowed her virginity to God and persevered in her holy resolution, ordered Matthew to be put to death as he was celebrating the holy mysteries at the altar. Thus on September 21, he fulfilled the apostolic office with the glory of martyrdom. His body was translated to Salerno, and in the time of the supreme Pontiff Gregory VII, it was laid in a church dedicated in his name, where it is piously honored by a great concourse of people.

From the Commentary of St. Gregory, Pope, on the Prophet Ezechiel

The prophet gives a minute description of the four holy living creatures, which he foresaw in the spirit as being to come, when he says: Every one had four faces, and every one four wings. What is signified by face, if it be not celebrity; or by wings, unless it be the power of flight? For it is by the face that a man is recognized; but by their wings the bodies of birds are raised in the air. Thus the face pertains to faith, the wings to contemplation. For in our faith we are known by almighty God, as He says of His sheep: I am the good shepherd; and I know Mine, and Mine know Me. And again He says: I know whom I have chosen.

For by contemplation we are raised above ourselves, as it were, to heaven. Every one, then, had four faces: for if thou inquirest what Matthew held concerning the Incarnation of the Lord, he assuredly held the same doctrine as Mark, Luke, and John. If thou askest what John held, it was undoubtedly that which was held by Luke, Mark, and Matthew. If thou askest what Mark held, it was the same as that of Matthew, John, and Luke. If thou askest what Luke held, it was the same as that of John, Matthew, and Mark.

R. Blessed are ye when men shall revile and persecute you and speak all that is evil against you, untruly, for My sake: * Be glad and rejoice, for your reward is very great in heaven. V. When men shall hate you and when they shall separate you and reproach you and cast out your name as evil, for the Son of man's sake. Be glad. Glory. Be glad.

III Nocturn
The reading of the holy Gospel
according to St. Matthew

At that time: Jesus saw a man sitting in the custom-house, named Matthew; and He saith to him: Follow Me. And so forth.

Homily of St. Jerome, Priest

The other Evangelist, out of reverence and respect for Matthew, would not call him by his ordinary name, but said: Levi, for he had two names. But Matthew himself (according to the words of Solomon: The just is first accuser of himself; and in another place; Confess thy sins that thou mayest be justified) calls himself both Matthew and a publican, to show his readers that no one should despair of salvation if he be converted to a better life, since he himself was suddenly changed from a publican to an Apostle.

Porphyry and Julian Augustus argue in this passage either the ignorance of a lying historian, or the folly of those who followed the Savior immediately, as though they had followed without reason this Man who had called them; yet there is no doubt that the Apostles had seen such great works of power and such great miracles as had already been done before they believed.

Certainly that brightness and majesty of the hidden divinity, which shone even in His human face, was able to attract at first sight those who saw Him. For if the loadstone and amber are said to have the power of attracting rings and straws and stalks, how much more can the Lord of all creatures draw to Himself those whom He calls?

And it came to pass as He was sitting at meat in the house, behold, many publicans and sinners came and sat down with Jesus. They saw that the publican, converted from sin to better things, had found a place of repentance; and so they themselves also did not despair of salvation. Nor did they come to Jesus persisting in their former vices, as the Pharisees and Scribes complained, but doing penance, as the following words of the Lord show: I will have mercy and not sacrifice. For I am not come to call the just, but sinners. But the Lord went to the banquet of sinners in order to have an opportunity of teaching and to give spiritual food to His hosts.

R. These are the holy men whom the Lord hath chosen in charity unfeigned ,and hath given them everlasting glory: * Whose teaching enlightens the Church, as the moon by the sun. V. By faith the Saints conquered kingdoms and wrought justice. Whose. Glory. Whose.

✠ Continuation of the holy Gospel according to St. Matthew.—At that time: Jesus saw a man sitting in the custom-house, named Matthew, and He saith to him, Follow Me. And he rose up and followed Him. And it came to pass as He was sitting at meat in the house, behold, many publicans and sinners came and sat down with Jesus and His disciples. And the Pharisees seeing it, said to His disciples, Why doth your Master eat with publicans and sinners? But Jesus hearing it, said? They that are in health need not a physician; but they that are ill. Go then, and learn what this meaneth, I will have mercy, and not sacrifice. For I am not come to call the just, but sinners.

LET US PRAY

May we be assisted by the prayers of Thy blessed Apostle and Evangelist Matthew, we beseech Thee, O Lord, that what we cannot obtain by our own merits, may be given to us by his intercession. Through our Lord.

September 29
DEDICATION OF ST MICHAEL
THE ARCHANGEL

I Nocturn

From the Book of Daniel, c. 7, 9 - 11; c. 10, 4 - 14

II Nocturn

Sermon of St. Gregory, Pope

We speak of nine choirs of Angels because we know, by the testimony of the holy words, that there are, to wit: Angels, Archangels, Virtues, Powers, Principalities, Dominations, Thrones, Cherubim, and Seraphim. For nearly every page of holy Writ speaks of Angels and Archangels. And the books of the prophets, as is well known, often mention the Cherubim and Seraphim. The Apostle Paul also enumerates to the Ephesians the names of four orders, saying: Above all Principality, and Power, and Virtue, and Dominion. Again, in writing to the Colossians, he says: Whether Thrones or Dominations or Principalities, or Powers. Now, therefore, to those four choirs whom he named to the Ephesians, if the Thrones be added, there are five choirs; and when we join to these the Angels, Archangels, Cherubim and Seraphim, it is quite clear that there are nine choirs of Angels.

We must know, however, that the word *Angel* is the name of the office, not of the nature. For those holy Spirits of the heavenly fatherland are indeed always Spirits, but can by no means always be called Angels; for they are Angels only when some message is sent through them. Whence also it is said by the Psalmist: Who maketh His spirits Angels; as if to say clearly: These whom He always has as Spirits, He also makes, when He will, Angels.

And those who announce things of lesser importance are Angels; those who bring important messages are called Archangels. And thus it is that to the Virgin Mary was sent, not any ordinary Angel, but the Archangel Gabriel. For it was just that for this supreme ministry of bearing the greatest of all tidings, the greatest Angel should be chosen. For that reason also they are designated by individual names, that these words may designate their individual powers. For Michael means: *Who is like to God?* Gabriel: *Strength of God;* Raphael: *Medicine of God.*

And whenever any work of great power is to be done, Michael is brought forward to be sent; that by that very act and name we may understand that no one can do what God alone has power to do. Hence when that old enemy, who through pride desired to be like unto God, saying: I will ascend into heaven, I will exalt my throne above the stars of heaven, I will be like the Most High; shall be, at the end of the world, left to his own might and cast into everlasting punishment, he is presented to us as being about to enter into combat with Michael the Archangel, as it is said by John: There was a battle with Michael the Archangel. To Mary, in like manner, Gabriel is sent, who is named *Strength of God*: for indeed, he came to announce Him who deigned to appear as humble, in order to vanquish completely the powers of the air. Raphael, as we have said, is interpreted in like maner *Medicine of God;* namely, because touching the eyes of Tobias by way of healing, he dispelled the darkness of his blindness.

R. The Archangel Michael, to whose care God had entrusted the souls of the blessed, came with a multitude of Angels, * To lead them to the joys

of Paradise. V. From heaven, O Lord, send forth
Thy Holy Spirit: the Spirit of wisdom and of
understanding. To lead. Glory. To lead.

III Nocturn

The reading of the holy Gospel
according to St. Matthew

At that time: The disciples came to Jesus, saying: Who, thinkest Thou, is the greater in the
kingdom of heaven. And so forth.

Homily of St. Jerome, Priest

After the finding of the stater, after the paying
of the tribute, what does this sudden question of
the Apostle mean? Who, thinkest Thou, is the
greater in the kingdom of heaven? Because they
had seen the same tribute paid for Peter and the
Lord, they concluded from the equality of the payment that Peter, who was placed upon the same
footing with the Lord in the paying of the tribute,
was preferred above all the Apostles; and so they
ask who is the greater in the kingdom of heaven.
And Jesus, seeing their thoughts and perceiving the
causes of the error, wishes to correct the desire of
glory by the contrast of humility.

And if thy hand or thy foot scandalize thee, cut
it off, and cast it from thee. For it must needs
be that scandals come, but woe to that man who, by
his own sins, makes himself the cause of that which
must necessarily be in the world. Therefore, let

every affection and every intimacy be cut off, lest, by the opportunity of affection, even one of the believers should be open to scandals.

If, He says, it is the case that anyone is so closely united to thee as hand, or foot, or eye, and is useful and careful and of acute perception, but scandalizes thee and by his contrary way of life drags thee down to hell, it is better for thee to be without his friendship and worldly advantages, lest, while thou art desiring to gain thy relatives and friends, thou findest an occasion of ruin.

I say to you that their Angels in heaven always see the face of My Father. He had said before that the hand, foot, and eye, that is, all relationships and friendships, which could be a cause of scandal, must be cut off; but He now modifies the austerity of the sentence by adding a commandment, saying: See that you despise not one of these little ones. I so command severity, He says, as teaching that it must be united with mercy. For their Angels in heaven always see the face of the Father. Great is the dignity of souls, that each should have from the hour of its birth an Angel deputed to guard it. Hence we read in the Apocalypse of St. John: Unto the Angel of Ephesus and of the other churches, write these things. And the Apostle Paul also orders women to be veiled in the churches because of the Angels.

R. The Archangel Michael came to the help of God's people: * He stood to defend the souls of the just. V. The Angel stood at the altar of the temple having a golden censer in his hand. He stood. Glory. He stood.

✠ Continuation of the holy Gospel according to St. Matthew.—At that time: The disciples came to Jesus, saying: Who, thinkest Thou, is the greater in the kingdom of heaven? and Jesus, calling unto Him a little child, set him in the midst of them, and said: Amen, I say to you, unless you be converted and become as little children, you shall not enter into the kingdom of heaven. Whosoever, therefore, shall humble himself as this little child, he is the greater in the kingdom of heaven: and he that shall receive one such little child in My name receiveth Me; but he that shall scandalize one of these little ones that believe In Me, it were better for him that a mill-stone should be hanged about his neck, and that he should be drowned in the depth of the sea. Woe to the world because of scandals; for it must needs be that scandals come; but nevertheless, woe to that man by whom the scandal cometh. And if thy hand or thy foot scandalize thee, cut it off and cast it from thee. It is better for thee to go into life maimed or lame, than having two hands or two feet to be cast into everlasting fire. And if thy eye scandalize thee, pluck it out and cast it from thee. It is better for thee having one eye to enter into life, than having two eyes to be cast into hell fire. See that you despise not one of these little ones; for I say to you, that their Angels in heaven always see the face of My Father, who is in heaven.

LET US PRAY

O God, who dost wonderfully arrange the duties of both Angels and men; mercifully grant that our life here upon earth may be protected by those who always serve Thee in heaven. Through our Lord.

October 2
THE HOLY GUARDIAN ANGELS
I Nocturn

From the Book of Exodus, c. 23, 20 - 23 and from Zacharias the Prophet, c. 1, 7 - 11 and 13 - 16; c. 2, 1 - 5

II Nocturn
Sermon of St. Bernard, Abbot

He hath given His angels charge over thee. A marvelous condescension, and a high expression of affection. For who hath given the charge? Unto whom? Over whom? And what charge? Let us attentively consider, brethren, let us carefully bear in mind this great charge. For who hath given the charge? To whom do the Angels belong? Whose commands do they obey? Whose will do they serve? For indeed, He hath given His Angels charge over thee, to keep thee in all thy ways. Nor are they remiss, for they even bear thee up in their hands.

It is the Highest Majesty, therefore, that gives this charge unto the Angels, and even to His own Angels. Unto these beings, so lofty, so blessed, set so near to Himself, yea, even of His own household, He hath given charge over thee. Who art thou? What is man, that Thou art mindful of him? or the son of man that Thou visitest him? Even as though man were not rottenness and the son of man a worm? But what charge, thinkest thou, has He given over thee? To keep thee.

How mightly should these words work in thee to induce reverence, to produce devotion, to conduce to confidence! Reverence for their presence, devotion for their kindness, confidence in their guardianship. Walk carefully, as one with whom are Angels, who have been given charge to keep thee in all thy ways. In every lodging, in every nook, have reverence for thine Angel. Dare not to do in his presence what thou wouldst not dare to do in mine. And dost thou doubt that he is present because thou dost not see him? What if thou didst hear him? What if thou didst touch him? What if thou didst perceive him by the sense of smell? For observe that not by sight alone is the presence of things attested.

Then let us, brethren, dearly love His angels as those with whom we shall some day be co-heirs, and who in the meantime are tutors and guardians appointed and set over us by the Father. With such powerful guardians what have we to fear? They who keep us in all our ways cannot be overcome or led away, much less can they lead us away. They are trusty, they are prudent, they are mighty; of what shall we be afraid? Only let us follow them and cleave to them, and we shall abide under the protection of the God of heaven. As often, then, as thou dost perceive that a very heavy trial presseth heavily upon thee and the violence of tribulation hangs over thee, call upon him who guards thee, who guides thee, thy helper in time of trouble and tribulation: invoke him and say: Lord, save us, we perish.

R. In all their affliction He was not troubled; * And the Angel of His presence saved them. V. In His love and in His mercy He redeemed them, and He carried them and lifted them up all the days of old. And the Angel. Glory. And the Angel.

III Nocturn
The reading of the holy Gospel
according to St. Matthew

At that time: The disciples came to Jesus, saying: Who, thinkest Thou, is the greater in the kingdom of heaven? And so forth.

Homily of St. Hilary, Bishop

The Lord teaches that only those who have returned to the nature of children shall enter into the

kingdom of heaven; that is, through childlike simplicity the vices of our body and soul are to be
done away with. To all who believe in that faith
which cometh by hearing He gave the name of
children. For these follow their father, they love
their mother, they know not how to wish evil to
their neighbor, they care nothing about riches;
they are not haughty, they do not hate, they do not
lie, they believe what is said, and what they hear
they hold for true.

Therefore we must return to the simplicity of
babes; because if we are established in that simplicity, we shall bear about with us an image of the
Lord's humility. Woe to this world because of
scandals. The abasement of the Passion is a scandal to the world. For in this most of all is the
ignorance of man held fast, that because of the disgrace of the Cross it would not receive the Lord of
eternal glory. And what is so dangerous to the
world as not to have accepted Christ.

Therefore indeed did He say it must needs be
that scandals come; because to accomplish the
mystery of giving back to us eternal life, all the
abasement of the Passion must be made complete
in Him. See that you despise not one of these
little ones that believe in Me. A most fitting bond
of mutual love did He impose especially upon those
who had truly believed in the Lord. For the Angels

of these little ones daily see God because the Son of man came to save that which was lost.

Therefore the Son of man saves, the Angels of the little ones see God, and preside over the prayers of the faithful. For Angels to be over anything means absolute authority. The Angels, then, daily offer to God the prayers of those who are saved through Christ. Therefore it is dangerous to despise him whose desires and entreaties are carried to the eternal and invisible God by the attentive service and ministry of Angels.

R. In the sight of the Angels * I will sing unto Thee, O my God. V. I will worship towards Thy holy temple and give glory unto Thy name. I will sing. Glory. I will sing.

Gospel as on the Feast of the Dedication of St. Michael, page 843

LET US PRAY

O God, who in Thy wonderful providence deignest to send Thy holy Angels to protect us, grant that those who pray to Thee may be defended on earth by Thy Angels and rejoice for all eternity in their company. Through our Lord.

October 5
ST. PLACID
I Nocturn

From the Epistle of St. Paul the Apostle to the Romans, c. 8, 12 - 19 and 28 - 39

II Nocturn
Sermon of St. Augustine, Bishop

Whenever, dearly beloved brethren, we keep the feasts of the holy Martyrs, let us, through their intercession, hope so to obtain from the Lord good things in this life that, by imitating the Martyrs themselves, we may deserve gifts which endure forever. They who follow the example of the Martyrs are able to keep those holy Martyrs' feasts with sincerity.

For the feasts of the Martyrs are exhortations to martyrdom, that we may not be loath to imitate what we delight to honor. For we wish to rejoice with the Saints, but we do not wish to suffer tribulation with them in this world. And yet he who will not, as far as he is able, imitate the holy Martyrs, will never attain to their blessedness.

For thus the Apostle Paul preaches, saying: If we have been partakers of the sufferings, we shall also be of the consolations. And the Lord says in the Gospel: If the world hate you, know ye that it hath hated Me before you. He who will not endure hatred in company with the Head, thereby refuses to be in the body.

But someone will say: And who can follow in the footsteps of the blessed Martyrs? To this I reply that we can imitate, if we will, not only the Martyrs, but also, with the help of His grace, the Lord Himself. Hear not me, but the Lord Himself crying out to mankind: Learn of Me, because I am meek and humble of heart. Hear also the admonition of the Apostle Peter: Christ suffered for us, leaving us an example that we should follow His steps.

R. As gold in the furnace the Lord hath proved His chosen ones, and as a victim of a holocaust He hath received them; and in time there shall be respect had to them, * For grace and peace is to the elect of God. V. They that trust in Him, shall understand the truth: and they that are faithful in love shall rest in Him. For. Glory. For.

III Nocturn
The reading of the holy Gospel
according to St. John

At that time: Jesus said to His disciples: Amen, amen, I say unto you, unless the seed falling into the earth die, itself remaineth alone. And so forth.

Homily of St. Augustine, Bishop

Your faith recognizes the seed which falls into the earth, dies, and is multiplied. I say that your faith recognizes this seed because it dwells in your minds. What Christ has said concerning Himself applies also to the Christian. But evidently from

that seed which has died and was multiplied, many
seeds were scattered abroad over the earth. Moreover, we have the happiness of seeing, rejoicing,
and of being among the harvest which that scattered seed has yielded, if only we enjoy the grace
of being gathered into the barns. For not all the
grain in the field is to be gathered into the barns.
Indeed the rain is used for nourishment by all until
the wheat gets ripe. But not all that grew so well
is fit to be gathered, although it all grew in the
same field and was ripened by the same air.

But now comes the reaping time, and the separation of the wheat from the chaff. Just as the grain
is cleansed when thrown into the air, so let there
be a separation in our lives of the good from the
bad habits before the Eternal Reaper comes. Listen
to me, ye holy grains, for I do not doubt that you
are such; for if I doubt, neither shall I myself
be a grain; hear me therefore, listen to the Chief
Grain who speaks through me. You should not
love your lives in this world. If you have loved
them, love them no longer; so that by not loving
your lives you may serve Him better and love Him
more. He that loveth his life in this world shall
lose it. Thus speaks the Grain which has fallen
into the earth and died in order to be multiplied.
Hear Him, for He lieth not. What He admonishes
us to do, He Himself has done; what He has taught
by His commandments, He has surpassed by His

example. Christ did not love His earthly life, because for this very reason did He come, to give it up, to lay it down for us. And when He so willed, He took it up again.

Surely we all, dearest brethren, desire life and truth. Yet, where will we find them? Where shall we search for them? By whatever way we may go—although we can not attain to actual possession, but only have them in our mind by faith—yet we always stretch forward towards the Life and Truth. Now this is Christ. Do you want to know the way? I am the Way, He says. To whom do you want to go? I am the Truth and the Life. Behold, this is what the Martyrs loved, and this is why they despised present and transitory things. We need not wonder at their fortitude, because love conquers all pain. Therefore, following the footsteps of the Martyrs and our eyes intently fixed upon their Head, Christ, let us not fear this hard path if we truly desire to come to so great a good. He who has promised it cannot deceive us, for He is truth and fidelity itself.

Let us therefore show a clean conscience: Because of the words of Thy mouth, O Lord, I have kept on hard ways. Why do you fear hard ways, sufferings and trials? He Himself has trod them. Perhaps you reply: But He was God. The Apostles have trod them. You answer: But they were Apostles. Granted, but I reply: many men have trod them after them, and women also. Blush therefore. If you have passed through suffering in old age, fear not death, for you are already near to it. If you are young, many youths also, both boys and girls, who had hoped to live, have passed through it. How, then, does the way which so many have marked out for us still seem hard. Hence on this feast day I most earnestly admonish you not to celebrate the feasts of these Martyrs in vain. But what we celebrate in their feasts out of love, we must also strive to imitate and be like in faith and practice.

R. The souls of the just are in the hands of God, and the torments of death shall not touch them: In the eyes of the unwise they seemed to die: * But they are in peace. V. God tried them and found them worthy of Himself. But they. Glory. But they.

✠ Continuation of the holy Gospel according to St. John.—At that time: Jesus said to His disciples: Amen, amen I say to you, unless the grain of wheat falling into the ground die, itself remaineth alone. But if it die, it bringeth forth much fruit. He that loveth his life shall lose it; and he that hateth his life in this world, keepeth it unto life eternal. If any man minister to Me, let him follow Me; and where I am, there also shall My minister be. If any man minister to Me, him will My Father honor.

LET US PRAY

O almighty and eternal God, who dost make us glad by the many feasts of Thy Saints, grant that we may be protected by those Saints in whose memory we rejoice. Through our Lord.

October 7
THE MOST HOLY ROSARY
I Nocturn

From the Book of Ecclesiasticus, c. 24, 11 - 22 and 24 - 31

II Nocturn

While the Albigensian heresy impiously increased throughout the district of Toulouse and daily thrust its roots deeper, the holy Dominic, who had recently constructed the foundations of the Order of Preachers, became entirely intent on rooting up that heresy. That he might more successfully accomplish this, he besought with earnest prayers the help of the Blessed Virgin, whose dignity was shamelessly attacked by these errors, and to whom it is given to destroy all heresies throughout the world. By whom (as it has been recorded) he was admonished to proclaim the Rosary to the people as a singular protection against heresies and vices; it is remarkable with what great fervor of soul and with what happy results he carried out this duty enjoined upon him. Now the Rosary is a fixed form of prayer which we divide into fifteen decades of the Angelical salutation with the Lord's prayer inserted between each decade, and throughout at each one of them we reflect in pious meditation on a certain mystery of our Redemption. Therefore from that time this pious method of prayer began to be marvelously promoted and propagated by St. Dominic. The supreme Pontiffs in apostolic letters have from time to time affirmed that Dominic himself was its founder and its author.

Henceforth countless products have been spread abroad throughout the Christian world from this most salutary observance. Among which may well be reckoned that famous victory which the most holy Pontiff, Pius V, and the Christian princes whose zeal he had evoked obtained over the most powerful tyranny of the Turks at Lepanto. For as this victory was gained on the very day on which the Confraternities of the most holy Rosary throughout the world were offering the prayers appointed according to custom, there is no doubt that it was due to these prayers. Indeed, Gregory XIII also testified in favor of it; he proclaimed that, for so singular a blessing, perpetual thanks should be offered everywhere on earth to the Blessed Virgin under the title of the Rosary, and that in all churches in which there was an altar of the Rosary, its Office should be celebrated in perpetuity according to the rite of a greater double; other Pontiffs also have granted almost innumerable indulgences to those reciting the Rosary and to confraternities of that Rosary.

Clement XI, however, considering the fact that in 1716 a great victory over the innumerable forces of the Turks was gained in the kingdom of Hungary by Charles VI, emperor elect of the Romans, on that day on which the feast of the Dedication of our Lady of the Snow was celebrated, and that almost at the same time the Confraternity of the most holy Rosary was offering public and solemn prayer in the beautiful City of Rome, in which an immense concourse of people took part, and with great devotion poured forth fervent prayers to God for the overthrow of the Turks, and humbly implored the powerful intercession of the Virgin Mother of God for the help of the Christians; owing to all this, the Pope devoutly held the opinion that that victory, as also the relief a short time afterwards of the island of Corcyra which was being besieged by those same Turks, was to be ascribed to the intercession of that same Blessed Virgin.

Wherefore also, in order that the unceasing recollection of and thanksgiving for so extraordinary a favor should be conspicuous forever, he extended the feast of the most holy Rosary to the universal Church to be celebrated by the same rite. All these things Benedict XIII ordered to be inserted into the Roman Breviary. Moreover, Leo XIII, at a very disturbed period of the history of the Church when

for a long time a tempest of very pressing evils
had raged, vehemently exhorted the faithful in the
world by a succession of apostolic letters to the
frequent use of the Rosary of Mary, more especially
during the month of October, and also increased the
rank of the rite of the annual feast and added to the
Litany of Loreto the invocation: Queen of the most
holy Rosary; he also granted a proper Office for
the same feast to the universal Church. Let us,
therefore, ever honor the Most holy Mother of God
by this devotion which is so very acceptable to her;
that she, who so many times has been prevailed
upon by the prayers of Christ's faithful in the
Rosary to bring their earthly enemies to destruction and ruin, may likewise grant that they may
overcome the powers of hell.

R. A great sign appeared in heaven: a woman
clothed with the sun, and the moon under her feet,
* And on her head a crown of twelve stars. V. Increase of graces shall be given to thy head, and a
noble crown shall protect thee. And on. Glory.
And on.

III Nocturn
The reading of the holy Gospel
according to St. Luke

At that time: The angel Gabriel was sent from
God into a city of Galilee, called Nazareth, to a
virgin espoused to a man whose name was Joseph,

of the house of David; and the Virgin's name was
Mary. And so forth.

Homily of St. Bernard, Abbot

For the commending of His grace and the overthrow of human wisdom, God deigned to take flesh
from a woman and a virgin that He might give
back like to like, heal opposite by opposite, pluck
forth the deadly thorn, and most effectively blot out
the handwriting of sin.

Eve was a thorn; Mary showed herself a rose.
Eve was a thorn in wounding; Mary, a rose, in
soothing the affections of all. Eve was a thorn
fastening death upon all; Mary, a rose, giving
back to all the destiny of salvation. Mary was a
rose, white by virginity, ruddy by love; white in
flesh, ruddy in soul; white in seeking after virtue,
ruddy in trampling upon vice; white in purifying
her affection, ruddy in mortifying her flesh; white
in loving God, ruddy in pitying her neighbor.

The Word was made flesh, and now dwells among
us. He dwells in our memory, He dwells in our
thought, for He descends even as far as our imag-
ination itself. In what way, sayest thou? Truly,
lying in the crib, resting in the Virgin's lap, preaching on the mountain, passing the night in prayer,
hanging on the cross, growing pale in death, free
among the dead, and ruling in the nether world, as
also rising again on the third day, and showing the
Apostles the places of the nails, the signs of

victory; lastly, mounting in their presence to the mysteries of heaven. Which of these things may we not think on truly, lovingly, and holily?

Whichever of these I think on, I think on God; and throughout all things is my God. Meditating on these, I have called it wisdom; and, giving forth the memory of their sweetness, I have judged it prudence; for of such kernels the priestly rod brought forth an abundance, which Mary, drawing up into the highest, poured back more plentifully upon us. Clearly she is in the highest and beyond the Angels, she, who received the Word from the very heart of the Father.

R. Arise, make haste, my love; for winter is now past, the rain is over and gone; * The flowers have appeared in our land. V. The Lord will give goodness, and our earth shall yield her fruit. The flowers. Glory. The flowers.

✠ Continuation of the holy Gospel according to St. Luke.—At that time: The Angel Gabriel was sent from God into a city of Galilee, called Nazareth, to a Virgin espoused to a man whose name was Joseph, of the house of David; and the Virgin's name was Mary. And the Angel being come in, said unto her: Hail, full of grace, the Lord is with thee: blessed art thou among women. Who, having heard, was troubled at his saying and thought with herself what maner of salutation this should be. And the Angel of the Lord said to her:

Fear not, Mary, for thou hast found grace with God. Behold thou shalt conceive in thy womb and shalt bring forth a Son and thou shalt call His name Jesus. He shall be great and shall be called the Son of the Most High, and the Lord God shall give unto Him the throne of David His father: and He shall reign in the house of Jacob forever, and of His kingdom there shall be no end. And Mary said to the Angel: How shall this be done, because I know not man? And the Angel, answering, said to her: The Holy Ghost shall come upon thee and the power of the Most High shall overshadow thee. And therefore also the Holy which shall be born of thee shall be called the Son of God. And behold thy cousin Elizabeth, she also hath conceived a son in her old age; and this is the sixth month with her that is called barren: because no word shall be impossible with God. And Mary said: Behold the handmaid of the Lord, be it done to me according to thy word.

LET US PRAY

O God, whose only begotten Son has merited for us by His Life, Death and Resurrection the rewards of eternal life, grant we beseech Thee, that honoring these mysteries in the holy Rosary of the Blessed Virgin Mary, we may both imitate what they contain and receive what they promise. Through the same our Lord.

October 11
MATERNITY OF THE BLESSED VIRGIN
I Nocturn
From the Book of Ecclesiasticus, c. 24, 5 - 23
II Nocturn
Sermon of St. Leo, Pope

A royal Virgin of the race of David is chosen to be pregnant with the sacred progeny, and to conceive the divine and human Offspring first in mind, then in body; and lest in ignorance of the heavenly counsel she should tremble at so strange an utterance, she learned from converse with the Angel that what is to be wrought in her is of the Holy Ghost, and she did not believe it loss of honor that she was soon to be the Mother of God. For why should she be in despair over the novelty of such a conception since the power of the Most High had been promised to effect it? Her implicit faith is confirmed also by the attestation of a foregoing miracle. Elizabeth receives unexpected fecundity in order that there might be no doubt that He who had given conception to the barren would give it even to a Virgin. Therefore the Word of God, the Son, who was with God in the beginning, through whom all things were made and without whom nothing was made, in order to set man free from eternal death became man.

Jesus Christ our Lord enters these lower parts, coming down from the heavenly throne, and yet not quitting His Father's glory, begotten in a new order, by a new nativity. In a new order, because being invisible in His own nature, He becomes visible in ours; the incomprehensible willed to be comprehended; abiding before all time, He began to exist in time. And by a new birth He was begotten: conceived by a Virgin, born of a Virgin, without the concupiscence of a paternal body, without injury to the maternal chastity; since such an origin was seemly for the future Savior of men who should at the same time possess in Himself the substance of human nature and also be ignorant of the stain of human lust. The origin is unlike, but the nature is like; He is free, as we believe, from the use and wont of mankind; but by the power of God was it brought about that a Virgin conceived, a Virgin brought forth and a Virgin she remained.

From the Acts of Pope Pius XI

When in the year 1931, amid the applause of the whole Catholic world, solemn rites were celebrated at the completion of the fifteenth century after the blessed Virgin Mary, of whom Jesus was born, had, at the Council of Ephesus in opposition to the heresy of Nestorius, been acclaimed as the Mother of God by the Fathers under the leadership of Pope Celestine, the Supreme Pontiff Pius XI wished

by a lasting proof of his piety to perpetuate the
memory of this most auspicious event. He therefore by his own munificence caused to be tastefully
restored that noble monument of the proclamation
of Ephesus already existing in the City, the triumphal arch in the basilica of St. Mary Major on
the Esquiline Hill, which had been decorated by his
predecessor, Sixtus III, with mosaics of marvelous
workmanship, and which was falling to pieces with
the decay of ages, together with the transept of
that basilica.

Moreover, narrating the true history of the Ecumenical Council of Ephesus in an encyclical letter,
he expounded fully and faithfully the ineffable prerogative of the divine Motherhood of the blessed
Virgin Mary in such a way that the doctrine of this
lofty mystery might sink deeper into the hearts of
the faithful. In it he likewise sets forth Mary,
the Mother of God, blessed among all women, and
the family of Nazareth as the most noble example
above all others to be followed, as well for the dignity and holiness of chaste wedlock, as for the holy
education that should be given to youth. Finally,
in order that no liturgical memorial should be lacking, he ordered that a feast of the divine Motherhood of the blessed Virgin Mary, with a proper
Mass and Office, under the rite of a double of the
second class should every year on October 11, be
celebrated by the universal Church.

R.   Blessed art thou among women and blessed is the fruit of thy womb: * Whence is this to me that the Mother of my Lord should come to me? V. He hath regarded the lowliness of His handmaid, and He that is mighty hath done great things to me. Whence. Glory. Whence.

III Nocturn
The reading of the holy Gospel
according to St. Luke

At that time: When they returned, the Child Jesus remained in Jerusalem, and His parents knew it not. And so forth.

Homily of St. Bernard, Abbot

Mary calls God, the Lord of Angels, her Son when she says: Son, why hast Thou done so to us? Which of the Angels would dare this? It is enough for them, and they hold it a great honor, that being by nature spirits they are by grace made and called Angels, according to the words of David: He that maketh His Spirits Angels. Mary then, knowing that she was His mother, with confidence named as her Son Him whom those Angels serve with reverence; nor did God disdain to be called that which He had deigned to become. For a little further on the Evangelist adds: and He was subject to them. Who? To whom? God to man? God, I say, to whom the Angels are subject, whom the Principalities and Powers obey, was subject to Mary.

Wonder at which of the two you please, and choose the one you admire the more, either the most kindly condescension of the Son, or the most sublime worthiness of the Mother. In both cases there is amazement, in both a marvel. That God should obey a woman shows an unprecedented humility; and that a woman should rule God, a peerless exaltation. In praise of virgins is it especially sung that they follow the Lamb whithersoever He goeth. Of what praises then, do you think, must she be worthy who even leadeth the Lamb? Learn, O man, to obey; learn, O earth, to be subject; learn, O dust, to comply. The Evangelist, speaking of thy Creator, says: And He was subject to them. Blush, O proud ashes: God humbleth Himself and dost thou exalt thyself? God submitted Himself to men, and dost thou, striving to domineer over men, set thyself before thy Creator?

Happy Mary, who lacked neither humility nor virginity; and truly so singular a virginity, which feared not fruitfulness, but honored it. And none the less remarkable humility, which was made illustrious, rather than detracted from, by that fruitful virginity; and an altogether incomparable fecundity, which was accompanied by both virginity and humility. Which of these is not a marvel? Which not incomparable? Which not singular? Indeed, the wonder is if thou dost not hesitate, when weighing these things, as to which thou deemest the more

worthy of wonder; namely, to wonder the more
at the fruitfulness of the Virgin, or at the virginity of the Mother; the sublimity of the Offspring,
or the humility accompanying that great sublimity;
save that all those things together are undoubtedly
to be preferred to any one of them singly, and it is
incomparably more preferable and more auspicious
to have received all of them than only a few.

And why is it astonishing if God, concerning
whom it is seen and read that He is wonderful in
His Saints, should show Himself still more wonderful in His Mother? Therefore, ye married folk,
revere this integrity of the flesh in corruptible
flesh; and you, holy virgins, revere fecundity in
the Virgin. All men, imitate ye the humility of the
Mother of God.

R. Blessed art thou, O Virgin Mary, Mother of
God, who hast believed the Lord: those things were
accomplished in thee that were spoken to thee *
Therefore hath God blessed thee forever. V. Grace
is poured forth on thy lips: intercede for us with
the Lord our God. Therefore. Glory. Therefore.

✠ Continuation of the holy Gospel according to
St. Luke.—At that time: When they returned, the
Child Jesus remained in Jerusalem, and His parents
knew it not. And thinking that He was in the company, they came a day's journey, and sought Him
among His kinsfolk and acquaintance. And not
finding Him, they returned into Jerusalem, seeking

Him. And it came to pass that after three days they found Him in the Temple, sitting in the midst of the doctors, hearing them, and asking them questions. And all that heard Him were astonished at His wisdom and His answers. And seeing Him, they wondered. And His mother said to Him: Son, why hast Thou done so to us? Behold Thy father and I have sought Thee sorrowing. And He said to them: How is it that you sought Me? Did you not know that I must be about My Father's business? And they understood not the word that He spoke unto them. And He went down with them and came to Nazareth, and was subject to them.

LET US PRAY

O God, who hath willed that Thy Word should become Man in the womb of the Virgin Mary at the message of an Angel, grant that Thy servants who truly believe she is the Mother of God may be aided by her intercession with Thee. Through our Lord.

October 18
ST. LUKE THE EVANGELIST
I Nocturn

From the Book of Ezechiel the Prophet, c. 1, 1 - 13
II Nocturn

From the Book of St. Jerome, Priest, on Ecclesiastical Writers

Luke, a physician of Antioch, as is shown by his writings, and skilled in the Greek tongue, was a

follower of the Apostle Paul and accompanied him
in all his journeys. He wrote a Gospel whereof the
same Paul says: We have sent with him the brother whose praise is in the Gospel through all the
churches. And to the Colossians: Luke, the most
dear physician, saluteth you. And to Timothy:
Only Luke is with me.

He also put forth another excellent volume whose
title, *Acts of the Apostles*, is already known;
wherein the history is brought down as far as
Paul's sojourn of two years at Rome, that is, to the
fourth year of Nero. From this we infer that the
book was compiled in that same city. Consequently, we class the journeys of Paul and Thecla and the
whole fable of the baptized Leo among the apocryphal writings. For is it possible that the Apostle's
inseparable companion should know everything concerning him except this one thing?

Moreover, Tertullian, who lived near to those
times, relates that a certain priest in Asia, an ad-
mirer of the Apostle Paul, was clearly proved by
John to have been the author of that book, which he
confessed he had done out of love for Paul, and was
on that account deprived of his position. Some are
of the opinion that whenever Paul in his epistles
says: According to my Gospel; he means that of
Luke.

Luke, however, was instructed in the Gospel not
only by the Apostle Paul, who had never been with

the Lord in the flesh, but also by the other Apostles; this he himself also declares in the beginning of his work, saying: According as they have delivered them unto us, who from the beginning were eye-witnesses and ministers of the Word.   He wrote a Gospel, then, from what he had heard; ~~but he com-piled the Acts of the Apostles from what he had heard~~; but he compiled the Acts of the Apostles from what he had himself seen.   He lived eighty-four years and was never married.   He was buried at Constantinople, to which city his bones were translated from Achaia, together with the relics of Andrew the Apostle, in the twentieth year of Constantine.

R.   I saw men standing together, clad in shining garments;   and the Angel of the Lord spoke to me, saying: * These holy men became the friends of God.   V.   I saw a mighty Angel of God, flying through the midst of heaven, crying out with a loud voice and saying. These holy men. Glory. These holy men.

III Nocturn
The reading of the holy Gospel according to St. Luke

At that time: The Lord appointed also other seventy-two; and He sent them two and two before His face into every city and place whither He Himself was to come.   And so forth.

Homily of St. Gregory, Pope

Our Lord and Savior, dearest brethren, admonishes us at one time by His words, at another time by His works. For His very deeds are precepts; for though He utters no word, He shows us clearly what we ought to do. Behold, He sends His disciples forth to preach, two by two; for the precepts of charity are two, namely, the love of God, and the love of our neighbor; for love cannot be said to exist at all unless there be two parties.

No one can properly be said to have charity towards himself; for the name of charity can be applied only to love which tends outward to another. Behold, the Lord sends forth His disciples to preach, two by two; and in so doing teaches us, without any need of words, that he who has not charity towards his neighbor ought by no means to undertake the office of preaching.

It is rightly said that He sent them before His face into every city and place whither He Himself was to come. For the Lord follows His preachers. First comes preaching and afterwards the Lord comes to the dwelling-place of our soul; the words of exhortation go before, and by them truth is taken into the mind.

Hence therefore Isaias says to the same preachers: Prepare ye the way of the Lord, make straight the paths of our God. Hence the Psalmist cries to his children: Make a way for Him who ascend-

eth upon the west. The Lord does indeed ascend
upon the west; for whereas he set, as it were, in
His Passion, on the other hand He rose with
greater glory in His Resurrection. He ascends
upon the west evidently in that, by rising from the
dead, He tramples upon the death which He had
suffered. So we make a way for Him who ascends
upon the west when we set forth His glory before
the eyes of your minds in order that He, following
after us, may enlighten you by the presence of His
love.

R. These are the holy men whom the Lord hath
chosen in charity unfeigned, and hath given them
everlasting glory: * Whose teaching enlightens
the Church, as the moon by the sun. V. By faith
the Saints conquered kingdoms and wrought justice. Whose. Glory. Whose.

✠ Continuation of the holy Gospel according to
St. Luke.—At that time: The Lord appointed also
other seventy-two; and He sent them two and two
before His face into every city and place whither
He Himself was to come. And He said to them:
The harvest indeed is great, but the laborers are
few: pray ye therefore the Lord of the harvest,
that He send laborers into His harvest. Go, behold
I send you as lambs among wolves. Carry neither
purse, nor scrip, nor shoes; and salute no man by
the way. Into whatsoever house you enter, first
say: Peace be to this house, and if the son of peace

be there, your peace shall rest upon him; but if not, it shall return to you. And in the same house remain, eating and drinking such things as they have: for the laborer is worthy of his hire. Remove not from house to house. And into what city soever you enter, and they reecive you, eat such things as are set before you, and heal the sick that are therein, and say to them: The kingdom of God is come nigh unto you.

LET US PRAY

We beseech Thee, O Lord, may blessed Luke Thy Evangelist, intercede for us, who, for the honor of Thy name, always bore the sufferings of the Cross in his own body. Through our Lord.

Last Sunday of October
FEAST OF OUR LORD JESUS CHRIST THE KING

I Nocturn

From the Epistle of blessed Paul the Apostle to the Colossians, c. 1, 3 - 23

II Nocturn

From the Encyclical Letter of Pope Pius XI

Since the Holy Year has provided more than one opportunity to enhance the glory of the kingdom of Christ, we deem it to be in the highest degree in, keeping with our Apostolic office to accede to the prayers of many Cardinals, Bishops and faithful, made known to Us both individually and collective-

ly, by closing this very year with the insertion into
the ecclesiastical liturgy of a special feast of Our
Lord Jesus Christ the King. It has long been a
common custom to give to Christ the metaphorical
title of King, because of the high degree of perfection whereby He excels and surpasses all created
beings. For as it is the case that He is said to
reign "in the hearts of men," not so much by reason
of the keenness of His intellect and the extent of
His knowledge, as that He Himself is the Truth;
so it is from Him that truth must be drawn and
obediently received by all mankind. He reigns,
likewise, "in the wills of men," since not only does
the integrity and the obedience of the human will
accord exactly and precisely with the holiness of the
divine will in Him, but also by His grace and inspiration, He substitutes this for our free will,
whereby we may be enkindled to every noblest deed.
In a word, Christ is acknowledged as the "King of
Hearts" on account of His "charity which sur-
passeth understanding," and of His mercy and kindness which draw unto Him the souls of men; for
never has it happened that anyone has been loved as
much at any time as Christ Jesus is loved by so
many different races, or will it happen in time to
come that anyone shall be so loved.

But, if we ponder this matter more deeply, we
cannot but see that the title and the power of a
King is rightly claimed for Christ as man in the
strict and proper sense of the word. For only in

so far as He is man can He be said to have received
"the power and the glory and the kingdom" from
the Father, seeing that the Word of God, which is
of the same substance as the Father, cannot fail to
have all things in common with the Father, and
therefore has in Itself the highest and most absolute dominion over all things created. And the
source from which the power and dignity of our
Lord is established Cyril of Alexandria fittingly
indicates: "He possesses dominion, if I may use
the word, over all creatures, a dominion not seized
by violence nor usurped from anyone, but His by
essence and by nature"; it is evident that His dominion is gloriously manifested in that marvelous
union which is called hypostatic.

From this it follows, not only that Christ is to be
adored as God by Angels and by men, but also that
Angels and men are obedient and subject to His
dominion as Man; indeed, that even by the doctrine of the hypostatic union alone, Christ possesses
power over all created things. And now, that we
may in a few words explain the import and the
nature of His headship, it is hardly necessary to
say that it consists in a threefold power; if this
power were lacking, the headship could scarcely be
discerned. The testimonies deduced from and announced by the sacred Scriptures concerning the
universal dominion of our Redeemer make that very
thing more than clear enough, and it is an article

of the Catholic faith that Christ Jesus was given
to mankind especially as a Redeemer for those who
put their faith in Him, but at the same time as a
Lawgiver for those who obey Him. And not only
do the Gospels relate that He established laws, but
they exhibit Him in the very act of establishing
laws; and truly, whosoever shall keep these commandments, they indeed are said by the divine
Master, in other passages and in other words, to
demonstrate their love for Him and to remain in
His love. But Jesus Himself announces the judi-
ciary power assigned to Him by the Father, when
accused by the Jews of having broken the Sabbath
day of rest, by the miraculous cure of a sick man:
"For neither doth the Father judge any man, but
hath given all judgment to the Son." And therein
it is understood (because the case is inseparable
from the judgment) that by His law He may confer
rewards and punishments upon men still living.
But moreover, that power which is called executive
power is also to be attributed to Christ, seeing
that it is necessary that all men obey His rule, and,
indeed, it is made clear to the refractory by the
imposition of penalties which no man can escape.

But, nevertheless, a kingdom of this nature, in
a certain special manner, is both a spiritual one and
also pertains to spiritual things, as these words
which we have quoted above from the Bible most
distinctly indicate, and moreover, as Christ the

Lord affirms by reason of His own actions. Inasmuch as on more than one occasion when the Jews, yea, when even the Apostles themselves, erroneously imagined that it was imminent that the Messias would set the people at liberty and would restore the Kingdom of Israel, He Himself both dispelled and destroyed this fond hope. Disclaiming the title of King from an encompassing multitude of admirers, He refused both the name and the honor by fleeing from them and by lying hid. In the presence of the Roman governor, He declared that His Kingdom "is not of this world." It is such a Kingdom indeed that is represented in the gospels, into which men prepare to enter by doing penance; but they cannot enter except by faith and by baptism, which, although it is an external rite, nevertheless denotes and produces an interior regeneration; it is opposed in a very special manner to the kingdom of Satan and to the powers of darkness, and it demands from its followers not only that, with their souls detached from riches and from worldly affairs, they display mildness of character and hunger and thirst after justice, but also that they deny themselves and take up their cross. But since Christ as Redeemer has both purchased the Church with His own Blood, and as Priest offered His very self as a sacrifice for sin, and so offers Himself in perpetuity, is it not evident to all that His kingly office assumes and participates in the nature of both the one and the other office? On the other hand, one errs in a most unseemly manner if he takes away from Christ as man all authority over any kind of civil affairs whatever, since He obtains from the Father such a highly absolute jurisdiction over created things that all things are placed under His power. Therefore, by Our apostolic authority, we appoint the feast of Our Lord Jesus Christ the King to be annually observed everywhere in the world on the last Lord's day in the month of October, that is, on the Sunday which immediately precedes the Feast of All Saints. Likewise we enjoin that the dedication of the human race to the most Sacred Heart of Jesus be annually renewed upon that selfsame day.

R. He must reign, for God hath put all things under His feet: * That God may be all in all. V. When all things shall be subdued unto Him, then the Son Himself shall also be subject unto the Father. That God. Glory. That God.

III Nocturn
The reading of the holy Gospel
according to St. John
At that time: Pilate said to Jesus? Art Thou the King of the Jews? Jesus answered: Sayest thou this thing of thyself, or have others told it thee of Me? And so forth.

Homily of St. Augustine, Bishop
What great thing was it for the King of ages to become the King of men? For Christ was not King

of Israel to exact tribute, or to arm a body of men with the sword, or to subdue visible foes; but King of Israel that He might rule souls, and counsel them regarding eternity; that He might lead to the kingdom of heaven such as believe in Him, hope in Him, and love Him. Accordingly, that the Son of God, equal with the Father, the Word by whom all things were made, should wish to be the King of Israel was a condescension on His part, and no advancement for Himself; it betokened His mercy, it did not increase His power. For He who on earth was called King of the Jews, is, in heaven, Lord of the Angels. But is Christ King of the Jews only, or also of the Gentiles? Yea, also of the Gentiles. For when He said in prophecy: But I am appointed by Him King over Sion, His holy mountain, preaching the commandment of the Lord; lest anyone should say, on account of mount Sion, that He was appointed King of the Jews alone, He immediately added: The Lord hath said to Me: Thou art My Son, this day have I begotten Thee; ask of Me, and I will give Thee the Gentiles for Thy inheritance, and the utmost parts of the earth for Thy possession.

Jesus answered: My kingdom is not of this world. If My kingdom were of this world, My servants would certainly strive that I should not be delivered to the Jews; but now My kingdom is not from hence. This is what the good Master would have us know; but first it had to be shown us how vain was that notion concerning His kingdom that was current among men, whether Gentiles or Jews, from whom Pilate had heard this; as if He ought to have been punished with death on the grounds of aspiring to an unlawful kingdom; or because reigning monarchs are wont to be jealous of those likely to reign; or as if, for example, there was need to beware lest His kingdom should be adverse either to the Romans or the Jews.

The Lord could indeed have answered: My kingdom is not of this world, to the first question put to Him by the governor, when he said: Art Thou the King of the Jews? But He, asking in His turn whether he (Pilate) said this of himself, or if he had heard it from others, wished to show by Pilate's answer that He had been charged with this as a crime by the Jews; thus laying open to us the thought of men, which He knows that they are vain; and to them, after Pilate's reply, He answers now more fittingly and more opportunely for both Jews and Gentiles; My kingdom is not of this world.

The twelfth lesson is taken from the last paragraph of the Homily of the occurring Sunday

R. The kingdom of this world is become the kingdom of our Lord and of His Christ: * And He shall reign forever and ever. V. All the kindreds of the Gentiles shall adore in His sight; for the kingdom is the Lords. And He shall reign. Glory. And He shall reign.

✠ Continuation of the holy Gospel according to St. John.—At that time: Pilate said to Jesus: Art Thou the King of the Jews? Jesus answered: Sayest thou this thing of thyself, or have others told it thee of Me? Pilate answered: Am I a Jew? Thine own nation and the chief priests have delivered Thee up to me; what hast Thou done? Jesus answered: My kingdom is not of this world. If My kingdom were of this world, My servants would certainly strive that I should not be delivered to the Jews; but now My kingdom is not from hence. Pilate therefore said to Him: Art Thou a King then? Jesus answered: Thou sayest that I am a King. For this was I born, and for this came I into the world, that I should give testimony to the truth. Everyone that is of the truth, heareth My voice.

LET US PRAY

O almighty and eternal God, who hast willed to re-establish all things in Thy beloved Son, the King of all; mercifully grant, that all the families of the nations, torn away by the wound of sin, may be subjected to His gentle rule; Who liveth and reigneth with Thee.

October 27
VIGIL OF SS. SIMON AND JUDE
The reading of the holy Gospel according to St. John

At that time: Jesus said to His disciples: I am the true vine; and My Father is the husbandman. And so forth.

Homily of St. Augustine, Bishop

This passage of the Gospel, brethren, where the Lord says that He is the vine and His disciples are the branches, speaks of Him according as He is the Head of the Church, and we His members; He is the mediator between God and men, the man Christ Jesus. For a vine and its branches are of one nature. And therefore, since He was God, of whose nature we are not, He was made man that in Him might be found the vine of human nature, whereof it might be possible that we men should be the branches.

What, then, does this mean: I am the true vine? Surely when He adds the word true, He does not refer to a real vine, from which He has taken this figure? For the word vine is used by similitude, not in its actual sense; as elsewhere He is called a sheep, a lamb, a lion, a rock, the cornerstone, and other things of a like kind; which are themselves rather the true ones, from which these are drawn as similitudes, not as realities.

I am the true vine; He distinguishes Himself from that other vine, of which it is said: How art thou turned into bitterness, O strange vine? For how can that vine be true which, when one looked that it should bring forth grapes, brought forth thorns? I am the true vine, He says, and My Father is the husbandman. Every branch in Me that beareth not fruit, He will take away; and everyone that beareth fruit, He will purge it, that it may bring forth more fruit.

October 28
SS. SIMON AND JUDE, APOSTLES
I Nocturn
From the Catholic Epistle of blessed Jude the Apostle c. 1, 1 - 13
II Nocturn

Simon, who is also called Zelotes, was a Chanaanite; and Thaddeus, also called Jude, the brother of James in the Gospel, was the writer of one of the Catholic Epistles; Simon went through Egypt preaching the Gospel, and Thaddeus did the same in Mesopotamia. They afterwards met together in Persia, where they begot countless children in Jesus Christ, and propagated the faith in those far-spreading countries among barbarous peoples by their teaching and miracles; and finally, by a glorious martyrdom, they together rendered honor to the most holy name of Jesus Christ.

Sermon of St. Gregory, Pope

It is written: The spirit of the Lord hath adorned the heavens. For the ornaments of the heavens are the virtues of preachers. Which ornaments are thus enumerated by Paul in the words: To one, by the Spirit is given the word of wisdom; to another, the word of knowledge, according to the same Spirit; to another, faith in the same Spirit; to another, the grace of healing in one Spirit; to another, the working of miracles; to another, prophecy; to another, the discerning of spirits; to another, diverse kinds of tongues; to another, interpretation of speeches. But all these things one and the same Spirit worketh, dividing to everyone according as He will.

The heavens, therefore, have as many ornaments as preachers have virtues. Wherefore, it is also written: By the word of the Lord the heavens were established. For the Word of the Lord is the Son of the Father. But that we may know that these heavens, that is, the holy Apostles, at the same time display the work of the whole Trinity, there is added at once, in reference to the divinity of the Holy Ghost: And all the power of them by the Spirit of His mouth. Therefore the power of the heavens is taken from the Holy Ghost; for they would not have dared to withstand the powers of this world if the Holy Ghost had not confirmed them with His fortitude.

We know what these Doctors of the holy Church were before the coming of the Spirit, and we see how they were endowed with that fortitude after He had descended upon them. Indeed, this very shepherd of the Church near whose most holy remains we are assembled displayed such great weakness and such great timidity, as we may learn if we ask the serving-maid who kept the door. For he was so stricken with terror at the mere voice of a woman that, in fear of death, he denied the Life.

R. These are the conquerors and the friends of God, who, despising the orders of princes, merited an everlasting reward: * Now they are crowned, and they receive the palm. V. These are they who have come out of great tribulation, and have washed their robes in the Blood of the Lamb. Now. Glory. Now.

III Nocturn
The reading of the holy Gospel according to St. John

At that time: Jesus said to His disciples: These things I command you, that you love one another. If the world hate you know ye that it hath hated Me before you. And so forth.

Homily of St. Augustine, Bishop

In the Gospel lesson which precedes this one the Lord had said: You have not chosen Me: but I have chosen you, and have appointed you that you should go and should bring forth fruit, and your fruit should remain; that whatsoever you shall ask of the Father in My name, He may give it you. But here He saith: These things I command you, that you love one another. And by this we are to understand that this is our fruit, of which He saith: I have chosen you, that you should go and should bring forth fruit, and your fruit should remain.

And whereas He adds: That whatsoever you shall ask of the Father in My name, He may give it to you; it means that He will assuredly give it to us, if we love one another; for this very thing He has given us, in choosing us when we had no fruit, because we had not chosen Him; and in appointing us, that we should bring forth fruit, that is, that we should love one another. Our fruit, therefore, is charity, which the Apostle defines to be: From a pure heart, and a good conscience, and an unfeigned faith. By this we love one another. By this we love God. For we cannot love one another with a true love unless we love God. For if one love God, he also loves his neighbor as himself. Since if he does not love God, he does not love himself; for on these two comandments of charity depend the whole law and the prophets. This is our fruit.

Therefore giving us commandments as to the fruit, He says: These things I command you, that you love one another. In the same way the Apostle Paul when, in contrast to the works of the flesh, he would commend the works of the spirit, put this as the head: The fruit of the spirit, he says, is charity; and then he wove the others together, as if they were springing from that head and bound up in it, namely, joy, peace, longanimity, benignity, goodness, faith, mildness, continency, chastity.

Who, indeed, rejoices aright that loves not the good whereof he rejoices? Who can have true peace, unless with him whom he truly loves? Who is long-suffering in perseveringly continuing in good, unless he be fervent in love? Who is benign, unless he loves the one he is aiding? Who is good, except he be made so by loving? Who is sound in the faith, without that faith which works by love? Who can be mild to any purpose, if he is not guided by love? Who is continent from that which is ignoble, except he love that which ennobles? With good reason, therefore, does the good Master so often insist upon love, as though it alone needed to be enjoined, as the boon without which other good things cannot profit, and which one cannot have without bringing the other good things by which a man is made truly good.

R. Blessed are ye when men shall revile and persecute you, and speak all that is evil against you, untruly, for My sake: * Be glad and rejoice for your reward is very grcat in heaven. V. When men shall hate you, and when they shall separate you, and shall reproach you, and cast out your name as evil, for the Son of man's sake. Be glad. Glory. Be glad.

✠ Continuation of the holy Gospel according to St. John.—At that time: Jesus said to His disciples: These things I command you, that you love one another. If the world hate you, know ye that it hath hated Me before you. If you had been of the world, the world would love its own: but because you are not of the world, but I have chosen you out of the world, therefore the world hateth you. Remember My word that I said to you: The servant is not greater than his Master. If they have persecuted Me, they will also persecute you: If they have kept My word, they will keep yours also. But all these things they will do to you for My name's sake, because they know not Him that sent Me. If I had not come and spoken to them, they would not have sin; but now they have no excuse for their sin. He that hateth Me, hateth My Father also. If I had not done among them the works that no other man hath done, they would not have sin; but now they have both seen and hated both Me and My Father. But that the word may be fulfilled which is written in their law: They hated Me without cause.

Let Us Pray

O God, who didst bring us to a knowledge of Thy name by Thy blessed Apostles Simon and Jude, grant us to celebrate their eternal glory by increasing in virtue, and by celebrating this feast to really increase in virtue. Through our Lord.

October 31
VIGIL OF ALL SAINTS
The reading of the holy Gospel according to St. Luke

At that time: Jesus, coming down from the mountain, stood in a plain place, and the company of His disciples, and a very great multitude of people from all Judea and Jerusalem, and the sea coast, both of Tyre and Sidon. And so forth.

Homily of St. Ambrose, Bishop

Mark well all things, how Jesus ascends with His Apostles, but descends unto the multitude. For how could the multitude behold Christ unless He come to a lower place? They do not follow Him aloft, they cannot rise to great heights. And thus, in coming down, He finds the weakly ones, since because of their infirmity they cannot attain the heights.

Matthew also tells us that the sick are healed in a lower place. For each one must first be healed that, little by little, as he gains in strength, he may climb the mountains; and He heals them in that lower place; that is, He recalls them from lust, He delivers them from blindness. He comes down to our wounds that, imparting to us some of the riches of His own nature, He may make us partakers with Him in the kingdom of heaven.

In the eyes of the foolish
the saints seem to die, but
they are in peace. Their
bodies are buried in peace
and they live forever.

Blessed are ye poor, for yours is the kingdom of God. St. Luke mentions only four of the Lord's beatitudes, while St. Matthew has eight; yet the four are included in the eight, and the eight in the four. The four may be taken as embracing the cardinal virtues; the number eight in itself contains a mystery. Many of the Psalms bear as a title: For the octave; and when thou art commanded to give a portion to eight, perhaps this may signify the beatitudes. For as the eight beatitudes are the perfection of our hope, so also are they the sum of all virtues.

November 1
FEAST OF ALL SAINTS
I Nocturn

From the Book of the Apocalypse of blessed John the Apostle, c. 4, 2 - 8; c. 5, 1 - 14

II Nocturn
Sermon of St. Bede the Venerable, Priest

Today, dearly beloved, we celebrate the feast of all the Saints with one solemn rejoicing; in whose fellowship heaven is glad, in whose patronage the earth rejoices, with whose triumphs holy Church is crowned. Whose confession is the more glorious in honor as their agony was the more intense; since, as the fight grew fiercer, it increased the glory of those who fought, and their manifold sufferings adorned the triumph of their martyrdom; for the greater the torments, the greater were the rewards.

While our Mother, the Catholic Church, spread far and wide throughout the whole world, has been taught in Christ Jesus, Her Head, not to fear shame, nor cross, nor death, having become stronger and stronger, not by resisting, but by enduring, she has inspired all those whom the cruel prison immured in a glorious band to carry on the conflict with an equal and similar fire of courage in order to gain the triumphal glory.

O truly blessed mother Church, whom the glory of the divine condescension so illumines, whom the glorious blood of the victorious Martyrs adorns, whom the white garment of virginity clothes with an inviolate confession! Neither roses nor lilies are wanting to thy garlands. And now, dearly beloved, let each and every one strive that they may gain the highest dignity of one or the other of these honors, either the white crowns of virginity, or the red crowns of martyrdom. In the heavenly camps, both peace and war have their own garlands with which the soldiers of Christ are crowned.

For the ineffable and boundless goodness of God has also provided this, that the period of labors and of struggles should not indeed be drawn out, should not be made long or without end, but brief, and, so to speak, momentary; so that in this short and fleeting life there are labors and struggles, but in that which is eternal, crowns and rewards of merits; that the labors indeed should soon be over, but the rewards of merits should last forever; that after the darkness of this world, they are to see an exceedingly bright light, and are to receive blessedness greater than the bitterness of all their torments, as the Apostle bears witness to this when he says: The sufferings of this time are not worthy to be compared with the glory to come, that shall be revealed in us.

R. In the sight of the Angels I will sing praise to Thee, * And I will worship towards Thy holy temple and give glory to Thy name, O Lord. V. For Thy mercy and Thy truth: for Thou hast magnified Thy holy name above all. And I will worship. Glory. And I will worship.

III Nocturn
The reading of the holy Gospel according to St. Matthew

At that time: Jesus, seeing the multitudes, went up into a mountain; and when He was sat down, His disciples came unto Him. And so forth.

Homily of St. Augustine, Bishop

If it is asked what the mountain means, it may well be understood to mean the greater precepts of righteousness, for there were lesser ones which were given to the Jews. Yet it is one God who, by His holy prophets and servants, according to a most well-arranged distribution of times, gave the lesser precepts to a people which had need to be still bound by fear; and who, by means of His Son, gave the greater ones to a people whom it was expedient now to set free by love. Moreover, when the lesser are given to the lesser, and greater to the greater, they are given by Him who alone knows how to present to the human race the remedy suited to the occasion.

For need we be surprised that the greater precepts are given for the kingdom of heaven, and lesser ones for an earthly kingdom, by the one same God who made heaven and earth? With respect, therefore, to this righteousness which is greater, it is said by the prophet: Thy justice is as the mountains of God; and this may well mean that the Master, who alone is fit to teach matters of so great importance, teaches on a mountain.

Then, too, He teaches sitting, which belongs to the dignity of the instructor's office. And His disciples draw near to Him, in order that they might be nearer in body to hear His words, as they also had approached in spirit to fulfil His precepts. And opening His mouth, He taught them, saying. This redundant expression which is written: And opening His mouth; perhaps, by its very delay in coming to the point, intimates that the discourse will be somewhat more extensive, unless, perchance, it is not without meaning that He, who under the old Law was accustomed to open the mouth of the prophets, is said to have opened His own mouth.

What, then, does He say? Blessed are the poor in spirit; for theirs is the kingdom of heaven. We read in Scripture about striving after temporal goods: All is vanity, and presumption of spirit. Presumption of spirit means audacity and pride. The proud are commonly said to have high spirits; and rightly, since this wind also is called spirit. Whence it is written; Fire, hail, snow, ice, stormy winds (spirits). But who does not know that the proud are spoken of as puffed up, as if distended with wind? And hence that other saying of the apostle: Knowledge puffeth up, but charity edifieth. Therefore the poor in spirit are rightly understood here as meaning the lowly and God-fearing, that is, those whose spirit is not puffed up.

R. The Precursor of the Lord cometh, of whom He, the Lord, giveth testimony: * Amongst those born of women there is not a greater than John the Baptist. V. He is a prophet and more than a prophet, of whom the Savior said. Amongst. Glory. Amongst.

✠ Continuation of the holy Gospel according to St. Matthew:—At that time: Jesus, seeing the multitudes, went up into a mountain; and when He was sat down, His disciples came unto Him. And opening His mouth, He taught them, saying: Blessed are the poor in spirit; for theirs is the kingdom of heaven. Blessed are the meek; for they shall possess the land. Blesed are they that mourn; for they shall be comforted. Blessed are they that hunger and thirst after justice; for they shall have their fill. Blessed are the merciful; for they shall obtain mercy. Blessed are the clean of heart; for they shall see God. Blessed are the peacemakers, for they shall be called the children of God. Blessed are they that suffer persecution for justice sake; for theirs is the kingdom of heaven. Blessed are ye when they shall revile you, and persecute you, and speak evil against you, untruly, for My sake; be glad and rejoice, for your reward is very great in heaven.

LET US PRAY

O almighty and eternal God, who dost grant us to honor the merits of all Thy Saints in one feast; we beseech Thee, that increasing the number of our intercessors, Thou wouldst also increase Thy mercy for which we long. Through our Lord.

November 2
(or, if it should fall on Sunday, November 3)
COMMEMORATION OF ALL THE FAITHFUL DEPARTED

I Nocturn

From the Book of Job, c. 7, 16 - 21; c. 14, 1 - 6; c. 19, 20 - 27

II Nocturn

From the Book of St. Augustine, Bishop, on Care to be had for the Dead.

The embalming of the corpse, the site of the tomb, the display in the funeral procession, are more of a consolation to the living than an assistance to the dead. Yet it follows not that the bodies of the departed are to be despised and flung aside, especially the bodies of just and faithful men, which their spirits have used holily as organs and vessels for all their good works. For if a father's garment and ring, and whatever such like, is the more dear to those whom they leave behind the greater is their affection towards their parents, in no wise are the bodies themselves to be spurned, which truly we wear in more familiar and close conjunction than any garment. For these pertain not to ornament or aid which is applied from without, but to the very nature of man. Whence also the funerals of the just men of old were cared for with dutiful piety, their obsequies celebrated, and sepulture provided; and they themselves, while they were yet alive, gave strict charge to their sons concerning the burial, or even the translation, of their bodies.

The remembrance and the prayers which are the signs of true affection, when they are displayed towards the departed by the faithful who were most dear to them, without doubt must profit them who, while living in the body, merited that such things should profit them after this life. But even if any emergency should prevent the bodies from being buried at all, or at least from being buried in holy places for lack of proper facilities, yet the supplications for the spirits of the dead should not be omitted. Moreover, the Church has taken it upon herself that these supplications be made for all who have departed in Christian and Catholic fellowship, even without mentioning their names, under a general commemoration, so that they who lack for this purpose parents or sons or whatever kindred or friends, may have the same afforded unto them by the one pious mother which is common to all. But if there were a lack of these supplications which are made with right faith and piety for the dead, I do not think that it would profit their spirits anything, no matter in how holy a place their lifeless bodies should be deposited.

Which things being so, let us not think that anything reaches those dead for whom we have a care except that which we solemnly supplicate by sacrifices either of the Altar, or of prayers, or of alms; although they do not profit all those for whom they are done, but only those whom, while they lived, merited that they should be profitable to them. But because we cannot discern who these are, it is meet to do them for all regenerate persons, that none of them may be passed by to whom these benefits may and ought to reach. For it is better that these things should be done superfluously to those whom they neither hinder nor help than to be lacking to those whom they help. However, each man doth these things more diligently for his own near and dear friends in order that they may be likewise done unto him by his friends. But as for the burying of the body, whatever is bestowed on it is no aid to salvation, according to that affection by which "no man ever hateth his own flesh." Whence it is fitting that he take whatever care he can for the flesh of his neighbor when he who bore it has passed away. And if they who believe not in the resurrection of the flesh do these things, how much more ought they who do believe to do the same; that so an office of this kind bestowed upon a body, dead, but yet to rise again and to remain for all eternity, may also be in some sort a testimony of the same faith.

R. O Lord, when Thou shalt come to judge the earth, where shall I hide myself from the face of Thy wrath? * For I have sinned exceedingly in my life. V. I dread my misdeeds, and blush before

Thee: do not condemn me, when Thou shalt come
to judge. For. Eternal rest give unto them, O
Lord: and let perpetual light shine upon them. For.

III Nocturn
From the first Epistle of blessed Paul
the Apostle to the Corinthians

Now if Christ be preached that He arose again
from the dead, how do some among you say that
there is no resurrection of the dead? But if there
be no resurrection of the dead, then Christ is not
risen again. And if Christ be not risen again, then
is our preaching vain, and your faith is also vain.
Yea, and we are found false witnesses of God, because we have given testimony against God, that
He hath raised up Christ: whom He hath not
raised up if the dead rise not again. For if the
dead rise not again, neither is Christ risen again.
And if Christ be not risen again, your faith is vain,
for you are yet in your sins. They also that are
fallen asleep in Christ have perished. If in this life
only we have hope in Christ, we are of all men most
miserable. But now Christ is risen from the dead,
the first-fruits of them that sleep. For by a man
came death, and by a man the resurrection of the
dead. And as in Adam all die, so also in Christ all
shall be made alive.

But some man will say: How do the dead rise
again? Or with what manner of body shall they
come? Senseless man, that which thou sowest is

not quickened, except it die first. And that which thou sowest, thou sowest not the body that shall be, but bare grain, as of wheat, or of some of the rest. But God giveth it a body as He will; and to every seed its proper body. All flesh is not the same flesh: but one is the flesh of men, another of beasts, another of birds, another of fishes. And there are bodies celestial, and bodies terrestrial; but one is the glory of the celestial, and another of the terrestrial. One is the glory of the sun, another the glory of the moon, and another the glory of the stars. For star differeth from star in glory: so also is the resurrection of the dead. It is sown in corruption, it shall rise in incorruption. It is sown in dishonor, it shall rise in glory. It is sown in weakness, it shall rise in power. It is sown a natural body, it shall rise a spiritual body.

Behold I tell you a mystery. We shall all indeed rise again: but we shall not all be changed. In a moment, in the twinkling of an eye, at the last trumpet: for the trumpet shall sound, and the dead shall rise again incorruptible; and we shall be changed. For this corruptible must put on incorruption: and this mortal must put on immortality. And when this mortal hath put on immortality, then shall come to pass the saying that is written: Death is swallowed up in victory. O death, where is thy victory? O death, where is thy sting? Now the sting of death is sin: and the power of sin is the law. But thanks be to God who has given us the victory through our Lord Jesus Christ. Therefore, my beloved brethren, be ye steadfast and unmoveable; always abounding in the work of the Lord, knowing that your labor is not vain in the Lord.

R. O Lord, judge me not according to my deeds: for I have done nothing worthy in Thy sight: therefore I beseech Thy majesty, * That Thou, O God, mayest blot out my iniquity. V. Wash me, O Lord, yet more from my injustice, and cleanse me from my sin. That Thou. Eternal rest give unto them, O Lord: and let perpetual light shine upon them. That Thou.

LET US PRAY

O God, the Creator and Redeemer of all the faithful, to the souls of Thy servants and of Thine handmaidens grant the pardon of all their sins, that through our devout prayers they may rejoice in the full forgiveness for which at all times they have hoped: who livest and reignest with God the Father.

November 3
III DAY WITHIN THE OCTAVE OF ALL SAINTS

From a Sermon of St. Bede the Venerable, Priest

Then there shall never be discord anywhere, but all shall be accord; since there shall be one concord

of all the Saints, all peace and joy are contained in
it; all things are calm and at rest. A perennial
splendor, not that which now is, but as much
brighter as it is more blessed; since, as we read,
that city needs not the light of the sun, but the
Lord almighty shall enlighten it, and the Lamb is
the lamp thereof. There the Saints shall shine like
stars for all eternity, and they who have taught
many shall be as the brightness of the sky.

And so there shall be no night there, no darkness, no gathering of clouds, no extremes of heat or
cold. But there shall be some such tempering of
things as no eye has seen, nor ear heard, neither
hath it entered into the heart of man, save only of
those who have been found worthy to enjoy it,
whose names are written in the book of life, and
who have washed their robes in the Blood of the
Lamb, and are before the throne of God, serving
Him day and night. There is not any old age there,
nor misery of old age, for all are come to perfect
manhood, unto the measure of the age of the fulness of Christ.

But yet, it is far above all these things to be in
fellowship with the hosts of Angels and Archangels,
to enjoy the companionship likewise of Thrones and
Dominations, Principalities and Powers and all the
heavenly Virtues on high, and to behold the army of
the Saints shining more gloriously than stars, of
the Patriarchs glowing with faith, of the Prophets

rejoicing in hope, of the Apostles judging the world in the twelve tribes of Israel, of the Martyrs resplendent in their ruddy crowns of victory, and to look upon the choirs of Virgins wearing garlands of the purest white.

November 4
IV DAY WITHIN THE OCTAVE OF ALL SAINTS

From a Sermon of St. Bede the Venerable, Priest

But of the King who presides in the midst of these Saints no word can say enough: for He defies all description, and this comeliness, this beauty, this power, this glory, this magnificence, this majesty surpasses all understanding of the human mind. For it is beyond all the glory of the Saints to look upon His Majesty. For would that we daily had to bear torments and even to endure hell itself for a short time in order that we might be worthy to see Christ coming in glory and to be associated in the number of His Saints! Would it not be fitting to suffer all that is disconcerting in order that we may be reckoned partakers of so great a good and of such great glory?

What will be, dearly beloved brethren, the glory of the Just, how intense the gladness of the Saints, when each countenance shall shine as the sun, when, in their proper ranks, the Lord has begun to number His people in the kingdom of His Father, and to bestow the promised rewards for the merits and

works of each one; to replace heavenly things for
things earthly; eternal for temporal; and an
abundance for mere handfuls; to lead the Saints
into the presence of the paternal glory, and to make
them sit in the midst of the heavenly company,
that God may be all in all, and to give eternity and
immortality to His lovers; and finally to bring
back to paradise those whom He has restored by
the new life of His Blood, and in the fidelity and
truth of His promise to open the kingdom of
heaven?

May these things cling firmly to our senses, may
they be understood with great faith, may they be
loved with the whole heart, may they be acquired
by the generosity of untiring labors. This thing
is placed within the power of him who works, for
the kingdom of heaven suffereth violence. This
thing, O man, namely, the kingdom of heaven, demands no other price save thyself; it is worth as
much as you. Give yourself and you will have it.
Why are you disturbed over the price? Christ delivered up Himself that He might gain you as a
kingdom for His Father; so too, give yourself that
you may be His kingdom; and let not sin reign in
your mortal body, but the Spirit, unto the obtaining
of life.

November 5
V DAY WITHIN THE OCTAVE OF ALL SAINTS

From a Sermon of St. Bede the Venerable, Priest

Therefore let it be our delight to attain to this prize of good works. Let us strive cheerfully and readily; let us all run in the contest of justice, in the sight of God and of Christ; and let us, who have already begun to rise above the things of time and of the world, delay our course for no worldly desires. If the last day shall find us ready and running swiftly in the race of good works, the Lord will never fail to reward us as we deserve.

He, who will give a purple crown for suffering in persecution, will give a white one to those who conquer in peace, as a reward of their righteousness. For neither Abraham, Isaac, nor Jacob were put to death, and yet for their faith and justice they merited to be honored as the first among the Patriarchs; and everyone who is found faithful, just, and praiseworthy is gathered together to their banquet. We must be mindful to do God's will, not our own; for he who does God's will abides forever, even as God abides forever.

Therefore, dearly beloved, with a pure soul, a firm faith, a solid virtue, and a perfect charity, let us be ready for whatever God wills, bravely keeping the Lord's commandments; having innocence in simplicity, concord in charity, modesty in humility, diligence in ministering, watchfulness in helping those who toil, mercy in succoring the poor, constancy in defending the truth, severity in the keeping of discipline, lest we should fail in any way to set an example of good deeds. For these are the footprints which the Saints have left us as they went on their way to their fatherland, that we, treading in their steps, might follow them into their joy.

November 6
VI DAY WITHIN THE OCTAVE OF ALL SAINTS
Sermon of St. Bernard, Abbot

Since today, dearly beloved, we are celebrating the feast of All Saints, who are indeed most worthy to be remembered with the utmost devotion, I think it worth while, with the help of the Holy Spirit, to address to your charity some discourse concerning the happiness which is their common lot, the blessed rest which they now enjoy, and that future consummation which they are awaiting. Truly, this is a faithful saying and worthy of all acceptation, that we should follow those to whom we render solemn veneration by imitating their conduct; we pronounce them most blessed, we should strive with all eagerness to attain to the same beatitude; we are delighted to hear their praises, we should be upheld by their protection.

What, then, is our praise to the Saints? What, our homage? What, this very feast of ours? What are earthly honors to those whom, according to the true promise of the Son, the heavenly Father is honoring? What are our eulogies to them? They are full. In a word, dearly beloved, the matter stands thus: the saints have no need of our goods, and our devotion adds nothing to them. Clearly our honoring their memory redounds to our interest, not to theirs. Would you know how greatly it is to our interest? I confess that when I think of this, I fell myself on fire with a great longing, even a threefold longing.

It is a common saying: For what the eye does not see, the heart does not grieve. My eye is my memory; and to think about the Saints is, in a measure, to see them. Such indeed is our portion in the land of the living; nor truly is it a small portion if, as is fitting, love be yet joined to memory. So, I say, our conversation is in heaven. But yet ours is not such as theirs. For they are there substantially, but we, by desire; they are there by their presence, we, by our thought.

November 7
VII DAY WITHIN THE OCTAVE OF ALL SAINTS
Sermon of St. John Chrysostom

He who wonders with reverential love at the merits of the Saints and who speaks with frequent

praise of the glory of the just ones should imitate
their saintly manners and their righteousness; for
he who takes pleasure in the merit of any Saint
should equally take pleasure in obedience as regards
the service of God. Wherefore, if he praises him,
he ought to imitate him; and if he is not ready to
imitate him, he ought not to praise him. Let him
who praises another make himself worthy of like
praise; and let him who admires the merits of the
Saints, become himself worthy of admiration by
holiness of life. For if we love those who are good
and faithful because we respect the goodness and
fidelity in them, we also may become what they are
if we do what they do.

For it is not difficult for us to imitate what is
done by them when we observe such deeds as they
did of old without any foregoing example; they did
not become emulous of others, but themselves afforded an example of virtue to be emulated by us;
so that while we derive advantage from them, and
others from us, Christ in His servants may thus be
ever glorified in His holy Church. Hence, from the
beginning of the world, blameless Abel was slain,
Enoch, who pleased God, was taken away, Noe was
found righteous, Abraham was found faithful,
Moses was distinguished for meekness, Josue was
chaste, David was mild, Elias was taken up, Daniel
was holy, and the three children were rendered victorious.

The Apostles, the disciples of Christ, are held to be the teachers of believers; taught by them, the most valiant confessors give battle, the excellent Martyrs triumph, and the Christian hosts, armed by God, ever prevail against the devil. All these have been men of like valor and glorious victories, though they fought dissimilar warfare. Therefore thou, O Christian, art but an effeminate soldier if thou thinkest thou canst conquer without battle, that thou canst triumph without a struggle. Put forth thy strength, contend manfully, struggle fiercely in this battle. Remember thy engagement, give heed to thy situation, know thy warfare; namely, the engagement to which thou hast pledged thyself, the situation in which thou findest thyself, the warfare in which thou hast enlisted.

November 8
OCTAVE DAY OF ALL SAINTS
I Nocturn
Lessons from the occurring Scripture
II Nocturn

From the book of St. Cyprian, Bishop and Martyr, on Mortality

We ought to consider, dearly beloved brethren, and repeatedly to ponder, that we have renounced the world, and are meanwhile living here as strangers. Let us reflect upon the day which assigns each of us to his own home, and after rescuing us from this life and freeing us from the snares of earth, restores us to paradise and to the kingdom of heaven. What man who finds himself in a far country does not hasten to return to his native land? Who that is hastening on a sea voyage to his friends does not long with the greater eagerness for a favorable wind, that he may all the sooner embrace those who are dear to him.

Heaven we look upon as our native land; we already begin to hold the Patriarchs as our kinsfolk. Why should we not hasten and run that we may see our country and greet our kinsfolk? There, a great number of dear ones await us; parents, brothers, children, a manifold and numerous assembly are longing for us; they are now in security as regards their own eternal life, but are still anxious as to our salvation.

What a mutual gladness, both for them and for us, in the hour when we are come into their sight and embrace! What sort of delight will there be there in the heavenly realms, where death can never terrify and life can never end! What perfect and perpetual bliss! There, the glorious choir of the Apostles, there, the band of the exultant Prophets, there, the countless multitude of the Martyrs, crowned for victory in sufferings and strife.

There are the triumphant Virgins who brought the concupiscence of the flesh and body under the curb of continence. The merciful, who have fulfilled the works of righteousness by nourishing and giving to the poor, and, by keeping the commandments of the Lord, have transferred their earthly inheritance into the treasuries of heaven, receive their reward. To these, dearly beloved brethren, let us hasten with eager longing and let us desire to be speedily with them, so that it may be our lot to come speedily to Christ.

R. In the sight of the Angels I will sing praise to Thee, * And I will worship towards Thy holy temple and give glory to Thy name, O Lord. V. For Thy mercy and for Thy truth: for Thou hast magnified Thy holy name above all. And I will worship. Glory. And I will worship.

III Nocturn

The reading of the holy Gospel
according to St. Matthew

At that time: Jesus, seeing the multitudes, went up into a mountain; and when He was sat down, His disciples came unto Him. And so forth.

From a Homily of St. Augustine, Bishop

Blessed are ye, He says, when they shall revile you, and persecute you, and speak all that is evil against you, untruly, for My sake; be glad and rejoice, for your reward is very great in heaven. Let anyone who is seeking the delights of this world and the riches of temporal things in the Christian name notice that our happiness is within;

as it is said by the mouth of the prophet concerning the soul of the Church: All the beauty of the king's daughter is from within.

For outside, there are promised revilings, and persecutions, and detractions; yet from all these things there is a great reward in heaven, which is felt in the heart of those enduring them, of those who can already say: We glory in tribulations, knowing that tribulation worketh patience; and patience trial; and trial hope; and hope confoundeth not; because the charity of God is poured forth in our hearts, by the Holy Ghost who is given to us.

For it is not simply the bearing of these things that is meritorious, but bearing them for the name of Christ, not only with a tranquil mind, but also with joy. For many heretics, deceiving souls by means of the Christian name, endure many such things; but are excluded from the reward because it is not said merely: Blessed are they who suffer persecution; but it is added: For justice' sake.

Now, where faith is not sound there can be no righteousness; for: The just man lives by faith. Neither let schismatics promise themselves anything of that reward; for there also, where there is no love, there cannot be righteousness. For: The love of our neighbor worketh no evil; and if they possessed it, they would not tear asunder the body of Christ, which is the Church.

R.   O most holy Confessor of Christ, St. Benedict, Father and Guide of monks: * Intercede for
the salvation of ourselves and of all men. V. Help
thy devoted people with thy holy intercession, that
aided by thy prayers, they may attain to the heavenly kingdom. Intercede. Glory. Intercede.

✠ Continuation of the holy Gospel according to
St. Matthew.—At that time: Jesus, seeing the multitudes, went up into a mountain; and when He
was sat down, His disciples came unto Him, And
opening His mouth, He taught them, saying:
Blessed are the poor in spirit; for theirs is the
kingdom of heaven. Blessed are the meek; for
they shall possess the land. Blessed are they that
mourn; for they shall be comforted. Blessed are
they that hunger and thirst after justice; for they
shall have their fill. Blessed are the merciful; for
they shall obtain mercy. Blessed are the clean of
heart; for they shall see God. Blessed are the
peacemakers, for they shall be called the children of
God. Blessed are they that suffer persecution for
justice's sake; for theirs is the kingdom of heaven.
Blessed are ye when they shall revile you, and persecute you, and speak all that is evil against you,
untruly, for My sake; be glad and rejoice, for your
reward is very great in heaven.

LET US PRAY

O almighty and eternal God, who dost grant us
to honor the merits of all Thy Saints in one feast;

we beseech Thee, that increasing the number of our intercessors, Thou wouldst also increase Thy mercy for which we long.   Through our Lord.

November 9
DEDICATION OF THE BASILICA OF THE MOST HOLY SAVIOR
I Nocturn
From the Book of the Apocalypse of blessed John the Apostle, c. 21, 9 - 18
II Nocturn

The rites which are observed by the Roman Church in consecrating Churches and altars were first instituted by the blessed Pope Sylvester. For although from the age of the Apostles places were dedicated to God, and called oratories by some persons and churches by others, and in them the Christian people assembled on the sabbath, and were wont to pray, to hear the word of God, and receive the Holy Eucharist, yet hitherto they were not consecrated by a solemn rite, and up to that time an altar was not erected in the church, which, anointed with chrism, symbolizes our Lord Jesus Christ, who is our altar, our victim, and priest.

But when the emperor Constantine had received health and salvation by the Sacrament of Baptism, then for the first time, by an edict published by him, it was ordained throughout the whole world that the Christians might build churches; and he encouraged this holy building by his own example as well as by this edict. Thus, in his Lateran palace, he dedicated a Church to the Savior, and adjacent to it he founded a basilica in the name of St. John the Baptist, on the very spot where he himself had been baptized by Pope Sylvester and cleansed from the leprosy of infidelity, this basilica, the same Pope consecrated on November 9. The memory of this consecration is celebrated today whereon for the first time a church was publicly consecrated in Rome, and there appeared to the Roman people an image of the Savior, painted on the wall.

Although later on, when consecrating the altar of the Prince of the Apostles, the blessed Sylvester decreed that thenceforward all altars should be built of stone, yet the altar of the Lateran basilica was built of wood. This, however, is not surprising. For from the time of St. Peter down to Sylvester persecution prevented the pontiffs from having any fixed abode; so that they offered the holy Sacrifice either in crypts or in cemeteries or in the houses of the faithful, or wherever necessity compelled them, upon the said wooden altar, which was hollow like a chest.

When peace was restored to the Church, the holy Sylvester placed this altar in the first church, the Lateran; and in honor of the Prince of the Apostles, who is said to have offered the holy Sacrifice upon it, and of the other pontiffs who had used it up to that time for the celebration of the holy Myste-

ries, he decreed that no one should thereafter celebrate Mass upon it except the Roman Pontiff. This
same church, having been injured and made ruinous
in consequence of fires, pillaging, and even of earthquakes, and repaired by the unremitting care of the
supreme Pontiffs, was afterwards restored by re-
building afresh, and the supreme Pontiff, Benedict
XIII, of the Order of Preachers, on April 28, 1726,
consecrated it by solemn rite, and ordered the commemoration of that consecration to be celebrated on
this present day. But that work which Pius IX
had counted worthy of accomplishment, Leo XIII
took charge of, the lengthening and widening by
vast building operations of the main structure
which was falling apart with age; the ancient
mosaic, which had already been restored in many
parts, was restored in accordance with the ancient
design and transferred to the new apse, which was
handsomely and richly decorated. In the year 1884,
he ordered the transept to be embellished and the
ceiling and the woodwork to be renewed; a sacristy,
a residence for the canons, and a continuous portico
to the baptistery of Constantine were also added.

R. If they pray in this place, * Forgive the sins
of Thy people, O Lord, and show them the good
way wherein they should walk and give glory in
this place. V. Give ear, O Thou that rulest Israel,
Thou that leadest Joseph like a sheep, Thou that sittest upon the Cherubim. Forgive. Glory. Forgive.

III Nocturn
The reading of the holy Gospel
according to St. Luke

At that time: Jesus, entering in, walked through Jericho. And behold, there was a man named Zacheus, who was the chief of the publicans, and he was rich. And so forth.

Homily of St. Ambrose, Bishop

Zacheus, of low stature, that is, not eminent with any dignity of hereditary rank, and, like most people, of slight merit, hearing that the Lord and Savior was at hand, greatly desired to see Him whom His own had not received. But no man can easily see Jesus; no man, if he stay upon the ground, can see Jesus. And, since he had neither the law nor the prophets as a recommendation for his bodily shape, he climbed up into a sycamore tree, setting his foot, as it were, upon the vanities of the Jews, and correcting the errors of his former life. And thus he came to receive Jesus as a guest into his house.

And rightly did he climb up into a tree, that the good tree might bring forth good fruit, and that he, cut out of the wild olive tree, which was natural to him, and, contrary to nature, grafted into the good olive tree, might bring forth the fruits of the law. For the root was holy, though the branches were barren; which barren glory the common people of the Gentiles greatly surpassed by their faith in the resurrection, as if by a physical climbing up.

Therefore Zacheus was in the sycamore tree, the blind man upon the highway; for the one, the Lord stood waiting that He might show him mercy; the other, He made celebrated by the fame of his house. Of the one He asked a question when about to heal him; to the other He offered Himself, though uninvited, as a guest. For He knew how rich would be the reward of such hospitality. For though He heard no words of invitation, He saw the man's good will.

But now, lest we should seem to hurry past the blind man in our haste to reach the rich man, as though impatient of poor folk, let us stand and wait for him, as the Lord stood and waited; let us ask him a question, as Christ also questioned him. But let us ask because we are ignorant; Christ asked because He knew. Let us interrogate him that we may know how he came to be healed; Christ asked him a question that, by the example of one man, we, who are many, might learn how we may merit to behold the Lord. For Christ asked that question that we might believe that no man, unless he confess Him, can be saved.

R. All thy walls are of precious stones, * And the towers of Jerusalem shall be built up with jewels. V. The gates of Jerusalem shall be built of sapphire and of emerald, and round about the

walls thereof of precious stones. And the towers.
Glory. And the towers.

✠ Continuation of the holy Gospel according to
St. Luke.—At that time: Jesus, entering in, walked
through Jericho. And behold, there was a man
named Zacheus, who was the chief of the publicans,
and he was rich. And he sought to see Jesus who
He was; and he could not for the crowd, because
he was low of stature. And running before, he
climbed up into a sycamore tree, that he might see
Him; for He was to pass that way. And when
Jesus was come to the place, looking up, He saw
him, and said to him; Zacheus, make haste and
come down; for this day I must abide in thy house.
And he made haste and came down, and received
Him with joy. And when all saw it, they murmured, saying, that He was gone to be a guest with
a man that was a sinner. But Zacheus, standing,
said to the Lord: Behold, Lord, the half of my
goods I give to the poor; and if I have wronged
any man of anything, I restore him fourfold. Jesus
said to him: This day is salvation come to this
house; because he also is a son of Abraham. For
the Son of man is come to seek and to save that
which was lost.

LET US PRAY

O God, who each year dost renew the day on
which Thy holy temple was consecrated and dost
continue to bring us safely to the Sacred Mysteries,

hear the prayers of Thy people and grant that all who enter this temple to ask Thy favors may rejoice because they have asked all from Thee. Through our Lord.

November 13
ALL SAINTS OF THE BENEDICTINE ORDER
I Nocturn
From the Book of Ecclesiasticus, c. 44, 1 - 15
II Nocturn
From a Sermon of St. John Damascene

Blessed and thrice blessed are they who have burned with the love of God, and out of love for Him have considered all possessions as nothing. They have shed profuse tears, and day and night have lived in mourning that they might obtain eternal consolation: They have suppressed themselves here on earth that they might there be lifted upon high. They have subdued their flesh by hunger, thirst, and vigils in order to enjoy the delights and joy of paradise.

Through their purity of heart they have been the tabernacle of the Holy Ghost, as it is written: I shall dwell in them, and move in them. They have crucified themselves to the world that they might stand at Christ's right hand; they have girded their loins in truth and they have held their lamps in readiness, awaiting the arrival of the Immortal Spouse. Since they were endowed with the eyes of

the mind, they were always looking forward to that
dreadful day; and they so bore the contemplation
both of future blessings and of future punishment
fixed in their heart that they were never without
it. They were zealous in laboring here, that they
might be sharers of eternal glory, and tried by
troubles as were the angels, they now exult with
them whose life they have imitated.

Blessed and thrice blessed are they because with
the steadfast eyes of the mind they have seen the
vanity of present things as well as the uncertain-
ness and inconstancy of human prosperity; and,
rejecting them, they have laid up for themselves
eternal goods and have taken for themselves that
life which never dies, that life which is not interrupted by death. Though unworthy and despicable,
we strive to imitate, therefore, these admirable and
holy men. We by no means seek the heights of
their heavenly life, but we imitate their life in proportion to our weakness and miserable ability; we
are also in the same state of life as they were, even
if we do not attain to their works. For we hold as
true that this divine profession wards off sin and
that it is a companion and a helper of that incorruption which is granted to us through Baptism.

R. This is the true brotherhood, which can
never be violated by strife: the saints have given
their blood for Christ and have followed Him. *
They have despised the glitter of this world and

have therefore come to the heavenly kingdom. V. Behold how good and how pleasant it is for brethren to dwell together in unity. They have despised. Glory. They have despised.

III Nocturn
The reading of the holy Gospel according to St. Matthew

At that time: Peter said to Jesus: Behold, we have left all things and have followed Thee: what, therefore, shall we have? And so forth.

Homily of St. Bernard, Abbot

Brethren, in the Gospel you have just heard our Lord making a promise to His disciples, saying to them: You shall sit on seats judging the twelve tribes of Israel. Behold! The restfulness of being seated and the honor of passing judgment are promised. Now our Lord Himself was unwilling to receive these rewards except by humility and labor. Wherefore He was condemned to a most shameful death, loaded with torments, filled with opprobrium; so has He done, together with all who imitate and accompany Him on the way, in order that the enemy might be confounded. He it is, O wicked creature, He it is who will be seated on the throne of His Majesty, like to the most High and coequal to Him. The angels considered this when, at the fall of the evil one, they did not consent to his apostasy, thereby leaving us an example that as they chose to serve, so should we also.

Let those who fly labor and seek honor know that they imitate the devil who sought for himself power and majesty, and if his crime does not terrify them, his punishment should. The Saints of God, who indeed will be seated in judgment, have given us an example of prudence in avoiding these vices; they, I say, (in their own esteem) wretched worms of the earth, will sit in judgment. Do you not know, says the Apostle, that we will judge even the angels? They indeed who went forth weeping, sowing their seed, will come with joy, carrying their sheaves. They who have sown labor and humility reap honor and rest. For "for their double confusion and shame they will receive double in their land." Wherefore also a certain one has said: Behold my lowliness and sorrow.

Not only life itself, but also the promise of eternal life and the eager anticipation of it is a joy for the just, and a joy so great that anything to be desired cannot be compared with it. At the time when the followers of the wisdom of this world, which is indeed foolishness in God's sight, and of the prudence of the flesh, which worketh death and is inimical to God, withdraw from Christ, the Holy Apostles sowed the seed of prudence for us, since they clung to our Lord. Manifestly the Martyrs sowed fortitude; the Confessors followed justice throughout their lives. The same comparison exists between the martyrs and Confessors as between

Peter leaving all things and Abraham using the wealth of this world for good purposes. For as the Martyrs, having become perfect in a short time, filled out a long time, so did the Confessors endure long and varied martyrdoms. Plainly the Virgins who thus trod upon lust sowed temperance.

Our heavenly father and guide, master and legislator, Benedict, also instructs us in this doctrine and directs our steps along the way of peace. Moreover, he strengthens and animates us for a life of justice in such a way, that we are so much the more impelled to practice what he taught since we are certain that he taught not otherwise than he acted. The example of works is indeed a living and effective sermon making what is spoken most persuasive because it shows that that which is urged is possible. In this regard his sanctity comforts us, his piety instructs us, his justice strengthens us. With what great piety was he not animated who provided not only for his children then present, but was also solicitous for those of the future! He nourishes us by his life, his teaching, and his intercession. Being always thus helped, dearly beloved, strive to become fruitful, since "for this were you appointed that you should go and should bring forth fruit." Let us imitate him because for this end he came, that he might give us the example and show us the way.

R. Ye priests of God, bless the Lord * O ye holy and humble of heart praise God. V. Ye spirits and souls of the Just, sing a hymn to our God. O ye holy. Glory. O ye holy.

✠ Continuation of the holy Gospel according to St. Matthew.—At that time: Peter said to Jesus: Behold, we have left all things and have followed Thee: what, therefore, shall we have? And Jesus said to them: Amen I say to you, that you, who have followed Me, in the regeneration when the Son of Man shall sit on the seat of His majesty, you also shall sit on twelve seats, judging the twelve tribes of Israel. And everyone that hath left house, or brethren, or sisters, or father, or mother, or wife or children, or lands, for My name's sake, shall receive a hundred fold and shall possess life everlasting.

LET US PRAY

Grant, we beseech Thee, O almighty God, that the examples of the holy Monks may urge us to a better life, that we may imitate the virtues of those whose solemn feast we celebrate. Through our Lord.

November 17
ST. GERTRUDE OF OUR ORDER, VIRGIN
I Nocturn
From the Canticle of Canticles, c. 2, 1 - 5; c. 8, 1 - 7
II Nocturn

The virgin Gertrude was born at Isleben in the neighborhood of Mansfield of most illustrious parents. When she was fifteen years of age, her parents took her to the Benedictine monastery in Rodard, because already at that tender age she had consecrated her virginity to her Spouse, Jesus Christ. From the time of her entrance into religion she applied herself to the angelical life, and by the aid of human knowledge, which she cultivated especially for the divine gifts, she came to that perfection of doctrine which only the most learned arrive at. Most exalted was her contemplation in which she was enlightened by many revelations and heavenly visions by God. In consequence of this she wrote books filled with divine wisdom.

Although she shone because of such gifts of nature and grace and enjoyed divine intercourse, and was renowned because of the gifts of prophecy and many miracles, yet she esteemed herself so vile that, amid the miracles of divine power, she believed it the greatest miracle that the earth would sustain so vile a sinner, as she thought herself to be. When she was thirty years old, she was elected abbess first of the monastery in which she had re-

ceived her habit, then of Elpedian. For forty years she filled this office with such charity, prudence, and integrity of regular discipline that her convent seemed to be a city of God where angels lived in the body under their mistress, Gertrude. And although she was the mother of all, she nevertheless made herself the servant of all.

The heavenly Spouse found His delight in her most pure heart in which the divine Lover also imprinted the stigma of His wounds with the fiery stylus of His love. Henceforward she spoke of nothing but Christ, whom she entertained in her heart, and who said that He would be found nowhere except in the Sacrament of the Altar and in the heart and soul of this, His beloved one. He confirmed the sanctity of His most dear spouse by a revelation of His own mouth by attesting that at that time there lived not a soul on the earth that was more united to Him, and thus more gracious and acceptable to Him.

With an especial piety she honored the Virgin Mother given to her, as a special privilege, by Christ as mother and procuratrix, whom, together with many other citizens of heaven, she entertained frequently. She was moved with devotion to the Sacrament of the Holy Eucharist and the Passion with such ardor of love and gratitude that she melted into a flood of tears. She inspired the souls of her charges to the flames of devotion by her daily

remembrance and fervent prayers. She literally burned with zeal for promoting the divine honor and the salvation of her neighbor. At length, Christ, accompanied by His most holy Mother, the beloved disciple, and a choir of virgins, came to her, though she languished more from the most fervent love than from any sickness, and took her soul, released from the shackles of the body and already received by a wonderful expansion into the innermost part of His Heart, with Him into the Heavenly bride-chamber.

R. With Christ I am fixed to the cross: * For I bear the marks of the Lord Jesus in my heart. V. I live now, not I, but Christ liveth in me. For. Glory. For.

III Nocturn
The reading of the holy Gospel
according to St. Matthew
At that time: Jesus spoke to His disciples this parable: The kingdom of heaven shall be like to ten virgins, who, taking their lamps, went out to meet the bridegroom and the bride. And five of them were foolish, and five wise. And so forth.

Homily of St. Augustine, Bishop.
Let us understand, dearly beloved, that this parable refers to all of us, that is, to the universal Church; not only the Hierarchy, nor to the people alone, but rather to all. Those five virgins are the souls of all Christians. But I will tell you what we

feel from God's inspiration; they are not any souls whatsoever, but such souls as have the Catholic faith and seem to perform good works in the Church of God; and yet five of them are prudent and five are foolish.

Let us see first why five are named, and why virgins are named. Every soul in a body is indicated by the number five, because it uses five senses. Whosoever, therefore, abstains from illicit looks, from illicit hearing, from illicit odors, from illicit tasting, from illicit touches, because of that integrity, receives the name of virgin. But if it is good to abstain from illicit motions of the senses, on whch account each Christian soul receives the name of virgin, why are five admitted and five rejected?

Yet they that are rejected are virgins also. It is a small thing that they are virgins and that they have lamps. They are virgins because they abstain from illicit use of the senses; they have lamps because of their good works, of which works the Lord says: Let your works shine before men. Likewise He says to His disciples: Let your loins be girt and your lamps burning in your hands. By girded loins is signified virginity; by burning lamps, good works. If therefore abstinence from illicit things is good, whence virginity receives its name, and if good works, which are signified by the lamps, are praiseworthy, why are five admitted and five rejected?

The ones He called prudent, the others foolish. By what shall we judge? How shall we distinguish? By the oil. Oil signifies something great, and that very great. Do you think it is charity? We express our opinion inquiringly; we will not insist on our solution. I will tell you why it seems to me that charity is designated by oil. The apostle says: But I will show you yet a more excellent way. If I speak with the tongues of men and angels and have not charity, I am become as sounding brass and as a tinkling cymbal. That is the more excellent way; that is, charity, which is rightly symbolized by oil, for oil excels all liquids in power to heal, illuminate, and smoothness of action.

R. With an eternal love the Lord loved Gertrude, therefore He drew her from her very infancy and led her into His solitude * And He spoke to her heart: V. He espoused her to Himself in faith and in mercy forever. And. Glory. And.

✠ Continuation of the holy Gospel according to St. Matthew.—At that time: Jesus spoke to His disciples this parable: The kingdom of heaven is like to ten virgins, who, taking their lamps, went out to meet the bridegroom and the bride. And five of them were foolish, and five wise: but the five foolish, having taken their lamps, did not take oil with them: but the wise took oil in their vessels with the lamps. And the bridegroom tarrying, they all slumbered and slept. And at midnight

there was a cry made: Behold the bridegroom
cometh, go ye forth to meet him. Then all those
virgins arose and trimmed their lamps. And the
foolish said to the wise: Give us of your oil, for
our lamps are gone out. The wise answered, saying: Lest perhaps there be not enough for us and
for you, go ye rather to them that sell, and buy for
yourselves. Now whilst they went to buy, the bridegroom came: and they that were ready went in
with him to the marriage, and the door was shut.
But at last came also the other virgins, saying:
Lord, Lord, open to us. But he answering, said:
Amen I say to you, I know you not. Watch ye therefore, because you know not the day nor the hour.

LET US PRAY

O God, who in the most pure heart of blessed
Gertrude Thy virgin didst prepare a pleasing dwelling for Thyself; by her merits and intercession
mercifully cleanse our hearts from all stain of sin
that we also may merit to become a worthy temple
of Thy divine Majesty. Through our Lord.

November 18
DEDICATION OF THE BASILICAS OF
SS. PETER AND PAUL

I Nocturn

*From the Book of the Apocalypse of blessed John
the Apostle, c. 21, 18 - 27*

II Nocturn

Among the holy places venerated of old by the
Christians, those were the most honored and most
frequented in which the bodies of the Saints were
preserved, or some relic or memorial of the Martyrs. Chief among the number of these holy places
has ever been noteworthy that part of the Vatican
hill which was called the Confession of St. Peter.
For Christians from all parts of the world flocked
thither as to the rock of the faith and the foundation of the Church, and honored with the greatest
reverence and piety the spot hallowed by the sepulchre of the Prince of the Apostles.

Thither on the eighth day after he received baptism came the emperor Constantine the Great; and
taking off his diadem, he prostrated himself on the
ground and shed abundant tears. Then taking a
hoe and a two-pronged mattock, he broke up the
earth, and from the place there were taken away
twelve basketfuls of earth, in honor of the twelve
Apostles; and on the site thus marked out he
build a church, the basilica of the Prince of the
Apostles. The holy Pope Sylvester dedicated it on

November 18, just as he had consecrated the Lateran church on November 9, and erected in it a stone altar which he anointed with chrism; he decreed that also thenceforward all altars should be made of stone.

The same blessed Sylvester dedicated the basilica of St. Paul the Apostle on the Ostian Way, which had also been most magnificently constructed by the Emperor Constantine. The same emperor enriched these basilicas by grants of many estates and decorated them with most abundant gifts. Thereafter, the Vatican basilica, already for a long time in a ruinous condition through age, was on that acount rebuilt from its foundations on a more extensive and magnificent scale through the piety of many Popes, and Urban VIII consecrated it by solemn rite on this same recurring day in the year 1626.

But the Basilica on the Ostian Way, when it had been entirely consumed by the terrible power of the flames in 1823, was rebuilt more magnificently than before by the unwearied energy of four Popes, and, as it were, restored from utter ruin; Pius IX, seizing the most auspicious occasion when the dogma of the Immaculate Conception of the blessed Virgin Mary, recently proclaimed by him, had drawn to Rome an immense number of cardinals and bishops from even the most distant parts of the Catholic world, solemnly dedicated this basilica on December

10, 1854, in the midst of this great circle of em-
purpled fathers and bishops, and decreed that the
commemoration of this festival should be observed
on this day.

R. My house shall be called the house of prayer,
saith the Lord; therein everyone that asketh, receiveth; and he that seeketh, findeth; * And to him
that knocketh it shall be opened. V. Ask, and it
shall be given you; seek and you shall find. And
to him. Glory. And to him.

III Nocturn

The reading of the holy Gospel
according to St. Luke

At that time: Jesus, entering in, walked through
Jericho. And behold, there was a man named
Zacheus, who was the chief of the publicans, and he
was rich. And so forth.

Homily of St. Gregory, Pope

If we would be truly wise and would contemplate
wisdom herself, we should humbly acknowledge ourselves to be fools. Let us cast aside hurtful wisdom;
let us learn praiseworthy foolishness. Hence it is
written: The foolish things of the world hath God
chosen that He may confound the wise. Again it is
said: If any man among you seem to be wise in
this world, let him become a fool, that he may be
wise. To this also the words of the Gospel story
bear witness, telling how Zacheus, when he could

see nothing for the crowd, climbed a sycamore tree that he might see the Lord passing by. Now the sycamore is called the foolish fig tree.

Little Zacheus, then, climbed the sycamore and saw the Lord; thus, they who in humility chose the foolish things of this world have a keen insight into the wisdom of God Himself. It is the crowd that hinders our littleness from seeing the Lord; for the tumult of worldly cares oppresses the weakness of the human mind lest it should gaze upon the light of truth.

But we wisely climb a sycamore if we are careful to keep our minds upon that foolishness which God has commanded. For what is greater folly in the eyes of the world than to refrain from seeking what we have lost, to yield our goods to robbers, never to inflict an injury for an injury received, yea, and to meet with patience all other such mischances? The Lord bids us, as it were, to climb a sycamore where He says: Of him that taketh thy goods, ask them not again: If one strike thee upon the right cheek, turn to him also the other.

From the sycamore the Lord may be seen passing by: since through this wise foolishness, even though as yet we see not face to face, in the light of contemplation we may gain, as if in passing, a sight of the wisdom of God, that wisdom which they who seem to themselves to be wise can never see. For they are hampered by the jostling crowd of their own lofty imaginations, and have found as yet no sycamore tree.

R.   Bless, O Lord, this house which I have built unto Thy name: of those who shall come unto this place * Hear Thou the prayers from the throne of Thy glory on high.   V.   O Lord, if Thy people shall turn and pray towards Thy sanctuary.   Hear. Glory.   Hear.

✠ Continuation of the holy Gospel according to St. Luke.—At that time: Jesus, entering in, walked through Jericho.   And behold, there was a man named Zacheus, who was the chief of the publicans, and he was rich.   And he sought to see Jesus who He was;   and he could not for the crowd, because he was low of stature.   And running before, he climbed into a sycamore tree, that he might see Him;   for He was to pass that way.   And when Jesus was come to the place, looking up, He saw him, and said to him: Zacheus, make haste and come down;   for this day I must abide in thy house. And he made haste and came down, and received Him with joy.   And when all saw it, they murmured, saying, that He was gone to be a guest with a man that was a sinner.   But Zacheus, standing, said to the Lord: Behold, Lord, the half of my goods I give to the poor;   and if I have wronged any man of anything, I restore him fourfold.   Jesus said to him: This day is salvation come to this house, because he also is a son of Abraham.   For the Son of man is come to seek and to save that which was lost.

LET US PRAY

O God, who each year dost renew the day on which Thy holy temple was consecrated and dost continue to bring us safely to the Sacred Mysteries, hear the prayers of Thy people and grant that all who enter this temple to ask Thy favors may rejoice because they have asked all from Thee. Through our Lord.

November 21
PRESENTATION OF THE BLESSED VIRGIN

I Nocturn

From the Proverbs of Solomon, c. 8, 12 - 25 and 34 - 36; c. 9, 1 - 5

II Nocturn

From the Book of St. John Damascene on the Orthodox Faith

Joachim joined himself in matrimony to that most excellent woman, Anne, one worthy of the greatest praise. And even as that former Anna, when laboring under the affliction of barrenness, gave birth to Samuel by means of a prayer and a promise; so in like manner, by an entreaty and a promise, this woman received from God the Mother of God, that in this also she might not be inferior to any of the illustrious matrons. Therefore grace (for such is the meaning of the name Anne) brings forth the Lady (for this is the meaning of the name Mary). For indeed she became the Mistress of all created things since she was the Mother of the Creator.

She first sees the light in the house of Joachim by Probatica, and thence is brought to the temple. And then, planted in the house of God and nourished by the Spirit, like to the fruitful olive, she becomes the abode of all virtues; so that she withdrew her mind from every desire of this life and of the flesh, and thus preserved both soul and body in virginity, as was becoming to her who was to receive God into her bosom.

From the Book of St. Ambrose, Bishop, on Virgins

Such was Mary that her single life may be a lesson to all. If then the author displease us not, let us approve the works, that whatever woman desires her reward may follow her example. What a great splendor of virtue shines forth in one Virgin! The secrecy of modesty, the standard of faith, the reverence of devotion; a virgin in the home, a companion in service, a mother in the temple. O, how many virgins has she assisted! How many hath she embraced and brought to the Lord, saying: Here is one who has kept with spotless purity the couch and nuptial chamber of my Son!

Why, therefore, should I proceed to speak of her frugality in food, of her abounding industry at her duties; the latter above nature's capacity, the former almost below nature's needs; her labor knowing no rest, her fasts continuing two days together? And when she fain would eat, she partook of any food that was at hand, not for the pleasure it gave her, but to ward off death. She slept not from desire, but from necessity; and even when her body rested, her soul watched; for often, while asleep, she either repeated what she had read, or continued what sleep had interrupted, or reviewed what had been done, or talked of what had yet to be done.

R. Truly happy art thou, O holy Virgin Mary, and worthy of all praise: * For from thee hath dawned the Sun of justice, Christ, our God. V. Pray for the people, mediate for the clergy, intercede for all devout women; may all experience thy help who celebrate thy holy Presentation. For from thee. Glory. For from thee.

III Nocturn
The reading of the holy Gospel
according to St. Luke

At that time: As Jesus was speaking to the multitude, a certain woman from the crowd, lifting up her voice, said to Him: Blessed is the womb that bore Thee. And so forth.

Homily of St. Bede the Venerable, Priest
It is clear that this was a woman of great faith and devotion, for while the scribes and Pharisees

were both tempting and blaspheming the Lord, she alone above all the rest so truly understood His Incarnation, and so boldly confessed it, that she confounded at once both the falsehoods of the great men there present, and the faithlessness of the heretics who were yet to come. For the Jews of that time, blaspheming the work of the Holy Ghost, denied that He was the true Son of God, consubstantial with the Father. And in like manner the heretics of a later day, denying that by the power and operation of the Holy Ghost, Mary, ever a Virgin, did verily give of her own flesh and blood in bringing forth the human Body of the only-begotten Son of God, have maintained that He ought not to be acknowledged as the true Son of man, consubstantial with His Mother.

But if the flesh of the Word of God, born according to the flesh, had no connection with the flesh of His Virgin Mother, without reason do we call blessed the womb that bore Him and the paps that gave Him suck. But the Apostle says: For God sent His Son, made of a woman, made under the law. Neither are we to listen to them who would read the passage thus: Born of a woman, made under the law; but made of a woman; for being conceived in the womb of a Virgin, He took not flesh from nothing, nor from elsewhere, but He partook of His Mother's flesh. Otherwise He could not truly have been the Son of man, since He would have had no origin from mankind.

Let us therefore in condemnation of the doctrine of Eutyches lift up our voices together with the Catholic Church, whereof this woman is a figure, and let us lift up our minds from the midst of the multitude, saying to the Savior: Blessed is the womb that bore Thee, and the paps that gave Thee suck. Yea, blessed indeed is that parent, whereof a certain one has said: She has given birth to the King who rules forever over heaven and earth.

Yea, rather, blessed are they who hear the word of God and keep it. The Savior graciously gives His approval to the woman's testimony, saying that not only she was blessed who merited to give birth to the Word of God according to the flesh, but all they also who, by hearing the same Word and conceiving in faith according to the spirit, strive by good works to bring it forth, and, as it were, nourish it either in their own hearts or in those of their neighbors. For the Mother of God was blessed indeed in that she gave flesh to the Word of God in time, but still more blessed in that she ever keeps that same Word in her love, throughout eternity.

R. All generations shall call me blessed * Because the Lord who is mighty hath done great things to me, and holy is His name. V. And His mercy is from generation unto generation to them that fear Him. Because. Glory. Because.

✠ Continuation of the holy Gospel according to St. Luke.—At that time: As Jesus was speaking to the multitudes, a certain woman from the crowd, lifting up her voice, said to Him: Blessed is the womb that bore Thee and the paps that gave Thee suck. But He said: Yea, rather, blessed are they who hear the word of God and keep it.

LET US PRAY

O God, who didst decree that on this day the blessed Mary ever Virgin, the temple of the Holy Ghost, shouldst be presented in the temple; grant, we beseech Thee, that through her intercession we may merit to be presented in the temple of Thy glory. Through our Lord ... in the unity of the same Holy Ghost.

ALPHABETICAL INDEX
OF THE SANCTORAL CYCLE